WITHDRAWN

A CD-ROM accompanies this book. Please ensure it is enclosed when the book is returned.

Eve is a

is a

a C

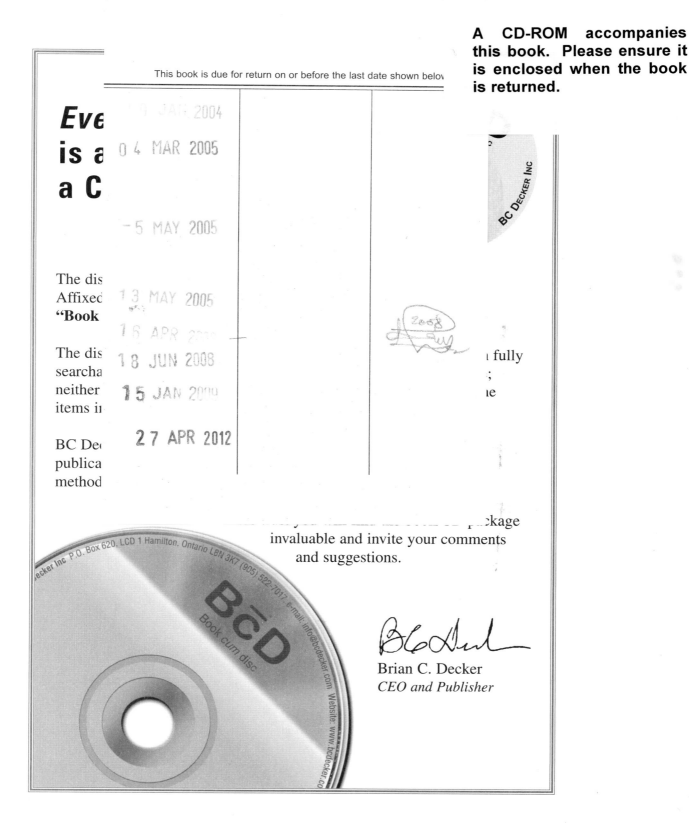

The dis

Affixed

"Book

The dis
searcha
neither
items in

BC Dec
publica
method

... fully

invaluable and invite your comments
and suggestions.

Brian C. Decker
CEO and Publisher

American Cancer Society
Atlas of
Clinical Oncology

Published

Blumgart, Fong, Jarnagin	*Hepatobiliary Cancer (2001)*
Cameron	*Pancreatic Cancer (2001)*
Carroll, Grossfeld	*Prostate Cancer (2002)*
Char	*Tumors of the Eye and Ocular Adnexa (2001)*
Clark, Duh, Jahan, Perrier	*Endocrine Tumors (2003)*
Eifel, Levenback	*Cancer of the Female Lower Genital Tract (2001)*
Ginsberg	*Lung Cancer (2002)*
Grossbard	*Malignant Lymphomas (2001)*
Ozols	*Ovarian Cancer (2003)*
Pollock	*Soft Tissue Sarcomas (2001)*
Posner, Vokes, Weichselbaum	*Cancer of the Upper Gastrointestinal Tract (2001)*
Prados	*Brain Cancer (2001)*
Shah	*Cancer of the Head and Neck (2001)*
Silverman	*Oral Cancer (1998)*
Silverman	*Oral Cancer 5th Edition (2003)*
Wiernik	*Adult Leukemias (2001)*
Willett	*Cancer of Lower Gastrointestinal Tract (2001)*
Winchester, Winchester	*Breast Cancer (2000)*

Forthcoming

Droller	*Urothelial Tumors (2003)*
Fuller, Seiden, Young	*Uterine and Endometrial Cancer (2003)*
Raghavan	*Germ Cell Tumors (2003)*
Richie, Steele	*Kidney Tumors (2004)*
Volberding	*Viral and Immunological Malignancies (2004)*
Yasko	*Bone Tumors (2004)*

American Cancer Society
Atlas of
Clinical Oncology

Editors

GLENN D. STEELE JR, MD
Geisinger Health System

THEODORE L. PHILLIPS, MD
University of California

BRUCE A. CHABNER, MD
Harvard Medical School

Managing Editor

TED S. GANSLER, MD, MBA
Director of Health Content, American Cancer Society

American Cancer Society
Atlas of
Clinical Oncology

Ovarian Cancer

Robert F. Ozols, MD, PhD
Senior Vice President, Medical Science
Fox Chase Cancer Center
Philadelphia, Pennsylvania

2003
BC Decker Inc
Hamilton • London

BC Decker Inc
P.O. Box 620, LCD 1
Hamilton, Ontario L8N 3K7
Tel: 905-522-7017; 1-800-568-7281
Fax: 905-522-7839; 1-888-311-4987
E-mail: info@bcdecker.com
www.bcdecker.com

ISBN 1–55009–096–8
Printed in Spain

Sales and Distribution

United States
BC Decker Inc
P.O. Box 785
Lewiston, NY 14092-0785
Tel: 905-522-7017; 800-568-7281
Fax: 905-522-7839; 888-311-4987
E-mail: info@bcdecker.com
www.bcdecker.com

Canada
BC Decker Inc
20 Hughson Street South
P.O. Box 620, LCD 1
Hamilton, Ontario L8N 3K7
Tel: 905-522-7017; 800-568-7281
Fax: 905-522-7839; 888-311-4987
E-mail: info@bcdecker.com
www.bcdecker.com

Foreign Rights
John Scott & Company
International Publishers' Agency
P.O. Box 878
Kimberton, PA 19442
Tel: 610-827-1640
Fax: 610-827-1671
E-mail: jsco@voicenet.com

Argentina
CLM (Cuspide Libros Medicos)
Av. Córdoba 2067 – (1120)
Buenos Aires, Argentina
Tel: (5411) 4961-0042/(5411) 4964-0848
Fax: (5411) 4963-7988
E-mail: clm@cuspide.com

Japan
Igaku-Shoin Ltd.
Foreign Publications Department
3-24-17 Hongo
Bunkyo-ku, Tokyo, Japan 113-8719
Tel: 3 3817 5680
Fax: 3 3815 6776
E-mail: fd@igaku-shoin.co.jp

U.K., Europe, Scandinavia,
Middle East
Elsevier Science
Customer Service Department
Foots Cray High Street
Sidcup, Kent
DA14 5HP, UK
Tel: 44 (0) 208 308 5760
Fax: 44 (0) 181 308 5702
E-mail: cservice@harcourt.com

Singapore, Malaysia, Thailand,
Philippines, Indonesia, Vietnam,
Pacific Rim, Korea
Elsevier Science Asia
583 Orchard Road
#09/01, Forum
Singapore 238884
Tel: 65-737-3593
Fax: 65-753-2145

Australia, New Zealand
Elsevier Science Australia
Customer Service Department
STM Division
Locked Bag 16
St. Peters, New South Wales, 2044
Australia
Tel: 61 02 9517-8999
Fax: 61 02 9517-2249
E-mail: stmp@harcourt.com.au
Web site: www.harcourt.com.au

Mexico and Central America
ETM SA de CV
Calle de Tula 59
Colonia Condesa
06140 Mexico DF, Mexico
Tel: 52-5-5553-6657
Fax: 52-5-5211-8468
E-mail: editoresdetextosmex@prodigy.net.mx

Brazil
Tecmedd
Av. Maurílio Biagi, 2850
City Ribeirão Preto – SP – CEP: 14021-000
Tel: 0800 992236
Fax: (16) 3993-9000
E-mail: tecmedd@tecmedd.com.br

Contents

Preface

Ovarian cancer is the leading cause of death from gynecologic malignancies in the Western world. The majority of patients are diagnosed with advanced-stage disease primarily due to peritoneal seeding from the primary tumor, which leads to peritoneal carcinomatosis without specific signs or symptoms. In addition, screening strategies have not yet been proven effective in increasing the number of patients diagnosed at earlier stages. Combined-modality therapy with surgery followed by chemotherapy has been the cornerstone of management in the past two decades. While substantial progress has been made and although more and more patients are living longer with their disease, the majority of patients with advanced ovarian cancer are not cured.

In the past two decades, there has been significant progress in the approach to ovarian cancer. When the "war on cancer" was declared in 1974, little was known about the biology of ovarian cancer, and few women were entering clinical research protocols. Since that time, major progress has been made in understanding the biology and the molecular genetics of ovarian cancer, which are summarized in this volume. In addition, ovarian cancer patients have benefited from a series of randomized clinical trials, many of which were performed by the Gynecologic Oncology Group. Important issues in the use of chemotherapeutic agents, such as dose intensity, different routes of administration, maintenance therapy, and the incorporation of novel new agents, have been carefully studied. In regard to early-stage disease, a group of patients for whom chemotherapy is not required (since 90% of these patients are cured by a comprehensive surgical procedure) has been identified. In patients with advanced-stage disease, current chemotherapy is associated with significantly less toxicity, and patients enjoy a better quality of life. The molecular basis for hereditary ovarian cancer has been established hereditary ovarian cancer patients currently represent only about 5% of all patients with advanced ovarian cancer. Understanding how mutations in *BRCA1* and *BRCA2* lead to the development of ovarian cancer has important therapeutic implications, for both the hereditary form and the sporadic form of this disease.

The majority of the authors of this volume work or have worked at Fox Chase Cancer Center or are involved in the Specialized Programs in Research Excellence (SPORE) Program in Ovarian Cancer, sponsored by the National Cancer Institute. It is particularly fitting that this Atlas has been published during the tenure of Robert C. Young as president of the American Cancer Society. Dr. Young has been instrumental in championing the importance of research in ovarian cancer and has been responsible for the development of new therapies in patients with both early-stage and advanced-stage disease. Many of the contributors to this Atlas have benefited from Dr. Young's mentorship and guidance. This volume is dedicated to Dr. Young, for his dedication to ovarian cancer patients, and to the patients themselves.

Robert F. Ozols, MD, PhD
December, 2002

Contributors

CYNTHIA A. BERGMAN, MD
Department of Surgical Oncology
Fox Chase Cancer Center
Philadelphia, Pennsylvania
Diagnosis and Staging and *Screening*

MATTHEW P. BOENTE, MD
Department of Obstetrics, Gynecology,
    and Women's Health
University of Minnesota
Fairview University Medical Center
Minneapolis, Minnesota
*Surgical Cytoreduction, Palliative Surgery,
Germ Cell Tumors*, and *Ovarian Sex
    Cord-Stromal Tumors*

MICHAEL A. BOOKMAN, MD
Department of Medical Oncology
Fox Chase Cancer Center
Philadelphia, Pennsylvania
Developmental Chemotherapy

MELISSA A. BURKE, MD
Department of Pathology
Thomas Jefferson University Hospital
Philadelphia, Pennsylvania
Pathology

LINDA F. CARSON, MD
Division of Gynecologic Oncology
University of Minnesota
Minneapolis, Minnesota
Surgical Cytoreduction

GEORGE COUKOS, MD, PhD
Division of Gynecologic Oncology
University of Pennsylvania Medical Center
Philadelphia, Pennsylvania
Advances in Biologic Therapy

MARY B. DALY, MD, PhD
Division of Population Science
    and of Medical Oncology
Fox Chase Cancer Center
Philadelphia, Pennsylvania
Epidemiology and *Genetic Counseling*

JEFFREY DIMASCIO, DO
Department of Medical Oncology
Fox Chase Cancer Center
Philadelphia, Pennsylvania
Early Stage Management

LEVI DOWNS, MD
Division of Gynecologic Oncology
University of Minnesota
Minneapolis, Minnesota
Germ Cell Tumors

ANDREY FROLOV, MS
Department of Medical Oncology
Fox Chase Cancer Center
Philadelphia, Pennsylvania
Genetics

MELISSA A. GELLER, MD
Department of Gynecologic Oncology
University of Minnesota
Minneapolis, Minnesota
Palliative Surgery

ANDREW K. GODWIN, PhD
Department of Medical Oncology
Fox Chase Cancer Center
Philadelphia, Pennsylvania
Genetics

HEIDI J. GRAY, MD
Department of Obstetrics and Gynecology
University of Pennsylvania Medical Center
Philadelphia, Pennsylvania
Advances in Biologic Therapy

THOMAS C. HAMILTON, PhD
Department of Medical Oncology
Fox Chase Cancer Center
Philadelphia, Pennsylvania
Biology

RAJESH V. IYER, MD
Department of Radiation Oncology
Monmouth Medical Center
Long Branch, New Jersey
Radiation Therapy

PATRICIA L. JUDSON, MD
Department of OB-GYN—Women's Health
University of Minnesota
Minneapolis, Minnesota
Ovarian Sex Cord-Stromal Tumors

CARL H. JUNE, MD
Department of Pathology and Laboratory Medicine
University of Pennsylvania School of Medicine
Abramson Cancer Center at the University of
   Pennsylvania
Philadelphia, Pennsylvania
Advances in Biologic Therapy

NANCY L. LEWIS, MD
Department of Medical Oncology
Fox Chase Cancer Center
Philadelphia, Pennsylvania
High-Dose Chemotherapy

ROBERT F. OZOLS, MD, PhD
Department of Medical Science
Fox Chase Cancer Center
Philadelphia, Pennsylvania
Primary Chemotherapy Regimens

ARTHUR S. PATCHEFSKY, MD
Department of Pathology
Fox Chase Cancer Center
Philadelphia, Pennsylvania
Pathology

CHRISTOS PATRIOTIS, PhD
Department of Medical Oncology
Fox Chase Cancer Center
Philadelphia, Pennsylvania
Biology

WAYNE H. PINOVER, DO
Department of Radiation Oncology
Abington Memorial Hospital/Rosenfeld Cancer
   Center
Abington, Pennsylvania
Radiation Therapy

AMANDA PROWSE, PhD
Nuffield Department of Obstetrics and Gynaecology
University of Oxford
John Radcliffe Hospital
Oxford, UK
Genetics

HERNANDO SALAZAR, MD, MPH
Department of Surgical Pathology
Fox Chase Cancer Center
Philadelphia, Pennsylvania
November 21, 1938 – July 16, 2001
Biology

RUSSELL J. SCHILDER, MD
Department of Medicine
Temple University School of Medicine
Department of Medical Oncology
Fox Chase Cancer Center
Philadelphia, Pennsylvania
Early Stage Management and *High-Dose
   Chemotherapy*

XIANGXI XU, PhD
Department of Medical Oncology
Fox Chase Cancer Center
Philadelphia, Pennsylvania
Biology

Pathology

MELISSA A. BURKE, MD
ARTHUR S. PATCHEFSKY, MD

Tumors of the ovary form a varied group of neoplasms. The surface epithelium, stroma, and germ cells each give rise to an array of histogenetically distinctive tumors that can occur in pure or combined forms and that represent one of the most extensive arrays of tumor types in solid-tumor pathology (Table 1–1).[1]

This chapter will present a necessarily condensed review of the pathology of these tumors, together with illustrations of their more common phenotypes. The reader is referred to a number of excellent general sources for more detailed discussion.[2–7]

SURFACE EPITHELIAL TUMORS

Surface epithelial tumors account for over half of all ovarian neoplasms.[4] They are derived from cystic invaginations of modified pelvic mesothelium that normally covers the ovarian surface and pelvic peritoneum. This surface lining is multipotential and can differentiate into müllerian and other types of epithelium, including endometrial, endocervical, intestinal, and tubal types, which helps explain the wide variety of epithelial tumors observed in the ovary and peritoneal surface. Surface epithelial tumors are classified according to cell type and are stratified as benign, borderline, or malignant, based on the degree of cellular proliferation, nuclear atypia, and presence or absence of stromal invasion. Their categorization is of obvious importance as it has a direct bearing on prognosis and treatment decisions.

Serous Tumors

Serous lesions comprise approximately 25% of all ovarian tumors.[2–4] They show a biologic spectrum ranging from benign to malignant and share histologic features that include tubal-type epithelium, papillary architecture, and the presence of psammoma bodies. Up to 50% of serous tumors are bilateral. In general, they are microscopically uniform throughout, in contrast to mucinous tumors that often show a spectrum of benign and malignant change within the same tumor.

Serous cystadenoma is benign and accounts for 60% of serous tumors.[2–4] It occurs most commonly in women of reproductive age, and 10 to 25% are bilateral. Grossly, tumors are smooth thin-walled unilocular or multilocular cysts that contain clear fluid (Figure 1–1).

Serous cystadenomas can sometimes attain large size. Microscopically, there is a single layer of benign appearing cuboidal to columnar epithelium, often with cilia (Figure 1–2). Architecturally, small papillae and psammoma bodies may be present (Figures 1–3 and 1–4). By definition, there is no cytologic atypia and no stromal invasion. Outside the ovary, the presence of benign serous inclusions in pelvic peritoneum, lymph nodes, and elsewhere is termed endosalpingiosis[8] (Figure 1–5). It reflects in situ metaplastic transformation of pelvic mesothelium and is not an adverse feature of serous tumors of the ovary.

A variant of benign serous tumor is *serous cystadenofibroma*. Histologically, it shows a microcys-

Table 1–1   HISTOLOGIC CLASSIFICATION OF OVARIAN TUMORS*

Surface epithelial–stromal tumors
  Serous tumors
    Benign
    Borderline (low malignant potential)
    Malignant
  Mucinous tumors (endocervical-like and intestinal types)
    Benign
    Borderline (low malignant potential)
    Malignant
  Endometrioid tumors
    Benign
    Borderline (low malignant potential)
    Malignant
  Epithelial-stromal and stromal tumors
    Adenosarcoma
    Mesodermal mixed tumor
    Stromal sarcoma
  Clear cell tumors
    Benign
    Borderline (low malignant potential)
    Malignant
  Transitional cell tumors
    Brenner tumor
    Brenner tumor of borderline malignancy
    Transitional cell carcinoma (non-Brenner type)
  Mixed epithelial tumors (specify types)
    Benign
    Borderline (low malignant potential)
    Malignant
  Undifferentiated carcinoma
Sex cord–stromal tumors
  Granulosa stromal cell tumors
  Granulosa cell tumors
    Adult
    Juvenile
  Thecoma-fibroma group
    Thecoma
    Fibroma
    Fibrosarcoma
    Unclassified

Sertoli stromal cell tumors (androblastomas)
  Well-differentiated tumors
    Sertoli cell tumor (tubular androblastoma)
    Sertoli-Leydig cell tumor
    Leydig cell tumor
  Sertoli-Leydig cell tumor of intermediate differentiation
  Sertoli-Leydig cell tumor, poorly differentiated (sarcomatoid)
  Retiform tumor
Sex cord tumor with annular tubules
Gynandroblastoma
Unclassified
Steroid (lipid) cell tumors
    Leydig cell tumor
    Unclassified (not otherwise specified)
Germ Cell Tumors
  Dysgerminoma
  Yolk sac tumor (endodermal sinus tumor)
    Polyvesicular vitelline variant
    Hepatoid variant
    Glandular variant
  Embryonal carcinoma
  Polyembryoma
  Choriocarcinoma
  Teratomas
    Immature
    Mature: with secondary tumor (specify type)
    Monodermal
      Struma ovarii
      Carcinoid tumor
      Strumal carcinoid tumor
      Mucinous carcinoid tumor
      Others
  Mixed germ cell tumor (specify type)
Gonadoblastoma
Tumors of uncertain origin and miscellaneous tumors
    Small cell carcinomas
    Others
Gestational trophoblastic diseases
Unclassified malignant tumors

*Abridged from the World Health Organization (WHO) classification.

tic pattern of benign serous glands imbedded in cellular fibrous tissue (Figure 1–6). This tumor generally is firm and solid grossly, in contrast to serous cystadenoma, which is cystic.

Serous borderline low malignant tumors account for 10% of serous neoplasms. Twenty-five to 30% are bilateral.[9] Borderline tumors tend to be larger than cystadenomas; are more often multicystic, containing clear or thinly mucoid fluid, and more frequently show papillary excrescences on the cyst wall or on the surface. Microscopically, papillary structures are seen to be composed of stratified layers of epithelial cells with varying degrees of nuclear atypia and cell tufting (Figure 1–7). These may

appear as free floating cell clusters in the cyst lumen. Psammoma bodies are common. By definition, there is no frank stromal invasion although one or more foci of microinvasion (< 10 mm^2) may be seen (Figure 1–9). Microinvasion appears to have no adverse effect on prognosis.[10–13]

Up to 60% of borderline tumors are associated with peritoneal implants. It may actually be impossible to assess whether these represent metastatic tumor from the ovary or de novo peritoneal transformation through the process of "field cancerization." By convention, they are nevertheless referred to as "implants." Peritoneal implants are classified as invasive or noninvasive, which has a direct bearing

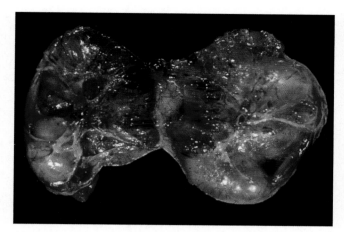

Figure 1–1. Serous cystadenoma. Multiloculated thin-walled cysts containing thin fluid are characteristic.

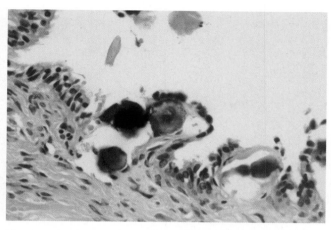

Figure 1–4. Serous cystadenoma. Psammoma bodies composed of laminated calcium deposits may be present in all types of serous tumors (original magnification ×200).

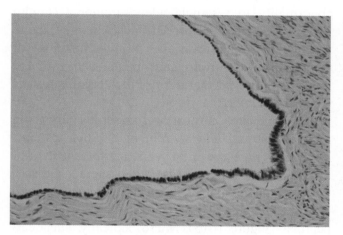

Figure 1–2. Serous cystadenoma. Cystic structure is lined by a single layer of benign cuboidal cells (original magnification ×100).

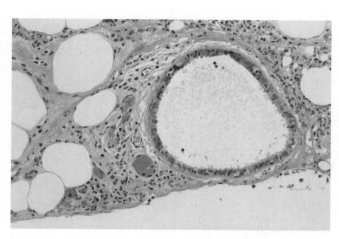

Figure 1–5. Endosalpingiosis of peritoneum. Simple serous inclusion is lined by a single layer of bland cuboidal cells with cilia (original magnification ×100).

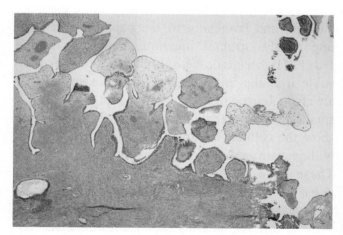

Figure 1–3. Serous cystadenoma. Broad-based simple papillae composed of stroma and lined by a layer of nonproliferating serous epithelium project into the lumen of a cyst tumor (original magnification ×40).

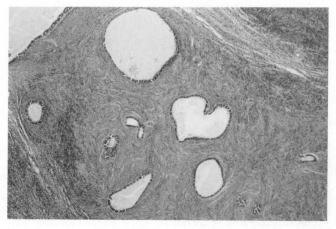

Figure 1–6. Serous adenofibroma. Abundant fibrous stroma containing simple microcysts define this tumor (original magnification ×40).

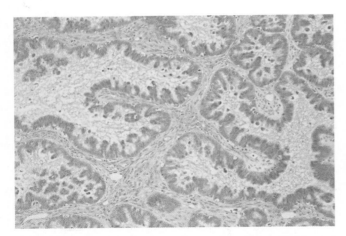

Figure 1–7. Serous borderline tumor. Complex proliferation of papillary epithelium shows piling up of several cell layers (original magnification ×40).

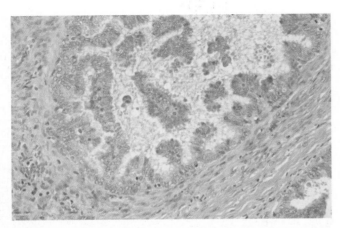

Figure 1–8. Borderline serous tumor. Higher magnification shows mildly atypical cells forming discohesive clusters in the glandular spaces. Stromal invasion is absent (original magnification ×100).

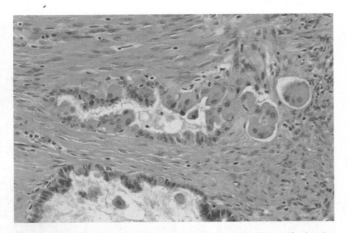

Figure 1–9. Borderline serous tumor showing the focus of microinvasion. Distorted invasive cell clusters with artifactual separation from the ovarian stroma is characteristic of early stromal invasion. Such foci should not exceed 3.0 × 3.0 mm to qualify as microinvasive (original magnification ×100).

on prognosis.[14] This distinction is important but is by no means easy to make in all cases. Tumors with noninvasive implants behave indolently, similar to borderline tumors without implants, whereas those with invasive implants pursue a course similar to that of low-grade serous carcinoma. Histologically, noninvasive implants resemble the primary borderline tumor and sit on the peritoneal surface or within the confines of normal tissue planes of the omental fat lobules, without invasion (Figures 1–10 and 1–11). There may be a fibrotic stromal reaction (noninvasive desmoplastic implants) (Figure 1–12). In contrast, invasive implants have a more diffuse and haphazard relationship to the underlying tissues (Figure 1–13). Implants histologically may show minimal atypia, or they may demonstrate sufficient abnormality to resemble adenocarcinoma (Figure 1–14). This generally correlates with the presence or absence of stromal invasion.[14] It is the histology of the tumor in the ovary and not the nature of the implants, however, that defines the classification of the primary tumor.

Approximately 30% of ovarian serous tumors are recognizable as *adenocarcinomas*. Such patients have an average age of 56 years, but the age distribution is wide. Two-thirds are bilateral. Grossly, tumors look malignant, being predominantly solid or cystic and papillary with areas of hemorrhage and necrosis (Figure 1–15). Microscopically, adenocarcinomas are differentiated from borderline tumors by increased nuclear atypia, a greater number of mitoses and greater cellular density, more complex budding and branching of the papillae, and most importantly, stromal invasion (Figure 1–16 and 1–17). Higher-grade serous tumors often demonstrate irregular anastamosing seivelike spaces that are characteristic of this tumor type (Figure 1–18). A small controversial subgroup of serous tumors that show the cellular features of serous carcinoma but without stromal invasion has been described.[15] These have been termed *micropapillary carcinoma*[16,17] (Figure 1–19). As a group, they are most often stage I, and the prognosis is favorable.[15–17]

Well-differentiated serous adenocarcinomas contain well-formed papillary structures and numerous psammoma bodies whereas more poorly differentiated tumors show predominantly solid sheets of cells

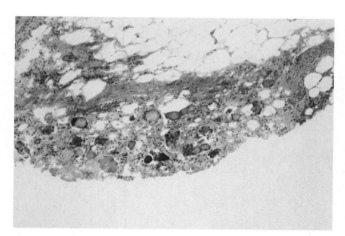

Figure 1–10. Noninvasive surface serous implant on peritoneum. Clusters of bland papillary serous tumor with psammoma bodies occupy the peritoneal surface without invasion (original magnification ×40).

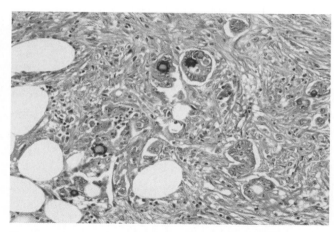

Figure 1–13. Invasive serous implant. Nests of serous tumor with psammoma bodies haphazardly infiltrating peritoneal fat without relationship to the surface, or fat lobules (original magnification ×100).

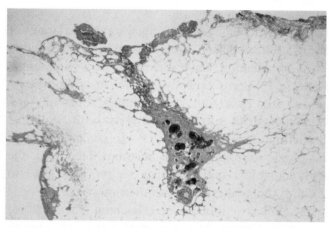

Figure 1–11. Noninvasive serous implant involving the connective-tissue septum of omental fat. The outline of the fat lobule is maintained with little or no stromal reaction, which indicates the absence of invasion (original magnification ×40).

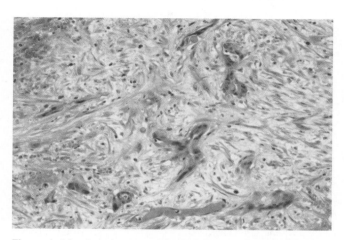

Figure 1–14. Invasive serous implant from borderline tumor. This example demonstrates severe cellular atypia that is indistinguishable from serous adenocarcinoma(original magnification ×200).

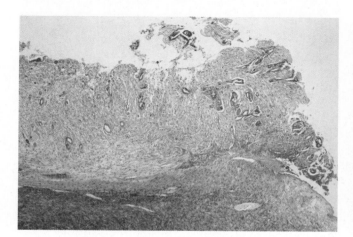

Figure 1–12. Noninvasive desmoplastic serous implant. Deposits of serous epithelium evoke a fibrotic stromal response on the peritoneal surface but do not invade the peritoneal fat (original magnification ×40).

Figure 1–15. Serous adenocarcinoma. Tumor has a predominantly solid appearance, with small cysts and hemorrhagic discoloration.

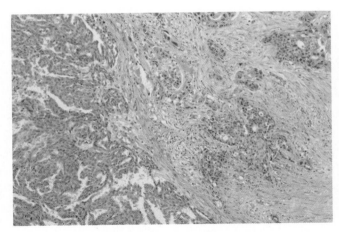

Figure 1–16. Papillary serous adenocarcinoma. This photomicrograph shows complex and partially solid papillary tumor proliferation associated with irregular nests of carcinoma invading ovarian stroma (original magnification ×40).

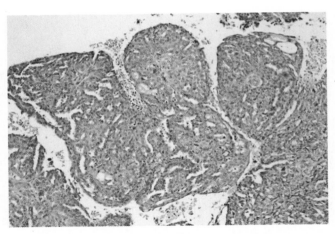

Figure 1–18. Papillary serous adenocarcinoma. Solid proliferation of tumor shows complex, elongated, and mazelike configuration of residual gland spaces due to fusion of papillae. This pattern is a characteristic of serous carcinoma, even in metastatic sites (original magnification ×40).

and fewer psammoma bodies. Anaplasia may be extreme in high-grade lesions (Figure 1–20).

Immunohistochemical stains for CA 125 are positive in the majority of serous tumors while carcinoembryonic antigen (CEA) is negative, which contrasts with mucinous tumors. The 5-year survival rate of serous tumors is stage related, with that of stage I borderline tumors being between 90 and 99% in most series, in contrast to 75% as seen with carcinoma.[9,18]

Mucinous Tumors

Mucinous tumors of the ovary arise from surface epithelium that shows differentiation toward endocervical (Figure 1–21), gastrointestinal (Figure 1–22), or

combined elements. As a group, they are the largest of the ovarian neoplasms, weighing up to 4,000 g. Ten to 20% are bilateral, fewer than observed with serous tumors.[2–4] Microscopically, greater histologic variation is seen than with serous tumors; areas of frank malignancy not infrequently coexist with benign or borderline areas (Figure 1–23). To ensure thorough histologic sampling, it is recommended that the pathologist take one histologic section for each 1 to 2 cm of the greatest tumor dimension.

Mucinous cystadenomas account for 75% of mucinous tumors. They are most commonly seen in

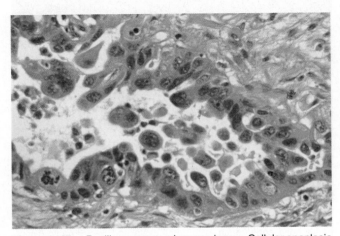

Figure 1–17. Papillary serous adenocarcinoma. Cellular anaplasia may be extreme in some cases (original magnification ×200).

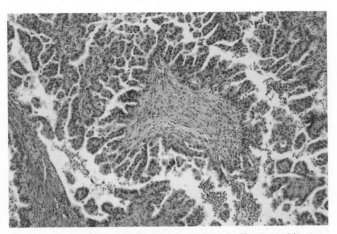

Figure 1–19. Micropapillary serous carcinoma. Tumor architecture reveals discohesive clusters of proliferating cells with extensive micropapillary stratification but without evidence of stromal invasion. Prognosis in stage I is comparable to that of ordinary borderline tumor, but these tumors have a greater tendency for invasive peritoneal implants (original magnification ×100).

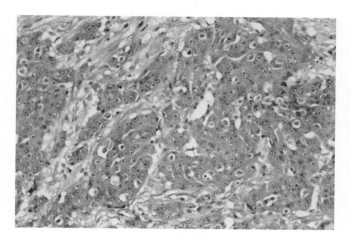

Figure 1–20. Solid anaplastic tumor in an otherwise recognizable papillary serous adenocarcinoma (original magnification ×100).

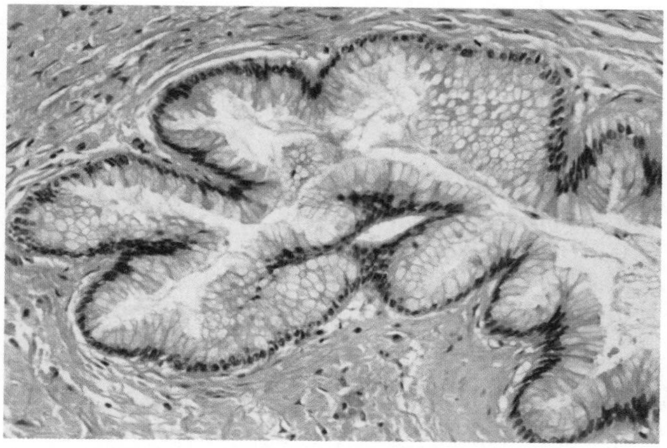

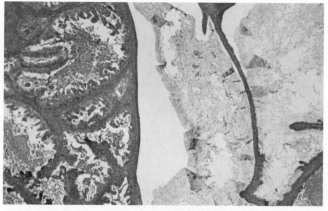

Figure 1–22. Mucinous cystadenoma with gastrointestinal-type benign goblet cells(original magnification ×100).

the fourth to sixth decades. Only 5% of cases are bilateral. Grossly, multiloculated thin-walled mucin filled cysts are characteristic. Microscopically, a single row of benign mucin-producing epithelial cells without atypia is most often seen (Figure 1–24). Papillary formations may be present. Microscopic rupture of the cysts may cause mucin to escape and dissect into the stroma (pseudomyxoma ovarii). This has a strong association with pseudomyxoma peritonei but should not be interpreted as stromal invasion (Figure 1–25).[4]

Approximately 10% of mucinous neoplasms are classified as borderline tumors. Patients are usually in the fifth decade. Grossly, there are multicystic loculations of varying size, with coarsely papillary and solid areas. Microscopically, the tumor is composed

of mucinous epithelium of intestinal or endocervical type, arranged in multiple cell layers with complex tufting and mild to moderate cytologic atypia[19] (Figure 1–26). By definition, there is no stromal invasion, but this can be very difficult to evaluate in mucinous neoplasms. As with serous tumors, microinvasion that does not affect prognosis may be present in mucinous borderline lesions[20] (Figure 1–27). Other features, such as the degree of nuclear atypia, mitotic rate, and epithelial layering, may be more reliable in separating borderline tumors from carcinomas in some cases.[21,22] Following this approach, some pathologists have defined a category of noninvasive borderline tumors with intraepithelial carcinoma that have excellent survival and that only rarely prove fatal (Figure 1–28).[20,23,24]

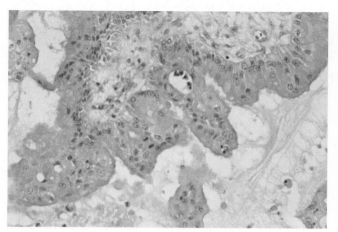

Figure 1–21. Mucinous cystadenoma composed of a single layer of benign-appearing endocervical-type tall columnar epithelium(original magnification ×200).

Figure 1–23. Mucinous cystadenoma adjacent to a more complex borderline mucinous tumor. Such juxtaposition of benign, borderline, and frankly malignant areas is common in mucinous tumors (original magnification ×40).

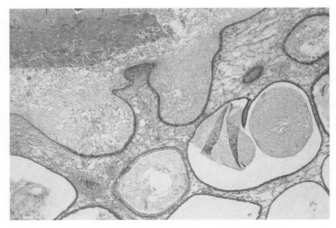

Figure 1–24. Mucinous cystadenoma. Multiloculated cysts are lined by a single layer of benign mucinous epithelium (original magnification ×40).

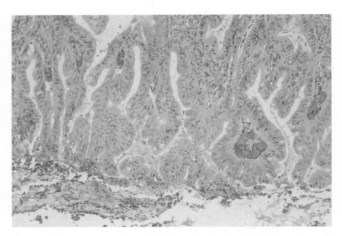

Figure 1–26. Borderline mucinous tumor. This tumor has a more complex locular arrangement of microcysts and greater tendency for nuclear stratification than is seen in cystadenoma (original magnification ×40).

Mucinous adenocarcinomas account for approximately 15% of mucinous tumors, and like borderline tumors, are seen usually in the fifth decade. Grossly, they are solid and cystic neoplasms with significant areas of hemorrhage and necrosis. Microscopically, severe cellular atypia, increased mitoses, nuclear stratification, and stromal invasion distinguish adenocarcinomas from borderline tumors (Fig.). Recently, two forms of invasive growth with expansile or infiltrating patterns have been described (Figures 1–29 and 1–30).[20] The prognosis of tumor with expansile growth is excellent and similar to that of borderline tumors. The malignant cells may have the appearance of endocervical, intestinal, or less well-differentiated

epithelium. Some tumors contain signet-ring cells and must be distinguished from metastases from the gastrointestinal tract or elsewhere (Kruckenberg's tumor). Similarly, distinction from metastatic tumor from the colon is sometimes difficult.[22] The rare pure endocervical type tumor has an excellent prognosis, even in cases with peritoneal and lymph node spread.[19] The combination of frank tumor invasion, high-grade nuclei, and tumor rupture have been shown to predict recurrence in stage I carcinoma of intestinal type.[23] Immunohistochemical stains typically are positive for CEA and EMA and negative for CA 125.

Borderline mucinous tumors of the ovary, most often with simultaneous mucinous tumors of the

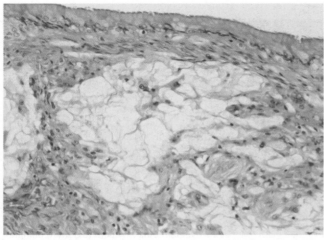

Figure 1–25. Pseudomyxoma ovarii. Mucinous cystadenoma shows rupture of microcysts, with dissection of acellular mucin in ovarian stroma (original magnification ×200).

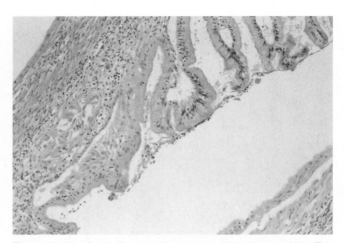

Figure 1–27. Borderline mucinous tumor with microinvasion. The orderly pattern of papillary architecture is disrupted by irregular islands of atypical glands that infiltrate ovarian stroma and evoke a fibrotic stromal reaction (original magnification ×100).

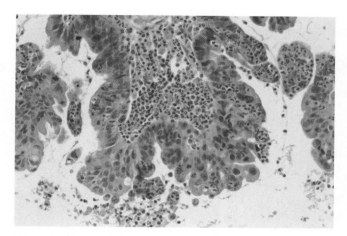

Figure 1–28. Borderline mucinous tumor with intraepithelial carcinoma. A proliferation of highly atypical malignant-appearing cells show extensive piling up on the surface, but without stromal invasion (original magnification ×100).

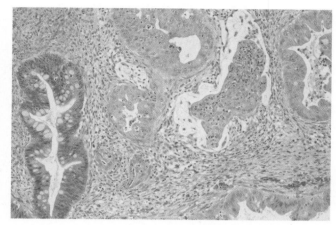

Figure 1–30. Mucinous adenocarcinoma with an irregular invasive pattern into stroma. Tumors with this pattern of invasion tend to be aggressive (original magnification ×40).

appendix, may be associated with pools of mucin in the peritoneal cavity (pseudomyxoma peritonei). Localized surface collection of mucin in the right lower quadrant caused by rupture of appendiceal mucocele or benign mucinous tumor has an excellent prognosis whereas invasive peritoneal mucin due to spread of borderline tumor or carcinoma containing cells with significant atypia is predictive of a malignant clinical course.[20,25] Cytogenetic studies have shown that simultaneous mucinous tumors in the appendix and ovary that are associated with pseudomyxoma peritonei most often represent primary borderline or low-grade malignant mucinous tumors of the appendix that

have spread to the ovary (Figure 1–31, 1–32, and 1–33).[20,26,27] Isolated examples of mucinous tumors may show solid mural nodules that can be reactive or malignant in nature (Figure 1–34).[28–30] The prognosis of mucinous tumors is strongly dependent on stage. The 5-year survival rate of stage I borderline mucinous tumor and mucinous carcinoma is excellent, exceeding 95% in most well-staged series.[20]

Endometrioid Tumors

Endometrioid tumors account for approximately 5% of ovarian neoplasms. Patients are usually post-

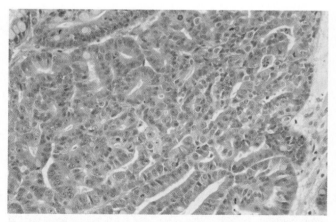

Figure 1–29. Mucinous adenocarcinoma. Expansile or confluent pattern of stromal invasion showing crowded back-to-back glands without intervening stroma and with a smoothly contoured epithelial interface. The prognosis for such tumors in stage I is excellent (original magnification ×100).

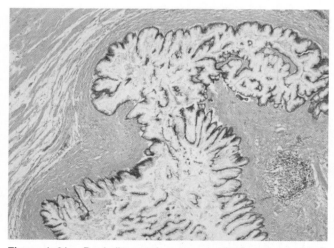

Figure 1–31. Borderline mucinous tumor of the appendix. Mucinous epithelium shows delicate papillae without cellular atypia (original magnification ×40).

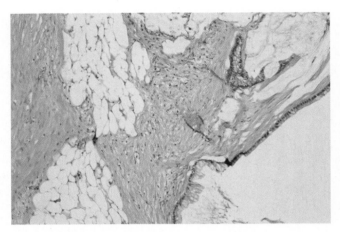

Figure 1–32. Borderline mucinous tumor of the appendix, with penetration of muscularis into peritoneal soft tissue. There is a desmoplastic reaction to tumor in fat (original magnification ×40).

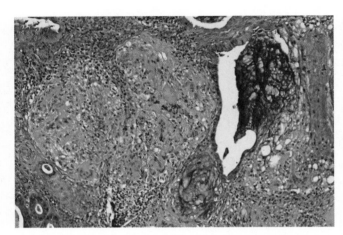

Figure 1–34. Borderline mucinous tumor with a solid mural nodule composed of benign giant cells in response to a ruptured mucinous cyst (original magnification ×40).

menopausal. Rarely, benign and borderline types are recognized; adenocarcinomas being by far the most common endometrioid tumors.[2–4]

Endometrial cystadenoma is rare and difficult to separate conceptually and pathologically from endometriosis. Endometrioid adenofibroma, on the other hand, is more easily recognizable and is the most frequent benign endometrioid tumor. It is similar to its serous counterpart and consists of a predominantly solid tumor composed of proliferating benign endometrial-type glands in abundant fibrous stroma (Figure 1–35).[2]

Endometrioid borderline tumors are not easily separated from adenocarcinomas. They are usually solid lesions composed of atypical proliferating or cytologically malignant endometrial-type glands but without stromal invasion (Figure 1–36).

Endometrioid adenocarcinomas account for 10 to 20% of ovarian malignancies.[2–4] Grossly, they are solid and cystic, often with areas of necrosis. Microscopically, most are differentiated and resemble low- to intermediate-grade endometrial adenocarcinoma. Malignant glands lined by atypical stratified columnar epithelium invade the ovarian stroma, which defines these tumors as carcinomas. Squamous metaplasia in the form of morules or more irregular foci of keratinization are frequently identified (Figure 1–37).

Some lesions closely resemble Sertoli cell tumors and are composed of compact cords and nests of

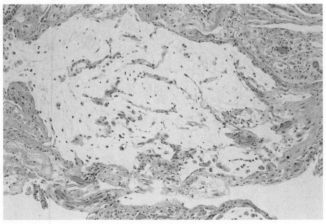

Figure 1–33. Pseudomyxoma peritonei. The acellular mucin pool in the peritoneum is the result of the tumor of the appendix seen in Figure 1–32 (original magnification ×100).

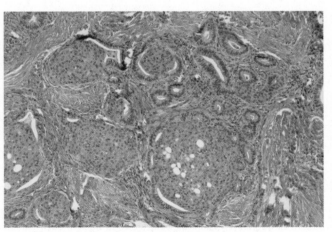

Figure 1–35. Endometrioid adenofibroma. Solid tumor is composed of benign endometrial glands with squamous metaplasia (squamous morules) within fibrotic ovarian stroma (original magnification ×40).

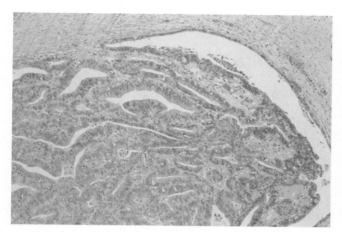

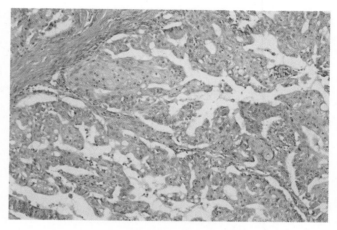

Figure 1–36. Borderline endometrioid tumor. This tumor is composed of a complex proliferation of endometrial-type glands separated by intervening fibrosis stroma and projecting into a microcystic space. There is a similarity to complex endometrial hyperplasia. There is no stromal invasion (original magnification ×100).

Figure 1–37. Endometrial adenocarcinoma. Irregularly shaped glands lined by moderately atypical cells with focal squamous metaplasia infiltrate the stroma. Glandular structures show little or no stroma and form secondary lumens, which is a feature of carcinoma (original magnification ×100).

Sertoli's cell–like tubules imbedded in fibrous stroma (Figure 1–38). Unlike true Sertoli cell tumors, however, they are immunohistochemically positive for estrogen and progesterone receptors, EMA, and keratin and are negative for inhibin.[31–33]

Minor areas of clear cell carcinoma can be seen in some cases. Approximately 20% of endometrioid carcinomas are associated with endometriosis in the ovary or elsewhere in the pelvis.[34] About the same number of cases have a simultaneous adenocarcinoma of the endometrium, shown by loss of heterozygosity (LOH) studies to represent an independent lesion rather than metastases.[35] Endometrioid carcinomas sometimes may be histologically confused with higher-grade serous carcinoma. The latter lesions, however, characteristically lack squamous or clear cell areas and do not have associated endometriosis. The 5-year survival rate of stage I carcinoma is 78%.[19]

Clear Cell Carcinomas

Clear cell carcinomas are high-grade aggressive tumors that make up 6% of primary ovarian carcinomas.[2–4,9] They most commonly occur in women between the ages of 40 and 60 years. Approximately 25% of these tumors are associated with endometriosis of the same ovary, and 25% have areas of coexisting endometrioid adenocarcinoma;[36,37] 10% are bilat-

eral. Adenomas and borderline clear cell tumors are rare and almost invariably behave as benign lesions.

Grossly, clear cell carcinomas may be solid or cystic and contain mucinous, serous, or hemorrhagic fluid.

Microscopically, tumor cells show anaplastic high-grade nuclei with abundant clear cytoplasm and show a distinctive "hobnailed" pattern with cells that protrude into the gland lumens like upholsterer's nails (Figure 1–39). Papillary and solid patterns are common, and some examples contain hyaline bodies similar to yolk sac tumors (Figures 1–40 and 1–41). Most cases present with disease already outside the ovary. The overall 5-year survival rate for stage I clear cell carcinoma is 70%, which is worse than that of other surface epithelial tumors.[38–40] Positive immunohistochemical staining with LeuM1 and negative staining with α-fetoprotein help separate these lesions from yolk sac tumors, and positive staining for B72.3 helps in distinguishing them from clear cell carcinoma of the kidney; both of these tumors may closely resemble clear cell carcinoma of the ovary.[4]

Malignant Mixed Müllerian Tumors

Malignant mixed müllerian tumors (MMMTs) represent less than 1% of ovarian malignancies.[4,41–43] Like their uterine counterparts, these tumors gener-

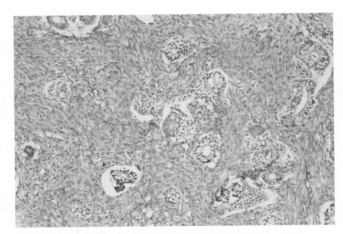

Figure 1–38. Endometrial adenocarcinoma with features similar to those of Sertoli cell tumors. Small hollow tubules composed of tall columnar cells with only mild atypia infiltrate the ovarian stroma. Elsewhere, more typical endometrioid adenocarcinoma was observed. Rarely, endometrial tumors may consist entirely of this pattern (original magnification ×40).

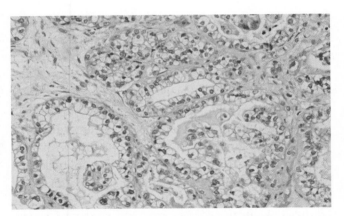

Figure 1–39. Clear cell adenocarcinoma. Malignant glands of varying sizes are lined by cuboidal cells having abundant clear cytoplasm (original magnification ×100).

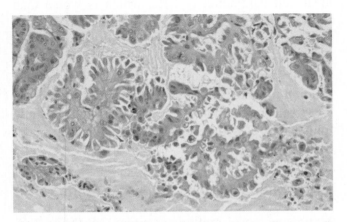

Figure 1–40. Clear cell adenocarcinoma, showing fibrous papillary structures covered by pink "hobnailed" epithelium (original magnification ×100).

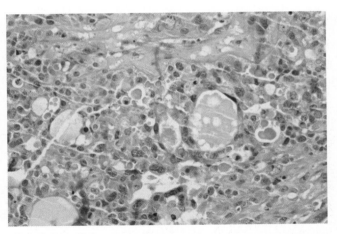

Figure 1–41. Clear cell adenocarcinoma, showing glands with pleomorphic cells containing intraluminal and intracytoplasmic hyaline bodies (original magnification ×200).

ally occur in postmenopausal women and are most often of high stage at diagnosis. Approximately one-third are bilateral. The prognosis is poor.

Grossly, MMMTs are solid or partly cystic and appear fleshy with areas of hemorrhage and necrosis. Microscopically, they are composed of malignant stromal and epithelial elements in proportions that vary widely from case to case. The epithelial component is usually high-grade and resembles serous, endometrioid, or less differentiated carcinoma whereas the stromal component may be homologous, resembling cellular ovarian mesenchyme (carcinosarcoma), or may contain heterologous elements such as malignant cartilage, bone, skeletal muscle, and adipose tissue (Figures 1–42 and 1–43). Pure carcinoma, sarcoma, or mixtures may be seen in metastatic sites. Neural elements are not observed, which helps distinguish MMMT from malignant teratoma.

TRANSITIONAL CELL TUMORS

Transitional cell tumors include Brenner tumor and transitional cell carcinoma and are felt to originate from the surface epithelium of the ovary in most cases, (excepting rare cases associated with dermoid cyst).[2–4]

Brenner tumors make up 2 to 3% of ovarian neoplasms. They are most commonly incidental findings in women between the ages of 40 to 60 years.

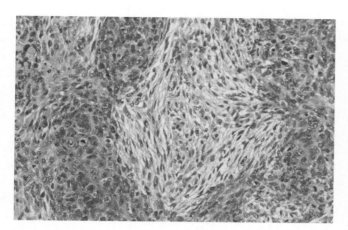

Figure 1–42. Malignant mixed müllerian tumor, homologous type (carcinosarcoma). Poorly differentiated solid carcinoma shows abrupt transition from noncommitted spindle cell sarcoma (original magnification ×200).

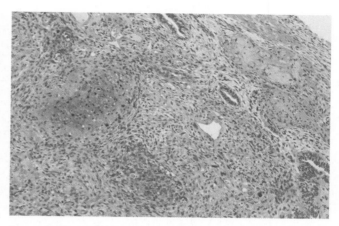

Figure 1–43. Malignant mixed müllerian tumor, heterologous type. Malignant cartilage is associated with a sarcomatous spindle cell component and atypical glands (original magnification ×100).

The tumors often are associated with mucinous cystic neoplasms or (rarely) are a component of dermoid cysts.

Grossly, these tumors are tan, solid, well circumscribed, and most often < 2 cm in greatest dimension. Bilateralism is rare.

Microscopically, Brenner tumors consist of discreet nests of transitional cell–type epithelium within dense fibrous stroma. Some nests may be cystic and contain mucinous or ciliated glandular cells with eosinophilic fluid material or calcifications. Nuclei are typically oval with a longitudinal groove. Immunohistochemical stains are positive for CEA, EMA, and pan-cytokeratin but are usually negative for cytokeratin-20, in contrast to transitional cell tumors of the urinary tract.[44]

Borderline and malignant Brenner tumors are extremely rare, accounting for 3 to 5% of all Brenner tumors;[45,46] by definition, they must be seen in association with their benign counterpart (Figure 1–44). Microscopically, papillary or solid nests of transitional cells similar to low-grade transitional cell carcinoma of the urinary bladder characterize these tumors.

There is no stromal invasion in borderline tumors whereas invasion and cellular anaplasia define the malignant Brenner tumor. Pure transitional cell carcinoma accounts for less than 1% of ovarian carcinomas and differs from malignant Brenner tumor only by the absence of coexistent benign Brenner tumor.[47] Metastases from transi-

tional cell carcinoma of the urinary bladder must be distinguished from primary transitional cell carcinoma of the ovary.

Small Cell Carcinomas

Hypercalcemic Type

Hypercalcemic-type small cell carcinoma is extremely rare.[2–4] It occurs in young women at an average age of 23 years and is almost always unilateral. What sets this tumor apart from most others is the finding that two-thirds of cases have associated paracrine hypercalcemia thought to be due to the secretion of a parathormone-like protein. Despite apparently limited disease at diagnosis, extraovarian spread is common and the prognosis is poor. Grossly, the tumor is solid, with hemorrhage and necrosis. Microscopically, it is composed of poorly differentiated mitotically active small cells that are arranged in a diffuse or nesting pattern and that may contain intracytoplasmic hyaline globules (Figure 1–46). Localized areas that show a follicular arrangement are frequent.[48–50]

Immunohistochemically, the tumor may express EMA, keratin, vimentin, and parathyroid hormone–related protein. As seen by electron microscopy, the cells do not contain the dense core granules that are characteristically found in pulmonary-type small cell carcinoma or in other neuroendocrine tumors.

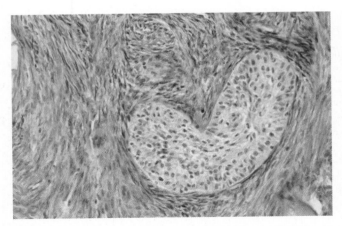

Figure 1–44. Benign Brenner tumor component of malignant Brenner tumor shows well-circumscribed nests of bland solid epithelial nests in fibrous stroma (original magnification ×100).

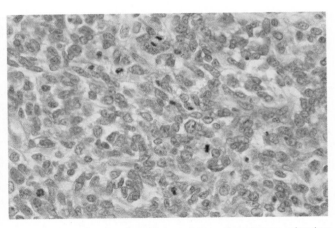

Figure 1–46. Small cell carcinoma, hypercalcemic type, showing anastamosing ribbons and small glandlike formations of pale pink cells with an open pattern of nuclear chromatin and frequent mitoses (original magnification ×200).

Pulmonary Type

Pulmonary-type small cell carcinoma is very rare and has a much wider age distribution than to the hypercalcemic type.[51] Microscopically, it resembles small cell carcinoma of the lung, with small undifferentiated tumor cells containing hyperchromatic nuclei with stippled chromatin, inconspicuous nucleoli, and scant cytoplasm that usually shows crush artifact (Figure 1–47). It is sometimes seen in combination with other epithelial tumors, such as endometrioid adenocarcinoma. Immunohistochemical stains demonstrate expression of keratin, EMA, neuron specific enolase (NSE), and (sometimes) chromogranin. The prognosis is poor.

SEX CORD–STROMAL TUMORS

Ovarian sex cord–stromal tumors are derived from the mesenchymal stroma and account for most hormonally functioning tumors. They are rare, making up only about 8% of all ovarian neoplasms.[52,53] Morphologically, tumors recapitulate the appearance of the primitive sex cords and ovarian mesenchyme. Differentiated lesions are recognized as of ovarian type, (granulosa and theca cell tumors) or of testicular type, (Sertoli-Leydig cell tumors). Classification of individual cases is sometimes difficult, however, as some tumors may show varying combinations and degrees of differentiation.

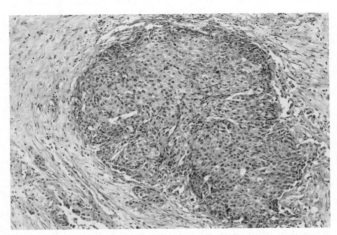

Figure 1–45. Malignant Brenner tumor: irregularly shaped infiltrating nest of mildly atypical transitional cell carcinoma that composed the major portion of the tumor shown in Figure 1–44 (original magnification ×100).

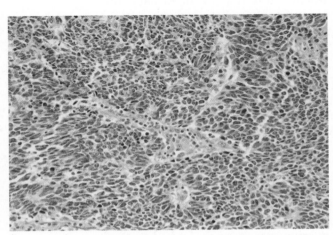

Figure 1–47. Small cell carcinoma, pulmonary type. Nests of anaplastic small tumor cells with elongated nuclei having finely granular chromatin, arranged in nests and rosettes, are identical to small cell carcinoma of the lung (original magnification ×100).

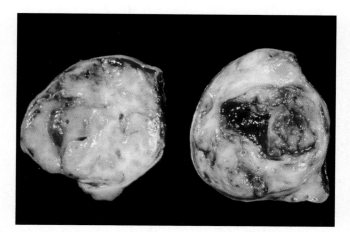

Figure 1–48. Adult granulosa cell tumor. Tumor is well circumscribed and yellow-white, with a focal area of hemorrhage and necrosis.

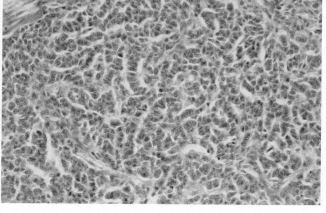

Figure 1–50. Adult granulosa cell tumor, showing a trabecular pattern (original magnification ×100).

Poorly differentiated examples may be impossible to categorize accurately. Granulosa and theca cell tumors are the most common, accounting for 99% of the group.[52]

Granulosa Cell Tumors

Granulosa cell tumors are composed of cells resembling the granulosa cells of the ovarian follicle. They are of two types, adult and juvenile.[3,4,7]

Adult granulosa cell tumors constitute 95% of these tumors.[54–56] The majority of patients are postmenopausal; the tumor is rarely diagnosed in women younger than 30 years. Approximately 75% of cases produce estrogen; 95% are unilateral.

Grossly, tumors may be predominantly solid, cystic, or a combination of these. They are usually encapsulated with a yellow to tan hemorrhagic cut surface (Figure 1–48). Microscopically, granulosa cell tumors may show variable appearances that include a microfollicular pattern, characterized by small follicles that contain eosinophilic material and that resemble the normal graafian follicle (Call-Exner bodies), as well as macrofollicular, diffuse, trabecular, and solid types (Figure 1–49 to 1–53). The background consists of spindled thecoma or fibroma elements. Combinations of microscopic patterns are common.

These tumor cells have pale oval nuclei with characteristic longitudinal grooves and scant cyto-

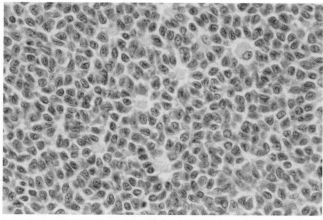

Figure 1–49. Adult granulosa cell tumor, showing a classic microfollicular pattern with clear spaces surrounded by monotonous cells having elongated "coffee bean" grooved nuclei (original magnification ×200).

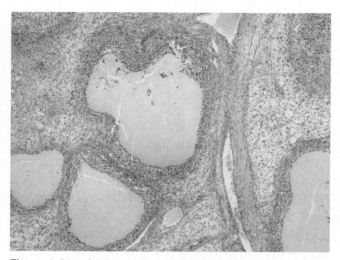

Figure 1–51. Adult granulosa cell tumor, macrofollicular variant (original magnification ×40).

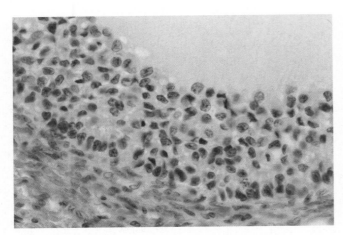

Figure 1–52. Adult granulosa cell tumor, macrofollicular variant. Cells lining the tumor follicles are almost indistinguishable from granulosa cells of the normal graafian follicle (original magnification ×200).

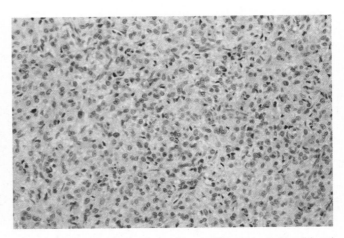

Figure 1–53. Adult granulosa cell tumor. This example is solid and poorly differentiated. Nuclei remain reasonably bland and show occasional nuclear grooves (original magnification ×100).

plasm, which creates a "coffee bean" appearance. Cellular pleomorphism varies. Mitotic figures are rare in well-differentiated tumors but may be frequent in more poorly differentiated examples. Immunohistochemical studies show that most tumors are positive for vimentin, desmoplakin, and smooth-muscle actin. Keratin is positive in one-third to one-half of cases, and S-100 is positive in about half of cases. A high proportion of all stromal tumors, including granulosa cell lesions, stain with the antibody to inhibin, which is very useful in distinguishing these tumors from other types.[57–59] The prognosis is generally favorable. Up to 90% of cases present in stage I. Decreased survival is associated with bilaterality, advanced clinical stage, increased size, tumor rupture, nuclear atypia, lymphatic-space invasion, and mitotic activity.[60–62] Ten-year survival rates range from 60 to 90%.[4] Recurrences may occur decades after treatment, with survival declining to 62% after 20 years.[63]

Juvenile granulosa cell tumor is far less common than the adult type, (5% of the group). It is usually diagnosed before age 30 years. Prepubertal patients often present clinically with isosexual precocity. Tumors are nearly always unilateral and confined to the ovary. Rare cases have been associated with Ollier's disease and Maffucci's syndrome.[64,65] Microscopically, they most commonly have a follicular pattern but may be solid or mixed (Figure 1–54).

In contrast to the adult tumor, the cells of juvenile granulosa cell tumor contain round nuclei without grooves and with abundant eosinophilic cytoplasm. The prognosis for the juvenile form is much better than for the adult type. The vast majority are stage I tumors and are almost always cured.

Fibromas and Thecomas

Fibromas are common ovarian tumors that most often occur in older persons. They are generally unilateral and may be associated with Meigs' syndrome, in which a large tumor (usually > 10 cm) is associated with ascites and unilateral pleural effusion that subside following removal of the tumor. Grossly, the tumors are lobulated and firm and have a pink/white whorled cut surface (Figure 1–55). Microscopically, bland spindled cells are arranged in a storiform or fascicular pattern and are associated with thick bands of collagen.

Thecomas also most frequently occur in postmenopausal women but, unlike fibroma, show estrogenic effects, most commonly postmenopause bleeding. Less than 10% of thecomas are bilateral. Grossly, the cut surface is firm and yellow to white. Microscopically, there are plump spindle cells with ample lipid-rich cytoplasm, little nuclear atypia, and usually few mitoses. Only rare examples of malignant thecoma and fibrosarcoma have been reported.[66] Positive staining with inhibin antibody has been reported for this group.[67]

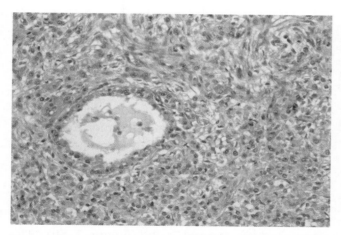

Figure 1–54. Juvenile granulosa cell tumor. Small follicular structures are commonly seen. Tumor nuclei are more rounded and lack the longitudinal grooves seen in adult granulosa cell tumor (original magnification ×100).

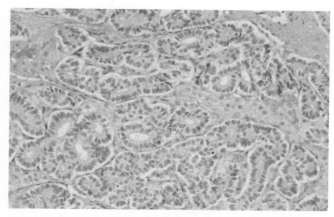

Figure 1–56. Well-differentiated Sertoli-Leydig cell tumor. A uniform proliferation of well-formed open tubules makes up this tumor type. An elongated solid nest of pink Leydig cells is seen near the middle of the picture (original magnification ×100).

Sertoli Cell Tumors

Pure Sertoli cell tumors are extremely rare and almost always benign.[4] Sertoli-Leydig cell tumors are more common but still make up less than 1% of sex cord–stromal tumors and represent only 0.2% of all ovarian neoplasms.[68–70] The average age of the patient at diagnosis is 25 years; less than 5% of cases are bilateral. About one-third of patients experience virilization, and one-half are nonfunctioning.[69] The remaining tumors secrete estrogen or progesterone. About 20% of patients have an elevated serum α-fetoprotein.[71] Tumor size ranges from microscopic to 20 cm. Histologically, tumors may be well differentiated, intermediate, or poorly differentiated (sarcoma-

tous), and this directly relates to survival. Well-differentiated tumors show hollow and solid tubules lined by lipid-rich Sertoli cells accompanied by variable numbers of Leydig cells (Figure 1–56). Mitoses are rare. Intermediate-grade tumors account for half of the tumors and are characterized by solid cords and sheets of more primitive Sertoli cells (Figure 1–57). Poorly differentiated or sarcomatoid tumors show a diffuse spindled cell pattern with numerous mitoses in which it may be difficult to recognize typical Sertoli or Leydig cell elements. Rarely, tumors may contain heterologous elements such as gastrointestinal epithelium, cartilage, and striated muscle or contain formations of cuboidal cells that resemble the rete testis.[72] Prognosis is dependent on stage, occurrence

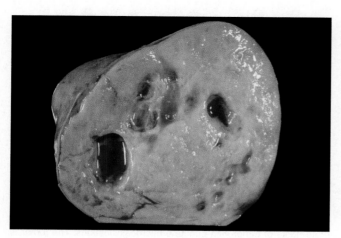

Figure 1–55. Fibroma. Firm yellowish white fibrous tumor shows focal cystic degeneration.

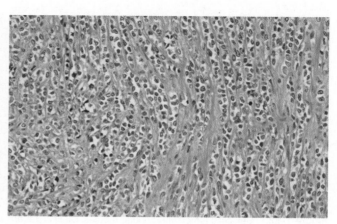

Figure 1–57. Intermediate-grade Sertoli cell tumor composed of elongated nests and cords of immature Sertoli cells (original magnification ×100).

of tumor rupture, and degree of differentiation. In approximately 20% of cases, the tumors are clinically malignant; most of these are poorly differentiated.[69]

Sex Cord Tumor with Annular Tubules

Sex cord tumors with annular tubules combine histologic features of granulosa and Sertoli cell tumors. One-third of cases are associated with Peutz-Jeghers syndrome, in which case the ovarian lesion is often an incidental finding.[73] The remaining cases are sporadic and present clinically with a mass in the pelvis. Adenoma malignum of the cervix has also been described.[74] Grossly, the tumors associated with Peutz-Jeghers syndrome are bilateral, multifocal, frequently calcified, and < 3 cm in diameter. Sporadic cases are usually unilateral large solid tumors. Microscopically, there are simple and complex tubules lined by columnar cells oriented like rosettes around the center, which contains rounded globules of eosinophilic basement membrane–like material (Figure 1–58). Tumors stain positively with inhibin.[75] Occasional cases show areas of granulosa or Sertoli cell tumor. The tumors associated with Peutz-Jeghers syndrome are clinically benign whereas approximately 20% of the sporadic tumors are malignant.

Gonadoblastomas

Gonadoblastomas are mixed germ cell–sex cord tumors that occur exclusively in patients with gonadal dysgenesis. Most patients are under age 15 years and are phenotypically female but possess a Y chromosome (xy gonadal dysgenesis). The tumors may produce steroid hormones, which can cause either virilization or feminization. Although pure gonadoblastoma is a benign tumor, over half of the cases have a malignant germ cell tumor component, most commonly consisting of dysgerminoma.[76,77]

Grossly, gonadoblastomas range from microscopic to large and have abundant calcification. Histologically, there are two cell populations, with dysgerminoma-type germ cells surrounded by Sertoli or granulosa-type stromal cells (Figure 1–59). The prognosis is excellent for cases with superimposed dysgerminoma.

Leydig Cell and Steroid Cell Tumors

Leydig cell and steroid cell tumors are composed entirely of steroid-producing cells of the ovarian stroma. The Leydig cell tumor is almost always benign and is the most common. Most patients are postmenopausal, and 80% of the tumors are associated with virilization.[4,7] Microscopically, large pink cells with crystals of Reinke classify the tumor as a Leydig cell tumor. Steroid cell tumors (not otherwise classified) may show fine cytoplasmic fat vacuoles. Malignancy has been reported in as many as 43% of these tumors and is correlated with large size, necrosis, nuclear atypia, and mitoses.[78]

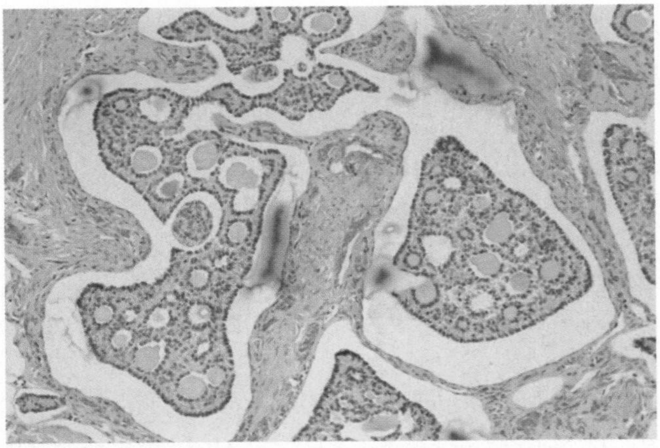

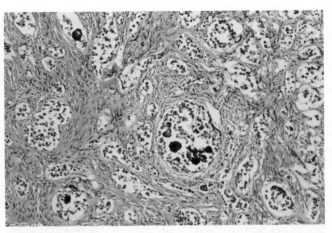

Figure 1–58. Sex cord tumor with annular tubules. Classic pattern shows well-demarcated nests of gonadal stromal cells arranged in a rosettelike fashion around hyalinized eosinophilic material (original magnification ×40)

Figure 1–59. Gonadoblastoma. Characteristic pattern shows discrete nests of tumor with punctate microcalcifications. The tumor is composed of a dual population of germ cells and granulosa-like gonadal stromal elements (original magnification ×40).

GERM CELL TUMORS

Germ cell tumors account for 20 to 30% of all ovarian tumors. Approximately 95% are benign cystic teratomas (dermoid cysts); the majority of the rest are malignant. In Western countries, these tumors make up 1 to 3% of ovarian malignancies. Malignant germ cell tumors are most common in children and young adults. Most are pure (one cell type); however, approximately 10% are mixed-cell types that require thorough histologic sampling to identify. In general, the prognosis of a mixed tumor is related to the most malignant component; choriocarcinoma and embryonal carcinoma are the worst, followed by yolk sac tumor, immature teratoma, and seminoma.[3–5,79]

Dysgerminomas

Dysgerminomas account for about 50% of malignant ovarian germ cell tumors. Over 80% of patients are under the age of 30 years at the time of diagnosis. About 5% of dysgerminomas are associated with gonadoblastoma and testicular feminization syndrome. Rarely, dysgerminoma may have hormonal manifestations and may mimic pregnancy, due to elaboration of β–hCG.[4] Rarely, hypercalcemia may be observed.[80]

Approximately 85% of these tumors are unilateral. Grossly, they may weigh up to 1,000 g and are predominantly solid, tan yellow, and homogenous appearing. Hemorrhage and necrosis are far less prominent than in the other types of germ cell tumors. Microscopically, the tumor is made up of uniform primitive germ cells with glycogen-rich clear or pink cytoplasm and a large round central nucleus with clumped chromatin and one or more prominent nucleoli. Cell membranes are distinct. The tumor is generally arranged in nests separated by bands of fibrous stroma, often containing lymphocytes and epithelioid cell granulomas, which creates a lobulated appearance (Figure 1–60). There is often diffuse infiltration by mature, T lymphocytes (mostly), with or without epithelioid cell granulomas. Approximately 3% of dysgerminomas contain scattered β–hCG–positive syncytiotrophoblasts, which may be associated with increased serum β–hCG.[4,81]

Immunohistochemically, dysgerminomas are characteristically positive for placental-like alkaline phosphatase (PLAP) and vimentin. They are characteristically negative for EMA and CEA but may stain positively with cytokeratins.[82] The prognosis is excellent, with a survival rate of almost 100% for stage I disease.[83]

Yolk Sac Tumors

Yolk sac tumors (endodermal sinus tumors) account for 20% of malignant germ cell tumors. They occur in children and young adults at a mean age of 19 years.[4,5] Patients typically present with a rapidly enlarging abdominal mass and an elevated serum α-fetoprotein level. The tumors are most often unilateral, but in rare cases, there is a dermoid cyst in the opposite ovary. Metastases to peritoneum and retroperitoneal lymph nodes are often present at diagnosis.

Grossly, yolk sac tumors are large, with an average diameter of 15 cm, and show a smooth outer surface. The cut surface is solid and cystic with conspicuous areas of hemorrhage and necrosis (Figure 1–61). Microscopically, there are a wide variety of patterns. The characteristic histologic feature of yolk sac tumors is the Schiller-Duval body. This structure consists of a papillary fibrovascular structure covered by primitive columnar cells within a glandular space, making it reminiscent of a renal glomerulus (Figure 1–62). Another feature of yolk sac tumors is

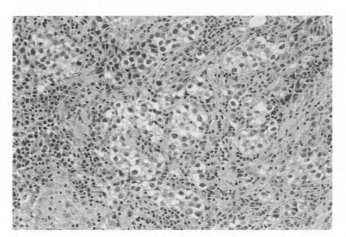

Figure 1–60. Dysgerminoma. Nests of primitive germ cells with clear cytoplasm are surrounded by lymphocyte-rich stroma (original magnification ×100).

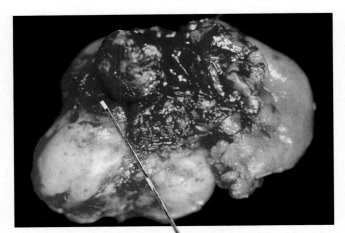

Figure 1–61. Yolk sac tumor, a large solid and cystic tumor with darker areas of hemorrhage and necrosis.

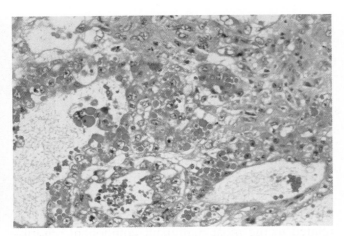

Figure 1–63. Yolk sac tumor. The tumor cells show numerous intracytoplasmic hyaline bodies (original magnification ×40).

the presence of intracytoplasmic eosinophilic, periodic acid–Schiff (PAS)–positive hyalin droplets. These may be positive for α-fetoprotein or may contain α₁-antitrypsin (Figure 1–64). Architecturally, a reticular pattern is seen in most tumors, characterized by communicating epithelial spaces of varying sizes lined by primitive clear glycogen-rich cells associated with loose myxoid stroma (Figure 1–65). Mitotic figures are numerous.

Other histologic variants of yolk sac tumor are rare and include the polyvesicular-vitelline, hepatoid, and glandular types.[84] The hepatoid pattern shows polygonal cells with abundant eosinophilic cytoplasm, resembling liver. The glandular variant contains struc-

tures resembling enteric or endometrial epithelium and may easily be mistaken for müllerian types of adenocarcinoma, particularly clear cell carcinoma.

Immunohistochemical staining of a yolk sac tumor may be helpful in diagnosis, especially when a glandular or hepatoid pattern predominates. Stains for α-fetoprotein, α₁-antitrypsin, and cytokeratin are nearly always positive in the tumor cell cytoplasm. Epithelial membrane antigen is usually negative.[85–87] Stains for CEA are positive in the intestinal-type glands. About one-half of tumors are positive for PLAP. Tumors commonly have retroperitoneal lymph node or peritoneal metastases at presentation; in older series, the prognosis was grave for these patients.

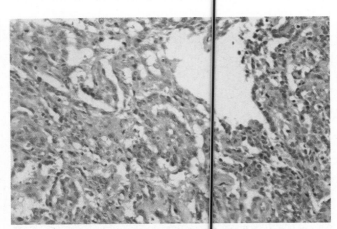

Figure 1–62. Yolk sac tumor. Primitive immature germ cells are arranged in anastamosing cords and irregularly shaped spaces. A Schiller-Duval body is in the center. The characteristic papillary-glomeruloid arrangement of stroma and epithelial cells is seen exclusively in this tumor type (original magnification ×100).

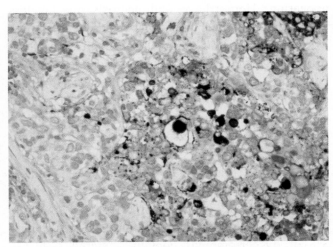

Figure 1–64. Yolk sac tumor. Immunohistochemical stain for α₁-antitrypsin shows positive reaction in hyaline bodies (original magnification ×200).

Modern chemotherapy has greatly improved survival; up to 95% of stage I patients survive their disease, and higher-stage patients have cure rates of up to 50%.[88,89]

Embryonal Carcinoma

Embryonal carcinoma is rare and accounts for only about 3% of malignant germ cell tumors of the ovary. Like yolk sac tumors, it is a malignancy of children and young adults with a median age of 12 years.[90,91] Unlike yolk sac tumors, however, embryonal carcinomas may produce precocious puberty, amenorrhea, and virilizing symptoms. Serum hCG and (less commonly) α-fetoprotein (AFP) levels are high. All reported cases have been unilateral. Patients commonly present in advanced clinical stages, but long-term survival has been reported.[89,92]

Grossly, the tumors are large and predominantly solid, with cysts, necrosis, and hemorrhage. Microscopically, they are composed of large cells with amphophilic cytoplasm and large vesicular nuclei with prominent nucleoli arranged in sheets, glands, and papillary formations (Figure 1–66). Mitotic figures are numerous. Syncytiotrophoblast giant cells are often scattered throughout the tumor.

Immunohistochemical stains for cytokeratin, PLAP, NSE, and alkaline phosphatase are positive. Stains for EMA are generally negative. AFP is expressed in some cases. β-hCG is expressed by the syncytiotrophoblast cells.[4]

Choriocarcinoma

Pure choriocarcinoma of the ovary is extremely rare, being most often part of a mixed germ cell tumor.[93,94] Exceptionally, a metastasis from uterine gestational choriocarcinoma or an ectopic primary tumor in the adnexa is encountered. Pure nongestational choriocarcinomas occur in children and young adults and account for less than 1% of malignant germ cell tumors. Contralateral germ cell tumors have been described.[95]

Grossly, the tumors are solid, with large areas of hemorrhage and necrosis. Microscopically, there is a characteristic mixture of cytotrophoblasts and intermediate trophoblasts with multinucleated syncytiotrophoblasts (Figure 1–67). Gestational and nongestational tumors look identical; their differentiation relies on patient age and the presence of other germ cell elements in the tumor. Chromosome analysis may be required.[96]

Immunohistochemically, the cytotrophoblast expresses cytokeratin, the intermediate trophoblast shows human placental lactogen (HPL) as well as cytokeratin, and the syncytiotrophoblast shows positivity with cytokeratin, β-hCG, and HPL.[97]

Immature Teratoma

Immature teratomas account for 20% of malignant germ cell tumors.[98] They generally occur in children

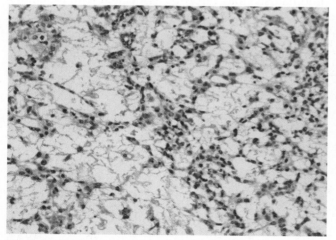

Figure 1–65. Yolk sac tumor. Reticular pattern shows thin strands of primitive germ cells arranged in loose myxoid stroma (original magnification ×100).

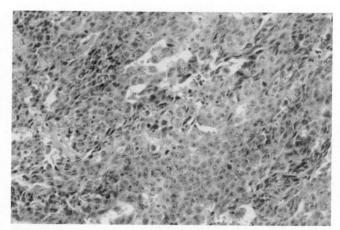

Figure 1–66. Embryonal carcinoma, showing a solid and trabecular arrangement of malignant germ cells having purple cytoplasm, large nuclei with prominent nucleoli, and a filigree pattern of individual cell degeneration. Necrosis is common in this tumor (original magnification ×100).

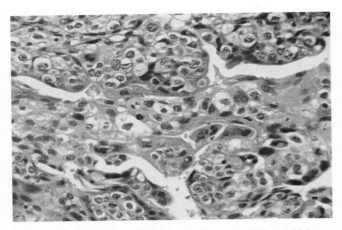

Figure 1–67. Choriocarcinoma. A multinucleated syncitial trophoblast is seen in intimate association with less pleomorphic, monotonous collections of clear cell cytotrophoblast (original magnification ×200).

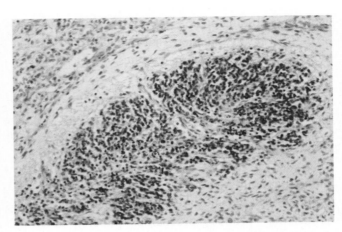

Figure 1–69. Immature teratoma. Higher magnification of Figure 1–68 shows primitive neuroblasts arranged in a loosely nested pattern with incipient pseudorosettes (original magnification ×100).

and adolescents and generally present as a painful abdominal mass. Occasionally, tumors occur in older women.[99] Over 50% of patients have an elevated serum AFP level at diagnosis.

Grossly, the tumors are large. The cut section shows predominantly solid gray-tan soft tissue with necrotic cystic areas. In about 25% of cases, there is a grossly evident dermoid cyst component. Microscopically, immature teratomas are composed of mature and immature tissues representative of all three germ layers. Grading is based predominantly on the amount of immature neural tissue present[98,100] (Figures 1–68, 1–69, and 1–70).

Grade I tumors consist mostly of mature tissues, and the immature neural component of the tumor may not exceed one high-power field per slide. Grade II tumors have immature neural tissue not exceeding four high-power fields per slide, and grade III tumors are predominantly immature, with primitive neural elements making up greater than four high-power fields per slide. This grading scheme might appear abitrary, but it has been demonstrated to have clinical relevance.[101] Over 90% of patients treated currently may be expected to have a long-term remission, even with disseminated tumor.[102,103]

Immunohistochemical stains for S-100 protein and glial fibrillary acid protein can be useful in identifying both immature and mature neural tissue. Peritoneal and lymph node implants of mature glial tissue (gliomatosis) may rarely be associated with immature

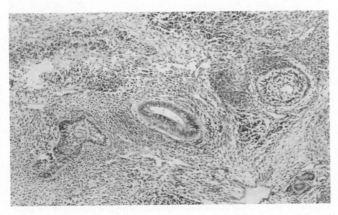

Figure 1–68. Immature teratoma. Immature-fetal type solid and glandular epithelium is seen in loose mesenchymal stroma. Areas with small dark cells represent primitive neural differentiation (original magnification ×40).

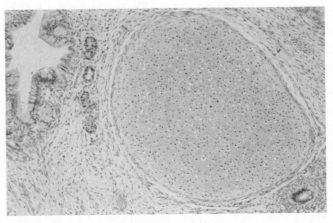

Figure 1–70. Immature teratoma (same tumor as in Figures 1–68 and 1–69). An area of fetal cartilage is shown (original magnification ×40).

teratomas. Such glial implants are benign as long as they are composed entirely of mature tissue.

Carcinoma Arising in Mature Teratomas (Dermoid Cyst)

Mature teratomas make up 20 to 30% of all ovarian tumors. Grossly, the majority of mature teratomas show multiple cysts that contain sebaceous material, hair, and sometimes teeth. Microscopically, only mature tissues from all three germ layers are represented.

In approximately 1% of mature teratomas, however, there is malignant transformation. Most commonly, this is squamous cell carcinoma, adenocarcinoma, or carcinoid tumor, but other malignancies such as malignant melanoma have been described.[104–106]

Carcinoid Tumor

Primary carcinoid tumors of the ovary are unilateral and occur most commonly in peri- and postmenopausal women.[107–109] They can be divided into pure carcinoid tumors, strumal carcinoids, and mucinous carcinoids. Approximately one-third of pure carcinoid tumors are associated with carcinoid syndrome.[107]

Grossly, the tumors may be solid or may appear as a solid component of a cystic teratoma or mucinous tumor. Microscopically, the pure carcinoid tumor resembles carcinoids found in other locations and shows an insular, solid, trabecular, or combination growth pattern[107,109] (Figure 1–71). Immunohistochemistry shows positive staining with neuroendocrine markers such as chromogranin and synaptophysin (Figure 1–72). Dense core granules are present on ultrastructural examination. Strumal carcinoid tumors show a mixture of carcinoid tumor and thyroid tissue and may cause hyperthyroidism.[110,111] Mucinous carcinoid tumors are the least frequent and contain goblet cells and argyrophillic cells similarly to mucinous carcinoid tumors of the appendix.[112] Metastases to the ovary from an appendiceal or other primary site must be considered in the differential diagnosis, especially when carcinoid tumor is bilateral. The prognosis of most primary tumors is excellent. Only rare patients have died as the result of the tumor. Mucinous carcinoids are the most aggressive type, similar to their appendeceal counterparts.[113]

In this chapter, we have attempted to provide a pictorial overview of the more common malignant tumors of the ovary. Most of the other entities that have not been illustrated are so rare that we ourselves have not seen examples of them at our institutions.

For a complete treatment of ovarian tumors, the reader is referred to the chapters and texts listed in the References.

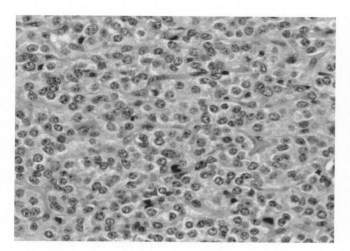

Figure 1–71. Carcinoid tumor, showing a solid proliferation of regular round cells having uniform rounded nuclei, granular cytoplasm, and fine fibrovascular stroma (original magnification ×100).

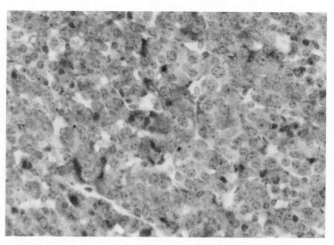

Figure 1–72. Carcinoid tumor shows strong granular cytoplasmic staining with chromogranin (original magnification ×200).

REFERENCES

1. Serov SF, Scully RE, Sobin LH. 1973 histological typing of ovarian tumors. International histological classification of tumors, No.9. Geneva: World Health Organization;

2. Seidman JD, Russell P, Kurman RJ. Surface epithelial-stromal tumors of the ovary. In: Kurman RJ, editor. Blaustein's pathology of the female genital tract. 4th ed. New York: Springer-Verlag; 2002. p. 791–904.

3. Russell P, Farnsworth A. Surgical pathology of the ovaries. 2nd ed. New York: Churchill Livingston; 1997.

4. Scully RE, Clement PE, Young RH. In: Rosai J, Sobin LH, editors. Atlas of tumor pathology: tumors of the ovary, maldeveloped gonads, fallopian tube and broad ligament. Washington (DC): Armed Forces Institute of Pathology, 1998.

5. Talerman A. Germ cell tumors of the ovary. In: Kurman RJ, editor. Blaustein's pathology of the female genital tract. 4th ed. New York: Springer-Verlag; 2002. p. 967–1033.

6. Talerman A. Nonspecific tumors of the ovary, including mesenchymal tumors and malignant lymphoma. In: Kurman RJ, editor. Blaustein's pathology of the female genital tract. 4th ed. New York: Springer-Verlag; 2002. p. 1035–61.

7. Young RH, Scully RE. Sex cord-stromal, steroid cell, and other ovarian tumors with endocrine, paracrine and paraneoplastic manifestations. In: Kurman RJ, editor. Blaustein's pathology of the female genital tract. 4th ed. New York: Springer-Verlag; 2002. p. 905–66.

8. Zinsser KR, Wheeler JE. Endosalpingiosis in the omentum: a study of autopsy and surgical material. Am J Surg Pathol 1982;6:109–17.

9. Pettersson F. Annual report of the results of treatment in gynecological cancer. Stockholm: International Federation of Gynecology and Obstetrics; 1991.

10. Bell DA, Scully RE. Ovarian serous borderline tumors with stromal microinvasion: a report of 21 cases. Hum Pathol 1990;21:397–403.

11. Kennedy AW, Hart WR. Ovarian papillary serous tumors of low malignant potential, (serous borderline tumors). A long-term follow-up study including patients with microinvasion, lymph node metastasis, and transformation to invasive serous carcinoma. Cancer 1996;78:278–86.

12. Nayer R, Siriaunkgul S, Robbins KM, et al. Microinvasion in low malignant potential tumors of the ovary. Hum Pathol 1996;27:521–7.

13. Tavassoli FA. Serous tumors of low malignant potential with early stromal invasion, (serous LMP with microinvasion). Mod Pathol 1988;1:407–14.

14. Bell DA, Weinstock MA, Scully RE. Peritoneal implants of ovarian serous borderline tumors. Histologic features and prognosis. Cancer 1988;62:2212–22.

15. Eichhorn JH, Bell DA, Young RH, et al. Ovarian serous borderline tumors with micropapillary and cribiform patterns. A study of 40 cases and comparison with 44 cases without these patterns. Am J Surg Pathol 1999;23:397–409.

16. Berks RT, Sherman ME, Kurman RJ. Micropapillary serous carcinoma of the ovary. Am J Surg Pathol 1996;20:1319–30.

17. Seidman JD, Kurman RJ. Subclassification of serous borderline tumors of the ovary into benign and malignant types. A clinicopathologic study of 65 advanced stage cases. Am J Surg Pathol 1996;20:1331–45.

18. Barnhill DR, Kurman RJ, Brady MF, et al. The behavior of stage I ovarian serous tumors of low malignant potential. A Gynecologic Oncology Group study. Trans Am Gynecol Obstet Soc 1995;12:35–42.

19. Rutgers JL, Scully RE. Ovarian mullerian mucinous papillary cystadenoma of borderline malignancy: a clinicopathologic analysis. Cancer 1988;61:340–8.

20. Lee KR, Scully RE. Mucinous tumors of the ovary. A clinicopathologic study of 196 borderline tumors (of intestinal type) and carcinomas, including an evaluation of 11 cases with "pseudomyxoma peritonei." Am J Surg Pathol 2000; 24:1447–64.

21. Hart WR, Norris HJ. Borderline and malignant mucinous tumors of the ovary: histologic criteria and clinical behavior. Cancer 1973;31:1031–45.

22. Hoerl HD, Hart WR. Primary ovarian mucinous cystadenocarcinomas. A clinicopathologic study of 49 cases with long-term follow-up. Am J Surg Pathol 1998;22:1449–62.

23. Riopel MA, Ronnette BM, Kurman RJ. Evaluation of diagnostic criteria and behavior of ovarian intestinal-type mucinous tumors. Am J Surg Pathol 1999;23:617–35.

24. Rodriguez IM, Prat J. Mucinous tumors of the ovary. A clinicopathologic analysis of 75 borderline tumors (of intestinal type) and carcinomas. Am J Surg Pathol 2002;26:139–52.

25. Ronnett BM, Kurman RJ, Zahn CM, et al. Pseudomyxoma peritonei in women: a clinicopathologic analysis of 30 cases with emphasis on site of origin, prognosis, and relationship to ovarian mucinous tumors of low malignant potential. Hum Pathol 1995;26:509–24.

26. Cuatrecasas M, Matias-Guiu X, Prat J. Synchronous mucinous tumors of the appendix and the ovary associated with pseudomyxoma peritonei. A clinicopathologic study of six cases with comparative analysis of C-Ki-ras mutations. Am J Surg Pathol 1996;20:739–46.

27. Szych C, Staebler A, Connolly DC, et al. Molecular genetic evidence supporting the clonality and appendiceal origin of pseudomyxoma peritonei in women. Am J Surg Pathol 1999;154:1849–55.

28. Prat J, Scully RE. Sarcomas in ovarian mucinous tumors. A report of two cases. Cancer 1979;44:1327–31.

29. Prat J, Scully RE. Ovarian mucinous tumors with sarcoma-like mural nodules. A report of seven cases. Cancer 1979; 44:1332–44.

30. Prat J, Young RH, Scully RE. Ovarian mucinous tumor with foci of anaplastic carcinoma. Cancer 1982;50:300–4.

31. Ordi J, Schammel DP, Rasekh L, et al. Sertoliform endometrioid carcinomas of the ovary: a clinicopathologic and immunohistochemical study of 13 cases. Mod Pathol 1999;12:933–40.

32. Roth LM, Liban E, Czernobilsky B. Ovarian endometrioid tumors mimicking Sertoli and Sertoli-Leydig cell tumors: sertoliform variant of endometrioid carcinoma. Cancer 1982;50:1322–31.

33. Young RH, Prat J, Scully RE. Ovarian endometrioid carcinomas resembling sex cord stromal tumors. A clinicopathologic analysis of 13 cases. Am J Surg Pathol 1982;6:513–22.

34. Czernobilsky B, Silverman BB, Mikuta JJ. Endometrioid carcinoma of the ovary: a clinicopathologic study of 75 cases. Cancer 1970;26:1141–52.

35. Shenson DL, Gallion HH, Powell DE, et al. Loss of heterozygosity and genomic instability in synchronous

endometrioid tumors of the ovary and endometrium. Cancer 1995;76:650–7.

36. Czernobilsky B, Silverman BB, Enterline HT. Clear cell carcinoma of the ovary. A clinicopathologic analysis of pure and mixed forms and comparison with endometrioid carcinoma. Cancer 1970;25:762–72.

37. Scully RE, Barlow JF. "Mesonephroma" of ovary. Tumor of mullerian nature related to endomterioid carcinoma. Cancer 1967;20:1405–16.

38. Crozier MA, Copeland LJ, Silva EF, et al. Clear cell carcinoma of the ovary: a study of 59 cases. Gynecol Oncol 1989;35:199–203.

39. Kennedy AW, Biscotti CV, Hart WR, et al. Ovarian clear cell adenocarcinoma. Gynecol Oncol 1989;32:342–9.

40. Norris HJ, Robinowitz M. Ovarian adenocarcinoma of mesonephric type. Cancer 1971;28:1074–81.

41. Hanjani P, Petersson RO, Lipton SE, et al. Malignant mixed mesodermal tumors and carcinosarcomas of the ovary: report of eight cases and review of the literature. Obstet Gynecol Surv 1983;38:537–45.

42. Morrow CP, d'Ablaing G, Brady LN, et al. A clinical and pathologic study of 30 cases of malignant mixed mullerian epithelial and mesenchymal ovarian tumors: a Gynecologic Oncology Group study. Gynecol Obstet 1984;18:278–92.

43. Terada KY, Johnson TL, Hopkins M, et al. Clinicopathologic features of ovarian mixed mesodermal tumors and carcinosarcomas. Gynecol Oncol 1989;32:228–32.

44. Soslow RA, Rouse RV, Hendrickson MR, et al. Transitional cell neoplasms of the ovary and urinary bladder: a comparative immunohistochemical analysis. Int J Gynecol Pathol 1996;15:257–65.

45. Hallgrimsson J, Scully RE. Borderline and malignant Brenner tumors of the ovary. A report of 15 cases. Acta Path Microbiol Scand (A) 1972;80 suppl 233:56–66.

46. Miles PA, Norris HJ. Proliferative and malignant Brenner tumors of the ovary. Cancer 1972;30:174–86.

47. Roth LM, Gersell DJ, Ulbright TM. Ovarian Brenner tumors and transitional cell carcinoma: recent developments. Int J Gynecol Pathol 1993;12:128–33.

48. Dickerson GR, Kline IW, Scully RE. Small cell carcinoma of the ovary with hypercalcemia: a report of eleven cases. Cancer 1982;49:188–97.

49. Matias-Guiu X, Prat J, Young RH, et al. Human parathyroid hormone-related protein in ovarian small cell carcinoma. An immunohistochemical study. Cancer 1994;73:1878–81.

50. Young RH, Oliva E, Scully RE. Small cell carcinoma of the ovary, hypercalcemic type. A clinicopathologic analysis of 150 cases. Am J Surg Pathol 1994;18:1102–16.

51. Eichhorn JH, Young RH, Scully RE. Primary ovarian small cell carcinoma of pulmonary type. A clinicopathologic, immunohistologic, and flow cytometric analysis of 11 cases. Am J Surg Pathol 1992;16:926–38.

52. Gee DC, Russell P. The pathological assessment of ovarian neoplasms. IV. The sex cord stromal tumors. Pathology 1981;13:235–55.

53. Young RH, Scully RE. Ovarian sex cord-stromal tumors. Problems in differential diagnosis. Pathol Annu 1988;23 (Pt I):237–66.

54. Evans AT, Gaffey TA, Malkasian GD Jr, et al. Clinicopathologic reivew of 118 granulosa and 82 theca cell tumors. Obstet Gynecol 1980;55:231–7.

55. Fox H, Agrawal K, Langley FA. A clinicopathological study of 92 cases of granulosa cell tumor of the ovary with special reference to the factors influencing prognosis. Cancer 1975;35:231–41.

56. Norris HT, Taylor HB. Prognosis of granulosa-theca tumors of the ovary. Cancer 1968;21:255–63.

57. Gebhart JB, Roche PC, Keeney GL, et al. Assessment of inhibin and p53 in granulosa cell tumors of the ovary. Gynecol Oncol 2000;77:232–6.

58. Hildebrandt RH, Rouse RV, Longacre TA. Value of inhibin in the identification of granulosa cell tumors of the ovary. Hum Pathol 1997;28:1387–95.

59. Rishi M, Howard LN, Bratthauer GL, et al. Use of monoclonal antibody against human inhibin as a marker for sex cord-stromal tumors of the ovary. Am J Surg Pathol 1997;21:583–9.

60. Bjorkholm E, Silversward C. Prognostic factors in granulosa cell tumors. Gynecol Oncol 1981;11:261–74.

61. Fujimoto T, Sakuragi N, Okuyama K, et al. Histopathological prognostic factors of adult granulosa cell tumors of the ovary. Acta Obstet Gynecol Scand 2001;80:1069–74.

62. Stenwig JC, Hazekamp JT, Beecham JB. Granulosa cell tumors of the ovary. A clinicopathological study of 118 cases with long term follow-up. Gynecol Oncol 1979;7:136–52.

63. Lauszus FF, Peterson AC, Greisen J, et al. Granulosa cell tumor of the ovary: a population-based study of 37 women with stage I disease. Gynecol Oncol 2001;81:456–60.

64. Calaminus G, Wessalowski R, Harms D, et al. Juvenile granulosa cell tumors of the ovary in children and adolescents: results from 33 patients registered in a prospective cooperative study. Gynecol Oncol 1997;65:447–52.

65. Young RH, Dickersin GR, Scully RE. Juvenile granulosa cell tumor of the ovary. A clinicopathologic analysis of 125 cases. Am J Surg Pathol 1984;8:575–96.

66. Azoury RS, Woodruff JD. Primary ovarian sarcomas. Report of 43 cases form the Emil Novak Ovarian Tumor Registry. Obstet Gynecol 1971;37:920–41.

67. McCluggage WG, Sloan JM, Boyle DD, et al. Malignant fibrothecomatous tumor of the ovary: diagnostic value of anti-inhibin antibody. J Clin Pathol 1998;51:868–71.

68. Roth LM, Anderson MC, Govan ADT, et al. Sertoli-Leydig cell tumors: a clinicopathologic study of 34 cases. Cancer 1981;48:187–97.

69. Young RH, Scully RE. Sertoli-Leydig cell tumors. A clinicopathologic analysis of 207 cases. Am J Surg Pathol 1985;9:543–69.

70. Zaloudek C, Norris HJ. Sertoli-Leydig cell tumors of the ovary. A clinicopathologic study of 64 intermediate and poorly differentiated neoplasms. Am J Surg Pathol 1984;8:405–18.

71. Gagnon S, Tetri B, Silva EG, et al. Frequency of alpha-fetoprotein production by Sertoli-Leydig cell tumors of the ovary: an immunohistochemical study of 8 cases. Mod Pathol 1989;2:63–7.

72. Young RH. Sertoli-Leydig cell tumors of the ovary: review and emphasis on historical aspects and unusual variants. Int J Gynecol Pathol 1993;12:141–7.

73. Scully RE. Sex cord tumor with annular tubules. A distinctive ovarian tumor of the Peutz-Jeghers syndrome. Cancer 1970;25:1107–21.

74. Young RH, Welch WR, Dickersin GR, et al. Ovarian sex cord

tumor with annular tubules: review of 74 cases including 27 with Peutz-Jeghers syndrome and 4 with adenoma malignum of the cervix. Cancer 1982;50:1384–402.

75. Stewart CJ, Jeffers MD, Kennedy A. Diagnostic value of inhibin immunoactivity in ovarian gonadal stromal tumors and their histological mimics. Histopathology 1997;31:67–74.

76. Hart WR, Burkons DM. Germ cell neoplasms arising in gonadoblastomas. Cancer 1979;43:669–78.

77. Scully RE. Gonadoblastoma. A review of 74 cases. Cancer 1970;25:1340–56.

78. Hayes MC, Scully RE. Ovarian steroid cell tumor (not otherwise specified): a clinicopathological analysis of 63 cases. Am J Surg Pathol 1987;11:835–45.

79. Kurman RJ, Norris HJ. Malignant germ cell tumors of the ovary: a clinical and pathologic analysis of 30 cases. Obstet Gynecol 1976;48:579–89.

80. Fleishhacker DS, Young RH. Dysgerminoma of the ovary associated with hypercalcemia. Gynecol Oncol 1994;52:87–90.

81. Bjorkholm E, Lundell M, Gyftodimos A, et al. Dysgerminoma. Radiumhemmet series 1929–1984. Cancer 1990;65:38–44.

82. Lifschitz-Mercer B, Walt H, Kushner I, et al. Differentiation potential of ovarian dysgerminoma. An immunohistochemical study of 15 cases. Hum Pathol 1995;26:62–6.

83. Ayhan A, Bildirici I, Gunala S, et al. Pure dysgerminoma of the ovary: a review of 45 well staged cases. Eur J Gynaecol Oncol 2000;21:98–101.

84. Young RH. New and unusual aspects of ovarian germ cell tumors. Am J Surg Pathol 1993;17:1210–24.

85. Kurman RJ, Norris HJ. Endodermal sinus tumor of the ovary: a clinical and pathologic analysis of 71 cases. Cancer 1976;38:2402–19.

86. Miettinen M, Waklstrom T, Virtanen I, et al. Cellular differentiation in ovarian sex cord-stromal and germ cell tumors studied with antibodies to intermediate filament proteins. Am J Surg Pathol 1985;9:640–51.

87. Neihans GA, Manivel JC, Copland GT, et al. Immunohistochemistry of germ cell and trophoblastic neoplasms. Cancer 1988;62:1113–23.

88. Kawai M, Kano T, Furuhashi Y, et al. Prognostic factors in yolk sac tumors of the ovary. A clinicopathologic analysis of 29 cases. Cancer 1991;67:184–92.

89. Nawa A, Obata N, Kikkawa M, et al. Prognostic factors of patients with yolk sac tumors of the ovary. Am J Obstet Gynecol 2001;184:1182–8.

90. Kurman RJ, Norris HJ. Embryonal carcinoma of the ovary: a clinicopathologic entity distinct from endodermal sinus tumor resembling embryonal carcinoma of the adult testis. Cancer 1976;38:2420–33.

91. Langley FA, Govan AD, Anderson MC, et al. Yolk sac and allied tumours of the ovary. Histopathology 1981;5:389–401.

92. Veda G, Abe Y, Yoshida M, et al. Embryonal carcinoma of the ovary: a six year survival. Int J Gynaecol Obstet 1990;31:287–92.

93. Goswami D, Sharma K, Zutshi V, et al. Nongestational pure ovarian choriocarcinoma with contralateral teratoma. Gynecol Oncol 2001;80:262–6.

94. Simsek T, Trak B, Tunc M, et al. Primary pure choriocarcinoma of the ovary in reproductive ages: a case report. Eur J Gynaecol Oncol 1998; 19:284–6.

95. Davis JR, Surgit EA, Garay J, et al. Sex assignment in gestational trophoblastic neoplasia. Am J Obstet Gynecol 1984;148:722–5.

96. Manivel JC, Neihans G, Wick MR, et al. Intermediate trophoblast in germ cell neoplasms. Am J Surg Pathol 1987;11:695–701.

97. Katsube Y, Berg JW, Silverberg SG. Epidemiologic pathology of ovarian tumors: a histopathologic review of primary ovarian neoplasms diagnosed in the Denver standard metropolitan statistical area, 1 July–December 1969 and 1 July–31 December 1979. Int J Gynecol Pathol 1982;1:3–16.

98. Doss BJ, Jacques SM, Qureshi F, et al. Immature teratomas of the genital tract in older women. Gynecol Oncol 1999;73:433–8.

99. Norris HJ, Zirkin HJ, Bensen WL. Immature teratoma of the ovary: a clinical and pathologic study of 58 cases. Cancer 1976;37:2359–72.

100. O'Conner DM, Norris HJ. The influence of grade on the outcome of stage I immature (malignant) teratoma and the reproducibility of grading. Int J Gynecol Pathol 1994;13:283–9.

101. Kojs Z, Urbanski K, Mitus J, et al. Pure immature teratoma of the ovary: analysis of 22 cases. Eur J Gynaecol Oncol 1997;18:534–6.

102. Baranzelli MC, Bouffat E, Quintana E, et al. Non-seminomatous ovarian germ cell tumors in children. Eur J Cancer 2000;36:376–83.

103. Bonazzi C, Peccatori F, Colombo N, et al. Pure ovarian immature teratoma, a unique and curable disease: 10 years' experience of 32 prospectively treated patients. Obstet Gynecol 1994;84:598–604.

104. Davis GL. Malignant melanoma arising in mature ovarian cystic teratoma (dermoid cyst). Report of 2 cases and literature analysis. Int J Gynecol Pathol 1996;15:356–62.

105. Peterson WF. Malignant degeneration of benign cystic teratomas of the ovary. A collective review of the literature. Obstet Gynecol Surv 1957;12:793–830.

106. Pins MR, Young RH, Daly WJ, et al. Primary squamous cell carcinoma of the ovary. Report of 37 cases. Am J Surg Pathol 1996;20:823–33.

107. Robboy SJ, Norris HJ, Scully RE. Insular carcinoid primary in the ovary. A clinicopathologic analysis of 48 cases. Cancer 1975;36:404–18.

108. Robboy SJ, Scully RE, Norris HJ. Carcinoid metastatic to the ovary: a clinicopathologic analysis of 35 cases. Cancer 1974;33:798–811.

109. Robboy SJ, Scully RE, Norris HJ. Primary trabecular carcinoid of the ovary. Obstet Gynecol 1977;19:202–7.

110. Szyfelbein WM, Young RH, Scully RE. Cystic struma ovarii. A frequently unrecognized tumor. A report of 20 cases. Am J Surg Pathol 1994;18:785–8.

111. Szyfelbein WM, Young RH, Scully RE. Struma ovarii simulating ovarian tumors of other types. A report of 30 cases. Am J Surg Pathol 1995;19:21–9.

112. Alenghat E, Okagaki T, Talerman A. Primary mucinous carcinoid tumor of the ovary. Cancer 1986;58:777–83.

113. Baker PM, Oliva E, Young RH, et al. Ovarian mucinous carcinoids, including some with a carcinomatous component: a report of 17 cases. Am J Surg Pathol 2001;25:557–68.

2

Biology

THOMAS C. HAMILTON, PhD
XIANGXI XU, PhD
CHRISTOS PATRIOTIS, PhD
HERNANDO SALAZAR, MD, MPH

Although cancers may arise from most of the many cell types of the ovary, the vast majority are believed to originate from the cells covering the ovarian surface (Figure 2–1). Sir Spencer Wells suspected this possibility as early as 1872. Since then, much observational data in support of this early notion have accumulated, and recently, experimental support has been generated. As such, efforts have been made over the years to understand the biology of the surface epithelium in the hope that such information might explain the propensity of these rela-

tively in numerous ovarian cells to undergo malignant transformation.

HOW OVARIAN CANCER DEVELOPS

The first hypothesis as to why the surface epithelium might be predisposed to malignant transformation was put forward by Fathalla in 1971.[1] This pathologist speculated that the process was somehow related to the rupture of the surface epithelium that happens when ovulation occurs. He based this theory on sev-

HISTOGENESIS OF OVARIAN NEOPLASMS

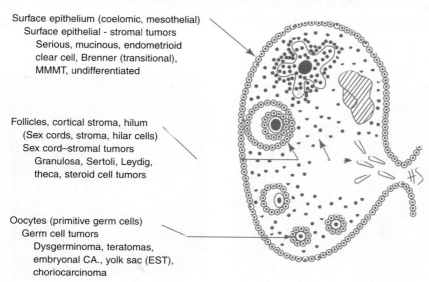

Surface epithelium (coelomic, mesothelial)
Surface epithelial - stromal tumors
Serious, mucinous, endometrioid
clear cell, Brenner (transitional),
MMMT, undifferentiated

Follicles, cortical stroma, hilum
(Sex cords, stroma, hilar cells)
Sex cord–stromal tumors
Granulosa, Sertoli, Leydig,
theca, steroid cell tumors

Oocytes (primitive germ cells)
Germ cell tumors
Dysgerminoma, teratomas,
embryonal CA., yolk sac (EST),
choriocarcinoma

Figure 2–1. Genesis of human ovarian cancer. (CA = cancer; EST = Embryonal yolk sac; MMMT = malignant mixed müllerian tumor.)

27

eral lines of evidence that mainly focused on epidemiologic studies that associated nulliparity (ie, frequent ovulations) with an increased risk of ovarian cancer. He also cited data that purported a high frequency of peritoneal carcinomatosis believed to be of ovarian origin in chickens forced to incessantly ovulate by the elimination of seasonal anovulatory rest.[2,3] The idea was that there must be something about the repetitious requirement of the surface epithelial cells to divide to repair the ovulatory wound that contributes to transformation. Of course, it is now known that the process of deoxyribonucleic acid (DNA) replication is mutagenic.[4] Before considering in more detail theories about why ovulation drives ovarian oncogenesis and why its inhibition is preventive, it is helpful to recall what is known about the normal surface epithelium and its transformed counterpart. This is especially true with regard to information about how the growth of the surface epithelium is regulated because repetitious growth of these cells figures so highly in ideas about how ovarian cancer arises.

The ovarian surface epithelial cells are modified peritoneal mesothelial cells and are contiguous with those cells that line the peritoneal cavity. It is of interest that these epithelial cells, even in their normal surface context, are often more differentiated than the peritoneal mesothelium (Figure 2–2). This may well be due to their proximity to the hormone and growth factor–producing components of the ovary for which they have receptors (see below) and is clearly evident when they become entrapped in the ovarian cortex

and form inclusion cysts[5,6] (Figure 2–3). The ovarian surface epithelium is related to other gynecologic tissues as well as the peritoneal mesothelium since these cells originate from the coelomic epithelium that overlies the gonadal ridge in the embryo.[7] Hence, they are of mesodermal origin and are developmentally closely related to the underlying stromal fibroblasts. As suggested above, the coelomic epithelium also gives rise to the müllerian ducts, which are the primordia for the epithelia of the fallopian tube, uterus, and endocervix. Thus, the embryonic coelomic epithelium in the urogenital region is competent to develop along many different pathways. The reexpression of this capacity is often apparent when the surface epithelium forms inclusion cysts in the ovarian cortex (see Figure 2–3) and is especially apparent when these cells become malignant (Figure 2–4). The tumors consisting of these malignant cells frequently differentiate along the lines of müllerian duct derivatives such that their histologic features are reminiscent of the appearance and epithelial cells of the endocervix (in the case of mucinous tumors), the endometrium (in the case of endometrioid tumors), and the fallopian tube (in the case of the most common serous tumors)[8,9] (see Figure 2–1).

OVARIAN SURFACE EPITHELIUM BIOLOGY AND GROWTH REGULATION

Numerous investigators have examined the surface epithelium at the histologic and ultrastructural level

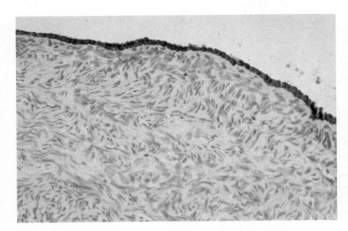

Figure 2–2. Micrograph of human ovary. Note the keratin staining of the cuboidal ovarian surface epithelium.

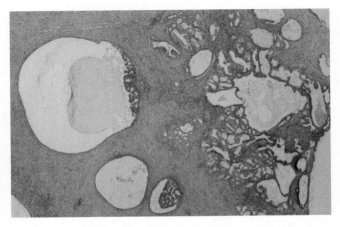

Figure 2–3. Hematoxylin and eosin–stained section of cancer-prone human ovary. Note the complex inclusion cysts.

and have described clear circumstantial evidence that these cells are under some form of autocrine, paracrine, and/or endocrine regulation. A series of detailed studies conducted in rabbits examined the appearance of the surface epithelium in the context of ovulation.[10] These studies provided a very strong indication that, in the rabbit at least, the surface epithelium actively participates in ovulation, with changes suggesting that the cells secrete proteolytic enzymes from their basal surface and aid in the breakdown of the tunica albuginea and in follicular rupture. Hence, it is logical to speculate that dysregulation of this process may be an early component of ovarian oncogenesis.[11–13] Several other investigators have performed less detailed studies in other species,[14] and these generally support studies in the rabbit. What is apparent is that the surface epithelium must be under paracrine or endocrine control in order for it to coordinately participate in the ovulatory process. Additional studies in the rabbit clearly support the notion that the rabbit surface epithelium is responsive to hormones. For example, it has been shown that chronic treatment of rabbits with estrogen or gonadotropins results in marked proliferation of the surface epithelium, which develops into complex papillary structures.[15] In summary, these data support the idea that the surface epithelium is responsive to paracrine and/or endocrine factors.

Some of the first direct evidence that the surface epithelium and its transformed counterpart had the capacity to respond to endocrine influences came from studies on ovarian tumors. This work showed that the tumors had receptors for estrogens, progestagens, and androgens.[16,17] Shortly thereafter, the presence of estrogen receptors was reported in the normal surface epithelium of the rat,[18,19] and more recently, these receptors were found in these cells of primates, including women.[20–24] This latter information is of academic interest since it infers that the presence of receptors in tumors is the result of the retention of a characteristic of their normal progenitor rather than a change associated with transformation. With regard to end effects of estrogens in ovarian tumor cells, it is apparent, based on work in cell lines, that the estrogen receptors are functional in some cases. Data indicate that the classic end effect of progesterone receptor induction occurs[25] and that the hormone is an extremely potent mitogen in a small subset of human

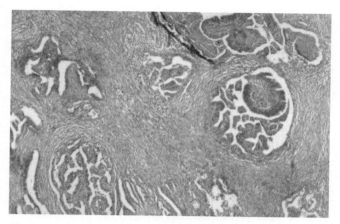

Figure 2–4. Hematoxylin and eosin–stained section from an invasive papillary serous cystadenocarcinoma of the ovary.

ovarian cancer cell lines.[26] However, there is some controversy as to whether the normal surface epithelium of humans can directly respond to estrogen, based on one recent report.[27] If, indeed, the normal surface epithelium of the human ovary is not responsive (in contrast to ovarian tumors), it would suggest that the pathways of estrogen action downstream of receptor presence become activated as part of the transformation process.

Both the peptide growth factors and the gonadotropins have been studied to some extent in the context of ovarian cancer cells and their normal progenitors. Substantial data are available on peptide growth factors, but it has only recently been shown that the surface epithelium has receptors for follicle-stimulating hormone (FSH).[28] There are, however, no conclusive studies on the effect of the interaction of FSH with its receptor in this cell type. In the case of peptide growth factors, extensive studies have investigated the role of epidermal growth factor (EGF) receptor signaling in both normal and malignant ovarian surface epithelial cells.[29]

Peptide growth factors, including EGF/transforming growth factor-α (TGF-α), are ubiquitous proteins that stimulate the proliferation, differentiation, and/or migration of a variety of cell types by binding to specific membrane receptors.[30] Unlike peptide hormones such as gonadotropins (luteinizing hormone [LH] FSH), which are synthesized by well-defined cells within specific glands and released into the circulation, peptide growth factors are produced by a variety of cells and act locally in the body via autocrine or paracrine mechanisms. Treatment of EGF/TGF-α–responsive cells with the growth factor results in the binding of the ligand to the EGF receptor (EGFR). This receptor-ligand interaction results in the variable activation of at least two signal transduction cascades (ie, Ras (or Ras-related)/MEK and PI3 kinase pathways) (Figure 2–5). This initiates a process that causes quiescent cells to advance into the first gap phase (G_1) of the cell cycle, traverse the G_1 phase, and then become committed to DNA synthesis or to the S phase.[30,31] EGF/TGF-α–responsive cells require sustained exposure to the growth factor for at least 6 to 8 hours before they are committed to DNA synthesis and transition through the G_1 phase.[32–35] Binding of the ligand to the EGFR results in activation of the receptor's kinase activity and leads to the autophosphorylation of several tyrosines in the receptor protein.[36] This is followed by induction of Ras signaling due to the association of the Shc-Grb2-SOS complex with the activated EGFR. Active GTP-bound Ras then binds the serine/threonine kinase Raf. These initial events trigger a phosphorylation cascade using mitogen-activated protein kinases (MAPKs).[30,37,38] These MAPKs (also called extracellular signal-regulated kinases [ERKs]) are themselves activated by phosphorylation by the MAPK-activating enzymes (MAPK/ERK kinases

[MEKs]).[30,37,38] They in turn phosphorylate a number of additional kinases and transcription factors that then affect cellular responses following growth factor stimulation. The Ras/MAPK pathway may cross-talk with an alternate signaling pathway of the EGFR (ie, PI3 kinase/AKT2). Data are emerging that show that ovarian cancers may have increased amounts of PI3 kinase[39] as well as AKT2[40–43] (see Figure 2–5).

Alterations in EGFR family signaling has perhaps been among the most frequently implicated effectors of human oncogenesis,[30] and many studies suggest that perturbations in EGFR signaling could also be a frequent component in ovarian surface epithelial oncogenesis. This view has its origins in the fact that DNA replication is a weak mutagen and in the finding that follicular fluid contains EGF, which is a mitogen to normal ovarian surface epithelial cells.[44,45] The notion is bolstered further by several studies in ovarian cancer. In cultured human ovarian cancer cells, the mitogenic response to EGFR ligands was found to be variable.[46–49] Similarly, studies on rat transformed ovarian surface epithelial cells indicated that there are variations in the growth responsiveness of the individual transformed cell lines to EGF.[50,51] Additionally, it is noteworthy that in estrogen-responsive ovarian cancer,[26] at least a part of the mitogenic effect uses the EGFR ligand, TGF-α, as an autocrine second mes-

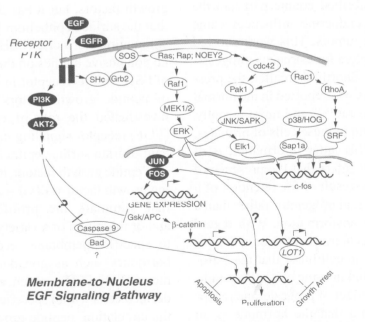

Figure 2–5. Signal transduction pathways believed to be involved in human ovarian cancer.

senger.[52] Furthermore, neutralization of TGF-α in ovarian cancer cells in tissue culture with a monoclonal antibody results in inhibition of proliferation, most probably by blocking a TGF-α/EGFR autocrine loop.[53] When mitogenic responsiveness to EGF is lost, it is not often because of decreased receptor expression. Therefore, the attenuated response may be due to alternations in the downstream signals generated after receptor and ligand interaction, such that proliferation does not require growth factor. This could occur in a variety of ways, including constitutive activation of some component along the EGFR-signaling cascades[30] or elimination of a growth-inhibitory signal in the absence of growth factor, such as inactivation of a growth or tumor suppressor gene.

Additional studies suggest the involvement of EGFR signaling in the clinical features of ovarian cancer. Laboratory studies have suggested that TGF-α might contribute to an aggressive tumor phenotype.[54] Clinical correlative studies would seem to support this concept since several authors have reported that EGFR expression in ovarian cancer is associated with a poor prognosis.[55-60] Additionally, clinical investigations have found that while TGF-α was not detectable in the normal pre- and postmenopausal ovaries, the majority of malignant epithelial tumors of the ovary did express this EGFR ligand.[61] TGF activity has also been found in effusions from ovarian cancer patients,[55,57] and EGF-like factors were present in ovarian tumors.[62,63] Another recent report indicated that serum TGF-α was detected in a greater proportion (62%) of patients with ovarian cancer than in those with benign ovarian tumors (28%).[31] TGF-α levels were even higher in serous and endometrioid ovarian cancers: 71% and 70%, respectively. In addition, decreased amounts of a soluble truncated form of the EGFR in serum correlates with the presence of ovarian cancer.[64,65] In summary, the above data suggest the frequent involvement of EGF/TGF-α signal transduction pathways in many aspects of the biology of ovarian cancer.

MOLECULAR GENETICS OF OVARIAN CANCER

Other studies have found additional evidence of strategies used by ovarian cancer cells to escape the need for growth factors in order to proliferate. For example, Ras activation was found in 50% of ovarian cancers tested, mostly resulting in constitutive activation of MAPK.[39] Mutations of the Ras oncoprotein have been observed frequently in mucinous ovarian cancers and in about 20 to 50% of epithelial ovarian tumors of low malignant potential.[66] Very recently, *NOEY2* (see Figure 2–5), a gene homologous to Ras and Rap G proteins, was discovered during an effort to find genes expressed in normal human ovary but not ovarian cancer. The report indicated a lack of *NOEY2* message in about 90% of ovarian cancer cell lines.[39] In an independent study with similar intent, DOC2 was discovered. DOC2 is an mDab2 homologue, and the gene product was suggested to bind Grb2, preventing the docking of SOS, which is required as an early event for tyrosine kinase–linked receptor signaling.[67]

Disabled-2 (Dab2), or DOC2, is thought to be a candidate tumor suppressor in ovarian and breast cancer[67,68] since its expression is lost or greatly diminished in 85% of breast and ovarian cancers analyzed,[68] and forced reexpression of Dab2 is able to suppress cell growth in vitro and tumorigenicity.[67,69] Gene deletions have been found to account for loss of Dab2 in a small percentage of tumors.[70]

Dab2 is one of the two mammalian orthologs of the *Drosophila disabled* gene, which was identified as one of the proteins genetically interacting with Abl kinase during neuronal development.[71] The three spliced forms of murine Dab2 complementary DNA (cDNA), p96, p93 and p67, were first isolated as signal phosphoproteins functioning in the macrophage colony-stimulating factor 1 (CSF-1) signal transduction pathway.[72] It is speculated that Dab2 may function as a tumor suppressor of ovarian cancer by negatively regulating Ras-mediated cell growth.[73] The C-terminal proline-rich domain of Dab2 binds Grb2, an adaptor protein that couples tyrosine kinase receptors to Sos (the activator of Ras) both in vitro and in vivo and competes with Sos for binding. Thus, in responding to extracellular signals, Dab2 may down-regulate Ras activation by preventing the docking of Sos to the receptor tyrosine kinase to activate Ras, and the loss of Dab2 may remove a regulatory site in Ras activation by growth factor receptor tyrosine kinase.[73]

Dab2 shows 30% sequence homology with dDab and is 45% identical and 60% homologous to Dab1, the other mammalian ortholog that is brain specific.[72,74] Dab1 functions in the positional organization of brain cells[75] and serves as an adaptor in a signal transduction pathway initiated from the extracellular matrix (ECM) signal consisting of reelin, to glycoprotein cell surface receptor, to Dab1, and to Src family kinases.[76] This signaling pathway is thought to sense the clue of the ECM proteins, such as reelin, in establishing the proper positioning of cortical neurons.[75,76] A similar function has been proposed for Dab2 in epithelial cell positioning control,[69] such that the ovarian surface epithelial cells can survive and proliferate only along the basement membrane (Figure 2–6). The epithelial cells that are not in close contact with the basement membrane are purged, thus maintaining the architecture of the ovarian surface epithelium. The loss of Dab2 and its signaling pathway may contribute to the basement membrane–independent and disorganized proliferation found in tumors[69] (Figure 2–7; see also Figure 2–6).

EXPERIMENTAL MODELING IN THE DEVELOPMENT OF OVARIAN CANCER

The data outlined above suggest that the ovarian surface epithelium actively participates in the ovulatory process. In addition, it is abundantly clear that after ovulation, return to continuity of the ovarian surface is achieved by the growth of these cells for repairing the ovulatory wound. Furthermore, it is apparent that the surface epithelium has in place the molecular machinery to respond to a variety of potential mitogens. As noted above, Fathalla hypothesized that the incessant or repetitious growth of the ovarian surface epithelial cells was the driving force in ovarian oncogenesis. Over the years since its inception, the incessant-ovulation hypothesis has been expanded and is often stated as dogma in reviews that cover the subject of ovarian cancer etiology.

Experimental support for the incessant-ovulation hypothesis has been presented.[50,51] Using the idea that repeated growth of surface epithelial cells might cause mutations leading to malignant transformation, surface epithelial cells from rat ovaries were isolated and subjected to the repetitious requirement for

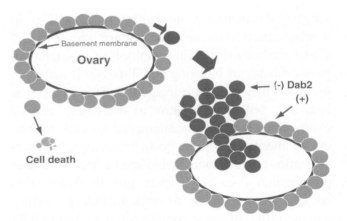

Figure 2–6. Ovarian surface epithelial cell positioning. The hypothesis is that Dab2 controls the positioning of epithelial cells attaching to the basement membrane on the surface of the ovary and that loss of Dab2 expression leads to invasive and metastatic tumorigenicity. Normal epithelial cells (Dab2-positive light-colored cells) that are detached from the basement membrane undergo apoptosis. Epithelial cells in which Dab2 expression is lost (darker cells) do not undergo apoptosis when membrane attachment is disrupted. The disorganized proliferation of Dab2-negative cells leads to tumorigenicity.

growth in vitro by repeated subculture. This strategy resulted in malignant transformation as assessed by tumorigenicity in ten of thirty independent attempts[51] (Figures 2–8 and 2–9). This rat ovarian surface epithelial cell transformation model is being used to identify genes that are differentially expressed in malignant versus normal cells. The characteristics of

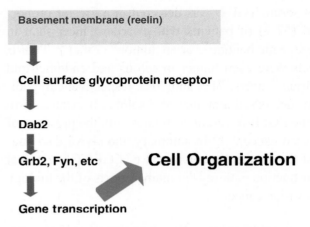

Figure 2–7. Dab2 in epithelial cell positioning: Dab2 signaling pathway functioning in positioning control. The proposed signaling pathway involving extracellular basement membrane protein such as reelin, cell surface receptors, Dab2 adapter, and downstream effectors are illustrated. This signaling pathway is thought to control the positioning organization of epithelial cells by basement membrane.

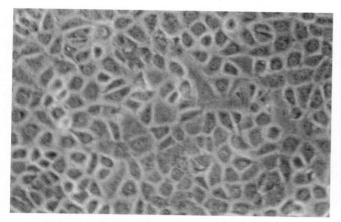

Figure 2–8. A confluent monolayer of rat ovarian surface epithelial cells.

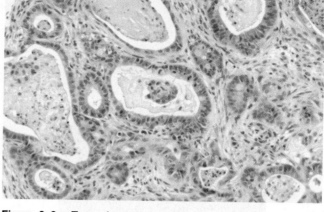

Figure 2–9. Tumor formed after injection of growth dependently transformed rat surface epithelial cells.

the model are summarized in Table 2–1. One of the genes identified so far is the growth suppressor gene *LOT1*[77] part of the EGFR signaling pathway (see above and Figure 2–5). The probable utility of this model to identify genes relevant to human ovarian cancer is suggested by data supportive of the involvement of *LOT1* in the human disease.[78] The characteristics of *LOT* are summarized in Table 2–2. Additionally, cathepsin B was found to be amplified and/or overexpressed in the transformed rat ovarian surface epithelial cells[79] (Figure 2–10). Cathepsin B is a peptidyl peptide hydrolase endopeptidase that has been found to be a prognostic factor in many solid tumors.[80] The data in this rat model were the first to suggest its possible involvement in human ovarian cancer. Others have reported similar results with ovarian surface epithelial cells.[81]

The epidemiologic data identified by Fathalla and the experimental data from the above-described rat model support the idea that frequent mitogenesis

of the ovarian surface cells is a critical component in ovarian oncogenesis. Some facets of the epidemiologic data are of special interest. It is apparent and noncontroversial that factors that limit the number of ovulations in a woman's life (ie, pregnancies and contraceptive pill use) decrease her relative risk of ovarian cancer. It is also clear that when viewed in a linear fashion, the decrease in risk is larger than is accounted for by the absolute decrease in ovulations. There are at least three explanations for this observation. The first possibility is that as with many biologic processes, the effect obeys a mathematical relationship that is other than linear.[82] A second reason may be that the process of a full-term pregnancy with associated hormonal fluctuations causes the surface epithelium to "differentiate" and to be less prone to transformation (Daniel Cramer, personal communication 04/99). The third reason relates to the possibility that oral contraceptive use decreases risk by a mechanism different from (or in addition to) inhibition of ovulation. This idea derives from a

Table 2–1. FEATURES OF RAT OVARIAN CANCER MODEL

Incidence: 10/30 (~30%)
Provides multiple independent episodes of transformation, with all malignant cell lines arising from cells initially with identical genetic constitution
Allows the recurrence of genetic changes leading to malignancy to be examined
Recurrence can be used to suggest causality and the need for thorough study.
Shows innate differences in drug sensitivity
Varies in aggressiveness
Nonimmunogenic

Table 2–2. CHARACTERISTICS OF *LOT1*

Frequent aberrant expression in human ovarian cancer
Maps to chromosome 6 at band 25 (a frequent site of LOH in ovarian cancer)
Is a nuclear transcription factor
Is part of the EGFR signaling pathway
Is a negative regulator of cell growth
Is an imprinted gene
Is a candidate for the cause of transient neonatal diabetes

EGFR = epidermal growth factor receptor; LOH = loss of heterozygosity.

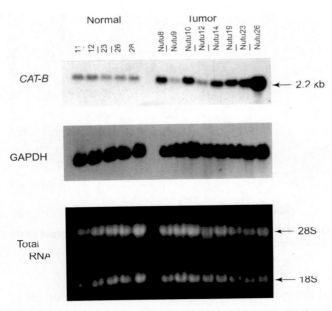

Figure 2–10.   Analysis of CAT-B gene expression in normal and malignantly transformed rat ovarian surface epithelial cells: Northern blot analysis of cathepsin B expression in normal and transformed rat ovarian surface epithelial cells. (RNA = ribonucleic acid.)

report describing the histologic analysis of the ovaries of cynomolgus monkeys that were treated for 2 years with an oral contraceptive containing the synthetic estrogen ethinyl estradiol, the synthetic progestin levonorgestrel, or a combination of these components.[83] The authors noted a marked increase in apoptosis of surface epithelial cells from animals treated with the combination contraceptive or with the synthetic progestin component. An important issue to be reconciled if these data are confirmed is why such a higher percentage of cells (14 to 25%) underwent apoptosis. The occurrence of apoptosis in genetically normal cells would seem counterproductive. Hence, it is tempting to speculate that the progestin is initiating apoptosis in surface epithelial cells that contain genetic damage. This idea is consistent with the notion that ovarian surface epithelial cells may be prone to genetic damage that is not repaired. Notably, these cells have not been under strong evolutionary pressure to develop the capacity for repeated wound repair as repetitious ovulation is a recent event in the darwinian sense; that is, until modern times, multiparity and a short life span were the norm. Furthermore, since the ovarian surface epithelium replicates as a generative stem cell,[84] it is

easy to see how there could be an accumulation of cells with mutations (Figure 2–11). In summary, there is abundant evidence to suggest that some aspect of repeated ovulation drives the process of malignant transformation of the ovarian surface epithelium. Recent preliminary data, however, suggest that multiparity and oral contraceptives may be exerting their protective effects by mechanisms different from (or in addition to) inhibition of ovulation.

OVARIAN PRENEOPLASIA

The information presented thus far in this review of ovarian cancer biology suggests that the process of malignant transformation of the ovarian surface epithelium is largely related to excessive proliferation of the cells and ultimate loss of normal growth regulatory mechanisms. This loss of growth control could occur through mutation in the genes whose products regulate growth or similarly, through their dysregulation by epigenetic phenomena. If these concepts are correct, one would speculate that recognizable histologic changes should occur in the ovary as the susceptible cells traverse the continuum between overtly normal and malignant. Indeed, several investigators have performed histologic studies on ovaries to determine if identifiable changes can be found. Many of the original studies evaluated the contralateral "normal" ovary of women with unilateral ovarian cancer and detected a range of changes.[85–88] Two recent studies used a slightly different approach. They evaluated ovaries removed from women who were at an inherited increased risk of ovarian cancer.[6,89] The first of these investigations revealed that cancer-prone ovaries contained two or

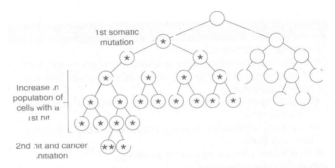

Figure 2–11.   Accumulation of genetic damage as ovarian surface epithelial cells replicate as generative stem cells.

more, in some investigations three or more, of the following histologic features: surface epithelial pseudostratification, surface epithelial papillomatosis (Figure 2–12), deep cortical invaginations (see Figure 2–12) of the surface epithelium, epithelial inclusion cysts, and increased stromal activity in 85% and 75% of cases (*n*=18), respectively.[6] These changes were observed far less frequently (and were less intense) in ovaries from women in the general population (two or more of these changes in 30% of cases and three or more in 10% of cases). These differences were statistically significant (*p* = .001 and *p* < .001). The authors suggested that these changes are an identifiable phenotye that is a fertile environment from which ovarian cancer may arise. The notion that human ovarian surface epithelial (HOSE) cells from individuals who are prone to ovarian cancer have acquired a distinct phenotype prior to the development of overt malignancy is also supported by work on these cells in tissue culture. For example, the HOSE cells from cancer-prone individuals, in comparison to those of individuals at normal risk, are more stable with regard to epithelial morphology and cancer antigen (CA 125) production.[90] Furthermore, the suggestion, by the histologic studies described above, of increased mitotic activity is supported by recent evidence that telomere length is shorter and rate of loss greater in the cells from individuals who are prone to ovarian cancer.[91] In contrast to this first study of cancer-prone ovaries, a second and smaller study did not support the findings of the original study. In this latter study, it is unclear that all ovaries were comprehensively sampled. Additionally, there is little information as to the penetrance of the disease in the families of individuals in the study. In the original report, most individuals came from families with high penetrance. This observation is based not only on the number of breast and ovarian cancer cases in those families but also on the fact that two adenocarcinomas were discovered in the prophylactically removed ovaries. It is logical that if the changes purported to be present in cancer-prone ovaries are real and relevant to the disease process, their presence and intensity should track with the relative likelihood of the disease's occurrence in the individual. Hence, future investigations aimed at resolving this discrepancy should carefully take penetrance into account and should thoroughly sample all portions of ovaries for signs of preneoplasia.

CONCLUSIONS

In conclusion, progress in unraveling how the biology of the surface epithelium may contribute to its propensity for malignant transformation has been slow. This slow progress has been caused by several factors, including the limited number of investigators in a sustained effort in the field, the difficulty of working with cells that are so limited in number, and the lack of well-characterized animal models of the disease. Nonetheless, momentum is building, and with the rapid advances in technologies that may be brought to bear on the problem, there should be optimism that the pace of progress will be more rapid in the future.

ACKNOWLEDGEMENTS

We are grateful to Natasha Salazar for creating the computer illustration for Figure 2–1 with her grandfather, Hernando Salazar.

Dr. Hamilton is supported by the Adler Foundation, the Evy Lessin Fund, appropriations from the Commonwealth of Pennsylvania and CA56919, CA84242, CA51228, CA83638, and CA06927. Dr. Patriotis is supported by the 5th District AHEPA, Cancer Research Foundation, Inc., CA83638, and CA73676. Dr. Xu is supported by CA79716 and CA75389.

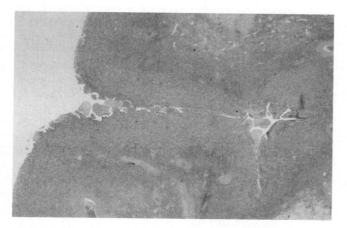

Figure 2–12. Section of cancer-prone human ovary. Note deep invaginations and papillomatosis.

REFERENCES

1. Fathalla M. Incessant ovulation—a factor in ovarian neoplasia? Lancet 1971;2:163.

2. Fredrickson TN. Ovarian tumors of the hen. Environ Health Perspect 1987;73:35–51.

3. Wilson J. Adeno-carcinomata in hens kept in a constant environment. Poultry Sci 1958;37:1253.

4. Preston-Martin S, Pike MC, Ross RK, et al. Increased cell division as a cause of human cancer. Cancer Res 1990;50:7415–21.

5. Radisavljevic S. The pathogenesis of ovarian inclusion cysts and cystomas. Obstet Gynecol 1976;49:424–9.

6. Salazar H, Godwin A, Daly M, et al. Microscopic benign and invasive malignant neoplasms and a preneoplastic phenotype in prophylactic oophorectomies. J Natl Cancer Inst 1996;88:1810–20.

7. Carmack D. Ham's histology. 9th ed. Philadelphia: Lippincott; 1987.

8. Fox H. Pathology of early malignant change in the ovary. Int J Gynecol Pathol 1993;12:153–5.

9. Scully R, Bell D, Abu-Jawdeh G. Update on early ovarian cancer and cancer developing in benign ovarian tumors. In: Sharp F, Mason P, Blackett T, Berek J, editors. Ovarian cancer 3. London: Chapman and Hall; 1995. p. 139–44.

10. Bjersing L, Cajander S. Ovulation and the role of the ovarian surface epithelium. Experientia 1975;31:605–8.

11. Ellerbroek SM, Fishman DA, Kearns AS, et al. Ovarian carcinoma regulation of matrix metalloproteinase-2 and membrane type 1 matrix metalloproteinase through beta 1 integrin. Cancer Res 1999;59:1635–41.

12. Fishman DA, Kearns A, Larsh S, et al. Autocrine regulation of growth stimulation in human epithelial ovarian carcinoma by serine-proteinase-catalysed release of the urinary-type plasminogen-activator N-terminal fragment. Biochem J 1999;341:765–9.

13. Stack MS, Ellerbroek SM, Fishman DA. The role of proteolytic enzymes in the pathology of epithelial ovarian carcinoma. Int J Oncol 1998;12:569–76.

14. Motta P, Van Blerkom J, Makabe S. Changes in the surface morphology of the ovarian 'Germinal' epithelium during the reproductive cycle and in some pathological conditions. J Submicro Cytol 1980;12:407–25.

15. Nicosia S, Nicosia R. Neoplasms of the ovarian mesothelium. In: Azar H, editor. Pathology of human neoplasms. New York: Raven Press; 1988. p. 435–86.

16. Hamilton T, Davies P, Griffiths K. Androgen and oestrogen binding of cytosols of human ovarian tumors. J Endocrinol 1981;90:421–31.

17. Holt J, Caputo T, Kelly K, et al. Estrogen and progestin binding in cytosols of ovarian adenocarcinomas. Obstet Gynecol 1979;53:50–8.

18. Adams A, Auersperg N. Autoradiographic investigation of estrogen binding in cultured rat ovarian surface epithelial cells. J Histochem Cytochem 1983;31:1321–5.

19. Hamilton T, Davies P, Griffiths K. Oestrogen receptor-like binding in the surface germinal epithelium of the rat ovary. J Endocrinol 1982;95:377–85.

20. Hild-Petito S, Stouffer R, Brenner R. Immunocytochemical localization of estradiol and progesterone receptors in the monkey ovary throughout the menstrual cycle. Endocrinology 1988;123:2896–905.

21. Hori K, Takakura K, Fujiwara H, et al. Immunohistochemical localization of androgen receptor in the human ovary throughout the menstrual cycle in relation to oestrogen and progesterone receptor expression. Hum Reprod 1992;7:184–90.

22. Lau L, Nathans D. Expression of a set of growth-related immediate early genes in BALB/c 3T3 cells: coordinate regulation with c-fos or c-myc. Proc Natl Acad Sci U S A 1987;84:1182–6.

23. Pujol P, Rey JM, Nirde P, et al. Differential expression of estrogen receptor-alpha and -beta messenger RNAs as a potential marker of ovarian carcinogenesis. Cancer Res 1998;58:5367–73.

24. Lau KM, Mok SC, Ho SM. Expression of human estrogen receptor-alpha and -beta, progesterone receptor, and androgen receptor mRNA in normal and malignant ovarian epithelial cells. Proc Natl Acad Sci U S A 1999;96:5722–7.

25. Hamilton T, Behrens B, Louie K, Ozols R. Induction of progesterone receptor with 17B-estradiol in human ovarian cancer. J Clin Endocrinol Metab 1984;59:561–3.

26. Nash J, Ozols R, Smyth J, Hamilton T. Estrogen and antiestrogen effects on the growth of human epithelial ovarian cancer in vitro. Obstet Gynecol 1989;73:1009–16.

27. Karlan B, Jones J, Greenwald M, Lagasse L. Steroid hormone effects on the proliferation of human ovarian surface epithelium in vitro. Am J Obstet Gynecol 1995;173:97–104.

28. Zheng W, Magid MS, Kramer EE, Chen YT. Follicle-stimulating hormone receptor is expressed in human ovarian surface epithelium and Fallopian tube. Am J Pathol 1996;148:47–53.

29. Berchuck A, Carney M. Human ovarian cancer of the surface epithelium. Biochem Pharmacol 1997;54:541–4.

30. Aaronson SA. Growth factors and cancer. Science 1991;254:1146–53.

31. Chien CH, Huang CC, Lin YH, et al. Detection of serum transforming growth factor-alpha in patients of primary epithelial ovarian cancers by enzyme immunoassay. Gynecol Oncol 1997;66:405–10.

32. Aharonov A, Pruss RM, Herschman HR. Epidermal growth factor. Relationship between receptor regulation and mitogenesis in 3T3 cells. J Biol Chem 1978;253:3970–7.

33. Carpenter G. Epidermal growth factor. Handbook Exp Pharmacol 1981;57:90–126.

34. Schechter Y, Hernaez L, Cuatrecasas P. Epidermal growth factor: biological activity requires persistent occupation of high-affinity cell surface receptors. Proc Natl Acad Sci U S A 1978;75:5788–91.

35. Weinberg RA. Tumor suppressor genes. Science 1991;254:1138–46.

36. Schlessinger J, Ullrich A. Growth factor signaling by receptor tyrosine kinases. Neuron 1992;9:383–91.

37. Ahn NG, Weiel JE, Chan CP, Krebs EG. Identification of multiple epidermal growth factor-stimulated protein serine/threonine kinases from Swiss 3T3 cells. J Biol Chem 1990;265:11487–94.

38. Zheng CF, Guan KL. Cloning and characterization of two distinct human extracellular signal-regulated kinase acti-

vator kinases, MEK1 and MEK2. J Biol Chem 1993;268: 11435–9.

39. Bast R Jr, Xu F, Yu Y, et al. Overview—the molecular biology of ovarian cancer. In Sharp F, Blackett T, Berek J, Bast R, editors. Ovarian cancer 5. Oxford (UK): Isis Medical Media; 1998. p. 87–97.

40. Bellacosa A, Franke T, Gonzalez-Portal M, et al. Structure, expression and chromosomal mapping of c-*akt*: relationship to v-*akt* and its implications. Oncogene 1993;8: 745–54.

41. Bellacosa A, de Feo D, Godwin AK, et al. Molecular alterations of the AKT2 oncogene in ovarian and breast carcinomas. Int J Cancer 1995;64:280–5.

42. Cheng J, Godwin A, Bellacosa A, et al. *AKT2*, a putative oncogene encoding a member of a subfamily of protein-serine/threonine kinases, is amplified in human ovarian carcinomas. Proc Natl Acad Sci U S A 1992;89:9267–71.

43. Liu AX, Testa JR, Hamilton TC, et al. AKT2, a member of the protein kinase B family, is activated by growth factors v-Ha-ras, and v-src through phosphatidylinositol 3-kinase in human ovarian epithelial cancer cells. Cancer Res 1998;58:2973–7.

44. Skinner MK, Lobb D, Dorrington JH. Ovarian thecal/interstitial cells produce an epidermal growth factor-like substance. Endocrinology 1987;121:1892–9.

45. Skinner MK, Keski-Oja J, Osteen KG, Moses HL. Ovarian thecal cells produce transforming growth factor-beta which can regulate granulosa cell growth. Endocrinology 1987;121:786–92.

46. Berchuck A, Olt G, Everitt L, et al. The role of peptide growth factors in epithelial ovarian cancer. Obstet Gynecol 1990;75:255–62.

47. Crew AJ, Langdon SP, Miller EP, Miller WR. Mitogenic effects of epidermal growth factor and transforming growth factor-alpha on EGF-receptor positive human ovarian carcinoma cell lines. Eur J Cancer 1992;28:337–41.

48. Singletary SE, Baker FL, Spitzer G, et al. Biological effect of epidermal growth factor on the in vitro growth of human tumors. Cancer Res 1987;47:403–6.

49. Zhou L, Leung BS. Growth regulation of ovarian cancer cells by epidermal growth factor and transforming growth factors alpha and beta 1. Biochim Biophys Acta 1992;1180:130–6.

50. Godwin A, Testa J, Handel L, et al. Spontaneous transformation of rat ovarian surface epithelial cells implicates repeated ovulation in ovarian cancer etiology and is associated with clonal cytogenetic changes. J Natl Cancer Inst 1992;84:592–601.

51. Testa J, Getts L, Salazar H, et al. Spontaneous transformation of rat ovarian surface epithelial cells results in well to poorly differentiated tumors with a parallel range of cytogenetic complexity. Cancer Res 1994;54:2778–84.

52. Nash J, Hall L, Ozols R, et al. Estrogenic regulation and growth factor expression in human ovarian cancer in vitro. Proc AACR 1989;30:299.

53. Stromberg K, Collins TJ IV, Gordon AW, et al. Transforming growth factor-alpha acts as an autocrine growth factor in ovarian carcinoma cell lines. Cancer Res 1992;52:341–7.

54. Morishige K, Kurachi H, Amemiya K, et al. Evidence for the involvement of transforming growth factor alpha and epidermal growth factor receptor autocrine growth mecha-

55. Arteaga CL, Hanauske AR, Clark GM, et al. Immunoreactive alpha transforming growth factor activity in effusions from cancer patients as a marker of tumor burden and patient prognosis. Cancer Res 1988;48:5023–8.

56. Berchuck A, Rodriguez GC, Kamel A, et al. Epidermal growth factor receptor expression in normal ovarian epithelium and ovarian cancer. I. Correlation of receptor expression with prognostic factors in patients with ovarian cancer. Am J Obstet Gynecol 1991;164:669–74.

57. Hanauske AR, Arteaga CL, Clark GM, et al. Determination of transforming growth factor activity in effusions from cancer patients. Cancer 1988;61:1832–7.

58. Kohler M, Janz I, Wintzer HO, et al. The expression of EGF receptors, EGF-like factors and c-myc in ovarian and cervical carcinomas and their potential clinical significance. Anticancer Res 1989;9:1537–48.

59. Sainsbury JR, Farndon JR, Needham GK, et al. Epidermal-growth-factor receptor status as predictor of early recurrence of and death from breast cancer. Lancet 1987;1: 1398–402.

60. Scambia G, Benedetti-Panici P, Ferrandina G, et al. Epidermal growth factor, oestrogen and progesterone receptor expression in primary ovarian cancer: correlation with clinical outcome and response to chemotherapy. Br J Cancer 1995;72:361–6.

61. Kommoss F, Wintzer H, vonKleist S, et al. In situ distribution of transforming growth factor alpha in normal human tissues and in malignant tumors of the ovary. J Pathol 1990; 162:223–30.

62. Bauknecht T, Kiechle M, Bauer G, Siebers JW. Characterization of growth factors in human ovarian carcinomas. Cancer Res 1986;46:2614–8.

63. Bauknecht T, Kohler M, Janz I, Pfleiderer A. The occurrence of epidermal growth factor receptors and the characterization of EGF-like factors in human ovarian, endometrial, cervical and breast cancer. EGF receptors and factors in gynecological carcinomas. J Cancer Res Clin Oncol 1989;115:193–9.

64. Lee H, Maihle NJ. Isolation and characterization of four alternate c-erbB3 transcripts expressed in ovarian carcinoma-derived cell lines and normal human tissues. Oncogene 1998;16:3243–52.

65. Baron AT, Lafky JM, Boardman CH, et al. Serum sErbB1 and epidermal growth factor levels as tumor biomarkers in women with stage III or IV epithelial ovarian cancer. Cancer Epidemiol Biomarkers Prev 1999;8:129–37.

66. Mok CH, Tsao SW, Bell DA, et al. Mutation of K-ras proto-oncogene in human ovarian epithelial tumors of borderline malignancy. Cancer Res 1993;53:1489–92.

67. Mok SC, Chan WY, Wong KK, et al. DOC-2, a candidate tumor suppressor gene in human epithelial ovarian cancer. Oncogene 1998;16:2381–7.

68. Fazili Z, Sun W, Mittelstaedt S, et al. Disabled-2 inactivation is an early step in ovarian tumorigenicity. Oncogene 1999; 18:3104–13.

69. Sheng Z, Sun W, Smith E, et al. Restoration of positioning control following disabled-2 expression in ovarian and breast tumor cells. Oncogene 2000;19:4847–54.

70. Fazili Z, Sun W, Mittelstaedt S, et al. Disabled-2 gene inacti-

vation by homozygous deletion in breast and ovarian tumors. 2000. [Unpublished data]

71. Hoffmann FM. *Drosphila* abl and genetic redundancy in signal transduction. Trends Genet 1991;7:351–5.

72. Xu XX, Yang W, Jackowski S, Rock CO. Cloning of a novel phosphoprotein regulated by colony-stimulating factor 1 shares a domain with the *Drosophila* disabled gene product. J Biol Chem 1995;270:14184–91.

73. Xu XX, Yi T, Tang B, Lambeth JD. Disabled-2 (D\ab2) is an SH3 domain-binding partner of Grb2. Oncogene 1998; 16:1561–9.

74. Howell BW, Gertler FB, Cooper JA. Mouse disabled (mDab1): a Src binding protein implicated in neuronal development. Embo J 1997;16:121–32.

75. Howell BW, Hawkes R, Soriano P, Cooper JA. Neuronal position in the developing brain is regulated by mouse disabled-1. Nature 1997;389:733–7.

76. Trommsdorff M, Gotthardt M, Hiesberger T, et al. Reeler/disabled-like disruption of neuronal migration in knockout mice lacking the VLDL receptor and ApoE receptor 2. Cell 1999;97:689–701.

77. Abdollahi A, Godwin A, Miller P, et al. Identification of a gene containing zinc-finger motifs based on lost expression in malignantly transformed rat ovarian surface epithelial cells. Cancer Res 1997;57:2029–34.

78. Abdollahi A, Roberts D, Godwin A, et al. Identification of a zinc-finger gene at 6q25: a chromosomal region implicated in the development of many solid tumors. Oncogene 1997;14:1973–9.

79. Abdollahi A, Getts L, Sonoda G, et al. Genome scanning detects amplification of the cathepsin B gene (CtsB) in transformed rat ovarian surface epithelial cells. J Soc Gynecol Investig 1999;6(1):32–40.

80. Keppler D, Saneni M, Moin K, et al. Tumor progression and angiogenesis: cathepsin B and company. Biochem Cell Biol 1996;74:799–810.

81. Roby KF, Taylor CC, Sweetwood JP, et al. Development of

syngeneic mouse model for events related to ovarian cancer. Carcinogenesis 2000;21:585–91.

82. Hamilton TC. Re: hormonal etiology of epithelial ovarian cancer, with a hypothesis concerning the role of androgens and progesterone [letter; comment]. J Natl Cancer Inst 1999;91:650–1.

83. Rodriguez GC, Walmer DK, Cline M, et al. Effect of progestin on the ovarian epithelium of macaques: cancer prevention through apoptosis? J Soc Gynecol Investig 1998;5:271–6.

84. Hamilton T. Ovarian cancer. Part I: Biology. Curr Probl Cancer 1992;16:1–57.

85. Deligdisch L, Einstein A, Guera D, Gil J. Ovarian dysplasia in epithelial inclusion cysts. Cancer 1995;76:1027–34.

86. Mittal K, Zeleniuch-Jacquette A, Cooper J, Demopoulos R. Contralateral ovary in unilateral ovarian carcinoma: a search for preneoplastic lesions. Int J Gynecol Pathol 1993;12:59–63.

87. Resta L, Russo S, Colucci G, Prat J. Morphologic precursors of ovarian epithelial tumors. Obstet Gynecol 1993;82:181–6.

88. Tresserra F, Grases PJ, Labastida R, Ubeda A. Histologic features of the contralateral ovary in patients with unilateral ovarian cancer: a case control study. Gynecol Oncol 1998; 71:437–41.

89. Stratton JF, Buckley CH, Lowe D, Ponder BA. Comparison of prophylactic oophorectomy specimens from carriers and noncarriers of a BRCA1 or BRCA2 gene mutation. United Kingdom Coordinating Committee on Cancer Research (UKCCCR) Familial Ovarian Cancer Study Group. J Natl Cancer Inst 1999;91:626–8.

90. Auersperg N, Maines-Bandiera S, Booth J, et al. Expression of two mucin antigens in cultured human ovarium surface epithelium: influence of a family history of ovarian cancer. Am J Obstet Gynecol 1995;173:558–65.

91. Kruk PA, Godwin AK, Hamilton TC, Auersperg N. Telomeric instability and reduced proliferative potential in ovarian surface epithelial cells from women with a family history of ovarian cancer. Gynecol Oncol 1999;73:229–36.

3

Epidemiology

MARY B. DALY, MD, PhD

Ovarian cancer is the leading cause of death from a gynecologic malignancy among women in the United States and is the fifth leading cause of cancer deaths among women overall after lung, breast, colorectal, and pancreatic. Every year, approximately 23,000 women are diagnosed, and about 14,000 women die from the disease.[1,2] While the understanding of the biology of ovarian cancer is slowly advancing, the precise molecular events that initiate and promote the carcinogenic process in the ovarian epithelium are still unknown. There is, however, a growing body of epidemiologic literature that has identified a number of factors related to a woman's risk for the disease. A thorough understanding of these risk factors may ultimately create possibilities for primary prevention, screening, and early detection.

GENERAL FEATURES

Epithelial ovarian cancer is a disease of older age; incidence rates increase with each decade of life and peak in the middle to late seventies (Figure 3–1). With the exception of the hereditary forms of the disease, ovarian cancer is rarely seen before the age of 40 years. Both age-adjusted incidence and mortality rates have remained relatively stable for the past 25 years (Figure 3–2).[3] Significant geographic and ethnic variations in incidence have been observed. Rates are highest for Caucasian women in the industrialized countries of northern and western Europe and North America and are lowest for women in Africa and Asia (Figure 3–3).[4] Within the United States, incidence rates for African American, Hispanic, and Native American women are

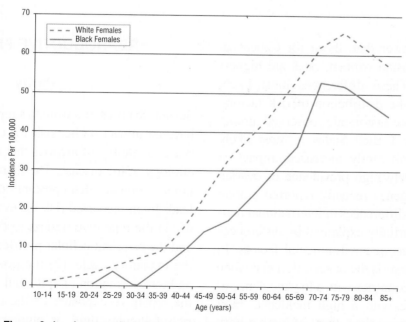

Figure 3–1. Age-specific incidence rates for ovarian cancer. Surveillance, Epidemiology and End Results (SEER) data, 1984 to 1988.

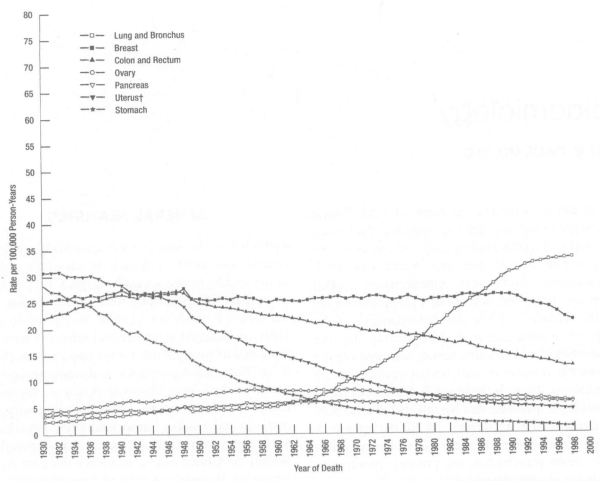

Figure 3–2. Age-adjusted mortality rates for female population by site in the United States, 1930 to 1995, highlighting ovarian cancer.[2]

approximately 40% lower than those for Caucasian women; among Caucasian women, rates are highest for Jewish women. These differences most likely reflect differences in the distribution of risk factors. The increased incidence historically observed among Jewish women in the United States is most likely explained by the significantly increased impact of family and the relatively high prevalence of ovarian cancer susceptibility genes recently reported among Ashkenazi Jews.[5] The differences in international incidence rates may be partially explained by differences in reproductive patterns or environmental factors. In support of this hypothesis is the observation that when women migrate from countries with a low incidence of ovarian cancer to one with a high incidence, their descendants' risk approaches that of native-born women within a few generations.

REPRODUCTIVE FEATURES

Parity

Several features of a woman's reproductive experience have an impact on her risk for ovarian cancer, giving rise to a number of theories that attempt to explain the etiology of the disease. The theory of "incessant ovulation" contends that constant uninterrupted ovulation leads to an increased risk for ovarian cancer by virtue of (1) the repetitive trauma to the ovarian epithelium and the resultant cellular proliferation associated with the ovulatory cycle, (2) the potential for entrapment and transformation of epithelial inclusion cysts, or (3) the repetitive exposure of the epithelium to steroid-rich follicular fluid or pituitary gonadotropins that may give rise to malignant transformation.[6] The actual

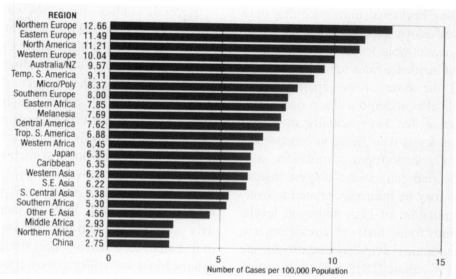

Figure 3–3. Incidence of ovarian cancer, by world region. Rates are higher for Caucasian women in the industrialized countries of northern and western Europe and in North America. Rates are lowest for women in Africa and Asia.

calculation of duration of ovulation has been correlated with ovarian cancer risk in a number of studies.[7,8] Further support for this theory is the association between parity and ovarian cancer. Pregnancy represents a prolonged period of anovulation. Women who have been pregnant have a 30 to 45% reduction in the risk of ovarian cancer compared to women who are nulliparous. Furthermore, there is a clear dose-response relationship, with each birth decreasing risk by 10 to 15%[9] (Figure 3–4). Breast-feeding, which suppresses ovulation less effectively than does pregnancy, adds additional modest protection. Failed pregnancies also protect against ovarian cancer although to

a lesser degree, depending on the length of the pregnancy.[10,11] When controlled for number of pregnancies, however, age at first pregnancy does not appear to affect risk, nor do most studies show any significant effect of age at menarche or at menopause, possibly due to subjects' imprecision in recalling age at first and last menses in most studies.

Endogenous Hormones

An alternative hypothesis to the "incessant ovulation" theory contends that the association of reproductive factors such as parity with ovarian cancer really rep-

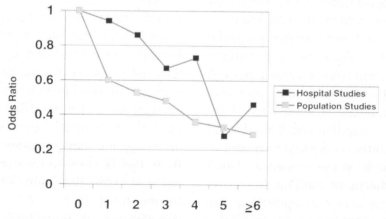

Figure 3–4. Parity decreases the risk of ovarian cancer and continues to decrease risk with each subsequent birth.

resents an underlying hormonal imbalance that may affect fertility as well as ovarian cancer risk. A role for altered pituitary gonadotropin levels is supported by the observation that incidence rates for ovarian cancer accelerate around the time of menopause, when gonadotropin levels also undergo a sharp rise. However, the few studies that have actually measured serum gonadotropin levels have failed to consistently support a role for gonadotropin stimulation as a causal factor in ovarian cancer and suggest instead that gonadotropins may be indirectly related to ovarian cancer by stimulation of high androgen levels. One prospective study found that high circulating levels of androstenedione, dehydroepiandrosterone (DHEA), and DHEA-sulfate (DHEA-S) were associated with an increased risk of ovarian cancer.[12] Although the exact function of androgens within the ovary is unknown, androgen receptors have been identified within ovarian epithelial cells, and androgens are present in ovarian follicular fluid, thus providing a source of exposure to epithelial cells trapped within stromal inclusion cysts. Ovarian cancer is significantly increased among women with polycystic ovarian syndrome, which is characterized by both high levels of luteinizing hormones and hypersecretion of adrenal androgens. Also, the use of oral contraceptives, which reduces risk, is known to suppress ovarian testosterone production and decrease the bioavailability of endogenous gonadal steroids.[13]

On the other hand, there is evidence for a possible protective role of endogenous progestins. The protection afforded by pregnancy, for example, may be partially related to the increase (greater than 10-fold) in circulating progesterone levels. Progestin-only oral contraceptives, which are less likely to suppress ovulation than are the estrogen/progestin combinations, still convey the same or possibly a higher degree of protection from ovarian cancer. A unique animal model using macaque monkeys showed a significant increase in apoptosis of the ovarian epithelium in a group that was administered a progestin over 35 months, compared to a control group.[14] Finally, there is some evidence that a genetic variant in the hormone-binding domain of the progesterone receptor in ovarian epithelium that decreases binding of progesterone is associated with an increased risk for ovarian cancer.[15]

Several studies have shown a significantly increased prevalence of a history of infertility among women diagnosed with ovarian cancer when compared to controls. The understanding of the association of infertility and ovarian cancer is also confounded by the use of fertility drugs, which have themselves been implicated in ovarian cancer etiology.

In a pooled analysis of studies of ovarian cancer, risk was increased among women who had used fertility drugs, with odds ratios of 4.0 among women with tumors of low malignant potential and 2.8 among women with invasive cancers.[16] However, data on drug type and duration of use were limited in this analysis. A case-cohort study of 3,837 women evaluated for infertility at participating sites in Seattle between 1974 and 1985 found that the use of clomiphene, an ovulation-stimulating agent, for 12 or more cycles was associated with an elevated risk of ovarian cancer.[17] Ovulation-stimulating agents could be active both by increasing the frequency of ovulation and by stimulating the endogenous production of pituitary gonadotropins. Data from 10 in vitro fertilization clinics in Australia, on the other hand, showed that ovarian cancers were more common than expected in women with unexplained infertility, irrespective of their treatment status.[18]

A pooled analysis of eight case-controlled studies in North America, Europe, and Australia found no association between fertility drug use and the overall risk of ovarian cancer. The analysis did reveal strong relationships among nulligravidity and prolonged attempts to become pregnant and ovarian cancer risk.

One study suggested an association of pelvic inflammatory disease (of which infertility may be a complication), with subsequent ovarian cancer, but a second study did not suggest an association.[19,20] Several case-control and case series studies have reported an increased risk for ovarian cancer among women with ovarian endometriosis, which may also be associated with infertility.[21,22] However, it is not clear if these cases represent primary ovarian cancer or malignant transformation of tissue transported from the uterus. Retrospective studies have also demonstrated a reduction in ovarian cancer risk following tubal ligation or hysterectomy.[23] Several mechanisms of protection have been proposed, including interruption of the utero-ovarian circulation, surgery-induced changes in estrogen secretion and/or growth factors, and reduced exposure of the ovaries to carcinogenic substances, by interruption of the passage from the uterus to the ovary.

Exogenous Hormones

One of the best-established findings in the epidemiologic literature of ovarian cancer is the risk reduction associated with the use of oral contraceptive pills (OCPs), whose effects mimic some of the physiologic changes induced by pregnancy, including anovulation. OCPs were first introduced in the United States in the 1960s. Most formulations include estrogen, progesterone, or a combination of the two. In addition to suppressing ovulation, OCPs also reduce pituitary secretion of gonadotropins. The use of OCPs appears to decrease a woman's risk for ovarian cancer by 30 to 60%. Risk reduction is apparent with as little as 3 months of use, increases in magnitude with increased duration of use (Figure 3–5), and persists for as long as 10 years after discontinuation of use. The risk reduction applies to nulliparous as well as parous women, to all histologic subtypes (including tumors of low malignant potential), and to women with a hereditary risk for ovarian cancer; it is also consistent across races and is independent of menopausal status or age at use.[9,11,24] Consistent with the proposed protective role of progestins, data from the Cancer and Steroid Hormone Study (CASH) showed that OCP formulations with high progestin potency offered the greatest protection from ovarian cancer.[25]

Although the use of hormone replacement therapy (HRT) might theoretically be expected to reduce the risk for ovarian cancer by lowering the relatively high gonadotropin levels of postmenopausal women, epidemiologic studies of the association between postmenopausal estrogen use and ovarian cancer have produced inconsistent findings. A collaborative analysis of 12 case-control studies conducted in the United States during the period from 1956 to 1986 failed to provide evidence of altered risk with HRT use.[11] However, the Cancer Prevention Study II, a large prospective study conducted by the American Cancer Society, recently reported an association of increased risk of ovarian cancer mortality with postmenopausal estrogen use. Both duration of use and recency of use were predictors of risk. Mortality from ovarian cancer was doubled in women who had used estrogens for 10 or more years within the 15 years prior to their enrollment in the study.[26] Similarly, a population-based case-control study that examined the role of combined estrogen and progestin therapy found an elevated risk for all histologic subtypes of epithelial ovarian cancer in women who had used estrogen, either unopposed or combined with sequential progestins. No change in risk was seen for women who used continuous estrogen/progestin combinations. Again, the highest risk was concentrated in women who used estrogen for 10 or more years.[27] Finally, long-term follow-up

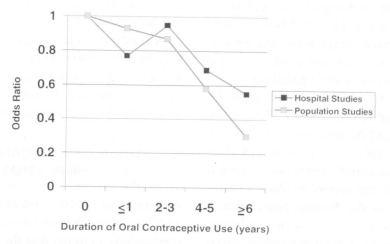

Figure 3–5. Oral contraceptive use has been shown to reduce ovarian cancer incidence. Risk reduction increases with duration of use.

of former participants in the nationwide Breast Cancer Detection Demonstration Project revealed a significant increased risk of ovarian cancer for women who used estrogen-only replacement therapy, particularly for those who used it for 10 or more years.[28] The potential mechanisms explaining an association between postmenopausal estrogen use and ovarian cancer are not known. Both a decrease in the level of gonadotropins associated with HRT and a direct effect of estrogen on epithelial cells have been proposed.

ENVIRONMENTAL FEATURES

Both the observed international and ethnic variations in rates and the shift in risk among migrant populations to that of the host country suggest a role for an environmental component, such as diet, in the etiology of ovarian cancer. Although there is no consistent association between either weight or dietary fat intake and ovarian cancer,[29,30] a positive association between risk and lactose consumption has been observed. The proposed mechanism of action is by way of impaired metabolism of galactose, a metabolite of lactose that may have adverse effects on the surface epithelium of the ovary. Women who suffer from galactosemia, an inborn error of metabolism that results in elevated levels of serum galactose, often develop premature ovarian failure and hypergonadotropic hypogonadism. Also, a series of animal studies has documented ovarian failure in rodents that have been fed a high-galactose diet.[31] The clinical implications of these findings are unclear at this point, particularly in view of the relatively high incidence of lactose intolerance among adults, which compromises the absorption of lactose-containing foods and would therefore decrease an individual's exposure to galactose.

Recently, evidence for a significant role in the growth and normal function of the ovary has begun to emerge for retinol and its derivatives. Vitamin A is essential for the maintenance of normal reproductive function in both male and female rats, and high concentrations of cellular retinol-binding protein have been identified in the human ovary. Fenretinide, a synthetic retinoid, has been shown to have a therapeutic effect against a human ovarian carcinoma cell line. Clinically, the benefit of fenretinide

was noted in a chemoprevention study in women with early-stage breast cancer. Women with breast cancer were randomized to either fenretinide or a placebo and were observed for 5 years. During the course of the study, six cases of ovarian cancer were diagnosed in the control group while none were diagnosed in the fenretinide group.[32] Further work on the potential mechanisms of action of the retinoids and the implications for prevention is currently under way.

Data on other dietary factors in relation to ovarian cancer are sparse and often contradictory. Total dietary fat, saturated fat consumption, serum cholesterol levels, dietary fiber, and selenium levels have been reported to be associated with ovarian cancer risk in small case-control studies. However, the inconsistencies among these studies and the lack of prospective data preclude any firm conclusions about the role of these dietary factors in ovarian cancer and underscore the need for further research.[33,34]

Several case-control studies have suggested a weak association between the use of talc-containing cosmetic products and risk for ovarian cancer. Talc is a specific hydrous magnesium silicate that is chemically related to asbestos. It has historically been a common component of cosmetic powders and is thought to gain access to the ovaries by retrograde transportation through the fallopian tubes. Embedded talc crystals have been documented histologically in ovaries removed for a variety of reasons, and their similarity to particles of asbestos, a known carcinogen in pleural and peritoneal tissues, lends some credibility to the potential risk of talc.[35,36] Industrial and household exposure to asbestos itself has also been linked to ovarian cancer risk. Asbestos fibers have been described in the ovarian tissue of exposed women, and the proposed association is supported by animal models of ovarian epithelial transformation by the intraperitoneal injection of asbestos.[37]

ROLE OF OVARIAN EPITHELIAL INFLAMMATION

Although the older epidemiologic literature often addressed the potential association between infection (particularly mumps) and the risk of ovarian cancer, the focus on an infectious etiology has lost favor over the years. Recently, however, renewed interest in the role of epithelial inflammation has surfaced in the context of a potential role for anti-inflammatory drugs as chemopreventive agents. Inflammation can be linked to several known or proposed risk factors for ovarian cancer. Inflammation may be an important component of the proposed repetitive trauma experienced by the ovarian epithelium during ovulation.[30] Exposure to talc and asbestos may represent an environmental trigger of epithelial inflammation that may either initiate or promote ovarian carcinogenesis. Endometriosis, which is associated with a local inflammatory reaction on the peritoneal surfaces, has been described as a site for the origin of ovarian tumors.[21,22] Pelvic inflammatory disease (PID), an infectious inflammation of the endometrium, fallopian tubes, and ovaries, has been linked to ovarian cancer risk in two case-control studies.[20,39] PID is also associated with subsequent infertility, another risk factor for ovarian cancer.

A role for chronic inflammation in ovarian carcinogenesis has biologic plausibility. Inflammation in general produces produces toxic oxidants that can cause direct damage to deoxyribonucleic acid (DNA), proteins, and lipids. Inflammation also leads to increased proliferation rates, which enhance the risk of mutagenesis. The induction of bioactive substances (such as growth factors, cytokines, and prostaglandins) that favor tumorigenesis is another feature of the inflammatory response. Finally, tubal ligation and hysterectomy, both of which decrease ovarian cancer risk, may act by preventing exposure of the ovarian epithelium to inflammatory products.[37] The use of anti-inflammatory drugs in the chemoprevention of ovarian cancer is discussed in Chapter 9.

GENETIC FEATURES

Although the majority of cases of ovarian cancer are sporadic, approximately 5 to 10% are thought to fit a hereditary pattern of autosomal dominant inheritance. Ovarian cancer in these families is characterized by multiple cases of ovarian and breast cancer in successive generations, an earlier age of onset, and evidence of both maternal and paternal transmission (Figure 3–6). Epidemiologic studies have estimated a two- to fourfold increase in risk among first-degree relatives of women with ovarian cancer. Recently, a number of genes that account for a large percentage of hereditary ovarian cancers and that allow more precise estimates of risk have been identified. (See Chapter 4 for a more detailed description of the genetics of ovarian cancer.) Since the identification of the *BRCA1* gene on chromosome 17q in 1994 and *BRCA2* on chromosome 13q in 1995, several hundred mutations in the genes have been characterized; many of these mutations lead to premature truncation of protein transcription and, therefore, to presumably defective gene products.[1] Ovarian cancer is also included in the phenotype of the recently described mismatch repair genes associated with the hereditary nonpolyposis colorectal cancer (HNPCC) syndrome.[38]

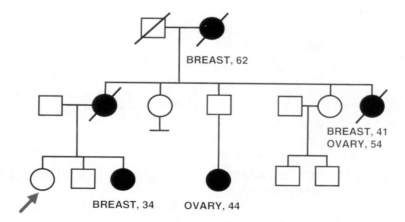

Figure 3–6. Family pedigree, illustrating multiple cases of ovarian and breast cancer in successive generations, earlier age of onset, and both maternal and paternal transmission. (Red arrow signifies the "proband.")

It has been estimated that 1 of 800 individuals in the general population may carry a mutation in the *BRCA1* gene. However, the frequency of both *BRCA1* and *BRCA2* mutations varies considerably by country of origin. For example, certain *BRCA1/2* mutations are found at a much higher frequency in Ashkenazi Jews whereas one of the *BRCA2* mutations is very common in the Icelandic population.[40,41] Decisions to pursue genetic testing for *BRCA1/2* should therefore consider both family history of cancer and ethnic background to determine the likelihood of a hereditary basis for ovarian cancer in a family. Similarly, the penetrance of a gene mutation (ie, the likelihood that a mutation will actually result in ovarian cancer) is estimated to range anywhere from 16 to 63%. Some mutations may be more specifically related to ovarian cancer risk than others. For example, an ovarian cancer cluster region (which is associated with a higher rate of ovarian cancer than other mutations in the gene) has been identified in exon 11 of *BRCA2* (Figure 3–7).[42] The wide variation observed may also reflect the interaction of the genetic mutation with other genetic and/or environmental factors and suggests that these genes may function as "gatekeepers" and that their loss allows other genetic alterations to accumulate.

The natural history of *BRCA*-related ovarian cancer is just beginning to be understood. In one study, OCP use conferred to *BRCA1*-positive women a degree of protection similar to that found in the general population.[43] Clinically, hereditary ovarian cancer appears to be characterized by an overrepresentation of serous histology. The majority of *BRCA*-related ovarian cancers are moderately to poorly differentiated. While a number of studies suggest superior survival for women with *BRCA*-related tumors, not all studies have found this association.[44] The functional role of the *BRCA* genes in DNA repair may provide a biologic mechanism for enhanced survival in mutation carriers by way of increased sensitivity to the DNA-damaging effects of chemotherapy. Efforts to also explore the role of acquired alterations of these genes in sporadic ovarian cancer are now under way.[45] As efforts to understand the precise function of these genes and their relation to the carcinogenic process continue to increase knowledge of ovarian cancer etiology, optimal treatment, and preventive strategies is likely to emerge.

OVARIAN TUMORS OF LOW MALIGNANT POTENTIAL

Ovarian tumors of low malignant potential (borderline ovarian tumors) make up approximately 15% of all epithelial ovarian tumors. They tend to occur earlier in life, with an average age at diagnosis of 49 years. Combined data from nine case-control studies indicate that despite differences in age distribution and prognosis, the risk profile for these tumors is similar to that of invasive ovarian cancer in terms of a protective effect of parity and lactation. The use of

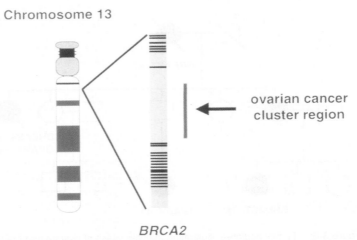

Figure 3–7.   Chromosome 13, the *BRCA2* gene, and the ovarian cancer cluster region.

fertility medications is more strongly associated with increased risk for these tumors whereas less protection appears to be afforded by OCP use.[46–48] The role of family history and genetic factors has not been well delineated in these tumors.

PRIMARY PERITONEAL TUMORS

Extraovarian primary peritoneal carcinoma is a relatively rare tumor that develops from the peritoneal lining of the pelvis and abdomen and that histologically resembles papillary serous ovarian cancer. It presents as advanced-stage epithelial ovarian cancer but is characterized by limited or no involvement of the ovaries and by the lack of a defined primary tumor. Some investigators speculate that primary peritoneal tumors develop from the malignant transformation of embryonic rest cells deposited along the gonadal pathway; others attribute the disease to field carcinogenesis of the coelomic epithelium lining the abdominal and pelvic cavities.[49] Of interest, there is a benign counterpart, endosalpingiosis, a condition in which glandlike structures lined by ciliated tubal-like epithelium are deposited beneath or on the peritoneal surface. Endosalpingiosis is most commonly associated with chronic salpingitis and ovarian serous borderline tumors and may, in some cases, represent a premalignant lesion for primary peritoneal cancer.[50]

Because of the small number of cases reported, the epidemiology of primary peritoneal cancer is poorly understood. However, it has been reported among *BRCA* carriers after bilateral prophylactic oophorectomy and is thought to represent one manifestation of hereditary breast-ovarian cancer syndrome.

REFERENCES

1. Daly M, Obrams GI. Epidemiology and risk assessment for ovarian cancer. Semin Oncol 1998;25(3):255–64.
2. Jemal A, Thomas A, Murray T, Thun M. Cancer Statistics 2002. Ca Cancer J 2002;52:23–47.
3. Ries LAG, Eisner MP, Kosary CL, et al (eds). 2002 SEER Cancer Statistics Review, 1973–1999, National Cancer Institutes. Bethesda, MD. Available at: http://www.seer.cancer.gov/csr/1973_1999/.htm (accessed October 21, 2002).
4. Parkin DM, Pisani P, Ferlay J. Global cancer statistics. CA Cancer J Clin 1999;49:33–64.
5. Steinberg KK, Pernarelli JM, Marcus M, et al. Increased risk for familial ovarian cancer among Jewish women: a population-based case-control study. Genet Epidemiol 1998; 15:51–9.
6. Fathalla MF. Incessant ovulation—a factor in ovarian neoplasia? Lancet 1971;2:163.
7. Casagrande JT, Louie EW, Pike MC, et al. "Incessant ovulation" and ovarian cancer. Lancet 1979;2:170.
8. Wu ML, Whittemore AS, Paffenbarger RS Jr, et al. Personal and environmental characteristics related to epithelial ovarian cancer. I. Reproductive and menstrual events and oral contraceptive use. Am J Epidemiol 1988;128:1216.
9. Barnes MN, Grizzle WE, Grubbs CJ, Patridge EE. Paradigms for primary prevention of ovarian carcinoma. CA Cancer J Clin 2002;52:216–25.
10. Riman T, Kickman PW, Nilsson S, et al. Risk factors for invasive epithelial ovarian cancer: results from a Swedish case-control study. Am J Epidemiol 2002;156:363–73.
11. Whittemore AS. Personal characteristics relating to risk of invasive epithelial ovarian cancer in older women in the United States. Cancer 1993;71:558–65.
12. Helzlsouer KJ, Alberg AJ, Gordon GB, et al. Serum gonadotropins and steroid hormones and the development of ovarian cancer. JAMA 1995;274:1926–30.
13. Schildkraut JM, Schwingl PJ, Bastos E, et al. Epithelial ovarian cancer risk among women with polycystic ovary syndrome. Obstet Gynecol 1996;88:554–9.
14. Rodriguez G, Walmer DK, Cline M, et al. Effect of progestin on the ovarian epithelium of macaques: cancer prevention through apoptosis? J Soc Gynecol Investig 1998;5:271–6.
15. Risch HA. Hormonal etiology of epithelial ovarian cancer, with a hypothesis concerning the role of androgens and progesterone. J Natl Cancer Inst 1998;90(23):1774–86.
16. Whittemore AS, Harris R, Itnyre J, and the Collaborative Ovarian Cancer Group. Characteristics relating to ovarian cancer risk: collaborative analysis of 12 case-control studies. II. Invasive epithelial ovarian cancer in white women. Am J Epidemiol 1992;136:1184–203.
17. Rossing MA, Daling JR, Weiss NS, et al. Ovarian tumors in a cohort of infertile women. N Engl J Med 1994;331:771–6.
18. Venn A, Watson L, Bruinsma F, et al. Risk of cancer after use of fertility drugs with in-vitro fertilization. Lancet 1999; 354:1586–90.
19. Ness RB, Cramer DW, Goodman MT, et al. Infertility, fertility drugs, and ovarian cancer: a pooled analysis of case-control studies. Am J Epidimiol 2002;155:217–24.
20. Risch HA, Howe GR. Pelvic inflammatory disease and the risk of epithelial ovarian cancer. Cancer Epidemiol Biomarkers Prev 1995;4:447–51.
21. Heaps JM, Nieberg RK, Berek JS. Malignant neoplasms arising in endometriosis. Obstet Gynecol 1990;75:1023–8.
22. Brinton LA, Gridley G, Persson I, et al. Cancer risk after a hospital discharge diagnosis of endometriosis. Am J Obstet Gynecol 1997;176:572–9.
23. Whittemore AS, Harris R, Itnyre J, and the Collaborative Ovarian Cancer Group. Characteristics relating to ovarian cancer risk: collaborative analysis of 12 US case-control studies. IV. The pathogenesis of epithelial ovarian cancer. Am J Epidemiol 1992;136:1212–20.
24. Ness RB, Grisso JA, Klapper J, et al. Risk of ovarian cancer in relation to estrogen and progestin dose and use charac-

teristics of oral contraceptives. Am J Epidemiol 2000; 152:233–41.

25. Schildkraut JM, Calingaert B, Marchbanks PA, et al. Impact of progestin and estrogen potency in oral contraceptives on ovarian cancer risk. J Natl Cancer Inst 2002;94:32–8.

26. Rodriguez C, Patel AV, Calle EE, et al. Estrogen replacement therapy and ovarian cancer mortality in a large prospective study of US women. JAMA 2001;285:1460–5.

27. Riman T, Dickman PW, Nilsson S, et al. Hormone replacement therapy and the risk of invasive epithelial ovarian cancer in Swedish women. J Natl Cancer Inst 2002;94:497–504.

28. Lacey JV, Mink PJ, Lubin KH, et al. Menopausal hormone replacement therapy and risk of ovarian cancer. JAMA 2002;288:334–41.

29. La Vecchia C. Tomatoes, Lycopene intake, and digestive tract and female hormone–related neoplasms. Biol Med 2002; 227:860–3.

30. Fairfield KM, Hakinson SE, Rosner BA, et al. Risk of ovarian carcinoma and consumption of vitamins A, C, and E, and specific carotenoids: a prospective analysis. Cancer 2001;92:2318–2.

31. Cramer DW, Muto MG, Reichardt JK, et al. Characteristics of women with a family history of ovarian cancer. I. Galactose consumption and metabolism. Cancer 1994;74:1309–17.

32. DePalo G, Veronesi U, Camerini T, et al. Can fenretinide protect women against ovarian cancer? J Natl Cancer Inst 1995;87:146–7.

33. Zhang M, Yang ZY, Binns CW, Lee AH. Diet and ovarian cancer risk: a case-control study in China. Br J Cancer 2002;86:712–7.

34. Huncharek M, Kupelnick B. Dietary fat intake and risk of epithelial ovarian cancer: a meta-analysis of 6,689 subjects from 8 observational studies. Nutr Cancer 2001;40:87–91.

35. Harlap S. The epidemiology of ovarian cancer. In: Markman M, Hoskins WJ, editors. Cancer of the ovary. New York: Raven Press Ltd; 1993.

36. Chang S, Risch HA. Perineal talc exposure and risk of ovarian carcinoma. Cancer 1997;79:2396–401.

37. Ness RB, Cottreau C. Possible role of ovarian epithelial inflammation in ovarian cancer. J Natl Cancer Inst 1999; 91:1459–67.

38. Watson P, Butzow R, Lynch HT, et al and the International Collaborative Group on HNPCC. The clinical features of ovarian cancer in hereditary nonpolyposis colorectal cancer. Gynecol Oncol 2001;82:223–8.

39. Shu XO, Brinton LA, Gao YT, Yuan JM. Population-based case-control study of ovarian cancer in Shanghai. Cancer Res 1989;49:3670–4.

40. Strewing JP, Hartge P, Wacholder S, et al. The risk of cancer associated with specific mutations of BRCA1 and BRCA2 among Ashkenazi Jews. N Engl J Med 1997;336:1401–8.

41. Johannesdottir G, Gudmundsson J, Bergthorsson JT, et al. High prevalence of the 995del5 mutation in Icelandic breast and ovarian cancer patients. Cancer Res 1996;56:3663–5.

42. Gayther SA, Mangion J, Russell P, et al. Variations of risks of breast and ovarian cancer associated with different germline mutations of the BRCA2 gene. Nature 1997;15:103–5.

43. Narod SA, Risch H, Moslehi R, et al. Oral contraceptives and the risk of hereditary ovarian cancer. Hereditary Ovarian Cancer Clinical Study Group. N Engl J Med 1998;339: 424–8.

44. Narod SA, Boyd J. Current understanding of the epidemiology and clinical implications of *BRCA1* and *BRCA2* mutations for ovarian cancer. Curr Opin Obstet Gynecol 2002;14:19–26.

45. Hilton JL, Geisler JP, Rathe JA, et al. Inactivation of *BRCA1* and *BRCA2* in ovarian cancer. J Natl Cancer Inst 2002; 94:1396–406.

46. Harris R, Whittemore AS, Itnyre J, and the Collaborative Ovarian Cancer Group. Characteristics relating to ovarian cancer risk: collaborative analysis of 12 US case-control studies. III. Epithelial tumors of low malignant potential in white women. Am J Epidemiol 1992;136:1204–11.

47. Menzin AW. Update on low malignant potential ovarian tumors. Oncology 2000;14:897–906.

48. Auranen A, Grenman S, Makinen J, et al. Borderline ovarian tumors in Finland: epidemiology and familial occurrence. Am J Epidemiol 1996;114:548–53.

49. Eltabbakh GH, Piver MS. Extraovarian primary peritoneal carcinoma. Oncology 1998;12:813–9.

50. Scully RE. The Eltabbakh/Piver article reviewed. Oncology 1998;12:820–6.

4

Genetics

AMANDA PROWSE, PHD
ANDREY FROLOV, MS
ANDREW K. GODWIN, PHD

Approximately 23,300 new cases of ovarian cancer will be diagnosed in the United States this year, and nearly 14,000 deaths will result from complications associated with this disease, according to the American Cancer Society. Ovarian cancer is the fifth most frequent cause of cancer death in women and accounts for 5% of all cancer deaths.[1] The death rate from ovarian cancer exceeds that from cervical and endometrial carcinoma combined. It has been estimated that in the United States, one woman in 58 will develop ovarian cancer in her lifetime and that one woman in 96 will die of this disease. Due to the asymptomatic nature of ovarian cancer in the initial stages, early detection is difficult, and by the time of diagnosis, more than 70% of these cancers have disseminated beyond the ovary, at which point the 5-year survival rate is less than 20%.[2] Despite the magnitude of this disease, little is known about the molecular events that occur during its development (Figure 4–1).

Epidemiologic studies have shown that endocrine, environmental, and genetic factors are important in the carcinogenesis of ovarian cancer. Age is the most significant risk factor, and family history, nulliparity, early menarche, and late menopause are also among the factors that increase the probability of having the disease. Oral contraceptives, breast-feeding, multiparity, and oopherectomy have been shown to decrease the risk of ovarian cancer.[2,3]

Epithelial ovarian cancers represent 87% of all ovarian cancers. It is the widely held view that these tumors arise from the surface epithelium or from the crypts or inclusion cysts developed from this surface epithelium.[2,3] These cells are modified peritoneal mesothelial cells that (as their name implies) cover the ovarian surface. Embryologically, they are related to other gynecologic tissues, and the malignant tumors often have histologic features that are reminiscent of epithelial cells of the endocervix (in the case of mucinous tumors), the endometrium (in the case of endometrioid tumors), and the fallopian tube (in the case of the most common serous tumors). These normal tissues, whose features are recapitulated in ovarian cancers, are derived from the coelomic epithelium. In the embryo, the ovarian surface epithelium also originates in the coelomic epithelium, which overlies the gonadal ridge. Ovarian surface epithelium is therefore of mesodermal origin and is developmentally closely related to the underlying stomal fibroblasts. For the purpose of this presentation, we will focus exclusively on the genetic alterations that contribute to common epithelial tumors of the ovary.

Common epithelial ovarian tumors are classified according to their cell type (serous, mucinous, endometrioid, and undifferentiated or of mixed histology), grade (borderline or low malignant potential [LMP]; well- to poorly differentiated), and stage (I to IV).[4] Differences at the molecular level most likely account for the heterogeneity seen in ovarian tumors, and a genetic classification system would be useful in determining treatment and outcome. The delineation of the molecular mechanisms involved in the development of ovarian cancer, its clinical behavior, and its response to treatment would undoubtedly help improve the overall management and outcome of the disease. Such information would be invaluable for the accurate assessment of the risk factors and genetic predisposition to the disease, an

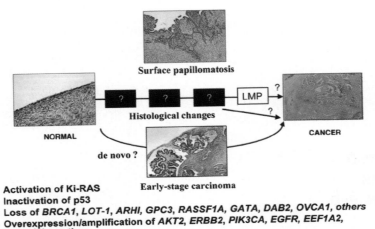

- Activation of Ki-RAS
- Inactivation of p53
- Loss of *BRCA1, LOT-1, ARHI, GPC3, RASSF1A, GATA, DAB2, OVCA1, others*
- Overexpression/amplification of *AKT2, ERBB2, PIK3CA, EGFR, EEF1A2, synucleins, others*
- Allelic losses on chromosomes 17p, 17q, 4q, 18q, 6q, 11q, 11p, 13q, etc.

Figure 4–1. A proposed scheme of ovarian carcinogenesis: is there a histologic continuum between the normal epithelium and overt ovarian cancer that can be defined by genetics? Epithelial ovarian cancer in the vast majority of cases develops from the malignant transformation of the surface epithelium (left panel). These cells are modified peritoneal mesothelial cells and cover the ovarian surface. However, the biologic mechanisms leading to their transformation remain unclear. It has been suggested that tumors of low malignant potential (LMP) are intermediate between adenoma and ovarian carcinoma; other studies have suggested that ovarian cancer arises from precursor lesions (*black boxes*; upper left panel) or de novo. This issue has considerable practical importance from the standpoint of defining the earliest genetic events in the process of malignant transformation of the ovarian surface epithelium. An analogy is provided from studies on the molecular genetics of colonic neoplasia, where knowledge of the histologic continuum between the normal colonic mucosa and overt colon cancer is clearly allowing progress in ordering the genetic changes leading to this disease. Among the greatest impediments to determining if there is a histologic continuum between the normal surface epithelium and ovarian cancer are the vague symptoms that generally lead to the diagnosis of ovarian cancer. This clinical feature means that this disease is most frequently diagnosed at advanced clinical stage. Hence, there has only been limited opportunity to examine stage I ovarian cancers (upper right panel) for genetic changes, and that even these tumors have often reached a substantial size to create the symptoms leading to their diagnosis. New techniques including laser capture microscopy, comparative genomic hybridization, and complementary deoxyribonucleic acid (cDNA) expression microarrays in combination with multivariate pattern-recognition analysis are being used to dissect the molecular genetic events associated with the early and late stages of ovarian oncogenesis.

earlier diagnosis, and the identification of novel targets for drug discovery. Information obtained along these lines would also facilitate the more rational design of adequate therapeutic strategies for ovarian cancer patients with poor prognosis. New techniques, including laser capture microdissection (LCM), comparative genomic hybridization (CGH), and complementary deoxyribonucleic acid (cDNA) expression microarrays in combination with multivariate pattern recognition analysis, are being used to dissect the molecular genetic events associated with ovarian oncogenesis (discussed below).

OVARIAN CARCINOGENESIS: ONCOGENES, TUMOR SUPPRESSOR GENES, AND MUTATOR GENES

Carcinogenesis is a multistep process that involves alterations in many specific genes. The normal cell has multiple independent mechanisms that regulate its growth and differentiation, and several separate events are required to override these control mechanisms. The fundamental mechanisms underlying the genetic basis of cancer are constantly being defined and involve alterations in three general categories of genes: (1) proto-oncogenes, which are involved in growth promotion (defects leading to cancer are a gain of function); (2) tumor suppressor genes, which are negative regulators of growth (a loss of function gives rise to cancer); and (3) DNA repair genes. DNA repair genes or "caretaker" genes help maintain the fidelity of the genome and, when functioning abnormally, can result in a mutator phenotype (ie, an enhanced frequency of unrepaired mutations) and, in turn, a predisposition to cancer (Figure 4–2). Progress is now being made in isolating these genes and the proteins they encode for, determining the normal cellular functions of the proteins, and investigating the mechanisms of tumorigenesis.

Oncogenes

Proto-oncogenes and oncogenes are a class of genes that encode for proteins that function to positively promote cell proliferation. The normal (nonmutant) versions are commonly referred to as proto-oncogenes while the mutant versions or inappropriately active forms are known as oncogenes. Mutations converting proto-oncogenes into their oncogenic forms are usually gain-of-function mutations, and these mutations include point mutations; structural alterations, such as insertions, deletions, inversions, and translocations; gene amplification; and hypomethylation of transcription regulatory elements.[3] Oncogenes were originally identified on the basis of their similarity to retroviral sequences, which were known to be able to transform rodent cells. The study of oncogenes in ovarian cancer has followed one or both of two general strategies: (1) determination of gene expression

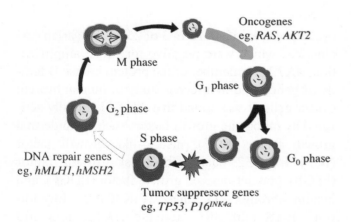

Figure 4–2. The three general categories of genes (ie, oncogenes, tumor suppressor genes, and deoxyribonucleic acid (DNA) repair genes) that give rise to cancer when mutated. Proto-oncogenes are genes that are involved in growth regulation. If a proto-oncogene is mutated or overexpressed, it becomes an oncogene and results in unregulated cell growth or transformation. Mutation in one allele is usually sufficient for a role in cancer development. Tumor suppressor genes suppress cell growth; both copies of a tumor suppressor gene must be lost or mutated to lead to cancer. DNA repair genes are a type of DNA damage response gene. The proteins they encode for act to recognize and repair mismatches in complementary base pairs in the normal DNA sequence. After the DNA is replicated, the mismatch repair proteins "proofread" the DNA to identify and correct such mismatches. If the mismatch repair protein is lost or nonfunctional, normal repair cannot take place, and mismatch errors accumulate in other genes, including oncogenes and tumor suppressor genes.

amounts at the ribonucleic acid (RNA) and/or protein level, and (2) examination of the genes for mutations, by nucleotide sequencing.

Many (at least 60) cellular oncogenes have been identified; however, their involvement in ovarian cancer has yet to be fully elucidated. Table 4–1 shows a few examples of studies evaluating alterations of proto-oncogenes in ovarian cancer. However, as can be seen, there is much variability between studies, and the relative importance of these oncogenes to the pathogenesis of ovarian cancer is therefore unknown.

Some recent reports have implicated three different genes—*RAS, AKT2,* and *PIK3CA*—whose protein products act within signal transduction pathways as being oncogenes involved in the pathogenesis of ovarian cancer (Figure 4–3). The *RAS* family of proto-oncogenes (*H-RAS, Ki-RAS,* and *N-RAS*) encode small guanosine triphosphate (GTP)–binding proteins sharing 90% amino acid identity, termed p21, that have key roles in multiple cytoplasmic signal transduction pathways.[4,5] They are commonly mutated in some cancers, including colon, pancreas, and lung cancers and some forms of leukemia, but not so commonly in others, such as breast, colorectal, and bladder cancers. The normal function of the p21 protein is to interact with tyrosine kinase receptors and other proteins to activate signal transduction pathways.[4,5] To do this, p21^{RAS} has to bind GTP and then hydrolyze it. *P21^{RAS}* mutated at codons 12 and 61 has been shown to have a structure that disfavors its ability to bind to the guanosine triphosphatase (GTPase)–activating protein (GAP), thus keeping p21^{RAS} in the GTP-bound activated mode.[4,5] Overexpression and amplification of the *Ki-RAS* oncogene have been found in a small percentage of ovarian cancer[6] and appear to be rare events. However, mutations in the *Ki-RAS* gene have been reported at a fairly high frequency in ovarian tumors, especially in mucinous tumors of low malignant potential (LMP) (see Table 4–1). In addition, a recent study suggested that the RAS pathway could be activated by other mechanisms.[7] In this study, it was found that in four of eight ovarian cell lines tested, 40 to 60% of p21^{RAS} was found in the active GTP complex, and that downstream targets of p21^{RAS} such as mitogen-activated protein (MAP) kinases p42 and p44 were acti-

Table 4-1. EXAMPLES OF STUDIES EVALUATING ALTERATIONS OF PROTO-ONCOGENES IN OVARIAN CANCER	
BRCA1 Interacting Protein or Complex	Function of Interacting Protein
RAD51	DSB repair
RAD50	DSB repair
BRCA2	DSB repair
BASC (ATM, BLM, MSH2, MSH6, MLH1, RCF)	Mismatch repair
ATP-MSH2	Mismatch repair
H2AX	Signal DNA damage
p53	Transcription factor. Tumor suppressor
PRB	Cell cycle regulator. Tumor suppressor
c-Myc	Transcription factor. Oncogene
ZBRK1	Transcription factor.
ATF	Transcription factor
STAT1	Signal transducer. Transcriptional activation
E2F	Transcription factor. Cell cycle regulator
RNA polymerase II holoenzyme	Transcription
RNA helicase A	Component of RNA polymerase II holoenzyme
Estrogen receptor	Ligand-responsive transcription factor
Androgen receptor	Ligand-responsive transcription factor
CtIP	Transcriptional co-repressor
p300/CBP	Transcriptional coactivator
SWI/SNF	Chromatin remodeling complex
HDAC 1 and 2	Histone deacetylation
BRAP2	Cytoplasmic retention
BARD1	Ubiquitination. Polyadenylation via CstF-50
BAP1	De-ubiquitinating enzyme
FANCD2	DNA repair
γ-Tubulin	Component of the centrosome

DNA = deoxyribonucleic acid; DSB = double-strand break; RNA = ribonucleic acid.

vated, ETS-2 was phosphorylated at position threonine 72, and RAS target genes such as *uPA* were transcribed. However, only one of these cell lines contained an activating point mutation in one of the *RAS* genes.[7] In contrast to *Ki-RAS*, mutations in the *H-RAS* gene have rarely been found in ovarian tumors. However, there is evidence that *H-RAS* is overexpressed in ovarian tumors, due to elevated binding of transcriptional enhancers, such as the glucocorticoid receptor (GR), the estrogen receptor (ER) and p53, to the *H-RAS* GR element, the ER element, and the p53 binding element, respectively.[8,9]

AKT2, which encodes a serine-threonine protein kinase, is a recently characterized oncogene located at chromosome 19q13.1-13.2. Cheng and colleagues first observed that the *AKT2* gene was amplified in 2 of 15 primary human ovarian carcinomas and in 2 of 8 ovarian cancer cell lines.[10] A larger study by Bellacosa and colleagues showed, by Southern blot analysis, amplification of the *AKT2* gene in 16 of 132 (12%) ovarian carcinomas.[11] *AKT2* alterations were not detected in 24 benign or borderline ovarian tumors. In addition, Northern blot analysis revealed overexpression of *AKT2* in 3 of 25 fresh ovarian carcinomas, which were negative for *AKT2* amplification. *AKT2* is a member of the protein kinase B family of genes, and in a recent study of human ovarian cancer cells, it was found that AKT2 is rapidly activated by mitogenic growth factors such as epidermal growth factor (EGF), insulin-like growth factor (IGF) I, IGF2 basic fibroblast growth factor (bFGF), platelet-derived growth factor (PDGF), and insulin, through PI3 kinase (PIK3CA).[12] In addition, RAS and SRC activate *AKT2* in a PI3 kinase–dependent manner (see Figure 4–3). *PIK3CA* has also been shown to have an increased copy number in approximately 77% (7 of 9) of ovarian cancer cell lines and in 58% (7 of 12) of ovarian cancers analyzed.[13] This increase in copy number was found to be associated with an increase in PIK3CA transcription, protein expression, and activity. PTEN is a tumor suppressor that acts by opposing the action of PI3-kinase by dephosphorylating the signaling lipid phosphatidylinositol triphosphate (Figure 4–3).[3–5] PTEN has been shown to be down regulated in a proportion of ovarian

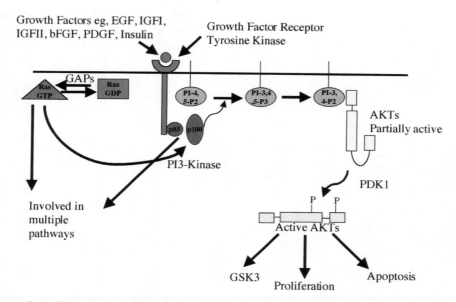

Figure 4–3. The activation of AKT by growth factors and by RAS through PI3 kinase. The activation of AKT through PI3 kinase pathway involves several steps. PI3 kinase phosphorylates membrane lipids, which, after subsequent modification, produce the second messengers PI-4,5-P2 and PI-3,4, 5-P3. AKT has a high affinity for these second messengers and is therefore recruited to the membrane, where PI-3,4,5-P3 promotes a conformational change in AKT that results in increased kinase activity. Phosphorylation (indicated by P) of AKT by both PI-3,4,5-P3–dependent protein kinase (PDK1) and mitogen-activated protein kinase activation protein kinase 2 is required for maximal activation. On its release from the membrane, AKT becomes available to phosphorylate downstream targets such as glycogen synthase kinase 3 (GSK3), leading to inactivation of GSK3 and stimulation of glycogen synthesis. (EGF = epidermal growth factor; IGF = insulin-like growth factor; bFGF = basic fibroblast growth factor; PDGF = platelet-derived growth factor; GAPs = guanosine triphosphatase-activating proteins; GTP = guanosine triphosphate; GDP = guanosine diphosphate.) (Adapted from Lynch HT et al; Tlsty TD.[55,274] A molecular blueprint for targeting cancer. Nat Genet 1999;21:64–5.)

tumors, and an inverse correlation between PTEN expression and activated (Phospho) AKT2 expression has been found.[14] Additional studies have shown elevated levels of AKT2 activity in 33 of 91 (36.3%) ovarian tumors, the majority of which were high-grade and stages III to IV.[15] Fifteen of these tumors showed high levels of PI3-kinase activity, and a further three tumors showed down regulation of PTEN. Therefore, this important pathway, that has been implicated in processes, including cell cycle, glucose transport and catabolism, cell adhesion, apoptosis, and RAS signaling; appears to be frequently disrupted in ovarian tumors by alterations in PTEN, PIK3CA and/or ATK2.

Further studies using the technique of CGH to look for regions of amplification have suggested that several other oncogenes may be involved in the pathogenesis of ovarian cancer. CGH is a powerful technique that can, in principle, reveal regions of amplification together with any regions of allele loss

or aneuploidy, in a single experiment. The CGH test uses a mixture of DNA from matched normal and tumor cells in competitive fluorescent in situ hybridization (FISH). With the aid of image-processing software, chromosomal regions can be picked out where the ratio of FISH signal deviates from expectation, marking regions of amplification or allele loss in the tumor (Figure 4–4). Sonada and colleagues analyzed 25 malignant ovarian carcinomas and two ovarian tumors of LMP.[16] They found that most of the carcinoma specimens displayed numerous imbalances, with the most frequent sites of copy number increases being 8q24.1, 20q13.2-qter, 3q26.3, 1q32, 20p, 9p21-pter, 12p, and 5p14-pter. DNA amplification was identified in 48% of the tumors examined, with the most frequent sites of amplification being at 8q24.1-24.2, 3q26.3, and 20q13.2-qter. Other recurrent sites of amplification included 7q36, 17q25, and 19q13.1-13.2. Candidate oncogenes that lie within these regions of amplification include *MYBL2* at

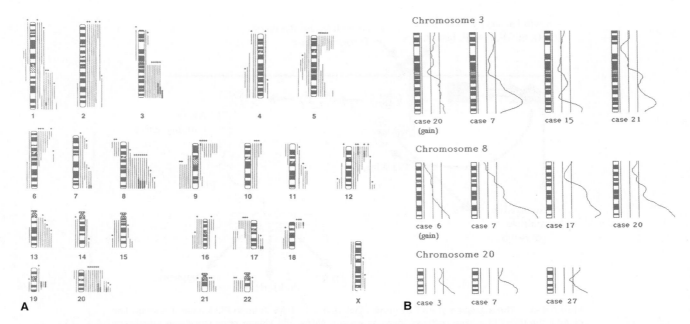

Figure 4–4. *A,* Summary of comparative genomic hybridization imbalances detected in 27 ovarian tumors. Vertical lines on the left side of each chromosome ideogram represent losses of genetic material in a given tumor whereas those on the right side correspond to gains and amplifications. Amplification sites are represented by solid bars. Imbalances observed in high-grade (grade 3) tumors are each indicated by a plus symbol (+) above the line. (Reproduced with permission from Sonoda G, et al.[16]) *B,* Average fluorescence ratio profiles of chromosomes 3, 8, and 20 in representative ovarian carcinomas exhibiting gains or amplifications of portions of these chromosomes. Each profile represents averages calculated from at least six metaphase spreads. The amplification sites overlap at 3q26.3, 8q24.1-24.2, and 20q13.2-qter. In case 15, the amplification peak of the chromosome 3 profile is distal to q26.3, suggesting the possibility of a second target region in this tumor. (Reproduced with permission from Sonoda G, et al.[16]).

20q13.1, *EVI1* at 3q26, and *c-MYC* at 8q24.[16] Analysis of the homogeneously staining region (HSR), a cytogenetic indicator of gene amplification, by micro-FISH has identified amplification of *c-MYC* as the origin of the HSR in ovarian carcinoma.[17] A recent study has shown that *c-MYC* overexpression is more common in serous adenocarcinomas and is associated with stage III disease, suggesting a role in disease progression.[18]

Several other oncogenes have been studied in ovarian tumors. Overexpression of the *ERBB2* (HER-2/neu) oncogene has been reported in 26% of human ovarian cancers and has been shown to be associated with poor prognosis in some studies[19] but not in others.[20] No relationship has been detected between *ERBB2* amplification and histologic grade.[21] Amplification of c-*ERBB2* has also been detected in two of eight ovarian carcinoma cell lines examined,[22] and a recent report associates experimental overexpression of the gene with paclitaxel (Taxol) resistance.[23] The proto-oncogene *c-FMS* codes for the receptor for colony-stimulating

factor-1 (CSF-1), a growth factor. An in situ hybridization study of 23 benign and malignant ovarian tumors showed that c-*FMS* expression is associated strongly with the clinicopathologic features (high grade and advanced stage) of ovarian cancers.[24] c-*FMS* expression was also observed in 57% of ovarian cancers in another study.[25] In addition, both the transcripts for c-*FMS* and its binding ligand (CSF-1) were detected in ovarian carcinoma cell lines[26] and surgically excised carcinomas,[27] suggesting an autocrine growth pathway in ovarian cancer cells. Expression of c-*FOS* has been detected in ovarian epithelial cancers.[28] Expression of transforming growth factor (TGF)-β and epidermal growth factor receptor (EGF-R) in ovarian carcinoma cell lines has also been described,[29] and limited work has suggested a relationship between EGF-R and prognosis.[20] One recent study has shown that transforming growth factor-β (TGF-β) receptor type I is mutated in a proportion of ovarian carcinomas.[30] The protein elongation factor EEF1A2 is amplified in a proportion of primary ovarian tumors and ovarian cell lines and has been shown to have oncogenic, properties such that it enhances focus formation, allows anchorage-independent growth, and decreases the doubling time of rodent fibroblasts.[31] Other proto-oncogenes have been examined in small numbers of ovarian cancer biopsy specimens and cell lines, including *L-MYC, c-MYB,* and *c-MOS*[20] and *N-MYC, c-SIS, N-RAS, c-ABL, c-FES, vascular endothelial growth factor (VEGF),* and *INT2.*[6,20,32] However, no amplification, deletion, re-arrangements, or point mutations have been observed in these genes.[33]

A candidate oncogene that has recently been identified through genetic screens (Figures 4–5 and 4–6) for genes overexpressed in ovarian cancer is *gamma (γ-) synuclein.* The synucleins (alpha, beta, gamma, and synoretin) are a family of small cytoplasmic proteins that are predominantly expressed in neurons.[34] *Synucleins* have not been previously shown to be oncogenes by the strictest of criteria; however, mutations in α-*synuclein* have been detected in some familial cases of Parkinson's disease.[34] Abnormal expression of α-synuclein has been observed in a number of neurodegenerative diseases.[34] The function of the synucleins are unclear; however, they exhibit weak homology to 14-3-3 proteins, a family of proteins known to function as adaptor/chaperone proteins. Bruening and colleagues reported that γ-synuclein is expressed in the majority (more than 80%) of late-stage ovarian carcinomas, but it is not expressed in normal ovarian surface epithelium.[35] Interestingly, γ-synuclein was also detected in some preneoplastic lesions, such as epithelial inclusions (entrapment or invagination of ovarian surface epithelium), and in cells with papillary projections from ovaries of high-risk women. Bruening and colleagues have also observed that when γ-synuclein is exogenously expressed in cell lines derived from ovarian tumors, the cells become highly motile (Bruening and Godwin, unpublished data). Furthermore, Pan and colleagues recently found that γ-synuclein can promote cell survival and inhibit stress- and chemotherapy drug-induced apoptosis by modulating the ERK and JNK pathways, suggesting that γ-synuclein is likely to be involved in the pathogenesis of ovarian cancer by promoting tumor cell survival under adverse

conditions and by providing resistance to certain anticancer drugs.[36] It is currently hypothesized that the up-regulation of γ-synuclein expression may occur at very early stages in ovarian cancers and that this abnormal expression contributes to the progression and metastatic spread of the disease. We (and others) have detected neither mutations or gene amplifications of *γ-synuclein* in ovarian

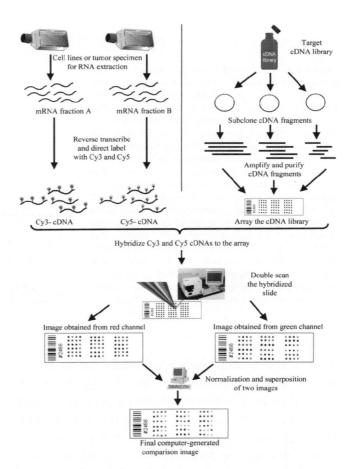

Figure 4–5. A schematic diagram showing glass complementary deoxyribonucleic acid (cDNA) microarray technology. Ribonucleic acid (RNA) extracted from two samples (eg, tumor and normal tissues) is reverse-transcribed and labeled with two fluorochromes, Cy3 (fluoresces in green light) and Cy5 (fluoresces in red light). cDNA arrays are fabricated by printing the cDNA fragments onto positively charged glass slides (polylysine-coated). Cy3- and Cy5-labeled cDNAs are combined and hybridized to a single slide. Following hybridization and processing, the arrays are scanned for each wavelength, and the separate images are obtained. The last step includes the normalization and superposition of two images, resulting in a final image. Black spots represent no detectable signal; yellow spots indicate that the genes are expressed at similar levels in both populations (red plus green); and red or green signals indicate that the genes are expressed at higher levels in one cell population than in the other. (mRNA = messenger RNA.)

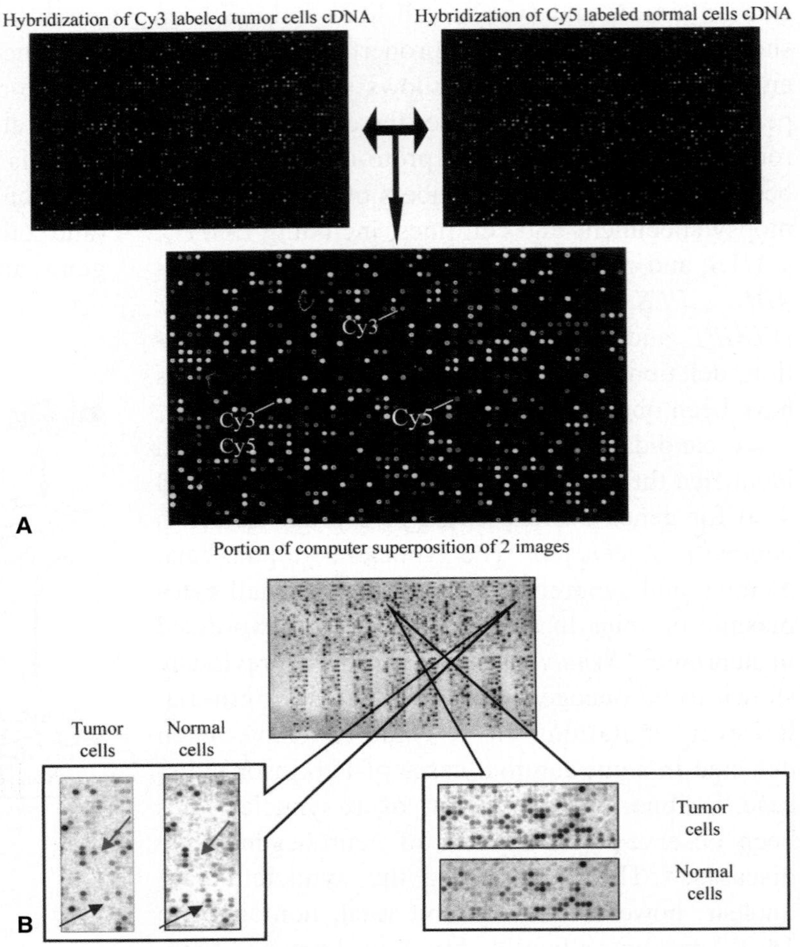

Hybridization of Cy3 labeled tumor cells cDNA   Hybridization of Cy5 labeled normal cells cDNA

A

Portion of computer superposition of 2 images

B

Figure 4–6. Examples of complementary deoxyribonucleic acid (cDNA) array technology. *A,* Glass cDNA microarray technology. Upper two panels show an individual's scans of Cy3-labeled tumor cells and Cy5-labeled normal cells (different colors represent different intensities of hybridization signal); lower panel shows the false color superposition of those two expression patterns, where red dots are genes expressed at higher levels in normal versus tumor cells, green dots are genes expressed at higher levels in tumor versus normal cells, and yellow dots represent genes expressed at similar levels in both cell populations. *B,* Membrane cDNA array technology. Comparison of two membranes hybridized with tumor and normal cells. The intensity of each spot is compared. Right enlarged area shows similar regions of expression, and left enlarged area shows genes expressed only in tumor cells (*red arrows*) or normal cells (*blue arrows*).

tumors and ovarian tumor cell lines, or in breast tumors and breast tumor cell lines[35] suggesting that the malignant phenotype observed correlates with high-level expression of wild-type γ-synuclein. Previous studies have shown that γ-synuclein messenger ribonucleic acid (mRNA) expression is regulated by oncostatin M, TGF-β, EGF, and TGF-α in breast cancer cells and in ovarian cancer cells.[37] In order to elucidate the molecular mechanisms that convert *γ-synuclein* from a silent gene in normal tissue to an actively transcribed gene in cancer, the 5′ promoter region of *γ-synuclein* was recently identified.[38] Liu and colleagues observed that transcription of *γ-synuclein* in breast cancer cells is controlled by DNA methylation-dependent and methylation-independent mechanisms. Analysis of the promoter has found that (1) intron 1 plays a critical role in the control of *γ-synuclein* transcrip-

tion through *cis*-regulatory sequences, (2) activator protein-1 (AP-1) is functionally involved in *γ-synuclein* transcription in breast cancer cells through its binding to an AP-1 motif located in intron 1, and (3) the exon 1 region of *γ-synuclein* gene contains a CpG island that is unmethylated in γ-synuclein–positive breast cancer cell lines but is densely methylated in γ-synuclein–negative breast tumor cells.[38,39]

Another interesting candidate oncogene, H-*ryk* is an unusual member of the receptor tyrosine kinase family, which is catalytically inactive due to amino acid substitutions of conserved residues in the catalytic domain.[40,41] H-Ryk has been shown to be overexpressed in borderline and malignant ovarian tumors,[42] and overexpression of H-Ryk in the mouse fibroblast cell line NIH 3T3 is transforming in vitro and in vivo.[43]

Tumor Suppressor Genes

The concept that genes can suppress cell growth came from early studies of somatic cell fusion.[44,45] In those experiments, fusion of tumorigenic cells with normal cells resulted in hybrids that could continue to grow in culture but were no longer tumorigenic in animals. Moreover, when some of the hybrid cells reexpressed the tumorigenic phenotype, that reexpression correlated with the specific loss of chromosomes derived from the normal nontumorigenic parental cell. In 1969, de Mars proposed that in certain familial cancers, gene carriers might be heterozygous for a recessive mutation and that the cancer appears because of subsequent somatic mutation causing an individual cell to become homozygous for the cancer-causing gene.[46] Epidemiologic analysis of retinoblastoma and Wilms' tumor provided important evidence for this theory[47,48] and led to what is now referred to as Knudson's "two-hit" hypothesis (Figure 4–7). Two forms of the disease were observed: patients with a family history of disease often presented with multiple bilateral lesions, and patients without a family history typically presented with single unilateral lesions and at a later age than did those with familial disease. Knudson and Strong speculated that the familial form of disease represented the inheritance of a mutation predisposing to neoplasia and that only one additional rate-limiting genetic event was necessary for tumorigenesis. Sporadic tumors, on the other hand, required two independent genetic lesions and would therefore be slower to develop. Since two independent lesions occurring in the same cell would be rare, only unilateral tumors would be expected. This hypothesis was confirmed at the molecular level with the isolation of the *retinoblastoma* (*RB1*) gene. The development of retinoblastoma has been shown to involve loss of both alleles at a single locus, with individuals with the hereditary form of *retinoblastoma* having one mutated allele in the germline.[49] The *retinoblastoma* gene is the prototypic tumor suppressor gene that conforms to the classic definition of Knudson's two-hit hypothesis.

Tumor suppressor gene studies have received far more attention than oncogene studies in ovarian cancer, but this is stated with the caveat that much of this work has focused on identifying the possible locations where tumor suppressor genes of relevance to the disease may reside in the ovarian tumor cell genome rather than on the actual study of known tumor suppressor genes. The most popular approach to identifying where tumor suppressor genes may reside in the cancer cell genome is examination for loss of heterozygosity (LOH). In accordance to Knudson's hypothesis, the first "hit" usually involves a mutation in one of the alleles of the gene while the second "hit," which leads to loss of function of the remaining normal copy of the gene, may occur by a variety of mechanisms, including mutation or deletion. This latter mechanism appears to be most com-

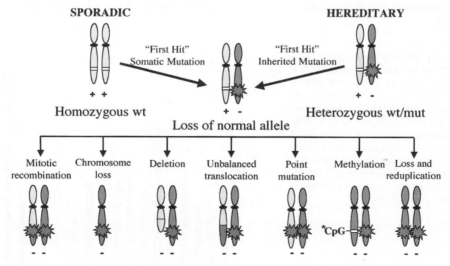

Figure 4–7.   Proposed mechanisms leading to loss of heterozygosity. (WT = Wud type; mut = mutant; * = methylation; CpG = Cpg island; c = cytosine; g = guonine.)

mon, and from it derives the way to determine where an unknown tumor suppressor gene may reside or if the locus for a known tumor suppressor gene is altered. Polymorphic markers distributed at high density throughout the genome can be used to distinguish the paternal and maternal contribution of DNA in normal tissues and tumor from the same individual. Loss of DNA from one chromosome in tumor cells is associated with the failure of the polymorphic marker to detect the heterozygosity characteristic of the individual's normal DNA at that locus, hence LOH. When a series of polymorphic markers, which cover sites throughout the genome, are used on a series of ovarian tumors and related constitutive DNA, the frequency of LOH in a given region of the genome can be determined. It is often stated that a frequency of LOH of approximately 30% suggests that this region of the genome contains a tumor suppressor gene targeted for inactivation by deletion, but it should be realized that this exact value has no special significance. At any rate, detection of such a frequently deleted region is generally followed by expanding the panel of tumors examined along with the density of polymorphic markers in the region. This refines the region where the gene may reside by defining the minimal region of deletion in the tumor series and sets the stage for positional cloning to identify candidate genes.[50,51] Of course, one may also use a limited number of polymorphic markers that reside in a region where a known tumor suppressor resides and gain some circumstantial evidence for the involvement of that gene in carcinogenesis.

As with most rules, there are always exceptions. As stated above, it has always been thought that both alleles of a tumor suppressor gene must be inactivated. However, it has now been shown that genes such as $p27^{KIP1}$ (a cyclin-dependent kinase inhibitor) and $Dmp1$ (a Cyclin D-binding Myb-like protein) are haploinsufficient for tumor suppression.[52,53] It is likely that these two examples are the first of a number of tumor suppressor genes in which haploinsufficiency, leading to reduced levels of a protein, will be sufficient for tumorigenesis.[54] Haploinsufficiency of other tumor suppressors (OVCA1, for example) has been suggested to be important in the pathogenesis of ovarian carcinoma (see below).

Increasingly, different mechanisms of mutation are being implicated in the inactivation of tumor suppressor genes leading to neoplasia. These include point mutations, deletions, insertions, hypermethylation, and alterations in genomic imprinting; loss of genetic material, leading to haploinsufficiency; dominant-negative mutations; and homozygous deletions (see Figure 4–7).

Numerous LOH studies have been performed on ovarian tumors. Whole genome allelotyping studies of a large number of ovarian cancers revealed that LOH has been observed on every chromosome arm. In one study, more than 30% of the tumors studied showed LOH on chromosomes 6, 9, 13q, 17, 18q, 19p, 22q, and Xp (Figure 4–8). The highest LOH rates were detected on 17p (13.3, 13.1), 17q (q21, q22-q23), 18q (q21.3-qter), 6q (q26-27), 11q (q23.3-qter), and 11p (p13-p15.5), in descending

Figure 4–8. Summary of allelic loss observed for polymorphic DNA markers in ovarian carcinomas. Allelotyping of a large number of ovarian cancers revealed that loss of heterozygosity (LOH) has been observed on every chromosome arm. Chromosome arms displaying greater than 30% LOH include chromosomes 6, 9, 13q, 17, 18q, 19, 22q, and Xp (histogram). LOH for the short arms of nonacrocentric chromosomes is depicted by blue bars; allelic loss on the long arm of chromosomes is represented by yellow bars. The chromosomal location for candidate ovarian tumor suppressor genes are indicated by arrows. (Adapted from Lynch HT et al.[55])

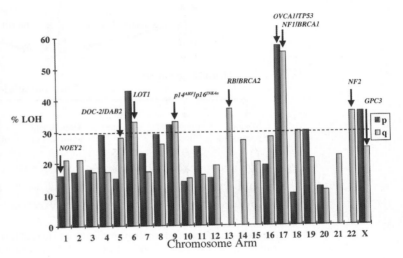

order.[55] These studies have suggested the existence of a large number of tumor suppressor genes, most of which have yet to be identified.

Other study groups have also concentrated on more specific chromosomal regions, using a large number of highly polymorphic markers to define a minimal region of allelic loss, and various candidate tumor suppressor genes have been suggested from these studies.

Multiple minimal regions of allelic loss were observed on chromosome 3p in epithelial ovarian tumors, at 3p25-26, 3p24-25, 3p14.2, and 3p12-13.[56,57] Candidate tumor suppressor genes within 3p include *VHL* (which is mutated in the majority of clear cell renal carcinomas), *FHIT, BAP-1* at 3p21.3 (which interacts with *BRCA1*),[58] *FUS1*,[59] and *SEMA3B* at 3p21.3,[60] *DUTT-1* at 3p12 (which was identified in a region that is homozygously deleted in a lung and a breast cancer cell line), *APPL* at 3p14.3-21 (encoding an adapter molecule that interacts with the AKT2 protein),[61] *RARb, TGFBR2,* and *PTPase.* Mutational analysis of the *VHL* gene and the *FHIT* gene has suggested their lack of involvement in ovarian carcinogenesis,[62,63] and the other candidate tumor suppressor genes have yet to be analyzed for mutations in ovarian tumors.

RASSF1A has recently been identified on 3p21.3 and was shown to be hypermethylated in 10 to 40% of primary ovarian tumors and 40% of ovarian tumor cell lines.[64,65] *RASSF1A* has also been shown to be inactivated in small cell lung carcinoma (SCLC), nonsmall cell lung carcinoma (NSCLC), malignant mesothelioma, renal cell carcinomas, nasopharyngeal carcinomas, and breast tumors.[64–76]

LOH studies concentrating on chromosome 12 mapped the chromosomal localization of two putative tumor suppressor genes.[77] Two regions showing common allelic losses were 12p12.3-13.1 and 12q23-ter and LOH was more commonly found in late-stage tumors. The region of LOH at 12p12.3-13.1 includes the genes that code for the ETS-family transcription factor (TEL) and p27[KIP1]. Mutational analysis of these two genes revealed no abnormalities, and the authors concluded that these two genes were not the relevant ovarian cancer tumor suppressor genes. However, in a recent immunohistochemical and Western blot analysis of 66 ovarian adenocarcinomas and 16 LMP tumors, loss of expression of p27[KIP1] was observed in 33% of ovarian adenocarcinomas versus 6% of LMP tumors.[78] In addition, cytoplasmic staining was observed in 55% of the 82 tumors analyzed with or without concomitant nuclear staining. The regulation of p27[KIP1] is complex, and the abundance of p27[KIP1] in the cell is determined either at or after translation, for example, as a result of phosphorylation by cyclin E/cyclin-dependent kinase 2 (CDK2) complexes, degradation via the ubiquitin (Ub)-proteasome pathway and proteolytic processing that rapidly eliminates the cyclin-binding domain, and sequestration by cyclin D2/CDK4 complexes upon activation of MYC.[79–81] A defect in any of these processes could contribute to a loss of p27[KIP1] expression. In addition, there is evidence that loss of the tumor suppressor gene Tuberin or binding to the transcriptional activator p38[JAB1] causes p27[KIP1] to be mislocalized to the cytoplasm, where it is rapidly degraded.[82] One study has shown that p38[JAB1] is over expressed in a proportion of ovarian tumors and this was inversely correlated with p27[K1P1] expression.[83] Furthermore, the recent finding that the murine gene *p27[KIP1]* is tumorigenic after loss of only one allele suggests that haploinsufficiency of p27[KIP1] could also lead to tumorigenesis.[52] Expression of p27[KIP1] has been reported to be positively associated with long-term survival of patients with epithelial ovarian cancer, and loss of expression of p27[KIP1] has been associated with a short time to progression; therefore, p27[KIP1] may have potential as a new prognostic marker.[84]

Two critical regions of deletion on chromosome 7q have been reported.[85] In addition, a re-arrangement in the *PAI-1* gene in one of the regions was identified. Plasminogen activator inhibitor (PAI)-1 inhibits plasminogen activators (PAs) and thus the PA-mediated breakdown of extracellular matrix proteins. It was hypothesized that inactivation of the *PAI-1* gene might disrupt the PA/PAI balance and favor the dissemination of tumor cells and the establishment of metastatic lesions. Contrary to this hypothesis, studies have found higher concentrations of PAI-1 in ovarian cancers than in benign ovarian tumors and normal ovaries, with especially elevated levels in high-grade tumors.[86,87] In addition, metastases of ovarian cancer have been found to have a higher PAI-1 content than the primary tumors,[86,88] and it has been shown that an elevated PAI-1 level is a poor prognostic factor for survival in advanced-stage epithelial ovarian cancer patients.[89] PAI-1 may therefore be protecting the cancer cells from proteolytic degradation.[89,90] Another possible candidate ovarian tumor suppressor gene, at 7q31.1, is the *caveolin-1* gene.[91] Caveolin-1 is a principal component of caveola membranes, vesicular invaginations of the plasma membrane that are thought to participate in vesicular trafficking events and signal transduction processes. It has been shown that caveolin-1 mRNA and protein expression are lost or reduced during cell transformation by activated oncogenes and targeted down-regulation of caveolin-1 in NIH 3T3 cells using antisense caveolin-1 is sufficient to drive cell transformation and hyperactivate the p42/44 MAP kinase cascade.[91] Two signaling pathways, Ras-p42/44 MAP kinase and protein kinase A, appear to be involved in transcriptionally down-regulating *caveolin-1* expression.[92] *Caveolin-1* was identified as a potential ovarian cancer tumor suppressor by the use of a microarray-based approach to identifying genes differentially regulated in ovarian carcinomas compared to a normal ovary.[93] *Caveolin-1* has been shown to be down-regulated in some ovarian cell lines and tumors, and overexpression of *caveolin-1* in OVCAR3 cells (which do not express *caveolin-1*) resulted in increased apoptosis.[93] Interestingly, caveolin-1 has

recently been identified as a positive regulator of estrogen receptor alpha (ER-alpha) signaling, whereby caveolin-1 drives ligand-independent nuclear translocation and activation of ER-alpha.[94] The *TES* gene, which also maps to 7q31.1, has been shown to be methylated in 7 of 10 ovarian carcinomas and all of 30 tumor-derived cell lines tested.[95] Furthermore, reexpression of *TES* in HeLa and OVCAR5 cells resulted in a significant reduction in growth potential, indicative of a tumor suppressor phenotype. The function of *TES*, however, is currently unknown.

Lu and colleagues defined 4 centimorgan (cM) and 11cM minimally deleted regions at 11p15.1 and 11p15.5-15.3 that are associated with high-grade nonmucinous epithelial ovarian carcinoma.[96] Region 11p15 has been shown to harbor multiple imprinted genes (ie, those that are expressed from a specific parental allele). Imprinted genes have now been implicated in the pathogenesis of tumors (Figure 4–9).[97] For example, it has been shown that many Wilms' tumors may not express H19 RNA, and this is due to either LOH or biallelic methylation of *H19*. In addition, IGF2 is overexpressed in Wilms' tumors, and this is correlated with a relaxation of imprinting.[98,99] Imprinted genes in this region include *TSSC3* (which is homologous to the mouse apoptosis gene *TDAG51*), *IGF2, H19,* p57[KIP2], and *KVLQTI*.[97,100] Loss of imprinting of *H19* and *IGF2* has been observed only in a few malignant serous cystadeno-

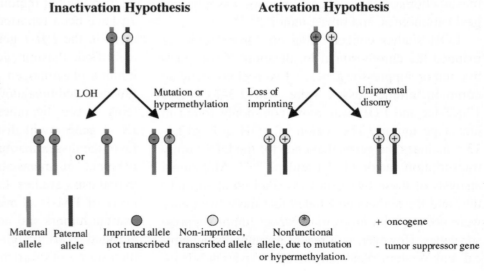

Figure 4–9. Alterations in imprinted tumor suppressor genes and oncogenes. The inactivation hypothesis involves loss of expression of a tumor suppressor gene. In this example, the maternal allele is inactivated by imprinting (the "first hit"), followed by loss of heterozygosity (LOH) or mutation or methylation of the paternal allele (the "second hit"). The activation hypothesis involves overexpression of an oncogene. Overexpression arises after loss of imprinting of the maternal allele or uniparental disomy of the paternal allele. (Adapted from Feinberg AP.[275] Genomic imprinting and gene activation in cancer. Nat Genet 1993;4:110–3.)

carcinomas and in benign mucinous cystadenomas and noncancerous endometritic cysts and is therefore unlikely to be of primary importance in the development of ovarian malignancy.[101] The *SRBC* gene, which was isolated in a yeast-2-hybrid screen for proteins interacting with BRCA1, maps to 11p15.5.[102] Interestingly, a frameshift mutation was identified in one of six ovarian cancer cell lines analyzed. Furthermore, *SRBC* expression was shown to be down-regulated in a proportion of breast and lung cancer cell lines. and this was associated with promoter-region hypermethylation. A study of the expression of SRBC in ovarian tumors will certainly be of interest, especially in light of the fact that SRBC may interact with BRCA1.

A region on the long arm of chromosome 11 also shows a high frequency of loss of heterozygosity (LOH) in ovarian tumors, and the *BARX2* gene that maps within this region has recently been shown to have the properties of a tumor suppressor in ovarian cancer: BARX2 was expressed in normal ovarian surface epithelium and in serous or mixed mesodermal tumors but had lower expression in endometrioid and clear cell carcinomas.[103] Mouse *Barx2* is a regulator of N–cell adhesion molecule (CAM) and L1-CAM, and it has been proposed that down-regulation of CAMs such as E-cadherin play a role in the loss of cell-to-cell and cell-to-matrix contact in the later stages of epithelial tumorigenesis. Interestingly, BARX2 expression was correlated with expression of the CAM cadherin 6 in ovarian tumors, and expression of BARX2 in a cell line that did not endogenously express BARX2 resulted in the suppression of cell invasion, migration, and adhesion.

LOH at the *p53* locus on 17-13.1 and at the *RB1* locus on 13q14 are two of the most common genetic alterations described thus far in human cancers (see Figure 4–8). Investigators have found that approximately 30% to 80% of the ovarian tumors examined show changes affecting the *RB1* or the *p53* gene loci.[104–111] However, in 95% of the tumors showing LOH for chromosome 13q polymorphisms defining the *RB1* locus, normal RB was expressed.[112,113] In epithelial ovarian carcinomas, *p53* mutation is present in about 30% of human ovarian cancers and in about 50% of stage II serous ovarian carcinomas.[111] Overexpression of the p53 protein has also been

observed in about 50% of ovarian cancers.[55,109] Mutation of the *p53* gene appears to be an early event in a distinct subset of ovarian cancers and occurs before the spread of cancer cells, as an identical pattern of mutation of the *p53* gene was observed in tumor cells collected from both the primary and metastatic sites.[110,114] This observation is in contrast to other data comparing early-stage versus late-stage tumors for *p53* mutations, which indicated that *p53* mutations were more common in late- than in early-stage disease.[115,116]

Chromosome 17 is one of the most frequently altered chromosomes reported in ovarian cancers, and LOH on chromosome 17p has been reported in more than 60% of ovarian tumors.[50,117–121] In addition to *p53*, chromosome 17 has a number of cancer-causing genes, including the *BRCA1* gene at 17q21, *prohibitin* and *NM23* at 17q23-24, and the proto-oncogene *ERBB2* at 17q21 (Figure 4–10); however, none of these have been clearly shown to be important in the development of sporadic forms of ovarian cancer.[55] The *NF1* gene at 17q11 is a putative tumor suppressor gene. NF1 contains a GAP-related domain (GRD) that accelerates the hydrolysis of RAS-bound GTP to GDP, thereby converting the RAS oncogene from its active form to its inactive form. There are two forms of the NF1 GRD transcript (type I and type II) that have been shown to be differentially expressed between normal human ovarian surface epithelial (HOSE) and malignant ovarian cell lines, with a significant decrease in type II isoform expression and an increase in type I expression in ovarian cancer cells and tumor tissue, relative to HOSE cells.[122] An increase in the type II-to-type I ratio was associated with a decrease in the cell proliferation rate in cancer cell lines. It has been suggested that the relative expression of the NF1 type I and type II isoforms affects cell growth and differentiation in certain cancer cell lines and that this might be due to differences in the catalytic activities of the two isoforms affecting their abilities to regulate *RAS* activity.[122]

Studies have reported a high frequency of LOH at 17p13.3 (see Figures 4–8 and 4–10) in early-stage ovarian tumors and in ovarian tumors possessing wild-type *p53*.[117,123,124] LOH at 17p13.3 has also been reported in breast tumors,[125–128] primitive neu-

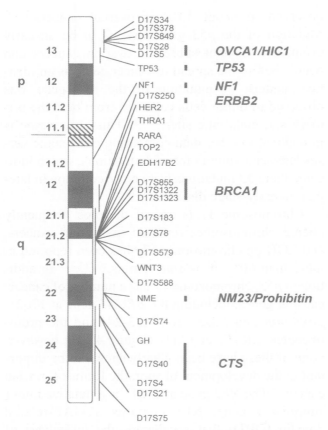

Figure 4–10. A summary of the candidate cancer genes and loci on chromosome 17. Loci that are frequently reported include *OVCA1* and *HIC1* at 17p13.3, *TP53* at 17p13.1, *NF1* at 17q11, *ERBB2* at 17q21, *BRCA1* at 17q12-21, *prohibitin* and *NM23* at 17q13-24, and candidate tumor suppressor (*CTS*) locus at 17q22-q23. The physical location and order of the several polymorphisms (Variable number of tandem repeats [VNTRs] and microsatellites) on chromosome 17 are shown. (Adapted from Godwin AK, Vanderveer L, Schultz DC, et al.[50] A common region of deletion on chromosome 17q in both sporadic and familial epithelial ovarian tumors distal to BRCA-1. Am J Hum Genet 1994;55:666–77.)

roectodermal tumors,[129] carcinoma of the cervix uteri,[130] medulloblastomas,[131] osteosarcomas, astrocytomas,[132] and lung tumors,[133] suggesting that genes on 17p13.3 may play a role in the development of multiple cancers. Schultz and colleagues defined a minimal region of allelic loss at 17p13.3 in ovarian tumors, and, by positional cloning within this region, identified two genes, *OVCA1* and *OVCA2*.[51] *OVCA1* is mutated in some ovarian tumor cell lines, and its protein levels are decreased or lost in nearly 40% of ovarian adenocarcinomas. Expression of low levels of exogenous OVCA1 results in dramatic growth suppression and decreased levels of cyclin D1.[134] *OVCA1* codes for a highly conserved

protein with no known function, but the C-terminal region of OVCA1 appears to interact with an RNA-binding motif protein named RBM8A.[135] RBM8, also referred to as Y14, has been shown to be a shuttling protein, which binds preferentially to spliced mRNA upstream of exon–exon junctions and remains in this position in the cytoplasm.[136–141] RBM8/Y14 may therefore be involved in communicating to the cytoplasm the location of exon and intron boundaries and might play an important role in postsplicing events such as mRNA transport and nonsense mediated delay.

The tumor suppressor gene *p16^INK4a/CDKN2* is located within a region of frequent LOH in ovarian tumors (see Figure 4–8).[142–145] However, studies have shown that inactivation of this gene by homozygous deletion, mutation, or hypermethylation of the promoter region is infrequent in ovarian tumors.[142,144–148] More recently, it has been found that there is another tumor suppressor gene at the same locus.[149,150] This gene, *p14^ARF*, actually shares the *p16* exon 2 and 3 (although in a different reading frame), and *p16^INK4a* and *p14^ARF* have an alternative exon 1 (referred to as 1α and 1β respectively). As described above, most human cancers show loss of growth regulation mediated by RB and p53, indicating that loss of both pathways is necessary for tumor development. RB, p53, and the transcription factor E2F proteins all have key roles in the regulation of the cell cycle. The E2F proteins act as transcription factors and are required for progression from the G_1 phase of the cell cycle to the S phase. This effect is inhibited by RB, which in turn is temporarily inactivated at different stages in normal cells, as a result of phosphorylation by cyclin-dependent kinases or inhibition by Human homolog of "mouse double minute 2" (MDM2). In cancer cells, RB is inappropriately inactivated by various mechanisms, including the inactivation of the cyclin-dependent kinase inhibitor p16^INK4a (Figure 4–11). Thus, E2F continues to be activated, and cells proliferate excessively. The gene product p53 prevents cells with potentially oncogenic changes or with DNA damage from progressing to S phase. It has recently been shown that E2F-1 directly activates expression of p14^ARF, which binds to the MDM2/p53 complex and prevents p53 degradation.[151–153] Therefore, if p14^ARF is inacti-

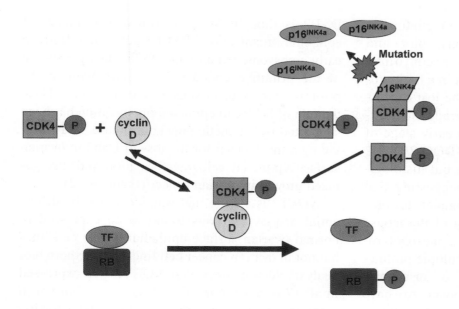

Figure 4–11. *p16^INK4a* has an essential role as a cell cycle inhibitor in the retinoblastoma (RB) pathway. *p16^INK4* acts to inhibit the activities of the cyclin D–dependent kinases, CDK4 and CDK6 and thus prevents phosphorylation of the retinoblastoma protein (RB). Hypophosphorylated RB represses genes that are dependent on the E2F family of transcription factors (TFs) and blocks G_1 to S phase progression. In cancer cells, RB is inappropriately inactivated by various mechanisms, including mutation of *p16^INK4*. Thus, E2F continues to be activated, and cells proliferate excessively.

vated, it will effect the p53 pathway, and if p16^INK4a is inactivated, it will effect the RB pathway.[154] To date, the *p14^ARF* gene has not been extensively analyzed in ovarian cancer and remains a candidate tumor suppressor gene.

Alternative techniques to LOH are also being used to identify oncogenes and tumor suppressor genes. Using the molecular biologic technique of differential RNA display, gene expression differences between normal rat ovarian surface epithelial cells and transformed cells that gave rise to moderately to well-differentiated tumors were examined. RNA differential display is a form of reverse transcription polymerase chain reaction (RT-PCR) in which reverse transcriptase catalyses cDNA synthesis by using a modified oligo (dT) primer, which binds to the poly (A) tail of a subset of mRNAs. Using this approach, a gene, *Lot1*, was identified that showed lost or decreased expression in five of eight independently transformed rat surface epithelial cell lines, compared to normal progenitor cells.[155] The mouse homologue of the *Lot1* gene has also recently been cloned (*Zac1*).[156] The human *LOT1/ZAC1* gene, which is maternally imprinted,[157] has now been cloned by two groups and resides within a region of LOH in ovarian tumors, on chromosome 6q25 (see Figure 4–8).[158,159] LOT1/ZAC1 is a nuclear zinc finger protein, which appears to act as a transcriptional coactivor for p53.[159–161] LOT1/ZAC1 shows trans-

activation and DNA-binding activity and inhibits tumor cell proliferation through the induction of both apoptosis and cell cycle arrest.[159] Overexpression of LOT1 in the ovarian cancer cell line A2780 results in growth suppression, indicative of a tumor suppressor.[160] In addition, LOT1/hZAC expression is reduced or lost in some breast cancer cell lines. Treatment of the cell lines that had no LOT1/ZAC1 expression with the methylation-interfering agent 5-azacytidine induced LOT1/hZAC reexpression, suggesting that aberrant hypermethylation of the *LOT1/hZAC* promoter is the predominant method for inactivating this putative tumor suppressor.[162]

An RNA fingerprinting strategy and Northern blot analysis identified a cDNA (*DOC2*, also named *DAB2*) that was differentially expressed in epithelial ovarian cancer cells, compared to normal human ovarian surface epithelial (HOSE) cells.[163] DOC-2/DAB2 is the human ortholog of the mouse p96/mDab2 phosphoprotein and has a phosphotyrosine interaction domain and multiple SH3-binding motifs.[163] Western blot analysis showed that the 105 kD DOC-2/DAB2 protein was down-regulated in all of the carcinoma cell lines examined, and in situ immunohistochemistry performed on normal ovaries and on benign, borderline, and invasive tumor tissues also showed down-regulation of the DOC-2/DAB2 protein, particularly in serous ovarian tumor tissues. Stable transfectants of DOC-2/DAB2 in the ovarian cell line SKOV3 showed a reduced growth rate and the ability to form tumors in nude mice. Additional Western blot and immunohistochemistry studies have confirmed that DOC-2/DAB2 expression is lost in a high proportion of ovarian carcinomas.[164] The lost expression did not correlate with tumor grade, suggesting that DOC-2/DAB2 is lost in an early stage of tumorigenicity, and indeed, loss of DOC-2/DAB2 protein occurs in hyperproliferative but histologically benign ovarian epithelium, suggesting that loss of DAB2 occurs in premalignant lesions. DOC2/DAB2 is the human ortholog of the mouse p96/mDab2 phosphoprotein and has a phosphotyrosine interaction domain (PID) and multiple proline-rich SH3 binding motifs, indicative of an adaptor molecule.[165,166] DOC2/DAB2 appears to have important functions in at least two major signaling pathways: RAS-mediated signaling pathways and TGF-β signaling pathways, where it may function as an adaptor molecule, connecting the TGF-β receptor complex to the Smad pathway.[167–169] The regulatory mechanism of DAB2 on the RAS/MAPK pathway has been further investigated, and it was concluded that DAB2 acts to uncouple RAS/MAPK activity from c-FOS expression, thus suppressing cell proliferation and tumorigenicity.[168]

In an examination of ovarian epithelia connecting morphologically normal and neoplastic lesions, it was found that the loss of DAB2 expression closely correlates with the morphologic transformation of the ovarian surface epithelial cells; thus,

DAB2 is thought to be a critical determinant of epithelial organization.[170] Dab2 deficiency leads to early embryonic lethality due to the disorganization of the primitive endoderm, an epithelium in the primitive egg cylinder stage of the embryo.[171] Thus, the role of DAB2 in epithelial organization has been supported by a genetic knockout mouse study, providing a mechanism for the loss of Dab2 in ovarian surface epithelial cell transformation and disorganized growth in ovarian cancer (Figure 4-12).

NOEY2 is a gene that was identified by differential display and was found to be expressed in normal ovarian surface epithelial (OSE) cell lines but not in ovarian cancer cell lines.[172] Northern blot analysis demonstrated that NOEY2 was expressed in all 17 primary normal OSE cell lines but not in eight of nine ovarian cancer cell lines. Transfection of *NOEY2* into three ovarian cancer cell lines resulted in a suppression of growth. *NOEY2*, which was localized to 1p31 (a region that shows LOH in ovarian cancers) (see Figure 4–8), was found to be maternally imprinted, and in four of five informative cases showing LOH, it was the nonimprinted functional allele that was lost. In one case, however, the methylated allele was lost, suggesting that there are also other genes on 1p that are important for the development of ovarian cancer.

The *GPC3* gene, which encodes a glypican integral membrane protein and is mutated in Simpson-Golabi-Behmel syndrome, was analyzed as a candidate tumor suppressor gene in ovarian cancer

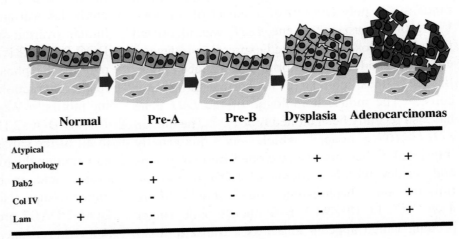

Figure 4-12. Model for neoplastic transformation of ovarian surface epithelium. Stages of ovarian surface epithelium transformation can be recognized by molecular markers and morphologic changes. In stage Pre-A, collagen IV (Col IV) and laminin (Lam) in the basement membrane of the epithelium are lost; in stage Pre-B, DAB2 protein is lost in the epithelial cells; in the dysplasia stage, the epithelium undergoes dysplastic morphologic transformation; and in adenocarcinoma, collagen IV and laminin are restored in the basement membrane lining the established adenomas of the transformed epithelium. Orange cells represent DAB2-positive cells, and blue cells represent DAB2-negative cells. The red line represents collagen IV and laminin-positive basement membrane. (Adapted from Yang DH et al.[170]).

	Normal	Pre-A	Pre-B	Dysplasia	Adenocarcinomas
Atypical Morphology	-	-	-	+	+
Dab2	+	+	-	-	+
Col IV	+	-	-	-	+
Lam	+	-	-	-	+

since it localizes to Xq26, a region frequently deleted in advanced ovarian cancers (see Figure 4–8).[173] Although no intragenic mutations were found in 13 ovarian cell lines analyzed, its expression was lost in four of the cell lines. In one of these cases, the promoter was found to be hypermethylated, and treatment with the demethylating agent 5-aza-2'-deoxycytidine resulted in reexpression of GPC3. In addition, ectopic expression of GPC3 resulted in a suppressed growth phenotype in a colony formation assay.

HEREDITARY OVARIAN CANCER

It is estimated that about 10% of all epithelial ovarian carcinoma cases result from a hereditary predisposition, with germline inheritance of a mutant gene conferring autosomal dominant susceptibility with variable penetrance. Epidemiologic studies and detailed analysis of familial ovarian cancer pedigrees have consistently confirmed the existence of two distinct manifestations of hereditary ovarian cancer. The first is the breast-ovarian cancer syndrome, in which these cancers are seen in excess, sometimes in the same individual. This has been linked to the *BRCA1* gene at chromosome 17q12-21 and, to a lesser extent, to the *BRCA2* gene at chromosome 13q (Figure 4–13). The second manifestation is ovarian cancers associated with an excess of colorectal and endometrial cancers that define the hereditary nonpolyposis colorectal cancer (HNPCC) syndrome, also known as Lynch syndrome II[55] (see Figure 4–13). Lynch syndrome I, the other variant of HNPCC, gives rise to site-specific colorectal cancer with early age of onset, predilection for the proximal colon, and an excess of synchronous and metasynchronous colorectal cancer.

Breast-Ovarian Cancer Syndrome

Genetic transmission of an autosomal dominant factor responsible for the familial association of ovarian and breast carcinomas was first reported in the early 1970s.[174–177] The number of cancers in the families studied was far too great to be explained by chance or by environmental factors, considering the striking

feature of the early onset of breast cancer. The mode of transmission, autosomal dominant, implies a mode of genetic transmission in which a single mutant allele is sufficient to promote breast cancer. The allele is carried on the nonsex chromosome, so transmission can occur from either parent. In such a family, each child has a 50% chance of inheriting a mutant allele, and whole branches of the family may be unaffected while other branches contain multiple cases of breast and ovarian cancer. Remarkable progress in molecular genetics during the 1990s was heralded by the gene linkage study of Hall and colleagues,[178] which identified a link between a locus on chromosome 17q and site-specific breast cancer. Narod and colleagues[179] subsequently reported that this same locus was responsible for the hereditary breast-ovarian cancer syndrome. The culprit gene, now known as *BRCA1*, was then cloned.[180] At nearly the same time, a second breast cancer susceptibility locus, on chromosome 13q12-13, was identified by linkage analysis;[181] less than 2 years later, the gene, *BRCA2*, was cloned.[182,183]

BRCA1

BRCA1 is located on the long arm of chromosome 17, at band q21 (see Figure 4–10). The gene is composed of 24 exons, 22 that are coding, distributed over roughly 100 kilobase pairs (kbp) of genomic DNA (Figure 4–14). The 7.8 kb transcript is detected in numerous tissues, including breast and ovary, and

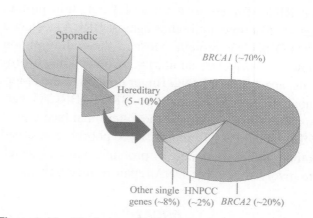

Figure 4–13. The incidence of hereditary ovarian cancer and the genes most commonly associated with cancer susceptibility (*BRCA1*, *BRCA2*, and hereditary nonpolyposis colorectal cancer (HNPCC)–related genes).

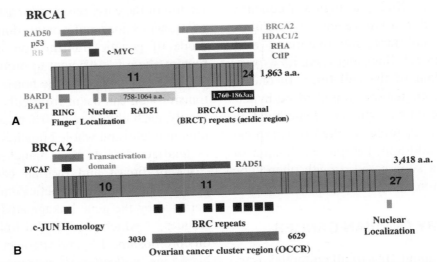

Figure 4–14. Functional and protein interaction domains of BRCA1 (*A*), and BRCA2 (*B*): BARD, BRCA1-associated RING domain 1 protein; BAP1, BRCA1-associated protein 1 (deubiquitinating enzyme); nuclear localization signal (NLS); BRCT, BRCA1 C-terminal repeats, HDAC, histone deacetylase 1 and 2; RHA, RNA helicase A; CtIP, CtBp-interacting protein; P/CAF, p300/CBP-associated factor (with histone acetylase activity).

encodes a predicted protein of 1,863 amino acids.[180] One of *BRCA1*'s exons, exon 11, is particularly large and codes for more than 50% of the protein. Much of *BRCA1* shows no homology to other known genes, with the exception of a 126-nucleotide sequence at the amino terminus, which encodes a really interesting new gene (RING) finger motif, a motif found in many other apparently functionally distinct proteins that, until recently, had no known function (Figure 4-14).[184] It has now been shown that the RING finger can specifically interact with E2 ubiquitin–conjugating enzymes, thereby promoting ubiquitination, and that RING fingers may act as E3 ubiquitin protein ligases. Multiple antibodies against BRCA1 detect a 220 kD nuclear protein. Most of the coding region shows no sequence similarity to other known proteins, apart from a RING finger domain at the N-terminal of the protein and two BRCT (BRCA1 carboxyl terminal) repeats at the C-terminal (see Figure 4–14). The BRCT repeat is a poorly conserved domain found in a range of proteins, many of which are involved in either DNA repair or metabolism.

BRCA2

BRCA2 is located on the long arm of chromosome 13, at band q12-13. The gene is composed of 27 exons, 26 that are coding, distributed over approximately 70 kbp of genomic DNA[182] (see Figure 4–14). The ~11,200- to 12,000-base transcript is ubiquitously expressed and encodes for a 3,418–amino acid protein with an estimated molecular weight of 384 kD.[185,186] Like BRCA1, the amino acid sequence of BRCA2 has given few clues to its function. An interesting feature is the presence of eight copies of a 30- to 80–amino acid repeat (BRC repeats) within exon 11, which are highly conserved between mammalian species (Figure 4–14; see also Figure 4–15). However, the functional significance of these repeats is presently unknown. Although the breast and ovarian cancer phenotypes that are associated with mutations in *BRCA1* and *BRCA2* are somewhat similar, the genes are not detectably related by sequence. However, the genomic parallels between the two genes are particularly striking: both genes span approximately 70 to 100 kbp of genomic DNA, and both have extremely large central exons encoding less than 50% of the protein. The primary amino acid sequence of BRCA2 has a weak similarity to that of BRCA1 over a restricted region.[182,183] Only a low level of homology is seen among other proteins, and human BRCA1 and BRCA2 have only a 60% homology with their murine counterparts (see Figure 4–15), which is somewhat unusual, given that

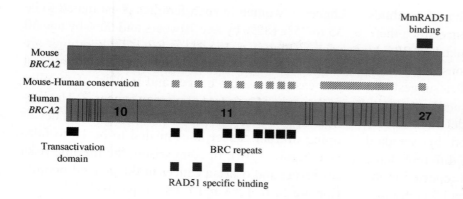

Figure 4–15. Homology between human BRCA2 and murine Brca2. At the amino acid level, less than 60% is conserved between human and mouse (*red hatched boxes*). However, the BRC repeats (*black boxes*) and RAD51 interaction domain (*blue boxes*) are well conserved between species.

most tumor suppressors appear to be more highly conserved across species than are *BRCA1* and *BRCA2*. This relatively low similarity may suggest a rapid evolution of these genes and proteins.[187]

Breast and Ovarian Cancer Susceptibility in Mutation Carriers

The fact that both *BRCA1* and *BRCA2* are such large genes has proven a hindrance to their study. In addition, mutations have been found across the entire length of both genes. Over 2,000 different sequence variants in *BRCA1* and *BRCA2* combined have been described (Figure 4–16). For the *BRCA1* gene, at least 1,237 total variants (including 373 missense, 66 unclassified variants, 135 splice-site, 154 non-sense, 446 insertion/deletions, and 60 common

polymorphisms) have been detected. To date, only a few of the missense changes have been determined to be associated with an increased risk of disease, mostly in the RING finger domain of *BRCA1*. The majority of deleterious mutations described thus far are nonsense, splice-site, and frameshift (ie, insertions and deletions) mutations, all leading to truncated forms of the protein. This may reflect the fact that it is very difficult to determine whether single base changes are disease causing or whether they are benign polymorphisms. Mutations in *BRCA2* are also prevalent. A total of at least 1,381 sequence variants (579 missense, 23 unclassified variants, 70 splice-site, 139 nonsense, 443 insertion/deletions, and 103 common polymorphisms) have been detected. However, recent studies have shown that not all *BRCA1* or *BRCA2* mutations are detected by

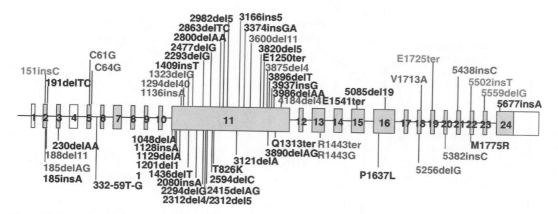

Figure 4–16. Schematic of the *BRCA1* gene and the location of a portion of the mutations detected in *BRCA1*. The gene is composed of 24 exons, 22 that are coding (*filled-in boxes*), distributed over roughly 100 kilobase pairs (kbp) of genomic DNA; 878 germline sequence variants (256 missense, 46 unclassified variants, 82 splice-site, 95 nonsense, 313 insertions/deletions, and 54 common polymorphisms) have been detected. Recurrent germline mutations (shown in blue) are relatively common. In comparison, somatic mutations (examples shown in green) are rare, occurring in less than 5% of ovarian tumors.

polymerase chain reaction (PCR)–based methods that focus primarily on coding sequence since there are a number of families strongly linked to *BRCA1* and *BRCA2* for which no mutations have been detected.[188] Furthermore, recent studies suggest that a substantial fraction of *BRCA1* (and potentially *BRCA2*) mutations may be large deletions or re-arrangements that are not detected by standard screening methods. Currently, 10 different large germline re-arrangements have been reported in the *BRCA1* gene in American, French, and Dutch families. Two of these large deletions account for 36% of all *BRCA1* mutations in Dutch breast cancer families[189] and are missed by PCR-based assays. To look specifically for mutations that span several kilobases of genomic DNA, Frolov and colleagues developed a fluorescent DNA microarray assay.[190] The microarray itself contains amplified and purified individual exons of the *BRCA1* and *BRCA2* genes. This assay rapidly and simultaneously screens for such re-arrangements along the entire gene.

Ovarian Cancer Risk in *BRCA1* and *BRCA2* Mutation Carriers**

Mutations in *BRCA1* account for breast cancer in about 50% of families with three or more cases of early-onset breast cancer. The lifetime risk of breast cancer in women in such families is estimated to be 35 to 85% (82% by age 70 years and 50% by age 50 years) (Figure 4–17).[191,192] *BRCA1* alterations are found in 76% of breast cancer families with at least one case of ovarian cancer and in 92% of families with two or more cases of ovarian cancer.[158] The lifetime risk of a woman with a *BRCA1* alteration developing ovarian cancer is estimated to be 15 to 60% (see Figure 4–17). In comparison, the lifetime risks for breast and ovarian cancer in the general population are 11 to 12% and 1.3%, respectively.[194]

The vast majority of breast cancer–related *BRCA1* mutations identified to date are germline mutations whereas somatic mutations are rarely found (< 10%) in human sporadic ovarian cancers.[195,196] The incidence of germline BRCA1 and BRCA2 mutations is especially high among the Ashkenazi Jewish population, a genetically distinct population whose ancestors lived in central and eastern Europe. The incidence of alterations is as high as 1 in 40 to 1 in 50, accounting for approximately 50% of early-onset breast cancer in Ashkenazi Jewish women (Figure 4–18).[197,198] Thus, 38% of Jewish women with breast cancer who are less than 30 years of age would be expected to have germline *BRCA1* or BRCA2 mutations.[199–201] The proportion of individuals in the general population who carry BRCA1 mutations is estimated to be approximately 1 in 800.[200,202]

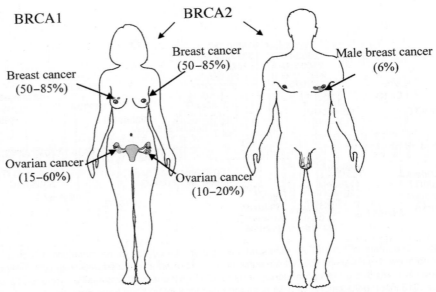

Figure 4–17.   Risk of breast (female or male) and ovarian cancer in *BRCA1* (left image) and *BRCA2* (left and right images) mutation carriers.

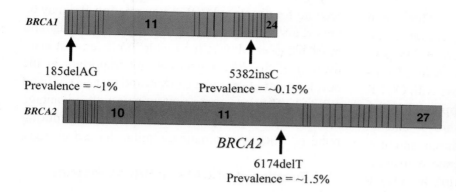

185delAG
Prevalence = ~1%

5382insC
Prevalence = ~0.15%

BRCA2

6174delT
Prevalence = ~1.5%

Figure 4–18. Recurrent mutations (shown in blue) are relatively common, especially those determined to be founders in certain ethnic populations, such as 185delAG (exon 2) and 5132insC (exon 20) in Ashkenazi Jewish individuals. An estimated 1 in 40 to 1 in 50 Ashkenazi Jewish individuals carry either a *BRCA1* (ie, 185delAG or 5382insC) or *BRCA2* (ie, 6174delT) mutation.

Women with *BRCA2* mutations appear to have a breast cancer risk similar to that of women with *BRCA1* mutations (35 to 85% by age 70 years).[200,202] The proportion of breast cancer attributable to *BRCA2* is roughly equal to that attributable to *BRCA1* (see Figure 4–17). Ovarian cancer risk appears to be increased with *BRCA2* mutations to a lesser degree than with *BRCA1* mutations; cumulative risk is estimated to be less than 10 to 20% by age 70 years (see Figure 4–17).[200] Also, in contrast to *BRCA1*, male carriers of mutated *BRCA2* have a 6% lifetime risk of developing breast cancer, a dramatic 100- to 200-fold increased risk as compared to the general population (see Figure 4–17).[203] It has been recently published that 14% of male breast cancers are attributed to *BRCA2* mutations; almost all of these patients have a family history of male or female breast cancer.[204,205] It is noteworthy, however, that these risk estimates are derived from families that are studied for research purposes, that are characterized by the early onset of cancer, multiple tumors, or both, and that have met stringent criteria for autosomal dominant inheritance of cancer predisposition. They are likely to represent a sample that is biased toward increased risk, and data derived from them may overestimate the cancer risk associated with *BRCA1* and *BRCA2* mutations.[206]

Several *BRCA1* and *BRCA2* mutations have been reported in more than one independently ascertained family, and analysis of polymorphic marker haplotypes within or close to the genes has shown that almost all of the recurrent mutations originate from a single founder. For example, in Ashkenazi Jews, two mutations in *BRCA1* (185delAG and 5382insC) and one in *BRCA2* (6174delT) account for 90% of

families who carry mutations in either *BRAC1* or *BRAC2* attributed to the two genes.[188] Evidence for a genotype-phenotype correlation for an elevated risk of ovarian cancer has been reported for both the *BRCA* genes, but this evidence is controversial. In terms of *BRCA1*, the ratio of ovarian cancer to breast cancer has been reported to be higher in families with truncating mutations toward the 5′ end of the *BRCA1* gene than in families with mutations close to the 3′ end, with a sharp demarcation point located between codons 1435 and 1443.[207] In this model, the position of the transition point suggests that the majority of *BRCA1* mutations confer a high ovarian risk and that the minority confer a lower ovarian risk. However, genetic linkage studies have suggested the opposite, namely, that a minority of families (29%) are associated with a high risk of ovarian cancer (42% by age 60 years) and that the majority (71%) have a lower risk (11% by age 60 years).[208] In addition, it has been reported that relatives of carriers of a *BRCA1* mutation 5382insC, close to the 3′ end, have a higher risk of ovarian cancer than do relatives of carriers of a *BRCA1* mutation 185delAG, close to the 5′ end of the gene, although the difference is not statistically significant.[209] Shattuck-Eidens and colleagues (1995) also suggested that 5′ mutations in the *BRCA1* gene confer a greater risk of ovarian cancer;[210] however, this was not confirmed by studies by Berman and colleagues[211] and by Serova and colleagues.[212] Additional studies are needed to resolve these discrepancies.

In *BRCA2*, truncating mutations located approximately between codons 1,000 and 2,000 have been reported to lead to a highly elevated risk of ovarian cancer relative to breast cancer risk, compared with mutations located 5′ or 3′ to this region.[213] This region has been designated the ovarian cancer cluster region (OCCR) (see Figure 4–14).[213] In support of this, penetrance analysis of families linked to *BRCA2* estimated the risk of ovarian cancer for those with OCCR mutations as 76% by age 70 years, as opposed to a risk of 26% and 5% for mutations that are 5′ and 3′, respectively, to the OCCR.[202] Neuhausen and colleagues also reported a higher incidence of ovarian cancer in families with mutations in the OCCR although this was not statistically significant.[214] In addition, despite the risk of ovarian cancer for those with *BRCA2* mutations being lower overall than for those *BRCA1* mutations, the recurrent *BRCA2* 6174delT mutation in Ashkenazi Jews confers a risk of ovarian cancer approximately equal to that of each of the two Ashkenazi Jewish *BRCA1* mutations.[209]

There is controversy over whether *BRCA1* and *BRCA2* may be involved in sporadic breast and ovarian cancer. LOH is commonly observed in the regions of 17q and 13q within which *BRCA1* and *BRCA2* are located; however, somatic mutations in *BRCA1* and *BRCA2* have rarely been detected in breast and ovarian tumors.[196,215–218] This may reflect the fact that other genes on 17q or 13q are important in the pathogenesis of these tumors. Alternatively, *BRCA1* and *BRCA2* may be inactivated by mechanisms other than somatic mutation, or there may be a role for haploinsufficiency of *BRCA1* and *BRCA2* in the development of breast and ovarian tumors. Initial studies reported that methylation of the promoter of BRCA1 was rarely detected in breast tumors.[219,220] However, immunohistochemical analysis of breast and ovarian specimens revealed that BRCA1 expression was reduced or undetectable in the majority of high-grade ductal breast carcinomas and in 40% of ovarian cancers analyzed.[221] More recent studies have found that the *BRCA1* promoter is hypermethylated in 15% of ovarian tumors that are judged to be sporadic and that this change is associated with decreased levels of BRCA1 expression.[222–224] Chan and colleagues reported that BRCA2 levels may be elevated in ovarian tumors, relative to normal tissue. Aberrant expression of BRCA2 in these tumors was attributed to hypomethylation at CpGs in the *BRCA2* promoter.[233] Haploinsufficiency or an alternate mechanism of inactivating the *BRCA1* gene could also account for decreased BRCA1 expression and may be important in the development of sporadic breast and ovarian cancers. It is still possible, however, that inactivation of the *BRCA* genes is not important in the development of sporadic cancers and that *BRCA1* and *BRCA2* mutations may confer a growth advantage only if they are present at a critical period (eg, during puberty, when few somatic mutations have occurred).

Function of BRCA1 and BRCA2 Proteins

Since *BRCA1* and *BRCA2* are such large genes, with distinct functional domains, it is likely that they have multiple functions. Analysis of BRCA1 and BRCA2 knockout mouse models, identification of BRCA1 and BRCA2 interacting proteins, and analysis of their functional domains have all helped to elucidate the functions of these molecules.[188] Under these approaches, both BRCA1 and BRCA2 have consistently been implicated in in DNA damage repair, including the repair of double-strand breaks by homologous recombination and the repair of oxidative damage by transcription-coupled repair. Therefore, they may not act as direct tumor suppressors after all but may be involved in the maintenance of genome integrity; loss of the *BRCA1* or *BRCA2* genes leads indirectly to mutation of tumor suppressor genes or inappropriate activation of oncogenes. There has also been a substantial amount of work demonstrating the roles of BRCA1 and BRCA2 in transcription regulation, and BRCA1 has also been implicated in mRNA processing and as a cell cycle checkpoint protein.

BRCA1 and *BRCA2* Knockout Mouse Models

Mice that are nullizygous for *BRCA1* and *BRCA2* show embryonic lethality around the same time (E7.5 in *BRCA1* and E8.5 in *BRCA2*), and these genes therefore appear to be crucial for development.[225,226] In addition, *BRCA1* and *BRCA2* mutant embryos exhibit similar phenotypes; the mutant embryos are hypersensitive to gamma irradiation and exhibit chromosomal abnormalities, and they die at early postimplantation stages and show extended survival in p53-deficient backgrounds but also dramatic increases in genetic instability.[225,226] These observations provide important evidence for a role in maintaining genetic stability, with the embryonic lethality observed in the nullizygous embryos being secondary to chromosome damage, which activates a p53-dependent cell cycle checkpoint to prevent the accumulation of damaged DNA. In the p53-deficient background, embryos survive longer but at the expense of genetic stability. The genetic instability finally affects other genes that are essential for viability; thus, the embryos die but at a later stage. In support of these observations is the fact that BRCA1 and BRCA2 interact with RAD51 in vivo,[227,228] and RAD51 is important in homologous recombination and double-strand break repair. The interaction between BRCA2 and RAD51 appears to be direct, and BRCA1 seems to bind indirectly, possibly through an interaction with BRAC2 In mitotic cells, it has been shown that Rad51, BRCA1 and BRCA2 coexist in nuclear dot structures, which may be sites of checkpoint processing in S-phase cells (Figure 4–19).[229] Following exposure to DNA-damaging agents Rad51, BRCA1 and BRCA2 accumulate in proliferating cell nuclear antigen (PCNA)–containing replicating structures (Figure 4–20). BRCA1 and BRCA2 were also found to colocalize on axial elements of developing synaptonemal complexes, which is consistent with a role in recombination. It has also been shown that BRAC1 becomes phosphorylated by ATM, ChK2-Kinase, and Atr, in response to DNA damage.[230–234] Mouse *BRCA1* and *BRCA2* conditional mutants that specifically target mammary epithelial cells have provided information regarding a role of the *BRCA* genes in tumor formation. The *BRCA1* conditional knockout mice developed mammary tumors after a long latency period.[235] Prior to the development of tumors, there appeared to be an increase in apoptosis in the mammary gland. Analysis of the tumors revealed multiple genetic changes, including inactivation of p53.[235,236] The *BRCA1* conditional mutation in a p53 heterozygous background results in a significantly accelerated rate of tumorigenesis.[237] In one study, with targeted disruption of exons 3 and 4 of *BRCA2* in conditional *BRCA2* knockout mice resulted in a high incidence of breast tumors, which were associated with various chromosomal aberrations.[238] However, in another study, homozygous conditional deletion of exon 11 in mammary epithelial cells gave rise to mammary tumors only in females carrying both conditional *BRCA2* and *p53* alleles but not in mice carrying conditional *BRCA2* alleles alone.[239] These studies reiterate "caretaker" functions for BRCA1 and BRCA2 where loss of function of these genes leads to genomic instability. This initially activates control pathways such as apoptosis, but tumors finally develop after the disruption of these surveillance mechanisms, for example, after inactivation of p53. Interestingly, it has been reported that a high proportion of breast and ovarian tumors from *BRCA1* and *BRCA2* mutation carriers have *p53* mutations.[240–242]

BRCA1 AND BRCA2 INTERACTING PROTEINS

BRCA1 and BRCA2 have been shown to be associated with an overwhelming number of protein partners. A list of some of the proteins with which BRCA1 and BRCA2 are connected is shown in Table 4-2. BRCA1 and BRCA2 have been shown to exist in various large multiprotein complexes.[243] BRCA1 is associated with (1) the RNA polymerase II holoenzyme, which is a multi-subunit complex > 1 MD in size; (2) the BRCA1-associated genome surveillance complex (BASC), which is larger than

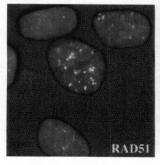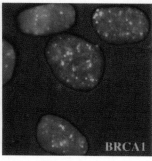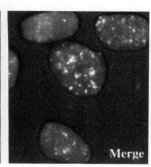

Figure 4–19. Colocalization of RAD51 (left panel, *green spots*) and BRCA1 (middle panel, *red dots*) by immunofluorescence. "Merge" panel shows that BRCA1 and BRCA2 (not shown) colocalize with RAD51 (mediates DNA strand-exchange functions). (Courtesy of Dr. D. Broccoli, Fox Chase Cancer Center, Philadelphia, PA.)

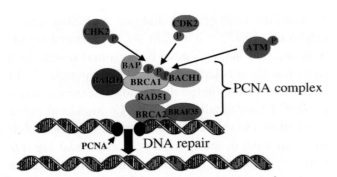

Figure 4-20. BRCA1 and BRCA2 in damage response. Following DNA damage, cell cycle checkpoints are activated, including *p53*. p53 induces *p21* and *CHK2* expression and signals cell cycle arrest until the damaged DNA can be repaired. Failure to repair leads to apoptosis, or programmed cell death. BRCA1 and BRCA2 participate in DNA repair by an unknown mechanism. BRCA1 is known to be phosphorylated (and activated) by ATM and CDK2 in a damage-free cell; BRCA1 is phosphorylated by CHK2 and ATR after damage; and phosphorylated BRCA1 associates with each of the proteins BARD1, RAD51, BRCA2, and PCNA during the processes of repair and replication. DNA damage is successfully repaired and normal cell growth proceeds. Mutant BRCA1 or BRCA2 proteins cause dysfunction in this repair/replication system; DNA repair fails, and proliferation continues with damaged DNA.

2 MD and which contains at least 15 subunits (including products of Bloom syndrome and ataxia telangiectasia [ATM] disease genes and subcomplexes implicated in DNA repair, such as Mre11-Rad50-Nbs1, the MSH2-MSH6 heterodimer, the MLH1-PMS2 heterodimer, and DNA replication factor C); and (3) the SWI/SNF-related complex, which has chromatin remodeling properties. BRCA2 is also associated with many different proteins (see Table 4-2) and has been shown to be a member of a large 2 MD complex that also contains BRAF35, a structural DNA-binding component containing a nonspecific DNA-binding HMG domain and a kinesin-like coiled domain.

BRCA1 and BRCA2 have both been shown to have functions in transcriptional regulation.[243,244] The N-terminal domains of BRCA1 interact with several different transcription factors, such as p53, c-myc, STAT1, estrogen receptor alpha, ATF1, and ZBRK1. Since BRCA1 binds to components of the RNA polymerase II holoenzyme, it has been suggested that it acts as a transcription coactivator and bridging factor to RNA polymerase II holoenzyme and thus alters the expression of target genes such as *GADD45* and *P21*. BRCA1 also binds to transcriptional repressors such as CtIP/CtBP, pRb, and the

histone deacetylases RbAp46, RbAp48, HDAC1, and HDAC2; therefore, BRCA1 may act as both positive and negative transcriptional regulator.

BRCA1 may have a role in mRNA processing as it has been found in a complex with the mRNA polyadenylation factor CstF and with BARD1.[245,246] Interestingly, the complex that contains BRCA1, BARD1, and CstF increases transiently following DNA damage and inhibits polyadenylation, thus providing a link between mRNA 3' processing and DNA repair.[245] This may be an important mechanism to prevent inappropriate RNA processing and the production of aberrant transcripts.

The RING Finger Domain and BRCA1's Role in Protein Degradation

An interesting feature of BRCA1 is the RING finger domain, a highly conserved structure found in more than 200 proteins. Originally thought to be important for DNA binding, it has recently been highlighted as having an important function in the ubiquitination pathway. Protein polyubiquitination is the method the cell uses to tag a protein for degradation by the 26S proteasome and is a key pathway for controlling the levels of many proteins with critical cellular functions. Ubiquitination occurs in steps and requires three different enzyme components.[247,248] First, the ubiquitin activating enzyme (E1) binds to ubiquitin (Ub), which is then transferred to the Ub conjugating enzyme (E2) ready to target a protein substrate. The Ub protein ligases (E3) are responsible for providing specificity to the Ub conjugation, interacting with E2 and promoting polyubiquitin ligation to a substrate. It has recently been shown that

Table 4-2. BRCA2-INTERACTING PROTEINS AND THEIR PUTATIVE FUNCTIONS	
BRCA2-Interacting Protein or Complex	**Function of Interacting protein**
RAD51	DSB repair
BRCA1	DSB repair
BRAF35	Chromatin condensation
DSS1	Cell cycle control
P/CAF	Histone acetyltransferase
hBUBR1	Mitotic checkpoint kinase

Adapted from Borg A244; Welcsh PL, King MC.273
DSB = double-strand break.

the RING finger can specifically interact with E2s, promoting ubiquitination, and that many RING finger proteins exhibit Ub ligase activity.[247,248] Although BRCA1 alone appears to have limited Ub ligase activity, BRCA1 combined with BARD1 (another RING finger protein) exhibits a very high level of activity.[249] In addition, mutations within the RING finger domain of BRCA1 can ablate this activity.[249,250] Although the specific substrates of the BRCA1/BARD1 E3 Ub ligase activity have yet to be identified, it is possible that the Ub ligase activity is key to many functions of BRCA1, including polyadenylation, DNA repair, and transcription regulation, and that it acts to regulate the abundance of proteins in many different protein complexes. There is clearly much work to be done to determine the precise functions of BRCA1 and BRCA2 and how a loss of functional BRCA1 and BRCA2 lead to breast and ovarian cancer. Important issues, such as why the breast and ovary are the primary organs affected by the inactivation of these genes and whether BRCA1 and BRCA2 are really involved in sporadic forms of breast and ovarian cancer, also remain to be resolved.

HNPCC and Ovarian Cancer Risk

The HNPCC syndrome arises from an inherited defect in any one of four known DNA mismatch repair genes: *hMSH2* (chromosome 2p), *hMLH1* (chromosome 3p), *hPMS1* (chromosome 2q), and *hPMS2* (chromosome 7p). The *hMSH2* and *hMLH1* genes appear to be the most predominantly affected genes. In a study of HNPCC syndrome families associated with either *hMSH2* or *hMLH1* mutations, it was found that there was a greater risk for endometrial and ovarian cancers in those families that carried *hMSH2* mutations.[55]

Global Genomic Approaches to Identifying the Molecular Genetic Events Associated with Ovarian Oncogenesis

As eluded to previously, the introduction of DNA microarray technology has opened new frontiers in understanding the etiology of ovarian cancer (see Figures 4-5 and 4-6). This powerful and robust "genocentric" approach has added an additional degree of freedom in the study of tumor classification and treatment. With the development of this technology, the work of scientists has evolved from descriptive genetic profiling (eg, genes expressed in normal tissue vs those expressed in tumor tissue) to the searching of new subgroups of cancers according to their genetic behavior. The rapidly growing field of bioinformatics has contributed to the visualization of these subgroups in multidimensional space and has introduced new criteria and tools for the classification of ovarian cancers.

One of the first common uses of microarray technology was in performing large scale expression profiling, comparing normal and malignant ovarian epithelial cells.[251,252] These studies attempted to determine global changes in gene expression during the onset and progression of ovarian cancer. Since little is known about the early stage of these carcinomas, such an approach can serve as a useful tool for elucidating candidate molecular markers of epithelial ovarian cancer. Additional studies have attempted to compare early- and late-stage ovarian tumors[253] in order to shed more light on the genetic changes that contribute to the progression and metastatic spread of this disease.

By the analysis of large amounts of expression data, it has become possible to determine genes that are specific for ovarian cancer.[254] This approach has given rise to the development of small specialized ovarian cDNA arrays. These arrays have several practical advantages and can reveal information that is lost in the "noise" generated by irrelevant genes present in the large arrays. This limited approach lacks the ability to find new genes that are specific for ovarian cancer, but it can be used as a versatile and rapid screening tool.

Another application of this method was to the comparison of various subgroups of ovarian cancers. Jazaeri and colleagues compared the expression profiles of *BRCA1*- and *BRCA2*-linked and sporadic carcinomas and observed that the greatest contrast in gene expression was between tumors with a *BRCA1* mutation and those with a *BRCA2* mutation.[255] Their study suggested that mutations in *BRCA1* and *BRCA2* might lead to carcinogenesis through distinct molecular pathways and that these same pathways also appear to be affected in sporadic disease. Schwartz and colleagues were among the first who tried to compare different types of ovarian carcinomas morphologically by expression profiling.[256] These types of studies can help design biologically and clinically meaningful tumor classification systems and provide the foundation for the development of new type-specific diagnostic and treatment strategies. Similar approaches can be taken to determine differences in the biologic behavior of carcinomas in regard to anticancer drugs as well as resistance to these drugs.[257]. With more data publicly available, and by increasing the number of clinical cases studied, it seems possible to apply microarray technology to the personalization of chemotherapy and even to the prediction of its therapeutic effect.

Microarray technology, however, cannot be used as the sole scientific approach to answering various questions about ovarian tumorigenesis, but it can be used as a first step in determining the direction of research. This method produces large amounts of data that need to be validated and scaled down for easy handling. Together with other techniques (ie, karyotyping and CGH), it has been shown to produce significantly smaller subsets of differentially expressed genes and to make future studies more executable.[258]

SUMMARY

There has been much progress in determining the genetics of ovarian cancer. The isolation of the *BRCA1* and *BRCA2* genes has certainly been of crucial importance although at present, it is only known that inactivation of these genes is important in those with an inherited predisposition to breast and ovarian cancer and that it is not important for the other 90% of sporadic cases. Studies on BRCA1 and BRCA2 are and continue to be important for the effective genetic counseling of patients. The identification of candidate oncogenes such as *AKT2, RAS, PIK3CA, TGF-β receptor I, γ-synuclein,* and *H-Ryk,* and tumor suppressor genes such as *LOT1, DOC2, GPC3, NOEY2, OVCA1* RASSF1A, SRBC, TES, and BARX2 have provided a foundation for further studies to determine the true importance of these genes in the development of ovarian cancer. With the

completion of the human genome project and the development and implementation of high-throughput screening methodologies such as cDNA microarray analysis, the isolation of genes that are important in the development of ovarian cancer will be quickly advanced. However, it will remain a challenge to be able to "see the forest for the trees" and to determine which genes and their respective proteins have a primary role in the development of ovarian cancer, how they carry out that role, and how an understanding of this can lead to improvements in the treatment of ovarian cancer.

REFERENCES

1. Jemal A, Thomas A, Murray T, Thun M. Cancer statistics, 2002. CA Cancer J Clin 2002;52:23–47.
2. Ries LA, Wingo PA, Miller DS, et al. The annual report to the nation on the status of cancer, 1973–1997, with a special section on colorectal cancer. Cancer 2000;88:2398–424.
3. Bishop JM. The molecular genetics of cancer. Science 1987; 235:305–11.
4. Krengel U, Schlichting L, Scherer A, et al. Three-dimensional structures of H-ras p21 mutants: molecular basis for their inability to function as signal switch molecules. Cell 1990;62:539–48.
5. Tong L, Milburn MV, de Vos AM, Kim SH. Structure of ras proteins. Science 1989;245:244.
6. Zhou DJ, Gonzalez-Cadavid N, Ahuja J. A uniform pattern of proto-oncogene abnormalities in ovarian adenocarcinoma. Cancer 1988;62:1573–9.
7. Patton SE, Martin ML, Nelsen LL, et al. Activation of the ras-mitogen-activated protein kinase pathway and phosphorylation of ets-2 at position threonine 72 in human ovarian cancer cell lines. Cancer Res 1998;58:2253–9.
8. Zachos G, Varras M, Koffa M, et al. Glucocorticoid and estrogen receptors have elevated activity in human endometrial and ovarian tumors as compared to the adjacent normal tissues and recognize sequence elements of the H-ras proto-oncogene. Jpn J Cancer Res 1996;87:916–22.
9. Zachos G, Spandidos DA. Transcriptional regulation of the c-H-ras1 gene by the P53 protein is implicated in the development of human endometrial and ovarian tumours. Oncogene 1998;16:3013–7.
10. Cheng JQ, Godwin AK, Bellacosa A, et al. AKT2, a putative oncogene encoding a member of a subfamily of protein-serine/threonine kinases, is amplified in human ovarian carcinomas. Proc Natl Acad Sci U S A 1992;89:9267–71.
11. Bellacosa A, de Feo D, Godwin AK, et al. Molecular alterations of the AKT2 oncogene in ovarian and breast carcinomas. Int J Cancer 1995;64:280–5.
12. Liu AX, Testa JR, Hamilton TC, et al. AKT2, a member of the protein kinase B family, is activated by growth factors, v-Ha-ras, and v-src through phosphatidylinositol 3-kinase in human ovarian epithelial cancer cells. Cancer Res 1998;58:2973–7.

13. Shayesteh L, Lu Y, Kuo WL, et al. PIK3CA is implicated as an oncogene in ovarian cancer. Nat Genet 1999;21:99–102.

14. Kurose K, Zhou XP, Araki T, et al. Frequent loss of PTEN expression is linked to elevated phosphorylated Akt levels, but not associated with p27 and cyclin D1 expression, in primary epithelial ovarian carcinomas. Am J Pathol 2001;158:2097–106.

15. Yuan ZQ, Sun M, Feldman RI, et al. Frequent activation of AKT2 and induction of apoptosis by inhibition of phosphoinositide-3-OH kinase/Akt pathway in human ovarian cancer. Oncogene 2000;19:2324–30.

16. Sonoda G, Palazzo J, du Manoir S, et al. Comparative genomic hybridization detects frequent overrepresentation of chromosomal material from 3q26, 8q24, and 20q13 in human ovarian carcinomas. Genes Chromosomes Cancer 1997;20:320–8.

17. Abeysinghe HR, Cedrone E, Tyan T, et al. Amplification of C-MYC as the origin of the homogeneous staining region in ovarian carcinoma detected by micro-FISH. Cancer Genet Cytogenet 1999;15:136–43.

18. Tashiro H, Miyazaki K, Okamura H, et al. C-myc overexpression in human primary ovarian tumours: its relevance to tumour progression. Int J Cancer 1992;50:828–33.

19. Berchuck A, Kamel A, Whitaker R, et al. Overexpression of HER-2/neu is associated with poor survival in advanced epithelial ovarian cancer. Cancer Res 1990;50:4087–91.

20. Godwin AK, Schultz D, Hamilton TC, Knudson A. Oncogenes and tumor suppressor genes. In: Hoskins W, Perez C, Young R, editors. Principles and practice of gynecological oncology. 2nd ed. . Philadelphia: J. B. Lippincott Company; 1997. p. 107–48.

21. Zheng J, Robinson W, Ehlen T, et al. Distinction of low grade from high grade human ovarian carcinomas on the basis of losses of heterozygosity on chromosome 3, 6 and 11 and HER-2/neu gene amplification. Cancer Res 1991;51:4045–51.

22. King BL, Carter D, Foellmer HG, Kacinski BM. Neu proto-oncogene amplification and expression in ovarian adenocarcinoma cell lines. Am J Pathol 1992;140:23–31.

23. Yu D, Liu B, Tan M, et al. Overexpression of *cerb*B-2/*neu* in breast cancer cells confers increased resistance to Taxol vis *mdr-1*-independent mechanisms. Oncogene 1996;13:1359–65.

24. Kacinski BM, Carter D, Kohorn EI, et al. Oncogene expression in vivo by ovarian adenocarcinomas and mixed-mullerian tumors. Yale J Biol Med 1989;62:379–92.

25. Tyson FL, Soper JT, Daly L, et al. Overexpression and amplification of the c-erbB-2 (Her 2/neu) proto-oncogene in epithelial ovarian tumors and cell lines. Am Assoc Cancer Res 1988;29:A1872.

26. Horiguchi J, Sherman ML, Sampson-Johannes A, et al. CSF-1 and C-FMS gene expression in human carcinoma cell lines. Biochem Biophys Res Commun 1988;157:295–401.

27. Kacinski BM, Carter D, Mittal K, et al. Ovarian adenocarcinomas express fms-complementary transcripts and fms antigen, often with coexpression of CSF-1. Am J Pathol 1990;137:135–47.

28. Tyson FL, Boyer CM, Kaufman R, et al. Expression and amplification of the HER-2/neu (c-erbB-2) protooncogene in epithelial ovarian tumors and cell lines. Am J Obstet Gynecol 1991;165:640–6.

29. Stromberg K, Collins TJ IV, Gordon AW, et al. Transforming growth factor-alpha acts as an autocrine growth factor in ovarian carcinoma cell lines. Cancer Res 1992;52:341–7.

30. Chen T, Triplett J, Dehner B, et al. Transforming growth factor-beta receptor type I gene is frequently mutated in ovarian carcinomas. Cancer Res 2001;61:4679–82.

31. Anand N, Murthy S, Amann G, et al. Protein elongation factor EEF1A2 is a putative oncogene in ovarian cancer. Nat Genet 2002;31:301–5.

32. Filmus J, Buick RN. Stability of c-K-ras amplification during progression in a patient with adenocarcinoma of the ovary. Cancer Res 1985;45:4468–75.

33. Auersperg N, Edelson MI, Mok, SC, et al. The biology of ovarian cancer. Semin Oncol 1998;25:281–304.

34. George JM. The synucleins. Genome Biol 2002;3: REVIEWS3002.

35. Bruening W, Giasson BI, Klein-Szanto AJ, et al. Synucleins are expressed in the majority of breast and ovarian carcinomas and in preneoplastic lesions of the ovary. Cancer 2000;88:2154–63.

36. Pan ZZ, Bruening W, Giasson BI, et al. Gamma-synuclein promotes cancer cell survival and inhibits stress- and chemotherapy drug-induced apoptosis by modulating MAPK pathways. J Biol Chem 2002;277:35050–60.

37. Liu J, Spence MJ, Zhang YL, et al. Transcriptional suppression of synuclein gamma (SNCG) expression in human breast cancer cells by the growth inhibitory cytokine oncostatin M. Breast Cancer Res Treat 2000;62:99–107.

38. Lu A, Gupta A, Li C, et al. Molecular mechanisms for aberrant expression of the human breast cancer specific gene 1 in breast cancer cells: control of transcription by DNA methylation and intronic sequences. Oncogene 2001;20:5173–85.

39. Gupta A, Godwin AK, Vanderveer L, et al. Hypomethylation of the synuclein gene CpG island promotes its aberrant expression in breast carcinoma and ovarian carcinoma. Cancer Res 2002. [In press]

40. Wang XC, Katso R, Butler R, et al. H-RYK, an unusual receptor kinase: isolation and analysis of expression in ovarian cancer. Mol Med 1996;2:189–203.

41. Katso RM, Russell R B, Ganesan TS. Functional analysis of H-Ryk, an atypical member of the receptor tyrosine kinase family. Mol Cell Biol 1999;19:6427–40.

42. Katso RM, Manek S, Ganjavi H, et al. Overexpression of H-Ryk in epithelial ovarian cancer: prognostic significance of receptor expression. Clin Cancer Res 2000;6:3271–81.

43. Katso RM, Manek S, Biddolph S, et al. Overexpression of H-Ryk in mouse fibroblasts confers transforming ability in vitro and in vivo: correlation with up-regulation in epithelial ovarian cancer. Cancer Res 1999;59:2265–70.

44. Harris H, Miller OJ, Klein G, et al. Suppression of malignancy by cell fusion. Nature 1969;223:363–8.

45. Stanbridge EJ. Suppression of malignancy in human cells. Nature 1976;260:17–20.

46. DeMars R. In: Wilkins WA, editor. 23rd annual symposium on fundamental cancer research. Baltimore: 1969. p. 105–6.

47. Knudson AG. Mutation and cancer: statistical study of retinoblastoma. Proc Natl Acad Sci U S A 1971;68:820–3.

48. Knudson AG, Strong LC. Mutation and cancer: a model for Wilms' tumor of the kidney. J Natl Cancer Inst 1972;48:313–24.

49. Marshall CJ. Tumor suppressor genes. Cell 1991;64:313–26.
50. Godwin AK, Vanderveer L, Schultz DC, et al. A common region of deletion on chromosome 17q in both sporadic and familial epithelial ovarian tumors distal to BRCA1. Am J Hum Genet 1994;55:666–77.
51. Schultz DC, Vanderveer L, Berman DB, et al. Identification of two candidate tumor suppressor genes on chromosome 17p13.3. Cancer Res 1996;56:1997–2002.
52. Fero ML, Randel E, Gurley KE, et al. The murine gene p27Kip1 is haplo-insufficient for tumour suppression. Nature 1998;396:177–80.
53. Inoue K, Zindy F, Randle DH, et al. Dmp1 is haplo-insufficient for tumor suppression and modifies the frequencies of Arf and p53 mutations in Myc-induced lymphomas. Genes Dev 2001;15:2934–9.
54. Quon KC, Berns A. Haplo-insufficiency? Let me count the ways. Genes Dev 2001;5:2917–21.
55. Lynch HT, Casey MJ, Lynch J, et al. Genetics and ovarian carcinoma. Semin Oncol 1998;25:265–80.
56. Fullwood P, Marchini S, Rader JS, et al. Detailed genetic and physical mapping of tumor suppressor loci on chromosome 3p in ovarian cancer. Cancer Res 1999;15:4662–7.
57. Lounis H, Mes-Masson AM, Dion F, et al. Mapping of chromosome 3p deletions in human epithelial ovarian tumors. Oncogene 1998;17:2359–65.
58. Jensen DE, Proctor M, Marquis ST, et al. BAP1: a novel ubiquitin hydrolase which binds to the BRCA1 RING finger and enhances BRCA1-mediated cell growth suppression. Oncogene 1998;16:1097–112.
59. Kondo M, Ji L, Kamibayashi C, et al. Overexpression of candidate tumor suppressor gene FUS1 isolated from the 3p21.3 homozygous deletion region leads to G1 arrest and growth inhibition of lung cancer cells. Oncogene 2001;20:6258–62.
60. Tomizawa Y, Sekido Y, Kondo M, et al. Inhibition of lung cancer cell growth and induction of apoptosis after reexpression of 3p21.3 candidate tumor suppressor gene SEMA3B. Proc Natl Acad Sci U S A 2001;98:13954–9.
61. Mitsuuchi Y, Johnson SW, Sonoda G, et al. Identification of a chromosome 3p14.3-21.1 gene, APPL, encoding an adaptor molecule that interacts with the oncoprotein-serine/threonine kinase AKT2. Oncogene 1999;18:4891–8.
62. Foster K, Osborne RJ, Huddart RA, et al. Molecular genetic analysis of the von Hippel-Lindau disease (VHL) tumour suppressor gene in gonadal tumours. Eur J Cancer 1995; 31A:2392–5.
63. Hendricks DT, Taylor R, Reed M, Birrer MJ. FHIT gene expression in human ovarian, endometrial, and cervical cancer cell lines. Cancer Res 1997;57:2112–5.
64. Agathanggelou A, Honorio S, Macartney DP, et al. Methylation associated inactivation of RASSF1A from region 3p21.3 in lung, breast and ovarian tumours. Oncogene 2001;20:1509–18.
65. Yoon JH, Dammann R, Pfeifer GP. Hypermethylation of the CpG island of the RASSF1A gene in ovarian and renal cell carcinomas. Int J Cancer 2001;94:212–7.
66. Astuti D, Agathanggelou A, Honorio S, et al. RASSF1A promoter region CpG island hypermethylation in phaeochromocytomas and neuroblastoma tumours. Oncogene 2001;20:7573–7.
67. Burbee DG, Forgacs E, Zochbauer-Muller S, et al. Epigenetic inactivation of RASSF1A in lung and breast cancers and malignant phenotype suppression. J Natl Cancer Inst 2001;93:691–9.
68. Byun DS, Lee MG, Chae KS, et al. Frequent epigenetic inactivation of RASSF1A by aberrant promoter hypermethylation in human gastric adenocarcinoma. Cancer Res 2001;61:7034–8.
69. Dammann R, Li C, Yoon JH, et al. Epigenetic inactivation of a RAS association domain family protein from the lung tumour suppressor locus 3p21.3. Nat Genet 2000;25: 315–9.
70. Dammann R, Takahashi T, Pfeifer GP. The CpG island of the novel tumor suppressor gene RASSF1A is intensely methylated in primary small cell lung carcinomas. Oncogene 2001;20:3563–7.
71. Dammann R, Yang G, Pfeifer GP. Hypermethylation of the cpG island of Ras association domain family 1A (RASSF1A), a putative tumor suppressor gene from the 3p21.3 locus, occurs in a large percentage of human breast cancers. Cancer Res 2001;61:3105–9.
72. Dreijerink K, Braga E, Kuzmin I, et al. The candidate tumor suppressor gene, RASSF1A, from human chromosome 3p21.3 is involved in kidney tumorigenesis. Proc Natl Acad Sci U S A 2001;98:7504–9.
73. Lee MG, Kim HY, Byun DS, et al. Frequent epigenetic inactivation of RASSF1A in human bladder carcinoma. Cancer Res 2001;61:6688–92.
74. Lo KW, Kwong J, Hui AB, et al. High frequency of promoter hypermethylation of RASSF1A in nasopharyngeal carcinoma. Cancer Res 2001;61:3877–81.
75. Morrissey C, Martinez A, Zatyka M, et al. Epigenetic inactivation of the RASSF1A 3p21.3 tumor suppressor gene in both clear cell and papillary renal cell carcinoma. Cancer Res 2001;61:7277–81.
76. Toyooka S, Pass HI, Shivapurkar N, et al. Aberrant methylation and simian virus 40 tag sequences in malignant mesothelioma. Cancer Res 2001;61:5727–30.
77. Hatta Y, Takeuchi S, Yokota J, Koeffle HP. Ovarian cancer has frequent loss of heterozygosity at chromosome 12p12.3-13.1 (region of TEL and Kip1 loci) and chromosome 12q23-ter: evidence for two new tumour-suppressor genes. Br J Cancer 1997;75:1256–62.
78. Masciullo V, Sgambato A, Pacilio C, et al. Frequent loss of expression of the cyclin-dependent kinase inhibitor p27 in epithelial ovarian cancer. Cancer Res 1999;59:3790–4.
79. Bouchard C, Thieke K, Maier A, et al. Direct induction of cyclin D2 by myc contributes to cell cycle progression and sequestration of p27. EMBO J 1999;18:5321–33.
80. Perez-Roger I, Kim SH, Griffiths B, et al. Cyclins D1 and D2 mediate myc-induced proliferation via sequestration of p27(Kip1) and p21. EMBO J 1999;18:5310–20.
81. Shirane M, Harumiya Y, Ishida N, et al. Down-regulation of p27(Kip1) by two mechanisms, ubiquitin-mediated degradation and proteolytic processing. J Biol Chem 1999;274:13886–93.
82. Tomoda K, Kubota Y, Kato J. Degradation of the cyclin-dependent-kinase inhibitor p27Kip1 is instigated by Jab1. Nature 1999;398:160–5.
83. Sui L, Dong Y, Ohno M, et al. Jab1 expression is associated

with inverse expression of p27(kip1) and poor prognosis in epithelial ovarian tumors. Clin Cancer Res 2001;7: 4130–5.

84. Newcomb EW, Sosnow M, Demopoulos RI, et al. Expression of the cell cycle inhibitor p27KIP1 is a new prognostic marker associated with survival in epithelial ovarian tumors. Am J Pathol 1999;154:119–25.

85. Kerr J, Leary JA, Hurst T, et al. Allelic loss on chromosome 7q in ovarian adenocarcinomas: two critical regions and a rearrangement of the PLANH1 locus. Oncogene 1996; 13:1815–8.

86. van der Burg ME, Henzen-Logmans SC, Berns EM, et al. Expression of urokinase-type plasminogen activator (uPA) and its inhibitor PAI-1 in benign, borderline, malignant primary and metastatic ovarian tumors. Int J Cancer 1996;69:475–9.

87. Speiser P, Mayerhofer K, Kucera E, et al. pS2 and PAI-1 in ovarian cancer: correlation to pathohistological parameters. Anticancer Res 1997;17:679–83.

88. Schmalfeldt B, Kuhn W, Reuning U, et al. Primary tumor and metastasis in ovarian cancer differ in their content of urokinase-type plasminogen activator, its receptor, and inhibitors types 1 and 2. Cancer Res 1995;55:3958–63.

89. Chambers SK, Ivins CM, Carcangiu ML. Plasminogen activator inhibitor-1 is an independent poor prognostic factor for survival in advanced stage epithelial ovarian cancer patients. Int J Cancer 1998;79:449–54.

90. Pyke C, Kristensen P, Ralfkiaer E, et al. The plasminogen activation system in human colon cancer: messenger RNA for the inhibitor PAI-1 is located in endothelial cells in the tumor stroma. Cancer Res 1991;51:4067–71.

91. Galbiati F, Volonte D, Engelman JA, et al. Targeted downregulation of caveolin-1 is sufficient to drive cell transformation and hyperactivate the p42/44 MAP kinase cascade. EMBO J 1998;17:6633–48.

92. Engelman JA, Zhang X, Razani B, et al. p42/44 MAP kinase-dependent and -independent signaling pathways regulate caveolin-1 gene expression. Activation of ras-map kinase and protein kinase a signaling cascades transcriptionally down-regulates caveolin-1 promoter activity. J Biol Chem 1999;274:32333–41.

93. Wiechen K, Diatchenko L, Agoulnik A, et al. Caveolin-1 is down-regulated in human ovarian carcinoma and acts as a candidate tumor suppressor gene. Am J Pathol 2001;159: 1635–43.

94. Schlegel A, Wang C, Katzenellenbogen BS, et al. Caveolin-1 potentiates estrogen receptor alpha (ERalpha) signaling. Caveolin-1 drives ligand-independent nuclear translocation and activation of ERalpha. J Biol Chem 1999;274:33551–6.

95. Tobias ES, Hurlstone AF, MacKenzie E, et al. The TES gene at 7q31.1 is methylated in tumors and encodes a novel growth-suppressing LIM domain protein. Oncogene 2001;20:2844–53.

96. Lu KH, Weitzel JN, Kodali S, et al. A novel 4-cM minimally deleted region on chromosome 11p15.1 associated with high grade nonmucinous epithelial ovarian carcinomas. Cancer Res 1997;57:387–90.

97. Joyce JA, Schofield PN. Genomic imprinting and cancer. Mol Pathol 1998;51:185–90.

98. Moulton T, Crenshaw T, Hao Y, et al. Epigenetic lesions at the H19 locus in Wilms' tumour patients. Nat Genet 1994; 7:440–7.

99. Steenman MJ, Rainier S, Dobry CJ, et al. Loss of imprinting of IGF2 is linked to reduced expression and abnormal methylation of H19 in Wilms' tumour. Nat Genet 1994;7: 433–9.

100. Lee MP, Feinberg AP. Genomic imprinting of a human apoptosis gene homologue, TSSC3. Cancer Res 1998;58:1052–6.

101. Kim HT, Choi BH, Niikawa N, et al. Frequent loss of imprinting of the H19 and IGF-II genes in ovarian tumors. Am J Med Genet 1998;80:391–5.

102. Xu XL, Wu LC, Du F, et al. Inactivation of human SRBC, located within the 11p15.5-p15.4 tumor suppressor region, in breast and lung cancers. Cancer Res 2001;61:7943–9.

103. Sellar GC, Li L, Watt KP, et al. BARX2 induces cadherin 6 expression and is a functional suppressor of ovarian cancer progression. Cancer Res 2001;61:6977–81.

104. Jones MH, Nakamura Y. Detection of loss of heterozygosity at the human TP53 locus using a dinucleotide repeat polymorphism. Genes Chromosomes Cancer 1992;5:89–90.

105. Kohler MF, Marks JR, Wiseman RW, et al. Spectrum of mutation and frequency of allelic deletion of the p53 gene in ovarian cancer. J Natl Cancer Inst 1993;85:1513–9.

106. Kupryjanczyk J, Thor A, Beauchamp R, et al. p53 gene mutations and protein accumulation in human ovarian cancer. Proc Natl Acad Sci U S A 1993;90:4961–5.

107. Li SB, Schwartz PE, Lee WH, Yang-Feng TL. Allele loss at the retinoblastoma locus in human ovarian cancer. J Natl Cancer Inst 1991;83:637–40.

108. Liu Y, Heyman M, Wang Y, et al. Molecular analysis of the retinoblastoma gene in primary ovarian cancer cells. Int J Cancer 1994;58:663–7.

109. Marks JR, Davidoff AM, Kerns BJ, et al. Overexpression and mutation of p53 in epithelial ovarian cancer. Cancer Res 1991;51:2979–84.

110. Mazars R, Pujol P, Maudelonde T, et al. p53 mutations in ovarian cancer: a late event? Oncogene 1991;6:1685–90.

111. Okamoto A, Sameshima Y, Yokoyama S, et al. Frequent allelic losses and mutations of the p53 gene in human ovarian cancer. Cancer Res 1991;51:5171–6.

112. Dodson MK, Cliby WA, Xu HJ, et al. Evidence of functional RB protein in epithelial ovarian carcinomas despite loss of heterozygosity at the RB locus. Cancer Res 1994;54: 610–3.

113. Kim TM, Benedict WF, Xu HJ, et al. Loss of heterozygosity on chromosome 13 is common only in the biologically more aggressive subtypes of ovarian epithelial tumors and is associated with normal retinoblastoma gene expression. Cancer Res 1994;54:605–9.

114. Mazars R, Sinardi L, BenCheikh M, et al. p53 mutations occur in aggressive breast cancer. Cancer Res 1992;52:918–23.

115. Berchuck A, Kohler MF, Hopkins MP, et al. Overexpression of p53 is not a feature of benign and early-stage borderline epithelial ovarian tumors. Gynecol Oncol 1994;52:232–6.

116. Kupryjanczyk J, Bell DA, Dimeo D, et al. p53 gene analysis of ovarian borderline tumors and stage I carcinomas. Hum Pathol 1995;26:387–92.

117. Phillips N, Ziegle M, Saha B, Xynos F. Allelic loss on chromosome 17 in human ovarian cancer. Int J Cancer 1993; 54:85–91.

118. Eccles DM, Granston G, Steel CM, et al. Allele losses on

chromosome 17 in human epithelial ovarian carcinoma. Oncogene 1990;5:1599–601.

119. Eccles DM, Russell SE, Haites NE, et al. Early loss of heterozygosity on 17q in ovarian cancer. The Abe Ovarian Cancer Genetics Group. Oncogene 1992;7:2069–72.

120. Foulkes WD, Black DM, Stamp GW, et al. Very frequent loss of heterozygosity throughout chromosome 17 in sporadic ovarian carcinoma. Int J Cancer 1993;54:220–5.

121. Lee JH, Kavanagh JJ, Wildrick DM, et al. Frequent loss of heterozygosity on chromosomes 6q, 11, and 17 in human ovarian carcinomas. Cancer Res 1990;50:2724–8.

122. Iyengar TD, Ng S, Lau CC, et al. Differential expression of NF1 type I and type II isoforms in sporadic borderline and invasive epithelial ovarian tumors. Oncogene 1999; 18:257–62.

123. Yang-Feng TL, Han H, Chen KC, et al. Allelic loss in ovarian cancer. Int J Cancer 1993;54:546–51.

124. Wiper DW, Zanotti KM, Kennedy AW, et al. Analysis of allelic imbalance on chromosome 17p13 in stage I and stage II epithelial ovarian cancers. Gynecol Oncol 1998; 71:77–82.

125. Coles C, Thompson AM, Elder PA, et al. Evidence implicating at least two genes on chromosome 17p in breast carcinogenesis. Lancet 1990;336:761–3.

126. Cornelis RS, van Vliet M, Vos CB, et al. Evidence for a gene on 17p13.3, distal to TP53, as a target for allele loss in breast tumors without p53 mutations. Cancer Res 1994; 54:4200–6.

127. Andersen TI, Gaustad A, Ottestad L, et al. Genetic alterations of the tumour suppressor gene regions 3p, 11p, 13q, 17p, and 17q in human breast carcinomas. Genes Chromosomes Cancer 1992;4:113–21.

128. Merlo GR, Venesio T, Bernardi A, et al. Evidence for a second tumor suppressor gene on 17p linked to high S-phase index in primary human breast carcinomas. Cancer Genet Cytogenet 1994;76:106–11.

129. Biegel JA, Burk CD, Barr FG, Emanuel BS. Evidence for a 17p tumor related locus distinct from p53 in pediatric primitive neuroectodermal tumors. Cancer Res 1992;52:3391–5.

130. Atkin NB, Baker MC. Chromosome 17p loss in carcinoma of the cervix uteri. Cancer Genet Cytogenet 1989;37:229–33.

131. Cogen PH, Daneshvar L, Metzger AK, et al. Involvement of multiple chromosome 17p loci in medulloblastoma tumorigenesis. Am J Hum Genet 1992;50:584–9.

132. Saxena A, Clark WC, Robertson JT, et al. Evidence for the involvement of a potential second tumor suppressor gene on chromosome 17 distinct from p53 in malignant astrocystomas. Cancer Res 1992;52:6716–21.

133. Konishi H, Takahashi T, Kozaki K, et al. Detailed deletion mapping suggests the involvement of a tumor suppressor gene at 17p13.3, distal to p53, in the pathogenesis of lung cancers. Oncogene 1998;17:2095–100.

134. Bruening W, Prowse AH, Schultz DC, et al. Expression of OVCA1, a candidate tumor suppressor, is reduced in tumors and inhibits growth of ovarian cancer cells. Cancer Res 1999;59:4973–83.

135. Salicioni AM, Xi M, Vanderveer LA, et al. Identification and structural analysis of human RBM8A and RBM8B: two highly conserved RNA-binding motif proteins that interact with OVCA1, a candidate tumor suppressor. Genomics 2000. [In press]

136. Kataoka N, Yong J, Kim VN, et al. Pre-mRNA splicing imprints mRNA in the nucleus with a novel RNA-binding protein that persists in the cytoplasm. Mol Cell 2000;6: 673–82.

137. Kataoka N, Diem MD, Kim VN, et al. A human homolog of Drosophila mago nashi protein, is a component of the splicing-dependent exon-exon junction complex. EMBO J 2001;20:6424–33.

138. Kim VN, Dreyfus G. Nuclear mRNA binding proteins couple pre-mRNA splicing and post-splicing events. Mol Cells 2001;12:1–10.

139. Kim VN, Kataoka N, Dreyfuss G. Role of the nonsense-mediated decay factor hUpf3 in the splicing-dependent exon-exon junction complex. Science 2001;293:1832–6.

140. Le Hir H, Izaurralde E, Maquat LE, Moore MJ. The spliceosome deposits multiple proteins 20-24 nucleotides upstream of mRNA exon-exon junctions. EMBO J 2000; 19:6860–9.

141. Le Hir H, Gatfield D, Izaurralde E, Moore MJ. The exon-exon junction complex provides a binding platform for factors involved in mRNA export and nonsense-mediated mRNA decay. EMBO J 2001;20:4987–97.

142. Campbell IG, Foulkes WD, Beynon G, et al. LOH and mutation analysis of CDKN2 in primary human ovarian cancers. Int J Cancer 1995;63:222–5.

143. Devlin J, Elder PA, Gabra H, et al. High frequency of chromosome 9 deletion in ovarian cancer: evidence for three tumour-suppressor loci. Br J Cancer 1996;73:420–3.

144. Rodabaugh KJ, Biggs RB, Qureshi JA, et al. Detailed deletion mapping of chromosome 9p and p16 gene alterations in human borderline and invasive epithelial ovarian tumors. Oncogene 1995;11:1249–54.

145. Schultz DC, Vanderveer L, Buetow KH, et al. Characterization of chromosome 9 in human ovarian neoplasia identifies frequent genetic imbalance on 9q and rare alterations involving 9p, including CDKN2. Cancer Res 1995;55:2150–7.

146. Ichikawa Y, Yoshida S, Koyama Y, et al. Inactivation of p16/CDKN2 and p15/MTS2 genes in different histologic types and clinical stages of primary ovarian tumors. Int J Cancer 1996;69:466–70.

147. Ryan A, Al-Jehani RM, Mulligan KT, Jacobs IJ. No evidence exists for methylation inactivation of the p16 tumor suppressor gene in ovarian carcinogenesis. Gynecol Oncol 1998;68:14–7.

148. Shih YC, Kerr J, Liu J, et al. Rare mutations and no hypermethylation at the CDKN2A locus in epithelial ovarian tumours. Int J Cancer 1997;70:508–11.

149. Quelle DE, Zindy F, Ashmun RA, Sherr CJ. Alternative reading frames of the INK4a tumor suppressor gene encode two unrelated proteins capable of inducing cell cycle arrest. Cell 1995;83:993–1000.

150. Kamijo T, Zindy F, Roussel MF, et al. Tumor suppression at the mouse INK4a locus mediated by the alternative reading frame product p19ARF. Cell 1997;91:649–59.

151. Bates S, Phillips AC, Clark PA, et al. p14ARF links the tumour suppressors RB and p53. Nature 1998;395:124–5.

152. Palmero I, Pantoja C, Serrano M. p19ARF links the tumour suppressor p53 to Ras. Nature 1998;395:125–6.

153. Stott FJ, Bates S, James MC, et al. The alternative product from the human CDKN2A locus, p14(ARF), participates

in a regulatory feedback loop with p53 and MDM2. EMBO J 1998;17:5001–14.

154. Sherr CJ, DePinho RA. Cellular senescence: mitotic clock or culture shock? Cell 2000;102:407–10.

155. Abdollahi A, Roberts D, Godwin AK, et al. Identification of a zinc-finger gene at 6q25: a chromosomal region implicated in development of many solid tumors. Oncogene 1997;14:1973–9.

156. Spengler D, Villalba M, Hoffmann A, et al. Regulation of apoptosis and cell cycle arrest by Zac1, a novel zinc finger protein expressed in the pituitary gland and the brain. EMBO J 1997;16:2814–25.

157. Piras G, El Kharroubi A, Kozlov S, et al. Zac1 (Lot1), a potential tumor suppressor gene, and the gene for epsilon-sarcoglycan are maternally imprinted genes: identification by a subtractive screen of novel uniparental fibroblast lines. Mol Cell Biol 2000;20:3308–15.

158. Abdollahi A, Godwin AK, Miller PD, et al. Identification of a gene containing zinc-finger motifs based on lost expression in malignantly transformed rat ovarian surface epithelial cells. Cancer Res 1997;57:2029–34.

159. Varrault A, Ciani E, Apiou F, et al. hZAC encodes a zinc-finger protein with antiproliferative properties and maps to a chromosomal region frequently lost in cancer. Proc Natl Acad Sci U S A 1998;95:8835–40.

160. Abdollahi A, Bao R, Hamilton TC. LOT1 is a growth suppressor gene down-regulated by the epidermal growth factor receptor ligands and encodes a nuclear zinc-finger protein. Oncogene 1999;18:6477–87.

161. Huang SM, Schonthal AH, Stallcup MR. Enhancement of p53-dependent gene activation by the transcriptional coactivator Zac1. Oncogene 2001;20:2134–43.

162. Bilanges B, Varrault A, Basyuk E, et al. Loss of expression of the candidate tumor suppressor gene ZAC in breast cancer cell lines and primary tumors. Oncogene 1999;18:3979–88.

163. Mok SC, Wong KK, Chan RK, et al. Molecular cloning of differentially expressed genes in human epithelial ovarian cancer. Gynecol Oncol 1994;52:247–52.

164. Fazili Z, Sun W, Mittelstaedt S, et al. Disabled-2 inactivation is an early step in ovarian tumorigenicity. Oncogene 1999;18:3104–13.

165. Mok SC, Chan WY, Wong KK, et al. DOC-2, a candidate tumor suppressor gene in human epithelial ovarian cancer. Oncogene 1998;16:2381–7.

166. Xu XX, Yang W, Jackowski S, Rock CO. Cloning of a novel phosphoprotein regulated by colony-stimulating factor 1 shares a domain with the *Drosophila* disabled gene product. J Biol Chem 1995;270:14184–91.

167. Hocevar BA, Smine A, Xu X-X, Howe PH. The adaptor molecule Disabled-2 links the transforming growth factor beta receptors to the Smad pathway. EMBO J 2001;20:2789–801.

168. He J, Smith ER, Xu X-X. Disabled-2 exerts its tumor suppressor activity by uncoupling c-Fos expression and MAP kinase activation. J Biol Chem 2001;276:26814–8.

169. Zhou J, Hsieh JT. The inhibitory role of DOC-2/DAB2 in growth factor receptor-mediated signal cascade. DOC-2/DAB2-mediated inhibition of ERK phosphorylation via binding to Grb2. J Biol Chem 2001;276:27793–8.

170. Yang DH, Smith ER, Cohen C, et al. Molecular events associated with dysplastic morphologic transformation and initiation of ovarian tumorigenicity. Cancer 2002;94:2380–92.

171. Yang DH, Smith ER, Roland IH, et al. Disabled-2 is essential for endodermal cell positioning and structure formation during mouse embryogenesis. Dev Biol 2002;251:27–44.

172. Yu Y, Xu F, Peng H, et al. NOEY2 (ARHI), an imprinted putative tumor suppressor gene in ovarian and breast carcinomas. Proc Natl Acad Sci U S A 1999;96:214–9.

173. Lin H, Huber R, Schlessinger D, Morin PJ. Frequent silencing of the GPC3 gene in ovarian cancer cell lines. Cancer Res 1999;59:807–10.

174. Lynch HT, Krush AJ. Carcinoma of the breast and ovary in three families. Surg Gynecol Obstet 1971;133:644–8.

175. Lynch HT, Krush AJ, Lemon HM, et al. Tumor variation in families with breast cancer. JAMA 1972;222:1631–5.

176. Lynch HT, Guirgis HA, Albert S, et al. Familial association of carcinoma of the breast and ovary. Surg Gynecol Obstet 1974;138:717–24.

177. Lynch HT, Conway T, Lynch J. Hereditary ovarian cancer. Pedigree studies, part II. Cancer Genet Cytogenet 1991;53:161–83.

178. Hall JM, Lee MK, Newman B, et al. Linkage of early-onset familial breast cancer to chromosome 17q21. Science 1990;250:1684–9.

179. Narod S, Lynch H, Conway T, et al. Increasing incidence of breast cancer in family with BRCA1 mutation [letter]. Lancet 1993;341:1101–2.

180. Miki Y, Swensen J, Shattuck-Eidens D, et al. A strong candidate for the breast and ovarian cancer susceptibility gene BRCA1. Science 1994;266:66–71.

181. Wooster R, Newhausen S, Mangion J, et al. Localization of a breast cancer susceptibility gene, *BRCA2*, to chromosome 13q12-13. Science 1994;265:2088–90.

182. Tavitigian S, Rommens J, Couch F, et al. The complete *BRCA2* gene and mutations in chromosomes 13q-linked kindreds. Nat Genet 1996;12:333–7.

183. Wooster R, Bignell G, Lancaster J, et al. Identification of the breast cancer susceptibility gene *BRCA2*. Nature 1995;378:789–92.

184. Lovering R, Hanson IM, Borden KLB, et al. Identification and preliminary characterization of a protein motif related to the zinc finger. Proc Natl Acad Sci U S A 1993;90:2112–6.

185. Bertwistle D, Ashworth A. Functions of the BRCA1 and BRCA2 genes. Curr Opin Genet Dev 1998;8:14–20.

186. Rahman N, Stratton MR. The genetics of breast cancer susceptibility. Annu Rev Genet 1998;32:95–121.

187. Lane TF, Deng C, Elson A, et al. Expression of BRCA1 is associated with terminal differentiation of ectodermally and mesodermally derived tissues in mice. Genes Dev 1995;9:2712–22.

188. Bove B, Dunbrack J, Godwin AK. *BRCA1*, *BRCA2*, and hereditary breast cancer. In: Pasqualini JR, editor. Breast cancer: prognosis, treatment, and prevention. New York: Marcel Dekker, Inc; 2002. p. 555–623.

189. Petrij-Bosch A, Peelen T, van Vliet M, et al. BRCA1 genomic deletions are major founder mutations in Dutch breast cancer patients. Nat Genet 1997;17:341–5.

190. Frolov A, Prowse AH, Vanderveer L, et al. DNA array-based method for detection of large rearrangements in the BRCA1 gene. Genes Chromosomes Cancer 2002;35:232–41.

191. Couch FJ, DeShano ML, Blackwood MA, et al. *BRCA1* mutations in women attending clinics that evaluate the risk of breast cancer. N Engl J Med 1997;336:1409–15.

192. Whittemore A, Gong G, Iitnyre J. Prevalence and contribution of *BRCA1* mutations in breast cancer and ovarian cancer: results from three US population-based case-control studies of ovarian cancer. Am J Hum Genet 1997;60:496–504.

193. Narod S, Ford C, Devilee P, et al. An evaluation of genetic heterogeneity in 145 breast-ovarian cancer families. Breast Cancer Linkage Consortium. Am J Hum Genet 1995;56:254–64.

194. Lynch HT, Watson P, Tinley S, et al. An update on DNA-based BRCA1/BRCA2 genetic counseling in hereditary breast cancer. Cancer Genet Cytogenet 1999;109:91–8.

195. Hosking L, Trowsdale J, Nicolai H, et al. A somatic *BRCA1* mutation in an ovarian tumour. Nat Genet 1995;9:343–4.

196. Merajver SD, Pham TM, Caduff RF, et al. Somatic mutations in the BRCA1 gene in sporadic ovarian tumours. Nat Genet 1995;9:439–43.

197. Bowcock AM. Breast cancer genes. Breast 1997;3:1–6.

198. Collins FS. *BRCA1*—lots of mutations, lots of dilemmas. N Engl J Med 1996;334:186–8.

199. Struewing JP, Abeliovich D, Peretz T, et al. The carrier frequency of the BRCA1 185delAG mutation is approximately 1 percent in Ashkenazi Jewish individuals. Nat Genet 1995;11:198–200.

200. Ford D, Easton D, Peto J. Estimate of the gene frequency of BRCA1 and its contribution to breast and ovarian cancer incidence. Am J Hum Genet 1995;57:1457–62.

201. Struewing J, Watson P, Easton D, et al. Prophylactic oophorectomy in inherited breast/ovarian cancer families. J Natl Cancer Inst Monogr 1995;17:33–5.

202. Ford D, Easton DF, Stratton M, et al. Genetic heterogeneity and penetrance analysis of the BRCA1 and BRCA2 genes in breast cancer families. The Breast Cancer Linkage Consortium. Am J Hum Genet 1998;62:676–89.

203. Weber B. Familial breast cancer. Recent Results Cancer Res 1996;140:5–16.

204. Couch FJ, Farid LM, DeShano ML, et al. BRCA2 germline mutations in male breast cancer cases and breast cancer families. Nat Genet 1996;13:123–5.

205. Roa B, Boyd A, Volcik K, Richards C. Ashkenazi Jewish population frequencies for common mutations in *BRCA1* and *BRCA2*. Nat Genet 1996;14:185–7.

206. Burke W, Daly M, Garber J, et al. Recommendations for follow-up care of individuals with an inherited predisposition to cancer. II. *BRCA1* and *BRCA2*. Cancer Genetics Studies Consortium. JAMA 1997;277:997–1003.

207. Gayther SA, Warren W, Mazoyer S, et al. Germline mutations of the BRCA1 gene in breast and ovarian cancer families provide evidence for a genotype-phenotype correlation. Nat Genet 1995;11:428–33.

208. Easton DF, Ford D, Bishop DT. Breast and ovarian cancer incidence in BRCA1-mutation carriers. Am J Hum Genet 1995;56:265–71.

209. Struewing JP, Hartge P, Wacholder S, et al. The risk of cancer associated with specific mutations of BRCA1 and BRCA2 among Ashkenazi Jews. N Engl J Med 1997;336:1401–8.

210. Shattuck-Eidens D, McClure M, Simard J, et al. A collaborative survey of 80 mutations in the BRCA1 breast and ovar-ian cancer susceptibility gene. Implications for presymptomatic testing and screening. JAMA 1995;273:535–41.

211. Berman DB, Wagner-Costalas J, Schultz DC, et al. Two distinct origins of a common BRCA1 mutation in breast-ovarian cancer families: a genetic study of 15 185delAG-mutation kindreds. Am J Hum Genet 1996;58:1166–76.

212. Serova O, Montagna M, Torchard D, et al. A high incidence of BRCA1 mutations in 20 breast-ovarian cancer families. Am J Hum Genet 1996;58:42–51.

213. Gayther SA, Mangion J, Russell P, et al. Variation of risks of breast and ovarian cancer associated with different germline mutations of the BRCA2 gene. Nat Genet 1997; 15:103–5.

214. Neuhausen SL, Godwin AK, Gershoni-Baruch R, et al. Haplotype and phenotype analysis of nine recurrent BRCA2 mutations in 111 families: results of an international study. Am J Hum Genet 1998;62:1381–8.

215. Kerangueven F, Eisinger F, Noguchi T, et al. Loss of heterozygosity in human breast carcinomas in the ataxia telangiectasia. Cowden disease and BRCA1 gene regions. Oncogene 1997;23:339–47.

216. Foster KA, Harrington P, Kerr J, et al. Somatic and germline mutations of the BRCA2 gene in sporadic ovarian cancer. Cancer Res 1996;56:3622–5.

217. Lancaster JM, Wooster R, Mangion J, et al. BRCA2 mutations in primary breast and ovarian cancers. Nat Genet 1996;13:238–40.

218. Nagai MA, Yamamoto L, Salaorni S, et al. Detailed deletion mapping of chromosome segment 17q12-21 in sporadic breast tumours. Genes Chromosomes Cancer 1994;11: 58–62.

219. Collins N, Wooster R, Stratton MR. Absence of methylation of CpG dinucleotides within the promoter of the breast cancer susceptibility gene BRCA2 in normal tissues and in breast and ovarian cancers. Br J Cancer 1997;76:1150–6.

220. Dobrovic A, Simpfendorfer D. Methylation of the BRCA1 gene in sporadic breast cancer. Cancer Res 1997;57:3347–50.

221. Wilson CA, Ramos L, Villasenor MR, et al. Localization of human BRCA1 and its loss in high-grade, non-inherited breast carcinomas. Nat Genet 1999;21:236–40.

222. Baldwin RL, Nemeth E, Tran H, et al. BRCA1 promoter region hypermethylation in ovarian carcinoma: a population-based study. Cancer Res 2000;60:5329–33.

223. Chan KY, Ozcelik H, Cheung AN, et al. U. S. Epigenetic factors controlling the *BRCA1* and *BRCA2* genes in sporadic ovarian cancer. Cancer Res 2002;62:4151–6.

224. Hilton JL, Geisler JP, Rathe JA, et al. Inactivation of BRCA1 and BRCA2 in ovarian cancer. J Natl Cancer Inst 2002; 94:1396–406.

225. Deng CX, Brodie SG. Knockout mouse models and mammary tumorigenesis. Semin Cancer Biol 2001;11:387–94.

226. Brodie SG , Deng CX. BRCA1-associated tumorigenesis: what have we learned from knockout mice? Trends Genet 2001;17:S18–22.

227. Scully R, Chen J, Plug A, et al. Association of BRCA1 with Rad51 in mitotic and meiotic cells. Cell 1997;88:265–75.

228. Sharan SK, Morimatsu M, Albrecht U, et al. Embryonic lethality and radiation hypersensitivity mediated by Rad51 in mice lacking Brca2. Nature 1997;386:804–10.

229. Chen J, Silver DP, Walpita D, et al. Stable interaction between

the products of the BRCA1 and BRCA2 tumor suppressor genes in mitotic and meiotic cells. Mol Cell 1998;2:17–28.

230. Tibbetts RS, Cortez D, Brumbaugh KM, et al. Functional interactions between BRCA1 and the checkpoint kinase ATR during genotoxic stress. Genes Dev 2000;14:2989–3002.

231. Li S, Ting NS, Zheng L, et al. Functional link of BRCA1 and ataxia telangiectasia gene product in DNA damage response. Nature 2000;406:210–5.

232. Gatei M, Scott SP, Filippovitch I, et al. Role for ATM in DNA damage-induced phosphorylation of BRCA1. Cancer Res 2000;60:3299–304.

233. Lee JS, Collins KM, Brown AL, et al. hCds1-mediated phosphorylation of BRCA1 regulates the DNA damage response. Nature 2000;404:201–4.

234. Cortez D, Wang Y, Qin J, Elledge SJ. Requirement of ATM-dependent phosphorylation of brca1 in the DNA damage response to double-strand breaks. Science 1999;286:1162–6.

235. Xu X, Wagner KU, Larson D, et al. Conditional mutation of Brca1 in mammary epithelial cells results in blunted ductal morphogenesis and tumour formation. Nat Genet 1999;22:37–43.

236. Brodie SG, Xu X, Qiao W, et al. Multiple genetic changes are associated with mammary tumorigenesis in Brca1 conditional knockout mice. Oncogene 2001;20:7514–23.

237. Xu X, Qiao W, Linke SP, et al. Genetic interactions between tumor suppressors Brca1 and p53 in apoptosis, cell cycle and tumorigenesis. Nat Genet 2001;28:266–71.

238. Ludwig T, Fisher P, Murty V, Efstratiadis A. Development of mammary adenocarcinomas by tissue-specific knockout of Brca2 in mice. Oncogene 2001;20:3937–48.

239. Jonkers J, Meuwissen R, van der Gulden H, et al. Synergistic tumor suppressor activity of BRCA2 and p53 in a conditional mouse model for breast cancer. Nat Genet 2001;29:418–25.

240. Crook T, Crossland S, Crompton MR, et al. p53 mutations in BRCA1-associated familial breast cancer. Lancet 1997;350:638–9.

241. Rhei E, Bogomolniy F, Federici MG, et al. Molecular genetic characterization of BRCA1- and BRCA2-linked hereditary ovarian cancers. Cancer Res 1998;58:3193–6.

242. Greenblatt MS, Chappuis PO, Bond JP, et al. TP53 mutations in breast cancer associated with BRCA1 or BRCA2 germ-line mutations: distinctive spectrum and structural distribution. Cancer Res 2001;61:4092–7.

243. Kerr P, Ashworth A. New complexities for BRCA1 and BRCA2. Curr Biol 2001;11:R668–76.

244. Borg A. Molecular and pathological characterization of inherited breast cancer. Semin Cancer Biol 2001;11:375–85.

245. Kleiman FE, Manley JL. The BARD1-CstF-50 interaction links mRNA 3' end formation to DNA damage and tumor suppression. Cell 2001;104:743–53.

246. Kleiman FE, Manley JL. Functional interaction of BRCA1-associated BARD1 with polyadenylation factor CstF-50. Science 1999;285:1576–9.

247. Freemont PS. RING for destruction? Curr Biol 2000;10:R84–7.

248. Jackson PK, Eldridge AG, Freed E, et al. The lore of the RINGs: substrate recognition and catalysis by ubiquitin ligases. Trends Cell Biol 2000;10:429–39.

249. Hashizume R, Fukuda M, Maeda I, et al. The RING heterodimer BRCA1-BARD1 is a ubiquitin ligase inactivated by a breast cancer-derived mutation. J Biol Chem 2001;276:14537–40.

250. Ruffner H, Joazeiro CA, Hemmati D, et al. Cancer-predisposing mutations within the RING domain of BRCA1: loss of ubiquitin protein ligase activity and protection from radiation hypersensitivity. Proc Natl Acad Sci U S A 2001;98:5134–9.

251. Tapper J, Kettunen E, El-Rifai W, et al. Changes in gene expression during progression of ovarian carcinoma. Cancer Genet Cytogenet 2001;128:1–6.

252. Welsh JB, Zarrinkar PP, Sapinoso, LM, et al. Analysis of gene expression profiles in normal and neoplastic ovarian tissue samples identifies candidate molecular markers of epithelial ovarian cancer. Proc Natl Acad Sci U S A 2001;98:1176–81.

253. Shridhar V, Lee J, Pandita A, et al. Genetic analysis of early-versus late-stage ovarian tumors. Cancer Res 2001;61:5895–904.

254. Sawiris GP, Sherman-Baust CA, Becker KG, et al. Development of a highly specialized cDNA array for the study and diagnosis of epithelial ovarian cancer. Cancer Res 2002;62:2923–8.

255. Jazaeri AA, Yee CJ, Sotiriou C, et al. Gene expression profiles of BRCA1-linked, BRCA2-linked, and sporadic ovarian cancers. J Natl Cancer Inst 2002;94:990–1000.

256. Schwartz DR, Kardia SL, Shedden KA, et al. Gene expression in ovarian cancer reflects both morphology and biological behavior, distinguishing clear cell from other poor-prognosis ovarian carcinomas. Cancer Res 2002;62:4722–9.

257. Sakamoto M, Kondo A., Kawasaki K, et al. Analysis of gene expression profiles associated with cisplatin resistance in human ovarian cancer cell lines and tissues using cDNA microarray. Hum Cell 2001;14:305–15.

258. Bayani J, Brenton, JD, Macgregor PF, et al. Parallel analysis of sporadic primary ovarian carcinomas by spectral karyotyping, comparative genomic hybridization, and expression microarrays. Cancer Res 2002;62:3466–76.

259. Chenevix-Trench G, Kerr J, Hurst T, et al. Analysis of loss of heterozygosity and KRAS2 mutations in ovarian neoplasms: clinicopathological correlations. Genes Chromosomes Cancer 1997;18:75–83.

260. Cuatrecasas M, Erill N, Musulen E, et al. K-ras mutations in nonmucinous ovarian epithelial tumors: a molecular analysis and clinicopathologic study of 144 patients. Cancer 1998;82:1088–95.

261. Mok SC, Bell DA, Knapp RC, et al. Mutation of K-ras protooncogene in human ovarian epithelial tumors of borderline malignancy. Cancer Res 1993;53:1489–92.

262. Katsaros D, Theillet C, Zola P, et al. Concurrent abnormal expression of erbB-2, myc and ras genes is associated with poor outcome of ovarian cancer patients. Anticancer Res 1995;15:1501–10.

263. Harlozinska A, Bar JK, Sobanska E, Goluda M. Epidermal growth factor receptor and c-erbB-2 oncoproteins in tissue and tumor effusion cells of histopathologically different ovarian neoplasms. Tumour Biol 1998;19:364–73.

264. Fajac A, Benard J, Lhomme C, et al. c-erbB2 gene amplification and protein expression in ovarian epithelial tumors:

evaluation of their respective prognostic significance by multivariate analysis. Int J Cancer 1995;64:146–51.

265. Meden H, Marx D, Rath W, et al. Overexpression of the oncogene c-erb B2 in primary ovarian cancer: evaluation of the prognostic value in a Cox proportional hazards multiple regression. Int J Gynecol Pathol 1994;13:45–53.

266. Tanner B, Hengstler JG, Luch A, et al. C-myc mRNA expression in epithelial ovarian carcinomas in relation to estrogen receptor status, metastatic spread, survival time, FIGO stage, and histologic grade and type. Int J Gynecol Pathol 1998;17:66–74.

267. Baker VV, Borst MP, Dixon D, et al. c-myc amplification of ovarian cancer. Gynecol Oncol 1990;38:340–2.

268. Bartlett JM, Langdon SP, Scott WN, et al. Transforming growth factor-beta isoform expression in human ovarian tumours. Eur J Cancer 1997;33:2397–403.

269. Cardillo MR, Yap E, Castagna G. Molecular genetic analysis of TGF-beta1 in ovarian neoplasia. J Exp Clin Cancer Res 1997;16:49–56.

270. Bartlett JM, Langdon SP, Simpson BJ, et al. The prognostic value of epidermal growth factor receptor mRNA expression in primary ovarian cancer. Br J Cancer 1996;73: 301–6.

271. Meden H, Marx D, Raab T, et al. EGF-R and overexpression of the oncogene c-erbB-2 in ovarian cancer: immunohistochemical findings and prognostic value. J Obstet Gynaecol 1995;21:167–78.

272. Di Renzo MF, Olivero M, Katsaros D, et al. Overexpression of the Met/HGF receptor in ovarian cancer. Int J Cancer 1994;58:658–62.

273. Welcsh PL, King MC. BRCA1 and BRCA2 and the genetics of breast and ovarian cancer. Hum Mol Genet 2001; 10:705–13.

274. Tlsty TD. A molecular blueprint for targeting cancer? Nat Genet 1999;21:64–5.

275. Feinberg AP. Genomic imprinting and gene activation in cancer. Nat Genet 1993;4:110–13.

5

Screening

CYNTHIA A. BERGMAN, MD

One of the biggest detriments to effective treatment for ovarian cancer is the failure to reliably identify early-stage disease. While cure rates for true stage I disease can be as high as 90%, most patients are asymptomatic or have symptoms that are nonspecific, and generally attributed to benign conditions until metastatic disease has developed, when survival rates are under 30%. Clearly, an effective form of screening for ovarian cancer would significantly impact outcome.

SCREENING CHARACTERISTICS

Screening is the use of tests or examinations to identify disease before it becomes clinically obvious. Hulka[1,2] created a timeline of disease development (Figure 5–1) to illustrate the temporal utility of screening modalities. Initially, there is some inciting event, such as deoxyribonucleic acid (DNA) mutation or a particular infection, which begins the disease process. Usually, at some later date, patients will develop symptoms, which leads to appropriate investigation and, ultimately, diagnosis of the disease process. For cancer diagnoses, outcome at this point is largely predetermined by stage at diagnosis. Predating this point, however, is a period of "preclinical disease." Identification of cancer during this period could lend an opportunity for earlier disease diagnosis and thus potentially improved treatment efficacy. The key, then, is to identify markers of this "disease in progress" that are evident prior to the appearance of symptoms.

The target population for screening tests includes people without related disease symptomatology. This may range from a specific at-risk population to the entire population at large, depending on characteristics of the disease being screened for, as well as the test modality itself. Ultimately, the goal is to reduce complications and mortality from that particular cancer among the persons undergoing screening. The cancer type, then, must be sufficiently dangerous to warrant screening efforts. Routinely diagnosed ovarian cancers, are usually of advanced stage, leading to serious complications and high mortality rates. For an effective screening program, treatment that is more effective in the preclinical disease state must also be available. If no treatment exists, earlier detection is not only ineffective but also psychologically damaging. For ovarian cancers, treatment of early-stage disease is over three times as effective as treatment for advanced disease, making early diagnosis highly beneficial. Finally, the preclinical disease state must in some way be detectable; an adequate marker must be identified to signify the "disease in progress" before the appearance of symptoms. For example, the identification and treatment of cervical cancer precursor lesions has reduced morbidity and mortality from frank cervical carcinoma. For ovarian

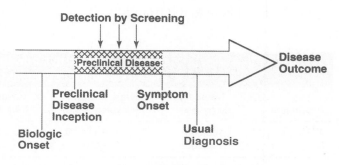

Figure 5–1. Timeline for usefulness of screening tests.

cancers, however, the pathologic changes occurring during disease development are not yet known; therefore, the preclinical state remains elusive.

An effective screening test also has specific prerequisites. The test must be sufficiently easy, both for patients and physicians. A modality causing significant discomfort or a large time commitment is not likely to be widely accepted as most people will test negative and therefore not directly benefit. Similarly, a test requiring intensive training or the time of many office staff members will be difficult to implement, particularly in this day of managed care. The test must have adequate sensitivity and specificity, and the positive predictive value must be sufficiently high, reflecting the number of people with positive test results who will actually have the disease. A positive screening test requires a diagnostic evaluation to determine whether or not the disease is actually present. An effective screening test, then, has a useful method in place for follow-up of positive results. Hemoccult-positive stools, for example, can be further evaluated by endoscopic procedures to identify neoplastic lesions. For ovarian cancers, however, the only definitive diagnostic procedure to date is surgical excision of the ovary for pathologic analysis. Follow-up of any positive screening test for ovarian cancer can therefore be both expensive and risky.

Several useful statistical parameters exist to evaluate the efficacy of screening tools. Ultimately, an effective screening program will show a shift in stage distribution of detected cancers towards earlier and more treatable lesions. Consequently, the site-specific mortality rate should decrease within the screened population as curability increases, and the case fatality rate should drop within the screened population since any given patient with the disease should be less likely to die from it.

RATIONALE

Available data support the concept of screening for ovarian cancer. Each year in the United States, approximately 23,300 women are diagnosed with an ovarian malignancy and 13,900 women die of this disease.[3] Although physicians have long known the devastating effects of ovarian cancer, public awareness has recently ballooned. In 1989, comedian and actress Gilda Radner's death from ovarian cancer enlightened the public about her illness and its difficulty in diagnosis. Since that time, several centers for the study of ovarian cancer have opened, and September was recently designated as Gynecologic Cancer Awareness month. On the personal level, patients are looking to their physicians for education, early detection, and thus protection against this deadly disease.[4] It is the physician's responsibility to accurately relay information about the limitations of today's screening tests for ovarian cancer.

Statistically, the low prevalence of ovarian cancer in the general population makes effective screening nearly impossible. Table 5–1[5] shows the difference in positive predictive value of a screening test as related to disease prevalence. For a population with a 0.1% disease prevalence, positive predictive value of a test with 100% sensitivity and 99% specificity is only 9%, which is under a generally accepted 10% minimum standard. For ovarian cancer, which has a 0.04% prevalence, the positive predictive value of such a completely sensitive and highly specific screening test would be far less. In contrast, that same test applied to a population with a 1% disease prevalence would yield a 50% positive predictive value. One key strategy for ovarian cancer screening, therefore, is to identify select populations with higher disease prevalence, such as those with a significant family history.

Table 5–1. PREDICTIVE POWER OF A COMPLETELY SENSITIVE* HIGHLY SPECIFIC† SCREENING TEST FOR OVARIAN CANCER					
Population	Number Screened	Ovarian Cancer Prevalence (%)	Number of Cases Detected	Number of False-Positives	Positive Predictive Power
A	100,000	0.1	100	1,000	100/(100 + 1,000) = 9%
B	100,000	1.0	1,000	1,000	1,000/(1,000 + 1,000) = 50%

*100% of all women with cancer are positive on test.
†99% of all women without cancer are negative on test.

SPECIFIC TECHNIQUES

Ultrasound Examination

The limitations of pelvic examination for the detection of early ovarian enlargement and internal ovarian structural changes are obvious. Consequently, ultrasonography has emerged as a primary mode of evaluation for gynecologic pathology and specifically ovarian alterations. Transvaginal ultrasonography uses a tubular transducer that is inserted into the vagina, allowing for up close imaging of adnexal structures. This test meets the criteria for a good screening tool in its ease of application both for patient and physician. It is widely available and of relatively low cost, especially when compared to pelvic computed tomography (CT) or magnetic resonance imaging (MRI).

An ovary presumably enlarges in size concurrently with neoplastic changes. In 1982, Campbell and colleagues[6] evaluated ovarian volume in postmenopausal women by ultrasonography followed by confirmatory surgical assessment. Correlation between measured and actual volumes was excellent (coefficient = 0.97). A larger group was then examined by ultrasonography alone, showing average ovarian volume to be 4.33 cm³. Additionally, size variation between any one patient's ovaries was found to be low (correlation coefficient = 0.82), leading the authors to suggest that an ovary that is twice the size of its contralateral partner should also be viewed as suspicious. Goswamy and colleagues[7] later tabulated ovarian volume in over 2,000 normal postmenopausal women and defined volumes > 10 cm³ as abnormal, noting continually decreasing ovarian size with advancing age.

Changes in internal ovarian architecture also accompany neoplastic change. In 1989, Granberg and colleagues[8] compared macroscopic ultrasonographic ovarian appearance to subsequent pathologic findings in 1,017 women. Cyst complexity and size were confirmed to correlate closely with the likelihood of malignancy although neither was completely predictive (Figure 5–2). Papillary wall vegetations, however, were strongly associated with malignant findings (Figure 5–3). In fact, this was the only ominous finding in the sole malignancy of 296

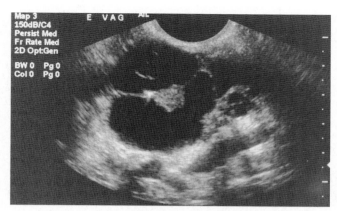

Figure 5–2. Transvaginal ultrasonography of a stage IA ovarian serous borderline tumor reveals a thick septation and mural nodularity.

identified unilocular cysts. DePriest and colleagues[9] presented a morphology index that assigned points for increasing size, complexity, and septal thickness of known ovarian tumors. A value of < 5 was found to be completely reassuring, and no cancers were seen in these 80 patients. In this retrospective evaluation of preoperative diagnostic sonograms, positive predictive value was 0.450 for malignancy in postmenopausal women scoring ≥ 5. Of the measured properties, wall structure was again the most predictive characteristic. These results suggest promise for ultrasonography as a screening tool, but targeted studies have not uniformly proven benefit.

Neovascularization is now accepted as a necessary component of tumorigenesis,[10] and color Doppler has therefore been proposed as a useful adjunct to transvaginal ultrasonography for the eval-

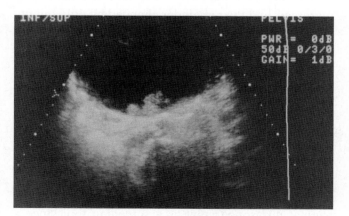

Figure 5–3. Transvaginal ultrasonography of a stage IC clear cell adenocarcinoma of the ovary shows mural papillations in a predominantly cystic lesion.

uation of blood vessels in ovarian tumors. As new blood vessels typically lack well-developed intramural smooth muscle, measurements of blood flow through such channels tend to reflect lower resistance and pulsatility. Timor-Tritsch and colleagues[11] measured the resistance index and pulsatility index of 115 adnexal masses scheduled for surgical removal and showed lower mean values for malignant lesions. Similarly, Kurjak and colleagues[12] imaged 14,317 women with vaginal color Doppler, 8,620 of whom were asymptomatic and 5,697 of whom had only suspected adnexal enlargement on pelvic examination. Resistance index was found to be highly predictive of malignancy, with values of ≤ 0.40 in 6 of 7 primary stage I ovarian tumors, all 9 metastatic lesions, and 39 of 40 advanced ovarian carcinomas. In contrast, resistance index measured > 0.40 in all but one of 624 benign tumors. Calculated positive predictive value was 98.2%, an unprecedented level that has yet to be replicated. Interestingly, all of the stage I primary ovarian tumors were < 4 cm in diameter, supporting Folkman's suggestion[10] that angiogenesis predates the development of clinically overt cancer. The usefulness of such blood flow measurements as a screening test, however, is currently unknown.

The largely reassuring natural history of cystic lesions in postmenopausal women limits the usefulness of transvaginal ultrasonography as a screening tool. Levine and colleagues[13] scanned 184 asymptomatic women and found 83 simple adnexal cysts over the study period. Of these, 72 were followed by repeat ultrasound examinations; over half spontaneously regressed, and the remainder changed by only minute measurements. Bailey and colleagues[14] agreed that nearly half of identified simple cysts resolve with no intervention and that the remainder represent benign lesions. Furthermore, in this population, over half of the complex adnexal masses also disappeared by the time of repeat ultrasound examination 60 days later. Of the persisting complex lesions, 6.1% represented malignancies; unfortunately, over two-thirds of these were advanced enough to require adjuvant chemotherapy. This nicely illustrates a limitation of transvaginal ultrasonography as a screening tool since a waiting period must be endured to define the natural history of a given postmenopausal cystic lesion.

Indeed, six of the seven cancers found in Bailey and colleagues' study increased in volume and complexity between the primary and follow-up scans; this may also have afforded opportunity for metastasis.

Cancer Antigen 125

Serum tumor markers have proven useful in the detection of existing disease in several cancer types. For epithelial ovarian cancers, cancer antigen 125 (CA 125) is the best studied of these. Initially, OC 125 monoclonal antibodies were used to bind to the CA 125 epitope on a high-molecular-weight glycoprotein expressed in coelomic epithelium and common to most nonmucinous epithelial ovarian carcinomas. More recently, the development of other related antibodies has created the more reliable CA 125-II assay. Several studies have confirmed the excellent correlation of elevated CA 125 values with active ovarian cancer. Jacobs and colleagues[15] demonstrated increased levels in more than 90% of patients with disease beyond the ovary, and Bast,[16] in his original article, showed a 93% correlation with documented disease activity.

Due to the relatively noninvasive nature of blood sampling, CA 125 has great appeal for screening programs. Furthermore, most studies show an elevation of this tumor marker in patients with a known history of ovarian cancer at least 3 months prior to the development of clinically detectable recurrence. Two additional studies[17,18] have shown that median CA 125 levels are higher in patients who later developed ovarian neoplasms than in to healthy controls up to 60 months preceding diagnosis. However, even the elevated levels were well within the established normal range, making prospective interpretation difficult if not impossible.

Still other problems are inherent to the wide distribution of CA 125. Nonovarian malignancies, benign gynecologic pathologies, and other nongynecologic pelvic diseases are known to elevate CA 125 levels. Many of these states are also accompanied by other symptoms, such as a mass or abdominopelvic discomfort, which can further mimic ovarian cancer. For example, Vuento and colleagues[19] observed 1,291 postmenopausal women for 3.5 years after baseline CA 125 determination and found only one ovarian cancer following a minimally elevated level (31 U/mL). In contrast, the 14 other patients with elevated CA 125 values (ranging from 30 to 1,210 U/mL) had noncancerous problems, including uterine fibroids, pancreatitis, and diverticulitis. In seven patients no pathology was ever identified. Such false-positive results are particularly problematic in the premenopausal population; common findings, including endometriosis, fibroids, pelvic inflammatory disease, and even menses, are known to elevate CA 125 readings.

Conversely, CA 125 levels are not reliably elevated in known early-stage ovarian disease. While there is good correlation with advanced malignancy, studies have shown that only 23 to 50% of patients with surgically staged stage I carcinomas have increased CA 125 readings preoperatively. Mann and colleagues[20] found that none of the studied patients

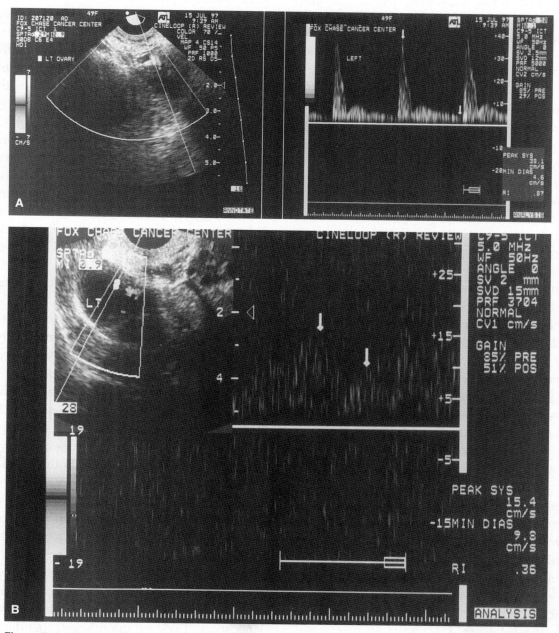

Figure 5–4. Transvaginal images by color flow Doppler. Peak systolic and diastolic waveform measurements (arrows) of a benign ovarian cyst (A) show a resistance index (RI) of 0.87. Similar measurements of a malignant lesion (B) show an RI of 0.36.

with stage IA tumors had levels > 35 U/mL. Clearly, additional or complementary tests are required to make CA 125 a useful component of a screening program. Woolas and colleagues[21] attempted to improve correlation with known early disease by using two other potential ovarian tumor markers and found that almost all patients with presumed stage I ovarian cancer had an elevation of at least one marker. Unfortunately, nearly one-third of the patients did not undergo lymph node dissection, which has been shown to understage a significant proportion of patients with apparently confined carcinoma.

SCREENING TRIALS

Several authors have used the above information to create screening programs. The following describes recent ovarian cancer screening trials that were conducted by three large groups involved in ongoing screening efforts.

Bourne and colleagues[22] studied 1,600 asymptomatic women with a family history of ovarian cancer by using transvaginal ultrasonography to assess morphology. Positive screening results were defined as abnormal morphology. Enlarged ovaries with normal morphology were reevaluated by reported ultrasonography until structural alterations were identified. The last 600 patients were additionally evaluated by pulsatility index. Follow-up was completed by phone over the subsequent 6 to 16 months. Six primary ovarian cancers were identified by the screening tests, five of which were stage IA. Three of the cancers were borderline tumors. Fifty-five other patients underwent surgery for positive screening tests, yielding a false-positive rate of 3.4%. The authors stated that all cancers were detected within the limits of the study, but two cancers were diagnosed within a year of a negative screen. Interestingly, these were primary peritoneal carcinomas, which, by lack of ovarian involvement, escape detection by such ultrasonographic assessment. Three additional cancers developed at 24, 41, and 44 months following a negative screen; the significance of this time interval is unclear. Overall, this screening scheme had a positive predictive value of 9.8%.

van Nagell and colleagues[23,24] enrolled 14,469 asymptomatic women in a screening trial. The patients were either over the age of 25 years, with a positive family history of ovarian cancer, or ≥ 50 years old. Patients were evaluated with transvaginal ultrasonography on a yearly basis; screens showing either abnormal ovarian volume or wall papillations were considered positive and were repeated in 4 to 6 weeks for confirmation. Cases of persistently abnormal ovaries were further evaluated with a morphology index and color flow Doppler measurements, and CA 125 levels were obtained prior to surgery. Seventeen primary invasive ovarian carcinomas were identified in the screened population, eleven of which were stage I. One patient actually had a negative confirmatory result on repeat ultrasound examination but underwent surgery for symptoms that developed soon thereafter. Another false-negative was found at prophylactic oophorectomy, 11 months after screening. One hundred sixty three patients underwent surgery and had no malignancy identified; positive predictive value was 9.4%. The authors found that their morphology index was highly representative, with no cancers scoring < 4. Conversely, low pulsatility index was not a reliable indicator of malignancy, and all of the identified carcinomas had CA 125 levels of < 20 U/mL, well within the normal range.

Finally, Jacobs and colleagues[25] presented a randomized controlled trial of ovarian cancer screening with the goal of assessing a possible impact on mortality. Of 22,000 women who had previously participated in their screening trials, nearly all agreed to be randomized to another screening program or to an unscreened control group. Screening involved three yearly CA 125 determinations, in which values ≥ 30 U/mL were deemed abnormal. Patients with elevated CA 125 levels were further evaluated by transvaginal ultrasonography for volume assessment. Abnormal morphologies were noted and were followed by ultrasonography every 3 months until volumes became abnormal. Six cancers were identified in the screened population, three of which were stage I. Twenty-three additional surgeries were performed for abnormal screening results, yielding a positive predictive value of 21%. During the ensuing 8-year follow-up period, 10 more patients were diagnosed with ovarian cancer. Lack of information regarding interval from screening precluded the calculation of a false-negative rate. The overall prevalence of primary ovarian cancers was identical in the control group. A higher percentage of stage I and II carcinomas were found in the screened population (31% vs 10%) although the difference was not statistically significant. Lower-grade tumors were more often found in the screened group, suggesting identification prior to anaplastic transformation. Ovarian cancer patients in the screened population had a longer median survival than those in the control group (73 months vs 42 months), possibly due to the subtle favorable shift in stage distribution. These measures begin to suggest the efficacy of such a screening program.

The study design as described above, however, discounts some of the fairly well accepted features of early ovarian cancer detection. Using CA 125 levels as an initial inclusion criterion disregards the low rate of CA 125 elevation in stage I tumors. Indeed, Bourne and colleagues[22] retrospectively evaluated their results by using CA 125 levels as a prescreening tool and found that nearly one-third of the identified cancers would have been missed if they had used CA 125 levels as a prescreening tool. Furthermore, in the study by Jacobs and colleagues, morphology alterations were of secondary importance and color flow Doppler assessments were not done. In contrast, Bourne and colleagues re-interpreted abnormal screens to include volume increase, morphology score ≥ 5 or pulsatility index < 1.0. This would have increased the positive predictive value to 29% in this population with a significant family history of the disease, suggesting the importance of these measurements in screening.

RECOMMENDATIONS

Currently, the best strategy for screening is to identify target patient populations that have a higher disease prevalence, to avoid the clinical and statistical pitfalls outlined above, obtaining a comprehensive family history to identify those at high risk is the first necessary step. For epithelial ovarian cancer, described hereditary syndromes include site-specific ovarian cancer syndrome, breast-ovarian cancer syndrome, and Lynch II syndrome. Family histories in which several members are affected with ovarian or breast cancers, therefore, are suspicious for such hereditary risk, particularly when the

age at diagnosis is earlier than is seen in the general population. In families with Lynch II syndrome, colonic and endometrial cancers predominate. Trained genetic counselors can also help with the time-consuming task of pedigree construction.

More recently, genetic testing has enabled physicians to tailor individual risk better, as patients who do not carry the gene in question are presumably not more likely than the general population to develop ovarian cancer.[26] As several known deleterious mutations have been recently characterized,[27] genetic testing can also identify patients who are at personal risk when their pedigrees are not completely supportive or comprehensive. Because of myriad physical, psychological, and social consequences of genetic risk determination, such testing must be accompanied by extensive patient education and counseling.

In 1994, the National Institutes of Health Consensus Development Conference on Ovarian Cancer[27] recommended that physical examination including a rectovaginal examination, CA 125 determination, and transvaginal ultrasonography be completed at least annually for patients undergoing screening. As improved screening modalities have yet to be developed, the authors similarly perform an annual pelvic examination with CA 125 testing, followed by transvaginal ultrasonography 6 months later. In this way, an ovarian assessment is completed every 6 months, and the screening modalities are divided throughout the year. Variations on this basic theme are likely to be equally acceptable.

FUTURE DIRECTIONS

While many screening programs have described successes with their various algorithms, none is completely satisfactory. The positive predictive value (PPV) in most studies is below 10%, even in populations with a family history of ovarian cancer. Jacobs and colleagues' promising calculation of a 21% PPV includes diagnoses of advanced-stage disease in half of the cases, which does not confer a survival advantage. Successful screening efforts must therefore be redirected. One strategy is to narrow the targeted population to a higher-risk group with a greater disease prevalence; another is to look to other markers of disease, such as macrophage colony-stimulating factor, lysophosphatidic acid,[28] osteopontin,[29] or more complex proteomic patterns.[30] Ideally, the processes that lead to malignant transformation will be better understood. Salazar and colleagues[31] identified a higher frequency of significant histologic abnormalities (including surface papillomatosis, papillary projections, and epithelial inclusion cysts) in ovaries of women who were at high risk for ovarian cancer. Other investigators have since agreed with these findings. Ultimately, advances in the molecular characterization of ovarian lesions may afford the best opportunity for screening.

REFERENCES

1. Hulka BS. Cancer screening. Degrees of proof and practical application. Cancer 1988;62(8 Suppl):1776–80.
2. Eyre HJ, Smith RA, Mettlin CJ. Cancer Screening and Early Detection. In: Bast RC, Kufe DW, Pollock RE, et al, editors. Holland Frei Cancer Medicine. Vol 5. 5th ed. Hamilton (ON): BC Decker Inc; 2000. p. 362–83
3. Jemal A, Thomas A, Murray T, Thun M. Cancer statistics, 2002. CA Cancer J Clin. 2002;52:23–47.
4. Andersen MR, Peacock S, Nelson J, et al. Worry about ovarian cancer risk and use of ovarian cancer screening by women at risk for ovarian cancer. Gynecol Oncol. 2002; 85:3–8.
5. Whittemore AS. Characteristics relating to ovarian cancer risk: implications for prevention and detection. Gynecol Oncol 1994;55(1):S15–S19.
6. Campbell S, Goessens L, Goswamy R, Whitehead M. Real-time ultrasonography for determination of ovarian morphology and volume. A possible early screening test for ovarian cancer? Lancet 1982;1(8269):425–6.
7. Goswamy RK, Campbell S, Royston JP, et al. Ovarian size in postmenopausal women. Br J Obstet Gynaecol 1988; 95(8):795–801.
8. Granberg S, Wikland M, Jansson I. Macroscopic characterization of ovarian tumors and the relation to the histological diagnosis: criteria to be used for ultrasound evaluation. Gynecol Oncol 1989;35(2):139–44.
9. DePriest PD, Shenson D, Fried A, et al. A morphology index based on sonographic findings in ovarian cancer. Gynecol Oncol 1993;51(1):7–11.
10. Folkman J, Watson K, Ingber D, Hanahan D. Induction of angiogenesis during the transition from hyperplasia to neoplasia. Nature 1989;339(6219):58–61.
11. Timor-Tritsch LE, Lerner JP, Monteagudo A, Santos R. Transvaginal ultrasonographic characterization of ovarian masses by means of color flow-directed doppler measurements and a morphologic scoring system. Am J Obstet Gynecol 1993;168(3 Pt 1):909–13.
12. Kurjak A, Zalud I, Alfirevic Z. Evaluation of adnexal masses with transvaginal color ultrasound. J Ultrasound Med 1991;10(6):295–7.
13. Levine D, Gosink BB, Wolf SI, et al. Simple adnexal cysts:

14. Bailey CL, Ueland FR, Land GL, et al. The malignant potential of small cystic ovarian tumors in women over 50 years of age. Gynecol Oncol 1998;69(1):3–7.
15. Jacobs I, Bast RC Jr. The CA 125 tumour-associated antigen: a review of the literature. Hum Reprod 1989;4(1):1–12.
16. Bast RC Jr, Klug TL, St John E, et al. A radioimmunoassay using a monoclonal antibody to monitor the course of epithelial ovarian cancer. N Engl J Med 1983;309(15): 883–7.
17. Helzlsouer KJ, Bush TL, Alberg AJ, et al. Prospective study of serum CA-125 levels as markers of ovarian cancer. JAMA 1993;269(9):1123–6.
18. Zurawski VR Jr, Orjaseter H, Andersen A, Jellum E. Elevated serum CA 125 levels prior to diagnosis of ovarian neoplasia: relevance for early detection of ovarian cancer. Int J Cancer 1988;42(5):677–80.
19. Vuento MH, Stenman UH, Pirhonen JP, et al. Significance of a single CA 125 assay combined with ultrasound in the early detection of ovarian and endometrial cancer. Gynecol Oncol 1997;64(1):141–6.
20. Mann WJ, Patsner B, Cohen H, Loesch M. Preoperative serum CA-125 levels in patients with surgical stage I invasive ovarian adenocarcinoma. J Natl Cancer Inst 1988;80(3):208–9.
21. Woolas RP, Xu FJ, Jacobs IJ, et al. Elevation of multiple serum markers in patients with stage I ovarian cancer. J Natl Cancer Inst 1993;85(21):1748–51.
22. Bourne TH, Campbell S, Reynolds KM, et al. Screening for early familial ovarian cancer with transvaginal ultrasonography and colour blood flow imaging. BMJ 1993; 306:1025–9.
23. van Nagell JR Jr, DePriest PD, Reedy MB, et al. The efficacy of transvaginal sonographic screening in asymptomatic women at risk for ovarian cancer. Gynecol Oncol. 2000; 77:350–6.
24. DePriest PD, Gallion HH, Pavlik EJ, et al. Transvaginal sonography as a screening method for the detection of early ovarian cancer. Gynecol Oncol 1997;65(3):408–14.
25. Jacobs IJ, Skates SJ, MacDonald N, et al. Screening for ovarian cancer: a pilot randomised controlled trial. Lancet 1999;353:1207–10.
26. Frank TS. Hereditary risk of breast and ovarian carcinoma: the role of the oncologist. Oncologist 1998;3:403–12.
27. National Institutes of Health Consensus Development Conference Statement. Ovarian cancer: screening, treatment, and follow-up. April 5–7, 1994. Gynecol Oncol 1994;55:S4–14.
28. Xu Y, Shen Z, Wiper DW, et al. Lysophosphatidic acid as a potential biomarker for ovarian and other gynecologic cancers. JAMA 1998;280(8):719–23.
29. Kim J-H, Skates SJ, Uede T, et al. Osteopontin as a potential diagnostic biomarker for ovarian cancer. JAMA 2002; 287:1671–9.
30. Petricoin EF, Ardekani AM, Hitt BA, et al. Use of proteomic patterns in serum to identify ovarian cancer. Lancet. 2002; 359(9306):57–7.
31. Salazar H, Godwin AK, Daly MB, et al. Microscopic benign and invasive malignant neoplasms and a cancer-prone phenotype in prophylactic oophorectomies. J Natl Cancer Inst 1996;88(24):1810–20.

6

Genetic Counseling

MARY B. DALY, MD, PhD

Recent advances in the field of molecular genetics have identified a series of germline mutations associated with a significantly increased risk for epithelial ovarian cancer and have led to a growing awareness of the familial nature of this disease. Women who are at risk and their health care providers are seeking information to better define their risk profiles and to develop appropriate preventive strategies. The technologic developments that have facilitated the location and isolation of cancer susceptibility genes have united the fields of oncology, cancer control, genetics, and genetic counseling, to create a new subspecialty of cancer risk counseling with an emphasis on the communication of risk information based on personal and family histories.

Ovarian cancer poses unique challenges and opportunities for the genetic counseling approach. Ovarian cancer is the second most common gynecologic cancer diagnosed in women in the United States but behind endrometrial cancer, because of its typically late stage at presentation causes the most deaths. A number of environmental and reproductive risk factors for ovarian cancer have been identified through epidemiologic studies. Genetic alterations in several genes (*BRCA1, BRCA2,* and the mismatch repair genes) have been associated with a hereditary risk for ovarian cancer, and while there is no clear consensus about optimal guidelines for women who are at risk, a number of promising preventive strategies are beginning to emerge. All of these factors contribute to the evolution of a multidisciplinary counseling strategy that can be used by health care practitioners to meet the needs of women facing an increased risk of ovarian cancer.

OBJECTIVES OF GENETIC COUNSELING FOR OVARIAN CANCER PATIENTS

Genetic counseling for ovarian cancer patients builds on the tradition of genetic counseling that relies on education, risk assessment, and risk management to help individuals and their families cope with a disorder or risk of a disorder. The specific goals of the ovarian cancer risk counseling process are to (1) provide accurate information on the genetic, biologic, and environmental factors related to the individual's risk of ovarian cancer; (2) provide a sufficient understanding of the genetic basis of ovarian cancer to assist in decisions regarding genetic testing; (3) provide a realistic assessment of personal risk both for the genetic syndromes and for the disease itself; (4) formulate appropriate options and recommendations for prevention and screening, and (5) offer psychosocial support appropriate to a family's culture, to facilitate adjustment to an altered risk perception and to promote adherence to the recommended actions. Ovarian cancer risk counseling uses a broad approach to place genetic risk in the context of other related risk factors, thereby customizing it to the experiences of the individual. The genetic counseling literature has shown that counseling is most likely to be effective if the presentation of information is tailored to the age and education of the counselees, their personal exposure to the disease, their level of risk, and their social environment. Positive and supportive involvement of the health care team is also an important determinant of satisfaction with counseling and of adherence to recommended health behaviors.

An individual's incentive to participate in ovarian cancer risk counseling ideally comes from consultation with her primary care provider, who is in the best position to identify individuals and families at risk and to facilitate decisions regarding primary or secondary prevention. The development of cancer risk counseling programs in close collaboration with the medical community helps to guarantee continuity of care to individuals who seek cancer risk counseling and to update professionals on new developments in risk identification and cancer control.

COMPONENTS OF A COUNSELING PROGRAM

The American Society of Human Genetics has defined genetic counseling as "a communication process which deals with the human problems associated with the occurrence, or risk of occurrence, of a genetic disorder in a family. The process involves an attempt by one or more appropriately trained persons to help the individual or family to (1) comprehend the medical facts including the diagnosis, probable course of the disorder, and the available management; (2) appreciate the way that heredity contributes to the disorder, and to the risk of recurrence (occurrence), in specific relatives; (3) understand the alternatives for dealing with the risk of recurrence (occurrence); (4) choose a course of action which seems to them appropriate in view of their risk, their family goals, and their ethical and religious standards and act in accordance with that decision; and (5) make the best possible adjustment to the disorder in an affected family member and/or to the risk of recurrence (occurrence) of that disorder."[1] This process has been tailored to the setting of cancer risk counseling and includes several components (Table 6–1).

Target Population

With the growing awareness of the familial nature of ovarian cancer, an increasing number of relatives of women with ovarian cancer are seeking information and advice about the disease, about their own potential risk, and about available preventive options. Women who seek counseling are often highly moti-

vated by a personal experience with ovarian cancer in their family and by concern for the risks faced by themselves and their close relatives. Women who have undergone prolonged fertility treatments with ovulation-stimulating drugs make up an additional group that may be at increased risk for ovarian cancer and are beginning to seek counseling to evaluate their risk and make medical management decisions. In addition, as physicians become more aware of the importance of family and reproductive history in determining a woman's risk for ovarian cancer, they are increasingly referring their patients for cancer risk counseling. While the general indication for participation in a cancer risk counseling program is a perception of increased risk based on family history and other recognized risk exposures, individual participants come to the process with a wide variety of experiences, health beliefs, expectations, and needs. An assessment of individual differences that can influence comprehension and compliance with appropriate health recommendations is therefore one of the primary goals of the counseling team. Although cancer risk counseling is often initiated by an individual concerned about her risk for cancer, it often has wide-reaching implications for the family, and the counseling process may ultimately include additional family members.

Counseling Team

Historically, the medical genetic counseling team has consisted of a medical geneticist, a genetic counselor, and (to a lesser extent) the referring pri-

Table 6–1. BASIC ELEMENTS OF CANCER GENETIC COUNSELING

Documentation of extended family medical history
Development of a family pedigree
Collection of medical records from proband and appropriate family members
Collection of information about other risk factors (biologic, environmental, lifestyle)
Careful assessment of risk
Education about cancer, genetics, and preventive options
Communication of risk estimate in clear and simple language
Development of individualized prevention and surveillance strategy
Attention to emotional and social needs and concerns of proband and family
Long-term follow-up and support

mary care physician. As the field of genetic counseling has expanded to include adult diseases such as cancer, practitioners of other disciplines, including oncology, gynecology, molecular genetics, social work, and psychology, have joined the team in order to provide the multidisciplinary approach needed. There is also a growing interest in genetics on the part of nurses, many of whom are beginning to seek specialized training in the field.[2] Genetic counselors and genetic advanced-practice nurses are now being trained to deliver medical and genetic risk information about familial forms of cancer and to counsel individuals and families about disease risk and management (Figure 6–1). Originally, ovarian cancer risk counseling programs were mainly situated in cancer centers and academic institutions, but increasingly these services are expanding to community hospitals, work sites, and health centers, where they are often one component of a more broadly based health promotion program. In fact, a growing consensus is that there is a baseline set of genetic services that all primary care physicians should provide; these include identifying individuals who are at increased genetic risk of cancer, counseling patients about their potential risk, and referring them to more-specialized services.[3]

Information Collection

The genetic counseling process begins with the collection of several components of information (Table 6–2). The first step in evaluating a woman's risk for ovarian cancer is to assess her worries, questions, concerns, beliefs, and reasons for seeking counseling, in order to guarantee that personal needs and priorities will be met in the counseling process. At this early stage of counseling, it is important to establish mutual trust and to negotiate a mutually agreeable agenda between the counselor and the individual seeking counseling. The counselor attempts to assess how realistic the individual's expectations of ovarian cancer risk are and to judge the risk of potentially adverse psychological reactions, by both the individual and her family, to the disclosure of risk information.

A detailed family history is the cornerstone of effective genetic counseling. The family history begins with the health of the proband and proceeds outward to include first-, second-, and third-degree relatives on both maternal and paternal sides. Information collected includes cancer diagnosis by primary site, age at onset, bilaterality when appropriate, and current age or age at death. It is important to include all relatives, both affected and unaffected, in the family history in order to judge the degree of penetrance of the disease. Ancestry and ethnicity are also important components of a family history because specific mutations (ie, founder mutations) occur with increased frequency in certain populations. Factors that limit the informativeness of the pedigree are small family size, adoption, uncertain paternity, early deaths in family members (precluding the possibility of developing adult diseases), prophylactic surgeries that remove an organ from subsequent risk of cancer (eg, total hysterectomy for uterine fibroids in which the ovaries are also removed), and incomplete information about the

Figure 6–1. A genetic counseling session.

Table 6–2.   COMPONENTS OF INFORMATION GATHERING

Establishment of needs, concerns, questions, and priorities
Assessment of psychosocial dimensions
Personal medical history
Detailed family history
Personal risk factor profile
Personal screening and health behavior history

Table 6–3.   FEATURES OF HEREDITARY CANCERS

Multiple cancers in close relatives
Multiple cancers in a single individual
Multiple cancers across generations
Early age of onset of cancer
Bilateral cancer in paired organs (eg, breasts)
The presence of precursor lesions known to be associated with the cancer phenotype (eg, multiple polyps in hereditary colon cancer)

health of other family members. Accuracy in reporting family history has been shown to differ by the type of cancer and by the degree of distance from the relative.[4] Whenever possible, cancer diagnoses are verified by obtaining medical records, pathology reports, or death certificates. Features of hereditary cancer are listed in Table 6–3. Family history data are then graphically represented on a pedigree, which follows standard nomenclature to illustrate family relationships and disease information in a graphic format (Figure 6–2).

The next step is to collect the pertinent medical and personal information that allows the counselor to estimate the contribution of other risk factors that may interact with or modify family history, to determine ovarian cancer risk. A history of prior medical conditions that may predispose an individual to ovarian cancer (such as polycystic ovarian syndrome); a thorough reproductive history, including the number of pregnancies and the duration of lactation; a history of infertility and fertility treatments, the use of exogenous hormonal agents (particularly oral contraceptive pills [OCPs]), and types of surgery; and a survey of lifestyle factors all contribute to an understanding of cancer risk. Finally, a record of past cancer screening and other health practices establishes a history of health promotion behavior and will help guide the counselor in making reasonable and appropriate health recommendations.

Education

Risk counseling for ovarian cancer must be preceded by a comprehensive educational component to provide a basis for understanding the etiology of ovarian cancer, the genesis of risk estimates, and the complex genetic changes associated with ovarian cancer. This preparation is necessary to provide effective risk communication and to facilitate health decision making. The normal anatomy and physiology of the female reproductive tract are explained, with an emphasis on the hormonal and biologic events that accompany ovulation (Figure 6–3). Reference is made to the physiologic process of ovulation to illustrate how parity and oral contraceptive use may modulate risk. This discussion provides an opportunity to explain the site of origin of ovarian cancer, its typical pattern of spread to involve both nodal tissue and peritoneal surfaces, and the rationale for its often late stage at presentation. This information also provides the framework for a subsequent discussion of the need for effective screening tests to detect the disease in its earlier and more curable stages.

The interaction of shared environmental, reproductive, and genetic factors among family members in relation to ovarian cancer risk is explored. The counselor introduces the concepts and language of chromosomes, genes, and deoxyribonucleic acid (DNA) and explains how genetic alterations can lead to cancer (Figure 6–4). Sample pedigrees can be used to illustrate the types of family cancer patterns and to demonstrate the concepts of vertical transmission through maternal or paternal lines, the significance of age at onset, and issues of penetrance. Within this context, the counselor can explain the role of the recently identified cancer susceptibility genes (*BRCA1* and *BRCA2*) and the mismatch repair genes that are related to an increased risk for ovarian cancer (Figure 6–5).

Cancer Risk Counseling

Risk Assessment

The first step in risk assessment is the determination of the level of risk perceived by the proband. Often this is colored by her experience with cancer, either

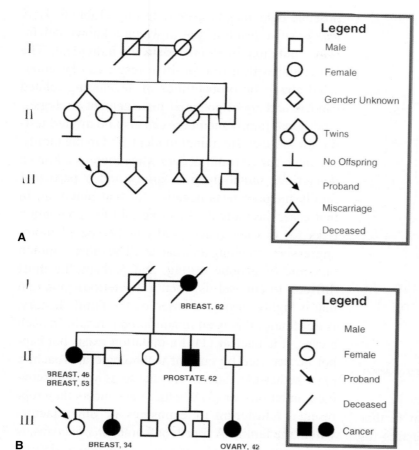

Figure 6–2. *A,* Family history data is graphically represented on this sample pedigree. The symbols in this pedigree follow standard recommended nomenclature to illustrate family relationships and other pedigree designations. *B,* Sample pedigree illustrating a family history of a hereditary family cancer pattern. This pedigree demonstrates vertical (autosomal dominant) transmission of cancers, showing early ages of onset, bilaterality of disease, and increased penetrance.

personally or in family members. While studies of health risk perception in the general population tend to report a sense of invulnerability and an underestimation of personal risk, experience with women from hereditary breast and ovarian cancer families has found a consistent overestimation of risk for these cancers; this can affect comprehension and response to information about risk.[5,6] Cancer risk counselors attempt to place the proband's risk of ovarian cancer within the context of population risk, in both quantitative and qualitative terms, in order to provide a rationale for recommended health behaviors. First, the counselor refers to the family pedigree to assign families into levels of risk. Most families will not exhibit the classic features of hereditary ovarian cancer but rather will illustrate the effect of multiple genetic and environmental factors that interact to increase ovarian cancer risk to a moderate degree. For these families, counselors often use empiric approaches based on epidemiologic data that indicate age-specific risks of ovarian

cancer in tabular formats that can incorporate several pertinent risk factors.[2] Risk estimates are most useful when placed within defined time frames, such as "in the next 5 years," or "in your lifetime." For families in which a hereditary pattern of cancer is suspected, the recent cloning of rare but highly penetrant cancer susceptibility genes such as *BRCA1* and *BRCA2* has made available the direct assessment of mutation status, thus obviating the need for empiric risk models.

Genetic Testing

The choice of appropriate candidates for genetic testing for either *BRCA1/2* or the hereditary non-polyposis colorectal cancer (HNPCC) genes is based on the personal and familial characteristics that determine the prior probability of being a mutation carrier. Mathematical models are available that, based on features of the family history, predict the likelihood of being a mutation carrier

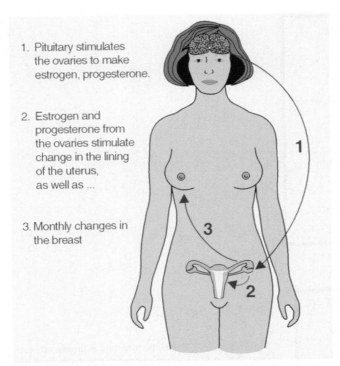

1. Pituitary stimulates the ovaries to make estrogen, progesterone.

2. Estrogen and progesterone from the ovaries stimulate change in the lining of the uterus, as well as ...

3. Monthly changes in the breast

Figure 6–3.   Hormonal and biologic events accompanying ovulation.

and that help the counselor and clinician further refine genetic testing decisions. Genetic testing for ovarian cancer susceptibility genes, its role, its benefits, and its limitations are discussed in the counseling session in order to assist family members in the decision-making process. The technical limitations of the testing process and the distinctions between positive, negative, inconclusive, and indeterminant test results are reviewed. Discussion of the probabilistic nature of genetic test results and the potential implications for other family members must be included in the counseling. A clear distinction is made between the probability of being a mutation carrier and the probability of developing cancer. Because estimates of penetrance of the gene (ie, the chance that a mutation will actually result in ovarian cancer in an individual) have been derived from small studies of narrowly defined families, they are difficult to apply to any particular individual unless she matches the characteristics of the families studied.

When possible, it is best to first consider testing an affected family member who meets the criteria for hereditary breast or ovarian cancer, as that individual is most likely to test positive. There are four possible outcomes to genetic testing (Table 6–4). A *true positive* result is that in which a known deleterious mutation is identified in an individual. The individual with a true positive result can be counseled about the probabilities of developing related cancers and about potential management strategies. Additional family members can also be offered testing for the specific mutation identified in the family. A *true negative* result occurs when there is a known deleterious mutation in a family and a particular family member tests negative for that mutation. In that case, the individual can be told the population risks for ovarian cancer and can be spared more-aggressive screening approaches. The most common outcome of genetic testing, and perhaps the most difficult to counsel, is when a deleterious mutation that is highly suspected based on the family history, is not found; this is an *indeterminate* result. In such a case, it is unclear (1) if a mutation exists but cannot be detected by current technologic approaches, (2) whether the cancers are due to as yet undiscovered mutations, or (3) whether the cancers they represent a clustering of exposures or other factors within the family. A fourth outcome, *inconclusive*, is the identification of variants of unknown significance. These are gene alterations whose clinical significance is uncertain. Individuals with these variants must be counseled that additional information about the alteration is needed before definitive risk estimates can be given. In these cases, counseling on the basis of the family history would seem to be the most prudent course.

In addition to these limitations, genetic testing is offered with caution because of the clinical limitations in altering risk once mutation status is known, as well as the potential for consequent discrimination on the part of insurers and employers. Long-term follow-up and support should be an integral part of the counseling protocol to monitor both psychosocial and medical outcomes of the testing process.

Management Strategies

One of the primary motivations for seeking cancer risk counseling is to identify ways to reduce or delay the risk of developing ovarian cancer or to improve the possibility of detecting it at an early curable stage. Recommendations fall into four general categories: increased surveillance, surgical prophylaxis, pharmacologic interventions (chemoprevention), and lifestyle changes.

The high case fatality rate consistently reported for ovarian cancer stems not from the lack of effective therapeutic modalities but rather from diagnosis at advanced stages of disease, when survival is poor.[7] The identification of an effective screening tool for identifying asymptomatic disease, therefore, could significantly affect mortality rates. Screening recommendations, however, are problematic for ovarian cancer as no test or series of tests have been found to be sufficiently sensitive and specific. After a careful review of the data, the 1994 National Institutes of Health Consensus Development Conference on Ovarian Cancer concluded that there was insufficient evidence to recommend routine screening for all women.[8] Despite these concerns, however, many practitioners have begun screening with the combination of pelvic examination, transvaginal ultrasonography, and assessment of levels of cancer antigen 125 (CA 125) in women with a family history of ovarian cancer. Although it is an important component of complete gynecologic care, the pelvic examination alone is clearly insufficient to detect most limited and early-stage epithelial ovarian tumors. Assessments of tumor markers such as CA 125 lack the sensitivity and specificity to serve as the sole form of screening. Although elevated in 50% of stage I cancers, CA 125 level is also elevated in several benign conditions, such as endometriosis.[7] A current study is evaluating the use of an algorithm that determines the risk of ovarian cancer on the basis of the trend of the CA 125 level rather than the absolute value.[9]

Studies using ultrasonography report sensitivities of approximately 95%, but the positive predictive value is in the range of only 3 to 5%, which results in a high rate of unnecessary surgical explorations. Benign and truly malignant abnormalities are often indistinguishable, and the visualization of the ovaries in postmenopausal women is often inadequate.[10] The combination of pulsed Doppler ultrasonography with real-time ultrasonography allows the location of deep vessels and the characterization of blood flow; however, attempts to use this modal-

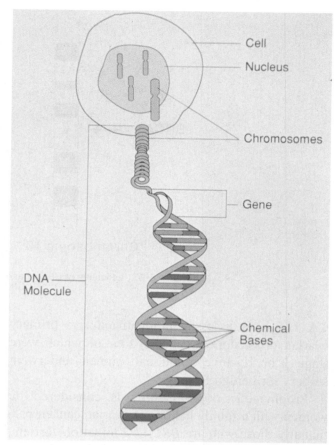

Figure 6–4. Illustration of a cell and the chromosome, showing its deoxyribonucleic acid (DNA) components. (Reproduced with permission from Jeanne Kelly, Aardvark Design Associates, Leesburg, VA.)

ity to distinguish malignant lesions have been disappointing.[11] A randomized trial of the combination of CA 125 level assessment and ultrasonography in average-risk women was unsuccessful in identifying early-stage cancers.[12] A recent paper described a proteomic approach to screening serum samples for patterns of protein expression that indicate early-stage ovarian cancer.[13] Although the high sensitivity and specificity rates reported (respectively 100% and 95%) are very promising, the low positive predictive value precludes this approach for the general population. Validation of these findings is currently under way. To date, there are randomized trials for screening women who have a hereditary risk for ovarian cancer. A clinical case series recently presented data on 251 women with documented mutations in *BRCA1/2*. Among 89 women who chose not to undergo prophylactic oophorectomy, screening with semiannual transvaginal ultrasonography and

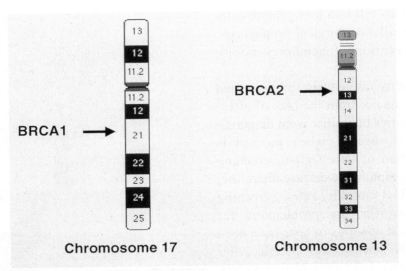

Figure 6–5. Locations of *BRCA1* and *BRCA2*.

CA 125 level assessment identified five primary ovarian or peritoneal cancers, four of which were stage I or II. Five additional women underwent surgery for benign findings.[14]

Prophylactic oophorectomy is considered by women with a family history of ovarian cancer, particularly those who are *BRCA1/2* mutation carriers, because of the uncertain nature of screening and because of the high case fatality rate of advanced-stage cancer. Data from the Gilda Radner Familial Ovarian Cancer Registry (obtained before the availability of genetic testing) suggested a significant reduction in incidence among women undergoing prophylactic oophorectomy because of a strong family history of ovarian cancer.[15] Two recent studies confirm this finding (Table 6–5). Kauff and colleagues[16] followed the cases of 170 women with documented *BRCA* mutations, for cancer outcomes. Among the 98 women who chose prophylactic oophorectomy, the hazard ratios for ovarian cancer and breast cancer were 0.15 and 0.32, respectively, compared to the women who chose surveillance. Three women were found to have early-stage tumors at the time of surgery. Similarly, Rebbeck and colleagues[17] compared breast and ovarian cancer rates for 259 *BRCA* mutation carriers who underwent prophylactic oophorectomy and 292 carriers who chose surveillance; hazard ratios for ovarian cancer and breast cancer were 0.04 and 0.47, respectively. In this study, six women were found to have ovarian cancer at the time of prophylactic surgery; all cancers were stage I. These two studies support the role of prophylactic surgery for women with known deleterious *BRCA* mutations. However, individuals considering this strategy must be counseled about the potential for primary peritoneal cancer. In the series of Piver and colleagues, the risk of subsequent peritoneal carcinomatosis was 1.9%.[15] Furthermore, premenopausal women who choose this option must consider the potential consequences of long-term hormone replacement therapy following surgically-induced menopause.

To date, there have been no randomized chemoprevention trials with OCPs to reduce risk of ovarian cancer. However, because of the strong epidemiologic association between oral contraceptive use and a reduction in ovarian cancer rates, many gynecolo-

Table 6–4. GENETIC TEST RESULTS	
Result	**Status of Person Tested**
True positive	Person is a carrier of an alteration in a known cancer-predisposing gene.
True negative	Person is not a carrier of a known cancer-predisposing gene that has been positively identified in another family member.
Indeterminant	Person is not a carrier of a known cancer-predisposing gene, and the carrier status of other family members is either also negative or unknown.
Inconclusive	Person is a carrier of an alteration in a gene that currently has no known significance.

gists are recommending OCP use for women with an increased risk due to either family history or nulliparity (Figure 6–6). Preliminary data from studies of women with *BRCA1/2* mutations suggest that they may enjoy the same degree of protection (approximately a 40% reduction) from OCPs as do women in the general population.[18] Both epidemiologic and experimental data suggest a role for the retinoids in the prevention of ovarian cancer. The retinoids inhibit growth, induce apoptosis, and promote cellular differentiation in ovarian cancer cell lines and in ovarian cancer heterographs in nude mice.[19] These data have led to the activation of a Gynecologic Oncology Group (GOG) randomized study of fenretinide in women who are planning to undergo prophylactic oophorectomy to evaluate the effect of the drug on intermediate markers of carcinogenesis. Finally, the potential role of chronic inflammation in ovarian carcinogenesis has led to inquiry about the effect of analgesic drugs on ovarian cancer rates. Two case-control studies have found an association between regular acetaminophen use and reduced risk for ovarian cancer.[20,21] An observed antigonadotropic effect may provide a biologic mechanism to explain the association.

High-risk individuals have an intense interest in opportunities to reduce their ovarian cancer risk by changes in diet or exercise or by other lifestyle modifications. There is concern, for example, about exposure to fertility drugs and their effect on ovulation. Unfortunately, most of the factors linked to ovarian cancer risk are reproductive in nature (eg, nulliparity), and their manipulation is therefore confounded by social concerns. The exact role of diet, micronutrient supplementation, and exercise remains elusive for ovarian cancer, and any recom-

mendations must be on the basis of general health and well-being.

Finally, comprehensive counseling for ovarian cancer risk must take into account the psychosocial needs of those at risk. Cultural beliefs, education level, and prior experiences can all affect comprehension and the motivation to alter health behaviors.[2] The experience of genetic risk counseling may be associated with levels of distress related to personal health threats, concerns about the risk for other family members, and the burden of having to share genetic risk information with relatives. Genetic counselors and nurses are routinely trained to identify individual coping strategies for dealing with stressful situations and to provide psychosocial assessment and support. Built into the process of counseling is the opportunity to process information, consider the implications of the information, and adjust to the emotional reactions generated. In addition to the assessment of the individual who is undergoing counseling, an assessment of the family circumstances (including patterns of communication within families, family cohesion, and family values) is an important component of the counseling situation. Counselors are also trained to give attention to the special circumstances of genetic information, including privacy and confidentiality issues.

FUTURE DIRECTIONS

A great deal of progress has been made in the understanding of the underlying etiology of ovarian cancer. Scientific advances, particularly in the field of genetics, have made it possible to better define the risk for ovarian cancer and to target cancer prevention and control strategies. Long-term follow-up of mutation carriers will help to explore the spectrum of cancer risk the clinical course of hereditary ovarian cancer, and response to treatment. Women are becoming increasingly aware of the role of family history in defining their own personal risk, and are seeking information and recommendations for risk reduction. The creation of multidisciplinary teams of health professionals to provide risk education, assessment, and counseling will complement the care of the ovarian cancer patient and may ultimately result in reductions in ovarian cancer morbidity and mortality.

Table 6–5. HAZARD RATIOS AFTER PROPHYLACTIC OOPHORECTOMY

Study	Ovarian Cancer	Breast Cancer
Kauff et al		
No. patients in analysis	170	131
Hazard ratio	0.15	0.25
(95% CI)	(0.02–1.31)	(0.08–0.74)
Rebbeck et al		
No. patients in analysis	551	241
Hazard ratio	0.04	0.47
(95% CI)	(0.01–0.16)	(0.29–0.77)

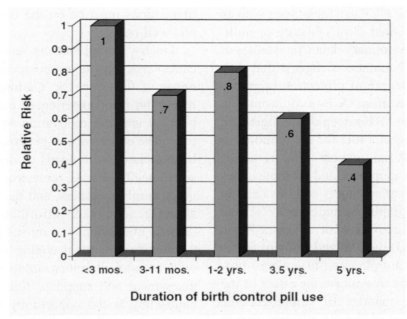

Figure 6–6. Correlation between birth control pill use and ovarian cancer risk. The risk decreases as the duration of birth control pill use increases.

REFERENCES

1. Epstein CJ, Childs B. Genetic counseling. Am J Hum Genet 1975;27:240–2.
2. Peters JA. Applications of genetic technologies to cancer screening, prevention, diagnosis, prognosis, and treatment. Semin Oncol Nurs 1997;13:74–81.
3. Emery J, Lucassen A, Murphy M. Common hereditary cancers and implications for primary care. Lancet 2001;358: 58–63.
4. Matloff ET. Complex decision-making for *BRCA1/2* carriers. Cancer J Sci Am 1999;5:266–8.
5. Stefanek ME. Counseling women at high risk for breast cancer. Oncology 1990;4:27–33.
6. Hoskins KF, Stopfer JE, Calzone KA, et al. Assessment and counseling for women with a family history of breast cancer. A guide for clinicians. JAMA 1995;273(7):577–85.
7. Brewer MA, Mitchell MF, Bast RC. Prevention of ovarian cancer. In Vivo 1999;13:99–106.
8. NIH Consensus Development Conference on Ovarian Cancer: screening, treatment, and followup. Bethesda (MD): National Institutes of Health, 1994. p. 1–30.
9. Skates SJ, Xu FJ, Yu YH, et al. Toward an optimal algorithm for ovarian cancer screening with longitudinal tumor markers. Cancer 1995;42:677–80.
10. Muto MG, Cramer DW, Brown DL, et al. Screening for ovarian cancer: the preliminary experience of a familial ovarian cancer. Gynecol Oncol 1993;51:12–20.
11. Carter JR, Lau M, Fowler JM, et al. Blood flow characteristics of ovarian tumors: implications for ovarian cancer screening. Am J Obstet Gynecol 1995;72:901–7.
12. Jacobs IJ, Skates SJ, MacDonald N, et al. Screening for ovarian cancer: a pilot randomised control trial. Lancet 1999; 353:1207–10.
13. Petricoin EF, Ardekani AM, Hitt BA, et al. Use of proteomic patterns in serum to identify ovarian cancer. Lancet 2002;359:572–7.
14. Scheuer L, Kauff N, Robson M, et al. Outcome of preventive surgery and screening for breast and ovarian cancer in BRCA mutation carriers. J Clin Oncol 2002;20:1260–8.
15. Piver MS, Jishi MF, Tsukada Y, Nava G. Primary peritoneal carcinoma after prophylactic oophorectomy in women with a family history of ovarian cancer. A report of the Gilda Radner Familial Ovarian Cancer Registry. Cancer 1993;71:2751–5.
16. Kauff ND, Satagopan JM, Robson ME, et al. Risk-reducing salpingo-oophorectomy in women with a *BRCA1* or *BRCA2* mutation. N Engl J Med 2002;346:1609–15.
17. Rebbeck TR, Lynch HT, Neuhausen SL, et al. Prophylactic oophorectomy in carriers of *BRCA1* or *BRCA2* mutations. N Engl J Med 2002;346:1616–22.
18. Narod SA, Risch H, Moslehi R, et al. Oral contraceptives and the risk of hereditary ovarian cancer. Hereditary ovarian cancer clinical study group. N Engl J Med 1998;339:424–8.
19. Barnes MN, Grizzle WE, Grubbs CJ, Partridge EE. Paradigms for primary prevention of ovarian carcinoma. CA Cancer J Clin 2002;52:216–25.
20. Cramer DW, Harlow BL, Titus-Ernstoff L, et al. Over-the-counter analgesics and risk of ovarian cancer. Lancet 1998;351:104–7.
21. Moysich KB, Mettlin C, Piver MS, et al. Regular use of analgesic drugs and ovarian cancer risk. Cancer Epidemiol Biomarkers Prev 2001;10:903–6.

7

Diagnosis and Staging

CYNTHIA A. BERGMAN, MD

DIAGNOSIS

The diagnosis of ovarian cancer is often elusive and frustrating to both patients and physicians alike. As no effective screening modality exists to date, diagnosis relies on the identification and work-up of symptoms that are often vague and misleading. Unfortunately, due to the free-floating position of the ovary in the peritoneal cavity, such symptoms often develop only when the neoplasm has become either very large or metastatic. Several authors have therefore attempted to raise awareness of this problem by reviewing symptom histories and reasons for delayed diagnosis. In 1985, Smith and Anderson[1] tabulated symptoms that were experienced by ovarian cancer patients and noticed that many real symptoms were not taken seriously by the patients themselves. In their study, they found that patients with early-stage lesions often noted urination problems but did not seek medical attention unless menstrual irregularities occurred. Patients with late-stage lesions developed abdominal swelling but were not likely to request evaluation unless pain was also present. Fifteen years later, these diagnostic difficulties unfortunately persist. Goff and colleagues[2] compiled the results of 1,725 retrospective symptom surveys from ovarian cancer patients and found that while 95% of patients felt they had experienced symptoms, almost half waited more than 3 months to be correctly diagnosed. The early performance of pelvic examination and imaging studies was helpful whereas incorrect diagnoses due to young age or overlapping symptoms led to further delays. Today, media efforts for public education on this issue are working to erase these confounding obstacles.

History

Complaints preceding a diagnosis of ovarian cancer vary in distribution, severity, and timing. Early-stage disease often begins as an enlargement of the ovary. Some presenting symptoms are therefore related to mass effect in the pelvis as the neoplastic ovary pushes on adjacent structures. The patient may sense pelvic pressure or fullness. Bladder compression may lead to changes in urinary patterns, including urgency and frequency. Pelvic pain may also develop, often as deep dyspareunia. Commonly, the mass extends posteriorly into the cul-de-sac (Figure 7–1) and compresses the rectum, causing narrowing of stool caliber or even severe constipation. In many ovarian cancers, especially the epithelial subtypes, these changes can occur gradually, over a period of weeks or even months. In stark contrast, germ cell malignancies have a rapid growth rate leading to the above changes and even visible protrusion of the enlarged ovary over a much shorter time period; this is detailed in a separate chapter. Conversely, sex cord–stromal tumors behave differently, due to slower characteristic growth patterns. Additionally, these tumors can have other symptomatology related to hormone production (reviewed in a later chapter).

Other presenting symptoms of ovarian cancer are related to the presence of intra-abdominal disease. These tumors primarily metastasize by exfoliation, in which tumor cells fall off of the primary lesion

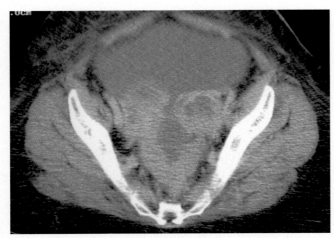

Figure 7–1. Stage IIIC ovarian adenocarcinoma. Bilateral tumor masses surrounded by ascites are seen extending down both sides of the pelvic peritoneum to fill the cul-de-sac.

and into the peritoneal cavity. Malignant ascites forms as seedlings develop on the peritoneal lining, and patients note slow increases in abdominal girth that often necessitate a change in clothing size. Early satiety and even respiratory compromise can ensue as pressure increases on the stomach and diaphragm (Figure 7–2). Note that primary peritoneal adenocarcinoma, a closely related malignancy, has no primary organ to expand and to create mass effect with and therefore almost always presents in this more advanced manner. Tumor deposits on the small bowel can cause local compression or kinking (Fig-

ure 7–3), leading to nausea and vomiting. Similar nodules on the colonic surfaces cause diarrhea and, later, constipation. Such metastases can also cause frank obstruction or even perforation, although actual invasion into the bowel wall is uncommon.

Physical Examination

On physical examination, an abnormal pelvic mass is the primary finding. Average ovarian size in the premenopausal population is only 4 to 5 cm, and ovaries in a postmenopausal female are too small to be appreciated on examination. Consequently, adnexal fullness in a woman of reproductive age should prompt further evaluation, and any palpable ovary in a postmenopausal female is suspect. Contour and mobility are further contributory characteristics. While smooth mobile masses more commonly represent functional or benign cystic enlargements, nodularity and fixation imply a more ominous process (Figure 7–4). Typically, the mass is not tender although the patient may experience pain from traction on surrounding structures. Associated vaginal discharge is unusual; important exceptions to this include germ cell and sex cord–stromal tumors, which often cause abnormal bleeding, and fallopian tube cancers, which can be associated with a watery vaginal discharge of uncertain composition. It should be noted that pelvic examination must

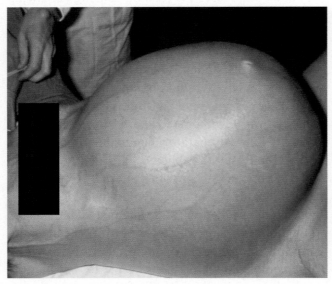

Figure 7–2. A patient with obvious ascites filling the abdomen. Note the additional surrounding evidence of body mass wasting.

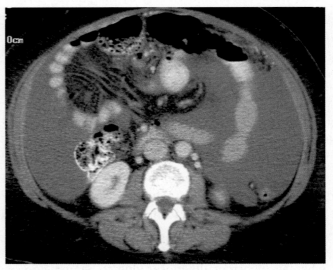

Figure 7–3. Stage IIIC ovarian adenocarcinoma. A loop of small bowel shows thick mesenteric stranding and pronounced tethering typical of peritoneal studding and subsequent fixation.

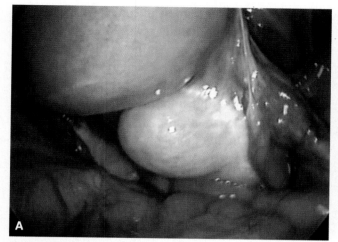

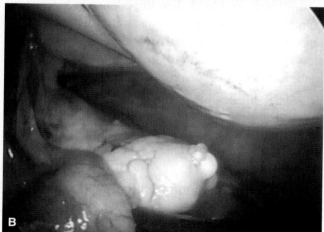

Figure 7–4. Laparoscopic views of adnexal masses. *A,* Right ovary is enlarged with a smooth thin-walled cystic fullness. *B,* Left ovary has a nodular thick capsule and is partially adherent to its ovarian fossa.

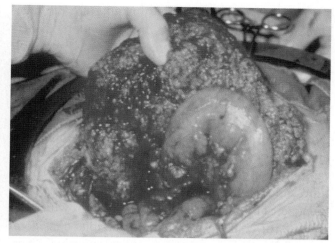

Figure 7–5. Stage III ovarian cancer. The omentum is nodular and firm, with tumor infiltration.

region (disease of which is known as Sister Mary Joseph's nodule).

Imaging Studies

Ultrasonography

Various imaging modalities have emerged as important contributors to the diagnosis of ovarian cancer. When symptoms or findings are localized to the pelvis, ultrasonography plays a primary role. The ini-

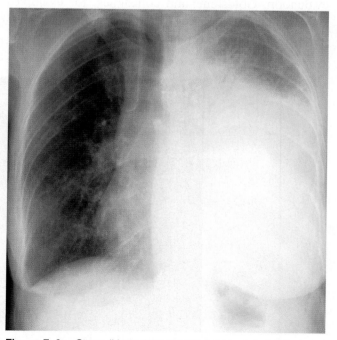

Figure 7–6. Stage IV ovarian cancer. A large left-sided pleural effusion is evident.

include bidigital rectovaginal examination in order to appreciate the characteristics outlined above.

In more-advanced disease stages, abdominal examination reveals protuberance. A fluid wave and shifting dullness on percussion may be noted if ascites is present. Large ovarian masses may be felt arising out of the pelvis. Decreased bowel sounds or gaseous distention may be present if obstruction is imminent. Malignant infiltration of the omentum (Figure 7–5) creates discrete masses or even a confluent "cake" of tumor that can float in the anterior abdomen and be palpated by ballotement. In even more-advanced cases, pulmonary examination may reveal a pleural effusion (Figure 7–6). Rarely, a lymph node survey can show disease in the supraclavicular, inguinofemoral, or inferior umbilical tial goals of ultrasonographic imaging are the measurement of ovarian size and the delineation of internal ovarian structure (Figure 7–7). Pavlik and colleagues[3] neatly documented declining measurable ovarian volumes with advancing age, with an upper limit of 20 cm^3 in premenopausal patients and a mean volume of 2.2 cm^3 in postmenopausal patients. For enlarged ovaries in a premenopausal patient, the absence of characteristic complexities on ultrasonography as outlined below is reassuring and can sometimes allow conservative close follow-up. For postmenopausal patients, any evidence of growth in an ovary is of concern and warrants serious consideration of direct assessment by surgical excision. Thus, the additional benefit of transvaginal pelvic ultrasonography is that it allows the assessment of lesion complexity. Several investigators have shown that volume, septation thickness, and the presence of papillary projections are important predictors of malignant histology (Figure 7–8). The University of Kentucky Medical Center, for example, uses a morphology index that incorporates size and lesion characteristics in an effort to accurately predict pathologic findings.[4,5] While this index is primarily used to stratify ultrasonographic screening results, other studies have used size and lesion characteristics to help determine which lesions may not require surgical evaluation. Goldstein[6] and colleagues, for example, showed that unilocular cysts < 5 cm in diameter seen in postmenopausal women had an extremely low incidence of malignancy; Bailey and colleagues[7] reported similar findings for unilocular cysts of up to 10 cm in diameter. Although surgery might still be necessary for symptoms or removal of benign neoplasms, the extent of the procedure can sometimes be limited, given more reassuring ultrasonographic characteristics. In contrast, findings of a large mass or lesion complexity including mural nodularity should prompt more expeditious surgery along with the availability of subspecialty gynecologic oncology services.

Color Doppler views of the vascular supply can further clarify the nature of the pathology. As new blood vessels forming in growing tumors contain less smooth muscle, blood flow impedence is lower. Calculated values such as the pulsatility index and resistance index provide quantitative descriptions of blood flow that can help sort out the likelihood of benign or malignant disease. Several authors[8,9] have attempted to identify limits of normal that can assist in the diagnosis of ovarian pathology, but to date, none of these measurements have successfully supplanted the value of surgery for diagnostic and therapeutic purposes.

Computed Tomography

For evaluation of the remainder of the peritoneal cavity, computed tomography (CT) remains the mainstay. While early small ovarian cancers are not best identified in this manner, larger primary masses can be seen quite well. Such three-dimensional views also allow

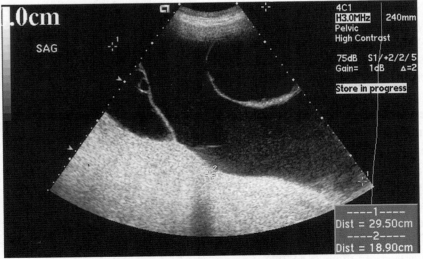

Figure 7–7. Transvaginal sonogram of a huge ovarian mass with multiple septations that was ultimately found to be a 35 cm combined Brenner tumor and mucinous cystadenoma.

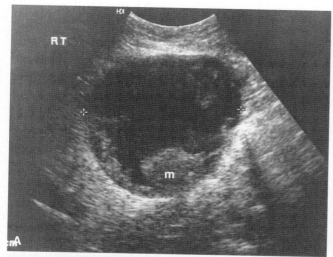

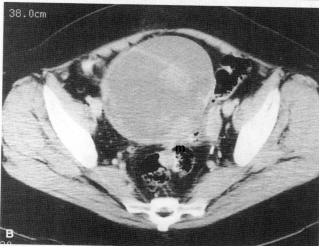

Figure 7–8. A 10 cm cystadenocarcinoma of the ovary. *A,* Ultrasonography demonstrates mural nodularity (m) and papillations. *B,* Similarly, pelvic computed tomography shows cystic and solid components with a thick septation and mural nodules (m).

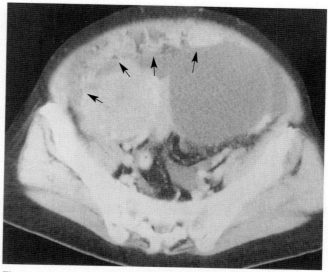

Figure 7–9. Stage IIIC ovarian adenocarcinoma. Large cystic and solid masses are evident in the pelvis, and an omental cake (*arrowheads*) is seen beneath the anterior abdominal wall.

CT to assess the likelihood of successful tumor debulking; for maximizing patient survival, however, imaging alone can rarely substitute for a judicious and aggressive primary surgical approach.[11]

Magnetic Resonance Imaging

In the last several years, magnetic resonance imaging (MRI) has become more useful for the evaluation of ovarian masses (Figure 7–14). Tissue parameters such as magnetic susceptibility and chemical shift allow for MRI to further characterize lesions beyond mea-

the assessment of structures neighboring the pelvic mass, such as bowel, bladder, and ureters. An omental cake of sufficient size can often be appreciated under the anterior abdominal wall (Figure 7–9). Other sites of disease that can also be visualized on CT include peritoneal surface deposits (Figure 7–10), retroperitoneal lymph nodes (Figure 7–11), and visceral parenchyma (Figure 7–12), as described in a recent report from the Radiological Diagnostic Oncology Group.[10] Administration of oral contrast can elucidate signs of bowel compromise, allowing for appropriate patient education and counseling regarding not only symptom control but also the timing and scope of the intended procedure (Figure 7–13). Some physicians have additionally advocated

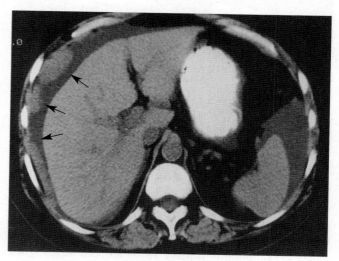

Figure 7–10. Stage IIIC ovarian adenocarcinoma. Computed tomography shows perihepatic ascites and large tumor deposits (*arrowheads*) on the right hemidiaphragm.

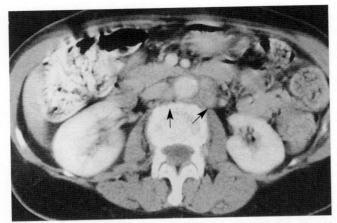

Figure 7–11. Metastatic para-aortic lymphadenopathy. Computed tomography of the abdomen demonstrates enlarged lymph nodes lateral to the aorta and between the aorta and vena cava (*arrowheads*).

surements of size and complexity.[12] Blood and lipids, for example, have distinguishing features on MRI that would appear only as nonsolid collections on a sonogram or CT scan (Figure 7–15).[13] Outwater and colleagues showed that standard and gadolinium-enhanced magnetic resonance (MR) images can help differentiate benign processes such as dermoid cysts, ovarian fibromas, and endometriomas.[14] Rieber and colleagues similarly reported particular success in identifying dermoid or endometrial cysts by MRI although the overall diagnostic accuracy of MRI was only 83%. The appropriate diagnostic role of MRI for ovarian lesions, therefore, still requires careful clinical correlation and continues to be defined.[15]

Laboratory Studies

Few laboratory studies are diagnostic of ovarian cancer, except in the specific case of germ cell tumors, in which tumor markers have unparalleled sensitivity and specificity for disease activity. For epithelial tumors, however, the value of laboratory information is less clear.

Cancer antigen (CA 125), an antigenic determinant on a high-molecular-weight glycoprotein, is expressed by many epithelial ovarian neoplasms.[16] An elevated CA 125 level can confirm suspicion of ovarian cancer in a postmenopausal woman, particularly in the presence of a pelvic mass. A normal level, however, cannot be taken as a guarantee against malignancy as up to 25% of epithelial ovarian cancers are marker negative.[17] Furthermore, the interpretation of CA 125 lev-

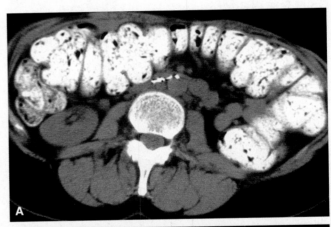

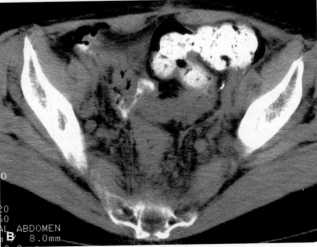

Figure 7–13. Comuted tomography scans of stage IIIC ovarian cancer. The transverse colon shows marked dilatation (*A*), which can be followed directly down to the level of the constricting lesion encircling the sigmoid colon (*B*).

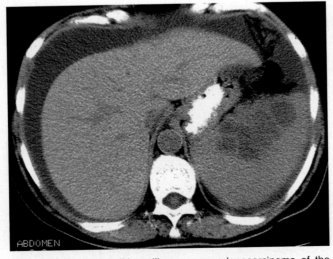

Figure 7–12. Stage IV papillary serous adenocarcinoma of the ovary. A large intrasplenic metastasis was still present after initial surgery and adjuvant chemotherapy. This was the only remaining site of the disease on second-look surgery including splenectomy.

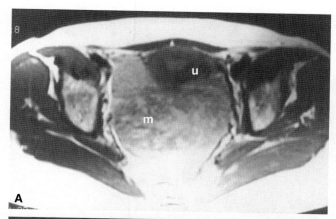

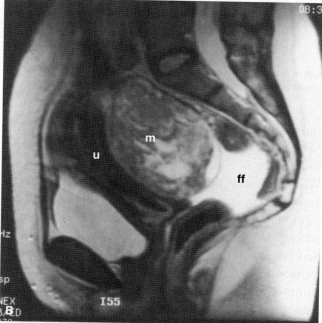

Figure 7–14. Magnetic resonance image of an 11 cm papillary and endometrioid ovarian adenocarcinoma. *A,* Axial image reveals a large complex mass (m) filling the posterior pelvis. *B,* Saggital view again shows the mass (m) to be posterior to the uterus (u) and additionally demonstrates enhancing free fluid (ff) in the cul-de-sac.

els in the premenopausal patient is hampered by low specificity since a multitude of common benign processes also cause abnormal readings. Examples include uterine leiomyomas, endometriosis, and pregnancy, all of which can additionally be associated with an abnormal pelvic mass. Liver disease, lung pathology, and other malignancies can also cause elevations in CA 125 levels, further limiting its use as a primary diagnostic tool. Other markers, such as CA 19-9, OVX1, and lysophosphatidic acid are still being evaluated.[1,18] Most recently, an iterative searching algorithm was used by Petricoin and colleagues at the

National Institutes of Health, to identify a cluster serum proteomic pattern that might segregate cancer from noncancer. A small set of key protein values was discovered that distinguished neoplastic from nonneoplastic ovarian disease with a promising positive predictive value of 94%.[18] At present, laboratory data can enhance or decrease a suspicion of ovarian cancer, but the primary use of surgery is unchanged.

Cytology

The prototypical cytologic finding associated with serous ovarian cancer is the psammoma body, a calcified deposit usually found in the midst of papillary tissue architecture. Obtaining such a cytologic specimen, however, is not always straightforward or clinically appropriate. For example, although a pelvic examination is important in the diagnostic work-up for ovarian cancer, Pap smear cytology is rarely helpful. Spatula and brush specimens identify cervical neoplastic processes with regularity, but the majority of patients with ovarian cancer will have normal Pap test results. An important but rare exception, however, is the smear that contains psammoma bodies (Figure 7–16). Reports show a prevalence of < 0.05% for this finding, but correlation with an ultimate diagnosis of extracervical gynecologic malignancy can be seen in up to one-half of these cases.[19,20] Cancers of the ovary, peri-

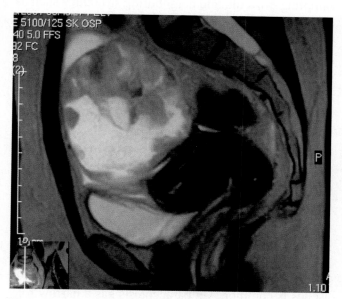

Figure 7–15. Stage IIIC clear cell carcinoma of the ovary. Magnetic resonance imaging of the ovarian mass shows a heterogeneous internal structure, with hemorrhage, mucin, and solid-growth areas.

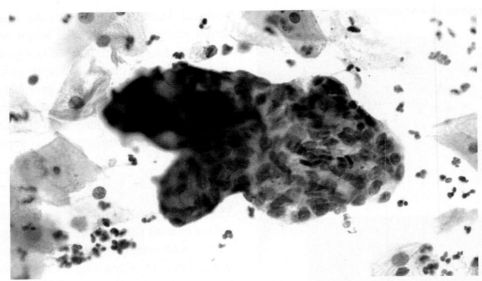

Figure 7–16. A routine Pap smear from a woman with a family history of ovarian cancer reveals psammoma bodies among atypical glandular cells of undetermined significance.

toneum, or fallopian tube were more likely to be found in postmenopausal patients and women with an abnormal history or physical examination. In any case, the unexpected appearance of psammoma bodies on a Pap test smear should prompt further evaluation.

Although direct sampling of a primary lesion in question aids in treatment planning by confirming the diagnosis in many cases, ovarian cancers should never be sampled directly as an initial form of evaluation. The free-floating nature of the ovary makes needle sampling difficult, and neighboring structures such as bowel, bladder, and blood vessels add significant risk. The fluid found in the cystic cavities of early ovarian cancers does not always harbor malignant cells and is thus of low diagnostic utility. Most importantly, however, fine-needle aspiration or biopsy of an actual ovarian cancer allows the spillage of tumor cells into the peritoneal cavity, which is a known receptive environment. As outlined elsewhere, ovarian cancers that are confined to the ovary have an excellent prognosis, often needing only surgery. Rupture of a contained stage I ovarian cancer at least requires the consideration of adjuvant chemotherapy that would otherwise not be necessary and at worst, may additionally worsen survival potential for the patient.[21]

In more-advanced cases, the accumulation of ascites is common, yet paracentesis has a narrow role in the diagnostic work-up for ovarian cancer. The primary use of this test is to differentiate malignant causes of ascites from non-neoplastic causes. This is particularly useful when additional abnormal mass lesions are not identified, as is commonly the case WITH primary peritoneal carcinomas. On cytology, ascites in the ovarian cancer patient will show adenocarcinoma cells (Figure 7–17), papillary formations, and (often) psammoma bodies.[22] Additionally, therapeutic paracentesis can be useful for alleviating symptoms when ascitic fluid accumulates sufficiently to compromise oral intake or respiratory function. The risks that are associated with paracentesis, however, are greater in the ovarian cancer population. Injuries, including blood vessel or organ perforation, are made more likely by the presence of metastatic disease, which can distort anatomy and cause adhesions of organs to each other and to the abdominal wall. Seeding of the skin and subcutaneous tissues with malignant cells can occur along the needle tract,[23] and the evacuation of malignant ascites depletes valuable albumin and other proteins trapped in the ascitic exudate.[24] In most cases, therefore, the diagnosis of ovarian cancer is best made on surgical exploration, when treatment can also begin at the same instant.

STAGING

The staging system for ovarian cancer, designed by the International Federation of Gynecology and Obstetrics (FIGO) (Table 7–1), reflects the current

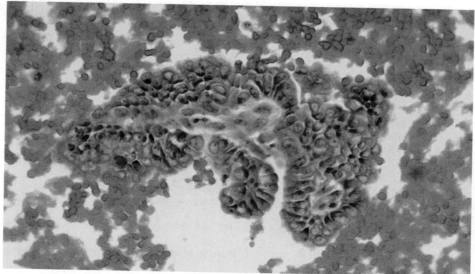

Figure 7–17. Cytology sample from a diagnostic paracentesis shows adenocarcinoma cells, confirming a suspicion of ovarian cancer.

understanding of the major patterns of disease spread: direct extension, exfoliation, and lymphatic dissemination. Staging of ovarian cancer is therefore accomplished by a systematic surgical procedure to obtain targeted tissues for microscopic assessment. At the time of surgical exploration, advanced disease will often be immediately evident. The goals of the procedure then shift to therapeutic cytoreduction, which is outlined in detail in a chapter 8. When disease is grossly confined to the ovary, however, a detailed staging procedure is mandatory to determine the actual extent of disease (Figure 7–18). Studies have shown that up to 30% of patients with apparent early-stage disease in fact have metastases outside the ovary, often to retroperitoneal lymph nodes. This has important prognostic implications; whereas up to 90% of patients with true stage I disease will survive, less than one-third of patients with spread outside the ovary are curable.[25] Furthermore, accurate staging is the only way to correctly define which patients can expect benefit from adjuvant therapy. Young and colleagues showed that well-differentiated or moderately differentiated cancers confined to the ovary carry an excellent prognosis that is not further improved by chemotherapy.[26] Accurate staging information, then, can spare this subset of patients dangerous toxicities as well as the financial and psychological investments associated with adjuvant treatment.

A staging laparotomy is best performed through a generous vertical midline incision allowing access to the upper abdominal cavity.[27] Ascites should be evacuated, or washings should be taken of the peritoneal cavity for cytologic review. Needed confirmation of ovarian malignancy is provided by frozen-section analysis, which is completed by histologic assessment of an abnormal ovary. An encapsulated mass should be removed intact because intraoperative rupture of a malignant cyst results in up-staging and may place the patient at risk of disease dissemination. For most patients, the remaining adnexal structures and the uterus should be removed. Pelvic and para-aortic lymph node dissections are completed, and omentectomy is performed. All peritoneal surfaces should be carefully inspected for evidence of tumor deposits (Figures 7–19 and 7–20); if none are found, random biopsies of dependent regions including colonic gutters and cul-de-sac are performed. Adhesions should be sampled or at least carefully noted. Last, the right hemidiaphragm is sampled by biopsy or scraping.

In some instances, tissue samples cannot be obtained as described above because of the patient's inability to withstand the necessary surgical procedure. With advancing age, cardiopulmonary comorbidities may compromise tolerance; other complications of a cancer diagnosis, such as pulmonary embolism might necessitate delay. In such cases, the diagnosis can be confirmed by cytologic or histo-

Table 7–1.   STAGING FOR PRIMARY CARCINOMA OF THE OVARY*

Stage	Description
I	Growth limited to the ovaries.
IA	Growth limited to one ovary; no ascites. No tumor on the external surface; capsule intact.
IB	Growth limited to both ovaries; no ascites. No tumor on the external surfaces; capsule intact.
IC	Tumor either stage IA or IB but with tumor on surfaces of one or both ovaries; or with capsule ruptured; or with ascites present containing malignant cells or with positive peritoneal washings.
II	Growth involving one or both ovaries with pelvic extension.
IIA	Extension and/or metastases to the uterus and/or tubes.
IIB	Extension to other pelvic tissues.
IIC	Tumor either stage IIA or IIB, but with tumor on surface of one or both ovaries; or with capsule(s) ruptured; or with ascites present containing malignant cells or with positive peritoneal washings.
III	Tumor involving one or both ovaries with peritoneal implants outside the pelvis and/or positive retroperitoneal or inguinal nodes. Superficial liver metastasis equals stage III. Tumor is limited to the true pelvis but with histologically proven malignant extension to small bowel or omentum.
IIIA	Tumor grossly limited to the true pelvis with negative nodes but with histologically confirmed microscopic seeding of abdominal peritoneal surfaces.
IIIB	Tumor of one or both ovaries with histologically confirmed implants of abdominal peritoneal surfaces, none exceeding 2 cm in diameter. Nodes are negative.
IIIC	Abdominal implants greater than 2 cm in diameter and/or positive retroperitoneal or inguinal nodes.
IV	Growth involving one or both ovaries, with distant metastases. If pleural effusion is present, there must be positive cytology to allot a case to stage IV. Parenchymal liver metastasis equals stage IV.

*Staging system designed by the International Federation of Gynecology and Obstetrics (FIGO).
Adapted from Gershenson DM, Wharton JT. Surgery for ovarian cancer. In: Gershenson DM, DeCherney AH, Curry SL, editors. Operative gynecology. Vol. 1. Philadelphia: W.B. Saunders Company; 1993.

logic assessment of appropriate areas. While biopsy of an isolated ovarian mass is rarely indicated, a fine-needle aspirate or biopsy specimen of a clearly metastatic lesion (such as an omental cake) is commonly useful.[28] Imaging such as CT can help with biopsy guidance and can provide further information regarding the extent of disease (Figure 7–21). Pleural effusions due to transit across the diaphragm or due to the accumulation of tumor cells on the pleural lining can be sampled by thoracentesis, to confirm stage IV disease (Figure 7–22). Similarly, percutaneous guided biopsy of an intrahepatic metastatic deposit can be clinically useful. With the advent of neoadjuvant chemotherapy, the careful documentation of such advanced disease can assist in accurately identifying select patients who might

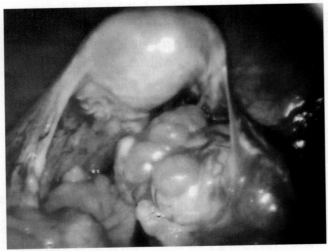

Figure 7–18. Laparoscopic view of a right ovarian mass. Subsequent complete staging laparotomy revealed a stage IIC undifferentiated ovarian adenocarcinoma with involvement of the adjacent pelvic peritoneum and a positive result on peritoneal cytology examination.

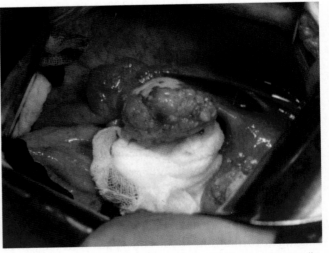

Figure 7–19. Stage IIIB ovarian serous cystadenoma of low malignant potential. The left ovary is covered by multiple surface papillations. The posterior uterine serosa and right ovary exhibit similar exophytic tumor processes.

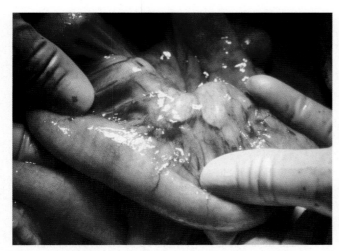

Figure 7–20. Stage IIIB papillary serous ovarian adenocarcinoma. Complete evaluation of the peritoneal cavity and its contents revealed 1.5 cm metastatic nodules in the small-bowel mesentery.

benefit from therapeutic variations, in an effort to limit morbidity and maximize outcome.

Unfortunately, accurate staging of ovarian cancer is not always completed for every patient. Due to unanticipated operative findings, knowledge deficiencies, and problematic changes in health care, many women are not managed correctly at the time of disease diagnosis. Over a decade ago, McGowan and colleagues found that initial surgery for almost one-half of ovarian cancer cases did not include comprehensive staging.[29] Most of the deficiencies stemmed from surgery being performed by surgeons without specific training in the management of ovarian cancers. In 1997, a study from the National Cancer Institute reviewed patterns of care for women diagnosed

with ovarian cancer, showing that these deficiencies have not been corrected; only 10% of patients with apparent early-stage disease were appropriately staged, and patient age was a significant contributor.[30] More complete education of both physicians and patients should help to ensure that patients with ovarian cancer have appropriate access to specialized care.

An important exception to standard staging procedures is the concept of conservative surgery, which primarily applies to younger patients who wish to preserve fertility.[31–33] Ideally, a detailed discussion is held preoperatively to outline specific procedures to be included in the surgery, depending on intraoperative findings. However, true malignancy is rarely encountered during surgery for an adnexal mass in patients under the age of 40 years; consequently, a diagnosis of cancer in a young patient is often a surprise to both the patient and her physician. When epithelial malignancy is identified by frozen-section analysis, the remainder of the abdomen and pelvis must be explored thoroughly. If no additional abnormalities are apparent, full staging, as described above, with preservation of the uterus and contralateral ovary may be appropriate. Still, the final pathology report may ultimately suggest consideration of completion surgery if metastatic disease is identified. For germ cell malignancies that are markedly chemosensitive, the decision for conservative surgery is more straightforward. Additionally, the majority of germ cell tumors present as stage I disease, making preservation of the uterus and contralateral ovary less risky. This is also true of sex cord–stromal tumors although,

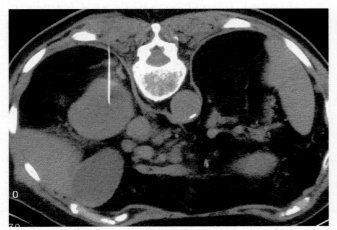

Figure 7–21. Computed tomographic guidance is used to obtain fine-needle aspirate of retroperitoneal mass.

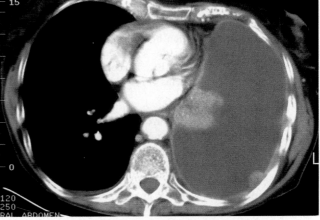

Figure 7–22. Stage IV ovarian cancer. Computed tomography shows pleural-based tumor and a large effusion in the left hemithorax.

fortunately, several specific types of these tumors are essentially benign and do not even require staging. Specifics regarding the management of these ovarian tumor subtypes are presented in subsequent chapters.

REFERENCES

1. Smith EM, Anderson B. The effects of symptoms and delay in seeking diagnosis on stage of disease at diagnosis among women with cancers of the ovary. Cancer 1985;56: 2727–32.
2. Goff BA, Mandel L, Muntz HG, Melancon CH. Ovarian carcinoma diagnosis. Cancer 2000;89:2068–75.
3. Pavlik EJ, DePriest PD, Gallion HH, et al. Ovarian volume related to age. Gynecol Oncol 2000;77:410–2.
4. DePriest PD, Shenson D, Fried A, et al. A morphology index based on sonographic findings in ovarian cancer. Gynecol Oncol 1993;51:7–11.
5. DePriest PD, Varner E, Powell J, et al. The efficacy of a sonographic morphology index in identifying ovarian cancer: a multi-institutional investigation. Gynecol Oncol 1994; 55:174–8.
6. Goldstein SR, Subramanyam B, Snyder JR, et al. The postmenopausal cystic adnexal mass; the potential role of ultrasound in conservative management. Obstet Gynecol 1989;73:8–10.
7. Bailey CL, Ueland FR, Land GL, et al. The malignant potential of small cystic ovarian tumors in women over 50 years of age. Gynecol Oncol 1998;69:3–7.
8. Kurjak A, Zalud I, Alfirevic Z. Evaluation of adnexal masses with transvaginal color ultrasound. J Ultrasound Med 1991;10:295–7.
9. Timor-Tritsch LE, Lerner JP, Monteagudo A, Santos R. Transvaginal Ultrasonographic characterization of ovarian masses by means of color flow-directed Doppler measurements and morphologic scoring system. Am J Obstet Gynecol 1993;168:909–13.
10. Tempany CM, Zou KH, Silverman SG, et al. Staging of advanced ovarian cancer: comparison of imaging modalities—report from the Radiological Diagnostic Oncology Group. Radiology 2000;215:761–7.
11. Nelson BE, Rosenfield AT, Schwartz PE. Preoperative abdominopelvic computed tomographic prediction of optimal cytoreduction in epithelial ovarian carcinoma. J Clin Oncol 1993;11:166–72.
12. Siegelman ES, Outwater EK. Tissue characterization in the female pelvis by means of MR imaging. Radiology 1999; 212:5–18.
13. Forstner R, Hricak H, White S. CT and MRI of ovarian cancer. Abdom Imaging 1995;20:2–8.
14. Outwater EK, Dunton CJ. Imaging of the ovary and adnexa: clinical issues and applications of MR imaging. Radiology 1995;194:1–18.
15. Rieber A, Nussle K, Stohr I, et al. Preoperative diagnosis of ovarian tumors with MR imaging: comparison with transvaginal sonography, positron emission tomography, and histologic findings. AJR Am J Roentgenol 2001;177:123–9.
16. Bast RC Jr, Klug TL, St John E, et al. A radioimmunoassay using a monoclonal antibody to monitor the course of epithelial ovarian cancer. N Engl J Med 1983;309:883–7.
17. Mann WJ, Patsner B, Cohen H, Loesch M. Preoperative serum CA-125 levels in patients with surgical stage I invasive ovarian adenocarcinoma. J Natl Cancer Inst 1988;80:208–9.
18. Petricoin EF, Ardekani AM, Hitt BA, et al. Use of proteomic patterns in serum to identify ovarian cancer. Lancet 2002; 359:572–7.
19. Parkash V, Chacho MS. Psammoma bodies in cervicovaginal smears: incidence and significance. Diagn Cytopathol 2002;26:81–6.
20. Zreik TG, Rutherford TJ. Psammoma bodies in cervicovaginal smears. Obstet Gynecol 2001;97:693–5.
21. Sainz de la Cuesta R, Goff BA, Fuller AF Jr, et al. Prognostic importance of intraoperative rupture of malignant ovarian epithelial neoplasms. Obstet Gynecol 1994;84:1–7.
22. Tauchi PS, Caraway N, Truong LD, et al. Serous surface carcinoma of the peritoneum: useful role of cytology in differential diagnosis and follow-up. Acta Cytol 1996;40:429–36.
23. Kruitwagen RF, Swinkels BM, Keyser KG, et al. Incidence and effect on survival of abdominal wall metastases at trocar or puncture sites following laparoscopy or paracentesis in women with ovarian cancer. Gynecol Oncol 1996; 60:233–7.
24. Lifshitz S, Buchsbaum HJ. The effect of paracentesis on serum proteins. Gynecol Oncol 1976;4:347–53.
25. Young RC, Decker DG, Wharton JT, et al. Staging laparotomy in early ovarian cancer. JAMA 1983;250:3072–6.
26. Young RC, Walton LA, Ellenberg SS, et al. Adjuvant therapy in stage I and stage II epithelial ovarian cancer. Results of two prospective randomized trials. N Engl J Med 1990; 322:1021–7.
27. Gershenson DM, Wharton JT. Surgery for ovarian cancer. In: Gershenson DM, DeCherney AH, Curry SL, editors. Operative gynecology. Philadelphia: W. B. Saunders Company; 1993. p. 523.
28. Pombo F, Rodriguez E, Martin R, Lago M. CT-guided coreneedle biopsy in omental pathology. Acta Radiol 1997; 38:978–81.
29. McGowan L, Lesher LP, Norris HJ, Barnett M. Misstaging of ovarian cancer. Obstet Gynecol 1985;65:568–72.
30. Munoz KA, Harlan LC, Trimble EL. Patterns of care for women with ovarian cancer in the United States. J Clin Oncol 1997;15:3408–15.
31. Gonzalez-Lira G, Escudero-De Los Rios P, Salazar-Martinez E, Lazcano-Ponce EC. Conservative surgery for ovarian cancer and effect on fertility. Int J Gynaecol Obstet 1997; 56:155–62.
32. Morice P, Wicart-Poque F, Rey A, et al. Results of conservative treatment in epithelial ovarian carcinoma. Cancer 2001;92:2412–8.
33. Zanetta G, Chiari S, Rota S, et al. Conservative surgery for stage I ovarian carcinoma in women of childbearing age. Br J Obstet Gynaecol 1997;104:1030–5.

8

Surgical Cytoreduction

MATTHEW. P. BOENTE, MD
LINDA F. CARSON, MD

Epithelial ovarian carcinoma is the second most common gynecologic malignancy and the leading cause of death from gynecologic cancer in the United States. Only lung, breast, colorectal carcinoma and pancreatic cancer account for more deaths in women than does ovarian carcinoma. The etiology of ovarian cancer is unknown, and despite significant advances in molecular biology, cytotoxic chemotherapy, and surgery, an estimated 13,900 American women will die from this malignancy in 1998.[1] The principle reason for this is that at the time of diagnosis, 75% of patients have disease outside the ovary. Unfortunately, the disease causes only a vague constellation of symptoms, such as indigestion, bloating, constipation, or diarrhea. There is no effective screening modality, and the cornerstone of treatment continues to be aggressive cytoreductive surgery followed by dose-intense cytotoxic chemotherapy with carboplatin and paclitaxel.

PROGNOSTIC FACTORS

The patient's prognosis is largely determined by the extent of disease present at the time of the initial operation (stage) and by the inherent biology of the tumor (grade). Both of these prognostic indicators have been extensively studied, and the patient's overall prognosis is inversely proportional to the increasing stage and grade of the tumor.[2–4] Unfortunately, there is no way for a physician to control the stage or grade of a tumor. It does appear, however, that the amount of residual disease remaining at the end of the initial debulking procedure may be influenced by an aggressive surgical approach, resulting in significant prognostic improvement.[5,6] Surgical debulking

offers numerous practical and theoretical advantages. Specifically, patient comfort is usually improved. Additionally, the risk of bowel obstruction interrupting induction chemotherapy is reduced. More importantly, the debulking of large tumor masses, which are typically necrotic and poorly vascularized, may facilitate the elimination of large numbers of tumor cells that would be difficult to eradicate with chemotherapy because of the aforementioned reasons. These large tumor masses typically harbor cells that have a low growth fraction, making them inherently insensitive to chemotherapy. Finally, the removal of large tumor masses probably decreases the development of drug-resistant clones, which develop partly from spontaneous mutations that are related to the total number of tumor cells present as well as to their growth rate (Figures 8–1 to 8–4).[7]

Young and co-workers at the National Cancer Institute in 1978 were the first to report this surgical cytoreduction prior to chemotherapy. His group reported a randomized trial showing that patients who were surgically reduced to minimal disease were more likely to achieve a complete clinical response with adjuvant chemotherapy, as well as a complete surgical response, as compared with patients who did not have optimal surgical debulking.[8] It should be further noted that investigators have documented that the smaller the residual disease, the more likely the patient is to have a complete clinical remission following cytotoxic chemotherapy. Specifically, patients with stage III ovarian cancer who are able to have all of their residual disease removed will typically outperform patients who are considered to have an optimal cytoreduction but who have gross residual disease at the end of their initial surgery (Figure 8–5).

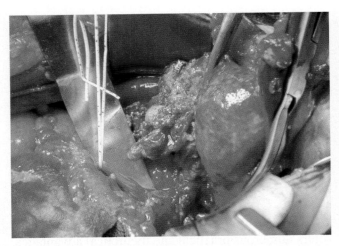

Figure 8–1. A 58-year-old with stage IIIC ovarian cancer covering all pelvic peritoneal surfaces and distorting all pelvic anatomy. The ureter is shown with a vessel loop.

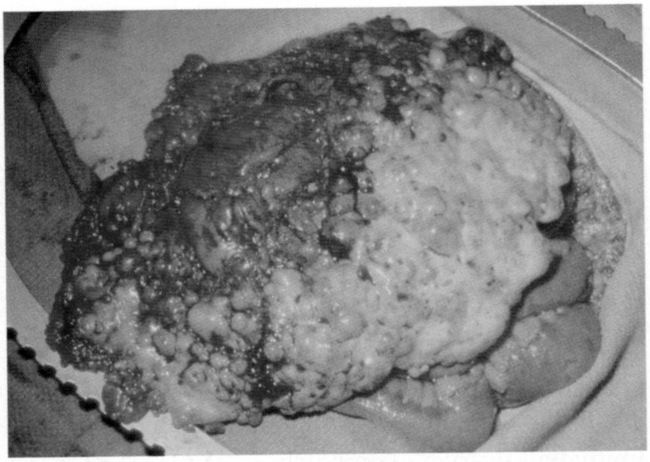

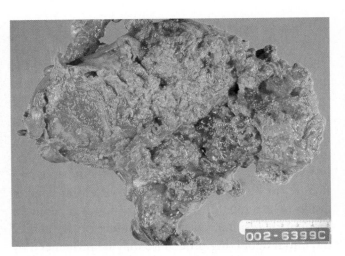

Figure 8–3. Photograph of same patient shows large-volume omental disease.

TREATMENT

In patients with advanced disease, resection of the primary tumor (total abdominal hysterectomy with bilateral salpingo-oopherectomy [TAH-BSO]) is typically accomplished through a retroperitoneal approach. Unfortunately, due to the advanced nature of these carcinomas, much of the normal pelvic architecture is often obscured by tumor growth. The only effective way to approach advanced pelvic disease of this nature is to establish anatomic landmarks via a retroperitoneal approach. One can thus identify the ureters bilaterally and can open as many avascular spaces as possible (pararectal, paravesical, pre-

sacral, and vesicouterine) to encircle the tumor-bearing tissues; the retroperitoneal identification of the iliac vessels, lower rectosigmoid colon, and bladder are much more readily made. In the majority of patients resection of a pelvic tumor can be achieved through the retroperitoneal approach (Figure 8–6).

Several techniques have proven effective in achieving optimal debulking, including the use of the (Cavitron Ultrasonic Surgical Aspirator (CUSA), the argon-beam coagulator, and the carbon dioxide (CO_2) laser to produce a complete elimination of all gross tumors.[9] Resection of the pelvic tumor, however, can require a rectosigmoid resection, partial cystectomy, and peritoneal stripping. This should be

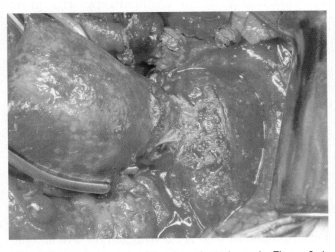

Figure 8–2. Photograph of same patient shown in Figure 8–1, shows tumor on the bladder peritoneum.

Figure 8–4. A necrotic and poorly vascularized left ovary from the same patient shown in Figure 8–1.

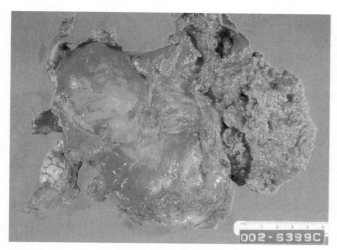

Figure 8–5. Specimen from the same patient shown in Figure 8–1. A radical hysterectomy, BSO, and radical peritonectomy resulted in a complete surgical resection of the tumor.

done when the rectosigmoid colon is near obstruction or when this portion of the procedure will render the patient optimal (Figures 8–7 and 8–8).[10] Preoperative computed tomography (CT) may assist the gynecologic oncologist in predicting who might need a retrosigmoid resection (Figure 8–9). The majority of patients having a rectosigmoid resection during their primary debulking surgery can be reanastomosed when they have been properly prepared with preoperative bowel preparation and antibiotics.

In addition, small-bowel resection, paritonectomy,[11] retroperitoneal lymphadenectomy,[12] and splenectomy[13] can also be used to achieve an adequate surgical debulking.

However, it is difficult to justify aggressive surgery such as this in all patients. Considerable judgment and experience in the operative theater is necessary to avoid excessive morbidity in trying to achieve optimal surgical debulking (< 1 cm). The literature varies considerably with regard to the frequency with which a gynecologic oncologist can achieve optimal cytoreduction. Large studies from reputable investigators estimate this figure to be in the 20 to 30% range,[14,15] and a thorough review of this literature has been recently published.[16–18]

Several additional caveats should be noted with regard to the tumor's inherent biology and how this relates to resectability and to judgments made in the operative arena. It has long been thought, although never proven, that a tumor's resectability is related as much to the biology of the disease as to the skill of the surgeon. Recently, several papers have documented that patients who required extensive cytoreduction to achieve minimal residual disease have a poorer prognosis than patients who have similar "de novo" residual disease without cytoreduction.[20] This would lend evidence to the fact that biology is perhaps more important than debulking. A recent large randomized series, however, evaluating the differences between carboplatin/paclitaxel and carboplatin/docetaxel in patients with high risk for ovarian cancer recurrence, showed that patients undergoing more-extensive surgery, which is typically done in the United States, had improved progression-free intervals as compared with patients receiving the

Figures 8–6. *A,* and *B,* The desired end result after a radical pelvic dissection. *A* and *B* refer to a 65-year-old woman with advanced papillary serous adenocarcinoma of the ovary (*A*) who subsequently underwent a radical pelvic dissection and debulking (*B*) including a TAH, BSO, and radical peritoniectomy.

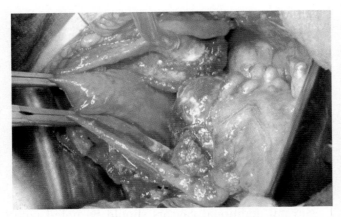

Figure 8–7. A 42-year-old woman with bilateral ovarian involvement and extensive colonic involvement.

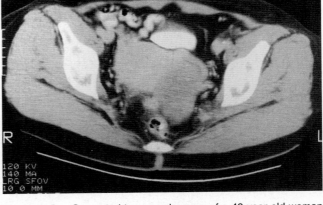

Figure 8–9. Computed tomography scan of a 42-year-old woman with suspected ovarian carcinoma.

same chemotherapy but less-radical (more conservative) surgery done in the United Kingdom.[21]

In elderly patients with significant comorbidities, consideration should be given to more-conservative surgery (TAH-BSO, omentectomy only) followed by induction chemotherapy since a large percentage of these cancers are chemosensitive. If the patient then does well, consideration can be given to an interval debulking or secondary cytoreduction following completion of the induction chemotherapy. In the

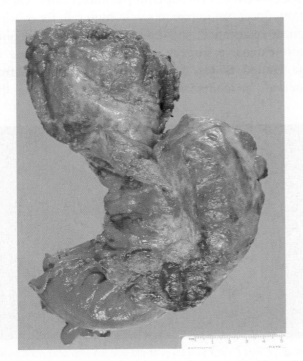

Figure 8–8. Photograph from same patient shown in Figure 8–7, after rectosigmoid resection.

vast majority of elderly patients, this can be accomplished safely and usually removes greater than 90% of the bulky tumor (Figure 8–10).

Recently, data from a large prospective randomized trial showed that interval debulking can improve survival in patients with advanced ovarian carcinoma.[22] This large, controvesial, randomized multicentered European trial showed a statistically significant improvement in progression-free and median overall survivals for patients who had interval surgery following three cycles of chemotherapy, as compared with patients who had no interval surgery. In general, the surgery was well tolerated and much less radical than the procedures discussed earlier in this chapter. This trial has been looked upon more skeptically in the United States. Many believe that the survival benefits in the interval debulking group were only slightly better than in patients who had chemotherapy alone.[23] In addition, the authors did not measure the patient's quality of life, therefore making it difficult to determine the true palliative effect of the surgery. In reality, approximately one-third of these patients could not be further debulked in an optimal fashion. Another one-third were already debulked by the chemotherapy given, rendering the surgery essentially diagnostic. And a third of the patients were debulked to an optimal level. The final analysis did show statistical significance, but one must carefully consider all of these factors when reviewing this data. The GOG is currently evaluating interval debulking in a similar randomized trial in the United States.

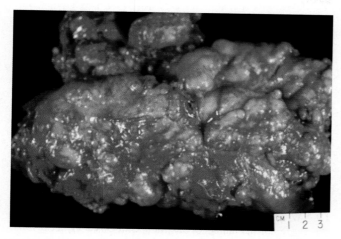

Figure 8–10. An omentum removed from a 92-year-old woman with stage IIIC ovarian cancer. Operative time was 15 minutes.

Patients with stage IV ovarian carcinoma were previously thought to have a particularly dismal prognosis in spite of efforts at cytoreduction. Recently, however, there appears to be evidence that aggressive cytoreduction benefits patients with stage IV disease.[24] Although careful evaluation is needed in the preoperative setting, no patient should be denied a debulking procedure based only on radiographic evidence of stage IV disease.

Much has been written and discussed about the role of intraperitoneal chemotherapy for ovarian carcinoma. The use intraperitoneal therapy remains one of the most controversial topics in the treatment of ovarian carcinoma. The results of randomized trials

that used chemotherapy in this arena will be discussed elsewhere in this publication. Suffice it to say that one of the problems inherent to this type of therapy is the difficulty with delivery of the intraperitoneal drug, specifically as it relates to catheter complications. In a recent report from Memorial Sloan-Kettering Cancer Center in New York, Barakat and colleagues reported significant complications with the use of chemotherapy in approximately 22% of 433 patients who received intraperitoneal chemotherapy at that institution in the largest study of its kind. The majority of these complications were due to catheter malfunction although sepsis, emesis, significant neuropathy, and abdominal pain were also reported. In this series, there was one case of peritonitis reported from bowel perforation.[25]

Similarly, the GOG has performed several large randomized trials evaluating intraperitoneal chemotherapy, predominantly with cisplatin. Markman and colleauges recently reported on the phase III trial comparing standard-dose intravenous cisplatin and paclitaxel versus moderately high-dose carboplatin and intravenous paclitaxel and intraperitoneal cisplatin in small-volume stage III ovarian carcinoma. In the cooperative group setting, 6.8% of patients randomized to the experimental arm did not receive any intraperitoneal therapy, and 18.3% of the patients received only two courses or less of a planned six courses of the intraperitoneal delivery. The reasons for this at this point are only specula-

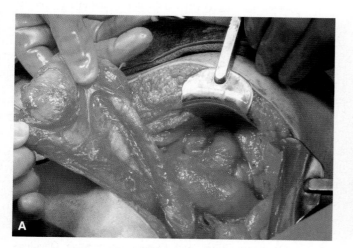
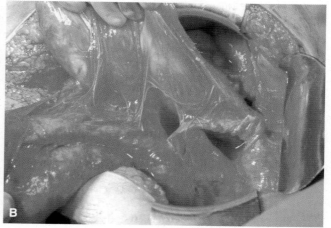

Figure 8–11. *A* figure is a 35-year-old woman with a small-bowel obstruction secondary to adhesions related to intraperitoneal cisplatin and catheter-related bacterial infection. Subsequent cultures revealed staph aureus to be the related organisms. *B,* Dense adhesions were found throughout the abdomen and pelvis, presumably related to the peritoritis and the intraperitoneal cisplatin.

tive. Suffice it to say that delivery of an intraperitoneal drug is cumbersome and that 20 to 30% of patients receiving this type of therapy will have significant complications (Figure 8–11).[26]

In conclusion, aggressive cytoreduction continues to be the hallmark of initial treatment of advanced ovarian carcinoma. However, considerable judgment and experience are necessary to accomplish this safely, and in selected cases, less aggressive surgery may be appropriate for very elderly patients with multiple comorbidities. Arguments for neoadjuvant chemotherapy without initial cytoreduction continue to be flawed by the absence of any prospective randomized data. In addition, proponents of this philosophy should continue to keep in mind that they are treating patients without a definitive histologic diagnosis and that proposing this outside of a clinical trial could deprive a patient of surgery that may improve her comfort, nutrition, and long-term survival.

REFERENCES

1. Greenlee RT, Hill-Harmon MB, Murray T. Cancer Statistics 2001. Cancer J Clin 2001;51:15–36.
2. Young RC, Walton LA, Ellenberg SS, et al. Adjuvant therapy in stage I and II epithelial ovarian cancer: results of two prospective randomized trials. N Engl J Med 1990;322:1021–7.
3. Young RC, Decker DG, Wharton JT, et al. Staging laparotomy in young early ovarian cancer. JAMA 1983;250:3072.
4. Partridge EE, Gunter B, Gelder M, et al. The validity and significance of substages in advanced ovarian carcinoma [abstract]. Gynecol Oncol 1992;45:9.
5. Griffiths CT. Surgical resection of tumor bulk in the primary treatment of ovarian carcinoma: seminars on ovarian cancer. NCI Monogr 1975;42:101.
6. Griffiths CT, Barker LM, Fuller AF. Role of cytoreductive surgical treatment in the management of advanced ovarian cancer. Cancer Treat Rep 1979;63:235.
7. Goldie JH, Coldman AJ. A mathematic model for relating the drug sensitivity of tumors to their spontaneous mutation rate. Cancer Treat Rep 1979;63:1727–33.
8. Young R, Chabner B, Hibbard S, et al. Advanced ovarian carcinoma. A prospective randomized trial of melphalan (L-PAM) versus combination chemotherapy. N Engl J Med 1978;299:1261–6.
9. Eisenkop SM, Nalick RH, Wang HJ, Teng NN. Peritoneal implant elimination during cytoreductive surgery for ovarian cancer: impact on survival. Gynecol Oncol 1993;51:224–9.
10. Soper JT, Couchman G, Berchuck A, et al. The role of partial sigmoid colectomy for debulking epithelial ovarian carcinoma. Gynecol Oncol 1991;41:239–44.
11. Montz FJ, Schlaerth JB, Berek JS. Resection of diaphragmatic peritoneum and muscle: role in cytoreductive surgery for ovarian cancer. Gynecol Oncol 1989;35:338–40.
12. Burghardt E, Pickel H, Lahousen M, et al. Pelvic lymphadenectomy in operative treatment of ovarian cancer. Am J Obstet Gynecol 1986;155:315–9.
13. Deppe G, Zheila EA, Skogerson K, Dumitru I. The rare indication for splenectomy as part of cytoreductive surgery in ovarian cancer. Gynecol Oncol 1983;16:282–7.
14. Smith J, Day T. Review of ovarian cancer at the University of Texas System Cancer Center, M.D. Anderson Hospital and Tumor Institute. Am J Obstet Gynecol 1979;135:984–93.
15. Wharton J, Edwards C. Cytoreductive surgery for common epithelial tumors of the ovary. Clin Obstet Gynecol 1984;10:235.
16. Boente MP, Chi DS, Hoskins WJ. The role of surgery in the management of ovarian cancer: primary and interval cytoreductive surgery. Semin Oncol 1998;25(3):326-34.
17. Piver MS, Lele SB, Marchetti DL. The impact of aggressive debulking surgery in cisplatin chemotherapy from progression-free survival in stage III and IV ovarian carcinoma. J Clin Oncol 1988;6:983–9.
18. Hacker NF, Berek JS, Lagasse LD, et al. Primary cytoreductive surgery for epithelial ovarian cancer. Obstet Gynecol 1983;61:413–20.
19. Hoskins WJ, Chi DS, Boente MP, Rubin SC. State of the art surgical management of ovarian cancer. Cancer Res Therapy Control 1999;9:373–82.
20. Hoskins WJ, McGuire WP, Brady MF, et al. The effect of diameter of largest residual disease on survival after primary cytoreductive surgery in patients with suboptimal residual epithelial ovarian carcinoma. Am J Obstet Gynecol 1994;170:974–9.
21. Kaye SB, Vasey PA. Docetaxel in ovarian cancer: phase II perspectives and future development. Semin Oncol 2002;29(3 Suppl 12):22–7.
22. van der Burg ME, van Lent M, Buyse M, et al. The effect of debulking surgery after induction chemotherapy on the prognosis in advanced epithelial ovarian cancer. N Engl J Med 1995;332:629–34.
23. Berek JS. Interval debulking of ovarian cancer—an interim measure. N Engl J Med 1995;332:675–7.
24. Curtin JP, Malik R, Venkatraman ES, et al. Stage IV ovarian cancer: impact of surgical debulking. Gynecol Oncol 1997;64:9–12.
25. Barakat RR, Sabbatini P, Bhaskaran D, et al. Intraperitoneal chemotherapy for ovarian carcinoma: results of long-term follow-up. J Clin Oncol 2002;20(3):694–8.
26. Markman M, Bundy BN, Alberts DS, et al. Phase III trial of standard-dose intravenous cisplatin plus paclitaxel versus moderately high-dose carboplatin followed by intravenous paclitaxel and intraperitoneal cisplatin in small-volume stage III ovarian carcinoma: an intergroup study of the Gynecologic Oncology Group, Southwestern Oncology Group, and Eastern Cooperative Oncology Group. J Clin Oncol 2001;19(4):1001–7.

9

Primary Chemotherapy Regimens

ROBERT F. OZOLS, MD, PHD

Approximately 90% of all patients with ovarian cancer are treated by surgery followed by chemotherapy. Chemotherapy is required because surgery, while removing bulk disease, cannot eradicate the microscopic and macroscopic disease that is frequently present due to the pattern of metastases that results in peritoneal carcinomatosis in most patients. The only patients who do not require chemotherapy as part of their initial treatment approach are those patients with early-stage disease who have no adverse prognostic factors as described in Chapter 11. These patients have a > 95% survival rate following surgery alone and consequently do not benefit from the addition of any postoperative treatment.[1]

COMPONENTS OF EFFECTIVE COMBINATION CHEMOTHERAPY

Ovarian cancer is a chemosensitive tumor for which numerous chemotherapeutic agents can produce objective remissions. Over the past 25 years, multiple combination chemotherapy regimens have also been tested as part of initial treatment approaches in patients with advanced ovarian cancer.[2,3] Currently, the best chemotherapeutic regimen consists of the combination of a platinum compound (primarily carboplatin) and paclitaxel.[4]

Platinum Compounds

Figure 9–1 shows the structure of the two most commonly used platinum compounds in ovarian cancer, carboplatin and cisplatin. Cisplatin was the platinum compound that was initially used in clinical trials, and carboplatin was developed as a less toxic alter-

native.[5] Both drugs are prodrugs and, after administration, undergo hydrolysis to produce the same active intermediates. The aquated forms of platinum damage deoxyribonucleic acid (DNA) by producing intrastrand and interstrand adducts that limit the tumor cells' ability to divide successfully. Multiple mechanisms of resistance have been identified in platinum-resistant ovarian cancer cell lines (Table 9–1).[5] Clinical trials have been performed with agents that inhibit DNA repair or decrease cellular

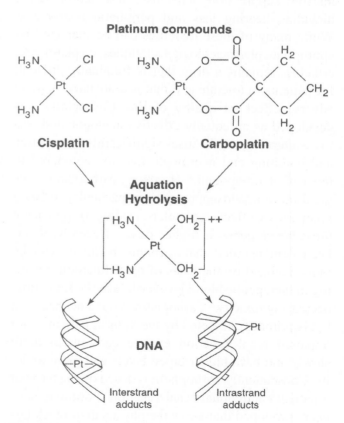

Figure 9–1. Platinum compounds.

Table 9–1. MECHANISMS OF RESISTANCE TO PLATINUM COMPOUNDS

Decreased cellular drug accumulation
  Enhanced efflux
  Impaired influx
Intracellular inactivation: reaction with thiol-containing
  compounds (primarily glutathione [GSH]) inactivates
  platinum and prevents DNA binding.
Enhanced DNA repair
  DNA damaged by PT can be repaired.
  Removal of PT-DNA adducts
  DNA repair synthesis
Proto-oncogenes and suppressor genes
  Overexpression of *c-ras*, *c-fos*, and *c-myc*
  Nonfunctional *P53*

DNA = deoxyribonucleic acid; PT = platinum.

thiol levels, based on demonstration that resistance to platinum compounds can be reversed in relevant experimental model systems of ovarian cancer.[6,7] Currently, however, there is no evidence that cisplatin resistance can be clinically reversed in ovarian cancer patients by any pharmacologic agents.

The primary toxicities of cisplatin include nephrotoxicity, severe nausea and vomiting, bone marrow suppression, hair loss, and neurotoxicity, including hearing loss and peripheral neuropathy. While many of these toxicities can be managed by appropriate pharmacologic techniques, cisplatin nevertheless remains a drug that is frequently difficult for patients to tolerate and that is associated with an adverse effect on quality of life. Carboplatin was developed as an equally effective analogue and less toxic alternative and causes significantly less nausea and vomiting and neurologic toxicity, compared to the parent compound.[5] However, carboplatin does yield more myelosuppression; in particular, it has a greater toxic effect on platelets, leading to significant thrombocytopenia at higher doses. Recently, it has been demonstrated that carboplatin dosing can be individualized on the basis of renal function, resulting in therapeutic blood levels while at the same time decreasing toxicity.[8] Carboplatin is not a nephrotoxin but is primarily excreted by the kidney. Patients with impaired renal function excrete carboplatin more slowly and have higher blood levels and more toxicity. Consequently, carboplatin is dosed on the basis of a patient's individual renal function. Formulas have been developed that allow the physician to reach targeted blood levels that are dependent on glomerular

filtration.[8] These blood levels, termed area under the curve (AUC), are a measure of carboplatin blood levels over time (Figure 9–2). It has been demonstrated that there is a relationship between a patient's response to treatment and the carboplatin AUC (Figure 9–3).[9] Renal function markedly deteriorates with age, to the point at which a woman in her forties may have a two- to threefold increased ability to clear carboplatin from her blood compared to a woman in her seventies. The formulas allow the calculation of drug doses that will be markedly different (in terms of total milligrams) for a woman in her seventies than for a woman in her forties but that will result in the same AUC in both patients and will consequently optimize the likelihood of response with acceptable toxicity. Based on the relationship between the probability of response and carboplatin AUC (see Figure 9–3), most patients are now dosed to an AUC of between 5.0 and 7.5 mg/mL/min.

Taxanes

The taxanes are a relatively new class of agents (Figure 9–4) that have been demonstrated to be among the most active chemotherapeutic agents available for a wide variety of malignancies, including ovarian, breast, and lung cancers. Paclitaxel was the initial taxane brought to clinical trial partly on the basis of a unique mechanism of action that demonstrated

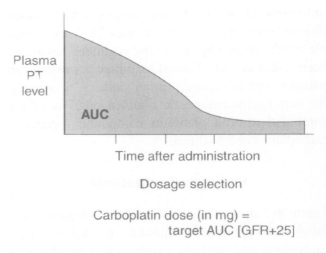

Figure 9–2. Carboplatin dosing. Glomerular filtration rate (GFR) can be measured, or creatine clearance can be substituted. (AUC - area under the curve; PT = platinum.)

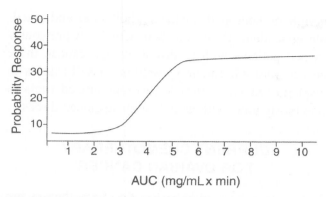

Figure 9–3. Probability of response and carboplatin area under the curve (AUC). (Reproduced with permission from Jodrell DI.[9])

that the taxanes bind to tubulin polymers (microtubules). Docetaxel shares the same tubulin binding site as paclitaxel but induces tubulin-assembly and polymerization in a concentration that is somewhat lower than that induced by paclitaxel, making docetaxel a more potent taxane analogue. Microtubules are essential for cell division, and the taxanes exert their cytotoxic effect primarily by disrupting normal microtubule dynamics. The taxanes induce tubulin polymerization, and this stability inhibits the dynamic reorganization of the microtubule network, resulting in a disruption of mitosis, inducing a sustained mitotic block at the metaphase-anaphase boundary.[10,11] Along with many other chemotherapeutic agents, the taxanes induce apoptosis in tumor cells. The molecular mechanisms by which tubulin-binding agents lead to programmed cell death remain to be fully elucidated. It has been postulated that genes that protect against apoptosis (including mutant *p53, BCL2,* and *BCLX*) may induce resistance to tubulin-binding agents.[10] It has also been

demonstrated that paclitaxel may modulate some of the genes involved in apoptotic regulation.[10]

Multiple mechanisms of resistance to antitubulin-binding agents, such as the taxanes, have been described (Table 9–2), and resistance to paclitaxel may be part of the multidrug-resistance (MDR) phenotype, in which tumor cells, after exposure to a natural product, develop cross-resistance to a variety of agents with different structure. This broad cross-resistance is frequently characterized by overexpression of the *MDR1* gene and its protein product, P-glycoprotein, which is a 170 kD membrane glycoprotein that acts as an efflux pump in reducing the intracellular accumulation of natural products, including paclitaxel. Other agents affected by this intracellular pump include anthracyclines, vinca alkaloids, and epipodophyllotoxins. It has also been shown that expression of β-tubulin, a major target for paclitaxel cytotoxicity, is also decreased in resistant cell lines.[10] As noted, paclitaxel also induces programmed cell death (apoptosis), and it has been demonstrated that mutant forms of the protein BCL2, which is involved in the regulation of apoptotic pathways, prevents paclitaxel-induced apoptosis. Resistance to MDR can be induced in experimental systems by inhibiting efflux and allowing increased intracellular levels of cytotoxic agents. Drugs that inhibit MDR include calcium channel blockers, calmodulin antagonists, hormonal agents, steroids, and cyclosporins. The Gynecologic Oncology Group (GOG) has evaluated valspodar (PSC 833), a nonimmunosuppressive analogue of cyclosporin D, in a phase II study in patients with resistance to paclitaxel.[12] This agent was shown to reverse MDR-associated resistance to natural products in preclinical systems. However, the clinical trial

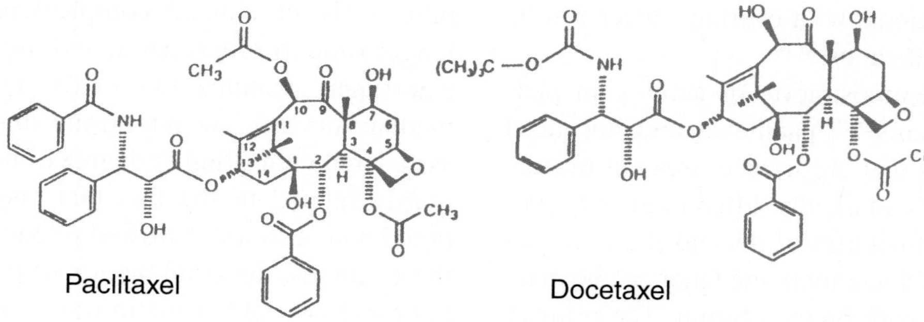

Paclitaxel

Docetaxel

Figure 9–4. Structure of paclitaxel/docetaxel.

Table 9–2. RESISTANCE TO TAXANES

Decreased intracellular accumulation (*MDR1* gene encodes for a 170-kD Pgp efflux pump)
Altered metabolism or subcellular distribution
Altered response to mitotic blockage-induced cell cycle arrest
Mutations in tubulin isotype genes

Pgp = Paycoprotein.

demonstrated that valspodar in combination with paclitaxel produced limited responses in patients with paclitaxel-resistant ovarian cancer. Nevertheless, an international randomized trial of paclitaxel and carboplatin, with or without valspodar, as first-line therapy in patients with previously untreated ovarian cancer is currently under way. This study has focused on attempts to prevent the development of drug resistance with this MDR inhibitor.

Paclitaxel, the first taxane developed for clinical use, was initially extracted from the bark of the western yew. At first, this was a severe limitation for the widespread clinical evaluation of paclitaxel, due to the relative scarcity of the slow-growing western yew. Recently, however, a semisynthetic procedure for extracting the taxane nucleus from the needle of the yew instead of the bark has been developed; consequently, the supply of paclitaxel is no longer a significant issue. Based on its novel mechanism of action and high degree of activity in relative preclinical models of human cancer, paclitaxel was evaluated in phase I and phase II trials in the 1970s. The clinical development of paclitaxel was initially threatened by the development of severe hypersensitivity reactions associated with short infusions of the drug. However, subsequent alterations in the length of the infusion, coupled with effective premedication regimens, have lowered the incidence of hypersensitive reactions to an acceptable level, and the vast majority of patients with ovarian cancer can be safely treated with taxanes.[13,14]

Based on the demonstration of activity in platinum-resistant patients[15,16] paclitaxel and docetaxel are the two taxanes that are used in treating ovarian cancer, and they have markedly different toxicity profiles. The primary toxicities of docetaxel are myelosuppression and fluid retention; the latter can be managed appropriately with premedication. The primary toxicity of paclitaxel relates to the development of peripheral neuropathy, which is both dose and schedule dependent. Based on their activity in previously treated patients with recurrent ovarian cancer, these agents were subsequently tested in phase I trials with cisplatin, which in turn led to randomized trials in previously untreated patients with advanced disease.

CURRENT CHEMOTHERAPY FOR OVARIAN CANCER

The current recommendations for chemotherapy are based on sequential prospective randomized trials in ovarian cancer. These trials were based on the analysis of earlier results that demonstrated that platinum combinations were superior to nonplatinum-based chemotherapy.[2,3] The demonstration that cisplatin could be combined safely with paclitaxel led to the landmark GOG 111 trial, which compared what was then considered standard therapy, cisplatin plus cyclophosphamide, to the new combination of cisplatin plus paclitaxel.[17] In this trial, paclitaxel was administered as a 24-hour infusion, after which cisplatin was administered at a standard dose of 75 mg/m^2. Almost 400 patients with suboptimal stage III and IV disease were randomized to six cycles of cisplatin/paclitaxel or six cycles of cyclophosphamide/cisplatin. Patients randomized to the paclitaxel combination showed improvement in both disease-free survival and overall survival (Figure 9–5). A subsequent intergroup trial (OV-10) performed in Canada and Europe[18] was similarly designed, with the exception that paclitaxel, when combined with cisplatin, was administered in a 3-hour infusion instead of a 24-hour infusion as in the GOG trial. Table 9–3 summarizes the results of these two trials. Both trials demonstrated that the paclitaxel/cisplatin combination had a higher response rate, a higher clinical complete remission rate, a longer time to progression, and most importantly, a significant prolongation of 10 to 14 months in median survival. The intergroup study, however, was associated with a higher degree of neurotoxicity, primarily related to the fact that cisplatin was combined with a shorter infusion of paclitaxel. Based on these studies, the combination of paclitaxel in a 24-hour infusion and cisplatin was considered to be the optimum chemotherapy in the mid-1990s.

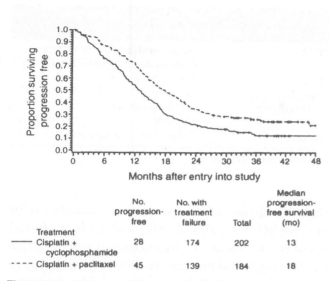
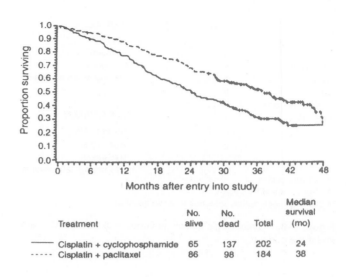

Treatment	No. progression-free	No. with treatment failure	Total	Median progression-free survival (mo)
—— Cisplatin + cyclophosphamide	28	174	202	13
---- Cisplatin + paclitaxel	45	139	184	18

Treatment	No. alive	No. dead	Total	Median survival (mo)
—— Cisplatin + cyclophosphamide	65	137	202	24
---- Cisplatin + paclitaxel	86	98	184	38

Figure 9–5. Outcomes of Gynecologic Oncology Group trial III.

However, recent clinical trials have established a new standard of care for patients with advanced ovarian cancer. Three randomized trials compared carboplatin plus paclitaxel[19] to cisplatin plus paclitaxel.[20–22] In particular, GOG 158 (Figure 9–6), was instrumental in establishing the safety, toxicity profile, and efficacy of carboplatin plus paclitaxel. GOG 158 was an equivalency study comparing carboplatin plus paclitaxel (CARBO/PAC) to cisplatin plus paclitaxel (CIS/PAC) in optimal stage III ovarian cancer patients. A previous study had demonstrated that CARBO/PAC could be successfully combined, using AUC dosing, particularly, when paclitaxel was administered in a 3-hour infusion.[19] In the phase II trial of CARBO/PAC, there was less toxicity than with CIS/PAC, primarily due to less nephrotoxicity,

nausea, and vomiting associated with cisplatin.[19] However, GOG 158 was necessary because there were concerns that the CARBO/PAC combination, even though less toxic, might potentially be inferior to cisplatin because carboplatin may have less efficacy than cisplatin in optimal stage III patients. There also was concern that a 3-hour infusion of paclitaxel was not as effective as a 24-hour infusion. Consequently, 802 patients were randomized to determine the relative risk ratios for progression-free survival and overall survival for CARBO/PAC versus CIS/PAC. The preliminary results of this study have been presented,[22] and more follow-up is required before a complete survival analysis can be performed. However, at this point, sufficient relapses have taken place that a statistical comparison can be made with regard

	GOG 111*		OV-10†	
Result	**PAC/CIS**	**CYCLO/CIS**	**PAC/CIS**	**CYCLO/CIS**
Response (%)	73	60	77	66
Clinical CR (%)	51	31	50	38
TTP (mo)	18	13	16	12
MS (mo)	38	24	35	25

Table 9–3. EPITHELIAL OVARIAN CANCER RANDOMIZED TRIALS OF CISPLATIN + CYCLOPHOSPHAMIDE VS CISPLATIN + PACLITAXEL

CR = complete remission; CYCLO/CIS = cyclophosphamide plus cisplatin; MS = median survival; PAC/CIS = paclitaxel plus cisplatin; TTP = time to progression.
*Gynecologic Oncology Group trial III.
†Intergroup trial OV-10.

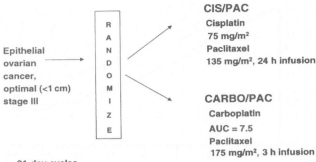

- 21-day cycles
- Six cycles of treatment
- Second-look option selected at randomization

Figure 9–6. Gynecologic Oncology Group trial 158. (AUC = area under the curve.)

Table 9–5. OUTPATIENT ADMINISTRATION OF CARBOPLATIN PLUS PACLITAXEL	
Drugs	Paclitaxel (175 mg/m^2 3 h infusion) Carboplatin (AUC 6.0–7.5 in 30 min)
Cycles	Every 21 days × 6
Hypersensitivity prophylaxis:	Decadron Diphenhydramine Cimetidine
Antiemetic	Granisetron or ondansetron

AUC = area under the curve.

to progression-free survival. The relative risk of failure is 0.86 when comparing CARBO/PAC to CIS/PAC. Thus, the likelihood of disease progression is 14% less if the patient is treated with CARBO/PAC rather than CIS/PAC. Consequently, the concerns that the CARBO/PAC regimen may not be as effective as CIS/PAC were dispelled by GOG 158, and due to the decreased toxicity associated with this regimen (Table 9–4), CARBO/PAC is now considered to be the standard of care for all patients with ovarian cancer. Two similar studies in Europe[20,21] also confirmed that there was no loss in efficacy with decreased toxicity for CARBO/PAC, compared to CIS/PAC.

Table 9–5 summarizes the manner in which CARBO/PAC is currently administered to patients with ovarian cancer. The other studies that demonstrated equivalency used lower AUC values of carboplatin, and many investigators have subsequently recommended that the AUC of carboplatin be dropped from 7.5 to a range of 5.0 to 6.0. There is no evidence of any benefit for more than six cycles of combination chemotherapy. Of patients with optimal

stage III disease after cytoreduction and six cycles of CARBO/PAC, almost 90% will be in a clinical complete remission. Unfortunately, the relapse rate remains high, and the median time to progression in GOG 158 was slightly less than 2 years. Consequently, most patients with advanced ovarian cancer, even if treated with what is currently the most effective chemotherapy regimen, will ultimately have disease progression. It is estimated that overall median survival will be greater than 50 months for patients treated with either CARBO/PAC or CIS/PAC.

Recently, a large randomized trial (ICON3) from Europe failed to confirm the previous reports of GOG-111 and OV10. The trial demonstrated that paclitaxel in combination with cisplatin improved survival compared to treatment with cisplatin plus cyclophosphamide. The ICON study reported no improvement in survival for patients treated with carboplatin compared to CARBO/PAC or the 3-drug CAP combination (cyclophosphamide plus adriamycin plus cisplatin).[22] The difference in results from the ICON study compared to GOG-111 and OV10 may be due to multiple factors, including protocol eligibility, drug delivery, and an imbalance in prognostic factors. Most investigators continue to recommend the use of CARBO/PAC as initial therapy and this combination remains the control treatment in ongoing prospective randomized trials evaluating new combination drug regimens.

APPROACH TO PATIENTS IN A CLINICAL COMPLETE REMISSION

Table 9–6 summarizes the outcomes that can be expected in patients with advanced ovarian cancer who receive chemotherapy and cytoreductive

Table 9–4. TOXICITY OF CISPLATIN/PACLITAXEL VERSUS CARBOPLATIN/PACLITAXEL		
Toxicity	Cisplatin/ Paclitaxel	Carboplatin/ Paclitaxel
Myelosuppression	↑	—
Neurotoxicity	—	↑
Allergy	↑	—
Stomatitis	↑	—
Diarrhea	↑	—
Myalgia/arthralgia	—	↑

Table 9–6.	OUTCOMES OF TREATMENT OF ADVANCED OVARIAN CANCER WITH SURGERY FOLLOWED BY CHEMOTHERAPY WITH A PLATINUM DRUG PLUS A TAXANE				
Disease Stage	Response Rate (%)	Clinical CR after Chemo (%)	Median DFS (mo)	Median OS (mo)	10-Year Survival (%)
Optimal stage III	NA	95	22	48	Pending (estimated at 30–35)
Suboptimal stage III and IV	75	50	18	38	~15

Overall for advanced-stage ovarian cancer: 75% of patients are in clinical complete remission following surgery and chemotherapy, but the majority of patients will relapse; 10-year survival will be 25 to 30%.

surgery. The patients are divided into two groups, optimal and suboptimal. Patients with optimal stage III disease have no remaining tumor nodule larger than 1.0 cm after initial surgery. Patients are considered to be suboptimal if they have stage IV disease or if a tumor nodule larger than 1.0 cm is left after initial surgery. As can be seen, there is a marked difference in prognosis for patients with either optimal or suboptimal disease. Patients with optimal disease have no measurable disease following initial cytoreductive surgery; that is, they have no tumor nodule that can be detected on imaging studies. Consequently, response rates to treatment cannot be accurately defined, and the end point of therapy is the percentage of patients who are in a clinical complete remission, which is defined as no evidence of disease on physical examination, normal imaging studies (such as computed tomography [CT]), and a normal level of serum CA 125. Almost 90% of patients with optimal stage III disease at the completion of six cycles of combination chemotherapy are in a clinical complete remission. In contrast, only 50% of patients with suboptimal disease are in a clinical complete remission. The median time to progression and median survival also are different between patients with optimal disease and patients with suboptimal disease. In patients with optimal disease, the median time to progression is approximately 2 years, and the median survival will be at least 4 years. In contrast, the median time to progression in patients with suboptimal disease, is approximately 14 months, and overall median survival ranges from 25 to 38 months, depending on additional prognostic factors. Long-term survival is possible for patients with either suboptimal and optimal disease although it appears that two to three times as many patients with optimal disease will be alive at 10 years, compared to patients with suboptimal disease.

The management of patients who are in clinical complete remission is an area of controversy. Some investigators have proposed that a second-look laparotomy be performed since approximately 50% of patients will be found to have residual ovarian cancer, even when they are felt to be in a clinical complete remission in which disease is not detected by noninvasive techniques. The rationale for a second-look procedure has been that the detection of residual disease would lead to immediate treatment, which theoretically would be more beneficial than waiting until the patients have recurrent disease with a larger volume of tumor.[23] However, there is no prospective evidence to support the routine use of second-look laparotomies since there is no evidence that treatment of patients who do have positive second-look laparotomies has an impact on survival or on time to progression.[22] Consequently, consensus panels do not recommend routine use of second-look laparotomies in patients who do achieve a clinical complete remission of ovarian cancer.[24] Furthermore, patients who undergo a second-look laparotomy and who are found to have no evidence of disease still remain at a high risk for recurrence, and at least 50% of these patients will ultimately have disease progression.[23]

The follow-up of patients who are in a clinical complete remission or a surgically confirmed complete remission remains an area of controversy as well. There is no evidence that the routine use of CT improves outcomes. In the United States, patients are frequently followed with routine tests of serum CA 125 levels, monthly or every other month. The GOG has accepted a marked rise in serum CA 125 levels (> 100 U) as being indicative of disease progression. Previous studies have demonstrated that the median time for clinical disease progression in the face of a rising CA 125 level ranges from 4 to 6 months.[25] Most patients who do have an elevated rise in their CA 125 will shortly thereafter have symptoms of recurrence, physical findings of recurrent disease, or detection of recurrence by imaging studies. However, a substantial subset of patients may have a rise in CA 125 for many months (and in some cases, years) before there is evidence of any clinical recurrence. The management of this group of patients remains controversial. Since the primary goal of treatment in patients with recurrent disease is palliation, it has been argued that the immediate institution of chemotherapy in an asymptomatic individual solely on the basis of elevated CA 125 is unnecessary. A randomized trial addressing the instituting of immediate chemotherapy for patients with rising CA 125 as opposed to the delaying of such treatment until the development of symptoms is currently in progress in Europe. Until the results of that study are known, it is likely that the management of patients with a rising CA 125 level will continue to be an area of debate. Many investigators will use tamoxifen, which has a defined response rate in ovarian cancer,[26] but is devoid of the toxicity associated with chemotherapy in those patients who have a rising CA 125 level but who have no other evidence of disease.[27]

OPTIMIZING CHEMOTHERAPY

Table 9–7 summarizes treatment approaches for improving chemotherapy in patients with ovarian cancer. Clinical trials to determine the optimum manner in which carboplatin should be used in combination with paclitaxel are still in progress. For example, it remains to be determined what the optimum carboplatin AUC is when carboplatin is used in combination with paclitaxel. In GOG 158, the AUC

Table 9–7.   TREATMENT APPROACHES FOR IMPROVEMENT OF OUTCOMES IN OVARIAN CANCER
Optimization of dose/schedule of active agents
High dose with hematologic support (autologous bone marrow transplantation or use of peripheral blood stem cells)
Intraperitoneal therapy
Maintenance therapy
Biologic agents and molecular targeting
New combinations of cytotoxic agents

was 7.5, which was higher than in the other studies comparing carboplatin plus paclitaxel to cisplatin plus paclitaxel.[22] In this study (ie, GOG158), the relative risk of failure was in favor of the carboplatin regimen whereas in the other trials, the risk ratio was slightly greater than 1 in favor of cisplatin plus paclitaxel.[20,21] Consequently, without the benefit of a randomized trial, it is not possible to conclude that an AUC of 7.5 is superior to a lower AUC. In patients who are initially treated with an AUC of 7.5, it is recommended that the dose be reduced if patients develop myelotoxicity and/or neurotoxicity. There also is no evidence that increasing the dose of paclitaxel is necessary. Recently, a randomized study from Italy[28] compared two different doses of paclitaxel (175 mg/m^2 vs 225 mg/m^2), and all patients received carboplatin at an AUC of 6.0. There was no significant improvement in overall survival in patients who received a higher dose of paclitaxel, and it is now accepted that a 175 mg/m^2 3-hour infusion is the optimum dose when administered on an every-3-week schedule together with carboplatin.

As previously described, based on pharmacologic in vitro studies, it is possible that docetaxel may be a more potent analogue than is paclitaxel. Based partly on these findings, a large randomized trial was performed with previously untreated patients who were randomized to carboplatin (AUC = 6.0) plus paclitaxel (175 mg/m^2 3-hour infusion) versus docetaxel (75 mg/m^2 1-hour infusion) and carboplatin (AUC = 6.0).[29] The preliminary results of this study demonstrated no difference in efficacy as disease-free survivals for both treatment arms were essentially identical. There was, however, a substantial difference in toxicity. Patients treated with docetaxel had more myelotoxicity, which led to more episodes of neutropenic fever, the necessity for antibiotics, colony-stimulating factors, and hospitalizations. In contrast, neurotoxicity was the primary toxicity in the patients who were treated with paclitaxel. This trial demonstrates that docetaxel plus carboplatin is an acceptable alternative chemotherapy regimen in appropriate clinical situations.

There has been a great deal of interest in exploring dose-response relationships of cytotoxic drugs in ovarian cancer. Pharmacologic modeling studies have demonstrated a possible advantage for certain cytotoxic agents when those agents are administered directly into the peritoneal cavity. This finding, together with the fact that the primary morbidity of ovarian cancer is peritoneal carcinomatosis, led to a series of phase II and phase III trials exploring the role of the intraperitoneal administration of drugs in patients with optimal stage III disease. In the most recent GOG study,[30] patients with optimal stage III disease were randomized to an experimental regimen consisting of two cycles of high-dose carboplatin (AUC = 9.0) followed by six cycles of intraperitoneal cisplatin (100 mg/m^2) together with paclitaxel (135 mg/m^2 24-hour infusion) or to the standard regimen of cisplatin plus paclitaxel (both drugs being administered intravenously). Despite the fact that the experimental treatment produced a statistically significant improvement in disease-free survival and a borderline improvement in overall survival, the severe toxicity associated with high-dose chemotherapy and intraperitoneal chemotherapy prohibited the further evaluation of this particular regimen. The GOG has completed a subsequent trial with optimal stage III patients; the control arm was intravenous cisplatin plus paclitaxel, and the experimental arm was intraperitoneal cisplatin and paclitaxel as well as intravenous paclitaxel. This study has completed accrual, but no survival data are available. Outside of a clinical trial, intraperitoneal therapy is not recommended for standard use in any subset of patients with ovarian cancer.

HIGH-DOSE CHEMOTHERAPY WITH HEMATOLOGIC SUPPORT

An alternative way to administer high-dose chemotherapy is to use autologous bone marrow transplantation or stem cell support to overcome the toxicity associated with high-dose intravenous chemotherapy. In the United States, no phase III trial of such an approach has been completed in patients with ovarian cancer. Phase II trials have suggested a high response rate and a longer disease-free interval than could be achieved with standard doses in patients with recurrent ovarian cancer, but selection criteria and phase II trials clearly limit any conclusions about efficacy.[31] In European registry studies,[32] the

outcomes from patients with advanced ovarian cancer treated with high-dose chemotherapy appear to be similar to those reported by the GOG for the use of chemotherapy at standard doses (see Table 9–6). Currently, there are no GOG prospective randomized trials comparing high-dose chemotherapy requiring autologous transplantation to standard-dose chemotherapy, but some clinical trials are still in progress in Europe.

NEW CHEMOTHERAPY COMBINATIONS

A series of drugs have been shown to have activity in patients with platinum-resistant disease (Table 9–8).[33–39] Some of these drugs have been evaluated as parts of new combination regimens for previously untreated patients. The SCOTROC trial of CARBO/PAC versus docetaxel/carboplatin has been described.[29] The largest experience with a three-drug combination has been with carboplatin combined with paclitaxel and gemcitabine. In a phase II trial in 24 previously untreated patients with advanced disease, Hanson and colleagues[40] reported an objective response rate of 100%. Based on this high level of activity, European investigators are performing a prospective randomized trial of CARBO/PAC versus the three-drug combination. Investigators at the European Organization for Research and Treatment of Cancer (EORTC) and the National Cancer Institute of Canada (NCIC) are performing a randomized trial of sequential doublets, in which patients are randomized to receive either CARBO/PAC or a regimen of four cycles of cisplatin plus topotecan followed by CARBO/PAC. This trial is based on a phase II trial in untreated patients with advanced ovarian cancer that reported a 78% response rate for a similar sequential-doublet

Table 9–8. CLINICALLY ACTIVE DRUGS IN PATIENTS WITH PLATINUM-RESISTANT OVARIAN CANCER

Drug	References	Response Rate (%)
Oral etoposide	33	33
Topotecan	34	12
Encapsulated doxorubicin	35	24
Gemcitabine	36, 37	18
Paclitaxel (Weekly)	38	25
Vinorelbine	39	17

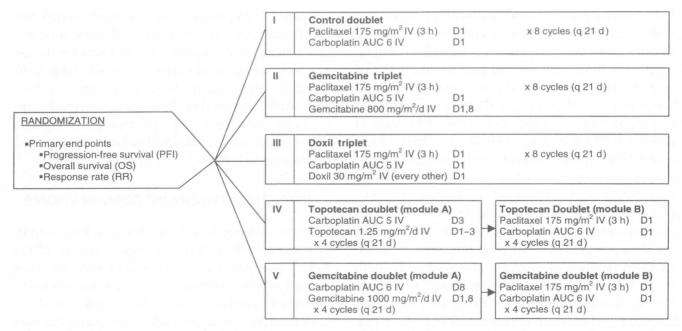

Figure 9–7. Schema for a phase III randomized trial of paclitaxel and carboplatin versus triplet or sequential doublet combinations in patients with epithelial ovarian or primary peritoneal carcinoma (Gynecologic Oncology Group trial 182). (AUC = area under the curve; IV = intravenously.)

approach although significant myelosuppression was observed.[41] European investigators have also performed a randomized trial of paclitaxel plus carboplatin versus a three-drug combination of paclitaxel plus epirubicin plus carboplatin. The preliminary results of that study[42] demonstrated that while the two-drug combination could be administered at full dose, there was no significant improvement in time to progression, and these investigators continue to use CARBO/PAC as the standard regimen.

Investigators from the GOG have taken the lead in performing the largest prospective randomized trial ever performed with previously untreated patients in advanced disease.[43] Patients in this trial will receive one of five different treatment approaches (Figure 9–7). The control arm consists of eight cycles of CARBO/PAC. There will be two three-drug combinations: (1) paclitaxel plus carboplatin and gemcitabine and (2) paclitaxel plus carboplatin plus encapsulated doxorubicin. The other two arms will be sequential doublets in which patients will receive either (1) carboplatin plus topotecan for four cycles followed by paclitaxel plus carboplatin for four cycles or (2) gemcitabine plus carboplatin for four cycles followed by paclitaxel

plus carboplatin for four cycles. Such randomized comparisons will determine whether the new three-drug combinations will improve outcomes, compared to treatment with standard CARBO/PAC.

MAINTENANCE THERAPY

As previously noted, while the majority of patients with advanced ovarian cancer achieve a clinical complete remission, at least 50% of patients will ultimately have a recurrence, at which point a cure is not a realistic possibility. Effective maintenance therapy

Table 9–9. RANDOMIZED TRIALS OF MAINTENANCE THERAPIES FOR OVARIAN CANCER	
Trial	Therapies Compared
GOG/SWOG*	3 vs 12 cycles of paclitaxel (175 mg/m² 3h)
AGO/GINECO	Observation vs topotecan
Italian trial	Observation vs paclitaxel
French trial	High-dose consolidation therapy vs "standard maintenance"
Antibody therapy trial	Antibody against CA 125 (OvaRex) vs placebo

AGO = Arbeitgemeinschaft gynäkologische Onko logie; GOG = Gynecologic Oncology Group; SWOG = .
*Study closed because of improved PFI with 12 cycles of paclitaxel.

should have an impact on both progression-free survival and overall survival. Clinical trials exploring the role of maintenance therapy in patients who do achieve a clinical complete remission with standard therapy are currently in progress (Table 9–9). The GOG trial compared three versus twelve cycles of standard paclitaxel in patients who achieved a clinical complete remission. No survival data are available,[44] but this study has been closed due to an improved time to progression with 12 cycles of treatment. A confirmatory trial in which patients are randomized to observation versus maintenance paclitaxel on an every-3-week schedule is currently in progress in Italy. The preliminary results of a French trial of maintenance therapy with high-dose chemotherapy with hematologic support versus maintenance therapy with standard doses of cytotoxic agents were recently reported.[45] In a subset of patients with drug-sensitive small-volume disease, an improvement in disease-free survival for patients treated with the high-dose regimen was observed. Immunotherapy also has been studied as maintenance therapy in patients who achieve a clinical complete remission. A placebo-controlled trial of an antibody against CA 125 has been completed with patients who achieved a clinical complete remission, but no long-term survival data are yet available from this trial.[46]

FUTURE STUDIES

Molecular-targeting therapies for ovarian cancer and other solid tumors are currently being investigated

Table 9–10. MOLECULAR-TARGETED THERAPY FOR OVARIAN CANCER
Angiogenesis
Matrix metalloproteinase
Signal transduction
Gene therapy
Immunotherapy

(Table 9–10). In particular, the epidermal growth factor receptor complex has been targeted by using either monoclonal antibodies against the receptor (C225) or small molecules that interfere with the adenosine triphosphate–binding sites of the associated tyrosine kinase (OSI774, ZD1839). One of these latter compounds (ZD1839) has recently entered a GOG phase II trial in patients with recurrent ovarian cancer.[47]

Most preclinical studies have demonstrated that molecular-targeted agents have synergistic effects with chemotherapy. In addition, these agents are likely to have the greatest effect when used in combination with chemotherapy in patients with a small volume of residual disease. Upon the completion of the prospective randomized trials in progress throughout the world that are evaluating the new chemotherapy regimens described above, subsequent clinical trials will combine chemotherapy with the molecular-targeted agents as initial therapy for patients with advanced ovarian cancer (Figure 9–8). It is probable that maintenance therapy with vaccines or molecular-targeted therapy will continue after chemotherapy is discontinued, in a further

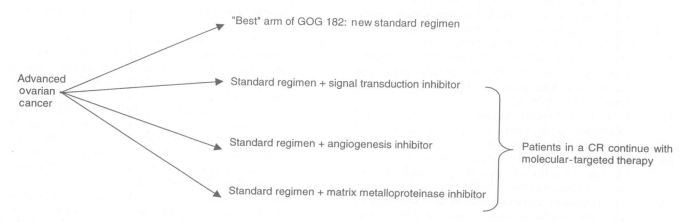

Figure 9–8. Future clinical trials in ovarian cancer. (CR = complete remission; GOG = Gynecologic Oncology Group.)

effort to prevent or delay recurrences. Such a new paradigm of treatment must be confirmed in prospective randomized trials, which await the completion of the current generation of ongoing studies.

REFERENCES

1. Young RC, Walton LA, Ellenberg SS, et al. Adjuvant therapy in stage I and stage II epithelial ovarian cancer. Results of two prospective randomized trials. N Engl J Med 1990; 322:1021–7.
2. Advanced Ovarian Cancer Trialists Group. Chemotherapy in advanced ovarian cancer: an overview of randomized clinical trials. BMJ 1991;303:884–93.
3. Aabo K, Adams M, Adnitt P, et al. Chemotherapy in advanced ovarian cancer: four systematic meta-analyses of individual patients data from 37 randomized trials. Advanced Ovarian Cancer Trialists Group. Br J Cancer 1998;78:1479–87.
4. Ozols RF. Update of the NCCN ovarian cancer practice guidelines. Oncology (Huntingt) 1997;11:95–105.
5. Go RS, Adjei AA. Review of the comparative pharmacology and clinical activity of cisplatin and carboplatin. J Clin Oncol 1999;17:409–22.
6. Lai GM, Ozols RF, Smyth JF, et al. Enhanced DNA repair and resistance to cisplatin in human ovarian cancer. Biochem Pharmacol 1988;37:4597–600.
7. Lai GM, Ozols RF, Young RC, et al. Effect of glutathione on DNA repair in cisplatin-resistant human ovarian cancer cell lines. J Natl Cancer Inst 1989;81:535–9.
8. Calvert AH, Newell DR, Gumbrell LA, et al. Carboplatin dosage: prospective evaluation of a simple formula based on renal function. J Clin Oncol 1989;7:1748–56.
9. Jodrell DI, Egorin MJ, Canetta RM, et al. Relationships between carboplatin exposure and tumor response and toxicity in patients with ovarian cancer. J Clin Oncol 1992;10:520–8.
10. Dumontet C, Sikic BI. Mechanisms of action of and resistance to antitubulin agents: microtubule dynamics, drug transport, and cell death. J Clin Oncol 1999;17:1061–70.
11. Rowinsky EK, Tolcher AW. Antimicrobule agents. In: DeVita VT, Rosenberg SA, Hellman S, editors. Cancer: principles and practice of oncology. 6th ed. Philadelphia: Lippincott, Williams and Wilkins 2001. p. 431.
12. Fracasso PM, Brady MF, Moore DH, et al. Phase II study of paclitaxel and valspodar (PSC 833) in refractory ovarian carcinoma: a Gynecologic Oncology Group study. J Clin Oncol 2001;19:2975–82.
13. Rowinsky EK, Gilbert MR, McGuire WP, et al. Sequences of Taxol and cisplatin: a phase I and pharmacologic study. J Clin Oncol 1991;9:1692–703.
14. Bookman MA, Kloth DD, Kover PE, et al. Short-course intravenous prophylaxis for paclitaxel-related hypersensitivity reactions. Ann Oncol 1997;8:611–4.
15. Piccart MJ, Gore M, ten Bokkel Huinink, et al. Docetaxel: an active new drug for treatment of advanced epithelial ovarian cancer. J Natl Cancer Inst 1995;87:676–81.
16. Thigpen JT, Blessing JA, Ball H, et al. Phase II trial of paclitaxel in patients with progressive ovarian carcinoma after platinum-based chemotherapy: a Gynecologic Oncology Group study. J Clin Oncol 1994;12:1748–53.
17. McGuire WP, Hoskins WJ, Brady MR, et al. Cyclophosphamide and cisplatin compared with paclitaxel and cisplatin in patients with stage III and stage IV ovarian cancer. N Engl J Med 1996;334:1–6.
18. Piccart MJ, Bertelsen K, James K, et al. Randomized intergroup trial of cisplatin-paclitaxel versus cisplatin-cyclophosphamide in women with advanced epithelial ovarian cancer: three-year results. J Natl Cancer Inst 2000;92:699–708.
19. Bookman MA, McGuire WP, Kilpatrick D, et al. Carboplatin and paclitaxel in ovarian carcinoma: a phase I study of the Gynecologic Oncology Group. J Clin Oncol 1996;14:1895–902.
20. duBois A, Luenck HJ, Meier W, et al. Cisplatin/paclitaxel vs carboplatin/paclitaxel in ovarian cancer: update of an Arbeitsgemeinshaft Gynaekologische Onkologie (AGO) Study Group trial [Abstract 1374]. Proc Am Soc Clin Oncol 1999;18:356a.
21. Neijt JP, Engelholm SA, Tuxen MK, et al. Exploratory phase III study of paclitaxel and cisplatin versus paclitaxel and carboplatin in advanced ovarian cancer. J Clin Oncol 2000;18:3084–92.
22. The ICON3 Randomised Trial. Paclitaxel plus carboplatin versus standard chemotherapy with either single-agent carboplatin or cyclophosphamide, doxorubicin, and cisplatin in women with ovarian cancer. Lancet 2002;360:505–15.
23. Ozols RF, Rubin SC, Thomas G, Robboy SJ. Epithelial ovarian cancer. In: Hoskins WJ, Perez CA, Young RC, editors. Principles and practice of gynecologic oncology. 2nd ed. Philadelphia: JB Lippincott Co. 1997. p. 919–86.
24. National Institutes of Health Consensus Development Conference Statement. Ovarian cancer: screening, treatment and follow-up. Gynecol Oncol 1994;55:S4–S14.
25. Rustin GJS, Marples M, Nelstrop AE, et al. Use of CA-125 to define progression of ovarian cancer in patients with persistently elevated levels. J Clin Oncol 2001;19:4054–7.
26. Hatch KD, Beecham JB, Blessing JA, Creasman WT. Responsiveness of patients with advanced ovarian carcinoma to tamoxifen. Cancer 1991;68:269–71.
27. Van Der Velden J, Gitsch G, Wain GV, et al. Tamoxifen in patients with advanced epithelial ovarian cancer. Int J Gynecol Cancer 1995;4:301–5.
28. Scarfone G, Parazzini F, Sciatta C, et al. A multicenter randomized trial comparing two different doses of Taxol (T) plus a fixed dose of carboplatin (C) in advanced ovarian cancer (AOC) [abstract 816]. Proc Am Soc Clin Oncol 2001;20:205a.
29. Vasey P for the Scottish Gynaecologic Cancer Trials Group. Preliminary results of the SCOTROC trial: a phase III comparison of paclitaxel-carboplatin (PC) and docetaxel-carboplatin (DC) as first-line chemotherapy for stage Ic-IV epithelial ovarian cancer (EOC) [abstract 804]. Proc Am Soc Clin Oncol 2001;20:202a.
30. Markman M, Bundy BN, Alberts DS, et al. Phase III trial of standard-dose intravenous cisplatin plus paclitaxel versus moderately high-dose carboplatin followed by intravenous paclitaxel and intraperitoneal cisplatin in small-

volume stage III ovarian carcinoma: an intergroup study of the Gynecologic Oncology Group, Southwestern Oncology Group, and Eastern Cooperative Oncology Group. J Clin Oncol 2001;19:1001–7.

31. Stiff PJ, Veum-Stone J, Lazarus HM, et al. High-dose chemotherapy and autologous stem-cell transplantation for ovarian cancer: an autologous blood and marrow transplant registry report. Ann Intern Med 2000;133:504–15.

32. Ledermann JA, Herd R, Maraninchi D, et al. High dose chemotherapy in ovarian cancer: an analysis of the experience of the European Group for Blood and Marrow Transplant (EBMT) over 7 years [Abstract 1391]. Proc Am Soc Clin Oncol 1999;18:360a.

33. Rose PG, Blessing JA, Mayer AR, Homesley HD. Prolonged oral etoposide as second-line therapy for platinum-resistant and platinum-sensitive ovarian carcinoma: a Gynecologic Oncology Group study. J Clin Oncol 1998;16:405–10.

34. Bookman MA, Malmstrom H, Bolis G, et al. Topotecan for the treatment of advanced epithelial ovarian cancer: an open-label phase II study in patients treated after prior chemotherapy that contained cisplatin or carboplatin and paclitaxel. J Clin Oncol 1998;16:3345–52.

35. Muggia FM, Hainsworth JD, Jeffers S, et al. Phase II study of liposomal doxorubicin in refractory ovarian cancer: antitumor activity and toxicity modification by liposomal encapsulation. J Clin Oncol 1997;15:987–93.

36. Lund B, Paaske Hansen O, Theilade K, et al. Phase II study of gemcitabine (2',2'-difluorodeoxycytidine) in previously treated ovarian cancer patients. J Natl Cancer Inst 1994; 86:1530–3.

37. Markman M, Kennedy A, Webster K, et al. Phase 2 trial of single-agent gemcitabine (GEM) in platinum (PLAT)/ paclitaxel (PAC) refractory ovarian cancer (ROC) [Abstract 813]. Proc Am Soc Clin Oncol 2001;20:204a.

38. Markman M, Baker ME, Hall JB, et al. Phase 2 trial of weekly single agent paclitaxel (P) in platinum (PLAT) and paclitaxel-refractory ovarian cancer (OC) [abstract 1567]. Proc Am Soc Clin Oncol 2000;19:396a.

39. Bajetta E, DiLeo A, Biganzoli L, et al. Phase II study of vinorelbine in patients with pretreated advanced ovarian cancer: activity in platinum-resistant disease. J Clin Oncol 1996;14:2546–51.

40. Hansen SW, Anderson H, Boman K, et al. Gemcitabine, carboplatin, and paclitaxel (GCP) as first-line treatment of ovarian cancer FIGO stages IIB-IV [abstract 1379]. Proc Am Soc Clin Oncol 1999;18:357a.

41. Hoskins P, Eisenhauer E, Vergote I, et al. Phase II feasibility study of sequential couplets of cisplatin/topotecan followed by paclitaxel/cisplatin as primary treatment for advanced epithelial ovarian cancer: a National Cancer Institute of Canada Clinical Trials Group study. J Clin Oncol 2000;18:4038–44.

42. duBois A, Weber B, Pfisterer J, et al. Epirubicin/paclitaxel/ carboplatin (TEC) vs. paclitaxel/carboplatin (TC) in first-line treatment of ovarian cancer FIGO stages IIb-IV. Interim results of an AGO-GINECO Intergroup phase III trial [Abstract 805]. Proc Am Soc Clin Oncol 2001; 20:202a.

43. A phase III randomized trial of paclitaxel and carboplatin versus triplet or sequential doublet combinations in patients with epithelial ovarian or primary peritoneal carcinoma. Gynecologic Oncology Group Protocol 182 [ongoing 909 trial]. Study chair: Bookman MA.

44. Markman M, Liu PY, Wilczynski S, et al. Phase 3 randomized trial of 12 vs. 3 months of single agent paclitaxel in patients with advanced ovarian cancer who attained a clinically-defined complete response to platinum/paclitaxel-based chemotherapy: A Southwest Oncology Group and Gynecologic Oncology Group trial. proc Soc Gynecol Oncol 2002;66:1.

45. Cure H, Battista C, Guastalla J, et al. Phase III randomized trial of high-dose chemotherapy (HDC) and peripheral blood stem cell (PBSC) support as consolidation in patients (pts) with responsive low-burden advanced ovarian cancer (AOC): preliminary results of a GINECO/ FNCLCC/SFGM-TC study [abstract 815]. Proc Am Soc Clin Oncol 2001;20:204a.

46. Berek J, Ehlen T, Gordon A, et al. Interim analysis of a double blind study of Ovarex™ mAb B43.13 (OV) versus placebo (PBO) in patients with ovarian cancer [abstract 837]. Proc Am Soc Clin Oncol 2001;20:210a.

47. A phase II trial of ZD1839 (Iressa™) (NSC#715055) in the treatment of persistent or recurrent epithelial ovarian or primary peritoneal carcinoma. Gynecologic Oncology Group Protocol 170. Study chair: Schilder R.

10

Radiation Therapy

WAYNE H. PINOVER, DO
RAJESH V. IYER, MD

Epithelial ovarian cancer, in contrast to other pelvic malignancies, is unique in its predilection for dissemination throughout the peritoneal cavity. While pelvic radiation therapy (RT) (compared to observation alone) may decrease pelvic relapses, pelvic RT has not reduced the overall relapse rates due to relapses occurring throughout the peritoneal cavity.[1,2] In a small study by Hreshchyshyn and colleagues, recurrence outside the pelvis was noted in 3% of women receiving single-agent melphalan, compared to 26% of women receiving pelvic RT.[2] Subsequently, effective postoperative adjuvant RT must be directed toward the entire peritoneal cavity.

This review will discuss the use of whole abdominopelvic RT (WAR) and the intraperitoneal instillation of radioactive chromic phosphate (P32) in the treatment of ovarian cancer.

WHOLE ABDOMINOPELVIC RADIATION THERAPY

Whole Abdominopelvic RT Following Primary Debulking Surgery

Long-term single-institution experiences have demonstrated the potentially curative role of WAR.[3–6] Stanford University investigators reported on the use of WAR in 152 cases of stage I through stage III ovarian cancer. The 15-year freedom-from-relapse and overall survival rates were 44% and 32%, respectively. Independent predictors of relapse were tumor grade, age, amount of residual disease, stage, and histopathology. For women with no residual disease or minimal residual disease following surgery, the 15-year freedom-from-relapse rate was 62%, compared with a rate of 14% for those with gross residual disease.[5] Fuller and colleagues described the benefit of WAR over subtotal WAR in 106 cases of stage I through stage IIIA ovarian cancer. In a favorable group with no residual disease or minimal residual disease, total WAR resulted in a 71% 10-year actuarial relapse-free survival rate, compared to a 40% rate for those receiving subtotal WAR.[3] In a similar group of favorable stage I through stage III ovarian cancer cases treated with WAR at Yale University, the 10-year actuarial overall survival rate was 77%, with 87% local control of abdominopelvic disease.[4] These reports demonstrate that ovarian cancer patients can experience long-term survival following adjuvant WAR. For patients to benefit from WAR, treatment must include the entire peritoneal cavity and pelvis as demonstrated above, and its use must be limited to particular patient subsets.[3]

Essential to the use of WAR is the identification of those patients who are most likely to benefit from treatment. Patients with a low risk of relapse following total abdominal hysterectomy and bilateral salpingo-oophorectomy (TAH-BSO) are least likely to benefit from WAR. This would be true for stage IA Figo grade I ovarian cancer when the risk of relapse is approximately 0 to 10%.[2,7] Equally unlikely to benefit are women at significant risk for relapse in the peritoneal cavity and systemically, despite maximally tolerated doses of WAR, such as women with stage IV ovarian cancer or those cases in which significant amounts of residual disease remain after surgery.[2,7] Some of the most influential studies of adjuvant WAR for ovarian cancer have been published by Dembo and colleagues at the Princess Margaret Hospital (PMH) in Toronto, Canada.[7-17] These investigators fully described the prognostic factors in women who are receiving WAR and identified those subsets of ovarian cancer patients most likely to benefit from WAR. Multivariate analysis of prognostic factors for relapse-free rates in ovarian cancer patients at PMH who were receiving WAR revealed histopathology, stage, grade, and amount of residual disease following surgery to be independent predictors.[15] By using various combinations of these prognostic factors, patients could be placed into low-risk, intermediate-risk, and high-risk categories, as demonstrated in Table 10–1. The low-risk group demonstrated a 5-year relapse-free survival rate of 96% and included only patients with stage I grade I ovarian cancer without ascites or dense adhesions.[18] These patients have such a low risk of recurrence that adjuvant therapy is not warranted. High-risk patients have a 5-year relapse-free rate of approximately 30% and require therapy that is more aggressive than WAR used alone. The intermediate-risk group demonstrated a 67% disease-free survival rate at 10 years. These patients, who are most likely to benefit from WAR, include those with primarily stage I and stage II disease. Stage III disease is appropriate for WAR as long as it is well differentiated and there is < 2 cm of macroscopic residual tumor limited to the pelvis. Because of dose limitations of the upper abdominal structures, it is important that no macroscopic residual tumor remains in the upper abdomen and that pelvic residual disease is < 2 cm.

As mentioned, Fuller and colleagues described long-term results of WAR in 106 women with stage I through stage III disease.[3] Multivariate analysis showed that stage, technique, and the amount of residual tumor were the only important predictors of outcome. The women favored were those with stage I through IIIA disease, without postoperative residual disease or with < 0.5 cm of abdominal residual disease and/or < 2 cm of pelvic residual disease. When total WAR was used, this favorable group had a 10-year relapse-free survival rate of 71%. When radiotherapy techniques that omitted portions of the peritoneal cavity were used, this favorable group had a significantly reduced 10-year relapse-free survival rate of 40%. Toxicity was tolerable, with surgical bowel complications noted in 7% of women after WAR.

Weiser and colleagues reported the results of WAR in 84 women, 81% of whom had stage II or stage III ovarian cancer.[6] Important predictors of outcome were stage and residual tumor after laparotomy. Stage II patients demonstrated a 67% survival rate at 10 years, compared to 20% for stage III patients. However, the majority of stage II patients had no gross residual disease after surgery. In the stage II and stage III patients, the 10-year survival rate was 59% for patients with no gross residual disease, 42% for patients with residual disease of < 2 cm, and 10% for patients with residual disease of > 2 cm. The toxicity of WAR was significant, with a 17% rate of serious morbidity. Eight of the 14 patients experiencing serious morbidity required surgery for bowel obstruction without evidence of

Table 10–1. PROGNOSTIC SUBGROUPINGS IN OVARIAN CANCER STAGES I TO III, ACCORDING TO STAGE, GRADE, AND RESIDUUM				
Stage	Residuum (cm)	Grade 1	Grade 2	Grade 3
I	0	Low risk		
II	0		Intermediate risk	
II	< 2			
III	0			High Risk
III	< 2			

Adapted from Dembo AJ.[15]

recurrent or persistent tumor. This rate of morbidity is attributable to the technique of WAR. When open field techniques of WAR were used, the total dose delivered was 4,000 cGy, which is significantly higher than doses considered standard at present. In addition, more than one-third of patients were treated by moving-strip technique. The moving-strip technique has previously been associated with increased toxicity when compared to the open field technique.[8]

These reports of the long-term efficacy of WAR were justification for prospective randomized trials comparing WAR to chemotherapy after primary surgery. Table 10–2 summarizes the results of these trials. The prospective randomized trial from M.D. Anderson Hospital is important for a number of reasons.[19] Women with stages I to III ovarian cancer and with < 2 cm of residual disease were randomized to WAR (2,600 to 2,800 cGy WAR by moving-strip technique in 2.5 weeks, followed by 2,000 cGy pelvic RT in 2 weeks) or melphalan (0.2 mg/kg/d for 5 days, repeated every 4 weeks for 12 cycles). Preliminary 2-year no-evidence-of-disease results were reported along with 5-year survival rates despite few patients having been treated for more than 5 years. The general conclusion from the study was that the overall 5-year survival rates were essentially equivalent but that chemotherapy appeared to improve survival in patients with stage II and III ovarian cancer. Additionally, it was felt that increased toxicity and costs were associated with WAR. Criticisms of the M.D. Anderson study include short follow-up, inadequate RT technique, and the lack of stratification for the important predictors of outcome, such as stage, grade, and residual disease. The results of this trial, along with that of another influential study, led to the widespread abandonment of abdominopelvic RT in the definitive management of ovarian cancer in North America.

The second study that had a negative impact on the use of WAR was a prospective randomized trial from the National Cancer Institute of Canada (NCIC).[20] High-risk patients with stage I and IIA disease in addition to stage IIB and stage III disease confined to the pelvis were randomized to WAR (2,250 cGy in 10 fractions by open field or moving-strip technique, following 2,250 cGy in 10 fractions to the pelvis), pelvic RT (4,500 cGy in 20 fractions)

and melphalan (8 mg/m^2/d for 4 days, every 4 weeks for 18 months), or pelvic RT (4,500 cGy in 20 fractions) and intraperitoneal chromic phosphate (P32). The pelvic RT and P32 arm was discontinued due to increased late toxicities (31% bowel obstruction). There were equivalent 5-year survivals for all treatment arms, without any obvious benefit of WAR. However, the NCIC study demonstrated the importance of good technique, as poorer survival was seen in those who received inadequate coverage of the entire peritoneal cavity and pelvis. The major criticism of this study relates to the higher-than-expected incidence of suboptimal RT technique.

Dembo and colleagues reported the results of a prospective randomized trial at PMH, randomizing women with stage IB to III ovarian cancer to WAR (2,250 cGy in 10 fractions by moving-strip technique plus 2,250 cGy pelvic RT) or pelvic RT (4,500 cGy) with or without chlorambucil (6 mg/d for 2 years). Of the women who underwent TAH-BSO, a significant benefit in 5-year and 10-year survival was noted in favor of WAR. Patients with incomplete surgery fared poorly, without differences by treatment arm. Important points of this report are that treatment arms were comparable with respect to prognostic variables, pathology was reviewed by a single pathologist, and the study was performed at a single institution. A criticism of this study is that there is uncertainty in regard to the treatment arms with respect to stage because meticulous surgical staging was not performed.

In a phase III trial from the Danish Ovarian Cancer Group, women with Stage IB to II ovarian cancer were randomized to WAR (2,250 cGy pelvic RT in 10 fractions and 2,250 cGy WAR via a modified open field technique) or to pelvic RT (4,500 cGy in 20 fractions) and cyclophosphamide (200 mg/m^2 for 5 days, every 4 weeks for 12 cycles).[21] No significant differences in 4-year survival were detected. WAR was associated with an 8% incidence of gastrointestinal complication requiring surgery.

The Northwest Oncologic Cooperative Group (NOCG) performed the only study using more conventional modern chemotherapy.[22] Ovarian cancer patients with stage IA or IB disease with poor differentiation, stage IC disease, and stage II disease were randomized to WAR (4,320 cGy in 24 fractions to the pelvis and 3,020 cGy WAR) or chemotherapy (cis-

Table 10-2. EARLY-STAGE OVARIAN CANCER: RANDOMIZED TRIALS OF WHOLE ABDOMINOPELVIC RADIATION THERAPY

Trial	Period	Stage	F/U (yr)	Residual (CM)	Treatment Arms	No.	Technique	Outcome (%)	Toxicity
MDA (113)	1969–74	I	NS	<2	WAR vs melphalan	14	MS	85 (2 yr NED)	NR
						28		90	NR
		II	NS	<2	WAR vs melphalan	37	MS	55 (2 yr NED)	NR
						29		58	NR
		III	NS	<2	WAR vs melphalan	19	MS	53 (2 yr NED)	NR
						22		35	NR
		I – III	NS	<2	WAR vs melphalan	70	MS	70 (5 yr S)	25/70 GI complications
						79		~70 (5 yr S)	32/79 Myelosuppression
PMH (122)	1971–75	IB–III	7 min	None or small	WAR	50	MS	64 (10 yr S)	3% Bowel surgery
					Pelvic RT + chlorambucil	51		40*	3% Fatal leukemia
NCIC (56)	1975–84	I–IIA (high risk) IIB, III (pelvic dis only)	8 med	NR	WAR	107	MS or OF	62 (5 yr S)	7% Surgical bowel obstruction
					Pelvic RT + melphalan	106		61	4 Acute leukemia
					Pelvic RT + IP P32	44		66**	25% Bowel obstruction
Danish (110)	1981–87	IB, IC, II	NR	NR	WAR	60	OF†	63 (4 yr S)	8% Bowel surgery
					Pelvic RT + cyclophosphamide	58		55**	25% Hemorrhagic cystitis
NOCG (7)	1985–89	Ia+b G3, IC + II	5	NR	WAR	25	OF	68 (4 yr S)	28% G 3–4 diarrhea/enteritis
					Cisplatin + cyclophosphamide	44		73**	71% G 3–4 nausea/vomiting

†Modified open technique.
WAR = whole abdominopelvic radiation therapy; MDA = M. D. Anderson Hospital; MS = moving strip; OF = open field; NR = not reported; NS = not significant; NOCG = Northwest Oncologic Cooperative Group; PMH = Princess Margaret Hospital; IP P32 = intraperitoneal chromic phosphate; NED = no evidence of disease; S = survival; dis = disease; F/U = follow-up; G = grade; GI = gastrointestinal; med = median; min = minimum; RT = radiation therapy.
*p = .007; **p = not significant.

platin [50 mg/m^2] and cyclophosphamide [600 mg/m^2 per day, every 28 days for 6 cycles]). The use of 18 MV photons for WAR is of concern as this may underdose the superficial peritoneum. Due to poor accrual and serious protocol compliance problems, the trial was closed prematurely. Up to 15% of patients had incomplete surgical staging. While protocol compliance was 94% in the chemotherapy arm, it was only 67% in the WAR arm. When analyzed by intention to treat, survival and relapse-free survival rates were 71% versus 53% ($p = .16$) and 74% versus 50% ($p = .07$) for the chemotherapy and WAR arms, respectively. Considering the excessive protocol violations in the WAR arm, an analysis according to treatment received was performed. This secondary analysis demonstrated more comparable survival and relapse-free survival rates of 73% versus 68% ($p = .7$) and 73% versus 60% ($p = .3$) for chemotherapy and WAR, respectively. Of all the randomized trials, the NOCG trial had the greatest potential because the treatment arms being compared could be considered to be optimal chemotherapy and optimal RT. Unfortunately, the NOCG trial could not answer the question of which treatment is better for ovarian cancer because of poor accrual, low protocol compliance, and early termination of the trial.

In summary, pelvic RT following complete surgical staging is inadequate as the entire peritoneal cavity and pelvis are at risk for recurrence. The women who may benefit from WAR are those who are considered to be at intermediate risk for recurrence, as demonstrated by Dembo and colleagues.[15] The need for trials that compare WAR to platinum/paclitaxel chemotherapy regimens continues to exist. However, due to the existing prevailing biases that would likely preclude the completion of such a trial (as the NOCG experience demonstrated), such a comparison is not likely to be undertaken. Despite evidence of efficacy, WAR is not commonly used in the United States for ovarian cancer patients with intermediate-risk early-stage disease or optimally debulked advanced-stage disease.

Consolidative Whole Abdominopelvic RT after Chemotherapy

Despite the use of platinum-containing chemotherapy regimens, the 5-year overall survival rate in advanced ovarian cancer is only approximately 20%. Considering the known effectiveness of the three treatment modalities in particular subsets of ovarian cancer patients, it was natural to evaluate the combination of surgery, chemotherapy, and consolidative abdominopelvic RT in advanced disease. A number of investigators have evaluated WAR as consolidation after chemotherapy in poor-prognosis ovarian cancer.[23–28]

In a phase II study, PMH investigators documented the benefit of combined modality therapy compared to the outcome of a matched historical control group receiving WAR alone.[26] Forty-four high-risk optimally cytoreduced stage II or stage III ovarian cancer patients received six cycles of cisplatin/doxorubicin/cyclophosphamide chemotherapy, followed 4 to 6 weeks later by 2,500 cGy WAR with a 1,500 to 2,250 cGy pelvic boost. Compared to the historical control group, the median survival was extended from 2.4 to 5.7 years. There was a significant increase in the relapse-free survival rate, from 22% to 43% at 5 years. Although an improvement in cause-specific survival at 5 years was noted (32% vs 54%), this was not statistically significant, most likely due to the small patient numbers. Gastrointestinal toxicity was tolerable, with 6% of patients requiring surgery for bowel complications after combined therapy, compared to 2% of patients in the historical control RT alone group. Myelosuppression was the cause of delay in completing RT in 19 patients. However, this report could not determine whether combined-modality therapy was of more benefit than was chemotherapy alone. Pickel and colleagues prospectively randomized 64 women (85% with stage III disease) to WAR with pelvic boost or to observation following six cycles of carboplatin-based chemotherapy.[29] All of the women were without evidence of disease by clinical examination, computed tomography (CT), and tumor markers, including CA 125, prior to randomization. Second-look surgery was not performed. The toxicity of WAR was moderate; 17% of the patients discontinued treatment because of myelosuppression. A significant improvement in overall survival rate at 5 years was seen in those being treated with WAR (59% vs 33%). Similar significant benefits in relapse-free survival were seen.

Goldhirsch and colleagues reported the results of a nonrandomized trial of WAR after cisplatin/melphalan chemotherapy and second-look laparotomy.[30] Patients achieving a negative result on second-look laparotomy demonstrated a significantly improved 3-year progression-free survival rate of 83% following consolidative WAR, compared to 49% for those not receiving WAR. Temporary or permanent interruptions in WAR, noted in 8 of 24 patients, were associated with an increased relapse rate of 33%, compared to 8% for those patients whose WAR was completed without interruption. Benefit of WAR could not be demonstrated in women with residual disease found at second-look surgery.

Thomas, in a review of 28 trials (a total of 713 patients) that investigated the role of consolidative WAR following surgery and chemotherapy, found the results to be generally disappointing.[31] It was noted that a variety of factors limit the ability of these studies to answer the question of whether consolidative WAR is beneficial. These factors include inconsistent patient selection criteria and the diversity of surgical procedures, chemotherapy regimens, and RT techniques used in the studies. Although the data were incomplete in many of the studies, Thomas was able to show the importance of the extent of residual disease prior to RT. The disease-free survival rates at variable times were 76% for those without residual disease, 49% for those with microscopic or < 5 mm residual disease, and 17% for those with greater-than-microscopic residual disease.

In an effort to determine a possible role for WAR after limited cisplatin-based chemotherapy in women with < 1 cm residual disease after second-look laparotomy, the Gynecologic Oncology Group (GOG) performed a prospective phase II trial in 47 women with optimally cytoreduced stage III ovarian cancer. Hyperfractionated WAR was used, delivering 80 cGy twice daily, for a total dose of 3040 cGy. This was followed by a pelvic boost in 63% of the 35 patients completing WAR. The median survival for all eligible patients and for those completing WAR was 39 months and 46 months, respectively. WAR was acutely well tolerated, and the incidence of late complications (in the absence of recurrent disease) was 8.6%. Although women who received a pelvic boost experienced no pelvic failures (compared to a 15%

rate of pelvic failure when the pelvic boost was omitted), the pelvic boost had no impact on overall survival and was associated with a 50% incidence of subsequent gastrointestinal toxicity.[23]

Table 10–3 shows the results of three prospective randomized trials comparing consolidative chemotherapy with WAR after second-look laparotomy. In the West Midlands Ovarian Cancer Group trial reported by Lawton and colleagues,[27] patients were randomized to receive chlorambucil or to undergo WAR by moving-strip technique after second-look laparotomy. Despite the increased number of patients without residual disease who were receiving chemotherapy, a statistically significant improvement in survival could not be detected, especially when controlling for residual disease and initial stage. Twenty-eight percent of patients who received RT experienced a delay in treatment. A major criticism of this report is that 50% of patients were unable to complete the planned therapy. Despite the improved survival for patients receiving consolidative chemotherapy in the study reported by Bruzzone and colleagues, even the authors noted that the study was flawed by small numbers and an increased incidence of negative second-look surgeries in the chemotherapy arm.[24] In the North Thames Ovary Study trial reported by Lambert and colleagues, women were randomized to carboplatin chemotherapy or to WAR after negative second-look surgery.[28] No significant advantage was found in either treatment arm. However, as noted by Lanciano and colleagues, a pelvic boost of RT was used in only 8 of 58 patients, and this may have contributed to the negative results.[32] Presently, consolidative WAR after primary surgery and chemotherapy is of unproven benefit.

Salvage Whole Abdominopelvic RT

The majority of women with advanced ovarian cancer will unfortunately experience disease recurrence in the pelvis or in the peritoneal cavity. These women are candidates for salvage RT. Numerous investigators have reported the results of WAR for salvage of recurrent or persistent ovarian cancer after chemotherapy with platinum-containing chemotherapy agents.[31,33–39] These results are shown in Table 10–4.

Schray and colleagues reported a 30% disease-free survival rate at 3 years in 53 patients who were treated with WAR for residual or recurrent ovarian cancer following chemotherapy.[37] Seventy-five percent of the recurrences were in the abdomen. The subset of patients with the combination of high-grade tumor, initial residual disease of 2 cm before chemotherapy, and macroscopic tumor after second-look surgery did not benefit from WAR. Reddy and colleagues demonstrated an overall 4-year survival rate of 23% for patients with micro/macroscopic residual disease with significant differences according to whether patients were noted to have microscopic or macroscopic residual disease prior to WAR.[35] Despite the use of WAR, 90% of the recurrences involved the abdominopelvic cavity. There was absolutely no benefit seen in patients with residual disease in the upper abdomen. Similar findings were reported by Baker and colleagues; patients with disease limited to the pelvis had an overall 4-year survival rate of 60%, compared to 16% when the upper abdomen was involved.[38] Similar significant differences in outcome were seen according to the extent of residual disease. Sedlacek and colleagues reported a 15% overall survival rate at 5 years, with significant differences seen depending on the amount of residual disease prior to WAR.[36] The average survival for patients with microscopic residual disease was 63 months, compared to 9 months for those with > 2 cm residual disease. Stanford investigators described a 53% disease-specific survival rate at 5 years for women with < 1.5 cm residual disease, as opposed to 0% for patients with > 1.5 cm residual disease after WAR for platinum-refractory recurrent or persistent ovarian cancer.[39]

In an effort to decrease relapse rates and improve tolerance, altered RT fractionation schemes have been used. Eifel and colleagues treated 34 patients who had a positive second-look laparotomy with twice-daily split-course WAR.[34] A total of 30 Gy was delivered in 1.0 Gy twice-daily fractions, with a 3-week treatment break after 15 Gy. The 3-year overall and relapse-free survival rates were 24% and 15%, respectively. Patients with microscopic residual disease at second-look surgery had a 3-year survival rate of 50%; there were no survivors in the group of women with macroscopic < 2 cm residual disease. Recurrences in the abdominal cavity occurred in 87% of those patients who relapsed. Fourteen patients experienced small-

Table 10-3. EARLY-STAGE OVARIAN CANCER: RANDOMIZED TRIALS OF WHOLE ABDOMINOPELVIC RADIATION THERAPY VERSUS CONSOLIDATIVE CHEMOTHERAPY										
Trial (Reference No.)	Period	Median F/U (mo)	Second-Look Surgery	Consolidative Treatment Arms	No.	Stage III/IV (%)	Grade 2/3 (%)	No Residual† (%)	Overall Median Survival (mo)	Median Survival in Optimally Debulked Pts
West Midlands Ovarian Group (27)	1981–85	NS	Yes	Chlorambucil	53	92	68	38	20.6*	31 mo**
				WAR	56	95	63	13	15.5	21 mo
Bruzzone et al (24)	1985–88	22	Yes	Cisplatin	21	100	62	71	NR	100%†‡
				WAR	20	100	65	50	24	55%§
North Thames Ovary Group Study (28)	1985–89	NS	Yes	Carboplatin	59	86	85	71	32§	22 mo§
				WAR	58	84	78	69	32§	27 mo§

†Percent with no residual disease after second-look surgery.
‡Percent 2-year survival in optimally debulked patients.
§Estimates from curves.
F/U = follow-up; NR = not reported; NS = not significant; WAR = whole abdominopelvic radiation therapy.
*$p = .32$; **$p = .58$; ***$p = .04$; ****$p = .89$; *****$p = .69$.

Table 10–4. OUTCOMES IN SELECTED REPORTS OF SALVAGE WHOLE ABDOMINOPELVIC RADIATION THERAPY

Author (Reference No.)	N	Overall Survival (%)	Survival (%) by Extent of Residual Disease Prior to WAR		% Recurrences Involving Abdominopelvic Cavity
			Microscopic Residual	Macroscopic Residual	
Schray(37)	52	35 (3 yr)	54*	11	75
Reddy(35)	44	23 (4 yr)	37	9	90
Sedlacek(36)	27	15 (5 yr)	36	7	89
Baker(38)	47	32 (4 yr)	48	11	NR
Cmelak(39)	41	47 (5 yr)†	40‡	0	NR
Eifel(34)	34	24 (3 yr)	50	0	87
Fein(33)	28	21 (5 yr)	27	18	96

N = number of patients in each report; NR = not reported; WAR = whole abdominopelvic radiation therapy.
*< 2 cm vs > 2 cm.
†Disease-specific survival.
‡< 1.5 cm vs > 1.5 cm.

bowel obstruction, but all of these patients had known recurrent abdominal disease. No bowel obstruction was documented in the 5 patients who were thought to be disease free. Fein and colleagues delivered twice-daily hyperfractionated radiation to 28 women with stage III ovarian cancer who showed persistent disease at second-look surgery.[33] The 5-year actuarial overall survival rate was 21%, with significant differences depending on the extent of residual disease. Abdominopelvic recurrences were seen in 22 of the 23 patients who relapsed. Acute toxicity was tolerable, with only 2 patients requiring a treatment break. A 14% incidence of late bowel obstruction was noted, but half of these patients had evidence of recurrent abdominal disease.

Investigators at Memorial Sloan-Kettering Cancer Center reported on the use of limited RT fields for salvage of patients with recurrent or persistent disease.[40] Thirty-five patients received RT to a field encompassing only the site of disease. WAR was not used. The median and progression-free survivals were 40 months and 14 months, respectively. Abdominopelvic recurrence occurred in 78% of the patients who relapsed. Only 14% of patients experienced acute toxicity requiring a 1-week treatment break. The rate of serious bowel complications was 9%.

The acute toxicity of salvage WAR ranges from approximately 15 to 55%; 10 to 29% of patients experience acute toxicity that precludes the completion of WAR.[33–39] The incidence of serious late gastrointestinal toxicity (primarily bowel obstruction and fistula formation) ranged from 5 to 21% in women who had no evidence of recurrent disease as a source of the complication.[31,33–39]

The results of salvage WAR are generally disappointing. Patients with residual macroscopic disease or residual disease in the upper abdomen rarely benefit from salvage WAR. Unfortunately, the pattern of failure does not appear to be altered by treatment, and the toxicity of salvage WAR after chemotherapy and possibly multiple laparotomies is considerable. Firm conclusions regarding the use of salvage WAR cannot be drawn from these small uncontrolled studies.

Technique and Toxicity

A detailed discussion of the techniques of WAR is beyond the scope of this text. The principle of WAR is to deliver adequate doses of radiation to all peritoneal surfaces while respecting the tolerance dose limits of the kidneys, liver, apex of the heart, small bowel, and bone marrow.

In general, an open field technique is used. Parallel opposed anterior and posterior fields are used to treat a volume encompassing the entire peritoneal cavity. This typically extends from above the diaphragms during quiet respiration to the midobturator foramen inferiorly. Figure 10–1 demonstrates the standard field borders for WAR. Doses range from 2,500 cGy to 3,000 cGy in 100 to 180 cGy daily fractions. Care must be taken to limit the doses received by the kidneys, liver, and the apex of the heart. Posterior kidney blocks are used to limit the kidney dose to 1,800 to 2,000 cGy.

Following WAR, a pelvic boost is used to increase the total pelvis dose to 4,500 to 5,000 cGy. Attention to technique and appropriate coverage of the peritoneal cavity is important as inadequate coverage of the peritoneal contents with appropriate margin has been associated with significantly poorer survival.[20] The benefits of using CT-based treatment planning have been noted by LaRouere and colleagues.[41] Figure 10–2 is a digitally reconstructed radiograph (from a dedicated CT simulator) that shows the limits of the peritoneal cavity, the borders of the WAR treatment portal, and the organs of interest.

The acute and late toxicity of WAR in almost 600 patients was reported by Fyles and colleagues.[42] Acute gastrointestinal side effects included nausea and vomiting in 61% of the patients and diarrhea in 68%. Severe nausea and vomiting or diarrhea occurred in 6% of the patients. Myelosuppression was infrequent; mild leukopenia or thrombocytopenia occurred in approximately 10% of patients. Late complications of WAR included temporary hepatic enzyme elevations in 44% of patients, chronic diar-

rhea in 14%, and symptomatic basal pneumonitis in 4%. Small-bowel obstruction occurred in 4.2%, with surgery being necessary in 2.7%. One percent of the women died as a result of complications of WAR. Risk factors for increased complications following WAR include the use of the moving-strip technique, WAR doses greater than 2,250 cGy, and the use of second-look laparotomy.[42,43]

PALLIATIVE RADIATION THERAPY

Despite impressive response rates to initial paclitaxel/platinum-containing chemotherapy regimens, long-term disease-free survival is infrequent, and most women with advanced-stage disease develop progressive or recurrent disease. These patients typically succumb to their disease after the development

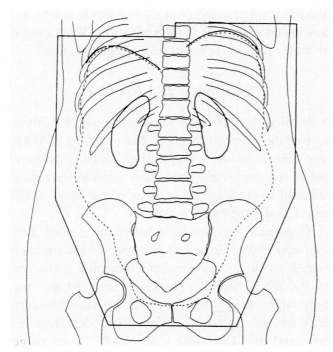

Figure 10–1. Line drawing from a simulator radiograph, showing the treatment volume for abdominopelvic radiotherapy. A generous margin is allowed between the treatment field edges and the peritoneum, indicated by the dotted line. Note that the field extends outside the iliac crests. The kidney shielding is from the posterior to keep the renal dose between 1,800 and 2,000 cGy. The pelvic boost is not shown. This is the posterior (prone) projection.

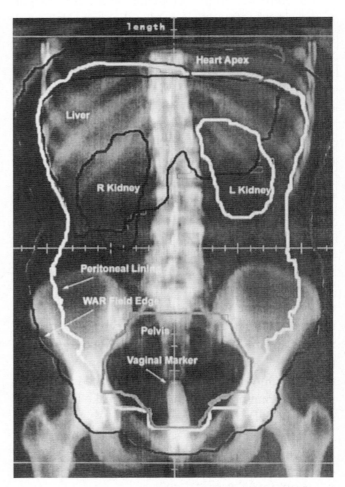

Figure 10–2. Digitally reconstructed radiograph from a dedicated computed tomography simulator demonstrating the limits of the peritoneal cavity, the borders of the whole abdominopelvic radiation therapy (WAR) treatment portal, and the organs of interest.

of persistent or recurrent ovarian cancer. For many of these women, RT can effectively palliate the symptoms of focally recurrent ovarian cancer.[44,45]

The palliative benefit of RT in 38 patients with recurrent disease following platinum-based chemotherapy was reported by May and colleagues.[44] Twelve courses of palliative RT were given for the prevention of impending difficulty from recurrent tumor. In this favorable group with a median survival of 15 months, RT prevented symptoms for a mean of 7.2 months. The palliative benefit of short-course RT was seen in women with (1) dyspnea due to pulmonary metastases, (2) vaginal bleeding or discharge due to vaginal recurrences, (3) central nervous system symptoms from brain metastases, (4) gastrointestinal obstruction secondary to abdominopelvic recurrences, and (5) localized pain secondary to recurrent tumor. Patients with vaginal recurrences were palliated for an average of 9 months and experienced a long median survival of almost 20 months.

Between 1987 and 1993, 556 women with ovarian cancer were evaluated at Fox Chase Cancer Center.[45] Palliative RT was eventually delivered to 47 sites in 33 women with symptomatic recurrent disease. The overall symptomatic response rate was 70%; 51% of patients experienced complete symptomatic response. Univariate analysis showed that higher Karnofsky performance scores, younger age, and higher RT doses are predictive of complete symptomatic response. Of patients receiving higher doses (biologically equivalent dose ≥ 44 Gy), 68% experienced complete symptomatic response, compared to 35% when lower doses were used. Palliative RT dose fractionation schedules might deliver 2,000 to 3,500 cGy over 1 to 3 weeks. Hypofractionated RT schedules (large fractional doses) that can provide adequate palliation are of particular interest for patients with a shortened life expectancy. Investigators at M. D. Anderson Hospital reported overall response rates of 55% for ovarian cancer patients with pain and 71% for those with bleeding after the delivery of large single fractions of RT (typically 1,000 cGy).[46] However, the large fraction size used may have been responsible for severe radiation injury in 6 of the 42 patients.

Patients with symptomatic recurrent ovarian cancer can be effectively palliated with RT. Short courses of palliative RT are associated with tolerable acute side effects and uncommon serious late complications.

TREATMENT WITH CHROMIC PHOSPHATE SUSPENSION

Overview

Intraperitoneal therapy with radioactive chromic phosphate (P32) suspension has been used in the treatment of ovarian carcinoma. This has been used both in early-stage patients who had no residual disease after surgery and in those patients with stage II/III disease who had negative second-look laparotomies and who received chemotherapy. Studies that have examined the role of P32 for these groups of patients as well as the physics of P32 will be reviewed.

Physics and Dosimetry

Radioactive chromic phosphate suspension undergoes pure beta decay and thus emits radiation in the form of electrons. Because it does not emit gamma irradiation, P32 does not pose as much of a radiation safety issue as do previously used isotopes such as radioactive gold. The depth of penetration of the radiation from P32 is approximately 1.4 to 3.0 mm, with a maximum of 8 mm.[47] Phosphorus 32 (P32) has a half-life of 14.3 days; its average energy is 0.69 MeV, with a maximum energy of 1.71 MeV. The typical dose used in clinical practice is 10 to 20 mCi. This is instilled into the peritoneum, and the patient is placed in various positions in order to evenly distribute the colloid over all peritoneal surfaces. The distribution can be verified either by imaging the bremsstrahlung photons that are emitted by the electrons given off by ^{32}P,[48] or by instilling technetium into the peritoneum and then imaging.

Vergote and colleagues reported a study of the intraperitoneal distribution of P32 in which 297 patients were studied by scintigraphic imaging.[49] Uneven distribution of P32 was seen in 16% of the patients, and leakage was seen in 3% while 53% of the patients showed accumulation in the thoracic lymph nodes. Furthermore, 46% of the patients who showed an even distribution on initial scintigraphy (performed on days 0 to 1) then had an uneven distribution on subsequent scintigraphy (performed on day 3 or 7). The authors do note that this should be interpreted cautiously because a homogeneous distribution on a gross scale, as seen by scintigraphy, does not necessarily imply a homogeneous distribution on the microscopic scale. In addition, this study did not find a correlation between a homogeneous distribution of P32 and the relapse of carcinoma or the location of small-bowel adhesions.

Currie and colleagues evaluated the distribution of P32 in a series of studies on phantoms, dogs, and human patients.[49] They found that the distribution of P32 as determined by technetium scanning correlated only approximately half of the time with the distribution as determined by detecting the bremsstrahlung photons. The use of thermoluminescent dosimetry in dogs allowed estimation of the dose to the peritoneal surfaces to be up to 10,000 cGy. However, retroperitoneal structures such as pelvic and para-aortic lymph nodes received only up to 200 cGy. Thus, according to this study, these latter structures would not be adequately treated by the instillation of P32.

Complications from intraperitoneal P32 have been reported by Walton and colleagues.[50] They detailed toxicity from a GOG study that randomized patients to melphalan or to P32. Most patients received 15 mCi, and 75% received the P32 within 20 days of their surgery. Sixteen patients experienced abdominal pain not requiring narcotic medication while 3% of the patients had more severe pain. Five of the patients required surgery for gastrointestinal (GI) injury although one of these was due to bowel injury at the time of laparoscopic catheter placement. These patients did not receive external beam radiation therapy in combination with instillation of P32. Pezner and colleagues reported increased toxicity by combining these two treatments.[51] A retrospective review was done of 48 patients who were treated with P32 alone versus 56 patients who received P32 in addition to external beam RT. The survivals of the two groups were similar. However, only 2% of the patients who received P32 alone had small-bowel complications, compared to 24% of those who received the combined treatment.

Spanos and colleagues have also reported complications from intraperitoneal P32.[52] Thirty-six patients were treated after primary surgery while 58 patients were treated after second-look laparotomies. Twelve percent of all of the patients experienced GI complications requiring surgery. The only significant predictor of toxicity was the timing of the delivery of P32 ($p = .05$); patients who received P32 more than 12 hours after surgery had an increased complication rate ($p = .007$).

Treatment of Stage I/II Ovarian Carcinoma with P32

A randomized trial involving P32 was performed by the GOG and was reported by Young and colleagues.[53] The study involved 141 women who had poorly differentiated stage I cancers or cancer outside the ovaries yet limited to the pelvis (stage II) and who were then randomized to melphalan or to a single intraperitoneal dose of P32 (15 mCi) given at the time of surgery. With a median follow-up greater than 6 years, the overall and disease-free survival rates were not significantly different (81% vs 78%, $p = .48$ and 80% vs 80%, respectively).

A second GOG study randomized 205 patients with early-stage ovarian cancer to 15 mCi of intraperitoneal P32 or to three cycles of cyclophosphamide/cisplatin (CP) chemotherapy. Although there were no statistically significant differences seen in the 5-year overall survival rates (84% for CP vs 76% for P32), a trend for an improvement in the 5-year recurrence-free interval with chemotherapy was seen (77% vs 66%, $p = .07$). Difficulties with P32 included poor distribution in 8 patients and bowel perforation in 2 patients during catheter insertion. Complications of cyclophosphamide/cisplatin chemotherapy included grade 3 to 4 hematologic toxicity in 67% of patients. Intraperitoneal P32 was felt to be inferior to cyclophosphamide/cisplatin chemotherapy and is no longer being evaluated in the protocol setting by the GOG.[54]

Another randomized trial was performed by the NCIC.[55] This again involved either poorly differentiated or pelvic contaminated stage I or IIA ovarian cancers. After 53 patients underwent total abdominal hysterectomy and bilateral salpingo-oophorectomy, they were randomized to WAR, pelvic RT followed by melphalan, or pelvic radiotherapy followed by intraperitoneal P32 in a single dose of 10 to 20 mCi. There were no significant differences between the three arms in terms of 5-year survival, but the P32 arm was closed early due to an increased incidence of bowel toxicity. In light of the other complication data presented above, this might not be unexpected.

A Norwegian randomized study, reported by Vergote and colleagues,[56] randomized 245 patients who were without any residual disease after laparotomy to intraperitoneal P32 or to cisplatin chemotherapy for six cycles. A small group of patients (17%) randomized to the P32 arm received whole-abdomen radiation instead of the P32, due to the presence of extensive adhesions. Again, between the P32 and cisplatin arms, no difference was seen in actuarial 5-year overall survival rates (81% vs 79%) or in disease-free survival rates (74% vs 76%). There was a significant difference in complications, favoring the cisplatin arm. Only 2% of the patients receiving cisplatin experienced bowel obstructions whereas 9% of those receiving P32 and 21% of those receiving whole abdomen radiation had bowel obstructions.

Bolis and colleagues reported the results of an Italian randomized study involving 161 patients with stage I ovarian cancer.[57] The treatment arms after radical surgery consisted of cisplatin for six cycles and P32 in a single dose (7 to 10 mCi). Note that this dose is lower than in the previous studies. Only one patient randomized to P32 developed an intestinal occlusion, but 20% of the patients did not receive the P32 because the isotope could not be instilled, due to the development of adhesions after surgery. These patients were included in the intention-to-treat analysis. The overall survival rates were not significantly different between the P32 and cisplatin arms (83% vs 81%, $p = .33$). There was a difference in disease-free survival, favoring the cisplatin arm (70% vs 83%, $p = .009$).

P32 as Adjuvant Therapy after Second-Look Laparotomy

A Norwegian randomized study reported by Vergote and colleagues randomized 50 patients to receive P32 as consolidative therapy after negative second-look surgeries or to no further treatment.[50] Of these women, 64% had stage I disease, 24% had stage II disease, and only 12% had stage III disease. The 5-year disease-free survival rate was 83% for those

who received P32 versus 97% for those who did not. This difference was not statistically significant ($p = .09$) due to the small numbers of patients involved. The study reported that two deaths could (at least in part) have been due to the P32 treatment.

There have been several phase II trials that have reported on this subset of patients. In 1987, Soper and colleagues reported on 65 patients with positive cytology who were treated with intraperitoneal P32.[58] Eighty percent of the patients had stage I disease, and 14% had stage II disease. Approximately 15 mCi of P32 was injected after initial technetium imaging to evaluate distribution. With a median follow-up of 25 months, the disease-free survival rate at 2 years was 89% for patients with clinical stage I disease and 94% for patients with pathologic stage I disease. This decreased to 25% and 33% in the small numbers of patients with stage II and III disease, respectively. There was a significant increase in bowel complications that required surgery among patients who received pelvic irradiation as compared to those who did not (29% vs 0%, $p < .001$). Another phase II trial, reported by Peters and colleagues, detailed 34 patients who received P32 after induction chemotherapy and negative second-look laparotomy.[59] Only 15% of patients had stage I disease, and 9% had stage II disease whereas 76% had stage III disease. All patients had a pretreatment technetium scan, followed by 12 to 15 mCi of P32. After a median follow-up of 31 months, the 2-year overall and disease-free survival rates were 68% and 42%, respectively. This difference from the results of the study reported by Soper and colleagues may represent the difference in stage distribution.[58] Rogers and colleagues described 51 patients who were treated with P32 after negative second-look surgery and chemotherapy.[60] These were compared with a matched group of 18 patients who did not receive P32, due to adhesions or physician preference. Of the patients who were treated with P32, 45% had stage I disease, 31% had stage II, and 24% had stage III disease. The median follow-up was 58 months. At 5 years, the overall survival in patients treated with P32 versus those who were not treated was 90% versus. 78%, and disease-free survival was 86% versus 67% ($p = .05$). Multivariate analysis confirmed that grade followed by use of P32 had independent prognostic significance.

Patients with stage III ovarian carcinoma were analyzed by Spanos and colleagues.[61] Fifty-two patients received 15 mCi of P32 after chemotherapy and second-look laparotomies whereas 4 received P32 as the only postsurgical treatment. One-half of the 52 patients receiving P32 had pathologic negative second-look surgeries; approximately 25% had microscopic residual disease, and another 25% had gross residual disease. Only 6% of the 52 patients had gross residual disease > 0.5 cm. After a median follow-up of 48 months, the actuarial 5-year overall survival rates were 77%, 48%, and 32% for the patients with no residual, microscopic residual, and gross residual disease, respectively. The four patients who received P32 as their only postsurgical treatment displayed a 100% actuarial 5-year survival rate.

In summary, intraperitoneal radioactive P32 suspension is a pure beta emitter (with a range of 1.4 to 3 mm) that is instilled into the peritoneum and then distributed about the peritoneal cavity. Prescanning with technetium or scanning of the P32 itself may aid in evaluating whether a homogeneous distribution of radioisotope has been achieved. Complications from treatment with P32 include abdominal pain and intestinal obstruction that may require surgery to correct. These bowel complications are increased if external beam RT is used in conjunction with P32.[51] The incidence of serious GI complications from P32 ranges from 2 to 12%.[51,52,56]

P32 has been used in the treatment of patients with high-risk early-stage ovarian carcinoma. Randomized studies of treatment with P32 versus chemotherapy (from the GOG, Canada, Norway, and Italy) have not shown a benefit in overall survival or disease-free survival from the use of P32.[53,55–57] Furthermore, in some of these studies, the patients in the P32 arm experienced more bowel complications than those in the chemotherapy arm, especially with the use of cisplatin-based chemotherapy.[55,56] Because of these results, the current GOG study no longer uses P32 as one of its treatment arms.

Patients with more advanced ovarian cancer have also been treated with P32 after initial surgery, chemotherapy, and negative second-look laparotomy. The one randomized trial involved small patient numbers but did not show a benefit for the use of P32.[49] Several phase II trials reported in the literature show that patients with stage I disease treated with P32 adjuvantly may expect 2-year disease-free survival rates of 89 to 94% whereas those with stage III disease have 5-year survival rates of 68 to 77% if there is no residual disease at the time of second-look laparotomy.[58,59,61] Presently, the role of intraperitoneal P32 in the management of ovarian cancer is not well defined.[60] Considering the difficulties with the intraperitoneal distribution of P32, the equivocal results of P32 in the above-noted prospective trials, the increased potential for serious GI complications, and the relatively favorable results of modern chemotherapy, there is likely a minimal potential role, if any, for the future use of intraperitoneal P32 in ovarian cancer treatment.

REFERENCES

1. Bush RS, Allt WEC, Beale FA, et al. Treatment of epithelial carcinoma of the ovary: operation, irradiation and chemotherapy. Am J Obstet Gynecol 1977;127:692–704.
2. Hreshchyshyn MM, Park RC, Blessing JA, et al. The role of adjuvant therapy in stage I ovarian cancer. Am J Obstet Gynecol 1980;138:139–45.
3. Fuller DB, Sause WT, Plenk HP, et al. Analysis of postoperative radiation therapy in stage I through III epithelial ovarian carcinoma. J Clin Oncol 1987;5:897–905.
4. Goldberg N, Peschel RE. Postoperative abdominopelvic radiation therapy for ovarian cancer. Int J Radiat Oncol Biol Phys 1988;14:425–9.
5. Martinez A, Schray MF, Howe AE, et al. Postoperative radiation therapy for epithelial ovarian cancer: the curative role based on a 24-year experience. J Clin Oncol 1985;3:901–11.
6. Weiser EB, Burke TW, Heller PB, et al. Determinants of survival of patients with epithelial ovarian carcinoma following whole abdomen irradiation (WAR). Gynecol Oncol 1988;30:201–8.
7. Dembo AJ, Bush RS, Beale FA, et al. The Princess Margaret Hospital study of ovarian cancer: stages I, II, and asymptomatic III presentations. Cancer Treat Rep 1979;63:249–54.
8. Dembo AJ, Bush RS, Beale FA, et al. A randomized clinical trial of moving strip versus open field whole abdominal irradiation in patients with invasive epithelial cancer of the ovary. Int J Radiat Oncol Biol Phys 1983;9:97.
9. Dembo AJ, Bush RS, Beale FA, et al. Ovarian carcinoma: improved survival following abdominopelvic irradiation in patients with a completed pelvic operation. Am J Obstet Gynecol 1979;134:793–800.
10. Dembo AJ, Van Dyk J, Japp B, et al. Whole abdominal irradiation by a moving-strip technique for patients with ovarian cancer. Int J Radiat Oncol Biol Phys 1979;5:1933–42.
11. Dembo AJ, Bush RS, DeBoer G. Therapy in stage I ovarian cancer. Am J Obstet Gynecol 1981;14:231–3.
12. Dembo AJ, Bush RS. Choice of postoperative therapy based

on prognostic factors. Int J Radiat Oncol Biol Phys 1982; 8:893–7.

13. Dembo AJ. Radiation therapy in the management of ovarian cancer. Clin Obstet Gynecol 1983;10:261–78.

14. Dembo AJ. Radiotherapeutic management of ovarian cancer. Semin Oncol 1984;11:238–50.

15. Dembo AJ. Abdominopelvic radiotherapy in ovarian cancer: A 10-year experience. Cancer 1985;55:2285–90.

16. Dembo AJ. The sequential multiple modality treatment of ovarian cancer. Radiother Oncol 1985;3:187–92.

17. Dembo AJ, Davy M, Stenwig AE, et al. Prognostic factors in patients with stage I epithelial ovarian cancer. Obstet Gynecol 1990;75:263–73.

18. Carey MS, Dembo AJ, Simm JE, et al. Testing the validity of a prognostic classification in patients with surgically optimal ovarian carcinoma: a 15-year review. Int J Gynecol Cancer 1993;3:24–35.

19. Smith JP, Rutledge FN, Delclos L. Postoperative treatment of early cancer of the ovary: a randomized trial between postoperative irradiation and chemotherapy. Nat Cancer Inst Monogr 1975;42:149–53.

20. Klaassen D, Shelley W, Starreveld A, et al. Early stage ovarian cancer: a randomized clinical trial comparing whole abdominal radiotherapy, melphalan, and intraperitoneal chromic phosphate. A National Cancer Institute of Canada clinical trials group report. J Clin Oncol 1988;6:1254–63.

21. Sell A, Bertelsen K, Andersen JE. Randomized study of whole-abdomen irradiation versus pelvic irradiation plus cyclophosphamide in treatment of early ovarian cancer. Gynecol Oncol 1990;37:367–73.

22. Chiara S, Conte P, Franzone P, et al. High-risk early-stage ovarian cancer. Am J Clin Oncol 1994;17:72–6.

23. Randall ME, Barrett RJ, Spirtos NM, et al. Chemotherapy, early surgical reassessment, and hyperfractionated abdominal radiotherapy in stage III ovarian cancer: results of a Gynecologic Oncology Group study. Int J Radiat Oncol Biol Phys 1996;34:139–47.

24. Bruzzone M, Repetto L, Chiara S, et al. Chemotherapy versus radiotherapy in the management of ovarian cancer patients with pathological complete response or minimal residual disease at second look. Gynecol Oncol 1990;38:392–5.

25. Arian-Schad KS, Kapp DS, Hackl A, et al. Radiation therapy in stage III ovarian cancer following surgery and chemotherapy: prognostic factors, patterns of relapse, and toxicity. A preliminary report. Gynecol Oncol 1990;39:47–55.

26. Ledermann JA, Dembo AJ, Sturgeon JFG, et al. Outcome of patients with unfavorable optimally cytoreduced ovarian cancer treated with chemotherapy and whole abdominal radiation. Gynecol Oncol 1991;41:30–5.

27. Lawton F, Luesley D, Blackledge G, et al. A randomized trial comparing whole abdominal radiotherapy with chemotherapy following cisplatinum cytoreduction in epithelial ovarian cancer: West Midlands Ovarian Cancer Group Trial II. Clin Oncol 1990;2:4–9.

28. Lambert HE, Rustin GJS, Gregory WM, et al. A randomized trial comparing single-agent carboplatin with carboplatin followed by radiotherapy for advanced ovarian cancer: a North Thames Ovary Group study. J Clin Oncol 1993; 11:440–8.

29. Pickel H, Lahousen M, Petru E, et al. Consolidation radio-

therapy after carboplatin-based chemotherapy in radically operated advanced ovarian cancer. Gynecol Oncol 1999; 72:215–9.

30. Goldhirsch A, Greiner R, Dreher E, et al. Treatment of advanced ovarian cancer with surgery, chemotherapy, and consolidation of response by whole-abdominal radiotherapy. Cancer 1988;62:40–7.

31. Thomas GM. Is there a role for consolidation or salvage radiotherapy after chemotherapy in advanced epithelial ovarian cancer? Gynecol Oncol 1993;51:97–103.

32. Lanciano R, Reddy S, Corn B, et al. Update on the role of radiotherapy in ovarian cancer. Semin Oncol 1998;25: 361–71.

33. Fein DA, Morgan LS, Marcus RB, et al. Stage III ovarian carcinoma: an analysis of treatment results and complications following hyperfractionated abdominopelvic irradiation for salvage. Int J Radiat Oncol Biol Phys 1994;29:169–76.

34. Eifel PJ, Gershenson DM, Delclos L, et al. Twice-daily, split-course abdominopelvic radiation therapy after chemotherapy and positive second-look laparotomy for epithelial ovarian carcinoma. Int J Radiat Oncol Biol Phys 1991;21:1013–8.

35. Reddy S, Hartsell W, Graham J, et al. Whole-abdomen radiation therapy in ovarian carcinoma: its role as a salvage therapeutic modality. Gynecol Oncol 1989;35:307–13.

36. Sedlacek TV, Spyropoulus P, Cifaldi R, et al. Whole-abdomen radiation therapy as salvage treatment for epithelial ovarian carcinoma. Cancer J Sci Am 1997;3:358–63.

37. Schray MF, Martinez A, Howes AE, et al. Advanced epithelial ovarian cancer: salvage whole abdominal irradiation for patients with recurrent or persistent disease after combination chemotherapy. J Clin Oncol 1988;6:1433–9.

38. Baker K, Reddy S, Lee MS, et al. Salvage whole abdominal radiation therapy for ovarian cancer: a twelve year experience. Int J Radiat Oncol Biol Phys 1996;36:176.

39. Cmelak AJ, Cox RS, Kapp DS. Long-term survival with whole abdominopelvic irradiation (WAI) in platinum-refractory ovarian cancer. Gynecol Oncol 1997;65:453–606.

40. Davidson SA, Rubin SC, Mychalczak B, et al. Limited-field radiotherapy as salvage treatment of localized persistent or recurrent epithelial ovarian cancer. Gynecol Oncol 1993;51:349–54.

41. LaRouere J, Perez-Tamayo C, Fraass B, et al. Optimal coverage of peritoneal surface in whole abdominal radiation for ovarian neoplasms. Int J Radiat Oncol Biol Phys 1989; 17:607–13.

42. Fyles AW, Dembo AJ, Bush RS, et al. Analysis of complications in patients treated with abdomino-pelvic radiation therapy for ovarian carcinoma. Int J Radiat Oncol Biol Phys 1992;22:847–51.

43. Whelan TJ, Dembo AJ, Bush RS, et al. Complications of whole abdominal and pelvic radiotherapy following chemotherapy for advanced ovarian cancer. Int J Radiat Oncol Biol Phys 1992;22:853–8.

44. May LF, Belinson JL, Roland TA. Palliative benefit of radiation therapy in advanced ovarian cancer. Gynecol Oncol 1990;37:408–11.

45. Corn BW, Lanciano RM, Boente M, et al. Recurrent ovarian cancer. Cancer 1994;74:2979–83.

46. Adelson MD, Wharton JT, Delclos L, et al. Palliative radio-

therapy for ovarian cancer. Int J Radiat Oncol Biol Phys 1987;13:17–21.

47. Hilaris BS, Clark DGC. The value of postoperative intraperitoneal injection of radiocolloids in early cancer of the ovary. AJR Am J Roentgenol 1971;112:749–54.

48. Currie JL, Bagne F, Harris C, et al. Radioactive chromic phosphate suspension: studies on distribution, dose absorption, and effective therapeutic radiation in phantoms, dogs, and patients. Gynecol Oncol 1981;12:193–218.

49. Vergote IB, Winderen M, DeVos LN, et al. Intraperitoneal radioactive phosphorus therapy in ovarian carcinoma. Cancer 1993;71:2250–60.

50. Walton LA, Yadusky A, Rubinstein L. Intraperitoneal radioactive phosphate in early ovarian carcinoma: An analysis of complications. Int J Radiat Oncol Biol Phys 1991;20:939–44.

51. Pezner RD, Stevens KR, Tong D, et al. Limited epithelial carcinoma of the ovary treated with curative intent by the intraperitoneal installation of radiocolloids. Cancer 1978;42:2563–71.

52. Spanos WJ, Day T, Abner A, et al. Complications in the use of intra-abdominal ^{32}P for ovarian carcinoma. Gynecol Oncol 1992;45:243–7.

53. Young RC, Walter LA, Ellenberg SS, et al. Adjuvant therapy in stage I and stage II epithelial ovarian cancer: results of two prospective randomized trials. N Engl J Med 1990;322:1021–7.

54. Young RC, Brady MF, Nieberg RM, et al. Randomized clinical trial of adjuvant treatment of women with early

55. Klaassen D, Starreveld A, Shelly W, et al. External beam pelvic radiotherapy plus intraperitoneal radioactive chronic phosphate in early stage ovarian cancer: a toxic combination. Int J Radiat Oncol Biol Phys 1985;11:1801–4.

56. Vergote IB, Vergote-DeVos LN, Abeler VM, et al. Randomized trial comparing cisplatin with radioactive phosphorus or whole-abdomen irradiation and adjuvant treatment of ovarian cancer. Cancer 1992;69:741–9.

57. Bolis G, Colombo N, Pecorelli S, et al. Adjuvant treatment for early epithelial ovarian cancer: results of two randomised clinical trials comparing cisplatin to no further treatment or chromic phosphate (^{32}P). Ann Oncol 1995;6:887–93.

58. Soper JT, Creasman WT, Clarke-Pearson DL, et al. Intraperitoneal chromic phosphate P32 suspension therapy of malignant peritoneal cytology in endometrial carcinoma. Am J Obstet Gynecol 1985;153:191–6.

59. Peters WA, Smith MR, Cain JM, et al. Intraperitoneal P-32 is not an effective consolidation therapy after a negative second-look laparotomy for epithelial carcinoma of the ovary. Gynecol Oncol 1992;47:146–9.

60. Rogers L, Varia M, Halle J, et al. 32P following negative second-look laparotomy for epithelial ovarian cancer. Gynecol Oncol 1993;50:141–6.

61. Spanos WJ, Day T Jr, Jose B, et al. Use of P-32 in stage III epithelial carcinoma of the ovary. Gynecol Oncol 1994;54:35–9.

(FIGO-I–IIA high risk) ovarian cancer—GOG #95. Proc Am Soc Clin Oncol ASCO 1999;18:357a.

11

Early Stage Management

JEFFREY DIMASCIO, DO
RUSSELL J. SCHILDER, MD

In 2001, the estimated number of new cases of epithelial ovarian cancer in the United States was 23,400, and there were approximately 13,900 deaths from ovarian cancer in the United States.[1] As in all malignancies, the diagnosis of ovarian cancer at an early stage portends an improved prognosis compared to that of advanced-stage disease. Unfortunately, only 30% of patients will present with early-stage disease as defined as stage I or stage II by the International Federation of Gynecology and Obstetrics (FIGO) (Table 11–1).[2] In contrast, approximately 90% of patients with breast cancer have localized or regional disease at the time of presentation.[2] This disparity exists because of the anatomy of the pelvis and abdominal cavity, the biology of epithelial ovarian cancer, and the lack of an effective screening program for ovarian carcinoma. The female pelvis and abdomen allow for the growth of masses and the accumulation of fluid, while maintaining the individual's ability to function with minimal symptoms. Epithelial ovarian cancers spread generally through exfoliation through the surface of the ovarian capsule, with subsequent implantation onto intraperitoneal surfaces as well as through lymphatic channels.[3] This biologic behavior does not generally induce early symptoms. In addition, epithelial ovarian cancers tend not to stretch or twist the infundibulopelvic ligament as do ovarian germ cell malignancies. The twisting and stretching of the ligament produces severe pain, resulting in an early-stage diagnosis for approximately 70% of germ cell ovarian carcinomas.[4] Indeed, 70 to 80% of patients with epithelial ovarian cancer will present at an advanced stage with vague complaints of abdominal discomfort or distention, gastrointestinal complaints, or signs and symptoms of a urinary-tract abnormality.[3] The pelvis and abdomen are relatively less amenable to physical and radiographic examination than is the breast. Despite a determined effort with various combinations of pelvic examination, ultrasonography, and serum levels of cancer antigen 125 (CA 125), there is currently no reliable method for the early detection of ovarian cancer. The introduction of new drugs and comprehensive surgical staging with cytoreduction have not changed the overall survival of patients with ovarian cancer over the last 20 years.[2] However, more patients are living longer with their disease. Five-year survival rates for patients with ovarian cancer have improved by approximately 13% in this time period (from 37% in 1974 to 1976 to 50% in 1989 to 1996).[1] The increase is likely a reflection of the more frequent performance of comprehensive surgical staging and cytoreduction and the now common use of platinum-based chemotherapy regimens. New chemotherapeutic agents also have contributed to the improved 5-year survival. The prognosis for patients with early-stage ovarian cancer (5-year survival rates of 70 to 90%) is vastly superior to that of patients with more advanced disease.[5] Unfortunately, the corollary is that 10 to 30% of women diagnosed with early-stage ovarian cancer will have recurrence and will eventually die of their disease. Appropriate surgical staging and cytoreduction is the first and most important step in managing a patient with a suspect ovarian or pelvic mass, and

Table 11–1.   STAGING SYSTEM FOR OVARIAN CANCER*

Stage I	Growth limited to the ovaries
IA	Growth limited to one ovary; no ascites; no tumor on the external surfaces, capsule intact
IB	Growth limited to both ovaries; no ascites; no tumor on the external surfaces, capsule intact
IC	Tumor either stage IA or IB but with tumor on the surface of one or both ovaries; or with capsule ruptured; or with ascites present, containing malignant cells or with positive peritoneal washings
Stage II	Growth involving one or both ovaries with pelvic extension
IIA	Extension and/or metastases to the uterus and/or tubes
IIB	Extension to other pelvic tissues
IIC	Tumor either stage IIA or IIB but with tumor on the surface of one or both ovaries; or with capsule(s) ruptured; or with ascites present containing malignant cells or with positive peritoneal washings
Stage III	Tumor involving one or both ovaries with peritoneal implants outside the pelvis and/or positive retroperitoneal or inguinal nodes; superficial liver metastases equals stage III; tumor is limited to the true pelvis but with histologically verified malignant extension to small bowel or omentum
IIIA	Tumor grossly limited to the true pelvis, with negative nodes with histologically confirmed microscopic seeding of abdominal peritoneal surfaces
IIIB	Tumor of one or both ovaries; histologically confirmed implants of abdominal peritoneal surfaces, none > 2 cm in diameter; nodes negative
IIIC	Abdominal implants > 2 cm in diameter and/or positive retroperitoneal or inguinal nodes
Stage IV	Growth involving one or both ovaries with distant metastases; if pleural effusion is present, there must be positive cytologic test results to allot a case to stage IV; parenchymal liver metastases equals stage IV

Adapted from Trope C et al.[31]
*International Federation of Gynecology and Obstetrics (FIGO) classification.

such women should be promptly referred to a gynecologic oncologist. The postoperative management of patients with early-stage ovarian cancer is guided by the tumor type, substage, and histologic grade. Carefully selected patients may be eligible for close observation. Other patients will require adjuvant therapy and have several options, including single- or multiagent chemotherapy, whole-abdomen radiotherapy, or intraperitoneal chemotherapy. This chapter will focus on the appropriate management of the patient with early stage epithelial ovarian cancer.

STAGING

Comprehensive surgical staging is the single most important determination of appropriate management of patients with early-stage ovarian cancer. A comprehensive staging laparotomy, which should be conducted through an adequate vertical incision to permit exploration of the entire abdominal cavity, is composed of the numerous procedures listed in Table 11–2. Inadequate surgical procedures can lead to understaging and potentially result in inappropriate postoperative treatment plans that could affect patient survival. Two studies from the early 1980s demonstrated that many women diagnosed with ovarian cancer had an initial surgical procedure that

would be considered incomplete by today's standard.[6,7] In one study published in 1983, Young and associates reported that only 25% of women had an incision that permitted a thorough exploration of the upper abdomen as an initial procedure. Of these patients, 31% were upstaged following repeat staging laparotomies, resulting in 77% of upstaged patients actually having stage III disease.[7]

A second study, by McGowan and co-investigators and published in 1985, described only 54% of 291 women who underwent ovarian cancer surgery as having received complete surgical staging.[6] Those patients who were explored by a gynecologic oncologist had complete staging 97% of the time, compared with 52% and 35% of patients who were explored by an obstetric gynecologist or a general surgeon, respectively. Even in the late 1980s, similar patterns of care were documented. In a more recent retrospective review involving 54 patients with stage I ovarian cancer, two groups of patients were identified on the basis of whether or not the initial surgery was conducted by a gynecologic oncologist.[8] The two groups were comparable in age, parity, gravidity, grade, and substage. Surgical staging was determined to be accurate in 100% of patients managed by a gynecologic oncologist, compared with 28% of patients who were not man-

Table 11–2.   COMPONENTS OF A COMPLETE STAGING LAPAROTOMY FOR OVARIAN CANCER
Vertical incision that gives sufficient access, to visualize and palpate the structures within the whole abdominal cavity and retroperitoneum
Inspection and palpation of all mesenteric and peritoneal surfaces
Peritoneal washings from pelvis and paracolic gutters
Scraping of samples from both hemidiaphragms
Biopsy of all lesions and adhesions
Removal of all visible tumor
Pelvic and para-aortic lymphadenectomy (inspection and palpation only are inadequate)
Appendectomy

aged by a gynecologic oncologist. Postoperative chemotherapy was prescribed in 79% of the cases managed by a gynecologic oncologist, versus 36% of the cases managed by a nongynecologic oncologist. The 6-year survival rate was 90% for the group managed by a gynecologic oncologist, compared to 68% for the other group.

Any patient suspected of having a gynecologic malignancy, especially a patient in the peri- or post-menopausal age group, would benefit from consultation with a gynecologic oncologist. Any post-menopausal women with an elevated CA 125 level and a pelvic mass should be referred directly to a gynecologic oncologist for appropriate surgical staging since the risk of having a malignancy in this population is high.

CONSERVATIVE SURGERY

For women with ovarian cancer, the standard surgical approach includes a total abdominal hysterectomy and bilateral salpingo-oophorectomy, in addition to the procedures previously outlined (see Table 11–2). Epithelial ovarian cancer is primarily a disease of older women; the median age at presentation is 63 years, but the disease can occur in women of child-bearing age. Conservative surgery may be considered in carefully selected patients who are interested in preserving fertility. There are no prospective randomized trials to draw upon in deciding which women are appropriate for such an approach. In one retrospective review, 56 patients, 40 years of age or younger, underwent fertility-sparing surgery for stage I ovarian cancer.[9] Thirty-two patients had stage

IA disease, and 22 had stage IC disease. No tumors were of clear cell histology. Thirty-five tumors were grade 1, 14 were grade 2 and the remainder were grade 3. Twenty women conceived, with 17 normal deliveries. With a median follow-up of 7 years, only 9% of the women had recurrence of their disease. In a multivariate analysis, age > 30 years, FIGO grade 2 to 3, FIGO stage IC, and conservative surgery predicted a shorter disease-free survival. Only tumor grade was of prognostic significance when evaluating the overall survival of these patients. There have also been reports suggesting an adverse effect of conservative surgery on survival. One study reported a lower survival rate of 50% for patients who only underwent unilateral oophorectomy, compared with women who had full debulking and surgical staging (80% vs 50%).[10] Contralateral normal-appearing ovaries have been shown to have visibly undetectable disease in 14% of cases.[11] Fertility-sparing surgery remains controversial and requires detailed discussions with the patient regarding the risk of less surgery for patients with early-stage ovarian cancer. Consideration should be given to complete total abdominal hysterectomy and oophorectomy after patients have completed their childbearing although the benefit of such an approach remains undefined.

PROGNOSTIC FACTORS

Traditional prognostic factors for patients with stage I disease are histologic grade, dense adhesions, and large-volume ascites (Table 11–3). Unfortunately, these factors are all somewhat subjective. Histologic grade is a visual description provided by a trained pathologist; it is the surgeon's description of the findings at the time of operation that defines "dense" vs "nondense" adhesions. Dense adhesions have been described, elsewhere, as those that require sharp dissection to free a tumor, as cyst rupture as a result of dissecting the adhesions, or when an erythematous area is left in the place of a dissected adherence.[3] A large retrospective review by investigators at the Princess Margaret Hospital identified these indicators and then validated them in a separate population from the Norwegian Radiation Hospital.[12] Patients with stage I disease with dense adhe-

Table 11–3.   CLINICAL CHARACTERISTICS OF PATIENTS NOT REQUIRING POSTOPERATIVE CHEMOTHERAPY

Traditional factors
  No ascites or cytologically negative washings
  Intact capsule or no tumor on external surface
  Tumor confined to ovaries
  Grade 1 or 2 histology
  Large volume prior to ascites
  No dense adhesions
Newer factors
  Diploid
  Low S phase
  No overexpression of VEGF
  Preoperative CA 125 < 65 U/mL

CA 125 = cancer antigen 125; VEGF = vascular endothelial growth factor.

sions had treatment results similar to those of patients with stage II disease. Factors that did not predict for relapse included substage (bilaterality or capsular integrity), age, type of postoperative treatment, time from diagnosis, and histologic cell type. The 5-year relapse-free survival for all stage I patients was 79%. In patients without large-volume ascites or dense adhesions, the 5-year relapse-free survival was 98%.

While these data were generated retrospectively, they have been validated in a separate large study population with a central pathologic review. Tumor grade has been identified as the most important prognostic factor in most studies of patients with stage I ovarian cancer. Studies have demonstrated that patients with stage I ovarian cancer with well-differentiated or moderately well differentiated carcinoma have a 90% survival rate with an appropriate surgery without adjuvant therapy.[13] Patients with poorly differentiated or clear cell histology have an inferior survival and should be considered for further therapy. Grading of malignancies is somewhat observer dependent. More objective and reproducible indicators are needed to improve the assessment of prognosis.

Recent data demonstrating the clinical significance of increased expression of vascular endothelial growth factor (VEGF) in early-stage ovarian carcinoma have emerged.[14] Tumor specimens of 68 patients with stage I and II tumors were assayed by in situ hybridization (Figure 11–1). As shown by these 68 specimens, 29 patients had tumor samples that overexpressed VEGF. The median disease-free

survival for the VEGF-positive group was 22 months, compared with greater than 108 months for the VEGF-negative group. When borderline tumors were eliminated from the analysis, the median survival of the VEGF-positive group decreased to 18 months and the median survival of the VEGF-negative group increased to greater than 120 months. Other common prognostic variables, including stage, grade, histologic subtype, size, and age, had minimal impact on disease-free survival. In a multivariate analysis, VEGF overexpression was the strongest independent predictor of poor prognosis. Thus, VEGF overexpression may eventually be used to determine which patients will require postoperative therapy and may also serve as a potential target for such therapy.

The deoxyribonucleic acid (DNA) content as measured by ploidy has been shown to correlate with survival. In a retrospective review of specimens from 157 patients, the relative risk of death was twofold higher in patients whose tumors had a single aneuploid cell population, and was sixfold higher in patients whose tumors had multiple aneuploid cell clones, compared with patients with diploid tumors, after adjusting for age, grade, treatment, amount of residual disease, stage, and histologic type[15] (Figure 11–2). Tumors with a DNA index of > 2.2 manifested more aggressive behavior. The DNA index, an S-phase fraction of > 16%, and the number of aneuploid clones were more prognostic together than ploidy alone.

All patients with more than one aneuploid cell population, even with stage I disease, died within 3 years of diagnosis. This marker may reflect a cell population that is more likely to manifest drug-resistant phenotypes. In a multivariate analysis, only stage, ploidy, S-phase fraction, and histologic cell type (undifferentiated carcinoma) were independent predictors of survival. There was no correlation between ploidy and any specific histologic subtype. In this study, all borderline tumors were diploid. In another study that contained patients with aneuploid borderline tumors, patients with these tumors had a worse prognosis than that of patients with borderline diploid tumors.[16] Ploidy was also shown to be an independent prognostic factor in a more recent and larger study with 279 patients with invasive stage I ovarian cancer.[17] The 5-year disease-free survival was 78%, with a median time to relapse of 16 months. Seventy-seven patients had stage I grade 1 diploid tumors and no relapses, and there were 62 relapses in the remaining 202 patients; 136 patients had nondiploid tumors. Grade did not correlate with ploidy: 32% of grade 1 patients had nondiploid tumors. Clear cell histology was a poor prognostic variable independent of ploidy. Substage was the most important predictor of relapse in patients with clear cell histology. In another recent study analyzing the effects of ploidy and its possible prognostic significance, Gajewski and colleagues examined ploidy analysis in patients with early-stage ovarian carcinoma. Of the patients with diploid tumors, 100% (nine) were alive after 10 years of follow-up, compared with 58% of patients with aneuploid tumors. This study also demonstrated that patients with a negative second-look laparotomy had 0% recurrence with diploid tumors and 43% recurrence with aneuploid tumors.[18]

The serum marker CA 125 is an antigenic determinant on a glycoprotein that is expressed in the adult by mesothelial cells of the pleura, pericardium, and peritoneum and in endometrial, endocervical, and tubal epithelium.[19] CA 125 has long been used to monitor the clinical course of patients with an established diagnosis of ovarian carcinoma. Its ability to function as a prognostic factor for survival in patients with stage I epithelial cancer was assessed retrospectively in 201 patients.[20] Patients with borderline tumors were excluded. In a univariate analysis of preoperative levels of CA 125 of > 65, substage and histologic grade were identified as predictors of decreased survival.

The presence of an initial elevated CA 125 levels enabled investigators to segregate good and poor risk in subgroups within each of the histologic grades. A multivariate analysis identified the preoperative CA 125 level as the most powerful prognostic factor for survival. The risk of dying of disease was greater than sixfold higher in patients with a preoperative CA 125 level of > 65 U/mL. Substage also was an independent prognostic factor; however, age and histologic grade were not independent prognostic factors in this study.

Mutation and overexpression of the nuclear protein p53 are known to have a negative prognostic

influence on outcome in many malignancies.[21] In a study of early-stage ovarian cancer, p53 overexpression was detected in 15% of stage IA/B cancers and 44% of stage IC/II cancers.[22] Furthermore, p53 overexpression was seen more commonly in larger tumors (> 10 cm) and in tumors with grade 3 histol-

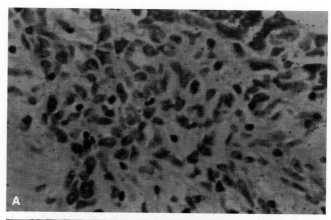
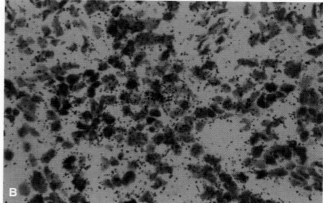
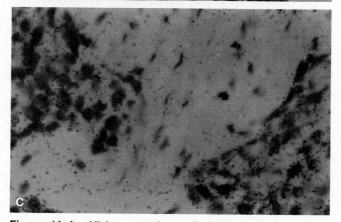

Figure 11–1. High-power views of a representative primary epithelial ovarian carcinoma. *A*, No significant labeling of tumor cells with the sense (control) probe; *B*, intense labeling of tumor cells with the antisense probe; and *C*, intense labeling of tumor cells, in comparison with stroma, with the antisense probe.

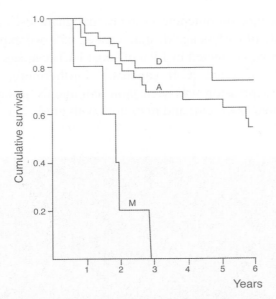

Figure 11–2. Survival in early-stage (stage I to II) ovarian cancer, with deoxyribonucleic acid (DNA) diploid (D, n = 47), single DNA aneuploid (A, n = 37), and multiploid (M, n = 5) tumors (p = .0001; Mantel-Cox test).

ogy. Recurrent disease developed in 35% of the 52 patients studied. No correlation was detected between p53 overexpression and recurrence rate or survival. Thus, overexpression of p53 did not segregate good-risk from poor-risk patients with early-stage ovarian cancer. More recent studies investigating p53 have been provided by Skirnisdottir and colleagues in 2001 and 2002.[23, 24] These studies investigated series of 113 and 109 patients, respectively, with FIGO stage 1A-IIC ovarian cancer and expression of p53. The patients had been optimally treated with surgery and adjuvant therapy. The first study examined p53 status and DNA content. The second study explored expression of several regulators of apoptosis, ie p53, BCL2, and BAX. Both studies demonstrated that p53 was associated with higher tumor grade and increased risk of recurrence. In the second study, p53 expression was associated with an increased risk of dying from the disease (p = 0.007). Expression of BCL2 and BAX were not associated with adverse prognosis, but co-expression of these proteins with p53 portended a worse outcome. P53 overexpression or mutation has also been implicated in resistance to platinum-based chemotherapy regimens.[25] Reles and colleagues studies p53 mutations and overexpression in 178

ovarian cancer samples. Ovarian cancer tumors had mutations in p53 in 56% of cases. These mutations were associated with significantly shortened time to progression and survival. Resistance to platinum based chemotherapy was significantly more frequent in patients with p53 overexpression and mutations. The difference in results of these newer studies, compared with earlier studies,[21, 22] likely reflects the decade that separates them, with the advances made in techniques of immunohistochemistry and DNA sequencing improving the detection of p53 overexpression and mutation. The more recent studies utilize mutational analysis of the gene for p53 as well as immunohistochemistry for detection of overexpression. Methods of analysis of genes and their proteins continue to improve and refine our understanding of the molecular and biochemical pathways involved in p53 expression and its impact on tumorigenesis and biology.

Flow cytometry, VEGF overexpression, over expression and mutation of p53, and elevated preoperative CA 125 are some of the newer prognosticators that may improve our ability to identify both patients with early-stage ovarian cancer who would benefit from aggressive management and (as importantly) those patients whose prognosis is so good that such therapy is not needed. These markers will need to be studied in prospective randomized trials.

CHEMOTHERAPY TRIALS

Patients with disease confined to the ovaries with an intact capsule, no ascites, grade 1 or 2 disease, and negative peritoneal-fluid cytology after comprehensive surgical staging are offered no further treatment. This recommendation is based on a seminal Gynecologic Oncology Group (GOG) trial by Young and colleagues, which randomized 81 such patients to oral melphalan versus no therapy.[13] The 5-year disease-free survival rate of 98% versus 91% and the overall survival rate of 99% and 94% were not statistically different (Table 11–4). The median follow-up was in excess of 6 years. Clear cell histology was identified as a poor risk factor. No patient receiving melphalan in this trial developed acute leukemia.

Other trials, however, have shown that prolonged administration of an alkylating agent is associated with the development of either myelodysplastic syndrome or acute myelogenous leukemia.[26]

A simultaneously conducted trial for higher-risk patients with early-stage ovarian cancer randomized 141 patients to receive either melphalan or intraperitoneal phosphorous 32 (^{32}P).[13] The patient groups were evenly matched for grade, stage, amount of residual disease, and age. The 5-year disease-free survival rate was 80% for both groups, with overall survival rates of 81% for the melphalan arm and 78% for the ^{32}P arm. Clear cell histology also was associated with a worse outcome. While only 17% of the patients had clear cell histology, 40% of the patients who relapsed had this cell type. Intraperitoneal ^{32}P was chosen for further study in high-risk patients, based on less toxicity with similar efficacy when compared with melphalan.

The next GOG trial compared intraperitoneal ^{32}P (15 mCi) to three cycles of cyclophosphamide (1,000 mg/m^2) and cisplatin (100 mg/m^2) every 21 days for three cycles for patients with stage IA/B (grade 3), IC, and II disease who had no macroscopic residual tumor after surgery.[27] Two hundred five patients with stage IA/B grade 3, IC, or II disease were randomized and were well balanced for age, performance, stage, histologic type, and grade. The relapse-free survival rate at 5 years was 77% for patients in the group treated with chemotherapy and 66% for patients who received intraperitoneal ^{32}P (see Table 11–4). The estimated recurrence rate was 31% less for the chemotherapy arm than for the intraperitoneal ^{32}P arm after adjusting for stage and grade. With a median follow-up of 6 years, the overall survival rate at 5 years was 83% for the chemo-

therapy arm and 76% for the ^{32}P arm. There was one treatment-related death in each arm. Myelosuppression was more frequent within the chemotherapy arm, with 67% of the patients having grade 3 or 4 toxicity. Of 98 patients randomized to the ^{32}P arm, 8 were unable to receive intraperitoneal therapy. The chemotherapy arm was deemed to have received the superior treatment despite there being no difference in survival, because of the improved progression-free interval and the late bowel-related toxicity associated with intraperitoneal ^{32}P. The 23% 5-year recurrence rate observed in this trial for early-stage disease with high-risk patients signified that three cycles of cisplatin and cyclophosphamide were still not sufficient therapy.

Paclitaxel now has an established role in the treatment of advanced ovarian cancer. Its superiority over cyclophosphamide was demonstrated in several large randomized trials.[28,29] A recently completed GOG trial (GOG 157) compared six cycles of paclitaxel (175 mg/m^2) and carboplatin (area under the curve [AUC] 7.5) every 21 days to three cycles of the same regimen, with the primary end point being survival and the secondary end points being progression-free survival and toxicity. Patients eligible for the study were patients with early-stage ovarian cancer who were deemed to be at high risk for failure with surgery alone. Patients included those with completely resected IC and II, clear cell, or poorly differentiated stage IA and IB epithelial cancer. The study is not yet unblinded, and 331 patients were evaluable for preliminary analysis. The two groups were well balanced for age, stage, histology, grade, and number of clear cell cancers. At a median follow-up of

Investigator	Patient Characteristics	n	Treatment	Median Follow-Up (yr)	5-Yr DFS (%)	5-Yr OS (%)
Young[13]	IA/B, grade 1/2	81	L-PAM vs observation	> 6	98 vs 91	98 vs 94
Bolis[28]	IA/B, grade 2/3	83	Cisplatin vs observation	> 6	83 vs 65	88 vs 82
Young[13]	IC, grade 3, II*	141	L-PAM vs ip P32	> 6	80 vs 80	81 vs 78
Bolis[28]	IC	152	Cisplatin vs ip P32	> 6	85 vs 65†	81 vs 79
Vergote[29]	I–III with no residual disease	347	Cisplatin vs ip P32	> 5	75 vs 81	81 vs 83
Young[24]	IC, grade 3, II*	205	Cisplatin/cyclophosphamide vs ip P32	> 5	77 vs 66	83 vs 76

Table 11–4. RANDOMIZED TRIALS REPORTING 5-YEAR RESULTS OF CHEMOTHERAPY FOR OVARIAN CANCER

DFS = disease-free survival; OS = overall survival; L-PAM = melphalan; ip = intraperitoneal; P32 = phosphorus 32.
*Stage at end, as defined by the International Federation of Gynecology and Obstetrics (FIGO).
†p = .008 (rest of pairs are not statistically significant).

3 years, 88% of the patients were alive and recurrence free; there have been 35 relapses and 19 deaths from disease. There was one treatment-related death in each arm of the study. One arm of this trial had more frequent grade 3 to 4 leukopenia, and the same arm had greater grade 2 to 4 neurologic toxicity.[30] No conclusions can be drawn from this early interim report, and only further analysis will determine the outcomes with respect to the very important question regarding the duration of therapy.

Many of the randomized trials in early-stage ovarian cancer, especially those conducted in the United States, have not had a no-treatment arm. However, such a trial has been conducted by the Italian Interregional Cooperative Group of Gynecologic Oncology.[31] This trial randomized patients to receive either 50 mg/m^2 of cisplatin every 28 days for six cycles or no further initial treatment. Patients in this study had stage IA or IB, grade 2 or 3 tumors. The disease-free survival rate for patients receiving cisplatin was 83%, compared to 65% for those patients who received no initial chemotherapy ($p = .05$) with a median follow-up in excess of 6 years. No overall survival advantage has yet been demonstrated due to the initiation of platinum-based chemotherapy at the time of relapse for the no-treatment population. Other potential explanations include the low dose of cisplatin, the use of single-agent chemotherapy, or the limited activity of the treatment. With only 41 and 42 patients in each arm, the study population may have been too small to detect small but significant differences between the two populations. In a companion study, patients with stage Ic disease were randomized to receive either cisplatin (50 mg/m^2) every 28 days for six cycles or one treatment of intraperitoneal ^{32}P.[31] The disease-free survival rate was 85% for the 77 patients treated with cisplatin and 65% for the 75 patients treated with ^{32}P ($p = .008$). No differences in overall survival between the two treatment groups was detected. On the basis of improved progression-free survival, cisplatin was deemed the superior therapy.

Another large trial also compared six cycles of cisplatin with intraperitoneal ^{32}P, similarly to the Italian trial.[32] Patients with stage I through stage III disease were eligible as long as they had no gross residual disease after surgery. One hundred seventy-one patients were randomized to receive cisplatin, and 169 patients were to receive the intraperitoneal ^{32}P. Twenty-eight patients in the ^{32}P arm had adhesions that precluded intraperitoneal administration and that were treated with external beam whole-abdomen irradiation. The median follow-up exceeded 5 years. The estimated 5-year disease-free survival rate was 81% for the ^{32}P patients and 75% for the cisplatin patients. There was no statistical difference in these values. No significant difference in survival was detected. The patients receiving ^{32}P had more bowel toxicity, and the investigators concluded that with no difference in efficacy and less toxicity, cisplatin was the preferred treatment.

Two other large cooperative European trials with a surgery-only arm in early-stage ovarian cancer were run in parallel and include the European Organization for Research and Treatment of Cancer trial (adjuvant chemotherapy in ovarian neoplasms [ACTION] trial) and the International Collaborative Ovarian Neoplasm (ICON-1) trial. These trials compared immediate platinum-based chemotherapy postoperatively in early-stage ovarian cancer to a delayed start of the same therapy at the time of recurrence. These trials were closed to accrual in January of 2000. An analysis with a median follow-up of 5.5 years was recently presented.[33] The ICON-1 trial initiated accrual in August of 1992 and enrolled 477 patients from 83 centers throughout five countries. The ACTION trial commenced in November of 1991 and enrolled 448 patients from 40 centers throughout Europe. These trials represent the largest effort to date, enrolling a total of 923 patients in a randomized setting to evaluate the efficacy of adjuvant chemotherapy for early-stage ovarian cancer. In the ICON-1 trial, eligibility included any patient for whom the clinician felt adjuvant therapy was indicated. The ACTION trial had more-stringent eligibility criteria enrolling patients with stage IA or IB disease with grade 2 or 3 tumors, and patients with all grades of stage IC and IIA cancers and all clear cell tumors. The studies were well balanced between the arms of each study and between the studies themselves for age, FIGO substage, and cell type. However, ICON-1 did include nine patients (2%) with stage III disease. The ICON-1 trial had 143 patients (32%) with grade I tumors, versus 54 (12%) in the ACTION trial. In these studies, patients could receive single-agent platinum-based chemotherapy or combination therapy using a platinum agent. In the ICON-1 trial, 170 (82%) of patients who were randomized to receive adjuvant therapy received single-agent carboplatin; 71 (33%) of patients in the ACTION trial were similarly randomized. The ACTION trial included 102 patients (47%) who received cisplatin-based combination chemotherapy, compared with 13 patients (6%) in the ICON-1 trial. Recurrence-free survival was similar in both studies at this interim analysis, with 351 patients without recurrence in the ICON-1 trial and 336 patients without recurrence in the ACTION trial (Table 11–5). There were 126 patients who had recurrence or who died in the ICON-1 trial and 112 such patients in the ACTION trial. Recurrence-free survival at 5 years was improved in both studies with the use of adjuvant therapy, and a meta-analysis of the two trials showed an absolute difference of 11% (65% in the observation arm vs 76% in the arm with immediate therapy, $p = .001$) (Table 11–6). An analysis of overall survival at 5 years showed an absolute difference of 7% (75% for observational therapy vs 82% for immediate therapy, $p = .01$) (see Table 11–6). In a hazard ratio analysis including age, FIGO substage, and histologic grade, there was no evidence that the effects of adjuvant therapy were smaller or larger in any subgroup. The Nordic Ovarian Cancer Study Group ran a trial that was similar to the ICON-1 study.[34] There was a 20% recurrence rate in the group not treated postoperatively, compared with the 13% recurrence rate for those patients who received carboplatin. These differences are not statistically significant. The small size of this trial (approximately 70 patients per arm) probably precluded the detection of any differences in outcome.

The current GOG trial (GOG 175) for patients with early-stage disease randomizes patients to receive weekly low-dose intravenous paclitaxel (40 mg/m^2) for 24 weeks or no further therapy after a uniform induction of three cycles of carboplatin (AUC 6) and paclitaxel (175 mg/m^2 over 3 hours). The use of low-dose weekly paclitaxel is based on preclinical findings that paclitaxel at these low doses has antiangiogenic properties.[35]

Early-stage ovarian cancer is a fertile area for research on the use of other antiangiogenic agents. Testing of other noncytotoxic strategies, such as vaccines (with or without dendritic cells) and targeted small molecules and monoclonal antibodies, are appropriate in this setting.

INTRAPERITONEAL THERAPY

Ovarian cancer remains clinically confined to the abdominal cavity for most if not all of the disease course. Intraperitoneal chemotherapy has been extensively studied in cases of ovarian cancer because of this property. It has been established that intraperitoneal chemotherapy is applicable only when there is minimal residual gross disease (ie, no single residual mass > 0.5 cm). Early-stage ovarian cancer is a good model for this form of treatment. Carboplatin has been shown to have a favorable ratio of peritoneal cavity concentration to plasma concentration (approximately 18).[36] Hematologic toxicity was still dose limiting in a phase I trial. The maximum tolerated dose was 500 mg/m^2 every 28 days. In a phase II trial by the same group of investigators, 47 patients with early-stage ovarian cancer were treated with four cycles every 28 days.[37] The median time to recurrence had not been reached with a median follow-up of 26 months. Relapse occurred in 23% of patients. The relapse rate was intra-abdominal in seven patients and outside the abdominal cavity in one. Two patients had recurrences both within

Table 11–5. RESULTS OF ICON-1* AND ACTION† TRIALS FOR EARLY-STAGE OVARIAN CANCER					
Trial	*N*	Recurrence	No Recurrence	Alive	Dead
ICON-1	477	126	351	375	102
ACTION	448	112	336	370	78

N = population size.
*International Collaborative Ovarian Neoplasm trial.
†Run by the European Organization for Research and Treatment of Cancer.

Table 11–6. RESULTS OF META-ANALYSIS OF ICON-1* AND ACTION† TRIALS

Timing of Therapy	Recurrence-Free Survival (%)	Overall Survival at 5 Years (%)
Immediate Treatment	76	82
Treatment at Recurrence	65	75

*International Collaborative Ovarian Neoplasm trial.
†Run by the European Organization for Research and Treatment of Cancer.

and outside the peritoneal cavity. Grade 4 leukopenia occurred in 6.8% of the patients, with grade 4 thrombocytopenia in 17.8% of patients. The treatment is safe but offers little advantage over the intravenous delivery of this drug.

Paclitaxel, given intraperitoneally, has a greater than 1,000 ratio of peritoneal cavity concentration to plasma concentration in relapsed disease.[38] The drug was detectable 1 week after intraperitoneal administration. A phase II trial of intraperitoneal paclitaxel used a dose of 60 mg/m^2 weekly for 16 weeks in 80 patients who required salvage therapy. Patients were required to have no residual site of disease > 0.5 cm. Eighty-six percent of patients were considered cisplatin sensitive. Due to catheter-related problems, 27 patients did not receive all 16 planned treatments, and abdominal pain was usually less than grade 2. Twenty-eight patients with microscopic disease at the start of treatment were assessable, 17 (61%) achieved a pathologic complete response. Conversely, of 31 assessable patients with small-volume macroscopic disease, 1 patient had a pathologic complete response and 4 others had surgical partial responses. The treatment regimen was active and tolerable. The impact of this therapy on survival would need to be determined by a randomized trial.

RADIOTHERAPY

Whole-abdomen irradiation has been evaluated as a postsurgical treatment in patients with early-stage ovarian carcinoma without large residual disease. The best experience has been reported by investigators at the Princess Margaret Hospital.[39] Whole-abdomen irradiation was superior to pelvic irradiation with or without chlorambucil. There was a statistically significant 10-year survival benefit

(64% vs 40%, $p = .0007$) in patients with less than 2 cm of residual disease; in patients with larger residual disease, no advantage was seen. This group used an open field technique, but other investigators have not demonstrated an improved outcome with this form of treatment.[40] Different techniques of radiation delivery may account for some of these differences.

One trial attempted to compare more-modern chemotherapy with whole abdomen irradiation.[41] Patients were randomized to receive either cisplatin (50 mg/m^2) and cyclophosphamide (600 mg/m^2) or whole abdomen irradiation with 30.2 Gy delivered to the abdomen and 43.2 Gy delivered to the pelvis. The trial was closed early because of low accrual and poor compliance. There is no trial currently examining a paclitaxel and platinum regimen compared to whole abdomen irradiation. Due to patient and investigator bias, it is doubtful that such a trial could be successfully completed in the United States.

CONCLUSION

In summary, patients with epithelial nonclear cell ovarian cancer who are found to have stage IA or IB disease and grade 1 or 2 tumors after comprehensive surgical staging have 5-year survival rates that exceed 90%, and no further treatment is appropriate for these patients. The preliminary results from the ICON-1 and ACTION trials have demonstrated an overall survival benefit for adjuvant therapy in early-stage ovarian cancer; however, a toxicity evaluation was not included, and long-term follow-up of this study with attention to the incidence of second malignancies will be of interest. We eagerly await full publication of these important studies.

A growing body of evidence supporting the hypothesis that adjuvant therapy increases progression-free survival exists. For the first time, there are data demonstrating a survival advantage for adjuvant chemotherapy in early-stage ovarian cancer. Patients with high-risk disease should be offered enrollment in a clinical trial if available. In the absence of an appropriate clinical trial, patients should be offered three to six cycles of a platinum-based chemotherapy regimen. Another alternative, although less popular, would be whole abdomen radiotherapy. In the United States, the standard treatment is platinum/taxane combination chemotherapy.

The future of therapy for early-stage ovarian carcinoma will be guided by randomized trials investigating novel prognostic factors for patient stratification as well as new targeted therapies aimed at the molecular mechanisms that control ovarian cancer cell proliferation.

REFERENCES

1. Greenlee RT, Hill-Harmon MB, Murray T, Thun M. Cancer statistics, 2001. CA Cancer J Clin 2001;51:15–37.
2. Landis SH, Murray T, Bolden S, Wingo PA. Cancer statistics, 1999. CA Cancer J Clin 1999;49:8–31.
3. Ozols RF, Rubin SC, Thomas GM, Robboy SJ. Epithelial ovarian cancer. In: Hoskins WJ, Perez CA, Young RC, editors. Principles and practice of gynecologic oncology. Philadelphia: Lippincott Williams & Wilkins, 2000.
4. Fishman DA, Schwartz PE. Current approaches to diagnosis and treatment of ovarian germ cell malignancies. Curr Opin Obstet Gynecol 1994;6:98.
5. Ozols RF. Ovarian cancer. Part II: Treatment. Curr Probl Cancer 1992;16:61–126.
6. McGowan L, Lesher LP, Norris HJ, et al. Misstaging of ovarian cancer. Obstet Gynecol 1985;65:568–72.
7. Young RC, Decker DG, Whaton JT, et al. Staging laparotomy in early ovarian cancer. JAMA 1983;250:3072–6.
8. Puls LE, Carrasco R, Morrow MS, Blackhurst D. Stage I ovarian carcinoma: specialty-related differences in survival and management. South Med J 1997;90:1097–100.
9. Zanetta G, Chiari S, Rota S, et al. Conservative surgery for stage I ovarian carcinoma in women of childbearing age. Br J Obstet Gynaecol 1997;104:1030–5.
10. Parker RT, Parker CH, Wilbanks GD. Cancer of the ovary: survival studies based on operative therapy, chemotherapy and radiotherapy. Am J Obstet Gynecol 1970;108:878–88.
11. Williams TJ, Dockerty MB. Status of the contralateral ovary in encapsulated low grade malignant tumors of the ovary. Surg Gynecol Obstet 1976;143:763–6.
12. Dembo AJ, Davy D, Stenwig AE, et al. Prognostic factors in patients with stage I epithelial ovarian cancer. Obstet Gynecol 1990;75:263.
13. Young RC, Walton LA, Ellenberg SS, et al. Adjuvant therapy in stage I and stage II epithelial ovarian cancer. N Engl J Med 1990;322:1021–7.
14. Paley PJ, Staskus KA, Gebhard K, et al. Vascular endothelial growth factor expression in early ovarian carcinoma. Cancer 1997;80:98–106.
15. Kallioniemi OP, Punnonen R, Jattila J, et al. Prognostic significance of DNA index, multiploidy, and S-phase fraction in ovarian cancer. Cancer 1988;61:334–9.
16. Kaern J, Trope C, Kjorstad KE, et al. Cellular DNA content as a new prognostic tool in patients with borderline tumors of the ovary. Gynecol Oncol 1990;38:452–7.
17. Vergote IB, Kaern J, Abeler VM, et al. Analysis of prognostic factors in stage I epithelial ovarian cancer. Am J Obstet Gynecol 1993;169:40–52.
18. Gajewski WH, Fuller AF, Pastel-Ley C, et al. Prognostic significance of DNA content in epithelial ovarian cancer. Gynecol Oncol 1994;53:5–12.
19. Kawabat SE, Bast RC Jr, Bhan AK, et al. Tissue distribution of a coelomic-epithelium-related antigen recognized by the monoclonal antibody OC125. Int J Gynecol Pathol 1983;2:275–85.
20. Nagele F, Petru E, Medl M, et al. Preoperative CA 125: an independent prognostic factor in patients with stage I epithelial ovarian cancer. Obstet Gynecol 1995;86:259–64.
21. Ruley HE. p53 and response to chemotherapy and radiotherapy. In: DeVita VT, Hellman S, Rosenberg SA, editors. Important advances in oncology. Philadelphia: Lippincott-Raven Publishers; 1996. p. 37–49.
22. Kohler MF, Kerns B-JM, Humphrey PA, et al. Mutation and overexpression of p53 in early-stage epithelial ovarian cancer. Obstet Gynecol 1993;81:643–50.
23. Skirnisdottir, I, Sorbe B, Karlsson M, Seidal T. Prognostic importance of DNA ploidy and p53 in early stages of epithelial ovarian carcinoma. Int J Oncol 2001;19:1295–1302
24. Skirnisdottir I, Seidal T, Gerdin E., Sorbe B. The prognostic importance of p53, bcl-2, and bax in early stage epithelial ovarian carcinoma treated with adjuvant chemotherapy. Int J Gynecol Cancer 2002;12:265–76.
25. Reles A, Wen WH, Schmider A, et al. Correlation of p53 mutations with resistance to platinum-based chemotherapy and shortened survival in ovarian cancer. Clin Cancer Res 2001;7:2984–97.
26. Greene MH, Boice JF, Greer BE, et al. Acute non-lymphocytic leukemia after therapy with alkylating agents for ovarian cancer: a study of five randomized clinical trials. N Engl J Med 1982;307:1416.
27. Young RC, Brady MF, Nieberg RM, et al. Randomized clinical trial of adjuvant treatment of women with early (Figo-I-IIA high risk) ovarian cancer—GOG #95 [abstract 1376]. Proc Am Soc Clin Oncol 1999;357a.
28. McGuire WP, Hoskins WJ, Brandy MF, et al. Cyclophosphamide and cisplatin compared with paclitaxel and cisplatin in patients with stage III and stage IV ovarian cancer. N Engl J Med 1996;334:1–6.
29. Mangioni C, Trope C, James K, et al. Updated analysis shows a highly significant improved overall survival (OS) for cisplatin-paclitaxel as first line treatment of advanced ovarian cancer: Mature results of the EORTC-GCCG, NOCOVA, NCIC CTG and Scottish Intergroup Trial. [abstract 1394] Proc Am Soc Clin Oncol 1998;17:361a.
30. Young RC. Three cycles versus six cycles of adjuvant paclitaxel (taxol)/carboplatin in early stage ovarian cancer. Semin Oncol 2000;27(3 Suppl 7):8–10.
31. Bolis G, Colombo N, Pecorelli S, et al. Adjuvant treatment for early epithelial ovarian cancer: results of two randomised clinical trials comparing cisplatin to no further treatment or chromic phosphate (^{32}P). Ann Oncol 1995;6:887–93.
32. Vergote IB, Vergote-De Vos LN, Abeler VM, et al. Randomized trial comparing cisplatin with radioactive phosphorus or whole-abdomen irradiation as adjuvant treatment of ovarian cancer. Cancer 1992;69:741–9.
33. Vergote IB, Trimbos BJ, Guthrie D, et al. Results of a randomized trial in 923 patients with high-risk early ovarian

cancer, comparing adjuvant chemotherapy with no further treatment following surgery. [abstract 802] Proc Am Soc Clin Oncol 2001;20:201a.

34. Trope C, Kaern J, Vergote I, et al. Randomized trial of adjuvant carboplatin versus no treatment in stage I high risk ovarian cancer by the Nordic Ovarian Cancer Study Group (NOCOVA) [abstract 1260]. Proc Am Soc Clin Oncol 1997;16:352a.

35. Klauber N, Parangi S, Flynn E, et al. Inhibition of angiogenesis and breast cancer in mice by the microtubule inhibitors 2-methoxyestradiol and taxol. Cancer Res 1997;57:81–6.

36. Malmstrom H, Larsson D, Simonsen E. Phase I study of intraperitoneal carboplatin as adjuvant therapy in early ovarian cancer. Gynecol Oncol 1990;39:289–94.

37. Malmstrom H, Simonsen E, Westberg R. A phase II study of intraperitoneal carboplatin as adjuvant treatment in early-stage ovarian cancer patients. Gynecol Oncol 1994;52:20–5.

38. Markman M, Brady MF, Spirtos NM, et al. Phase II trial of intraperitoneal paclitaxel in carcinoma of the ovary, tube and peritoneum: a Gynecologic Oncology Group study. J Clin Oncol 1998;16:2620–4.

39. Dembo AJ. Radiotherapeutic management of ovarian cancer. Semin Oncol 1984;11:238–50.

40. Schilder RJ, Boente MP, Corn BW, et al. The management of early ovarian cancer. Oncology (Huntingt) 1995;9:171–82.

41. Chiara S, Pierfranco C, Franczone P, et al. High-risk early-stage ovarian cancer: randomized clinical trial comparing cisplatin plus cyclophosphamide versus whole abdominal radiotherapy. Am J Clin Oncol 1994;17:72–6.

12

Palliative Surgery

MELISSA A. GELLER, MD
MATTHEW P. BOENTE, MD

Many patients with advanced ovarian carcinoma will ultimately have an intra-abdominal recurrence despite an initial response to cytoreductive surgery and cytotoxic chemotherapy. In fact, most patients with ovarian cancer will ultimately die of intestinal obstruction and the malnutrition that results from the patient's inability to digest and absorb nutrients. The majority of these women will experience subtle symptoms associated with disease progression. Initially these symptoms will be vague, usually in the form of indigestion, diarrhea, or constipation. Eventually, abdominal distention, nausea, and vomiting become overwhelming. Patients are usually not in severe pain and many times, unfortunately, undergo a number of useless diagnostic procedures when these symptoms initially present. Upper and lower endoscopies are rarely beneficial during the early periods of recurrent ovarian carcinoma. The mainstay of diagnosis continues to be CA 125 elevation, symptomatology, and abnormal radiographic appearances on computed tomography (CT) scans. Often, minor surgical procedures such as a paracentesis and thoracentesis may provide temporary relief. Medical management such as salvage chemotherapy can be initiated and may temporarily provide palliation for recurrent abdominal ascites, partial intestinal obstruction, or malignant pleural effusions. Many patients, however, will ultimately need major abdominal surgery to palliate their symptoms. Unfortunately, these types of surgeries are incredibly complex and are associated with serious complications. Surgical intervention is rarely successful in alleviating a patient's symptoms for long periods of time unless effective successful salvage chemother-

apy can be initiated as well; this has been previously published.[1] Unfortunately, there are no reliable prognostic factors that predict surgical success or, for that matter, responses to chemotherapy. This chapter will outline the role for surgery in relieving intestinal obstruction for patients with ovarian cancer and review what palliative measures may be offered in such circumstances. We hope to underscore the diagnostic and therapeutic dilemmas that present when a patient with advanced ovarian cancer has a bowel obstruction.

DIAGNOSIS

Most recently, GOG 158, a study by the Gynecologic Oncology Group (GOG) that randomized 840 patients to either paclitaxel and carboplatin or to paclitaxel and cisplatin showed a median survival advantage for patients receiving carboplatin (area under the curve [AUC] = 6) and paclitaxel (175 $\mu g/m^2/3$ h).[2] In addition, because of the ease of administration of the carboplatin and 3-hour paclitaxel regimen, this regimen is now considered the standard of care in patients with advanced ovarian carcinoma after initial cytoreductive surgery. Unfortunately, despite an initial response rate of around 70 to 80%, the disease of many of these patients will recur. In patients who initially had a suboptimal surgical debulking, these symptoms recur earlier. Many patients with a known diagnosis of ovarian cancer will present to their family practitioner or internist with vague and subtle complaints of fullness or indigestion. These symptoms do not warrant evaluation by upper and lower endoscopy. Ovarian carcinoma is predominantly a "surface tumor." The tumor spreads by coating the bowels and other intra-abdominal organs (Figures 12–1, 12–2, and 12–3). With early recurrences, rarely, will symptoms warrant upper and lower endoscopy. In situations in which patients report melena or have heme-positive stools, evaluation by a gastroenterologist accustomed to the problems of patients with ovarian cancer is appropriate. Many of these patients' recurrences can be diagnosed by serial CA 125 values, physical examination, or abnormalities detected on a CT scan of the abdomen and pelvis.

Many of the initial recurrences will not require surgical intervention for diagnosis or management. Rather, patients with such recurrences will be better served by the administration of second-line chemotherapy. The response rate for these agents are in the 20 to 25% range, with most of these responses being short-lived and partial in nature. Therefore, subsequent symptoms of nausea and vomiting will ultimately warrant a gastrointestinal work-up.

At the Fox Chase Cancer Center, our preference has been to perform a lower gastrointestinal series with gastrografin, followed by an upper gastrointestinal series with a small-bowel follow-through once the contrast has been evacuated from the large colon. Tap water enemas following the gastrografin enema are usually helpful in eliminating excess contrast. The lower and upper gastrointestinal studies, specifically in that order, are quite important to determine the location of the obstruction. If there is not obvious tumor on the CT scan and if serial

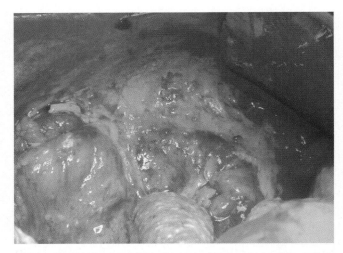

Figure 12–2. Same patient shown in Figure 12–1, with carcinomatosis obliterating the pelvis and normal pelvic anatomy.

CA 125 values are not suspicious for recurrent ovarian cancer, the differential diagnosis regarding the etiology of the obstruction must be entertained. The number one differential diagnosis should include adhesions resulting from previous surgery (Figures 12–4 and 12–5) or perhaps intraperitoneal chemotherapy or radiation (Figures 12–6 and 12–7). Although the use of radiation therapy as primary adjuvant therapy in this country has declined over the past several decades, it continues to be used for palliating local symptoms of ovarian cancer.[3] Therefore, intestinal injury secondary to previous radiation continues to be a potential problem. No patient

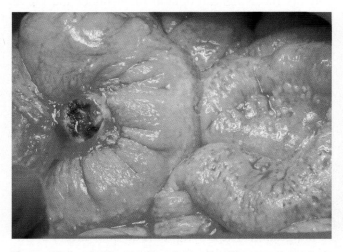

Figure 12–1. A 63-year-old patient with diffuse carcinamatosis distorting and encasing the transverse colon and small intestine.

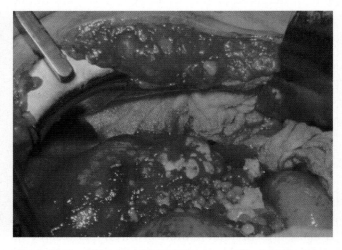

Figure 12–3. Diffuse carcinomatosis covering the right diaphragm in a 47-year-old woman.

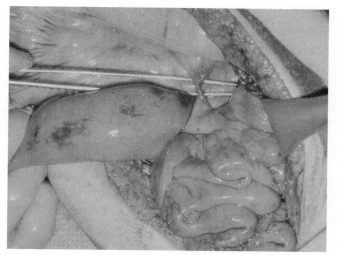
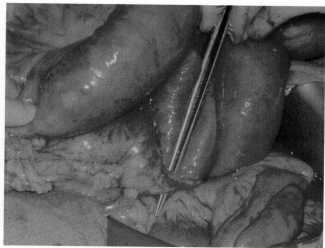

Figure 12–4 and 12–5. A 45-year-old woman with symptoms of small-bowel obstruction, a slightly elevated CA 125 level (102 μ/mL), and a normal appearing CT scan, 2.5 years after chemotherapy.

should be denied surgery when the diagnosis of recurrent disease is in question. CT-directed fine-needle aspirations of regions suspicious for recurrent disease have, for the most part, made these types of diagnostic dilemmas unusual. Between 5 and 24% of patients who undergo surgical intervention for a presumed small-bowel obstruction related to ovarian cancer or previous surgery for ovarian cancer will not have recurrent disease diagnosed. The surgical intervention in these patients is likely to be much more successful in the long term.[4]

Unfortunately, however, recurrent disease is the more common cause for obstruction, and major gas-

trointestinal surgery is often required to relieve or palliate these obstructions. A summary of the literature would show that approximately 57% of patients undergoing surgery for recurrent ovarian carcinoma with suspected bowel obstruction will have obstructions involving the small intestine. Approximately 30% will have a colonic obstruction, and approximately 13% will have a combined small- and large-bowel obstruction.[5] This underscores a major diagnostic principle. A simple loop colostomy, without exploration, will not palliate the majority of patients. The need for lower gastrointestinal radiography followed by upper gastrointestinal radiography is para-

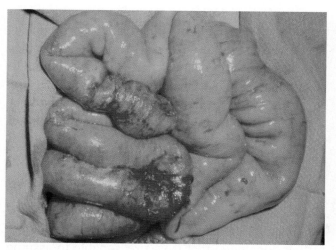
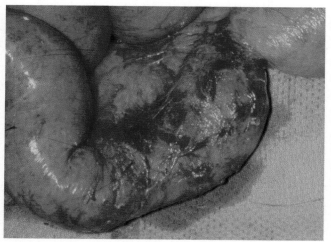

Figure 12–6 and 12–7. A 63-year-old woman with a history of stage IIIC ovarian cancer, an elevated CA 125 level (151 μ/mL), and symptoms of bowel obstruction. She had received whole-abdomen radiation 3.7 years earlier. No recurrence was found at the time of surgery.

mount to avoid multiple surgical procedures. Furthermore, the radiographic series are important to provide the gynecologic oncologist with a "road map" of the upper and lower gastrointestinal anatomy. This is necessary because of the fact that the intra-abdominal appearance of the gut in these advanced malignancies will humble even the most experienced and talented gynecologic oncologists (Figure 12–8). If a preoperative work-up reveals an intact lower colon but an obstructed terminal ileum (which is oftentimes the case), then a simple enteroenterostomy between identifiable areas of the small intestine and the colon can be accomplished without excessive morbidity. Without the radiologic studies, adequate identification of the anatomy and visualization of the exact areas of obstruction are not possible in most situations.

PROGNOSTIC FEATURES

A number of authors have tried to identify the clinical features of ovarian cancer that would most likely be associated with a successful surgical outcome in patients with advanced ovarian carcinoma presenting with bowel obstruction. Similarly, authors have tried to identify factors that would portend surgical failure. Unfortunately, at this time, there are no reliable prognostic factors in the preoperative setting that would universally predict either favorable or poor outcomes. Krebs and co-workers were the first to systematically evaluate clinical variables associated

Figure 12–8. Multiple loops of bowel obstructed by recurrent ovarian cancer in a 28-year-old woman.

with surgical outcome in patients with bowel obstructions secondary to recurrent ovarian carcinoma. These authors describe a successful outcome as a survival of 2 months from the date of surgery. In their hands, 65% of patients (118 surgeries) benefited. There were, unfortunately, 26 postoperative deaths, and 14 patients were found to be inoperable. The median survival was approximately 12.5 weeks, with a range of 1 to 78 weeks. The prognostic factors evaluated included age, nutritional deprivation, tumor spread, ascites, previous chemotherapy, and previous radiotherapy. The authors devised a scoring system that assigned points to each variable. The likelihood of successful surgery was determined from this point system.[6] The aforementioned variables were determined to be of prognostic significance in either evaluation. Unfortunately, these authors did not take into account the interaction between these variables (multivariate analysis), and numerous authors since then have been unable to validate this scoring system.[6–8]

Fernandes and co-workers studied diagnostic factors that were associated with survival 12 months after the onset of intestinal obstruction. In a univariate analysis, factors associated with prolonged survival included younger age, lower stage, no prior radiation therapy, the absence of ascites, and favorable radiographic findings. Higher serum albumin levels, normal urea nitrogen levels, and lower alkaline phosphatase levels were also associated with a favorable outcome.[8]

Clarke-Pearson and co-workers at the Duke University Medical Center more recently evaluated 36 perioperative variables and compared this to a postoperative survival of 60 days. One of these variables was the Krebs prognostic score, which was found to be predictive of survival in a univariate analysis. However, when the authors controlled for interaction between the multiple variables (multivariant logistic regression analysis), they found that clinical tumor status and serum albumin levels were of particular importance in predicting successful outcomes. This clinical tumor status is defined as the clinical detection of recurrent tumor based on physical examination and chest radiography. The authors further concluded that it was reasonable to assume that patients with clinical ascites and with advanced tumor spread detected by CT scan and elevated CA 125 would more accurately predict less favorable surgical outcomes.[9]

Since clinical tumor status cannot be altered in the acute setting of a bowel obstruction in patients with recurrent ovarian cancer, many authors have attempted to assign a role for total parenteral nutrition (TPN) in these patients, in an attempt to raise serum albumin levels. Clarke-Pearson and co-workers, however, did not show a perioperative survival advantage for patients who had received TPN in the preoperative setting. Similarly, operative morbidity has not been significantly altered when TPN has been given in a preoperative fashion.

The indications for perioperative use of TPN are complicated and poorly understood. They have been thoroughly reviewed elsewhere, but, to date, there have been no definitive prospective randomized trials to justify the perioperative use of TPN in patients with ovarian cancer.[10–13] However, when patients have been without food for 7 or more days or when patients undergo surgery that will likely interfere with adequate nutritional intake for this length of time, the use of TPN seems prudent. Unfortunately, the exact indications for its use will have to await the results of prospective randomized trials.

The Veterans Affairs Total Parenteral Nutrition Cooperative Study Group has prospectively evaluated the use of TPN in malnourished surgical patients. It should be noted that although none of these patients had ovarian cancer, this was a large randomized series of 395 malnourished patients, many of whom had gastrointestinal malignancies and required surgery for intestinal obstruction. There was no difference in the two groups with mild or moderate nutritional impairment with regard to major surgical postoperative complications or the overall 90-day postoperative mortality rate. The only benefit of TPN seemed to be in the severely malnourished patient subgroup, in which the number of postoperative noninfectious complications was found to be lower. Taken together, these studies would seem to indicate that there is a limited role for TPN in the perioperative setting, with exceptions being made for severely malnourished patients (serum albumin < 2.0) or for women who have already been without nutrition for 7 days preoperatively.[14]

MEDICAL MANAGEMENT

Many patients with advanced ovarian cancer who present with a small-bowel obstruction are managed conservatively with nasogastric decompression prior to any attempts at surgical intervention. The goal with these patients is to obtain the highest quality of life for the longest period of time. While no patient should be denied conservative management, it is extremely unlikely that nasogastric decompression will completely rid the patient of their intestinal obstruction symptoms for any significant period of time. Krebs and Goplerud reported their experience with the management of 96 women who had 165 episodes of bowel obstruction. Of these, 43 patients were managed conservatively with decompression and intravenous fluid. Unfortunately, only 32% had a significant enough improvement in symptoms to allow for discharge. The hospital stay ranged from 2 to 30 days, with a mean of 5 days. Furthermore, 12 of the 14 patients who were discharged returned to the hospital with recurrent intestinal obstruction in a mean time of 5.5 weeks. Conservative medical management, therefore, offers little for the prolonged palliation of symptoms.[15] Our experience has been that the best surgical candidates for relief of intestinal obstruction are patients who have had a long interval between the initial diagnosis of ovarian cancer and the onset of intestinal obstruction. Similarly, patients whose treatment-free interval has been 2 years or longer (since they were last administered chemotherapy) are usually better candidates for surgical intervention (Figures 12–9 and 12–10). In addition, these patients are more likely to respond to salvage chemotherapy than are patients with persistent disease and who have received three or four previous agents.

SURGICAL COMPLICATIONS

The prevention of surgical complications should be a major goal of the gynecologic oncologist attempting to relieve a patient of intestinal obstruction from ovarian carcinoma. Serious complications have been reported in each and every manuscript reviewing this topic. The rate of these complications is between 30 and 64%, and the operative mortality is reported to be

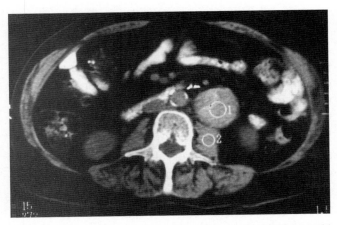

Figure 12–9. Enlarged left aortic lymph nodes in a 75-year-old with recurrent ovarian carcinoma 4 years from last dose of chemotherapy. The patient was optimally debulked (100%) and had no intraperitoneal disease at the exploration.

between 14 and 32%. The majority of these complications are related to wound healing, infection, and anastomotic breakdown. Fistulas are not uncommon, and a large percentage of these will never heal unless the patient has effective postoperative chemotherapy. Since the rate of response to chemotherapy in the salvage situation is in the range of 20 to 25%, the majority of patients who experience fistulization after these surgeries will retain the fistula for the remainder of their life. It is important to outline these complications to the patient prior to surgery. In addition, the patient should understand that there is a significant chance (15%), that she will never leave the hospital following the surgery. A detailed explanation of the

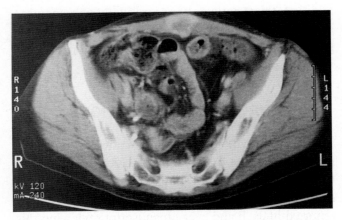

Figure 12–10. An anterior abdominal wall mass, 3.5 years since patient's last dose of chemotherapy; optimally debulked (99%), with small-volume (< 0.5 cm) carcinomatosis.

surgery and all of its potential complications should be given to the patient and her family in the preoperative setting. Ample time should be given for the patient to ask questions and receive honest answers. This is time well spent, both for the patient and the physician, so that there are reasonable expectations in the postoperative period.

MINIMALLY INVASIVE SURGICAL PALLIATION

A percutaneous endoscopic gastrostomy (PEG) tube should be considered when the patient is felt to be a poor surgical candidate for relief of bowel obstruction. Patients who are good candidates for PEG tubes are those who have undergone failed prior surgical procedures, have had multiple prior chemotherapies, and have a poor performance status or large-volume recurrent ascites. It should be noted that these tubes can be placed with intravenous sedation and a local anesthetic. They can provide significant relief of nausea and vomiting in the terminally ill patient. Malone and co-workers reported a series of 10 patients with advanced recurrent ovarian cancer in whom percutaneous gastrostomies were placed. The median length of survival following placement was 35 days, and this route of decompression seems to be much more "civilized" than the prolonged use of a nasogastric tube during the last days or weeks of a patient's life.[16]

The patient who is an appropriate candidate for a PEG tube may also be a candidate for a wall stent in the setting of a large-bowel obstruction. Metallic wall stents are often used as a treatment option in patients with esophageal and colorectal carcinomas. Recently they have been used not as a curative means, but as a palliative nonsurgical treatment of gastrointestinal obstructions in ovarian cancer patients. When patients have reached the stage of colonic obstruction, they often have advanced disease and are not operative candidates. In patients with end-stage malignancy, stent placement may offer palliation of obstructive symptoms. There are, however, complications associated with this procedure. Failure to relieve obstruction can occur due to the inability to get a guidewire through the area of stricture. In one series, this occurred 36% of the time.[17] Another potential risk is bowel perforation. With tumor encasing the bowel wall and with the inflammatory response that results, this risk becomes of great concern. In one series, the perforation rate was 15.4%.[18] Tamim's series reported no perforations when using a combined endoscopic and fluoroscopic technique. The vast differences in reported complications can most likely be attributed to the technical skill of the operator. An experienced endoscopist or interventional radiologist, or both, are required for fluoroscopic placement of these stents (Figure 12–11). A long-term complication is stent migration. Most ovarian cancer patients who have this procedure done

for palliation will, however, die before stent migration presents as an issue. This procedure is currently an option for patients with low rectosigmoid lesions. Patients who have more proximal lesions are not optimal candidates for wall stent placement because of the technical difficulty in placement.

Ascites is often a recurring problem in end-stage ovarian cancer patients, who may present with symptoms of obstruction. Ascites can cause the patient's significant abdominal distension, tachypnea, dyspnea and gastrointestinal upset. The respiratory difficulties that are often seen result from elevation of the

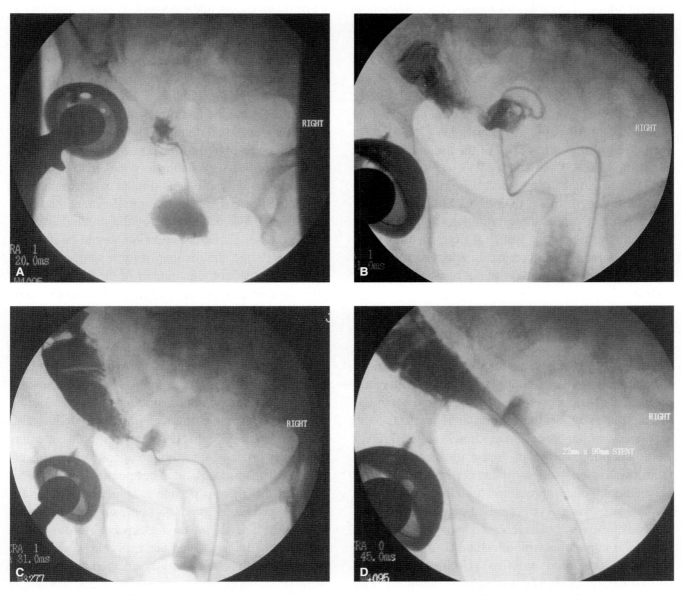

Figure 12–11. *A* to *D*, Fluoroscopic placement of an endoluminal colonic wall stent in a woman with distal colonic obstruction.

diaphragm from intra-abdominal fluid collection. Palliative treatment of symptomatic ascites can improve the quality of life for a patient. Parascentesis can acutely alleviate the patient's symptoms; however, the fluid generally recurs within a short period of time. Other palliative options such as a permanently implanted abdominal drains, peritoneovenous shunts and intraperitoneal chemotherapy have been used. Several trials have been performed, using intraperitoneal interferon-α or interferon-β. A pilot study performed by Sartori and colleagues[19] evaluated the efficacy of a standardized schedule of interferon-α_{2b} in 41 cancer patients, 12 of whom had ovarian cancer. This was administered at 6 million or 9 million units, depending on body weight ($\leq$ or $>$ 50 kg), via a catheter clamped for a total of 6 hours. Six courses were given at 4-day intervals. The highest rate of response was obtained in the 12 ovarian cancer patients. Six (50%) of the ovarian cancer patients had a complete response, defined as no fluid recurrence at 30 days. Three patients (25%) had a partial response, with $<$ 50% of the ascites recurring at 30 days, and 3 patients (25%) had no response 51% of the patients experienced mild flulike symptoms with fevers of up to 39.3°C, chills, myalgias, and fatigue. Despite these complaints, the patients tolerated the treatment well. Of note in this study, patients showing no decrease in ascites production after the first three courses did not respond to further courses.

INTESTINAL FISTULAS

The treatment of intestinal fistulas by using various therapeutic modalities continues to be a challenging problem for the gynecologic oncologist and continues to cause a great deal of suffering in patients with advanced ovarian cancer. Many times, surgical repair is not an option, secondary to the advanced nature of their disease as well as their performance status. Nasogastric decompression and treatment with somatostatin has had only limited success in the past. Recently, infliximab was reported to have healed 60% of fistulas in patients with intestinal fistulas that were caused by regional enteritis (Crohn's disease).[20] Infliximab, a chimeric monoclonal antibody that blocks tumor necrosis factor, has yielded remarkable

results. We have had a limited experience at the University of Minnesota with a handful of patients suffering from enterocutaneous fistulas and enterovesical fistulas from advanced gynecologic malignancies. In a small number of patients ($N = 6$), we have had a 67% response rate with this agent.

SUMMARY

The management of patients who develop bowel obstruction related to recurrent ovarian cancer is a complex problem and requires the total breadth of the skills of an experienced gynecologic oncologist. Unfortunately, the management of these patients is usually based on an institution's bias or, perhaps, the bias of an individual surgeon. These patients and their problems will humble the most skilled and the most experienced gynecologic oncologists. Fortunately, experience and the published literature offer some guidance despite the fact that the majority of the studies suffer from small numbers and retrospective analyses. Our philosophy has been one of a multidisciplinary approach. A gynecologic oncologist, a medical oncologist, and a radiologist trained in gastrointestinal procedures participate in the initial evaluation, carefully taking into account all of the previously mentioned factors. Particular attention should be given to the patient's age, the number of prior surgeries undergone by the patient, the number of prior chemotherapies administered to the patient, the patient's nutritional status (albumin ≥ 2.0), the amount of time elapsed since the patient's initial diagnosis of ovarian cancer, and the presence or absence of recurrent or refractory ascites. It has been our experience that long disease-free intervals or a long time period since a prior chemotherapy administration ($>$ 2 years) often portends a favorable surgical prognosis. It has also been our experience that despite the rigorous attempts to identify prognostic factors preoperatively, this exercise is often unsuccessful. These cases tend to be so complex that there is no one formula that would universally predict a good or poor surgical outcome. Many times, patients who are expected to do well do not whereas patients who are expected to do poorly surprise us. No patient should be denied an aggressive work up or surgical exploration, provided that she is willing to accept the risk-benefit ratio that is involved.

For patients who do not appear to be operative candidates, palliative care in this setting must be used. Placement of PEG tubes and rectal stents and alleviation of abdominal distension due to ascites are all means of improving the quality of life for patients with progressive ovarian cancer.

REFERENCES

1. Clarke-Pearson DL, Rodriguez GC, Boente M. Palliative surgery for epithelial ovarian cancer. In: Rubin SC, Sutton GP, editors. Ovarian cancer. Philadelphia: Lippincott, Williams & Wilkins; 2001. p. 329–44.
2. Ozols RF, Bundy BN, Fowler J, et al. Randomized phase III study of cisplatin (CIS)/paclitaxel (PAC) versus carboplatin (CARBO)/PAC in optimal stage III epithelial ovarian cancer (OC). Gynecologic Oncology Group trial (GOG 158). Proc Am Soc Clin Oncol 1999;18:3084–92.
3. Corn BW, Lanciano RM, Boente M, et al. Recurrent ovarian cancer: effective radiotherapeutic palliation after chemotherapy failure. Cancer 1994; 74(11):2979–83.
4. Lund B, Hansen M, Lundvall F, et al. Intestinal obstruction in patients with advanced carcinoma of the ovaries treated with combination chemotherapy. Surg Gynecol Obstet 1989;169(3):213–8.
5. Clarke-Pearson DL, Chin NO, DeLong ER, et al. Surgical management of intestinal obstruction in ovarian cancer. Clinical features, postoperative complications and survival. Gynecol Oncol 1987;26(1):11–8.
6. Krebs HB, Goplerud DR. Surgical management of bowel obstruction in advanced ovarian carcinoma. Obstet Gynecol 1983;61:327–30.
7. Rubin SC, Hoskins WJ, Benjamin I, Lewis JL Jr. Palliative surgery for intestinal obstruction in advanced ovarian cancer. Gynecol Oncol 1989;34(1):16–9.
8. Fernandes JR, Seymour RJ, Suissa S. Bowel obstruction in patients with ovarian cancer. A search for prognostic factors. Am J Obstet Gynecol 1988;158:244–9.
9. Clarke-Pearson DL, DeLong ER, Chin N, et al. Intestinal obstruction in patients with ovarian cancer: variables associated with surgical complications and survival. Arch Surg 1988;123(1):42–5.
10. Clarke-Pearson DL, Olt G, Rodriguez G, Boente M. Preoperative evaluation and postoperative management. In: Berek JS, Adashi EY, Hillard PA, editors. Novak's Gynecology. Baltimore: Williams & Wilkins; 1996. p. 543–617.
11. Clarke-Pearson DL, Olt G, Rodriguez GC, Boente M. Preoperative evaluation and preparation for gynecologic surgery. In: Copeland LJ, editor. Textbook of gynecology. 2nd ed. Philadelphia: W.B. Saunders Co.; 2000. p. 917–54.
12. Clarke-Pearson DL, Olt G, Rodriguez GC, Boente MP. Preoperative evaluation and preparation for gynecologic surgery. In: Copeland LJ, editor. Textbook of gynecology. Philadelphia: W.B. Saunders Co.; 1993. p. 641–69.
13. Clarke-Pearson DL, Olt G, Rodriguez GC, Boente MP. Preoperative and postoperative management. In: Gershenson DM, Decherney AH, Cury SL, editors. Operative Gynecology. Philadelphia: W.B. Saunders; 1993.
14. Veterans Affairs Total Parenteral Nutrition Study Group. Perioperative total parenteral nutrition in surgical patients. N Engl J Med 1991;325:525–32.
15. Krebs HB, Goplerud DR. The role of intestinal intubation in obstruction of the small intestine due to carcinoma of the ovary. Surg Gynecol Obstet 1984;158:467–71.
16. Malone JM Jr, Koonce T, Larson DM, et al. Palliation of small bowel obstruction by percutaneous gastrostomy in patients with ovarian carcinoma. Obstet Gynecol 1986; 68(3):431–3.
17. Tamim WZ, Ghellai A, Counhan TC, et al. Experience with endoluminal colonic wall stents for the management of large bowel obstruction for benign and malignant disease. Arch Surg 2000;135(4):434–8.
18. Canon CL, Baron TH, Morgan DE, et al. Treatment of colonic obstruction with expandable metal stents. AJR Am J Roentgenol, 1997;168(1):199–205.
19. Sartori S, Nielsen I, Tassinari D, et al. Evaluation of a standardized protocol of intracavitary recombinant interferon alpha-2b in the palliative treatment of malignant peritoneal effusions. Oncology 2001;61(3):192–6.
20. D'Haens GR. Infliximab (Remicade), a new biological treatment for Crohn's disease. Ital J Gastroenterol Hepatol 1999;31(6):5519–20.

13

Developmental Chemotherapy

MICHAEL A. BOOKMAN, MD

Despite improvements in median and overall survival with the use of a combination of platinum drugs and paclitaxel, long-term survival rates for patients with advanced epithelial ovarian carcinoma (EOC) remain disappointing, and the development of a more effective primary therapy remains a priority. In particular, several interesting chemotherapy agents have demonstrated activity individually in patients with recurrent EOC. Among these are gemcitabine, topotecan, liposomal doxorubicin, and prolonged oral etoposide. Preclinical models have suggested an advantage for combinations of these agents with platinum, which advantage has been attributed to the inhibition of pathways involved in deoxyribonucleic acid (DNA) repair. However, efforts to develop multidrug combinations with platinum and paclitaxel have encountered substantial bone marrow toxicity, prompting the exploration of alternative schedules and sequences of drug administration. In this regard, the Gynecologic Oncology Group (GOG) and other organizations have conducted pilot studies in previously untreated patients to define combinations that are suitable for group-wide phase III trials. With international collaboration, the GOG has launched a five-arm trial (GOG 0182-ICON5) that will compare these combinations against carboplatin/paclitaxel. The selection of candidate regimens for this trial illustrates the challenges of drug development for treatment of EOC.

EVOLUTION OF STANDARD THERAPY

The primary treatment of EOC has evolved from single alkylating agents (ie, melphalan) to cisplatin and platinum-based combinations, followed by incorpo-ration of paclitaxel, but this has not been without a degree of controversy. EOC is considered to be a chemoresponsive neoplasm; initial response rates to systemic therapy exceed 80%, prompting an active international program for drug development, evaluation, and registration. However, among women with advanced-stage disease at diagnosis, long-term survival remains poor due to eventual tumor recurrence and the emergence of drug-resistant disease.

In contrast to other advanced malignancies, an attempt at maximal cytoreductive surgery is a standard component of initial EOC management and, when successful, is associated with improved clinical outcomes. This ability to achieve cytoreduction reflects the tendency of ovarian cancer to remain clinically confined to the peritoneal cavity and to be characterized by superficial implants without distant metastatic or parenchymal disease. Thus, patients with tumors that can be readily cytoreduced will generally have more well-differentiated lesions without deep invasion or dense adhesions. This unusual biology has also prompted an evaluation of intraperitoneal treatment modalities and characterization of the local peritoneal milieu from the perspective of growth factors, angiogenesis, and the host immune response.

Preclinical models have been important for the initial identification of nonplatinum compounds that merit evaluation as single agents or platinum-based combinations. Several of these agents have demonstrated promising clinical activity in patients with recurrent and platinum-resistant EOC. In addition, preclinical models have also suggested an advantage for combinations of these agents with platinum, an advantage which has been attributed to the inhibition of pathways involved in DNA repair. Recent efforts have focused on combinations with topotecan, gemcitabine, liposomal doxorubicin, and oral etoposide as potential candidates for incorporation in frontline phase III trials. However, clinical efforts to develop multidrug combinations with platinum and paclitaxel have encountered substantial bone marrow toxicity, prompting the exploration of alternative schedules and sequences of drug administration. Unfortunately, existing preclinical models have not been predictive of clinical outcomes, including host toxicity, and clinical development has largely been based on empiric pilot studies.

PHASE III LEGACY

There are a number of scientific, statistical, clinical, and practical criteria that contribute to the adoption of new treatment regimens and changes in clinical practice. Although well-designed phase III randomized trials can have a substantial impact on treatment practices, community perception and acceptance are influenced by other factors, including toxicity, quality of life, costs, and complexity of treatment. These points are important to consider in the design of clinical trials to maximize long-term benefit and to use limited clinical resources most efficiently.

Each trial needs to be considered within the historical context in which it was developed. Although tempting, historical comparisons are usually not informative, due to evolving practices that have an impact on supportive care, including the timing and sensitivity of diagnostic studies to confirm disease recurrence, suitability for aggressive cytoreductive surgery, availability of alternative treatments, and extent of disease at recurrence.

In addition, the widespread use of cytoreductive surgery needs to be considered when evaluating the potential impact of chemotherapy administered in the postoperative setting. Frequently, patients have small-volume residual disease that is undetectable with routine imaging modalities. Thus, a decline in serum cancer antigen 125 (CA 125) and the achievement of a clinical complete remission may have more to do with the extent of initial cytoreductive surgery rather than the use of platinum-based chemotherapy. As such, overall survival and pro-gression-free survival are preferred endpoints although expected outcomes are influenced by the stage of disease and the extent of cytoreduction in the target population.

Taken together, these observations reinforce the role for carefully designed phase III trials to evaluate and compare clinical outcomes associated with new combination regimens.

The addition of doxorubicin to standard platinum-based chemotherapy is a case in point. Doxorubicin was evaluated in combination with cisplatin and cyclophosphamide for treatment of EOC and achieved a small but significant impact on long-term survival that was detectable in a meta-analysis of four randomized trials (Figure 13–1).[1] Although the magnitude of the benefit was small (a change in median survival of approximately 3 months), a significant *p* value of .02 was achieved owing to the large number of evaluable participants (*n* = 1,194). These data were published in 1991 and did not substantially alter clinical practice in the United States because of concerns about added toxicity and interest in the emerging data on paclitaxel.

The use of intraperitoneal chemotherapy is a second illustrative case. Two trials that incorporated intraperitoneal cisplatin documented a modest but statistically significant improvement in survival, compared to intravenous cisplatin in patients with optimal initial cytoreductive surgery (Figures 13–2

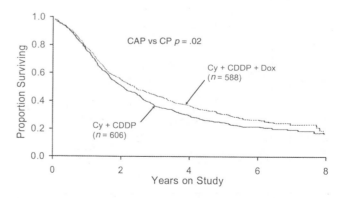

Figure 13–1. Results from the Ovarian Cancer Meta-Analysis Project. Based on the pooled analysis of four individual phase III trials, it was possible to demonstrate that the overall survival of patients who received CAP (a combination of cyclophosphamide [Cy], cisplatin [CDDP], and doxorubicin [Dox] was slightly superior to that of patients who received CP (a combination of cyclophosphamide and cisplatin.

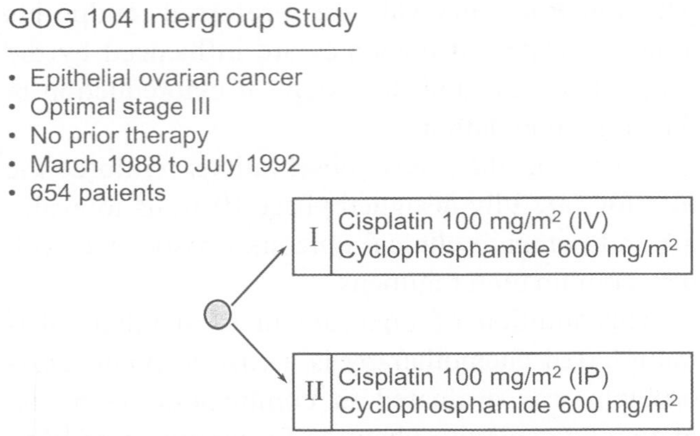

GOG 104 Intergroup Study

- Epithelial ovarian cancer
- Optimal stage III
- No prior therapy
- March 1988 to July 1992
- 654 patients

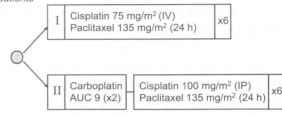

Figure 13–2. Intravenous (IV) versus intraperitoneal (IP) cisplatin. Schema for phase III intergroup protocol GOG 104.

GOG 114

- Epithelial ovarian cancer
- Optimal stage III (residual ≤ 1 cm)
- No prior therapy
- August 1992 to April 1995
- 462 patients

Figure 13–4. Intravenous (IV) versus intraperitoneal (IP) cisplatin. Schema for phase III protocol GOG 114, which also included two cycles of dose-intense carboplatin in the experimental arm. (AUC = area under the curve.)

to 13–5).[2,3] However, once again, these trials have not substantially altered clinical practice. The role of intraperitoneal therapy is subject to considerable scientific and clinical bias, and the use of a peritoneal catheter adds complexity and potential toxicity, even though it can reduce nonhematologic toxicities associated with intravenous cisplatin. In addition, with the widespread adoption of intravenous carboplatin, the nonhematologic toxicities associated with cisplatin are avoided, which negates any potential advantage afforded by intraperitoneal cisplatin. Unfortunately, the first trial accrued more slowly than expected and was expanded to include more patients with minimal residual disease. This prolonged the overall duration of the study, and

results were ultimately published after promising data on other new agents, such as paclitaxel, were already being disseminated. The second trial included two additional cycles of intravenous dose-intense carboplatin on the experimental arm, which complicates any analysis of potential benefit. A third randomized trial confirmed an advantage in disease-free survival but (again) at the expense of increased toxicity, and the role of intraperitoneal therapy remains unresolved.[4]

Bias can also occur in the opposite direction, promoting the early adoption of new regimens, such as carboplatin and paclitaxel, prior to mature results from phase III trials. Early experience with single-

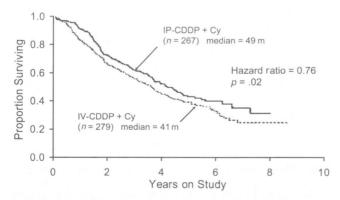

Figure 13–3. Intravenous (IV) versus intraperitoneal (IP) cisplatin. Overall survival documents a significant improvement in the hazard ratio, favoring intraperitoneal therapy. (CDDP = cisplatin; Cy = cyclophosphamide.)

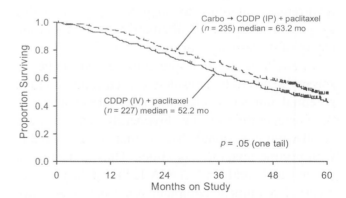

Figure 13–5. Intravenous (IV) versus intraperitoneal (IP) cisplatin. Overall survival in the GOG 114 trial, documented a significant improvement in favor of the experimental arm. (Carbo = carboplatin; CDDP = cisplatin.)

agent paclitaxel in recurrent disease generated considerable enthusiasm, and data from frontline trials were eagerly awaited. Empiric combinations with cisplatin were rapidly developed and evaluated in the GOG 111 trial (Figures 13–6 and 13–7), in which a total of 410 previously untreated women with suboptimal stage III and IV EOC were randomized to receive either cisplatin plus cyclophosphamide or cisplatin plus paclitaxel (at 135 mg/m² over 24 hours). The cisplatin-plus-paclitaxel regimen was judged to be superior, with increased median progression-free interval (18 months vs 13 months) and overall survival (38 months vs 24 months).[5] Favorable data were confirmed by a European-Canadian intergroup trial (OV10) with similar arms although paclitaxel was administered at 175 mg/m² over 3 hours.[6] In both trials, the use of paclitaxel, which was an investigational agent at the time, was largely restricted to initial protocol–mandated therapy, and only a small number of patients on the control arm ever received paclitaxel for management of recurrent or progressive disease. This control over the choice of subsequent chemotherapy tended to maximize any differences in clinical outcomes attributed to the use of paclitaxel in primary therapy and undoubtedly contributed to the positive results reported from these important randomized trials. Based on the favorable results and manageable toxicity, the combination of paclitaxel and cisplatin rapidly emerged as the standard of care for advanced-stage EOC. However, in view of the non-hematologic toxicity and required hydration associated with cisplatin, as well as the inconvenient 24-

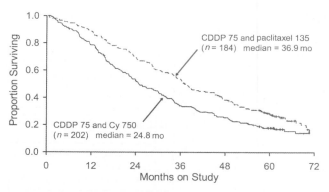

Figure 13–7. Improved survival with incorporation of paclitaxel in the GOG 111 trial. Impressive and significant improvement in median survival for the experimental arm was clearly demonstrated. However, it was uncertain if this was due to the specific drug combination, the addition of a non-cross-resistant active agent, or the elimination of a potentially antagonistic agent (cyclophosphamide). (CDDP = cisplatin; Cy = cyclophosphamide.)

hour infusion schedule for paclitaxel, there was early interest in switching to an outpatient regimen with carboplatin and 3-hour paclitaxel.

In spite of concern about bone marrow toxicity, combinations of paclitaxel and carboplatin proved relatively easy to develop. Phase I studies documented that both agents could be safely administered in combination at nearly full single-agent doses, without a requirement for hematopoietic growth factors. The relative convenience of this outpatient regimen led to its rapid adoption by the oncology community, even prior to the completion of phase III randomized trials. Ultimately, the GOG 158 trial documented that carboplatin plus paclitaxel (3 hours) was equally effective when compared to cisplatin plus paclitaxel (24 hours),[7] validating a regimen that had already been widely adopted within the community.

Meanwhile, other studies have suggested that single-agent or sequential therapy may have long-term outcomes that are equivalent to those of frontline combinations. For example, in the GOG 132 trial (Figure 13–8), patients with suboptimal (stages III to IV) disease were randomized to initial therapy with cisplatin (100 mg/m²), paclitaxel (200 mg/m² over 24 hours), or a combination of cisplatin (75 mg/m²) and paclitaxel (135 mg/m² over 24 hours).[8] Although not incorporated in the actual trial design, many patients on single-agent therapy crossed over to receive the other agent at the time of

GOG 111

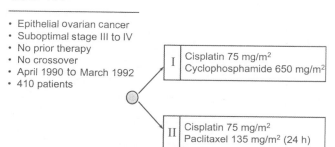

- Epithelial ovarian cancer
- Suboptimal stage III to IV
- No prior therapy
- No crossover
- April 1990 to March 1992
- 410 patients

I | Cisplatin 75 mg/m²
Cyclophosphamide 650 mg/m²

II | Cisplatin 75 mg/m²
Paclitaxel 135 mg/m² (24 h)

Figure 13–6. Schema for incorporation of paclitaxel in the GOG 111 trial. Note that paclitaxel remained an investigational agent for the duration of this trial, limiting the opportunities for crossover at disease progression.

GOG 132

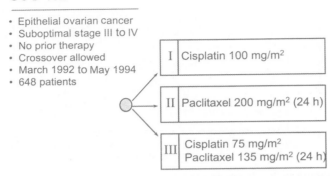

• Epithelial ovarian cancer
• Suboptimal stage III to IV
• No prior therapy
• Crossover allowed
• March 1992 to May 1994
• 648 patients

I Cisplatin 100 mg/m²

II Paclitaxel 200 mg/m² (24 h)

III Cisplatin 75 mg/m²
     Paclitaxel 135 mg/m² (24 h)

Figure 13–8. Single-agent versus combination therapy schema for the GOG 132 trial. Although many patients assigned to single-agent therapy (arms I and II) crossed over to the alternative agent at disease progression, this was not a formal component of the protocol design.

disease progression. Initial response rates to single-agent paclitaxel (43%) were inferior to each of the arms with cisplatin (67%). In addition, patients who received initial paclitaxel and progressed were still able to achieve a 60% response rate when treated with cisplatin as second-line therapy. Not surprisingly, progression-free survival favored the two arms with cisplatin, but overall survivals for all three arms were equivalent (Figure 13–9). This suggests that using sequential therapy with two active single agents in women with advanced disease is acceptable and perhaps equally effective as using a frontline combination. Further evidence along these lines is provided by the ICON3 trial, which randomized over 2,000 patients between a reference arm (either single-agent carboplatin or a combination of carboplatin, doxorubicin, and cyclophosphamide) and an experimental arm of carboplatin and paclitaxel.[9] No significant improvement in progression-free interval or overall survival was apparent with the combination, reinforcing the option of sequential single agents for some patients with advanced disease.

Thus, although phase III trials represent our best vehicle for the objective evaluation of new treatment strategies, the results of phase III trials will not always alter clinical practice, due to feasibility, toxicity, and complexity. In addition, by their design, large phase III trials often lag behind clinical advances and can sometimes be preempted by the early adoption of new interventions on the basis of extrapolation from smaller studies.

DEVELOPMENTAL THERAPY

Overview

Developmental therapy in the setting of ovarian cancer has focused on cytotoxic chemotherapy, which includes organoplatinum derivatives, taxanes, nontaxane antimicrotubular agents, nucleoside analogues, antifolates, and inhibitors of topoisomerase and other enzymes involved in DNA synthesis and repair, many of which are derived from natural sources (Figures 13–10 and 13–11). In view of the central role of platinum compounds, there has also been particular interest in nonplatinum agents that may accentuate the platinum response through the inhibition of DNA repair and through interference with the removal of platinum-DNA adducts (summarized in Table 13–1). In addition to examining these cytotoxic agents, recent studies have also targeted growth factors, cellular receptors, angiogenesis, signal transduction pathways, apoptosis, and cell cycle progression. With a variety of novel agents and more traditional compounds available, it is also important to consider how to evaluate single agents and combinations in a meaningful and efficient manner.

Although a major focus of the GOG has been the design and execution of definitive phase III trials to evaluate various aspects of frontline therapy, the GOG also maintains an active developmental chemotherapy program in collaboration with the National Cancer Institute (NCI) and the pharmaceutical industry. This effort is guided by scientific prioritization through committees to define new

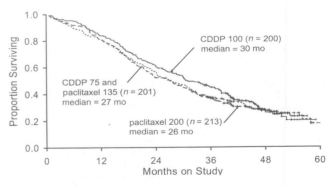

Figure 13–9. Single-agent versus combination therapy in the GOG 132 trial. There was no apparent difference in overall survival for single-agent therapy (with optional crossover), compared to combination therapy. (CDDP = cisplatin.)

Figure 13–10. Natural sources of cytotoxic agents for developmental therapy. Clockwise from top left: mayapple (etoposide); vinca (vinca alkaloids); Pacific forest growth zones for *Taxus brevifolia*, or western yew (paclitaxel); *taxus baccata*, or eastern yew (docetaxel); Chinese growth zones for *Camptotheca acuminata* (camptothecins, topotecan); and a specimen of *Camptotheca acuminata*.

regimens for evaluation in future phase III trials. Although there are nearly 25,000 new cases of ovarian cancer diagnosed in the United States each year, few individual centers manage enough patients to conduct their own phase II trials within a reasonable time frame. Regulatory, scientific, and administrative details require thoughtful prioritization of new concepts in the cooperative group setting, and the GOG provides an effective multicenter infrastructure to rapidly complete studies once they are activated. In general, new investigational agents will undergo initial phase I evaluation outside of the GOG but will then receive formal phase II evaluation in patients with recurrent disease. Agents with significant antitumor efficacy will then be selected for phase I studies in previ-

ously untreated patients, to develop safe and tolerable combinations with platinum and/or taxane derivatives (Figure 13–12).

Following successful phase I development, a regimen can move directly to a definitive phase III trial. In general, formal phase II evaluation of each new platinum-based combination is felt to be unwarranted as the expected response rate from platinum alone exceeds 75% in this population. While phase II studies in patients with newly diagnosed disease may provide valuable information on feasibility and toxicity, the importance of an non-comparative response rate or progression-free interval is difficult to assess. In part, this is due to the potential impact of patient selection factors and other sources of bias in a relatively small clinical trial.

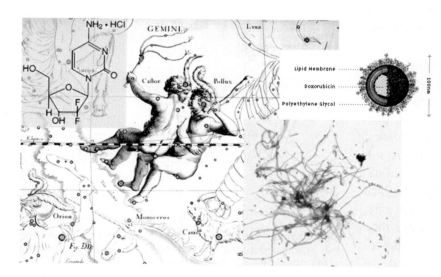

Figure 13–11. Other agents for developmental therapy. Clockwise from upper left: structure of gemcitabine, with the constellation Gemini, reflecting the "geminal" sites for fluorine, polyethylene glycol liposomal doxorubicin (Doxil), and *Streptomyces* (doxorubicin).

Table 13–1.   REPRESENTATIVE CYTOTOXIC AGENTS: TARGETS, MECHANISMS, SCHEDULE DEPENDENCE, RESISTANCES, AND TOXICITY

	Platinum	Paclitaxel	Topotecan	Gemcitabine
Target	DNA	β-tubulin	Topo-I	RN reductase, DNA
Mechanism	DNA adduct formation	Tubulin aggregation	Stabilize DNA complex	↓RNA, DNA synthesis
Schedule	Independent	Dependent (toxicity)	Dependent (efficacy)	Dependent (metabolism)
Resistance	↑GSH, ↑tolerance, ↓accumulation	↑MDR-MRP, tubulin mutations	↓Topo-I	↑RR
Toxicities	Cumulative, long-term	Noncumulative	Noncumulative	Noncumulative

DNA = deoxyribonucleic acid; GSH = reduced glutathione; MDR = multidrug-resistance glycoprotein; MRP = membrane-associated–resistance protein; RN = ribonucleotide; RNA = ribonucleic acid; RR = ribonucleotide reductase; Topo-I = topoisomerase-I.

In the setting of recurrent disease, patients have been divided into prognostic categories based on the platinum-free interval, which predicts for resistance to platinum compounds and other agents. With the incorporation of nonplatinum agents in frontline therapy, eligibility for phase II trials has been modified to reflect the treatment-free interval, which is defined as the time from the completion of chemotherapy to when there is clinical evidence of recurrent disease. Although not perfect, this simple categorization facilitates the design and interpretation of phase II trials with reference to the existing database of prior studies. Ideally, new agents are selected for evaluation in the specific patient population that will yield the most important clinical data, based on potential risks and benefits. For example, a new platinum compound that has been engineered to overcome drug resistance would have highest priority for evaluation in a chemotherapy-resistant population, provided that the risk of cumulative nonhematologic toxicity was acceptable. Conversely, a novel biologic agent that inhibits signal transduction is probably better evaluated for efficacy and molecular targeting in patients with longer treatment-free intervals and potentially chemoresponsive disease.

Several chemotherapeutic agents exhibit schedule-dependent host toxicities, but the impact of schedule on tumor response is less clear. Sometimes these relationships are defined through preclinical models or phase I studies, but in most cases, information on optimal dose and schedule is not available when planning phase II and III clinical trials. In addition, traditional phase I paradigms place undue emphasis on defining dose-limiting toxicity, which usually consists of neutropenia, rather than on the optimization of tumor biologic targeting or efficacy. As one might expect, the importance of

schedule dependencies or other treatment variables is accentuated during the development of combination regimens, particularly if there is any biologic interaction between the individual components. For example, combinations of platinum with either topotecan or gemcitabine have demonstrated sequence-dependent effects on hematologic toxicity, requiring a substantial reduction in initial drug dose levels and raising questions about adequate tumor exposure. Conversely, paclitaxel can be combined with carboplatin at full doses with an apparent reduction in hematologic toxicity, prompting some investigators to describe a "platelet-sparing" effect[10,11] and raising questions about the potential for negative tumor interactions.[12]

In view of the toxicity encountered with some drug combinations, investigators have evaluated alternative strategies for drug delivery, including weekly treatment with lower individual doses, abbreviated duration of treatment, cycle-by-cycle alternations, and the use of sequential doublets composed of different agents rather than a conventional fixed triplet

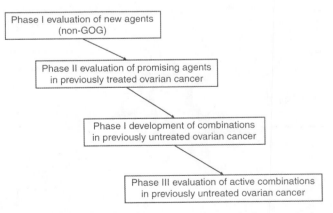

Figure 13–12. Developmental therapeutics pathway for screening new agents and for the incorporation of active agents in frontline phase III trials. (GOG = Gynecologic Oncology Group.)

regimen. The optimum approach has not been defined, and each strategy has potential limitations. Better preclinical models that are predictive of human drug interactions would be helpful to minimize host toxicity while maximizing antitumor effects.

Finally, our clinical trial paradigms are being challenged by a fast-growing panel of biologic and molecular-targeted reagents. In addition, it is widely anticipated that molecular profiling of tumor genotype, DNA methylation status, messenger ribonucleic acid (mRNA) expression, patterns of protein synthesis, and pharmacogenomic pathways of drug metabolism will better predict which tumors might respond to which reagents in which patients. These advances in drug development and tumor biology have the potential to overwhelm our traditional approach to clinical trials and will require increased attention as we move forward.

Role of Phase II Trials in Recurrent Disease

The GOG has used the phase II trial as a mechanism to screen new single agents or specific combinations for activity in women with recurrent disease. In general, these trials have employed a two-stage accrual design that allows for early stopping in the event of inactivity. The primary study hypothesis is usually based on a response rate "of interest" (to demonstrate activity) and a response rate of "no further interest" (consistent with inactivity), based on historical thresholds from prior studies. The sample size for each stage is determined by the desired precision (Type I error [α]) and power (Type II error [β]) of the analysis. For example, for patients with platinum-resistant disease, the response rate of interest for further development would typically be 25%, with a response rate of less than 10% being of no further interest. When combined with a desired precision of 0.1 and a power of 0.9, this yields a sample size of approximately 25 patients in the first stage and 20 to 25 additional patients in the second stage, which would be activated only if more than two responses are observed during the first stage.

With response rate (complete and partial) as the primary endpoint, patients are required to have measurable disease according to response evaluation criteria in solid tumors (RECIST) criteria, as adopted by the NCI and the GOG. The occurrence of disease sta-

bilization is reported as a favorable clinical outcome but is of uncertain significance in a small phase II study with variability in patient selection and natural history that may include indolent tumors.

It has been argued that tumor response rate may not be the best primary end point for the evaluation of newer targeted biologic or antiangiogenic compounds as these may exhibit cytostatic "growth-arresting" behavior rather than direct tumor cytotoxicity. The importance of this assertion is unclear; however, it has resulted in alternative phase II designs that emphasize the progression-free interval and disease stabilization rate, rather than the response rate. Historical baselines for these end points are less robust and were largely obtained in patients with bi-dimensional measurable disease, which likely has a different response rate and time to progression, compared to small-volume disease not measurable by radiographic criteria or to minimal disease that is detectable only on the basis of an elevated CA 125 level or other serum tumor marker. Nonetheless, as more of these studies are conducted, it will be possible to refine expectations and to apply these end points in the target patient population.

While the focus of this chapter is developmental chemotherapy, it should be noted that selected patients with recurrent disease may benefit from secondary cytoreductive surgery or palliative radiation. Due to the propensity for diffuse peritoneal spread, the extent of recurrent disease is often underestimated by conventional imaging modalities. This has led many oncologists to reserve surgery for symptomatic patients with localized bowel obstruction or other disease-related symptoms. However, some patients may develop a localized pelvic recurrence that is amenable to cytoreduction, which can be followed by chemotherapy or observation. In addition, it should be noted that radiation therapy can offer palliative management of pain or bleeding associated with bulky pelvic disease.

In any discussion of treatment of recurrent ovarian cancer, clinicians, patients, and family members can benefit from a shared understanding of basic goals in the setting of a chronic relapsing illness. While clinically meaningful objective and subjective responses can occur in patients with resistant disease, and while prolonged progression-free and overall survival may be observed in patients with platinum-sensitive disease, available data do not support the conclusion that therapy has a realistic potential to be curative in these settings. Thus, the evaluation of new treatment interventions in the context of clinical trials is appropriate and of a high priority.

Characterization of Phase II Populations

As already mentioned, one of the difficulties in interpreting the reported activity of individual agents in small phase II studies has been variability in the treated population. It is now well recognized that there is considerable heterogeneity among patients who receive second-line treatment and that this can lead to wide variations in the anticipated objective response rates to second-line platinum-based therapy, ranging from less than 10% to greater than 40%.[13] Characterization of the treated population makes it easier for results to be appropriately interpreted with reference to historical expectations.

"Platinum-sensitive" ovarian cancer is defined as the recurrence of active disease in a patient who has achieved a documented response to initial platinum-based treatment and has been off therapy for an extended period of time. For the purposes of study design and interpretation, the GOG has arbitrarily set the boundary between "sensitive" and "resistant" disease at 6 months.[14]

"Platinum-resistant" ovarian cancer is defined as disease that was surgically resected or responded to initial platinum-based chemotherapy but demonstrated recurrence within a relatively short period of time following the completion of treatment. Within GOG criteria, patients with documented recurrence within 6 months of completing initial therapy should be considered platinum resistant.

"Persistent" ovarian cancer is defined as residual disease in a patient who has completed (and perhaps partially responded to) initial chemotherapy. For example, findings indicating this would include a microscopically positive second-look laparotomy in a patient who began chemotherapy with suboptimal or optimal residual disease after initial cytoreductive surgery. However, over one-half of patients with advanced ovarian cancer begin chemotherapy in clinical complete remission after initial cytoreduc-

tive surgery. In this setting, the persistence of small-volume disease may actually represent resistant, rather than responsive, tumor deposits, which further contributes to heterogeneity in this population.

"Refractory" ovarian cancer occurs in a patient who has failed to achieve at least a partial response to platinum-based therapy. This includes patients with either stable disease or actual disease progression during primary therapy, which occurs in approximately 20% of cases. As might be expected, this group has the lowest response rate to platinum and other second-line interventions.

In many studies of second-line treatment, patients with resistant, persistent, and refractory disease are considered as one group while individuals with platinum-sensitive recurrent disease are considered separately. Even within these more resistant populations, there is still considerable heterogeneity with regard to overall drug sensitivity. Although the difference between drug-sensitive and drug-resistant disease was initially described in relationship to platinum-based therapy, these observations can be applied in a general sense to other chemotherapy regimens. However, the patterns of resistance and the mechanisms of action of many drugs (such as paclitaxel) are distinct from those of platinum drugs, and resistance to a combined regimen does not always imply resistance to the individual components. In addition, these definitions are largely based on the response to frontline therapy. With the diverse agents that are currently available for managing recurrent disease, the relevance of response to initial platinum-based therapy has become less clear.

Platinum, compounds however, remain the single most important drug employed in the therapy of advanced ovarian cancer, and selected patients with platinum-sensitive disease may benefit from retreatment with either cisplatin or carboplatin. Eventually, the majority of patients with recurrent ovarian cancer manifest platinum-resistant disease, in which case the potential risks of cumulative toxicity outweigh any potential benefits. In some cases, prolongation of the platinum-free interval can improve the likelihood of response to retreatment with platinum, due to a partial reversal of acquired drug resistance. This phenomenon has been documented in a small number of patients with cisplatin-refractory disease who have responded to retreatment with carboplatin after extension of the platinum-free interval using nonplatinum-based chemotherapy.[15] Fortunately, a number of agents with moderate activity against platinum-resistant disease have recently been described, and these agents may contribute to the extension of the platinum-free interval, opening an opportunity for eventual rechallenge with platinum.

Approaches in Defined Phase II Populations

Platinum-Sensitive Disease

There is no absolute treatment-free interval that completely separates individuals with regard to potential sensitivity to platinum or paclitaxel after response to initial therapy.[16,17] In general, the longer the platinum-free interval, the greater the expectation of a durable response to retreatment. Patients who remain disease free for more than 2 years following primary therapy have the greatest likelihood of benefit and are usually re-treated with a combination of platinum and paclitaxel,[18,19] as in de novo disease.

Although patients with a treatment-free interval of less than 12 months are frequently considered candidates for re-treatment with platinum and/or paclitaxel, there is currently no evidence from prospective randomized trials that combination chemotherapy achieves superior outcomes with regard to survival or quality of life, compared to the use of sequential single agents in this population. In addition, early re-treatment with platinum places the patient at risk for cumulative hematologic (carboplatin) and nonhematologic (cisplatin) toxicity that can limit further therapy and diminish the overall quality of life. Ideally, such patients should consider participation in phase II clinical trials to evaluate new treatment strategies as such patients are better able to tolerate multiple cycles of therapy and are more likely to respond to a given treatment regimen, compared to patients with more extensive prior therapy.

Persistent Disease

Patients with evidence of persistent disease after initial chemotherapy can be divided into at least two groups with different expectations and treatment

options. Patients with gross residual disease after initial surgery who then exhibit a major response are considered to have potentially chemoresponsive residual disease, and efforts have focused on consolidation to maximize the progression-free interval. In contrast, patients who have small-volume residual disease after initial surgery and who continue to have small-volume or microscopic disease after systemic chemotherapy are more likely to be chemoresistant, and efforts have focused on the development of noncross-resistant regimens.

Several treatment approaches can be considered for the chemoresponsive population. First, patients may continue to receive the drugs to which their disease has responded, with or without interval cytoreductive surgery. The optimal number of chemotherapy cycles to be administered in this setting is unknown, and it remains to be established whether continued treatment in responding patients will impact favorably on long-term clinical outcomes. Alternatively, patients may be treated with one of a number of agents that have been demonstrated to have activity in the second-line setting.

For patients who have achieved a major response to initial treatment but with the persistence of small-volume residual disease, it is not unreasonable to consider a dose-intensive approach in order to maximize response and extend the progression-free interval. Strategies that have been employed in this setting include intraperitoneal therapy[20] and high-dose intravenous chemotherapy with hematopoietic progenitor cell support.[21-23]

Again, it must be emphasized that there are no current data from randomized controlled trials to demonstrate that any therapeutic approach (including a variety of dose-intensity strategies) has curative potential in the second-line treatment of advanced ovarian cancer. As a result, the potential significant toxicities of these regimens must be kept in mind when considering possible strategies in this clinical setting.

Platinum-Resistant and Refractory Disease

Patients with platinum-resistant ovarian cancer that does not respond to initial therapy or who have disease that recurs after a short (less than 6 months) treatment-free interval following frontline or second-line therapy pose a particular challenge. In some cases, treatment options may be further compromised due to cumulative toxicity or declining nutritional and performance status as a consequence of progressive disease. However, through their participation in clinical trials, these patients have provided a valuable opportunity to rapidly screen promising agents for activity in a resistant population, and to select agents for potential integration with frontline therapy. The potential assignment of patients to phase II clinical trials within the GOG's framework is illustrated in Figure 13–13.

Within this resistant population with measurable disease, objective response rates (complete and partial) have ranged from 5 to 30%, with few agents exceeding 15%. While the duration of these responses has generally been short (less than 8 months), occasional patients may continue to respond or maintain stable disease for a more extended interval. In this palliative setting, the development of stable disease is also considered to be a positive, but limited, outcome that is achieved in an additional 25 to 40% of patients. In the absence of dose-limiting toxicity or clinical evidence of progressive disease, it is reasonable to continue therapy in such patients, depending on their overall quality of life and performance status.

In view of the number and diversity of active agents presently available for second-line treatment of ovarian cancer, clinicians and patients often consider treatment beyond the second-line setting. Palliative therapy in this setting requires adequate vital-organ function, hematologic reserve, and performance status. Unfortunately, there are limited data for predicting the activity of individual agents against tumors that are refractory to multiple chemotherapy regimens. In these circumstances, it is reasonable to choose an agent with a different mechanism of action and limited potential for serious toxicity. Response should be evaluated after two or three cycles. Once again, the attainment of stable disease with acceptable levels of toxicity is a valid clinical end point and would justify the continuation of therapy. Ultimately, it is anticipated that tumor molecular profiling, metabolic imaging, and/or enhanced drug sensitivity testing may help match patients with particular treatment regimens, not only in the frontline setting but also during the management of recurrent disease.

Role of Phase III Studies in Persistent or Recurrent Disease

Compared to the large number of single-arm phase II trials as well as frontline randomized phase III trials, there are only a small number of randomized phase III trials that have been completed in the set-

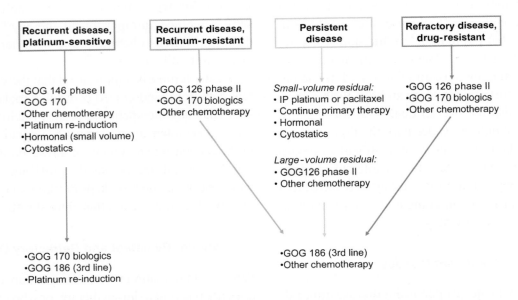

Figure 13–13. Phase II Gynecologic Oncology Group (GOG) clinical trial options for patients with recurrent or persistent disease, in accordance with the treatment-free interval following primary therapy. (IP = intraperitoneal.)

ting of recurrent disease. In part, this reflects the need to efficiently screen individual agents for activity and to then make efforts to quickly integrate active agents with frontline therapy. Although there are certainly valid scientific and clinical questions that would merit the expense and complexity of a large phase III trial, it has been difficult to support these efforts in the absence of pharmaceutical sponsorship, which has usually been focused on more-restrained designs geared toward specific Food and Drug Administration (FDA) drug registrations. Similarly, only a small number of trials have addressed important issues such as consolidation and maintenance following first remission or such as the management of small-volume residual disease following primary therapy, which remain the subject of considerable bias in the absence of definitive data.

From a logistics perspective, several of these ambitious studies have been difficult to complete because of evolving standards of care, limited insurance reimbursement, and stringent criteria for interim analysis. For example, based on promising phase II data with intraperitoneal interferon-α in patients with small-volume residual disease, the Southwest Oncology Group (SWOG) initiated a phase III trial of intraperitoneal interferon-α versus observation in patients with a laparotomy-documented complete remission following initial therapy. Due to declining rates of second-look surgery, accrual was slower than expected, even when joined by the GOG, and the trial was eventually closed as nonfeasible. In another example, an attempt was made to evaluate the role of high-dose consolidation with hematopoietic progenitor cell support in a prospective phase III randomized trial organized by the GOG and the NCI. However, after 2 years, the study was terminated due to poor accrual, reflecting physician bias and the limitations of insurance reimbursement for high-dose therapy for patients with solid tumors.

In a third example, the Southwest Oncology Group and the GOG jointly evaluated the role of maintenance therapy with paclitaxel (3 months versus 12 months) for patients in clinical complete remission following initial therapy (Figure 13–14). This trial accrued well but was terminated with 50%

accrual at the time of a planned interim analysis, based on a significant improvement in median progression-free survival for the patients who received 12 months of paclitaxel but demonstrated no benefit in overall survival or quality of life.[24] One could argue that a short-term benefit in progression-free survival was not unexpected, given the inequality in treatment duration between the two arms, and it is unfortunate that the trial was closed without an opportunity to evaluate and compare the overall survivals of the two populations.

Among the more innovative ongoing phase III trials is an attempt, sponsored by the Medical Research Council (MRC) in the United Kingdom, to address the timing of second-line therapy based on clinical evidence of disease progression versus early intervention on the basis of elevated CA 125. The GOG has also initiated an ambitious phase III trial with dual randomization to evaluate secondary cytoreductive surgery versus no further surgery, and carboplatin versus topotecan with crossover at the time of disease progression. Both of these trials address important clinical questions and will hopefully be successful in reaching their accrual goals, which will expand the opportunity for other phase III initiatives.

Evaluation and Integration of Individual Agents

Overview of GOG Development

Within the GOG, new agents and combinations are evaluated in the phase I and phase II settings. Generally, phase I studies are limited to the evaluation of new platinum-based combinations in patients with previously untreated disease. These studies use standard dose-escalating models, fixed-dose expanded cohorts to verify feasibility, and small pilot studies to examine issues such as high-dose therapy with stem cell support. Due to the known activity of platinum-based therapy in this setting, promising combinations that appear to be feasible can advance directly from phase I to phase III evaluation, without a formal phase II study.

In contrast, phase II trials have generally focused on the evaluation of new investigational agents in patients with recurrent disease, with sponsorship

SWOG 9701 (GOG 178)

- Epithelial ovarian cancer
- Stage III-IV with clinical CR after primary therapy
- Primary end point: PFS
- November 1997 to December 2001
- 222 patients (target 458)
- Terminated after interim analysis

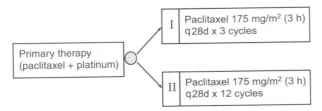

Figure 13–14. Schema for an intergroup trial (GOG 178) of maintenance paclitaxel for patients in clinical complete remission (CR) after primary therapy.[24] Although the trial was terminated early on the basis of an improvement in progression-free survival (PFS), there was no documented improvement in overall survival. (GOG = Gynecologic Oncology Group; SWOG = Southwestern Oncology Group.)

from the Cancer Therapy Evaluation Program of the NCI or from the pharmaceutical industry. These studies are sequentially activated in separate queues for patients with platinum-sensitive (ie, with a treatment-free interval longer than 6 months) and platinum-resistant (ie, with a treatment-free interval shorter than 6 months) disease. There is also a concurrent queue to evaluate biologicals, including monoclonal antibodies, antiangiogenesis agents, and other novel compounds. Recent, ongoing, and planned phase II studies using cytotoxic agents and

biologicals are summarized in Tables 13–2 (in platinum-resistant patients), 13–3 (in platinum-sensitive patients), and 13–4 (biologic and pilot studies). Table 13–5 provides a summary of phase I studies to evaluate dose, schedule, and feasibility of new combinations in patients without prior therapy.

Paclitaxel

Paclitaxel has been established as an important initial component of ovarian cancer chemotherapy and should also be considered in the management of patients with recurrence. Of interest, the mechanisms of acquired drug resistance are different between paclitaxel and platinum, and not all patients with platinum-resistant disease are resistant to paclitaxel, even if paclitaxel was included in their front-line treatment program.

As a component of initial platinum-based chemotherapy, paclitaxel is most commonly administered as a 3-hour intravenous infusion at 175 mg/m^2. In patients with recurrent disease, phase III randomized trials have evaluated dose intensity (135 versus 175 mg/m^2 and 175 versus 250 mg/m^2) and infusion duration (3 versus 24 hours) without finding a clear advantage for either higher doses or prolonged infusion.[25,26] In nonrandomized studies, a prolonged 96-hour infusion at a total dose of 120 to 160 mg/m^2 was reported to have good activity in breast cancer but was evaluated in recurrent ovarian cancer following

Study	Chair	Reagents	Response	Comment
126-D	Bookman	Pyrazolacridine	2/24 (8.4%)	Heme toxic
126-E	Fracasso	PSC833 + Paclitaxel	5/58 (8.6%)	Inactive
126-G	Hoffman	CI-958	1/25 (4%)	Inactive
126-H	Markman	Topotecan (24h, q21d)	1/25 (4%)	Inactive
126-I	Rose	Docetaxel	12/57 (21%)	Active
126-J	Miller	9-A-camptothecin (120 h)	6/25 (24%)	Active
126-K	Fracasso	Oxaliplatin	1/23 (4.3%)	Inactive
126-L	Brewer	Gemcitabine + CDDP		Under analysis
126-M	Spriggs	Epothilone-B		Accrual in progress
126-N	Markman	Weekly paclitaxel		Accrual in progress
126	Rose	Oral topotecan		Under development
126	Rose	Topotecan + etoposide		Under development
186-B	Grendys	9-Nitro-camptothecin		Under development
186-C	Sabbatini	PG-paclitaxel		Accrual in progress
186	Kavanagh	Kareniticin		Under development

Table 13–2. PHASE II STUDIES: PLATINUM-RESISTANT OVARIAN CANCER SERIES†

CDDP = cisplatin.
*Gynecologic Oncology Group (GOG) studies, recent and ongoing.

Table 13–3. PHASE II STUDIES: PLATINUM-SENSITIVE SERIES OVARIAN CANCER SERIES*

Study	Chair	Reagents	Response	Comment
146-C	McGuire	Topotecan	15/46 (33%)	Active
146-D	Plaxe	Pyrazolacridine	10/42 (23.8%)	Active
146-F	Markman	Topotecan (24h, q21d)	2/28 (7%)	Inactive
146-E	Hoffman	CI-958	1/23 (4%)	Inactive
146-H	Armstrong	Bryostatin	0/27; 1/25	
146-J	Hoffman	Dolastatin	1/28 (3.6%)	Inactive
146-K	Miller	Topotecan (3 d)	4/29 (14%)	Limited
146-L	Garcia	Capecitabine		Accrual in progress
146-M	Covens	Tirapazamine + CDDP		Accrual in progress

CDDP = cisplatin.
*Gynecologic Oncology Group (GOG) studies, recent and ongoing.

multiple prior therapies, achieving only a modest response rate.[27] Overall, it appears that variations in paclitaxel's dose and schedule have little bearing on tumor response but have a clear impact on the spectrum and severity of hematologic, mucosal, and neurologic toxicity (Table 13–6). Based on these data, the well-tolerated 3-hour infusion at 175 mg/m^2 has been commonly employed as a single agent for the management of recurrent disease.

However, the demonstration of a further reduction in toxicity and the apparent maintenance of efficacy among women with "paclitaxel-resistant" disease using a 1-hour weekly infusion at 60 to 90 mg/m^2 has raised considerable interest, even in the absence of randomized data.[28] This particular schedule is associated with minimal noncumulative hematologic and nonhematologic toxicity, including a reduction in alopecia. Peripheral neurotoxicity is not uncommon, particularly with higher cumulative doses in patients with preexisting neuropathy, but this can usually be managed with treatment breaks and/or dose reduction.

A number of studies are also being initiated with alternative formulations of paclitaxel as liposomes, polymer-based microspheres, polyglutamated conjugates, and albumin conjugates. In general, these formulations reduce or eliminate the need for Cremophor EL (a solubilizing agent containing ethyl alcohol and polyoxethylated castor oil), which is responsible for the majority of hypersensitivity reactions. In addition, alternative formulations may achieve more-prolonged serum or peritoneal concentrations after intermittent dosing. Thus far, although some of these agents may improve the toxicity profile associated with paclitaxel, none are thought to have clinical activity that is superior to native paclitaxel. Attention has also focused on entirely different compounds, such as the epothilones, which have the same molecular target but a different chemical source and structure.

Docetaxel

In addition to docetaxel's being of interest as an alternative taxane, preclinical data have suggested

Table 13–4. PHASE II BIOLOGIC AND PILOT STUDIES: RECURRENT OVARIAN CANCER*†

Study	Chair	Reagents	Response	Comment
160	Bookman	Trastuzumab	3/41 (7.3%)	Inactive
170-B	Hurteau	IL-12 (IV)	1/26 (3.8%)	Inactive
170-C	Schilder	Iressa (anti-EGFR-TK)		Under analysis
170-D	Monk	Bevacizumab (anti-VEGF)		Accrual in progress
170-E	Schilder	STI-571		Accrual in progress

IL = interleukin; IV = intravenous; EGFR-TK = epidermal growth factor receptor thymidine kinase; VEGF = vascular endothelial growth factor.
*Irrespective of platinum sensitivity.
†Gynecologic Oncology Group (GOG) studies, recent and ongoing.

Table 13–5. SUMMARY OF GYNECOLOGIC ONCOLOGY GROUP PHASE I AND PILOT STUDIES: NEW CHEMOTHERAPY COMBINATIONS*

Dose-escalating combinations (phase I)
  Paclitaxel and carboplatin (GOG9202)
  Paclitaxel, cisplatin, topotecan (GOG9602)
  Paclitaxel, cisplatin, doxorubicin (GOG9405)
  Paclitaxel, carboplatin, oral etoposide (GOG9603)
  Paclitaxel, carboplatin, liposomal doxorubicin (GOG9703)
Fixed-dose combinations
  Paclitaxel, carboplatin, gemcitabine (GOG9801)
  Topotecan/carboplatin → paclitaxel/carboplatin (GOG9906)
Multicycle high-dose therapy (stem cell support)
  High-dose carboplatin and paclitaxel (GOG9501)
  High-dose carboplatin, paclitaxel, topotecan (GOG9903)

*In patients who have had no prior therapy.

that docetaxel may have several potential advantages over paclitaxel, including increased potency, enhanced receptor binding,[29] and less induction of microsomal metabolic pathways. However, apparent clinical advantages have not readily translated into improvements in clinical outcomes (Table 13–7).[30] Docetaxel has been examined for the management of platinum-resistant ovarian cancer in several clinical trials, with an objective response rate of 20 to 35%.[31,32] This level of activity is comparable to that of paclitaxel, observed in a similar patient population. As a single agent, docetaxel was administered at 100 mg/m^2 every 3 weeks. Although lower doses and weekly treatment schedules have been developed, randomized studies to compare alternative dosing have not been performed. In general, docetaxel is well tolerated in this setting, the major toxicity being neutropenia and a capillary leak syndrome with fluid accumulation that is related to the cumulative dose and the number of cycles administered. Docetaxel has the advantage of a 1-hour infusion every 3 to 4 weeks, with a reduced risk of serious hypersensitivity reactions. Preliminary data suggest that some patients with resistance to paclitaxel may respond to subsequent therapy with docetaxel.[33] However, there are no direct randomized comparisons of docetaxel and paclitaxel as single agents for patients with recurrent disease.

In frontline combination therapy, data have been reported on clinical response rate, progression-free survival, and toxicity from a phase III trial (the Scottish Randomized Ovarian Cancer [SCOTROC] trial)

of the Scottish Gynaecological Cancer Trials Group (Figure 13–15) comparing carboplatin and docetaxel at 75 mg/m^2 (1-hour infusion) versus carboplatin and paclitaxel at 175 mg/m^2 (3-hour infusion).[34] There was a clear difference in the pattern of toxicity, with a reduction in neuropathy and an increase in myelosuppression among women who received docetaxel. However, there has been no apparent difference in clinical efficacy on the basis of response rate, reduction of CA 125, or progression-free survival.

Topoisomerase-I Inhibitors

Topotecan is a semisynthetic water-soluble analogue of camptothecin that acts through the inhibition of Topoisomerase-I, an enzyme that relieves torsional stress during DNA synthesis. Preclinical models have demonstrated that topotecan can enhance platinum-mediated cytotoxicity through the inhibition of DNA repair,[35] and the clinical development of platinum/topotecan combinations has been of high priority. After platinum and paclitaxel, topotecan is the agent that has undergone the most extensive testing to define a role as second-line therapy for recurrent ovarian cancer,[36,37] and it has been approved by the FDA for that indication. The standard 5-day topotecan regimen (1.5 mg/m^2/d) is inconvenient and results in considerable bone marrow suppression in previously treated patients, with 80% grade 4 neutropenia and 25% grade 4 thrombocytopenia,[38] but it can achieve a 33% response rate in patients with platinum-sensitive disease.[39]

Based on interpatient variability in drug clearance, frequency of dose-limiting hematologic toxic-

Table 13–6. RELATIONSHIP BETWEEN PACLITAXEL SCHEDULE, HOST TOXICITY, AND TUMOR RESPONSE

	Paclitaxel Schedule			
	1 h (qwk)	3 h	24 h	96 h
Dose (mg/m^2)	60–100	175	135	120–140
HSR	+*	+	+	−
Alopecia	−†	+	+	+
Neutropenia	−	+	++	+++
Mucositis	−	−	+	++
Neuropathy	++*	++	+	+
Myalgia	++	++	++	+
Efficacy	+++*	++	++	++

HSR = hypersensitivity reaction; qwk = every week; * = increased frequency or severity; † = reduced frequency or severity.

Table 13–7. COMPARISON OF PRECLINICAL AND CLINICAL CHARACTERISTICS OF DOCETAXEL AND PACLITAXEL

Characteristic	Docetaxel	Paclitaxel
Tubulin binding (ratio)	1.9	1.0
Maximum polymerization (μM)	0.2	0.7
BCL2 phosphorylation (ratio)	100	1
Uptake (pmol/10^6 cells)	6	2
T 1/2 efflux (min) P388 cells	135	45
Hepatic metabolism	CYP3A4	CYP3A4/2C8, SXR
Single-agent dosing	75 mg/m^2 q21d	175 mg/m^2 q21d
	30 mg/m^2/week	80 mg/m^2/week
Clinical toxicity	Hematologic	Neuropathy
Clinical efficacy	Fluid retention	Hematologic
	Equivalent	

pmol = prcomol.

ity, and the lack of evidence for a tight dose-response relationship, it has become common practice to initiate therapy at 1.25 mg/m^2/d for 5 consecutive days. The choice of starting dose is guided by toxicity, the extent of prior therapy, and the estimated renal clearance. Fortunately, as hematologic toxicity is noncumulative and generally emerges during the first cycle, it can be readily managed with dose reduction and/or the introduction of hematopoietic growth factors, which permits the safe continuation of therapy over multiple cycles.

In an attempt to improve the tolerability of single-agent topotecan and to facilitate the development of combination regimens, the GOG has conducted phase II studies of single-agent topotecan with alternative schedules of drug administration. Using a single 24-hour infusion of topotecan (8.5 mg/m^2) every 21 days, there was a similar frequency and severity of hematologic toxicity but an apparent reduction in efficacy, compared to prior phase II studies. In patients with platinum-sensitive disease,[40] the response rate was 7%; in patients with platinum-resistant disease, the response rate was only 4%.[41] The GOG is in the process of evaluating an intermediate 3-day regimen (2 mg/m^2/d) for patients with platinum-sensitive disease (GOG 146K). However, in platinum refractory disease, a similar 3-day regimen (1.5 mg/m^2/d) achieved a response rate of only 7%,[42] confirming the schedule-dependent efficacy of topotecan (Table 13–8). (Changes in schedule of topotecan used as a single agent can have a substantial impact on tumor response; however, at maximal tolerated doses,

there appears to be little impact on the spectrum or severity of host toxicity.) In view of this dependency on schedule, there has also been interest in prolonged (21-day) dosing by continuous intravenous or daily oral administration. Using an intravenous infusion at 0.4 mg/m^2/d, a favorable response rate of 35% was reported in a mixed population with both platinum-sensitive and -resistant disease,[43] but it has not been established that this is superior to the 5-day schedule, and it will likely prove more difficult to develop platinum-based combinations using a prolonged infusion.[44] Of note, a number of novel formulations and camptothecin analogues are under development for delaying clearance and achieving prolonged drug exposure after single-dose administration (Table 13–9).

SCOTROC Trial

- Epithelial ovarian cancer
- Stage I C to IV
- No prior therapy
- October 1998 to May 2000
- 1,077 patients

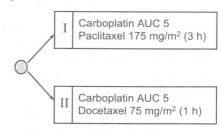

Figure 13–15. Schema for the Scottish Randomized Ovarian Cancer (SCOTROC) trial, comparing carboplatin with either paclitaxel or docetaxel. (AUC = area under the curve.) (Adapted from Vasey PA.[34])

Table 13–8.   RELATIONSHIP BETWEEN TOPOTECAN SCHEDULE, HOST TOXICITY, AND TUMOR RESPONSE

	Topotecan Schedule			
	21 d	Daily ×5	Daily ×3	24 h
Dose (mg/m²/d)	0.4	1.5	2.0	8.5
Neutropenia	+++*	+++	+++	+++
Thrombocytopenia	++*	++	++	++
Other toxicity	–†	–	–	–
Efficacy	+++	+++	++	–

* = increased frequency of severity; † = reduced frequency or severity.

Table 13–9.   CAMPTOTHECIN AND DERIVATIVES THAT ARE UNDER DEVELOPMENT

Camptothecin
  Parent compound from bark of *Camptotheca acuminata*
  Bladder toxicity, poor solubility, not further evaluated
Topotecan
  Water soluble intravenous and oral
  Dose-limiting hematologic toxicity, but noncumulative
Irinotecan (CPT-11)
  Dose-limiting gastrointestinal toxicity
  Converted to active metabolite (7-ethyl-10-hydroxy-
    camptothecin [SN-38])
Rubitecan (9-nitro-camptothecin, RFS2000)
  Oral formulation, 5 days per week
NX211 (liposomal lurtotecan, GI47211)
  Water-soluble analogue 10, 11-ethylenedioxy-20(S)-
    camptothecin
  Developed as a liposomal preparation to prolong clearance
9-Amino-camptothecin (9-AC)
  Evaluated at 25 μg/m²/h ×120 h as colloidal dispersion,
    weekly ×2
Karenitecin
  Lipid-soluble formulation with prolonged clearance

Preclinical studies with established cell lines have evaluated the optimal schedule and sequence of drug exposure, using various in vitro assays. In almost all cases, the combination of topotecan and cisplatin has exhibited synergistic toxicity. However, only a minority of cell lines have shown schedule dependence, generally favoring the administration of cisplatin prior to topotecan.[45] Other systems have favored synchronous drug administration[46] or have shown no difference.

Phase I trials have examined drug sequencing of doublets, including paclitaxel/topotecan[47] and topotecan/cisplatin, confirming that neutropenia and thrombocytopenia are the major dose-limiting toxicities. When the sequence of topotecan and cisplatin was alternately evaluated in the same patient, it was clear that administration of cisplatin on day 1 was more toxic than on day 5.[48] The mechanism for this effect was not entirely explained but was attributed to changes in topotecan clearance as a consequence of subclinical renal dysfunction after cisplatin administration, a finding that has not been confirmed. In a phase I trial using oral topotecan (5 days) in combination with cisplatin (75 mg/m² on day 1 or 5), hematologic toxicity was increased when cisplatin was administered on day 1, resulting in a recommended topotecan dose of 1.25 mg/m²/d compared to 2 mg/m²/d by the reverse sequence.[49] For the use of intravenous topotecan in patients with untreated lung cancer, a reverse sequence was recommended, with topotecan at 1.5 mg/m²/d for 5 days, followed by cisplatin at 50 mg/m² on day 5.[50]

As one might expect, attempts to develop a tolerable triplet combination have been more problematic. An ongoing phase I study (GOG 9602) is evaluating the combination of cisplatin, paclitaxel, and topotecan in previously untreated patients.[51] The starting dose of cisplatin was 50 mg/m², and that of paclitaxel was 175 mg/m², using a 3-hour infusion. The dose of topotecan could not be escalated above 0.5 mg/m²/d, which is one-third of the usual single-agent dose, and the study was revised to evaluate a shortened 3-day regimen of topotecan (Figure 13–16). Other studies have confirmed the increased hematologic toxicity of this triplet regimen. For example, Herben and colleagues recommended a phase II regimen with topotecan at 0.3 mg/m²/d (days 2 to 6), paclitaxel at 110 mg/m² (day 1), and cisplatin at 75 mg/m² (day 2), followed by mandatory granulocyte colony-stimulating factor (G-CSF).[52] Similar experiences have been encountered with carboplatin-based triplets, prompting some investigators to suggest that such combinations are impractical without hematopoietic stem cell support.[53] However, in spite of decreased dose intensity, some carboplatin-based triplets have shown promising activity in advanced ovarian cancer, as illustrated by a phase II trial of topotecan (1.00 mg/m²/d, days 1 to 3) followed by carboplatin (area under the curve [AUC] 5) and paclitaxel (175 mg/m² on day 3).[54] As an alternative, a weekly combination of paclitaxel (85 mg/m²), cisplatin (40 mg/m²), and topotecan (0.75 to 2.50 mg/m²) was tested in patients

GOG 9602 Pilot Study

- Ovarian and primary peritoneal carcinoma
- Conventional dose-escalating design to define MTD
- MTD exceeded at topotecan 0.60 mg/m²/d x5d, due to ↓ PLTs
- Amended to evaluate a 3-day topotecan schedule with G-CSF
- Recommended topotecan dose at 0.60 mg/m2/d x3 days

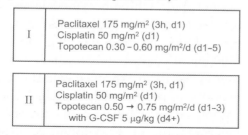

| I | Paclitaxel 175 mg/m² (3h, d1)
Cisplatin 50 mg/m² (d1)
Topotecan 0.30 – 0.60 mg/m²/d (d1–5) |
| II | Paclitaxel 175 mg/m² (3h, d1)
Cisplatin 50 mg/m² (d1)
Topotecan 0.50 → 0.75 mg/m²/d (d1–3)
with G-CSF 5 μg/kg (d4+) |

Figure 13–16. Schema for GOG 9602, a phase I study evaluating the combination of cisplatin, paclitaxel, and topotecan. Dose-limiting neutropenia and thrombocytopenia have required substantial reductions in the dose of all agents, as well as the incorporation of granulocyte colony-stimulating factor (G-CSF) MTD = maximal tolerated dose; PLTs = platelets.

with ovarian and lung cancer and achieving a favorable overall response rate with acceptable toxicity at a recommended phase II topotecan dose of 2.25 mg/m² per week.[55] Although phase I trials of weekly single-agent topotecan were inactive, a phase II study of an escalating-dose single agent in patients with recurrent ovarian cancer documented limited activity,[56] which would support the evaluation of a well-tolerated weekly combination regimen that might maximize synergistic interactions. As already suggested, full (or increased) doses of this triplet combination would require hematopoietic support. One promising high-dose combination can be safely administered over multiple cycles following a single harvest of peripheral blood progenitor cells[57] and is being formally evaluated in a pilot study with combined end points of feasibility and efficacy (GOG 9903).

In view of the difficulty of developing a well-tolerated platinum-based triplet combination, efforts have focused on the use of doublets, individually or in sequence, to maximize effective drug exposure. For example, a phase II trial of the National Cancer Institute of Canada (NCIC) found the combination of cisplatin (50 mg/m², day 1) and topotecan (0.75 mg/m²/d, days 1 to 5) to be feasible when administered over four cycles followed by four cycles of paclitaxel/cisplatin.[58] This is the basis of an ongoing NCIC/European Organization for Research and Treatment of Cancer (EORTC) phase III randomized trial (OV16) of cisplatin and topotecan for four cycles followed by four cycles of carboplatin and paclitaxel versus 8 cycles of carboplatin and paclitaxel (Figure 13–17).

In a phase I trial reported by Gordon and colleagues, a doublet of topotecan and carboplatin was alternated cycle-by-cycle with paclitaxel and carboplatin in newly diagnosed EOC patients.[59] Carboplatin (AUC 4 or 5) was given prior to a 3-day regimen of topotecan, in view of the reported synergy of this sequence. At a topotecan dose level of 1 mg/m²/d, two of six patients exhibited dose-limiting toxicity. Similar to the experience with cisplatin, postponing the administration of carboplatin was associated with more effective drug delivery at higher doses with decreased bone marrow toxicity,[60] but the preferred schedule for clinical development has not been established. Although it is clear that sequence has a substantial impact on hematologic toxicity, the potential impact of sequence on tumor response is unknown. The GOG evaluated both sequences of topotecan in combination with carboplatin to select the optimal doublet regimen for phase III studies (Figure 13–18). In this trial (GOG 9906), dose-limiting events were monitored over four cycles per patient, using 15 patients in each cohort. All cohorts included carboplatin at AUC 5, but the dose and sequence of topotecan was varied.

NCIC EORTC OV16

- Ovarian and primary peritoneal carcinoma
- Stage II B to IV
- Sequential couplet design, phase III
- Feasibility established in pilot study (with cisplatin/paclitaxel)
- Activated August 2001

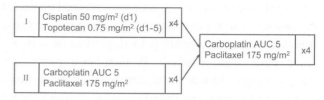

Figure 13–17. Schema for the National Cancer Institute of Canada/European Organization for Research and Treatment of Cancer (NCIC/EORTC)phase III trial OV16. This study is evaluating a combination of topotecan (once daily for 5 consecutive days and cisplatin, based on a pilot study in which the experimental regimen was followed by a combination of cisplatin and paclitaxel. (AUC = area under the curve.)

GOG 9906 Pilot Study

- Ovarian and primary peritoneal carcinoma
- Sequential doublet design, serial cohorts ($n = 15$)
- Modified phase I to evaluate cumulative DLT events over first four cycles
- FWD sequence not feasible with topotecan at 1.00 or 0.75 mg/m²/d x3d
- REV sequence not feasible with topotecan at 1.50 mg/m²/d x3d
- REV sequence feasible with topotecan at 1.25 mg/m²/d x3d
- G-CSF not required

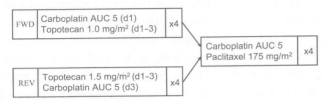

Figure 13–18. Schema for the GOG 9906 trial, which evaluated two sequences of carboplatin and topotecan followed by carboplatin and paclitaxel. Feasibility was defined on the basis of cumulative toxicity over four cycles of therapy, and the "reverse sequence" was selected for phase III evaluation, using a topotecan dose of 1.25 mg/m²/d for 3 days. (AUC = area under the curve; DLT = dose-limiting toxicity; FWD = forward; G-CSF = granulocyte colony-stimulating factor; REV = reverse.)

Two cohorts using the "forward" sequence (carboplatin on day 1 and topotecan on days 1 to 3) exhibited excessive hematologic toxicity, even at topotecan doses of 1.00 and 0.75 mg/m²/d for 3 days. However, cohorts with the "reverse" sequence (topotecan on days 1 to 3 and carboplatin on day 3) were well tolerated at topotecan doses of 1.50 and 1.25 mg/m²/d (M. Bookman, unpublished data), and this sequence was selected for the current phase III GOG intergroup trial (GOG 0182-ICON5).

Gemcitabine

Gemcitabine (2'2'-difluorodeoxycytidine) is sequentially phosphorylated after cellular uptake in vivo to its primary active metabolite, 2'2'-difluorodeoxycytidine-5'-triphosphate (dFdCTP), which can be incorporated into DNA, leading to masked chain termination[61] while the diphosphate can inhibit ribonucleotide reductase, leading to depletion of intracellular nucleoside pools.[62] It has been postulated, based on preclinical data, that gemcitabine might enhance platinum-mediated toxicity through inhibition of DNA repair.[63] Clinical activity has been demonstrated in patients with recurrent EOC, using doses of from 800 to 1,250 mg/m² (days 1, 8, and 15).[64,65] Following the experience of Greco and colleagues in lung cancer,[66] Look and colleagues

piloted a triplet regimen of carboplatin (AUC 5, day 1), paclitaxel (175 mg/m², day 1), and gemcitabine (1,000 mg/m², days 1 and 8) in patients with advanced EOC (GOG 9801) (Figure 13–19). Due to an unacceptable incidence of complicated neutropenia and grade 4 thrombocytopenia, the starting doses were reduced to carboplatin (AUC 5, day 1), paclitaxel (135 mg/m², day 1), and gemcitabine (800 mg/m², days 1 and 8), which was tolerable over four cycles in an expanded cohort of patients.[67] The majority of patients received eight complete cycles without dose modification, excessive delay, or incorporation of hematopoietic growth factors. However, it was not uncommon to omit gemcitabine on day 8 in the setting of transient grade 4 neutropenia. A similar triplet regimen was evaluated by Geertsen and colleagues in 19 patients with recurrent (platinum-sensitive) disease[68] and by Hansen and colleagues in 24 newly diagnosed EOC patients, using paclitaxel at 175 mg/m² and achieving 100% overall response rates but with somewhat increased bone marrow toxicity.[69]

Although the triplet regimen is feasible with acceptable activity in patients with EOC, there is concern that the overall therapeutic results might be compromised by the inability to deliver full doses of all active drugs. Sequential platinum-based doublets offer an alternative strategy for the incorporation of new agents at higher doses with acceptable toxicity.

GOG 9801 Pilot Study

- Ovarian and primary peritoneal carcinoma
- Serial cohorts ($n = 15$) with total of 51 patients (all cohorts)
- Modified phase I to evaluate cumulative DLT events over first four cycles
- First dose level not feasible, based on hematologic DLT
- Second level feasible, recommended for phase III evaluation

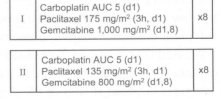

Figure 13–19. Schema for the GOG 9801 study, which evaluated a triplet combination of carboplatin, gemcitabine, and paclitaxel. Cumulative dose-limiting events were monitored over four cycles to establish feasibility for the second cohort, which was then recommended for incorporation in a phase III trial. (AUC = area under the curve; DLT = dose-limiting toxicity.)

In particular, several phase II trials have evaluated the combination of gemcitabine at 1,250 mg/m^2 (days 1 and 8) with cisplatin at either 75[70,71] or 100 mg/m^2 (day 1).[72] As expected, the major dose-limiting toxicity for each of these regimens was bone marrow suppression.

Doublet combinations with carboplatin are of interest because of reduced nonhematologic toxicity and increased patient convenience, but they have been more challenging to develop because of the increased risk of short-term and cumulative bone marrow toxicity, necessitating a reduction in drug dosing. For example, Arbeitsgemeinschaft Gynakologische Onkologie (AGO) conducted a dose-escalating phase I trial for patients with recurrent disease and a treatment-free interval of at least 6 months (Figure 13–20).[73] Its recommended dose, based on first-cycle toxicity, was carboplatin at AUC 4 (day 1) with gemcitabine at 1,000 mg/m^2 (days 1 and 8). This was followed by a phase III intergroup (AGO-NCIC) trial in recurrent disease, comparing single-agent carboplatin with the combination of carboplatin and gemcitabine. Accrual has been completed, but results are pending with regard to the primary end point of time to progression.

Alternative schedules have been applied to develop other feasible combinations with carboplatin that would be suitable for evaluation in a phase III trial. In this regard, Iaffaioli and colleagues reported a phase I/II study of gemcitabine at 1,100 mg/m^2 (days

1 and 8) with carboplatin at AUC 5 (day 8) in patients with nonsmall cell lung cancer.[74] The delayed administration of carboplatin on day 8 was associated with reduced bone marrow toxicity, compared to regimens with carboplatin on day 1.[75] These results are similar to the schedule-dependent effects observed with combinations of topotecan and platinum, suggesting that delayed administration of carboplatin offers a potential strategy for safely evaluating this doublet regimen in the setting of a multicenter phase III trial.

Liposomal Doxorubicin

Doxorubicin, a DNA-intercalating agent that inhibits Topoisomerase-II, was evaluated in combination with cisplatin and cyclophosphamide in patients with EOC, achieving a small but significant impact on long-term survival that was detectable in a meta-analysis of four randomized trials prior to the advent of paclitaxel.[1] However, in a large international trial, the combination of cisplatin, cyclophosphamide, and doxorubicin was not superior to carboplatin as a single agent, which was also less toxic than the combination.[76] Although this might suggest limited potential for benefit following the incorporation of doxorubicin, there are no comparative data regarding combinations of doxorubicin with platinum and paclitaxel. However, there have been two international phase III trials comparing paclitaxel (Taxol)/epirubicin/carboplatin (TEC) to paclitaxel/carboplatin.[77,78] Preliminary results from both studies demonstrate an expected increase in hematologic and mucosal toxicity with TEC and a minor increase in response rate but no significant improvement in progression-free or overall survival.

Stealth liposomal doxorubicin (Doxil) is a formulation of doxorubicin encapsulated in polyethylene glycol (PEG)–coated liposomes, associated with a dramatic alteration in pharmacokinetics characterized by a prolonged circulation time, reduced clearance, and a small volume of distribution[79,80] as well as increased localization in tumors. In a phase II study, PEG-liposomal doxorubicin (PLD) was studied in patients whose previous therapy with paclitaxel and platinum had failed. In this previously treated patient population, 9 (25.7%) of 35 patients responded to liposomal doxorubicin, with a median progression-

AGO Pilot Study

• Recurrent platinum-sensitive ovarian cancer
• Dose-escalating phase I/II trial
• MTD exceeded at 1,100 mg/m^2 (↓PLTs > ↓ANC)
• Recommended phase II with gemcitabine 1,000 mg/m^2 (d1,8)
• Evaluated in a phase III (trial compared to single-agent carboplatin)

I	Carboplatin AUC 4 (d1) Gemcitabine 800 – 1,100 mg/m^2 (d1,8)

Figure 13–20. Schema for the Arbeitsgemeinschaft Gynakologische Onkologie (AGO) pilot study of gemcitabine and carboplatin, as evaluated in patients with platinum-sensitive recurrent disease.[73] This study was followed by a phase III trial for patients with recurrent disease, comparing the doublet combination to single-agent carboplatin. (AUC = area under the curve; ANC = absolute neutrophil count; MTD = maximum tolerated dose; PLTs = platelets.)

free interval of 5.7 months.[81] This was followed by an industry-sponsored randomized phase III study of second-line therapy in patients with recurrent or progressive disease, comparing PLD (50 mg/m^2 every 4 weeks) with topotecan at the original FDA-approved dose (1.5 mg/m^2 daily for 5 days, repeated every 3 weeks).[82] Not surprisingly, greater hematologic toxicity was associated with this dose of topotecan, but efficacy was comparable, based on overall response rates and progression-free survival.

As with other agents, the integration of PLD with frontline platinum-based therapy has also been associated with dose-limiting hematologic toxicity at less than full single-agent doses. Within the GOG, Rose and colleagues have conducted a phase I evaluation of PLD in combination with carboplatin (AUC 5) and paclitaxel (175 mg/m^2) and defined a recommended dose for this triplet combination, using PLD (30 mg/m^2) administered every other cycle.[83]

Prolonged Oral Etoposide

A prolonged 21-day low-dose oral etoposide regimen (50 mg/m^2/d) results in a 25% objective response rate in the second-line setting in patients with EOC.[84,85] Rose and colleagues completed a frontline phase I study (GOG 9603) of oral etoposide with carboplatin (AUC 5) and paclitaxel (175 mg/m^2), establishing a recommended etoposide dose of 50 mg/m^2/d for 10 days.[86] In this study, 3 of 52 patients developed acute myelogenous leukemia between 16 and 35 months post therapy. Etoposide is known to carry a risk of secondary myelodysplasia and acute leukemia that is related to the cumulative dose and duration of therapy, but the incidence was surprising in this phase I trial, which used fairly low cumulative doses that were not expected to be associated with myelodysplasia. The impact of secondary leukemia in newly diagnosed patients receiving frontline therapy is worrisome, and further development will depend on a better understanding of potential risks and predictive factors.

Biologic Agents

Although high response rates are expected with primary chemotherapy in patients with EOC, as many as 80% of patients in clinical complete remission will ultimately relapse, and a number of biologic or molecular-targeted strategies for delaying or preventing recurrence are under active consideration. These include antibody targeting, inhibition of signal transduction pathways, antisense oligonucleotides, pro-apoptotic agents, selective hormonal modulation, vaccines, and inhibitors of tumor invasion and angiogenesis. Other areas of study, such as pharmacogenomics, tumor expression profiling, or drug sensitivity testing, could also contribute to the individualized selection of chemotherapy regimens. However, optimal strategies for prioritizing and evaluating these novel approaches in phase III trials have yet to be defined.

Phase III Integration

Designing the next generation of phase III trials remains challenging as we need to rapidly evaluate a number of interesting new compounds and treatment strategies as part of an ongoing effort to improve outcomes for women with advanced ovarian cancer. The development of new combinations will be characterized by biologic drug interactions with a definite impact on host toxicity and a potential impact on tumor response. In this regard, better and more predictive preclinical models would be helpful, together with improved clinical trial paradigms that address biologic targeting, to better guide our selection of key regimens that merit phase III evaluation.

A conventional randomized trial with two arms is generally designed to answer one primary question. A control arm is then carried forward and repeated, with modification, for each future trial. The ability to conduct a randomized trial with multiple experimental arms is appealing as it offers the best opportunity to simultaneously test several reagents and strategies while using a single reference (control) population, which is more efficient and potentially more informative. In the developing of the current phase III Gynecologic Cancer Intergroup (GCIG) trial (GOG 0182-ICON5), it was decided to include four experimental arms to evaluate the addition of three new drugs (topotecan, gemcitabine, and PEG-liposomal doxorubicin), using two different strategies for drug administration (sequential doublets and triplet combinations). In studying advanced ovarian cancer, a fully-powered phase III randomized trial with five arms could require as many as 4,000 patients to adequately address the primary end point of overall survival. Intergroup trials of this magnitude are feasible for early-stage breast cancer, lung cancer, and colorectal cancer. However, the typical GOG ovarian cancer trial has included only two or three arms and has been limited to between 400 and 800 patients. Of note, recent MRC ICON ovarian cancer trials have enrolled more than 2,000 patients, but have not had the degree of data management, auditing, and modality quality review charactistic of GOG studies.

Several factors have collectively enhanced our ability to mount a larger randomized trial at the present time. First, rather than running two concurrent studies, the GOG has decided to enroll all patients in one trial, regardless of the extent of residual disease (optimal or suboptimal) following initial cytoreductive surgery. Second, with the assistance of the NCI, the GCIG, and pharmaceutical-industry sponsors, the GOG has developed international collaborative relationships with colleagues in the United Kingdom, Italy, Australia, New Zealand, and Japan, with a number of investigators planning to join current phase II and III studies. Third, a method for performing an event-triggered interim analysis based on progression-free survival was developed, and this analysis will have the capability of selecting promising arms for full accrual while closing arms that appear unpromising, thus providing more-optimal control over the total number of patients required to complete an adequately powered study. Finally, a number of operational issues were adopted in the current trial in order to minimize interference with primary and secondary end points. These include the prohibition of second-look laparotomy and maintenance therapy, allowance for optional interval cytoreductive surgery (with stratification for intent), the adoption of international criteria for using CA 125 to declare progression of disease, and the modification of each arm (including the control arm) to equilibrate toxicity and the number of cycles across all arms.

In spite of substantial investigator bias, no evidence currently exists to indicate whether optimal combinations should use sequential single agents, doublets, or triplets. As illustrated, most triplet regimens have exhibited increased bone marrow toxicity, especially in combination with carboplatin. As a consequence, phase I trials have used individual drug doses that are much lower than those of comparable single agents or doublets, raising questions about compromised tumor efficacy. However, newer agents that inhibit DNA repair, such as topotecan and gemcitabine, are expected to enhance the effects of platinum, and it may not be necessary to use higher doses to achieve optimal therapeutic benefit. As already discussed, clinical data from phase III randomized trials support the use of sequential single agents, such as platinum and paclitaxel, in patients with advanced EOC. Although sequential single agents allow individual drugs to be administered at a full dose and schedule, their use effectively eliminates any possibility of biologic drug interaction or synergy. The use of sequential doublets generally permits higher doses of individual drugs but does so over a smaller number of cycles with each agent. Doublets are also appealing because the sequential use of more than one regimen with a different mechanism of action and/or pattern of resistance has been postulated to prevent the emergence of drug-resistant tumors. However, this remains an unproven hypothesis in the treatment of solid tumors, and triplet regimens may be equally effective in this setting.

Regardless as to whether the patient is receiving a triplet, doublet, or sequential doublet regimen, the optimal duration of chemotherapy for patients with advanced disease remains undefined. Of note, several randomized trials with platinum-based therapy have not documented any advantage associated with the prolongation of standard therapy beyond five cycles, but these studies were conducted prior to the incorporation of paclitaxel.[87–89] In addition, GOG 97 demonstrated equivalent long-term survival after four cycles of therapy with cyclophosphamide and higher-dose cisplatin (100 mg/m^2) compared to eight cycles of cyclophosphamide with lower-dose cisplatin (50 mg/m^2), suggesting that four cycles of platinum-based therapy may be adequate in this patient population.[90] Without actual data, it was assumed that each experimental regimen should be given for at least four cycles, to provide an opportunity to observe a treatment-related benefit, and that each arm should also contain at least four cycles of carboplatin and paclitaxel, to provide best standard care.

With these issues in mind, the reference arm for GOG 0182-ICON5 consists of eight cycles of carboplatin (AUC 6) and paclitaxel (175 mg/m²). Experimental triplets with gemcitabine and PLD will each consist of eight cycles although PLD will only be administered every other cycle, based on data from GOG-9703. A sequential doublet using topotecan (once daily for 3 consecutive days) will use the reverse sequence (carboplatin on day 3) for four cycles as piloted on GOG 9906, followed by four cycles of carboplatin and paclitaxel. Similarly, a sequential doublet with gemcitabine will also use the reverse sequence (carboplatin on day 8) for four cycles, followed by four cycles of carboplatin and paclitaxel, achieving a total of eight cycles on all five arms (Figure 13–21). This trial was opened to patient accrual in January 2001 and is expected to require between 3 and 4 years to complete accrual, depending on the interim analysis, final sample size requirements, and extent of international collaboration. Accrual within the GOG has been rapid and has exceeded 1,000 patients per year.

Future phase III trials will be driven by the rapid development of novel compounds, including antiangiogenic reagents, humanized monoclonal antibodies, selective hormonal agents, and small molecules that target key components in signal transduction pathways associated with cell growth, tumor vascularity, and invasive potential. New molecular targets continue to emerge, and new laboratory techniques are being applied to rapidly synthesize, screen, and identify vast numbers of candidates for preclinical testing. Thus, it becomes important to efficiently and decisively evaluate as many new agents as possible in the context of a high-priority randomized trials program. Although larger multiarm phase III trials appear feasible with international collaboration, it will also be important to consider other innovative strategies, such as dual randomization and/or bifactorial designs, randomized phase II programs, streamlined tools for data management and regulatory review, and core laboratory facilities, as well as appropriate sponsorship, with per capita reimbursement to enhance local accrual. A robust phase I/II

GO G0182-ICON5

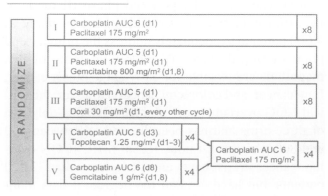

Figure 13–21. Schema for the international collaborative phase III trial GOG 0182-ICON5. This five-armed randomized trial opened to accrual in January 2001. Dose, schedule, and number of cycles were selected for each arm, based on feasibility without hematopoietic growth factors and the need to maintain overall equivalency in the number of platinum-based treatment cycles. (AUC = area under the curve.)

developmental therapeutics program will continue to be required in order to identify and evaluate promising new agents and develop feasible combinations for future phase III initiatives.

REFERENCES

1. Ovarian Cancer Meta-analysis Project. Cyclophosphamide plus cisplatin versus cyclophosphamide, doxorubicin, and cisplatin chemotherapy of ovarian carcinoma: a meta-analysis. J Clin Oncol 1991;9:1668–74.
2. Alberts DS, Liu PY, Hannigan EV, et al. Intraperitoneal cisplatin plus intravenous cyclophosphamide versus intravenous cisplatin plus intravenous cyclophosphamide for stage III ovarian cancer. N Engl J Med 1996;335:1950–5.
3. Markman M, Bundy BN, Alberts DS, et al. Phase III trial of standard-dose intravenous cisplatin plus paclitaxel versus moderately high-dose carboplatin followed by intravenous paclitaxel and intraperitoneal cisplatin in small-volume stage III ovarian carcinoma: an intergroup study of the Gynecologic Oncology Group, Southwestern Oncology Group, and Eastern Cooperative Oncology Group. J Clin Oncol 2001;19:1001–7.
4. Armstrong DK, Bundy BN, Baergen R, et al. Randomized phase III study of intravenous (IV) paclitaxel and cisplatin versus IV paclitaxel, intraperitoneal (IP) cisplatin and IP paclitaxel in optimal stage III epithelial ovarian cancer (OC): a Gynecologic Oncology Group trial (GOG 172) Proc Annu Meet Am Soc Clin Oncol 2002;21:A803.
5. McGuire WP, Hoskins WJ, Brady MF, et al. Cyclophosphamide and cisplatin compared with paclitaxel and cisplatin in patients with stage III and stage IV ovarian cancer. New Engl J Med 1996;334:1–6.
6. Piccart MJ, Bertelsen K, James K, et al. Randomized inter-

group trial of cisplatin-paclitaxel versus cisplatin-cyclophosphamide in women with advanced epithelial ovarian cancer: three-year results. J Natl Cancer Inst 2000;92:699–708.

7. Ozols RF, Bundy BN, Fowler J, et al. Randomized phase III study of cisplatin (CIS)/paclitaxel (PAC) versus carboplatin (CARBO)/PAC in optimal stage III epithelial ovarian cancer (OC): a Gynecologic Oncology Group trial (GOG 158). Proc Annu Meet Am Soc Clin Oncol 1999; 18:A1373.

8. Muggia FM, Braly PS, Brady MF, et al. Phase III randomized study of cisplatin versus paclitaxel versus cisplatin and paclitaxel in patients with suboptimal stage III or IV ovarian cancer: a Gynecologic Oncology Group study. J Clin Oncol 2000;18:106–15.

9. The International Collaborative Ovarian Neoplasm (ICON) Group. Paclitaxel plus carboplatin versus standard chemotherapy with either single-agent carboplatin or cyclophosphamide, doxorubicin, and cisplatin in women with ovarian cancer: the ICON3 randomised trial. Lancet 2002;360:505–15.

10. Pertusini E, Ratajczak J, Majka M, et al. Investigating the platelet-sparing mechanism of paclitaxel/carboplatin combination chemotherapy. Blood 2001;97:638–44.

11. de Graaff M, Malepaard M, Pluim D, et al. In vitro antagonistic cytotoxic interactions between platinum drugs and taxanes on bone marrow progenitor cell CFU-GM. Anticancer Drugs 1999;10:213–8.

12. Judson PL, Watson JM, Gehrig PA, et al. Cisplatin inhibits paclitaxel-induced apoptosis in cisplatin-resistant ovarian cancer cell lines: possible explanation for failure of combination therapy. Cancer Res 1999;59:2425–32.

13. Markman M, Hoskins W. Responses to "salvage" chemotherapy in ovarian cancer: a critical need for precise definitions of the treated population. J Clin Oncol 1992;10:513–4.

14. Thigpen JT, Blessing JA, Ball H, et al. Phase II trial of paclitaxel in patients with progressive ovarian carcinoma after platinum-based chemotherapy: a Gynecologic Oncology Group study. J Clin Oncol 1994;12:1748–53.

15. Kavanagh H, Tresukosol D, Edwards C, et al. Carboplatin reinduction after taxane in patients with platinum-refractory epithelial ovarian cancer. J Clin Oncol 1995;13:1584–8.

16. Markman M. "Recurrence within 6 months of platinum-therapy": an adequate definition of "platinum-refractory" ovarian cancer? Gynecol Oncol 1998;69:91–2.

17. Markman M, Kennedy A, Webster K, et al. Evidence a "treatment-free interval of < 6 months" does not equate with clinically defined platinum resistance in ovarian cancer or primary peritoneal carcinoma. J Cancer Res Clin Oncol 1998;124:326–8.

18. McGuire WP, Ozols RF. Chemotherapy of advanced ovarian cancer. Semin Oncol 1998;25:340–8.

19. Rose PG, Fusco N, Fluellen L, et al. Second-line therapy with paclitaxel and carboplatin for recurrent disease following first-line therapy with paclitaxel and platinum in ovarian or peritoneal carcinoma. J Clin Oncol 1998;16:1494–7.

20. Markman M. Intraperitoneal therapy of ovarian cancer. Semin Oncol 1998;25:356–60.

21. Stiff PJ, Bayer R, Kerger C, et al. High-dose chemotherapy with autologous transplantation for persistent/relapsed ovarian

cancer: a multivariate analysis of survival for 100 consecutively treated patients. J Clin Oncol 1997;15:1309–17.

22. Legros M, Dauplat J, Fleury J, et al. High-dose chemotherapy with hematopoietic rescue in patients with stage III to IV ovarian cancer: long-term results. J Clin Oncol 1997;15: 1302–8.

23. Morgan MA, Stadtmauer EA, Luger SM, et al. Cycles of dose-intensive chemotherapy with peripheral stem cell support in persistent or recurrent platinum-sensitive ovarian cancer. Gynecol Oncol 1997;67:272–6.

24. Markman M, Liu PY, Wilczynski S, et al. Phase 3 randomized trial of 12 vs. 3 months of single agent paclitaxel in patients with advanced ovarian cancer who attained a clinically-defined complete response to platinum/paclitaxel-based chemotherapy: a Southwest Oncology Group and Gynecologic Oncology Group study. Proc Annu Meet Soc Gynecol Oncol 2001;33:A1.

25. Eisenhauer EA, ten Bokkel Huinink WW, Swenerton KD, et al. European-Canadian randomized trial of paclitaxel in relapsed ovarian cancer: high-dose versus low-dose and long versus short infusion. J Clin Oncol 1994;12: 2654–66.

26. Omura GA, Brady MF, Delmore JE, et al. A randomized trial of paclitaxel (T) at 2 dose levels and filgrastim (G; G-CSF) at 2 doses in platinum (P) pretreated epithelial ovarian cancer (OVCA): a Gynecologic Oncology Group, SWOG, NCCTG and ECOG Study. Proc Annu Meet Am Soc Clin Oncol 1996;15:A755.

27. Markman M, Rose PG, Jones E, et al. Ninety-six-hour infusional paclitaxel as salvage therapy of ovarian cancer patients previously failing treatment with 3-hour or 24-hour paclitaxel infusion regimens. J Clin Oncol 1998;16: 1849–51.

28. Fennelly D, Aghajanian C, Shapiro F, et al. Phase I and pharmacologic study of paclitaxel administered weekly in patients with relapsed ovarian cancer. J Clin Oncol 1997; 15:187–92.

29. Riou JF, Naudin A, Lavelle F. Effects of Taxotere on murine and human tumor cell lines. Biochem Biophys Res Commun 1992;187:164–70.

30. Synold TW, Dussault I, Forman BM. The orphan nuclear receptor SXR coordinately regulates drug metabolism and efflux. Nat Med 2001;7:584–90.

31. Francis P, Schneider J, Hann L, et al. Phase II trial of docetaxel in patients with platinum-refractory advanced ovarian cancer. J Clin Oncol 1994;12:2301–8.

32. Piccart MJ, Gore M, ten Bokkel Huinink W, et al. Docetaxel: an active new drug for treatment of advanced epithelial ovarian cancer. J Natl Cancer Inst 1995;87:676–81.

33. Kavanagh JJ, Winn R, Steger M, et al. Docetaxel for patients with ovarian cancer refractory to paclitaxel, an update. Proc Annu Meet Am Soc Clin Oncol 1999;18:A1423.

34. Vasey PA for the Scottish Gynaecological Cancer Trials Group. Survival and longer-term toxicity results of the SCOTROC study: docetaxel-carboplatin (DC) vs. paclitaxel-carboplatin (PC) in epithelial ovarian cancer (EOC). Proc Am Soc Clin Oncol 2002;21:A804.

35. Chou TC, Motzer RJ, Tong Y, et al. Computerized quantitation of synergism and antagonism of taxol, topotecan and cisplatin against human teratocarcinoma cell growth: a

rational approach to clinical protocol design. J Natl Cancer Inst 1994;86:1517–24.

36. ten Bokkel Huinink W, Gore M, Carmichael J, et al. Topotecan versus paclitaxel for the treatment of recurrent epithelial ovarian cancer. J Clin Oncol 1997;15:2183–93.

37. Cremers GJ, Bolis G, Gore M, et al. Topotecan, an active drug in the second-line treatment of epithelial ovarian cancer: results of a large European phase II study. J Clin Oncol 1996;14:3056–61.

38. Bookman MA, Malmström H, Bolis G, et al. Topotecan for the treatment of advanced epithelial ovarian cancer: an open-label phase II study in patients treated after prior chemotherapy containing cisplatin or carboplatin and paclitaxel. J Clin Oncol 1998;16:3345–52.

39. McGuire WP, Blessing JA, Bookman MA, et al. Topotecan has substantial antitumor activity as first-line salvage therapy in platinum-sensitive epithelial ovarian carcinoma: a Gynecologic Oncology Group study. J Clin Oncol 2000;18:1062–7.

40. Markman M, Blessing JA, Alvarez RD, et al. Phase II evaluation of 24-h continuous infusion topotecan in recurrent, potentially platinum-sensitive ovarian cancer: A Gynecologic Oncology Group study. Gynecol Oncol 2000;77:112–5.

41. Markman M, Blessing JA, DeGeest K, et al. Lack of efficacy of 24-h infusional topotecan in platinum-refractory ovarian cancer: a Gynecologic Oncology Group trial. Gynecol Oncol 1999;75:444–6.

42. Markman M, Kennedy A, Webster K, et al. Phase 2 evaluation of topotecan administered on a 3-day schedule in the treatment of platinum- and paclitaxel-refractory ovarian cancer. Gynecol Oncol 2000;79:116–9.

43. Hochster H, Wadler S, Runowicz C, et al. Activity and pharmacodynamics of 21-day topotecan infusion in patients with ovarian cancer previously treated with platinum-based chemotherapy. New York Gynecologic Oncology Group. J Clin Oncol 1999;17:2553–61.

44. Lilenbaum RC, Miller AA, Batist G. Phase I and pharmacologic study of continuous infusion topotecan in combination with cisplatin in patients with advanced cancer: a Cancer and Leukemia Group B study. J Clin Oncol 1998;16:3302–9.

45. Ma J, Maliepaard M, Nooter K, et al. Synergistic cytotoxicity of cisplatin and topotecan or SN-38 in a panel of eight solid-tumor cell lines in vitro. Cancer Chemother Pharmacol 1998;41:307–16.

46. Romanelli S, Perego P, Pratesi G, et al. In vitro and in vivo interaction between cisplatin and topotecan in ovarian carcinoma systems. Cancer Chemother Pharmacol 1998;41:385–90.

47. O'Reilly S, Fleming GF, Baker SD, et al. Phase I trial and pharmacologic trial of sequences of paclitaxel and topotecan in previously treated ovarian epithelial malignancies: a Gynecologic Oncology Group study. J Clin Oncol 1997;15:177–86.

48. Rowinsky EK, Kaufmann SH, Baker SD, et al. Sequences of topotecan and cisplatin: phase I pharmacologic and in vitro studies to examine sequence dependence. J Clin Oncol 1996;14:3074–84.

49. de Jonge MJ, Loos WJ, Gelderblom H, et al. Phase I pharmacologic study of oral topotecan and intravenous cisplatin: sequence-dependent hematologic side effects. J Clin Oncol 2000;18:2104–15.

50. Sorensen M, Jensen PB, Herrstedt J, et al. A dose escalating study of topotecan preceding cisplatin in previously untreated patients with small-cell lung cancer. Ann Oncol 2000;11:829–35.

51. Armstrong DK, O'Reilly S, Bookman M, et al. A phase I study of topotecan (T), cisplatin (C), and paclitaxel (P) in newly diagnosed epithelial ovarian cancer, a Gynecologic Oncology Group (GOG 9602) study. Proc Annu Meet Am Soc Clin Oncol 1998;17:A1351.

52. Herben VM, Panday VR, Richel DJ, et al. Phase I and pharmacologic study of the combination of paclitaxel, cisplatin, and topotecan administered intravenously every 21 days as first-line therapy in patients with advanced ovarian cancer. J Clin Oncol 1999;17:747–55.

53. Cacciari N, Zamagni C, Martoni A. The addition of topotecan to carboplatin and paclitaxel as first-line therapy for advanced ovarian cancer; is it possible only with peripheral blood stem cell support? Eur J Gynaecol Oncol 2000;21:84–5.

54. Bolis G, Scarfone G, Sciatta C, et al. A phase II study of topotecan (T), carboplatin (C) and paclitaxel (P) as front line treatment in suboptimal advanced epithelial ovarian cancer (AEOC). Proc Annu Meet Am Soc Clin Oncol 2000;19:A1543.

55. Frasci G, Panza N, Comella P, et al. Cisplatin-topotecan-paclitaxel weekly administration with G-CSF support for ovarian and small-cell lung cancer patients: a dose-finding study. Ann Oncol 1999;10:355–8.

56. Homesley HD, Hall DJ, Martin DA, et al. Weekly bolus topotecan toxicity and dose response trial in second or third line therapy of epithelial ovarian carcinoma. Proc Am Soc Clin Oncol 2000;19:A1564.

57. Schilder RJ, Gallo JM, Millenson MM, et al. Phase I trial of multiple cycles of high-dose carboplatin, paclitaxel, and topotecan with peripheral-blood stem-cell support as front-line therapy. J Clin Oncol 2001;19:1183–94.

58. Hoskins P, Eisenhauer E, Vergote I, et al. Phase II feasibility study of sequential couplets of cisplatin/topotecan followed by paclitaxel/cisplatin as primary treatment for advanced epithelial ovarian cancer: a National Cancer Institute of Canada Clinical Trials Group Study. J Clin Oncol 2000;18:4038–44.

59. Gordon AN, Doherty M, Hancock KC, et al. Phase I study of topotecan (T) with carboplatin (C) alternating with paclitaxel (P) via 3 hour infusion in combination with carboplatin (C) in treatment of newly diagnosed ovarian cancer (OC) patients. Proc Annu Meet Am Soc Clin Oncol 1999;18:A1408.

60. Bowman A, Rye T, Ross G, et al. "Reverse-schedule" topotecan and carboplatin in relapsed ovarian cancer: a phase I/II dose-ranging study. Proc Eur Conf Clin Oncol 1999;10:A914f.

61. Guchelar HJ, Richel DJ, Van Knapen A. Clinical, toxicological and pharmacological aspects of gemcitabine. Cancer Treat Rev 1996;222:15–31.

62. Huang P, Chubb S, Hertel LW, et al. Action of 2',2'-difluorodeoxycytidine on DNA synthesis. Cancer Res 1991;51:6117–7.

63. Peters GJ, Bergman AM, Ruiz van Haperen VW, et al. Interaction between cisplatin and gemcitabine in vitro and in vivo. Semin Oncol 1995;22 Suppl 11:72–9.

64. Lund B, Hansen OP, Theilade K, et al. Phase II study of gemcitabine (2'2'difluorodeoxycytidine) in previously treated ovarian cancer patients. J Natl Cancer Inst 1994;86:1530–3.

65. Shapiro JD, Millward MJ, Rischin D, et al. Activity of gemcitabine in patients with advanced ovarian cancer: responses seen following platinum and paclitaxel. Gynecol Oncol 1996;63:89–93.

66. Greco FA, Burris HA 3rd, Hainsworth JD. Gemcitabine, paclitaxel, and carboplatin for advanced non-small-cell lung cancer. Oncology (Huntingt) 2000;14(7 Suppl 4):31–4.

67. Look KY, Bookman MA, Brady M, et al. Update of the phase I feasibility trial of carboplatin, paclitaxel, and gemcitabine in patients with previously untreated epithelial ovarian or primary peritoneal cancer (EOC/PPC): a Gynecologic Oncology Group (GOG) study. Proc Soc Gynecol Oncol 2000;32:A154.

68. Geertsen P, Hansen M, Strøyer I, et al. Combination chemotherapy with platinum, paclitaxel, and gemcitabine in patients with relapsed ovarian carcinoma. Proc Annu Meet Am Soc Clin Oncol 1999;18:A1395.

69. Hansen SW, Anderson H, Boman K, et al. Gemcitabine, carboplatin, and paclitaxel (GCP) as first-line treatment of ovarian cancer FIGO, stages IIB-IV. Proc Am Soc Clin Oncol 1999;18:A1379.

70. Krakowski I, Petit T, Kayitalire L, et al. Gemcitabine (Gemzar) in combination with cisplatin (CP) in advanced ovarian cancer (AOC): a phase II study. Proc Annu Meet Am Soc Clin Oncol 1998;17:A1373.

71. Bauknecht T, Grieshaber C, Breitbach G-P, et al. Gemcitabine (Gem) in combination with cisplatin (GP) in previously untreated patients ≥ 60 years with FIGO stage IIIc or IV epithelial ovarian cancer: a phase II study: preliminary results. Proc Annu Meet Am Soc Clin Oncol 1998;17:A1376.

72. Nogué M, Cirera M, Arcusa I, et al. Gemcitabine combined with cisplatin first line: a phase II study in patients with advanced epithelial ovarian cancer. Proc Annu Meet Am Soc Clin Oncol 1998;17:A1377.

73. du Bois A, Luck HJ, Pfisterer J, et al. Second-line carboplatin and gemcitabine in platinum sensitive ovarian cancer—a dose-finding study by the Arbeitsgemeinschaft Gynakologische Onkologie (AGO) Ovarian Cancer Study Group. Ann Oncol 2001;12:1115–20.

74. Iaffaioli RV, Tortoriello A, Facchini G, et al. Phase I-II study of gemcitabine and carboplatin in stage IIIB-IV non-small-cell lung cancer. J Clin Oncol 1999;17:921–6.

75. Pedersen AG. Phase I studies of gemcitabine combined with carboplatin or paclitaxel. Semin Oncol 1997;24(2 Suppl 7):64–8.

76. ICON collaborators. ICON2: randomised trial of single-agent carboplatin against three-drug combination of CAP (cyclophosphamide, doxorubicin, and cisplatin) in women with ovarian cancer. Lancet 1998;352:1571–6.

77. du Bois A, Weber B, Pfisterer J, et al. Epirubicin/paclitaxel/carboplatin (TEC) vs. paclitaxel/carboplatin (TC) in first-line treatment of ovarian cancer FIGO Stages IIb–IV.

Interim Results of an AGO–GINECO intergroup phase III trial. Proc Annu Meet Am Soc Clin Oncol 2001;20:A805.

78. Mirza E, Aavall-Lundquist AB, Lopez M, et al. First line treatment of ovarian cancer FIGO stages IIb-IV with paclitaxel/epirubicin/carboplatin (TEC) vs. paclitaxel/carboplatin (TC). Interim results of an NSGO-EORTC-NCIC CTG Gynecological Cancer Intergroup phase III trial. Proc Annu Meet Am Soc Clin Oncol 2002;21:805.

79. Gabizon A, Barenholz Y, Bialer M. Prolongation of the circulation time of doxorubicin encapsulated in liposomes containing a polyethylene glycol-derivatized phospholipid: pharmacokinetic studies in rodents and dogs. Pharm Res 1993;10:703–8.

80. Gabizon A, Catane R, Uziely R, et al. Prolonged circulation time and enhanced accumulation in malignant exudates of doxorubicin encapsulated in polyethylene-glycol coated liposomes. Cancer Res 1994;54:987–92.

81. Muggia FM, Hainsworth JD, Jeffers S, et al. Phase II study of liposomal doxorubicin in refractory ovarian cancer: antitumor activity and toxicity modification by liposomal encapsulation. J Clin Oncol 1997;15:987–93.

82. Gordon AN, Fleagle JT, Guthrie D, et al. Recurrent epithelial ovarian carcinoma: a randomized phase III study of pegylated liposomal doxorubicin versus topotecan. J Clin Oncol 2001;19:3312–22.

83. Rose P, Greer B, Markman M, et al. A phase I study of paclitaxel, carboplatin, and liposomal doxorubicin in ovarian, peritoneal, and tubal carcinoma: a Gynecologic Oncology Group study. Proc Annu Meet Am Soc Clin Oncol 2000;19:A1531.

84. Rose PG, Blessing JA, Mayer AR, et al. Prolonged oral etoposide as second-line therapy for platinum-resistant and platinum-sensitive ovarian carcinoma: a Gynecologic Oncology Group study. J Clin Oncol 1998;16:405–10.

85. Hoskins PJ, Swenerton KD. Oral etoposide is active against platinum-resistant epithelial ovarian cancer. J Clin Oncol 1994;12:60–3.

86. Rose PG, Rodriguez M, Waggoner S, et al. Phase I study of paclitaxel, carboplatin, and increasing days of prolonged oral etoposide in ovarian, peritoneal, and tubal carcinoma: a Gynecologic Oncology Group study. J Clin Oncol 2000;18:2957–62.

87. Bertelsen K, Jakobsen A, Stroyer J, et al. A prospective randomized comparison of 6 and 12 cycles of cyclophosphamide, adriamycin, and cisplatin in advanced epithelial cancer: a Danish Ovarian Cancer Study Group (DACOVA) trial. Gynecol Oncol 1993;49:30–6.

88. Hakes TB, Chalas E, Hoskins WJ, et al. Randomized prospective trial of 5 versus 10 cycles of cyclophosphamide, doxorubicin, and cisplatin in advanced ovarian carcinoma. Gynecol Oncol 1992;45:284–9.

89. Lambert HE, Rustin GJ, Gregory WM, Nelstrop NE. A randomized trial of five versus eight courses of cisplatin or carboplatin in advanced epithelial ovarian carcinoma: a North Thames Ovary Group study. Ann Oncol 1997;8:327–33.

90. McGuire WP, Hoskins WJ, Brady MF, et al. Assessment of dose-intensive therapy in suboptimally debulked ovarian cancer: a Gynecologic Oncology Group study. J Clin Oncol 1995;13:1589–99.

14

Advances in Biologic Therapy

GEORGE COUKOS, MD, PHD

HEIDI J. GRAY, MD

CARL H. JUNE, MD

Traditionally, standard first-line treatment of ovarian cancer has been surgical cytoreduction followed by platinum-based chemotherapy. Although incremental advances have been made in the field of chemotherapy, the 5-year overall survival rate for ovarian cancer remains approximately 25%, underscoring the need for innovative therapeutic strategies. Recent developments in cell and molecular biology have greatly contributed to our insight into the complex mechanisms surrounding cancer biology and have resulted in the development of biotechnological approaches to manipulating tumor cell growth, angiogenesis, and the immune system that hold promise for future therapeutics. More than 50% of patients with advanced ovarian cancer achieve complete clinical response following cytoreduction and chemotherapy; however, in most patients, disease is not eradicated, and most relapse and eventually develop chemoresistant disease. Patients with minimal disease appear to be excellent candidates for adjuvant biologic therapy aimed at suppressing disease recurrence. Lessons learned from biotherapeutic approaches in ovarian cancer and other tumors suggest that this subset of patients may maximally benefit from multimodality approaches (Figure 14–1).

There are three general biotherapeutic approaches that will be the focus of this review. Gene therapy entails the administration of recombinant deoxyribonucleic acid (DNA) into target tumor cells, causing cell differentiation or death. A second approach directly targets tumor cells by using recombinant viruses with oncolytic activity. A third approach tar-

gets antitumor immune mechanisms by enhancing immune recognition and immune-mediated tumor destruction through therapeutic vaccines, adoptive immunotherapy, biologic response modifiers, and monoclonal antibodies.

GENE THERAPY

Cancer gene therapy aims at altering the behavior of tumor cells or causing their death through the introduction of genetic material into tumor cells. To date, there have been several approaches to gene therapy used in ovarian cancer (Table 14–1). The first technique, termed cytotoxic or suicide gene therapy,

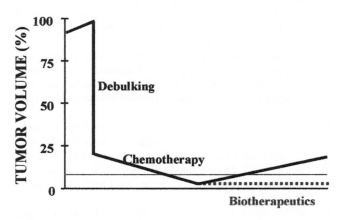

Figure 14–1. Multimodality approach to ovarian cancer treatment. The current standard for treatment of advanced-stage ovarian cancer is initial surgical debulking combined with chemotherapy as a first-line treatment to reduce tumor volume below clinical detection. Future strategies include the introduction of biotherapeutics with first-line treatment and/or as an adjuvant for the delivery of therapy at the molecular level to induce long-term tumor regression and/or eradication.

introduces genes into the host cell that encode enzymes that transform prodrugs into cytotoxic drugs. Transfected cells express the enzyme and become susceptible to cell death. The second approach, known as corrective gene therapy, involves transfecting host tumor cells with specific genes that can cause cell cycle arrest, induce programmed cell death, or cause the cell to be more susceptible to cytotoxic chemotherapy or radiation. A third approach entails the introduction of genes that cause the enhancement of immune recognition of the tumor cell and is termed immunopotentiating gene therapy.

Vectors

Gene therapy approaches have given highly promising results in vitro and in preclinical animal models but have been largely disappointing in subsequent clinical trials, probably because of a limitation of the vectors to achieve gene transfer. All vectors that have been investigated to date (Table 14–2) have limitations related to low efficacy, difficulty in penetrating tumor nodules, immune system inactivation, and undesirable side effects. Although a variety of vectors have been developed, viruses remain the most commonly used vectors because of their high transfection rate and ease of production. Through manipulation or deletion of portions of the viral genome involved in viral replication, vectors are usually made replication incompetent, which may be useful in limiting toxicity.

Replication-incompetent recombinant adenovirus vectors have been the most extensively studied vectors for use in cancer gene therapy.[1,2] The advantages to using these vectors include demonstrated stability in vivo, relative ease of mass production, high-efficiency transduction of a wide range of target cells (including nondividing cells), high expression levels of the delivered transgene, and the ability to be manufactured without contamination by replication-competent adenoviruses (RCAs).[3] The primary disadvantages to adenoviral vectors are that they produce only transient gene expression, as the inserted gene is not integrated into the human genome, and that the virions are highly immunogenic, producing a prominent inflammatory response locally and systemically. However, these features may prove to be an advantage in cancer gene therapy.

Herpes simplex–based vectors comprise another major category of gene therapy vectors. Herpes simplex virus (HSV) is a 152-kb enveloped virus that primarily infects epithelial cells of the skin and mucous membranes. Several features unique to this virus make it attractive as a vector in cancer gene therapy: (1) a large portion of its genome (up to 30 kb) can be replaced without impairing the virus's ability to replicate, (2) HSV has a higher efficacy of infection to tumors of epithelial origin (such as ovarian cancer), than does adenovirus,[4,5] and (3) antiherpetic drugs can be used to control undesired side effects.

Table 14–1. CLINICALLY TESTED GENE THERAPY APPROACHES TO OVARIAN CANCER*	
Gene	**Rationale**
HSVtk	Cancer cells transduced with thymidine kinase die following administration of ganciclovir. Bystander killing mechanisms mediated by toxic metabolites and cytokines amplify the toxic effect. A T-cell response may be triggered against the tumor.
P53	More than 50% of advanced ovarian cancers display loss of *P53*. Overexpression of *P53* induces apoptosis or cell cycle arrest and sensitizes cancer cells to chemotherapeutic drugs. Bystander mechanisms of cell killing and inhibition of angiogenesis may also occur.
BRCA1	Overexpression of *BRCA1* in sporadic ovarian cancer cells induces tumor growth suppression.
Adenoviral E1A	Approximately 30% of ovarian cancers overexpress *HER-2/neu* proto-oncogene. Adenoviral E1A gene product counteracts HER-2 protein and inhibits tumor growth in ovarian cancer cells overexpressing *HER-2/neu*.
Gene encoding an anti-HER-2/neu single-chain intracellular antibody	Expression of the gene results in decreased expression of surface HER-2 and induces growth suppression in ovarian cancer cells overexpressing *HER-2/neu*.

HSVtk = herpes simplex virus thymidine kinase.
*For an updated reference on current clinical trials, go to <www.ovarian.org/>; or <www. centerwatch.com/>; or <www.cancertrials.nci.nih.gov/>.

Table 14-2. GENE DELIVERY VECTORS
Viral vectors
Adenovirus
Adeno-associated virus
Herpes simplex virus
Vaccinia virus
Polyoma virus
Papilloma simian virus
Oncoretroviral vectors
Moloney murine leukemia virus
Harvey murine sarcoma virus
Avian spleen neurosis virus
Lentiviruses
Human immunodeficiency virus
Simian immunodeficiency virus
Feline immunodeficiency virus
Nonviral vectors
Cationic lipids
Cationic liposomes
Stealth liposomes
Naked plasmid DNA
Gene gun

DNA = deoxyribonucleic acid.

Retroviruses are ribonucleic acid (RNA) viruses that replicate in the host via DNA reverse transcription, and the subsequently transcribed DNA is integrated into the host genome in a pseudorandom fashion. Their main advantage as gene therapy vectors is long-term gene expression; their disadvantages relate to the possibility of insertional mutagenesis and incidental insertion of transgenes into the germ line.

Finally, there is growing interest in using liposomes as a nonviral vector delivery system for plasmid DNA. Liposomes are amphipathic lipids that can act as a vehicle for delivering plasmid DNA into mammalian cells. They can be produced on a large scale, they can carry large transgenes (up to 50 kb), and they are taken up efficiently by a variety of cells, including epithelial ovarian cancer (EOC).[6] Limitations to this system include (1) poor in vivo transduction, compared to viral vectors, and (2) transient transgene expression.

Cytotoxic Gene Therapy

The basic principle of cytotoxic (suicide) gene therapy involves introducing into tumor cells a specific gene that encodes for an enzyme, which converts a prodrug into a cytotoxic drug. Only cells expressing this transgene will then be susceptible to the toxic effects of the active metabolites. Although many enzyme/prodrug systems exist, the classic model is provided by the system involving the thymidine kinase of HSV (HSVtk). HSVtk allows for the phosphorylation of ganciclovir (GCV) into GCV monophosphate. Cellular enzymes subsequently phosphorylate GCV monophosphate twice, producing GCV triphosphate, which is a potent DNA and RNA, synthesis inhibitor.[7] GCV triphosphate incorporates into DNA and inhibits DNA polymerase, leading to fragmentation of the DNA and ultimately to cellular death, through apoptosis mechanisms (Figure 14–2).[8] This strategy is cell cycle-dependent as it requires the incorporation of GCV triphosphate into DNA during the S phase. In general, malignant cells exhibit higher mitotic rates than neighboring normal cells and are therefore preferentially susceptible to this therapy. Thus, after treatment with ganciclovir, tumor cells that have been transfected with HSVtk selectively undergo cell death (Figure 14–3).

When the initial studies using suicide gene therapy with the HSVtk/GCV system were performed, the expectation was that only transfected tumor cells would be affected. However, it was consistently observed that adjacent nontransfected cells were undergoing cell death as well. The phrase "bystander effect" was coined to describe these observations, which can be seen in other cytotoxic systems as well[9] (Figure 14–4). In the HSVtk/GCV system, GCV triphosphate diffuses through gap junctions into adjacent cells, accounting for the bystander effect.[10] Other hypotheses include the release of cytotoxic

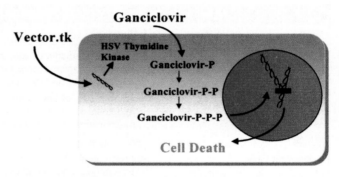

Figure 14–2. Cancer suicide gene therapy. A vector containing herpes simplex virus (HSV) thymidine kinase (vector.tk) is introduced into the tumor cell. The expressed transgene (*HSVtk*) allows for the phosphorylation of ganciclovir (GCV), ultimately producing GCV triphosphate, which incorporates into deoxyribonucleic acid (DNA), leading to DNA fragmentation and cell death.

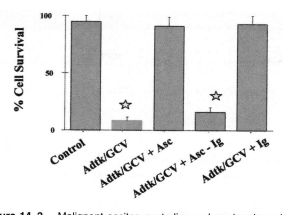

Figure 14–3. Malignant ascites neutralizes adenovirus-based suicide gene therapy. Malignant ascites from patients with advanced ovarian cancer was harvested and depleted of its immunoglobulin fraction, using a protein-A sepharose column. Ovarian carcinoma cells (SKOV3) were infected with an E1/E2-deleted adenoviral vector carrying herpes simplex virus thymidine kinase (Adtk) and exposed to 100 µM of ganciclovir (GCV). Significant cell death was observed after 4 days of the addition of GCV (Adtk/GCV). Ascites diluted at 30% (Asc) completely neutralizes the cytotoxic effect of Adtk (Adtk/GCV + Asc) whereas ascites containing a 100-fold lower amount of immunoglobulin (Ig) loses its neutralizing ability (Adtk/GCV + Asc-Ig). The immunoglobulin fraction of ascites alone retains the neutralizing ability of the ascites (Adtk/GCV + Ig). (*$p < .01$)

cytokines from the dying cells, inducing apoptosis in the neighboring cells,[11] and the possible recruitment of the Fas/Fas ligand mechanism.[12] Further studies on HSVtk-based gene therapy in immunocompetent

animals have suggested that the use of viral vectors could generate an intense immune response, which may lead to immune recognition of tumor-specific antigens,[13] potentiating the effects of cytotoxic gene therapy (Table 14–3).

Corrective Gene Therapy

Another key approach in cancer gene therapy aims at correcting specific genetic defects in tumor cells through gene replacement or neutralization. Certain tumors display a loss of specific tumor suppressor genes, offering the opportunity to control tumor growth through replacement of the wild-type gene. Other tumors may exhibit overexpression of oncogenes, providing specific molecular targets for neutralization[14] (Table 14–4). Mutations in the *P53* tumor suppressor gene are found in a large number of solid tumors, including 50 to 75% of ovarian carcinomas. Loss of functional p53 alters cell cycle control and enables tumor cells to resist apoptosis; in ovarian cancer, it may also contribute to resistance to chemotherapy and may be an independent measure of a poor prognosis.[15] Other genes involved in cell cycle control have been identified in ovarian cancer and include *P21*, and *P16*, which are cyclin inhibitors (Table 14–5). Patients with hereditary breast and ovarian cancer syndrome exhibit germline mutations in the *BRCA1* and *BRCA2* genes, which are thought to exert a tumor suppressor function.

The use of gene therapy strategies that target these tumor suppressor genes and other genes involved in control of the cell cycle has been studied in EOC and other solid malignancies. Studies involving the *P53* tumor suppressor gene by far dominate the field. Initial studies delivering wild-

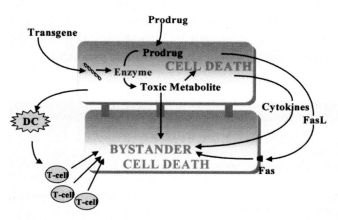

Figure 14–4. Bystander mechanisms in cancer suicide gene therapy. Some tumor cells are transduced by a transgene encoding a specific enzyme, becoming sensitive to a specific nontoxic prodrug by virtue of their ability to transform it into a cytotoxic metabolite. Toxic metabolites may diffuse into neighboring cells via gap junctions or membrane diffusion or transport mechanisms, causing cell death in nontransduced cells. Dying infected cells release toxic cytokines and Fas ligand (FasL), amplifying the cytotoxic cascade. Furthermore, infected or dying cells may display an enhanced presentation of tumor-specific antigens, triggering a tumor-specific cellular immune response. DC = Dentritic cell.

Table 14–3. MECHANISMS OF TUMOR IMMUNE RECOGNITION BY SUICIDE GENE THERAPY
↑ Class I MHC molecules
↑ Tumor-specific antigens
↑ Nonspecific enhancers (B7, ICAM)
↑ Heat shock proteins
↑ Cytokines promoting Th1 response (IL-1, IL-12, TNF-α, interferon-γ)

ICAM = intercelular adhesion molecule; IL = interleukin; MHC = major histocompatibility complex; TNF = tumor necrosis factor.

Table 14–4. GENES USED IN CORRECTIVE GENE THERAPY FOR CANCER	
Gene	Action
P53	Induces apoptosis (up-regulates Bax, down-regulates Bcl-2); induces cell cycle arrest (up-regulates *P21* and Gadd45); blocks DNA replication and transcription
P21	Induces cell cycle arrest (inhibits cyclin D kinase, inactivates retinoblastoma (RB) gene and *PCNA*)
P16	Induces cell cycle arrest downstream of *P21* (inhibits cyclin D)
BRCA1	Induces cell cycle arrest (interacts with *P21* and RB)
BAX	Induces apoptosis downstream of *P53* (induces activation of caspases)
ICE	Large family of proteases inducing apoptosis (cleave a large number of regulatory proteins)
RB	Induces cell cycle arrest and loss of in vivo tumorigenic potential (inhibits E2F transcription factor, c-myc, and c-fos)
BCL-X$_S$	Induces apoptosis (binds to and inhibits Bcl-2 or Bcl-x$_L$)

ICE = Interleukin-1β converting enzyme; DNA = deoxyribonucleic acid. PCNA = proliferating cell nuclear antigen.

type *P53* gene via a variety of vectors in vitro showed increased amounts of apoptosis and/or cell cycle arrest of EOC cells.[16–18] Additionally, tumor regression was noted in vivo in intraperitoneal xenograft mouse models.[16–18] Other studies have shown that cells transfected with wild-type *P53* gene exhibit increased sensitivity to platinum,[19] and a synergistic effect has been documented with adenovirus-delivered *P53* and paclitaxel[20] in vitro. Gene therapy with *P53* has elicited bystander effects in EOC cells involving decreased expression of vascular endothelial growth factor (VEGF)[21] and increased Fas/Fas ligand.[22]

Neutralization of oncogenes has been attempted via nucleic acid sequences or intracellular antibodies. Innovative approaches have been designed against oncogene *HER-2/neu* (c-erbB-2), which is overexpressed in breast cancer and approximately 30% of EOCs.[15,23] *HER-2/neu* encodes an epidermal growth factor–related protein that has tyrosine kinase activity[24] (Figure 14–5). DeShane and colleagues developed a gene therapy construct that encodes a single-chain humanized intracellular antibody (intrabody) directed at the HER-2 protein.[25] Transduced cells showed decreased cell-surface expression of HER-2 in vitro and showed regression of tumor nodules in vivo in a xenograft intraperitoneal tumor model for ovarian cancer.[26] A phase I clinical trial was completed at the University of Alabama, using an anti-erbB-2– encoding adenovirus in patients with erbB-2– overexpressing EOC, and reported disease stabilization in 38% (5 of 13) of patients after treatment.[27] Other studies have used the adenoviral *E1A* gene, whose protein product inhibits

Table 14–5. TARGETS OF GENE SUPPRESSIVE STRATEGIES	
Gene	Action
HER-2/neu	Encodes human epidermal growth factor receptor 2 (HER-2), a membrane tyrosine kinase receptor promoting cell replication. HER-2 overexpression is associated with malignant transformation. It is overexpressed in approximately 30% of ovarian cancers.
c-fos	Proto-oncogene encoding a portion of AP-1 transcription factor mediating postreceptor activation of mitogenic pathways normally activated in growth factor–stimulated cells; activates cell proliferation
c-myc	Proto-oncogene encoding a transcription factor activating mitogenic pathways
K-ras	Proto-oncogene encoding a GTP-binding protein mediating activation of mitogenic pathways, including activation of Raf protein-serine kinase and MAP kinase pathways; is overexpressed in ovarian mucinous adenocarcinomas
BCL-2	Major antiapoptotic factor; promotes cell survival by counteracting p53-dependent and p53-independent apoptosis; is implicated in chemotherapy resistance
BCL-X$_L$	Promotes cell survival and chemotherapy resistance; counteracts p53-dependent and p53-independent apoptosis
NF-κB	Transcription factor involved in lymphocyte activation; overexpressed in many solid tumors; inhibits apoptosis
VEGF	Promotes tumor angiogenesis; inhibits T-cell and dendritic cell maturation and function

GTP = guanosine triphosphate; AP-1 = activator protein-1; MAP = mitogen-activated protein.

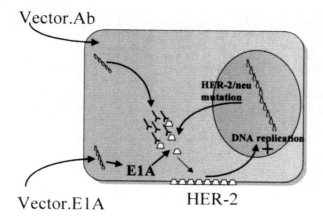

Figure 14–5. Anti-HER-2/*neu* corrective approaches in ovarian carcinoma. Intrabodies directed against HER-2/*neu* protein lead to decreased surface expression, inhibiting further deoxyribonucleic acid (DNA) replication. The adenoviral gene E1A protein product similarly inhibits HER-2 protein function. Ab = antibody.

HER-2 function. A dramatic reduction in the malignant phenotype was seen in the ovarian cancer cell line SKOV3.ip1 transfected with *E1A* gene.[28] In a phase I clinical trial completed at the M.D. Anderson Cancer Center at the University of Texas using adenoviral *E1A* gene delivered through liposomes for patients with metastatic breast or ovarian cancer with documented overexpression of *HER-2/neu*, 6 of 18 enrolled patients underwent molecular analysis and were found to have down-regulation of *HER-2/neu* expression and a decreased number of tumor cells in ascitic and pleural fluid. These promising results have led to the initiation of a phase II trial with this vector in patients with recurrent EOC (also at the M.D. Anderson Cancer Center).[29]

VIRAL ONCOLYTIC AGENTS

Early studies with viral oncolytic agents in the 1950s and 1960s entailed the injection of wild-type viruses into tumors. The underlying principle was that the introduction of replication-competent viruses would directly infect tumor cells and subsequently carry out a replicative cycle, leading to cell death. These techniques were abandoned briefly as they were met with limited success and an inability to molecularly modify the viruses.[30] With the advent of recombinant technology, mutated viruses were generated, renewing interest in viral oncolytic tumor therapies (Figure 14–6). Emerging evidence suggests that the use of

replication-competent viruses may generate antitumor immune responses based on an immunomodulatory function of viruses, which may induce the stimulation of dendritic cells (DCs), macrophages, and other accessory cells.

HSV is a 152 kb enveloped double-stranded DNA virus that primarily infects epithelial cells of the skin and mucous membranes. Initial work was carried out using recombinant replication-restricted HSV type 1 (HSV-1) for the treatment of tumors of the central nervous system (CNS).[31] The HSV gene *ICP34.5* is important for neurovirulence,[32,33] viral replication,[34] exit of the virus from infected cells,[35] and protein synthesis in infected cells.[36] *ICP34.5*-mutated viruses were shown to selectively infect and destroy malignant tumors in the CNS but not neighboring normal neurons. Two completed phase I clinical trials using stereotactic intratumoral injection of HSV in the brain have reported minimal toxicity. *ICP34.5*-mutated viruses have also been shown to be efficacious against a variety of extra-CNS malignancies, including melanoma, head and neck squamous cancer, mesothelioma, and breast, prostate, ovarian, and colon carcinoma.[37–42] Multiple lines of evidence have confirmed the safety of these strains following intratumoral or intraperitoneal injection (Table 14–6).

We investigated the use of recombinant HSV-1 lacking *ICP34.5* in the treatment of EOC. We found that EOC cell lines were highly susceptible to infection by recombinant HSV-1, with 99% of the cells infected at 1.5 multiplicities of infection.[4] Further-

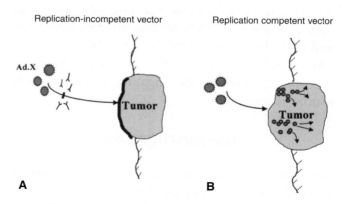

Figure 14–6. Intraperitoneal viral gene therapy. *A*, Replication-incompetent viral vectors such as Ad.X transduce only a few surface layers of tumor cells. Intraperitoneal antibodies further reduce gene transfer. *B*, Replication-competent viral vectors infect and propagate within tumor nodules, transducing a larger portion of the tumor.

TABLE 14–6. EVIDENCE FOR SAFETY OF ONCOLYTIC HERPES SIMPLEX VIRUS 1 MUTANTS
SCID mice show no toxicity following IP injection of 1×10^6 pfu *ICP34.5*-deficient HSV-1716 but are readily killed by 1×10^2 pfu wild-type HSV-1.
Human skin xenotransplants in SCID mice show no toxicity following inoculation of *ICP34.5*-deficient HSV-1716, but are rapidly lysed by wild-type HSV-1.
Following IP inoculation in the SCID mouse, *ICP34.5*-deficient HSV-1716 remains confined within tumor nodules and is not detected by immunohistochemistry or PCR in any normal murine tissues whereas wild-type HSV-1 rapidly spreads in extraperitoneal and distant tissues, including the brain.
ICP34.5/ICP6-deleted HSV-G207 causes no toxicity following systemic administration in HSV-sensitive nonhuman primates.
ICP34.5-deficient HSV-1716 and I*CP34.5/ICP6*-deleted HSV-G207 cause no peritonitis in the SCID mouse.
ICP34.5/ICP6-deleted HSV-G207 kills rapidly ovarian cancer cells but not normal peritoneal cells.

pfu = particle forming unit; IP = intraperitoneal; HSV = herpes simplex virus; PCR = polymerase chain reaction; SCID = severe combined immunodeficiency.

more, oncolytic HSV-1 killed primary ovarian carcinoma cultures more rapidly than established cell lines[4,43] and was equally efficacious in chemotherapy-sensitive and chemotherapy-resistant EOC in vitro and in vivo.[4,44] Additionally, EOC cell lines incubated with recombinant HSV-1 underwent a variable degree of apoptosis, which was not dependent on *P53* status.

ONYX-015 is a recombinant replication-competent adenovirus that lacks early (E) gene *E1B*. Tumor suppressor gene *P53* is up-regulated upon adenoviral infection and blocks adenoviral replication in normal cells, suppressing further viral spread. The protein product of *E1B* inactivates *P53* and allows adenoviral replication.[45] E1B-deleted adenovirus is therefore unable to replicate in normal diploid cells or cells with intact p53 function but can replicate in (and kill) cells that lack p53 function (such as tumor cells). This strategy confers tumor specificity to this oncolytic virus. Although controversy exists on the accuracy of this model of viral replication, significantly higher response rates and disease-free intervals have been seen in a phase II study treating patients with head and neck cancer with ONYX-015.[46] Because up to 75% of ovarian cancers exhibit loss of p53 function, this strategy warrants investigation in patients with ovarian carcinoma.

IMMUNOTHERAPY

The use of clinical immunotherapy has spanned many decades, and multiple approaches have been developed, including the use of systemic cytokines or biologic response modifiers, antibodies, therapeutic vaccines, and adoptive cell-based therapies using activated macrophages, natural killer (NK) cells, and T lymphocytes (Figure 14–7). Earlier clinical trials were designed empirically, without fundamental knowledge of the immune biology of solid tumors, and resulted in poor clinical responses. As advancements in molecular and cellular immunology continue to be made rapidly, there has been significant progress in our understanding of immune dysfunction caused by tumors and in our ability to manipulate the immune system in an effort to circumvent such dysfunction. The discovery and characterization of tumor-specific antigens has revealed that tumors are

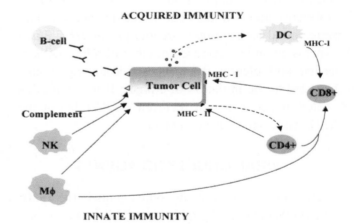

Figure 14–7. Antitumor immune mechanisms. Innate immunity is composed of both complement and major histocompatibility complex (MHC)–independent cytotoxic cell effectors such as macrophages (M) and natural killer (NK) cells. Acquired immunity responses include humoral antibody-mediated response (B cells) and MHC-dependent cellular responses (T cells). Antibodies may facilitate complement-mediated cell killing. Professional antigen-presenting cells such as dendritic cells (DCs) or macrophages phagocytose tumor debris and cross-present tumor-specific antigens on MHC class I sites. These are recognized by cytotoxic CD8+ T lymphocytes that then undergo clonal proliferation. Similarly, class II MHC (MHC-II) molecules are recognized by CD4+ helper T lymphocytes, which then produce cytokines to enhance the CD8+ cytotoxic response.

antigenic; that is, they may offer antigen determinants that may be recognized by the immune system in select patients. Lessons learned from melanoma[47,48] indicated that such antigens may vary in nature and may be tumor-specific peptides that are absent in all adult normal tissues except germline cells such as MAGE, BAGE, or GAGE. Other tumor rejection antigens were identified as tissue-specific differentiation antigens, which may be recognized as nonself by virtue of their temporally inappropriate expression within a specific tumor. Tumor-specific antigens result also from mutations such as those occurring in tumor suppressor genes and oncogenes, as seen in many malignancies (examples include p53, caspase-8, and bcr-abl). Overexpressed peptides may also represent tumor-specific antigens. An example is *HER-2/neu*, an oncogene overexpressed in approximately 30% of breast and ovarian cancers. Finally, cytotoxic lymphocytes may recognize epitopes of mucin, a surface glycoprotein containing multiple tandem repeats of 20 amino acids.[49] Although this protein is heavily glycosylated in normal cells, the peptide repeats are unmasked by underglycosylation in some tumors, including breast and ovarian carcinomas.[50] In ovarian carcinoma, antigen characterization has not been systematic, but evidence exists that tumor-associated antigens are present, and mounting circumstantial evidence indicates that EOC may be recognized and targeted by the immune system. Some ovarian carcinoma specimens harbor a brisk leukocyte infiltrate.[51–53] Isolated tumor-associated lymphocytes exhibit activation[51] and oligoclonal expansion,[54,55] recognize tumor-associated antigens,[56–62] and display antitumor activity ex vivo.[62–65] Occasionally, patients with ovarian carcinoma display autoimmune paraneoplastic cerebellar degeneration, due to tumor-specific T cells' recognizing onconeuronal protein cdr2, an antigen shared by EOC and cerebellar Purkinje cells.[66] These findings suggest that the manipulation of immune mechanisms may offer powerful therapeutic tools for treating ovarian carcinoma.

Significant progress has been made recently in our understanding of immune evasion mechanisms in ovarian carcinoma (Table 14–7). Such mechanisms may involve the antigen-presenting arm of the immune system. Immature HLA-DR-negative macrophages and lineage-negative immature DCs have been described in ascites.[67–69] Elevated levels of VEGF in tumor and ascites may be responsible for inhibiting the maturation of antigen-presenting cells, leading to tumor immunologic ignorance. Increasing evidence also suggests that immature DCs may present antigen in vivo and result in tolerance or anergy of T cells.[70,71] Ovarian carcinoma may also evade recognition and attack by T cells. Immune escape may be mediated by functional inactivation of tumor-infiltrating T cells, including down-regulation of the T-cell receptor, zeta chain (TCRζ);[72,75] adverse polarization due to elevated levels of interleukin-10 (IL-10)

Table 14–7.   IMMUNE ESCAPE MECHANISMS IDENTIFIED IN TUMORS

Humoral immunity
    Loss of antigenic determinants recognized by antitumor antibodies
    Escape from complement-mediated cytotoxicity
    Complement inactivation
Cellular immunity
    Loss of antigenic determinants recognized by tumor-specific T cells
    Down-regulation of MHC class I molecules (inhibition of TAP)
    Induction of T-cell anergy
        Loss of co-stimulatory signals (B7)
        Release of counterstimulatory signals (CTLA-4)
    Inhibition of T-cell function (by IL-10 and TGF-β)
    Loss of T-cell receptor (inhibition of NF-κB and loss of TCRζ)
    Inhibition of dendritic cell maturation (by VEGF)
    Induction of T-cell apoptosis (by tumor-released Fas ligand)
    Escape from T-cell-induced apoptosis (loss of apoptotic machinery, production of Fas ligand)

MHC = major histocompatibility complex; TAP = transporter associated with (antigen) processing; TCR = T-cell receptor; TGF = transforming growth factor; VEGF = vascular endothelial growth factor.

and transforming growth factor-β (TGF-β) secreted by tumor cells or immunosuppressive HLA-DR-negative macrophages and immature DCs;[67–69] or tolerance induction by regulatory CD4$^+$CD25$^+$ T cells secreting high amounts of IL-10 and TGF-β.[74] Although tumor-infiltrating lymphocytes (TILs) may undergo physiologic activation-induced cell death and may commit suicide upon activation by antigen,[75,76] ligands to members of the family of tumor necrosis factor receptors (TNFRs) (such as FasL, tumor necrosis factor-α [TNF-α], or TNF-related apoptosis-inducing ligand) may be expressed by tumor cells, resulting in contact-dependent apoptosis of TILs.[77–79] Ovarian carcinoma cells were found to express FasL ex vivo and induced Fas-mediated apoptotic cell death on activated T cells.[72,80,81] RCAS-1, a TNFR-unrelated death ligand that induces suppression and/or apoptosis of activated lymphocytes in vitro, has recently been described in solid tumors, including ovarian carcinoma.[82]

Tumor Vaccines

Recognizing that tumors may harbor specific antigenic targets and that tumor antigen presentation may be severely impaired within the tumor microenvironment, tumor vaccines are designed with the purpose of restoring tumor antigen presentation. In the absence of well-characterized tumor-specific antigens, many investigators have undertaken nonspecific vaccination using whole-tumor-cell preparations, but antigen-based vaccines have been tried also, especially for melanoma (Table 14–8). In the first investigations to use tumor cell extracts, extracts prepared by freezing and thawing tumor cells or whole-tumor extracts were injected into patients, with or without known immunologic adjuvants. These trials were met with varying success.[83] As the role of professional antigen-presenting cells, such as DCs, in antigen presentation to T cells was elucidated and as methodologies were developed to generate clinically meaningful

Table 14–8.   STRATEGIES FOR THE PREPARATION OF TUMOR VACCINES

Whole-cell vaccines
  Administration of autologous or allogeneic tumor cells
    Tumor cells modified with physical or chemical agents
      UV radiation
      Ionizing radiation
      Dinitrophenyl (DNP)
      Acetic acid
      Keyhole limpet hemocyanin
      Incomplete Freund's adjuvant
      Semustine
      Vibrio cholerae neuraminidase
    Tumor cells modified with biologic extracts
      Bacille Calmette-Guérin
      Corynebacterium parvum
      Candida antigens
    Tumor cells lysed by genetically modified virus
    Tumor cells infected by genetically modified *Salmonella typhimurium*
  Administration of autologous dendritic cells
    Dendritic cells incubated with whole-tumor cells modified by UV radiation, ionizing radiation, or cell fragmentation
    Dendritic cells incubated with whole-tumor cells
      Apoptotic bodies
      Total RNA
Antigen-based vaccines
  Administration of tumor-specific antigen
    Recombinant tumor-specific antigen enriched by adjuvants
  Administration of autologous dendritic cells
    Incubated with recombinant antigen
    Transduced with specific antigen cDNA
DNA vaccines
  Recombinant virus carrying tumor-specific antigen cDNA

DNA = deoxyribonucleic acid; cDNA = complementary DNA; RNA = ribonucleic acid; UV = ultraviolet.

quantities of DCs from peripheral blood precursors, DC-based vaccine approaches were designed. In the absence of known tumor antigens, patient-derived DCs may be "pulsed" with whole-tumor antigens ex vivo[84] (Figures 14–8 and 14–9).

Whole-Cell Vaccines

In the absence of well-defined tumor antigens, whole-cell vaccines have been used.[83] Whole-cell vaccines were initially developed because of their simplicity of preparation and the theoretical advantage of a broad tumor antigen repertoire from which to draw an immune response. Unfortunately, the disadvantages include high cost and the difficulty of gathering and isolating autologous tumor cells. One approach to increasing the immunogenicity of whole-cell tumor vaccines, is to associate the cells with specific adjuvant haptens, such as dinitrophenyl (DNP), that can provoke a strong inflammatory response. A recent clinical phase I trial using DNP-modified autologous ovarian tumor cells in stage III patients reported no acute toxicities. Some patients developed a measurable immune response although no clinically meaningful responses were observed.[85]

Another series of strategies using virus extract to make whole-cell vaccines more immunogenic were based on the observation that viruses can be potent inflammatory mediators. This led to the development

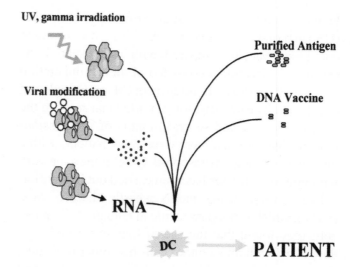

Figure 14–9. Methodologies to pulse dendritic cells (DCs) with tumor antigen for preparation of DC-based cancer vaccine. Whole-tumor antigen (left) may be prepared with ultraviolet- (UV) or gamma-irradiated apoptotic tumor cells, virally infected tumor cells, or whole-tumor ribonucleic acid (RNA). Tumor-associated antigens (right) may be used as purified peptides or in the form of nucleic acid, to load DCs.

of a variety of viral oncolysates for use in clinical trials for many different cancers, including melanoma, gastric carcinoma, and cervical, ovarian, vulvar, and renal cancers[86,87] (Table 14–9). Mechanisms that have been proposed to explain the antitumor immune response include the invoking of inflammatory cytokines or chemokines, which then activate immune cells;[88] viral/tumor antigen interactions that increase the uptake of tumor antigens by DCs; the activation of helper T cells by recall immune mechanisms against the viral antigens;[89] and increased immunogenicity through the release of heat shock protein–mediated pathways.[90] Clinical experimentation with viral oncolysates as vaccines has shown that antitumor immune response may be elicited in select patients, followed by partial clinical responses (Table 14–10).

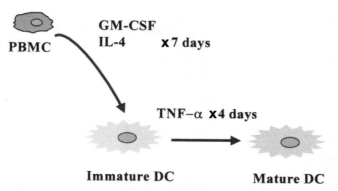

Figure 14–8. Ex-vivo generation of dendritic cells (DCs) from peripheral blood mononuclear cells (PBMCs). PBMCs extracted from patients, placed in culture, and incubated with granulocyte-macrophage colony-stimulating factor (GM-CSF) and interleukin-4 (IL-4) for 7 days differentiate into immature DCs (orange). Further incubation with tumor necrosis factor-α (TNF-α) for 4 days matures the DCs (green). Immature DCs specialize in antigen uptake whereas mature DCs specialize in T-cell activation.

Table 14–9. VIRUSES USED FOR ONCOLYSATE VACCINE PREPARATION
Herpes simplex virus
Newcastle disease virus
Polyoma virus
Vaccinia virus
Influenza virus
Friend leukemia virus
Vesicular stomatitis virus
Measles virus

Freedman and colleagues studied the use of ultraviolet (UV)-irradiated influenza A virus to produce oncolysate vaccine prepared with established EOC cell lines.[91] Treatment consisted of the administration of several courses of intraperitoneal or intrapleural oncolysate. The investigators reported that some of the patients experienced several months of progression-free survival and that there were a few patients with a documented complete response. Other important work with viral oncolysates has been carried out by the Heidelberg group, using the Newcastle disease virus (NDV), which is nonpathogenic in humans.[92] Remarkably, they found that the use of live inactivated low-dose NDV with intact tumor cells had superior results, compared to those achieved with tumor lysates,[93] and led to the generation of specific cytotoxic T lymphocytes with antitumor activity but no antiviral activity. In a subsequent phase II trial in Germany using repeated doses of NDV-modified autologous tumor cells, the Heidelberg group reported a 50% 2-year survival rate in 31 patients with advanced EOC.[94]

Antigen-Based Vaccines

The discovery of tumor-specific antigens raised hopes of molecularly targeted tumor vaccina-

Table 14–10. RESULTS OF CLINICAL TRIALS PERFORMED WITH VIRAL ONCOLYSATE FOR OVARIAN CANCER

Virus	Responses
Autologous	
Vaccinia*	Partial response in 9/23
Newcastle disease	50% 2-year survival with high-quality vaccine
Allogeneic	
Influenza A	Partial response in 9/40

*Also included other solid tumors.

tion.[95–98] Recent clinical trials have used peptides conjugated to a carrier protein adjuvant (such as keyhole limpet hemocyanin)[99] and directly administered to patients or used to pulse ex vivo autologous DCs that were subsequently injected to patients. While most of the antigen-based vaccine work has been carried out for melanoma,[100,101] several antigens have been discovered in EOC[102] (Table 14–11). HER-2/neu,[61] amino enhancer of split protein,[103] and the folate-binding protein,[104] sialylated TN (sTN), which is a mucin carbohydrate–derived antigen, are all examples. Recently, a clinical trial administered a synthetic analogue of sTN to patients with advanced-stage EOC. Investigators reported no acute toxicities and a documented

Table 14–11. TUMOR-ASSOCIATED ANTIGENS IDENTIFIED IN OVARIAN CANCER

Antigen Type	Ovarian Cancer (%)	MHC Restriction
Tumor-specific antigens		
MAGE-1	+ 28	HLA-A1
MAGE-3	+ 17	HLA-A1/2/B44
MAGE-6	—	HLA-Cw16
BAGE	+ 15	HLA-Cw16
GAGE-1,2	+ 31	HLA-Cw6
RAGE-1	—	HLA-B7
Mucins	—	Nonrestricted
Differentiation antigens		
CEA	+ 30	HLA-A2
Mutated antigens		
p53	+> 50	HLA-A2
Ras	—	—
MUM-1	Melanoma	HLA-B44
β-Catenin	—	HLA-A24
CASP-8	—	HLA-B35
Overexpressed antigens		
p53	+ 30–40	HLA-A2
HER-2/neu	+ 30	HLA-A2

CEA = carcinoembryonic antigen; HLA = human leukocyte antigen; MHC = major histocompatibility complex; CASP-8 = caspase-8.

immune response, with several patients maintaining stable disease for a prolonged time.[60] Other strategies being pursued include DNA-based vaccines in which DNA encoding for tumor-specific antigens may be inserted into recombinant viruses and transfected into DCs.[105–107]

Adoptive Immunotherapy

Over the past 40 years, a significant amount of research has focused on using T lymphocytes to attack established tumors. These approaches attempt to generate large amounts of activated T cells and to circumvent mechanisms of immune suppression within the tumor microenvironment (Table 14–12). Earlier strategies used peripheral blood lymphocytes, tumor-associated lymphocytes (eg, from ascites), or tumor-infiltrating lymphocytes, which were expanded and activated ex vivo. Typically, T-cell expansion was achieved with interleukin-2 (IL-2) stimulation. Bispecific antibodies were used in one trial to increase the targeting ability of re-infused lymphocytes. Antibodies directed against CD3 and the tumor-specific antigen folate-binding protein MOv18, which is overexpressed in 90% of ovarian carcinomas, were administered intraperitoneally together with T cells and recombinant IL-2, resulting in a 27% response rate and evidence of intraperitoneal immune response but no systemic immune response.[108]

Our current understanding of the critical importance of T-cell co-stimulation for proper T-cell activation and effector function may partially explain the failures of past trials. In fact, recent evidence suggests that in the absence of co-stimulatory signals such as those provided through the CD28 receptor pathway,[109,110] antigen presentation leads to T-cell anergy or apoptotic clonal deletion.[111] Co-stimulatory signaling to T cells may be provided artificially through monoclonal antibodies directed against the CD28 receptor.[112] Cross-linking of the T-cell receptor through monoclonal antibodies against CD3 linked to polymer beads in association with monoclonal antibodies directed against CD28 affords supraphysiologic stimulation of T cells ex vivo. Such treatment has been shown to restore the ability of tumor-infiltrating lymphocytes isolated from ovarian carcinoma to secrete type-1 effector cytokines in response to tumor antigens.[78] For therapeutic purposes, T cells could be procured from peripheral blood and activated ex vivo through CD3/CD28 co-stimulation, to generate potent effector cells. The use of natural antigen-presenting systems (such as DCs), or artificially engineered antigen-presenting systems to present tumor-specific antigens,[113] in combination with co-stimulatory molecules, could lead to the generation of oligoclonally expanded super-activated effector T cells that could be used for adoptive immunotherapy (Figure 14–10).

Allogeneic T cells have also shown efficacy in adoptive immunotherapy of solid tumors as they may recognize tumor-associated alloantigens, resulting in a graft-versus-tumor response. In a recent trial of nonmyeloablative allogeneic peripheral blood stem cell transplantation in 19 patients with refractory metastatic renal cell carcinoma, 50% of the patients experienced response with disease regression, and one-third of those patients experienced complete response.[114] Anecdotally, patients with ovarian carcinoma have experienced dramatic

Table 14–12.	T-CELL DEFICIENCY IN OVARIAN CANCER
Cause	**Effect**
Tumor microenvironment cytokines (IL-10, TGF-β, VEGF)	→ Inhibition of T-cell differentiation; decrease in Th1/Th2 ratio
Counterstimulatory signals; loss of co-stimulatory signals	→ T-cell anergy
Fas ligand	→ T-cell apoptosis
Cytotoxic chemotherapy	→ T-cell death (? deletion of tumor-specific clones)
Aging	→ Decreased T-cell reserve and replicative senescence

IL = interleukin; TGF = transforming growth factor; VEGF = vascular endothelial growth factor.

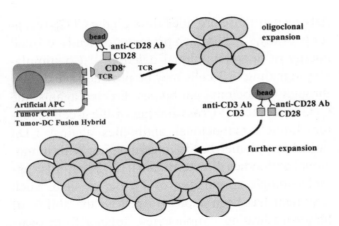

Figure 14–10. Hypothetical scheme of adoptive T-cell immunotherapy. Oligoclonal expansion of tumor-specific T cells may be achieved with artificial antigen-presenting cells, tumor cell–dendritic cell hybrids, or tumor cells expanding co-stimulatory molecules in association with CD28 co-stimulation. Further expansion and activation of T cells may be achieved through CD3 cross-linking and CD28 co-stimulation. (Ab = antibody; APC = antigen-presenting cell; DC = dendritic cell; TCR = T-cell receptor.)

responses to allogeneic bone marrow transplants in the presence of a nonlethal graft-versus-host disease.[115] Currently, a trial is being conducted (in our center) with nonmyeloablative stem cell transplantation followed by adoptive infusion of co-stimulated donor T lymphocytes. (For updates on other clinical trials on ovarian carcinoma, visit the following web sites: <www.ovarian.org>, <www.centerwatch.com>, and <www.cancertrials.nci.nih.gov>.)

Cytokines

Cytokines are regulatory peptides that control the function of immune cells. Stimulatory cytokines such as IL-2, IL-12, IL-18, TNF-α, interferon (IFN)-α, IFN-γ, and granulocyte-macrophage colony-stimulating factor can variably activate innate and adaptive antitumor immune mechanisms and have been used in the systemic or regional therapy of solid tumors[116] (Table 14–13). Seminal clinical work carried out in renal cell carcinoma, melanoma, and lymphoma underscored the power of specific cytokines, such as recombinant IL-2, in select patients who have experienced durable complete clinical responses.[117] Several cytokines that appeared to be therapeutically promising have been tested in ovarian cancer; these include IL-2, IL-12, IFN-α, and IFN-γ.[118,119] Based on evidence suggesting that IL-2 can promote the activation of effector cells, including NK cells and cytotoxic T cells, a phase I/II trial of intraperitoneal injection of IL-2 was carried out in patients with recurrent or progressive EOC. Out of 35 evaluable patients, an overall response rate of 25% was reported, as well as six complete responses.[120] The Gynecologic Oncology Group (GOG) currently has an open study protocol (170-B) evaluating the systemic administration of recombinant IL-12 to patients with recurrent or refractory EOC, while a four-institution trial of intraperitoneal IL-12 is currently being carried out at the M.D. Anderson Cancer Center (at the University of Texas), the University of Pennsylvania, the University of Pittsburgh, and the Massachusetts General Hospital. There have been several studies exploring IFN-α treatment of ovarian cancer, with intraperitoneal administration yielding more significant responses than to the intravenous route.[121,122] A recent GOG study using intraperitoneal IFN-α2b reported measurable responses (28% overall

Table 14–13.	EFFECTS OF IMMUNOSUPPRESSIVE TUMOR-DERIVED CYTOKINES		
Effect	TGF-β	IL-10	VEGF
Inhibition of T-cell growth or differentiation	Y	Y	Y
Induction of T-cell anergy	Y	N	N
Induction of T-cell cytotoxic activity	Y	Y	N
Inhibition of cytokine production	Y	Y	N
Inhibition of antigen presentation	Y	Y	N
Inhibition of Th1 response	Y	Y	N
Stimulation of Th2 response	Y	Y	N
Inhibition of co-stimulatory molecules	Y	Y	N
Inhibition of dendritic cell maturation	Y	N	Y

L = interleukin; N = no; TGF = transforming growth factor; VEGF = vascular endothelial growth factor; Y = yes.

response) and minimal toxicity selectively in patients, with minimal residual disease and a disease-free interval longer than 6 months.[123]

IFN-γ can potently stimulate innate as well as adaptive antitumor immune mechanisms, inhibit angiogenesis, and exert direct effects on tumor cells expressing the IFN-γ receptor (which has been documented in up to 70% of ovarian cancer cell lines), including up regulation of major histocompatibility complex (MHC) class I and class II molecules.[124,125] A recent European multicenter randomized phase III trial reported its results in patients with stage IC-IV ovarian cancer with subcutaneous systemic IFN-γ as adjuvant therapy to first-line cisplatinum and cyclophosphamide. A threefold prolongation of disease-free interval was seen in the experimental arm as compared to the control arm ($p = .031$), with a similar toxicity profile in each group.[126] Although this did not translate into an improved overall survival, the results are promising for the further use of biologic response modifiers as first-line treatment of ovarian carcinoma.

Antibodies

Another immunotherapeutic strategy is to target tumors through antibody-mediated mechanisms against tumor-specific antigens. Antibodies may enhance antitumor immune response or may be used as vehicles to deliver cell toxins, radioactive particles, or cytokines in a tumor-specific manner. Monoclonal antibodies with specificity against tumor antigens have been identified, and some have been tested clinically. Preclinical studies with a humanized monoclonal antibody against the extracellular domain of HER-2 receptor suggested that such an approach may have a promising efficacy against ovarian and breast carcinoma.[127–129] Trastuzumab (Herceptin, Genentech, San Francisco, CA), a recombinant humanized anti-HER-2 monoclonal antibody was tested in a phase II study in 46 patients with metastatic breast cancer and whose tumors overexpressed HER-2. The treatment was well tolerated, but an overall response rate of 11.6% was seen, along with one complete response out of 43 evaluable patients (2.3%). Similar results were recently reported by the GOG in protocol 160, a phase II study in which no complete responses were seen among 27 evaluable patients and in which a partial response rate of 7.4% was reported (GOG Statistical Report, January 2000). Based on the heterogeneity of protein overexpression among tumor cells within the same patients,[130] perhaps it is not surprising that monotherapy based on HER-2 was ineffective.

Antibody-mediated tumor therapy faces many limitations with respect to target specificity, tumor penetration kinetics, and half-life of administered antibodies. Although antibodies may be manufactured as partly humanized chimeric molecules, they may still elicit an antiantibody immune response. The specificity of the antibody is critical for safety issues as cross-reactivity with normal tissues may result in significant toxicity. The paradigm of onconeuronal antigens clearly illustrates this point.[131] Although antibodies against Purkinje cells have been identified in up to 3% of patients with EOC,[132] T cells recognizing the cdr2 antigen expressed by tumor and Purkinje cells are the main effectors of paraneoplastic cerebellar degeneration.[133] Nevertheless, these disorders illustrate the fact that ovarian tumors and normal human tissues may share immunodominant antigens. In the phase I trial of intraperitoneal OVB3-PE administration, dose-limiting toxicity at doses of 5 and 10 μg/kg was manifested by severe encephalopathy in 3 of 23 patients, resulting in one death.[134] In another phase I study of recombinant ricin administration, two patients developed progressive central neurologic toxicity, resulting in one death. Hemorrhagic necrotic vasculitis was seen within the basal ganglia.[135]

CONCLUSION

In summary, advances in molecular and cellular biology have translated into promising innovative strategies in cancer therapeutics. Based on the current studies reviewed here, cancer gene therapy and immunotherapy are best applied in patients with a minimal volume of disease. For epithelial ovarian cancer and many other solid tumors, a mulitmodality approach using a combination of cytoreductive surgery, chemotherapy, gene therapy, and immunotherapy is the direction of the future. Cancer gene therapy and immunotherapy are rapidly emerging fields and will continue to contribute promising therapeutic tools as more studies and clinical trials are performed.

REFERENCES

1. Wivel NA, Wilson JM. Methods of gene delivery. Hematol Oncol Clin North Am 1998;12:483–501.

2. Yeh P, Perricaudet M. Advances in adenoviral vectors: from genetic engineering to their biology. FASEB J 1997;11: 615–23.

3. Gao GP, Yang Y, Wilson JM. Biology of adenovirus vectors with E1 and E4 deletions for liver-directed gene therapy. J Virol 1996;70:8934–43.

4. Coukos G, Makrigiannakis A, Kang EH, et al. Use of carrier cells to deliver a replication-selective herpes simplex virus-1 mutant for the intraperitoneal therapy of epithelial ovarian cancer. Clin Cancer Res 1999;5:1523–37.

5. Wang M, Rancourt C, Navarro JG, et al. High-efficacy thymidine kinase gene transfer to ovarian cancer cell lines mediated by herpes simplex virus type 1 vector. Gynecol Oncol 1998;71:278–87.

6. Xing X, Zhang S, Chang JY, et al. Safety study and characterization of E1A-liposome complex gene-delivery protocol in an ovarian cancer model. Gene Ther 1998;5:1538–44.

7. Moolten FL. Tumor chemosensitivity conferred by inserted herpes thymidine kinase genes: paradigm for a prospective cancer control strategy. Cancer Res 1986;46:5276–81.

8. Wallace H, Clarke AR, Harrison DJ, et al. Ganciclovir-induced ablation non-proliferating thyrocytes expressing herpesvirus thymidine kinase occurs by p53-independent apoptosis. Oncogene 1996;13:55–61.

9. Freeman SM, Abboud CN, Whartenby KA, et al. The "bystander effect": tumor regression when a fraction of the tumor mass is genetically modified. Cancer Res 1993;53:5274–83.

10. Mesnil M, Piccoli C, Tiraby G, et al. Bystander killing of cancer cells by herpes simplex virus thymidine kinase gene is mediated by connexins. Proc Natl Acad Sci U S A 1996;93:1831–5.

11. Ramesh R, Marrogi AJ, Munshi A, et al. In vivo analysis of the "bystander effect": a cytokine cascade. Exp Hematol 1996;24:829–38.

12. Wei SJ, Chao Y, Shih YL, et al. Involvement of Fas (CD95/APO-1) and Fas ligand in apoptosis induced by ganciclovir treatment of tumor cells transduced with herpes simplex virus thymidine kinase. Gene Ther 1999;6:420–31.

13. Gagandeep S, Brew R, Green B, et al. Prodrug-activated gene therapy: involvement of an immunological component in the "bystander effect." Cancer Gene Ther 1996;3:83–8.

14. Stass SA, Mixson J. Oncogenes and tumor suppressor genes: therapeutic implications. Clin Cancer Res 1997;3:2687–95.

15. Berchuck A, Carney M. Human ovarian cancer of the surface epithelium. Biochem Pharmacol 1997;54:541–4.

16. Song K, Cowan KH, Sinha BK. In vivo studies of adenovirus-mediated p53 gene therapy for cis-platinum-resistant human ovarian tumor xenografts. Oncol Res 1999;11:153–9.

17. Kim J, Hwang ES, Kim JS, et al. Intraperitoneal gene therapy with adenoviral-mediated p53 tumor suppressor gene for ovarian cancer model in nude mouse. Cancer Gene Ther 1999;6:172–8.

18. Mujoo K, Maneval DC, Anderson SC, Gutterman JU. Adenoviral-mediated p53 tumor suppressor gene therapy of human ovarian carcinoma. Oncogene 1996;12:1617–23.

19. Song K, Li Z, Seth P, et al. Sensitization of cis-platinum by a recombinant adenovirus vector expressing wild-type p53 gene in human ovarian carcinomas. Oncol Res 1997;9: 603–9.

20. Nielsen LL, Lipari P, Dell J, et al. Adenovirus-mediated p53 gene therapy and paclitaxel have synergistic efficacy in models of human head and neck, ovarian, prostate, and breast cancer. Clin Cancer Res 1998;4:835–46.

21. Bouvet M, Ellis LM, Nishizaki M, et al. Adenovirus-mediated wild-type p53 gene transfer down-regulates vascular endothelial growth factor expression and inhibits angiogenesis in human colon cancer. Cancer Res 1998;58: 2288–92.

22. Owen-Schaub LB, Zhang W, Cusack JC, et al. Wild-type human p53 and a temperature-sensitive mutant induce Fas/APO-1 expression. Mol Cell Biol 1995;15:3032–40.

23. Meden H, Kuhn W. Overexpression of the oncogene c-erbB-2 (HER2/neu) in ovarian cancer: a new prognostic factor. Eur J Obstet Gynecol Reprod Biol 1997;71:173–9.

24. Semba K, Kamata N, Toyoshima K, Yamamoto T. A v-erbB-related protooncogene, c-erbB-2, is distinct from the c-erbB-1/epidermal growth factor-receptor gene and is amplified in a human salivary gland adenocarcinoma. Proc Natl Acad Sci U S A 1985;82:6497–501.

25. Deshane J, Loechel F, Conry RM, et al. Intracellular single-chain antibody directed against erbB2 down-regulates cell surface erbB2 and exhibits a selective anti-proliferative effect in erbB2 overexpressing cancer cell lines. Gene Ther 1994;1:332–7.

26. Deshane J, Siegal GP, Wang M, et al. Transductional efficacy and safety of an intraperitoneally delivered adenovirus encoding an anti-erbB-2 intracellular single-chain antibody for ovarian cancer gene therapy. Gynecol Oncol 1997;64:378–85.

27. Alvarez RD, Barnes MN, Gomez-Navarro J, et al. A cancer gene therapy approach utilizing an anti-erbB-2 single-chain antibody-encoding adenovirus (AD21): a phase I trial. Clin Cancer Res 2000;6:3081–7.

28. Hung MC, Matin A, Zhang Y, et al. HER-2/neu-targeting gene therapy—a review. Gene 1995;159:65–71.

29. Wang SC, Zhang L, Hortobagyi GN, Hung MC. Targeting HER-2/neu: recent developments and future directions for breast cancer patients. Semin Oncol 2001;6:21–29.

30. Sinkovics J, Horvath J. Cytotoxic human lymphocytes: from in vitro testing (1970s) to immunotherapy (1990s). Acta Microbiol Hung 1993;40:165–79.

31. Martuza R, Malick A, Markert J, et al. Experimental therapy of human glioma by means of a genetically engineered virus mutant. Science 1991;252:854–6.

32. Chou J, Kern E, Whitley R, Roizman B. Mapping of herpes simplex virus-1 neurovirulence to g_1 34.5, a gene nonessential for growth in culture. Science 1990;250:1262–5.

33. MacLean M, Ul-Fareed M, Roberson L, et al. Herpes sim-

plex virus type 1 deletion variant 1714 and 1716 pinpoint neurovirulence-related sequences in Glasgow strain 17+ between immediate early gene 1 and the "a" sequence. J Gen Virol 1991;72:633–9.

34. Bolovan CA, Sawtell NM, Thompson RL. ICP34.5 mutants of herpes simplex virus type 1 strain 17syn+ are attenuated for neurovirulence in mice and for replication in confluent primary mouse embryo cell cultures. J Virol 1994;68:48–55.

35. Brown S, MacLean A, Aitken J, Harland J. ICP34.5 influences herpes simplex virus type I maturation and egress from infected cells in vitro. J Gen Virol 1994;75:3679–86.

36. He B, Gross M, Roizman B. The gamma(1)34.5 protein of herpes simplex virus 1 complexes with protein phosphatase 1 alpha to dephosphorylate the alpha subunit of the eukaryotic translation initiation factor 2 and preclude the shutoff of protein synthesis by double-stranded RNA-activated protein kinase. Proc Natl Acad Sci U S A 1997;94:843–8.

37. Kucharczuk JC, Randazzo B, Elshami AA, et al. Use of a replication-restricted, recombinant herpes virus to treat localized human malignancy. Cancer Res 1997;57:466–71.

38. Randazzo B, Bhat M, Kesari S, et al. Treatment of experimental subcutaneous human melanoma with a replication-restricted herpes simplex virus mutant. J Invest Dermatol 1997;108:933–7.

39. Kooby DA, Carew JF, Halterman MW, et al. Oncolytic viral therapy for human colorectal cancer and liver metastases using a multi-mutated herpes simplex virus type-1 (G207). FASEB J 1999;13:1325–34.

40. Carew JF, Kooby DA, Halterman MW, et al. Selective infection and cytolysis of human head and neck squamous cell carcinoma with sparing of normal mucosa by a cytotoxic herpes simplex virus type 1 (G207). Hum Gene Ther 1999;10:1599–606.

41. Toda M, Rabkin SD, Martuza RL. Treatment of human breast cancer in a brain metastatic model by G207, a replication competent multimutated herpes simplex virus 1. Hum Gene Ther 1998;9:2173–85.

42. Advani SJ, Chung SM, Yan SY, et al. Replication-competent, nonneuroinvasive genetically engineered herpes virus is highly effective in the treatment of therapy-resistant experimental human tumors. Cancer Res 1999;59:2055–8.

43. Coukos G, Makrigiannakis A, Montas S, et al. Multi-attenuated herpes simplex virus-1 mutant G207 exerts cytotoxicity against epithelial ovarian cancer but not normal mesothelium, and is suitable for intraperitoneal oncolytic therapy. Cancer Gene Ther 2000;7:275–83.

44. Coukos G, Makrigiannakis A, Kang EH, et al. Oncolytic herpes simplex virus-1 lacking ICP34.5 induces p53-independent death and is efficacious against chemotherapy-resistant ovarian cancer. Clin Cancer Res 2000;6:3342–53.

45. Heise C, Sampson-Johannes A, Williams A, et al. ONYX-015, an E1B gene-attenuated adenovirus, causes tumor-specific cytolysis and antitumoral efficacy that can be augmented by standard chemotherapeutic agents. Nat Med 1997;3:639–45.

46. Kirn D, Hermiston T, McCormick F. ONYX-015: clinical data are encouraging. Nat Med 1998;4:1341–2.

47. Restifo NP, Rosenberg SA. Developing recombinant and synthetic vaccines for the treatment of melanoma. Curr Opin Oncol 1999;11:50–7.

48. Diederichs K, Boone T, Karplus PA. Novel fold and putative receptor binding site of granulocyte-macrophage colony–stimulating factor. Science 1991;254:1779–82.

49. Taylor-Papadimitriou J, Finn OJ. Biology, biochemistry and immunology of carcinoma-associated mucins. Immunol Today 1997;18:105–7.

50. Granowska M, Mather SJ, Jobling T, et al. Radiolabelled stripped mucin, SM3, monoclonal antibody for immunoscintigraphy of ovarian tumours. Int J Biol Markers 1990;5:89–96.

51. Santin AD, Hermonat PL, Ravaggi A, et al. Phenotypic and functional analysis of tumor-infiltrating lymphocytes compared with tumor-associated lymphocytes from ascitic fluid and peripheral blood lymphocytes in patients with advanced ovarian cancer. Gynecol Obstet Invest 2001;51:254–61.

52. Negus RP, Stamp GW, Hadley J, Balkwill FR. Quantitative assessment of the leukocyte infiltrate in ovarian cancer and its relationship to the expression of C-C chemokines. Am J Pathol 1997;150:1723–34.

53. Schondorf T, Engel H, Kurbacher CM, et al. Immunologic features of tumor-infiltrating lymphocytes and peripheral blood lymphocytes in ovarian cancer patients. J Soc Gynecol Investig 1998;5:102–7.

54. Halapi E, Yamamoto Y, Juhlin C, et al. Restricted T cell receptor V-beta and J-beta usage in T cells from interleukin-2-cultured lymphocytes of ovarian and renal carcinomas. Cancer Immunol Immunother 1993;36:191–7.

55. Hayashi K, Yonamine K, Masuko-Hongo K, et al. Clonal expansion of T cells that are specific for autologous ovarian tumor among tumor-infiltrating T cells in humans. Gynecol Oncol 1999;74:86–92.

56. Kooi S, Freedman RS, Rodriguez-Villanueva J, Platsoucas CD. Cytokine production by T-cell lines derived from tumor-infiltrating lymphocytes from patients with ovarian carcinoma: tumor-specific immune responses and inhibition of antigen-independent cytokine production by ovarian tumor cells. Lymphokine Cytokine Res 1993;12:429–37.

57. Kooi S, Zhang HZ, Patenia R, et al. HLA class I expression on human ovarian carcinoma cells correlates with T-cell infiltration in vivo and T-cell expansion in vitro in low concentrations of recombinant interleukin-2. Cell Immunol 1996;174:116–128.

58. Fisk B, Blevins TL, Wharton JT, Ioannides CG. Identification of an immunodominant peptide of HER-2/neu protooncogene recognized by ovarian tumor-specific cytotoxic T lymphocyte lines. J Exp Med 1995;181:2109–17.

59. Dadmarz RD, Ordoubadi A, Mixon A, et al. Tumor-infiltrating lymphocytes from human ovarian cancer patients recognize autologous tumor in an MHC class II-restricted fashion. Cancer J Sci Am 1996;2:263.

60. Peoples GE, Anderson BW, Fisk B, et al. Ovarian cancer-associated lymphocyte recognition of folate binding protein peptides. Ann Surg Oncol 1998;5:743–50.

61. Peoples GE, Goedegebuure PS, Smith R, et al. Breast and ovarian cancer-specific cytotoxic T lymphocytes recog-

nize the same HER2/neu-derived peptide. Proc Natl Acad Sci U S A 1995;92:432–6.

62. Peoples GE, Schoof DD, Andrews JV, et al. T-cell recognition of ovarian cancer. Surgery 1993;114:227–34.

63. Santin AD, Bellone S, Ravaggi A, et al. Induction of ovarian tumor-specific CD8+ cytotoxic T lymphocytes by acid-eluted peptide-pulsed autologous dendritic cells. Obstet Gynecol 2000;96:422–30.

64. Luiten RM, Warnaar SO, Sanborn D, et al. Chimeric bispecific OC/TR monoclonal antibody mediates lysis of tumor cells expressing the folate-binding protein (MOv18) and displays decreased immunogenicity in patients. J Immunother 1997;20:496–504.

65. Bouet-Toussaint F, Genetel N, Rioux-Leclercq N, et al. Interleukin-2 expanded lymphocytes from lymph node and tumor biopsies of human renal cell carcinoma, breast and ovarian cancer. Eur Cytokine Netw 2000;11:217–24.

66. Albert ML, Darnell JC, Bender A, et al. Tumor-specific killer cells in paraneoplastic cerebellar degeneration. Nat Med 1998;4:1321–4.

67. Loercher AE, Nash MA, Kavanagh JJ, et al. Identification of an IL-10-producing HLA-DR-negative monocyte subset in the malignant ascites of patients with ovarian carcinoma that inhibits cytokine protein expression and proliferation of autologous T cells. J Immunol 1999;163:6251–60.

68. Merogi AJ, Marrogi AJ, Ramesh R, et al. Tumor-host interaction: analysis of cytokines, growth factors, and tumor-infiltrating lymphocytes in ovarian carcinomas. Hum Pathol 1997;28:321–31.

69. Nash MA, Lenzi R, Edwards CL, et al. Differential expression of cytokine transcripts in human epithelial ovarian carcinoma by solid tumour specimens, peritoneal exudate cells containing tumour, tumour-infiltrating lymphocyte (TIL)-derived T cell lines and established tumour cell lines. Clin Exp Immunol 1998;112:172–80.

70. Mahnke K, Guo M, Lee S, et al. The dendritic cell receptor for endocytosis, DEC-205, can recycle and enhance antigen presentation via major histocompatability complex class II-positive lysosomal compartments. J Cell Biol 2000;151:673–84.

71. Jonuleit H, Schmitt E, Schuler G, et al. Induction of interleukin 10-producing, nonproliferating CD4(+) T cells with regulatory properties by repetitive stimulation with allogeneic immature human dendritic cells. J Exp Med 2000;192:1213–22.

72. Rabinowich H, Reichert TE, Kashii Y, et al. Lymphocyte apoptosis induced by Fas ligand-expressing ovarian carcinoma cells. Implications for altered expression of T cell receptor in tumor-associated lymphocytes. J Clin Invest 1998;101:2579–88.

73. Lockhart DC, Chan AK, Mak S, et al. Loss of T-cell receptor-CD3zeta and T-cell function in tumor-infiltrating lymphocytes but not in tumor-associated lymphocytes in ovarian carcinoma. Surgery 2001;129:749–56.

74. Woo EY, Chu CS, Goletz TJ, et al. Regulatory CD4(+)CD25(+) T cells in tumors from patients with early-stage non-small cell lung cancer and late-stage ovarian cancer. Cancer Res 2001;61:4766–72.

75. Zaks TZ, Chappell DB, Rosenberg SA, Restifo NP. Fas-mediated suicide of tumor-reactive T cells following activation

by specific tumor: selective rescue by caspase inhibition. J Immunol 1999;162:3273–9.

76. Restifo NP. Not so Fas: re-evaluating the mechanisms of immune privilege and tumor escape. Nat Med 2000;6:493–5.

77. Whiteside TL, Rabinowich H. The role of Fas/FasL in immunosuppression induced by human tumors. Cancer Immunol Immunother 1998;46:175–84.

78. Zheng L, Fisher G, Miller RE, et al. Induction of apoptosis in mature T cells by tumour necrosis factor. Nature 1995;377:348–51.

79. Chappell DB, Restifo NP. T cell-tumor cell: a fatal interaction? Cancer Immunol Immunother 1998;47:65–71.

80. Das H, Koizumi T, Sugimoto T, et al. Quantitation of Fas and Fas ligand gene expression in human ovarian, cervical and endometrial carcinomas using real-time quantitative RT-PCR. Br J Cancer 2000;82:1682–8.

81. Rabinowich H, Suminami Y, Reichert TE, et al. Expression of cytokine genes or proteins and signaling molecules in lymphocytes associated with human ovarian carcinoma. Int J Cancer 1996;68:276–84.

82. Nakashima M, Sonoda K, Watanabe T. Inhibition of cell growth and induction of apoptotic cell death by the human tumor-associated antigen RCAS1. Nat Med 1999;5:938–42.

83. Mastrangelo MJ, Maguire HC, Lattime EC, Berd D. Whole cell vaccines. In: De Vita VT, Hellman S, Rosenberg SA, editors. Biological therapy of cancer. 2nd ed. Philadelphia: J.B. Lippincott; 1996. p. 648–58.

84. Tarte K, Klein B. Dendritic cell-based vaccine: a promising approach for cancer immunotherapy. Leukemia 1999;13:653–63.

85. Berd D, Kairys J, Dunton C, et al. Autologous, hapten-modified vaccine as a treatment for human cancers. Semin Oncol 1998;25:646–53.

86. Sinkovics JG. Viral oncolysates as human tumor vaccines. Int Rev Immunol 1991;7:259–87.

87. Sivanandham M, Wallack MK. Viral oncolysates. In: De Vita VT, Hellman S, Rosenberg SA, editors. Biological therapy of cancer. Philadelphia: J.B. Lippincott; 1996.p. 659–67.

88. Howard OM, Oppenheim JJ, Wang JM. Chemokines as molecular targets for therapeutic intervention. J Clin Immunol 1999;19:280–92.

89. Boone CW, Paranjpe M, Orme T, Gillette R. Virus-augmented tumor transplantation antigens: evidence for a helper antigen mechanism. Int J Cancer 1974;13:543–51.

90. Melcher A, Todryk S, Hardwick N, et al. Tumor immunogenicity is determined by the mechanism of cell death via induction of heat shock protein expression. Nat Med 1998;4:581–7.

91. Ioannides CG, Den Otter W. Concepts in immunotherapy of cancer: introduction. In Vivo 1991;5:551–2.

92. Schirrmacher V, Ahlert T, Probstle T, et al. Immunization with virus-modified tumor cells. Semin Oncol 1998;25:677–96.

93. Schirrmacher V. Tumor vaccine design: concepts, mechanisms, and efficacy testing. Int Arch Allergy Immunol 1995;108:340–4.

94. Mobus V, Horn S, Stock M, Schirrmacher V. Tumor cell vaccination for gynecological tumors. Hybridoma 1993;12:543–7.

95. Kawakami Y, Rosenberg SA. Human tumor antigens recognized by T-cells. Immunol Res 1997;16:313–39.

96. Van den Eynde BJ, van der Bruggen PT. Cell defined tumor antigens. Curr Opin Immunol 1997;9:684–93.

97. Boon T, Coulie PG, Van den Eynde B. Tumor antigens recognized by T cells. Immunol Today 1997;18:267–8.

98. Wang RF, Rosenberg SA. Human tumor antigens for cancer vaccine development. Immunol Rev 1999;170:85–100.

99. Harris JR, Markl J. Keyhole limpet hemocyanin (KLH): a biomedical review. Micron 1999;30:597–623.

100. Rosenberg SA. The immunotherapy of solid cancers based on cloning the genes encoding tumor-rejection antigens. Annu Rev Med 1996;47:481–91.

101. Nestle FO, Alijagic S, Gilliet M, et al. Vaccination of melanoma patients with peptide- or tumor lysate-pulsed dendritic cells. Nat Med 1998;4:328–32.

102. Kuiper M, Peakman M, Farzaneh F. Ovarian tumour antigens as potential targets for immune gene therapy. Gene Ther 1995;2:7–15.

103. Babcock B, Anderson BW, Papayannopoulos I, et al. Ovarian and breast cytotoxic T lymphocytes can recognize peptides from the amino enhancer of split protein of the Notch complex. Mol Immunol 1998;35:1121–33.

104. Vanderkwaak TJ, Alvarez RD. Immune directed therapy for ovarian carcinoma. Curr Opin Obstet Gynecol 1999;11: 29–34.

105. Todryk S, McLean C, Ali S, et al. Disabled infectious single-cycle herpes simplex virus as an oncolytic vector for immunotherapy of colorectal cancer. Hum Gene Ther 1999;10:2757–68.

106. Diao J, Smythe JA, Smyth C, et al. Human PBMC-derived dendritic cells transduced with an adenovirus vectorinduce cytotoxic T-lymphocyte responses against a vector-encoded antigen in vitro. Gene Ther 1999;6:845–53.

107. Ishida T, Chada S, Stipanov M, et al. Dendritic cells transduced with wild-type p53 gene elicit potent anti-tumour immune responses. Clin Exp Immunol 1999;117:244–51.

108. Lamers CH, Bolhuis RL, Warnaar SO, et al. Local but no systemic immunomodulation by intraperitoneal treatment of advanced ovarian cancer with autologous T lymphocytes re-targeted by a bi-specific monoclonal antibody. Int J Cancer 1997;73:211–9.

109. Yang G, Mizuno MT, Hellstrom KE, Chen L. B7-negative versus B7-positive P815 tumor: differential requirements for priming of an antitumor immune response in lymph nodes. J Immunol 1997;158:851–8.

110. Greenfield EA, Nguyen KA, Kuchroo VK. CD28/B7 costimulation: a review. Crit Rev Immunol 1998;18:389–418.

111. Becker JC, Brabletz T, Czerny C, et al. Tumor escape mechanisms from immunosurveillance: induction of unresponsiveness in a specific MHC-restricted CD4+ human T cell clone by the autologous MHC class II+ melanoma. Int Immunol 1993;5:1501–8.

112. Levine BL, Ueda Y, Craighead N, et al. CD28 ligands CD80 (B7-1) and CD86 (B7-2) induce long-term autocrine growth of CD4+ T cells and induce similar patterns of cytokine secretion in vitro. Int Immunol 1995;7:891–904.

113. Maus MV, Thomas AK, Leonard DG, et al. Ex vivo expansion of polyclonal and antigen-specific cytoxic T lymphocytes by artifical APCs expressing ligands for the T-cell receptor, CD28 and 4-1BB. Nat Biotechnol 2002; 20:143–8.

114. Childs R, Chernoff A, Contentin N, et al. Regression of metatstatic renal-cell carcinoma after nonmyeloablative allogeneic peripheral-blood stem-cell transplantation. N Engl J Med 2000;343:750–8.

115. Bay JO, Choufi B, Pomel C, et al. Potential allogeneic graft-versus-tumor effect in a patient with ovarian cancer. Bone Marrow Transplant 2000;25:681–2.

116. Musiani P, Modesti A, Giovarelli M, et al. Cytokines, tumour-cell death and immunogenicity: a question of choice. Immunol Today 1997;18:32–6.

117. Rosenberg SA. Progress in human tumour immunology and immunotherapy. Nature 2001;411:380–4.

118. Simons JW, Mikhak B. Ex-vivo gene therapy using cytokine-transduced tumor vaccines: molecular and clinical pharmacology. Semin Oncol 1998;25:661–76.

119. Oppenheim JJ, Murphy WJ, Chertox O, et al. Prospects for cytokine and chemokine biotherapy. Clin Cancer Res 1997;3:2682–6.

120. Edwards RP, Gooding W, Lembersky BC, et al. Comparison of toxicity and survival following intraperitoneal recombinant interleukin-2 for persistent ovarian cancer after platinum: twenty-four-hour versus 7-day infusion. J Clin Oncol 1997;15:3399–407.

121. Abdulhay G, DiSaia PJ, Blessing JA, Creasman WT. Human lymphoblastoid interferon in the treatment of advanced epithelial ovarian malignancies: a Gynecologic Oncology Group study. Am J Obstet Gynecol 1985;152:418–23.

122. Berek JS, Hacker NF, Lichtenstein A, et al. Intraperitoneal recombinant alpha-interferon for "salvage" immunotherapy in stage III epithelial ovarian cancer: a Gynecologic Oncology Group study. Cancer Res 1985;45:4447–53.

123. Berek JS, Markman M, Stonebraker B, et al. Intraperitoneal interferon-alpha in residual ovarian carcinoma: a phase II Gynecologic Oncology Group study. Gynecol Oncol 1999;75:10–4.

124. Fruh K, Yang Y. Antigen presentation by MHC class I and its regulation by interferon gamma. Curr Opin Immunol 1999;11:76–81.

125. Mobus VJ, Asphal W, Knapstein PG, Kreienberg R. Effects of interferon gamma on the proliferation and modulation of cell-surface structures of human ovarian carcinoma cell lines. J Cancer Res Clin Oncol 1993;120:27–34.

126. Windbichler GH, Hausmaninger H, Stummvoll W, et al. Interferon-gamma in the first-line therapy of ovarian cancer: a randomized phase III trial. Br J Cancer 2000; 82:1138–44.

127. Carter P, Presta L, Gorman CM, et al. Humanization of an anti-p185HER2 antibody for human cancer therapy. Proc Natl Acad Sci U S A 1992;89:4285–9.

128. Lewis GD, Figari I, Fendly B, et al. Differential responses of human tumor cell lines to anti-p185HER2 monoclonal antibodies. Cancer Immunol Immunother 1993;37:255–63.

129. Jurianz K, Maslak S, Garcia-Schuler H, et al. Neutralization of complement regulatory proteins augments lysis of breast carcinoma cells targeted with rhumAb anti-HER2. Immunopharmacology 1999;42:209–18.

130. Rubin SC, Finstad CL, Hoskins WJ, et al. Analysis of antigen expression at multiple tumor sites in epithelial ovarian cancer. Am J Obstet Gynecol 1991;164:558–63.

131. Dropcho EJ. Autoimmune central nervous system paraneoplastic disorders: mechanisms, diagnosis, and therapeutic options. Ann Neurol 1995;37 Suppl 1:S102–13.

132. Drlicek M, Bianchi G, Bogliun G, et al. Antibodies of the anti-Yo and anti-Ri type in the absence of paraneoplastic neurological syndromes: a long-term survey of ovarian cancer patients. J Neurol 1997;244:85–9.

133. Okano HJ, Park WY, Corradi JP, Darnell RB. The cytoplasmic Purkinje onconeural antigen cdr2 down-regulates c-Myc function: implications for neuronal and tumor cell survival. Genes Dev 1999;13:2087–97.

134. Pai LH, Bookman MA, Ozols RF, et al. Clinical evaluation of intraperitoneal *Pseudomonas* exotoxin immunoconjugate OVB3-PE in patients with ovarian cancer. J Clin Oncol 1991;9:2095–103.

135. Bookman MA. Biological therapy of ovarian cancer: current directions. Semin Oncol 1998;25:381–96.

15

High-Dose Chemotherapy

NANCY L. LEWIS, MD
RUSSELL J. SCHILDER, MD

More than 23,000 estimated new cases of ovarian cancer were diagnosed in the United States in 2002.[1] With 13,900 estimated deaths, it remains the fifth leading cause of cancer-related mortality in women.[1] The 5-year overall survival rate for all stages is approximately 50%.[1] Despite recent surgical and chemotherapeutic advances, the 5-year overall survival rate for the 70 to 80% of patients who present with advanced stage III or stage IV disease remains 35% and 20%, respectively.[2]

Dose intensification has been considered one method for overcoming drug resistance, preventing the emergence of drug resistance by killing a larger fraction of tumor cells before the development of a resistant or clonal population. Myelosuppression is a significant dose-limiting toxicity for regimens containing platinum agents or taxanes. It has been shown that dose escalation can be achieved safely with the use of autologous hematopoietic cellular support and growth factors. The long-term efficacy of this treatment approach and the patient population most likely to benefit from high-dose therapy remain to be established. This chapter will provide an overview of the clinical trials evaluating high-dose chemotherapy in patients with ovarian cancer.

RATIONALE FOR HIGH-DOSE THERAPY

The rationale for dose-intensity is based on the finding that certain therapeutic agents demonstrate a steep log-linear relationship between dose and tumor cell, where that relatively small changes in dose can produce significant changes in therapeutic response. In 1987, Levin and Hryniuk[3] published a retrospec-

tive analysis of dose-intensity in single- and multiagent chemotherapy involving patients with advanced ovarian cancer. The analysis showed a highly significant correlation between relative dose intensity, clinical response, and (subsequently) median survival time. Multiagent regimens, particularly those containing cisplatin, were superior to single-alkylating-agent regimens. Further support for dose-intensity was provided by other investigators, who showed that 20 to 32% of patients who relapsed after treatment with conventional doses of cisplatin responded to higher doses.[4–6]

In large randomized trials, it has been shown that carboplatin and cisplatin provide equivalent response rates and overall survival (OS) in patients with advanced ovarian cancer when coadministered with cyclophosphamide[7,8] and (in subsequent trials) when given with paclitaxel.[9,10] Although carboplatin has increased myelosuppressive effects, its nonhematologic toxicities (neurologic, renal, and gastrointestinal) are more favorable as compared with cisplatin. Therefore, carboplatin has a better therapeutic index than cisplatin, making it a logical choice for trials evaluating high-dose chemotherapy with hematopoietic support using either autologous bone marrow or peripheral blood progenitor cells.

PHASE I TRIALS

There have been numerous phase I trials of high-dose chemotherapy with hematopoietic support that have included patients with refractory epithelial ovarian cancer. These studies are summarized in Table 15–1.[11–25] Most of the patients on these early trials

213

were heavily pretreated. The numbers of patients are small, but these studies demonstrate that partial response (PR) or complete response (CR) in patients with recurrent or refractory ovarian cancer can be achieved with upwards of 80% response rates and that high doses of active agents can be given safely with hematopoietic cell and cytokine support. Unfortunately, the duration of these responses were short-lived for the most part.

In one of the largest of these series reported by Weaver and colleagues,[11] 31 patients with stage III or IV ovarian cancer who had failed initial chemotherapy or had relapsed were treated with melphalan, mitoxantrone, and carboplatin with peripheral blood stem cell (PBSC) support on a phase I/II study. Of the 20 evaluable patients, 14 patients (70%) achieved a CR, and 7 patients (35%) are alive with a median disease-free survival of 20 months (range, 7 to 26 months). Similarly, high response rates were seen in 6 evaluable patients with refractory ovarian cancer treated with high-dose mitoxantrone, cyclophosphamide, and carboplatin.[12] Five patients had a CR lasting 3 to 30+ months, with a median progression-free survival (PFS) duration of 8 months and a median survival duration of 15 months. The other patient had a PR of 4 months' duration. Shea and colleagues

included 11 patients with previously treated refractory ovarian cancer in a phase I trial, using escalating doses of single-agent carboplatin with autologous bone marrow support. Six of the patients responded, one with a CR.[13]

HIGH-DOSE THERAPY IN PATIENTS WITH REFRACTORY OR RELAPSED OVARIAN CANCER

These response rates in Phase I trials were encouraging and led to phase II studies evaluating high-dose therapy with stem cell support specifically in patients with refractory or relapsed ovarian cancer (Table 15–2). Expected response rates with standard doses of chemotherapy in this population is approximately 30%.[26,27]

Investigators at Duke University[28] treated 12 patients who progressed on cisplatin-based therapy with cyclophosphamide, thiotepa, and intraperitoneal cisplatin. Autologous bone marrow was infused on the day following chemotherapy. Eight patients were considered radiographically evaluable for response. There were 6 PRs with a median response duration of 6 months (range, 3 to 9 months), with 1 nonresponder. Three toxic deaths were noted due to infection and/or renal failure. Despite the fact that this group

Table 15–1.	PHASE I TRIALS OF HIGH-DOSE THERAPY WITH HEMATOPOIETIC SUPPORT			
Investigator (Reference)	Evaluable Patients	Regimen	Response	Duration
Tobias[14]	6	doxo/cy	1 CR/3 PR	NR
Lazarus[15]	2	cy/LPAM	not measurable	5 mo/6.5 mo
Corringham[16]	2	cy/LPAM	1 SD/1 CR	8 wk/35 wk
Vriesendorp[17]	2	cy/VP-16	1 pCR/1 cCR	10+ mo
Maraninchi[18]	2	LPAM	1 CR	5 wk
Postmus[19]	1	cy/VP-16	1 CR	16+ mo
Antman[20]	2	cy/cis/BCNU	2 PR	3.8 mo/4.3 mo
Mulder[21]	1	LPAM/mito	1 CR	9+ mo
	4	cy/mito	2 PR/1 CR	13 mo/3 mo/9 mo
Williams[22]	1	cy/TT	PR	NR
Shea[13]	11	carbo	1 CR/5 PR	NR
Ellis[23]	3	cy/mito/TT	1 CR	NR
Stiff[12]	6	mito/cy/carbo	5 CR/1 PR	3, 7, 8, 22, 30+ mo/4 mo
Stemmer[24]	2	paclit/cy/cis	1 PR/1 sCR	< 5 mo
Weaver[11]	20	LPAM/mito/carbo	14 CR/3 PR	7+ – 26+ mo
Donato[25]	30	topo/mel/cy	15 CR/13 PR	NR
Total	94		44 CR/32 PR = 80% response	

doxo = doxorubicin; cy = cyclophosphamide; LPAM = melphalan; VP-16 = etoposide; cis = cisplatin; BCNU = carmustine; mito = mitoxantrone; TT = thiotepa; carbo = carboplatin; paclit = paclitaxel; NR = not reported; CR = complete response; PR = partial response; pCR = pathologic complete response; cCR = clinical complete response; sCR = cerologic clinical response; wk = weeks.

of patients was heavily pretreated with a median number of three prior regimens and a median number of 7.3 cycles of cisplatin, there was a 75% PR in this group of refractory patients.

Shea and colleagues enrolled 10 heavily pretreated patients with advanced ovarian cancer in a trial evaluating dose escalation of intravenous mitoxantrone and thiotepa and fixed doses of intraperitoneal etoposide and carboplatin.[29] A high response rate (50% CR and 20% PR) was reported. The median duration of response was only 8 months, however, and many patients progressed with disease outside of the peritoneal cavity.

Nine patients with stage III/IV ovarian cancer and who had persistent disease on second-look laparotomy (SLL) or progressed within 6 months of receiving platinum were treated with high-dose carboplatin/ifosfamide with autologous bone marrow support.[30] One toxic death due to ifosfamide-related renal and central nervous system toxicities was reported. In the remaining 8 patients, 5 patients had a CR, 2 patients had a PR, and 1 patient had stable disease. All eventually progressed, with response durations of 4, 5, 6, 8, and 23 months for the complete responders.

In their initial series, Stiff and co-investigators reported on 30 patients with refractory or progressive ovarian cancer and who had undergone a median number of two prior regimens.[31] The overwhelming majority (73%) had residual lesions > 1 cm; 67% had platinum-resistant disease, and the remaining 33% were thought to have platinum-sensitive disease. Of the 27 evaluable patients, 16 (59%) had a CR, 8 (30%) had a PR, and 3 (11%) had no response, giving an overall response rate of 89%. All platinum-sensitive patients responded, and 84% of the platinum-resistant patients responded. The overall 2-year

survival rate was 23%. For the platinum-sensitive patients, the median PFS was 10.1 months; for patients with platinum-resistant disease, the PFS was 5 months. Of those patients with minimal-bulk disease (< 1 cm), median OS was 20.7 months (range, 6 to 46 months) versus 12.5 months (range, 16 days to 49 months) for those with a disease bulk of > 1 cm.

These studies in heavily pretreated patients with progressive or clearly refractory ovarian cancer illustrate that high responses of 50 to 80%, including CRs, can be achieved in a salvage setting with high-dose chemotherapy and autologous hematopoietic support. With few exceptions, these responses are short-lived. Those patients with platinum-sensitive disease and a low tumor burden fared the best, suggesting that patients may benefit from high-dose therapy earlier in their course, before resistant clones emerge.

HIGH-DOSE THERAPY AS CONSOLIDATION

Since such high response rates can be attained in patients with refractory ovarian cancer, perhaps treating patients with high-dose therapy as consolidation, after surgical debulking, standard chemotherapy, and SLL could result in improved PFS and OS. Table 15–3[32–38] summarizes seven studies that evaluated patients treated with high-dose therapy in this setting.

One of the largest series published to date included 53 patients who were initially treated with surgery and a cisplatin-based regimen.[32] SLL was negative for cancer in 19 patients; 7 patients had microscopic residual disease, and 22 patients had macroscopic disease at second-look surgery. A second debulking procedure was undertaken in those patients with macroscopic residual disease; how-

Table 15–2.   PHASE II TRIALS OF HIGH-DOSE THERAPY WITH STEM CELL SUPPORT IN PATIENTS WITH REFRACTORY OR RELAPSED OVARIAN CANCER

Investigator (Reference)	Patients	Regimen	Response	Median Duration (mo)
Schpall (28)	8	cy/TT/IP cis	75% PR	6
Shea (29)	10	mito/TT/mel/VP-16/IP carbo	50% CR/20% PR	8
Broun (30)	8	carbo/ifos	62% CR/25% PR/12% SD	6
Stiff (31)	27	mito/carbo/cy	59% CR/30% PR	10

cy = cyclophosphamide; mel = melphalan; VP-16 = etoposide; cis = cisplatin; mito = mitoxantrone; TT = thiotepa; carbo = carboplatin; IP = intraperitoneal; CR = complete response; PR = partial response; SD = stable disease.

ever, 4 of those 22 patients still had macroscopic residual disease despite a second surgical debulking. Patients were then treated with either high-dose melphalan or high-dose carboplatin/cyclophosphamide with autologous stem cell support. At a median follow-up of 81.5 months, the 5-year OS was 59.9%, and the DFS was 23.6%. In the 19 patients with pathologic CRs at SLL (ie, the consolidation group), the expected 5-year OS and DFS rates were 74.2% and 32.8%, respectively. This implies that high-dose therapy may be beneficial despite PCR, as a recently published 10-year follow-up of ovarian cancer patients with negative SLLs reported only a 60% 5-year OS for stage III/IV patients who underwent initial debulking surgery and standard cisplatin-based chemotherapy.[39] For those undergoing high-dose therapy as "salvage", (ie, those 22 patients with macroscopic disease at SLL), the 5-year OS was 33.8% and the DFS was 19.2%, compared to an expected 5-year OS of 14.2% for similar patients.[40] This suggests that patient selection and the timing of high-dose chemotherapy have a major impact on outcome.

A group from the Netherlands[33] evaluated 11 patients after debulking and standard therapy with cisplatin-based regimens (1 patient had single-agent melphalan). All patients had residual disease at SLL, with macroscopic disease > 2 cm ($n = 3$), minimal disease < 2 cm ($n = 5$), or microscopic disease ($n = 3$) disease. They received high-dose cyclophosphamide and etoposide with autologous bone marrow support. Of the 11 patients, 6 (55%) achieved a CR with a median duration of response of 15 months. Two of the patients remained free of disease at 43 and 75 months. All CRs were seen in patients with minimal or microscopic disease; no responses were observed in those patients with bulky residual disease.

Most recently, preliminary results from the only phase III randomized trial to evaluate high-dose therapy in this setting was reported. Cure and associates randomized 110 patients with pathologic CRs or minimal residual disease on SLL to receive either high-dose carboplatin/cyclophosphamide with PBSC support or three cycles of standard-dose carboplatin/cyclophosphamide.[41] Of the 102 patients who were eligible for intention-to-treat analysis, the median DFS in the high-dose arm was significantly better than that seen in the standard-dose arm (22 months versus 10 months, respectively, $p = .033$) (H. Cure, personal communication, March 2002).

In summary, there may be a role for high-dose therapy as consolidation for those patients who remain at high risk for recurrence after surgical debulking and standard chemotherapy. High risk may be based on initial stage, findings at SLL, or an aggressive histology. Clearly, those patients who were negative on SLL fared better than patients with residual disease. Those who underwent a second optimal debulking procedure fared better than those patients who continued to have macroscopically residual disease even after SLL. Although high-dose therapy is not without significant risks and toxicities, it can be performed relatively safely overall. Less toxic conditioning regimens, the use of PBSC over stem cells harvested

Investigator (Reference)	Patients	Negative SLO	Macro SLO	Micro SLO	Therapy
Dauplat (34)	14	—	9	5	LPAM
Mulder (33)	11	—	3	8	cy/VP-16
Rebollo (35)	12	—	7	5	carbo/VP-16
Barnett (36)	5	NR	NR	NR	carbo/VP-16/LPAM
Cure (37)	57	21	23	8	LPAM/carbo/cy
Viens (38)	28	10	10	2	LPAM (3)
					cy/LPAM (9)
					carbo/VP-16/LPAM (12)
					TT/cy/carbo (4)
Legros (32)	53	19	22	7	LPAM/carbo/cy

Table 15–3. CONSOLIDATION AFTER SURGICAL DEBULKING AND STANDARD THERAPY WITH CISPLATIN-BASED REGIMEN

cy = cyclophosphamide; LPAM = melphalan; VP-16 = etoposide; TT = thiotepa; carbo = carboplatin; NR = not reported; SLO = second-look operation.

from bone marrow, and the use of hematopoietic growth factors all increase the tolerability and safety of this therapy. When compared to the 5-year OS of 20 to 30% when treated with standard salvage regimens, these poor-prognosis patients undergoing high-dose therapy with stem cell support have an improved 5-year OS of greater than 50% in some trials. Rates of relapse, however, continue to be high. Further randomized trials comparing high-dose therapy to conventional therapy will truly confirm these findings.

ADDITIONAL SINGLE-CYCLE HIGH-DOSE EXPERIENCE

Several groups of investigators have published their experiences with high-dose therapy in larger series of patients with ovarian cancer. Donato and colleagues recently presented the long-term results of a study of 102 patients with advanced ovarian cancer treated with a variety of high-dose regimens at the M.D. Anderson Cancer Center.[42] Patients were treated with HD therapy in a variety of settings: after three cycles of standard-dose induction ($n = 11$); after a positive second-look surgery ($n = 18$); with refractory disease ($n = 18$); in a second CR ($n = 15$); in a second PR ($n = 13$); with relapsed refractory disease ($n = 8$); and with untreated relapsed ovarian cancer ($n = 12$). Three different high-dose regimens were used: topotecan/melphalan/cyclophosphamide ($n = 73$), carboplatin/paclitaxel ($n = 23$), and cyclophosphamide/carmustine (BCNU)/thiotepa ($n = 5$). The 6-year OS for all patients was 40%. Those patients with a clear cell histology clearly had an inferior survival. Three groups emerged as having a more favorable prognosis, with a 6-year OS of 55%: those treated after standard-dose consolidation, those treated immediately after a positive second look, and those treated in a second CR.

A multivariate analysis of survival for 100 patients with ovarian cancer who consecutively underwent high-dose therapy with hematopoietic support at Loyola University was reported by Stiff and associates.[43] Several treatment regimens were used, including carboplatin/mitoxantrone/cyclophosphamide +/- cyclosporine ($n = 70$), melphalan/mitoxantrone +/- paclitaxel ($n = 25$), and thiotepa/cis-platin/cyclophosphamide ($n = 5$). Of these 100 patients, 66% were considered to have platinum-resistant disease, 61% had bulky disease at transplantation, and 70% had been heavily pretreated with two or more regimens prior to transplantation. Of the 100 patients, 87 were evaluable. The overall response rate was 74%; 52% achieved CR and 22% achieved PR. Cisplatin-sensitive patients had a CR rate of 88%, and resistant patients had a CR rate of 50%. The treatment-related mortality of 12% was higher than expected and included death from infection, renal failure, and cardiac events. Factors associated with increased OS included younger age, low tumor burden, platinum sensitivity, completion of second-look surgery, a history of CR to initial therapy, and longer survival from diagnosis to transplantation. The most important factor for both PFS and OS was tumor bulk.

These 100 patients, treated at a single institution, were included in a larger analysis of 421 patients identified through the Autologous Blood and Marrow Transplant Registry (ABMTR).[44] This larger observational study was undertaken to identify potential prognostic factors related to treatment outcome. Adverse prognostic factors that were associated with poor PFS and OS included age ≥ 48 years, Karnofsky performance status (KPS) < 90%, clear cell histology, and platinum-resistant disease (Figure 15-1). Although the overwhelming majority of these patients were treated while with relapsed or resistant disease, the best treatment outcomes were observed in patients who underwent high-dose therapy while in first or second remission. The optimal patient group to evaluate in further randomized clinical trials may be those patients with platinum-sensitive disease, with no lesion being > 1 cm at the time of transplantation.

MULTIPLE CYCLES OF HIGH-DOSE THERAPY WITH HEMATOPOIETIC SUPPORT

Despite very high initial responses and a slight increase in PFS and OS as a result of high-dose chemotherapy and stem cell support, frequent relapses continue to be problematic. Even in highly curable and more chemotherapy-sensitive malignan-

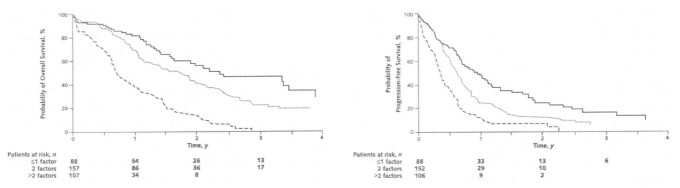

Figure 15–1. Adverse prognostic factors associated with poor progression-free and overall survival after high-dose therapy with autologous stem cell support. (Reproduced with permission from Stiff PJ et al.[44])

cies such as testicular cancer and lymphoma, multiple cycles of therapy are usually required for long-term PFS. The Norton-Simon model predicts that multiple rapidly cycled applications of high-dose chemotherapy are more likely to eradicate residual cancer cells than are single applications of high-dose therapy or multiple applications with long intertreatment periods.[45] This issue in ovarian cancer is being addressed with additional studies.

Multiple Cycles in the Refractory/Salvage Setting

Table 15–4 summarizes three studies that evaluated multiple cycles of high-dose therapy in the refractory/relapsed setting. A phase I feasibility trial for delivering repeated cycles of dose-intensive therapy with peripheral blood progenitor cell support was carried out by Shea and colleagues.[46] Of the 18 patients enrolled, 6 patients had platinum-resistant ovarian cancer. Three cycles of high-dose carboplatin (1,200 mg/m^2) were administered, supported with either sargramostin alone or sargramostin with PBSC. More than half of the patients receiving sargrastim alone did not complete the planned therapy because of toxicity or disease progression. In the patients who received PBSC support, a significant decrease in the duration of neutropenia, thrombocytopenia, length of hospital stay, days on intravenous antibiotics, and frequency of red cell and platelet transfusions was noted. This decrease in toxicity resulted in a 37% increase in the weekly dose intensity and a 56% increase in the total dose delivered, compared with the patients who did not receive

PBSC support. No cycle supported by PBSC resulted in hematologic dose-limiting toxicity, compared with 7 of 20 cycles supported by sargramostin alone. This study demonstrated that sequential cycles of high-dose therapy with stem cell rescue was feasible.

Lotz and colleagues published a study of 37 patients with stage III/IV advanced poor-prognosis ovarian cancer, who were treated with two cycles of high-dose teniposide/ifosfamide/carboplatin followed by bone marrow support.[47] This included 8 patients with disease that was refractory to standard first- or second-line therapy. Seven patients were treated in chemosensitive relapse, and 22 patients were treated in PR or CR after six courses of doxorubicin/cyclophosphamide/cisplatin and SLL. Of the 37 patients in the study, 29 received the two scheduled cycles. Eight patients failed to complete both cycles: 4 because of nonhematologic toxicity, 1 due to death secondary to infection, and 3 due to progressive disease. Sixteen patients were considered evaluable for response. Among the 8 refractory patients, 1 patient achieved a CR lasting 10 months, and 4 patients attained a PR lasting 5 to 10 months. The 2 patients treated in chemosensitive relapse had PRs lasting 7 and 12 months, respectively. For the 6 patients treated as consolidation, 1 patient attained a CR that lasted 57 months, and another had a PR lasting 10 months. The overall response rate in the 16 of the 37 patients who were evaluable for response, was 56%, with two CRs (12%) and seven PRs (44%). The overall 5-year survival was 32%.

Most of these studies used clinical response rates as end points although radiographically undetectable microscopic residual disease at the completion of

Table 15–4. MULTIPLE CYCLES OF HIGH-DOSE CHEMOTHERAPY IN THE REFRACTORY/SALVAGE SETTING

Investigator (Reference)	Evaluable Patients	Therapy	Response	Overall RR (%)
Shea (46)	16	Carbo/sargramostatin +/- PBSC	18% CR/50% PR	70
Lotz (47)	16	Tenopiside/ifos/carbo	12% CR/44% PR	56
Morgan (48)	7	Carbo/cy + PBSC and paclit	57% CR/14% PR	71

cy = cyclophosphamide; ifos = ifosfamide; Carbo = carboplatin; paclit = paclitaxel; CR = complete response; PR = partial response; RR = response rate.

therapy may explain these short durations of response. In a phase II trial conducted at the University of Pennsylvania, 14 patients with persistent or recurrent disease were treated with multiple high-dose cycles.[48] Six patients who had clinical CRs to cisplatin-containing regimens but who were found to have persistent disease at SLL were enrolled, as well as eight patients who had clinical evidence of recurrent cisplatin-sensitive ovarian cancer. Peripheral stem cells were harvested after mobilization with filgrastim and cyclophosphamide. The patients then underwent three cycles of carboplatin/cyclophosphamide given every 2 weeks with stem cell support. This was followed by paclitaxel, 250 mg/m², with filgrastim support. Of the 7 patients with measurable disease, 4 had a CR and 1 had a PR, making the total response rate 71%. One patient had progressive disease, and one had persistent disease. One patient completed only two cycles, secondary to hematuria. Of 8 patients with an elevated CA 125 level, 7 (88%) returned to normal levels. The pathologic CR rate, one of the end points of this study, was 2 of 14 (14%), which fell short of the desired pathologic CR rate of 40%. This study points out the difference between clinical CR and pathologic CR, the latter being the end point most likely to accurately predict a durable remission.

Multiple Cycles of High-Dose Chemotherapy as Frontline Treatment

Table 15–5 lists several studies evaluating multiple cycles of high-dose therapy as frontline treatment. Several studies were conducted by investigators at Memorial Sloan-Kettering Cancer Center, evaluating the role of paclitaxel as a component of high-dose chemotherapy for the treatment of patients with ovarian carcinoma. One phase I trial employed escalating doses of paclitaxel given in combination with high-dose carboplatin and PBSC support.[49] In this study, leukapheresis was performed on two occasions after mobilization with one or two cycles of cyclophosphamide (3 g/m²), paclitaxel (300 mg/m²) and filgrastim. Four courses of high-dose carboplatin (1,000 mg/m²) with escalating doses of paclitaxel (150 mg/m² to 300 mg/m²) were given 2 weeks apart, with PBSC rescue in cohorts of three patients. Eighteen patients with optimal (*n* = 11) or suboptimal (*n* = 7) surgically debulked advanced ovarian cancer were enrolled, and 15 patients were evaluable

Table 15–5. MULTIPLE CYCLES OF HIGH-DOSE CHEMOTHERAPY AS FRONTLINE TREATMENT

Investigator (Reference)	Study Phase	Drugs	Evaluable Patients	Response	Overall RR (%)
Fennelly (49)	I	cy/carbo/paclit	15	33% pCR/40% PR	73
Fennelly (50)	I	carbo/cy	27	18% pCR/59% PR	77
Fennelly (51)	I	cy/carbo/paclit	13	38.5% pCR/71% PR	100
Aghajanian (52)	II	cy/carbo/mel/paclit	42	36% CR/38% PR	74
Tepler (53)	II	cy/carbo	4	25% pCR/75% cCR	100
Murakami (54)	II	cy/doxo/cis	20	NR	100
Peccatori (55)	II	epi/doce/carbo/ifos/etop	13	46% pCR/54% PR	100
Prince (56)	I	carbo/paclit/topo	19	73% CR/22% PR	95
Schilder (57)	I	cy/etop/carbo/paclit	9	66% CR	100
Schilder (58)	I	cy/carbo/paclit/topo	13	15% pCR/23% CR/38% PR	85

cy = cyclophosphamide; etop = etoposide; mel = melphalan; cis = cisplatin; topo = topotecan; carbo = carboplatin; paclit = paclitaxel; doxe = docetaxel; NR = not reported; doxo = doxorubicin; ifos = ifosfamide; CR = complete response; pCR = pathologic CR; PR = partial response; RR = response rate.

for response. Five of the 18 patients (28%) completed only three cycles, as a result of toxicity or noncompliance, while the remaining 13 patients (75%) completed all four cycles. Of 15 patients, 5 demonstrated a pathologic CR, and 6 patients had microscopic disease, and two patients had macroscopic residual disease at SLL. Dose-limiting toxicities of diarrhea and hypotension were noted. Adequate numbers of PBSCs were obtained with one mobilization cycle, and this enabled further dose escalation of paclitaxel in subsequent cycles. In the group of patients with optimally debulked disease, the CR and PR rates appear to have been better than those achieved with standard therapy although this statement did not hold true for the suboptimally debulked population.

At the same institution, escalating doses of carboplatin were evaluated in a phase I trial.[50] Of the 31 patients enrolled, 29 had ovarian cancer. Stem cells were mobilized with multiple cycles of cyclophosphamide and filgrastim. These treatments were then followed by high-dose carboplatin in escalating doses given to successive cohorts of patients. The maximum tolerated dose of carboplatin was 1,000 mg/m^2, with dose-limiting ototoxicity occurring at 1,200 mg/m^2. The median interval between treatments was 15 days (range, 12 to 20 days). Of the 29 patients with ovarian cancer, 27 were evaluable. Five (18.5 %) pathologic CRs at SLL (including one patient with parenchymal liver metastases prior to high-dose therapy) remain in CR at a median of 16 months (range 15^+–25^+ months). In addition, 16 patients (59%) had PRs, and 5 patients (18.5%) had progressive disease. There were no treatment-related deaths. Twenty-two patients were alive at 13.7 to 30.3 months' follow-up.

In another phase I study conducted at Memorial Sloan-Kettering Cancer Center, 16 patients with stage IIc to IV ovarian cancer underwent optimal ($n = 6$) or suboptimal ($n = 10$) surgical debulking.[51] Two cycles of cyclophosphamide/paclitaxel were used to mobilize PBSC, and patients then underwent four sequential high-dose cycles of cyclophosphamide/carboplatin given every 2 weeks. All 16 patients completed the two mobilization cycles, and 12 patients completed all planned therapy. Of the 13 patients who were assessable surgically, 5 (38.5%) had pathologic CRs. Six patients (46%) had residual microscopic disease, and the remaining two patients had PRs.

To potentially decrease the number of patients with persistent disease at second look, these same investigators undertook a pilot study of 21 patients and added one cycle of high-dose melphalan after mobilization with one cycle of cyclophosphamide/paclitaxel/filgrastim and three cycles of high-dose carboplatin/paclitaxel. Taking all of their patients with ovarian cancer who received one of these four regimens, 56 patients were evaluated. A total of 44 patients underwent SLL; 15 of these patients (34%) had a pathologic CRs. The majority of these pathologic CRs (75%) were in patients who had platinum-sensitive disease and who had undergone optimal debulking, however. These studies showed that multiple cycles of high-dose carboplatin and paclitaxel can be safely administered but that this treatment was of no additional benefit over conventional treatment to patients with suboptimally debulked disease.[52] As a result, the Gynecologic Oncology Group initiated a similar phase II trial in patients with optimally debulked stage III ovarian cancer. However, only one pathologic CR was documented after nine patients were enrolled and evaluated, and the study was terminated.[53]

Tepler and associates treated women with suboptimally debulked stage III or stage IV ovarian cancer in a phase I study designed to determine whether four consecutive cycles of high-dose carboplatin could be administered in an outpatient setting.[54] Peripheral blood stem cells were mobilized with cyclophosphamide (4 g/m^2) and sargrastim, which were administered on an inpatient basis. Four weeks later, cyclophosphamide (600 mg/m^2) and carboplatin (600 mg/m^2) were given in the outpatient facility every 28 days for a maximum of four cycles. For the first cycle, sargrastim support alone was given; subsequent cycles were supported with sargrastim and PBSCs. Thirteen patients, nine of whom had suboptimally debulked ovarian cancer, were enrolled. Only 5 patients completed all four planned cycles. Of the 8 patients who came off the study, 3 left the study due to progressive disease, 2 left due to sargrastim toxicity, 2 left due to hematologic toxicity, and 1 left due to sepsis. Of the 9 patients with ovarian cancer, 4 completed all four planned cycles. Of these four, 3 achieved clinical CRs with respective durations of 1, 4, and > 7 months, and 1 had stable disease. This study showed that up to four consecutive cycles of high-dose (nonmyeloablative) treatment can be administered with hematopoietic stem cell support in a subset of patients in an outpatient setting, without extended intervals between cycles.

Murakami evaluated 42 previously untreated patients with stage Ic ($n = 8$), stage II ($n = 6$), stage III ($n = 18$), and stage IV ($n = 10$) ovarian cancer.[55] All patients underwent two sequential courses of cyclophosphamide (1,600 to 2,400 g/m^2), doxorubicin (80 to 100 mg/m^2), and cisplatin (100 to 150 mg/m^2) with autologous bone marrow rescue. The median interval between cycles was 6 weeks. Of the 22 patients who were treated after undergoing complete surgical debulking, 4 patients (18%) died of recurrent disease, and 18 patients were alive and disease free at 2 to 6 years. The 5-year OS for this group was 77 %. Of the 15 patients who were treated with residual disease, 10 patients (66%) died of recurrent disease, and 5 patients (33%) had a DFS of 2 to 6 years, with a 5-year OS of 26.3%. Five-year OS by stage was as follows: Ic, 100%; II, 66.7%; III, 53.9% (optimally debulked, 65.6%; suboptimally debulked, 42.7%); and IV, 0%. These results, particularly for stage III disease, are improved when compared with the 5-year OS of 35% after standard-dose therapy (2).[55]

Preliminary data was recently presented from a European study evaluating 17 patients with poor-prognosis advanced ovarian cancer.[56] Patients were treated with three cycles of standard-dose etoposide and docetaxel, followed by three cycles of high-dose ifosfamide/carboplatin/etoposide (ICE) with stem cell support. Of the 13 patients who completed therapy and underwent second-look surgery, 43% demonstrated pathologic CRs, and the remaining patients had PRs. With a median follow-up of 15.2 months, the OS is 76% for the entire group. Of those patients with a pCR, 71% were alive and disease free with a median follow-up of 23.6 months (range, 9.4 to 35.8 months).

A phase I study evaluating multiple cycles of topotecan, carboplatin, and paclitaxel in previously untreated patients with ovarian cancer was conducted in Australia.[57] Nineteen patients with previ-ously untreated stage IIIc or stage IV ovarian cancer after debulking surgery were treated with two cycles of standard-dose carboplatin and paclitaxel, followed by high-dose topotecan, paclitaxel, and carboplatin for three cycles with PBSC support. The clinical CR rate was 73%, and the overall response rate was 95%. Of the 14 patients with CRs, 13 underwent SLL, with 8 (61%) achieving pathologic CRs.

Similarly, Schilder and colleagues at Fox Chase Cancer Center treated 28 chemotherapy-naive patients with multiple cycles of paclitaxel (250 mg/m^2) and increasing doses of high-dose carboplatin (AUC of 12 to 20).[58] In the 12 patients with ovarian cancer, a response rate of 100% with a clinical CR rate of 67% was observed. Nine of these 12 patients had suboptimally debulked stage III or stage IV disease. The median duration of response was 49.5 weeks (range, 8 to > 142 weeks). Because of its activity in cases of ovarian cancer, topotecan has been added to this regimen, and a phase I trial evaluating multiple cycles of high-dose carboplatin, paclitaxel, and topotecan in previously untreated patients was undertaken.[59] Carboplatin (Area under the concentration-time curve [AUC] of 16), paclitaxel (250 mg/m^2), and escalating doses of topotecan (10 mg/m^2, 12.5 mg/m^2, and 15 mg/m^2) were used. The maximum tolerated dose of topotecan was 12.5 mg/m^2, administered as a 24-hour infusion given for three cycles. The dose-limiting toxicity was hemorrhagic stomatitis. Of the 13 patients assessable for response, 5 patients had CRs (2 had pathologic CRs) and 5 patients demonstrated PRs, for an overall response rate of 85%. The recommended phase II dose of topotecan is 10 mg/m^2, administered for four cycles. This combination drug regimen is now being evaluated in previously untreated patients with optimally debulked stage III ovarian cancer and primary peritoneal carcinoma as a pilot study within Gynecologic Oncology Group trial 9903 (GOG 9903) (Figure 15–2).

SUMMARY

Ovarian cancer, most frequently diagnosed in its later stages, claims approximately 14,000 lives each year. Relapses are common despite initial chemosensitivity. Multiple cycles of high-dose chemother-

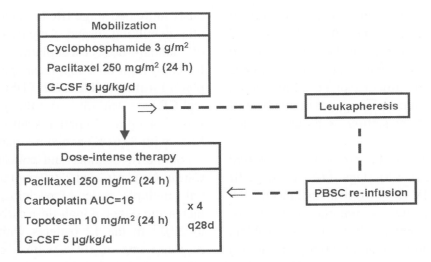

Figure 15–2. Gynecologic Oncology Group trial 9903 (GOG 9903), a phase II trial using multiple cycles of high-dose sequential carboplatin, paclitaxel, and topotecan with peripheral blood stem cell (PBSC) support as initial chemotherapy in patients with optimally debulked stage III ovarian carcinoma or primary peritoneal carcinoma. (G-CSF = granulocyte colony-stimulating factor; AUC = area under the concentration-time curve.)

apy with active agents can be administered safely with hematopoietic support, with higher response rates and longer disease-free intervals than historically expected with conventional regimens. A recent randomized trial in the United States to compare carboplatin and paclitaxel to high-dose carboplatin, mitoxantrone, and cyclophosphamide with stem cell support as consolidation (GOG 164) was closed due to poor accrual. Although preliminary results from a European randomized trial are encouraging,[41] the role of high-dose chemotherapy in the treatment of ovarian cancer remains unclear. Based on the available data, the patients most likely to benefit from this approach are those patients who have a minimal residual tumor burden after initial surgical debulking and whose tumors are platinum sensitive. The optimal conditioning regimens and the ideal timing of high-dose therapy remain to be determined. As such, high-dose therapy for ovarian cancer remains experimental, and patients should be treated within the context of a clinical trial.

REFERENCES

1. Jemal A, Thomas A, Murray T, et al. Cancer statistics, 2002. CA Cancer J Clin 2002; 52:23–47.
2. McGuire WP, Hoskins WJ, Brady MF, et al. Cyclophosphamide and cisplatin compared with paclitaxel and cisplatin in patients with stage III and stage IV ovarian cancer. N Engl J Med 1996;334:1–6.
3. Levin L, Hryniuk WM. Dose intensity analysis of chemotherapy regimens in ovarian carcinoma. J Clin Oncol 1987;5: 756–67.
4. Bruckner H, Wallach R, Cohen CJ, et al. High-dose cisplatin for the treatment of ovarian cancer. Gynecol Oncol 1981; 12:64–7.
5. Barker GH, Wiltshaw E. Use of high-dose cisplatin following failure on previous chemotherapy for advanced carcinoma of the ovary. Br J Obstet Gynecol 1981;88:1192–9.
6. Ozols R, Ostchega Y, Meyers C, et al. High-dose cisplatin in hypertonic aline in refractory ovarian cancer. J Clin Oncol 1985;2:1246–50.
7. Alberts DS, Green S, Hanningan EV, et al. Improved therapeutic index of carboplatin plus cyclophosphamide versus cisplatin plus cyclophosphamide: final report by the Southwest Oncology Group of a phase III randomized trial in stages III and IV ovarian cancer. J Clin Oncol 1992;10:706–17.
8. Swenerton K, Jeffrey J, Stuart G, et al. Cisplatin-cyclophosphamide versus carboplatin-cyclophosphamide in advanced ovarian cancer: a randomized phase III study of the National Cancer Institute of Canada Clinic Trials Group. J Clin Oncol 1992;10:718–26.
9. Ozols RF, Bundy BN, Fowler J, et al. Randomized phase III study of cisplatin (CIS)/paclitaxel (PAC) versus carboplatin (CARBO/PAC) in optimal stage III epithelial ovarian cancer (OC): a Gynecologic Oncology Group trial (GOG 158) [abstract 1373]. Proc Am Soc Clin Oncol 1999;18:356a.
10. Du Bois A, Lueck HJ, Meier W, et al. Cisplatin/paclitaxel vs. carboplatin/paclitaxel in ovarian cancer: update of an

Arbeitsgemeinschaft Gynaekologische Onkologie (AGO) study group trial [abstract 1374]. Proc Am Soc Clin Oncol 1999;18:356a.

11. Weaver CH, Greco FA, Hainsworth JD, et al. A phase I-II study of high-dose melphalan, mitoxantrone and carboplatin with peripheral blood stem cell support in patients with advanced ovarian or breast carcinoma. Bone Marrow Transplant 1997;20:847–53.

12. Stiff PJ, McKenzie S, Alberts DS, et al. Phase I clinical and pharmacokinetic study of high-dose mitoxantrone combined with carboplatin, cyclophosphamide and autologous bone marrow rescue: high response rate for refractory ovarian cancer. J Clin Oncol 1994;12:176–83.

13. Shea TC, Flaherty M, Elias A, et al. A phase I clinical and pharmacokinetic study of carboplatin and autologous bone marrow support. J Clin Oncol 1989;7:651–61.

14. Tobias JS, Weiner R, Griffiths CT, et al. Cryopreserved autologous marrow infusion following high-dose cancer chemotherapy. Eur J Cancer 1977;13:269–77.

15. Lazarus HM, Herzig RH, Graham-Pole J, et al. Intensive melphalan chemotherapy and cryopreserved autologous bone marrow transplantation for the treatment of refractory cancer. J Clin Oncol 1983;1:359–67.

16. Corringham R, Gilmore M, Prentice HG, et al. High-dose melphalan with autologous bone marrow transplant. Cancer 1983;52:1783–7.

17. Vriesendorp R, Aalders JG, Sleijfer DT, et al. Effective high-dose chemotherapy with autologous bone marrow infusion in resistant ovarian cancer. Gynecol Oncol 1984;17:271–6.

18. Maraninchi D, Abecasis M, Gastaut J-A, et al. High-dose melphalan with autologous bone marrow rescue for the treatment of advanced adult solid tumors. Cancer Treat Rep 1984;68:471–4.

19. Postmus PE, de Vries EG, de Vries-Hospers HG, et al. Cyclophosphamide and VP-16-213 with autologous bone marrow transplantation. A dose escalation study. Eur J Cancer Clin Oncol 1984;20:777–82.

20. Antman K, Eder JP, Elias A, et al. High-dose combination alkylating agent preparative regimen with autologous bone marrow support: the Dana-Farber Cancer Institute/Beth Israel Hospital experience. Cancer Treat Rep 1987;71:119–25.

21. Mulder POM, Sleijfer DT, Willemse PHB, et al. High-dose cyclophosphamide or melphalan with escalating doses of mitoxantrone and autologous bone marrow transplantation for refractory solid tumors. Cancer Res 1989;49:4654–8.

22. Williams SF, Bitran JD, Kaminer L, et al. A phase I-II study of bialkylator chemotherapy, high-dose thiotepa and cyclophosphamide with autologous bone marrow reinfusion in patients with advanced cancer. J Clin Oncol 1987;5:260–5.

23. Ellis ED, Williams SF, Moormeier JA, et al. A phase I-II study of high-dose cyclophosphamide, thiotepa and escalating doses of mitoxantrone with autologous stem cell rescue in patients with refractory malignancies. Bone Marrow Transplant 1990;6:439–42.

24. Stemmer SM, Cagnoni PJ, Shpall EJ, et al. High-dose paclitaxel, cyclophosphamide and cisplatin with autologous hematopoietic progenitor-cell support: a phase I trial. J Clin Oncol 1996;14:1463–72.

25. Donato ML, Gershenson DM, Wharton JT, et al. High-dose topotecan, melphalan, and cyclophosphamide (TMC) with stem cell support: a new regimen for the treatment of advanced ovarian cancer. Gynecol Oncol 2001;81:420–6.

26. Bruckner HW, Cohen CJ, Feuer E, et al. Prognostic factors: cisplatin regimens for patients with ovarian cancer after failure of chemotherapy. Obstet Gynecol 1987;69:114–20.

27. Thigpen JT, Blessing JA, Ball H, et al. Phase II trial of paclitaxel in patients with progressive ovarian carcinoma after platinum-based chemotherapy: a Gynecology Oncology Group study. J Clin Oncol 1994;12:1748–53.

28. Shpall EJ, Clarke-Pearson D, Soper JT, et al. High-dose alkylating agent chemotherapy with autologous bone marrow support in patients with stage III/IV epithelial ovarian cancer. Gynecol Oncol 1990;38:386–91.

29. Shea T, Wiley J, Serody J, et al. High-dose chemotherapy with melphalan, VP-16, carboplatin, thiotepa and mitoxantrone in patients with advanced epithelial ovarian cancer. Proc Am Soc Clin Oncol 1995;14:807.

30. Broun ER, Belinson JL, Berek JS, et al. Salvage therapy for recurrent and refractory ovarian cancer with high-dose chemotherapy and autologous bone marrow support: a Gynecologic Oncology Group pilot study. Gynecol Oncol 1994;54:142–6.

31. Stiff P, Bayer R, Camarda M, et al. A phase II trial of high-dose mitoxantrone, carboplatin, and cyclophosphamide with autologous bone marrow rescue for recurrent epithelial ovarian carcinoma: analysis of risk factors for clinical outcome. Gynecol Oncol 1995;57:278–85.

32. Legros M, Dauplat J, Fleury J, et al. High-dose chemotherapy with hematopoietic rescue in patients with stage III or IV ovarian cancer: long-term results. J Clin Oncol 1997;15:1302–8.

33. Mulder PO, Willemse PH, Aalders JG, et al. High-dose chemotherapy with autologous bone marrow transplantation in patients with refractory ovarian cancer. Eur J Cancer Clin Oncol 1989;25:645–9.

34. Dauplat J, Legros M, Condat P, et al. High-dose melphalan and autologous bone marrow support for treatment of ovarian carcinoma with positive second-look operation. Gynecol Oncol 1989;34:294–8.

35. Rebollo J, Henriquez I, Martin Algarra S, et al. High-dose combination of carboplatin and etoposide followed by peripheral blood stem cell transplantation in the treatment of ovarian cancer. Proc Am Assoc Cancer Res 1991;32:1025a.

36. Barnett MJ, Swenerton KD, Hoskins PJ, et al. Intensive therapy with carboplatin, etoposide and melphalan and autologous stem cell transplantation for epithelial ovarian carcinoma. Proc Am Soc Clin Oncol 1990;9:654.

37. Cure H, Legros M, Fleury J, et al. High-dose chemotherapy and autologous stem cell transplantation in advanced epithelial ovarian cancer. Bone Marrow Transplant 1996;18 Suppl 1:S34–5.

38. Viens P, Gravis G, Blaise D, et al. High-dose chemotherapy with bone marrow rescue for patients with FIGO stage III or IV common epithelial ovarian carcinoma responding to first line treatment. Proc Am Soc Clin Oncol 1995;13:811.

39. Rubin SC, Randall TC, Armstrong KA, et al. Ten-year follow-up of ovarian cancer patients after second-look laparotomy with negative findings. Obstet Gynecol 1999;93:21–4.

40. Hempling RE, Wesolowski JA, Piver MS. Second-look laparotomy in advanced ovarian cancer: a critical assessment of morbidity and impact on survival. Ann Surg Oncol 1997;4: 349–54.

41. Cure H, Battista C, Guastalla J, et al. Phase III randomized trial of high-dose chemotherapy (HDC) and peripheral blood stem cell (PBSC) support as consolidation in patients (pts) with responsive low-burden advanced ovarian cancer (AOC): preliminary results of a GINECO/FNCLCC/SFGM-TC study [abstract 815]. Proc Am Soc Oncol 2001;20:204a.

42. Donato ML, Aleman AS, Gershenson DM, et al. Long term results of 102 patients with advanced ovarian cancer treated with high-dose chemotherapy [abstract 814]. Proc Am Soc Oncol 2001;20:204a.

43. Stiff PJ, Bayer R, Kerger C, et al. High-dose chemotherapy with autologous transplantation for persistent/relapsed ovarian cancer: a multivariate analysis of survival for 100 consecutively treated patients. J Clin Oncol 1997;15:1309–17.

44. Stiff PJ, Veum-Stone J, Lazarus HM, et al. High-dose chemotherapy and autologous stem-cell transplantation for ovarian cancer: an autologous blood and marrow transplant registry report. Ann Intern Med 2000;133:504–15.

45. Norton L, Day R. Potential innovations in scheduling of cancer chemotherapy. In: DeVita VT Jr, Hellman S, Rosenberg SA, editors. Important advances in oncology. Philadelphia (PA): Lippincott; 1991. p. 57–72.

46. Shea TC, Mason JR, Storniolo AM, et al. Sequential cycles of high-dose carboplatin administered with recombinant human granulocyte-macrophage colony-stimulating factor and repeated infusions of autologous peripheral-blood progenitor cells: a novel and effective method for delivering multiple courses of dose-intensive therapy. J Clin Oncol 1992;10:464–73.

47. Lotz J-P, Boulenc C, Andre T, et al. Tandem high-dose chemotherapy with ifosfamide, carboplatin and teniposide with autologous bone marrow transplant for the treatment of poor prognosis common epithelial ovarian cancer. Cancer 1996;77:2550–9.

48. Morgan MA, Stadtmauer EA, Luger SM, et al. Cycles of dose-intensive chemotherapy with peripheral stem cell support in persistent or recurrent platinum-sensitive ovarian cancer. Gynecol Oncol 1997;67:272–6.

49. Fennelly DW, Aghajanian C, Shapiro F, et al. Dose escalation of paclitaxel with high-dose carboplatin using peripheral blood progenitor support in patients with advanced ovarian cancer. Semin Oncol 1997; 24 Suppl 2:S2–26–S2–30.

50. Fennelly D, Wasserheit C, Schneider J, et al. Simultaneous dose escalation and schedule intensification of carboplatin-based chemotherapy using peripheral blood progenitor cells and filgrastim: a phase I trial. Cancer Res 1994;54:6137–42.

51. Fennelly D, Schneider J, Spriggs D, et al. Dose escalation of paclitaxel with high-dose cyclophosphamide with analysis of progenitor-cell mobilization and hematologic support of advanced ovarian cancer patients receiving rapidly sequenced high-dose carboplatin/cyclophosphamide courses. J Clin Oncol 1995;13:1160–6.

52. Aghajanian C, Fennelly D, Shapiro F, et al. Phase II study of "dose-dense" high-dose chemotherapy treatment with peripheral-blood progenitor-cell support as primary treatment for patients with advanced ovarian cancer. J Clin Oncol 1998;16:1852–60.

53. Schilder RJ, Brady MF, Spriggs D, et al. Pilot evaluation of high-dose carboplatin and Paclitaxel followed by high-dose melphalan supported by peripheral blood stem cells in previously untreated advanced ovarian cancer. Gynecol Oncol (in press).

54. Tepler I, Cannistra SA, Frei E, et al. Use of peripheral-blood progenitor cells abrogated the myelotoxicity of repetitive outpatient high-dose carboplatin and cyclophosphamide chemotherapy. J Clin Oncol 1993;11:1583–91.

55. Murakami M, Shinozuka T, Kuroshima Y, et al. High-dose chemotherapy with autologous bone marrow transplantation for the treatment of malignant ovarian tumors. Semin Oncol 1994;21 Suppl 1:29–32.

56. Peccatori F, Colombo N, Griso C, et al. Multicycle sequential high-dose chemotherapy (HDCT): an effective regimen as first line treatment in poor prognosis advanced epithelial ovarian cancer (AOC). Proc Am Soc Clin Oncol 2001;20: 818.

57. Prince HM, Rischin D, Quinn M, et al. Repetitive high dose topotecan, carboplatin and paclitaxel with peripheral blood progenitor cell support in previously untreated ovarian cancer: results of a phase I study. Gynecol Oncol 2001;81:216–44.

58. Schilder RJ, Johnson, S, Gallo J, et al. Phase I trial of multiple cycles of high-dose chemotherapy supported by autologous peripheral-blood stem cells. J Clin Oncol 1999; 17:2198–207.

59. Schilder RJ, Gallo JM, Millenson MM, et al. Phase I trial of multiple cycles of high-dose carboplatin, paclitaxel and topotecan with peripheral-blood stem cell support as front-line therapy. J Clin Oncol 2001;19:1183–94.

16

Germ Cell Tumors

LEVI DOWNS, MD

MATTHEW P. BOENTE, MD

Ovarian germ cell tumors are rare but interesting cancers of the female reproductive tract. They constitute only about 2 to 3% of all ovarian cancers and typically affect women in their early twenties. Significant progress has been made in the past two decades concerning the diagnosis, surgical management, and chemotherapy of these unusual tumors that arise from primitive germ cells in the embryonic gonad. In many situations, even in the setting of advanced disease, patients can be cured.

DIAGNOSIS

Advances in serum tumor marker analysis have helped the preoperative triage of young women with malignant germ cell tumors. These tumors typically make human chorionic gonadotropin (HCG), α-fetoprotein (AFP), lactic dehydroxenase (LDH), or human placental lactogen (HPL) (Table 16–1).

In addition, improvements in imaging studies (transvaginal ultrasonography, computed tomography [CT], and magnetic resonance imaging [MRI]) have allowed clinicians to be appropriately suspicious in the preoperative setting, so that the patient can be referred to a gynecologic oncologist for definitive surgical staging. Unfortunately, many young patients with germ cell tumors are operated on in small community hospitals, where gynecologic oncologists are not available and where an experienced pathologist is not available for a frozen-section analysis.

Typically these patients leave the operative theater without being staged, or having been inappropriately castrated. It should be clearly understood

that these tumors are extraordinarily rare, are potentially lethal, and often can be cured with staging procedures that do not include hysterectomy and bilateral salpingo-oophorectomy.

HISTOLOGIC SUBTYPES

Dysgerminoma

Approximately 50% of malignant germ cell tumors are dysgerminomas. Dysgerminomas are typically fleshy, unilateral, and solid tumors (10% bilateral) that have a propensity to spread to the retroperitoneal lymph nodes, as opposed to their epithelial counterparts, which spread contiguously on the peritoneal surfaces[1] (Figures 16–1, 16–2, and 16–3). Precise surgical staging, including ipsilateral lymph node dissection, is imperative since the majority will be cured by either surgery alone or surgery plus adjuvant chemotherapy. Most dysgerminomas will manufacture LDH, and a small percentage will

Table 16–1. SERUM TUMOR MARKERS FOR GERM CELL TUMORS			
Histologic Subtype	HCG	AFP	LDH
Dysgerminoma	+/–	–	+
Endodermal sinus tumor	–	+	–
Immature teratoma	–	+/–	
Embryonal carcinoma	+	+/–	+/–
Choriocarcinoma	+	–	+/–
Polyembryoma*	+	+/–	–

AFP = α-fetoprotein; HCG = human chorionic gonadotropin; LDH = lactic dehydroxenate.
*May produce human placental lactogen.

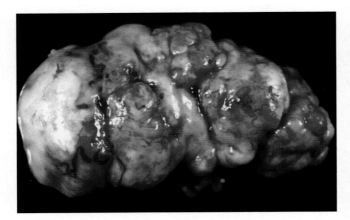

Figure 16–1. A completely excised stage IC dysgerminoma.

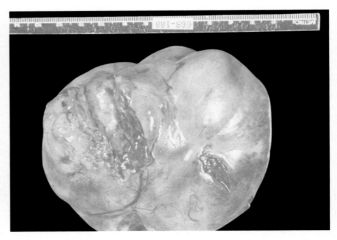

Figure 16–3. Dysgerminoma.

make HCG even though no mixed germ cell component will be identified microscopically.

The clinical presentation can vary, from an incidental finding on pelvic examination, to pelvic pain, to an acute abdomen secondary to rupture of the adnexal mass. Alternatively, young women may present with isosexual precocious puberty or, more rarely, hirsutism. It is particularly important in young amenorrheic patients to consider a karyotype analysis preoperatively when the diagnosis of dysgerminoma is being considered. Patients with a dysgenetic gonad (a Y chromosome) are at risk for malignant degeneration in up to 50% of cases, and although rare exceptions of a normal contralateral ovary have been reported, strong consideration should be given to removing the contralateral ovary in these cases.[2]

Yolk Sac Tumor

The second most common malignant germ cell tumor, the endodermal sinus tumor (EST), originates

from the embryonic "yolk sac." This tumor represents less than 1% of gynecologic malignancies but about 20% of malignant ovarian germ cell tumors. On examination, ESTs are solid friable masses and can be associated with ascites. They are often hemorrhagic and are frequently ruptured at the time of surgery[3] (Figures 16–4 and 16–5). Figure 16–6 shows the CT findings in a 16-year-old girl diagnosed with a large abdominal-pelvic mass, that was found to be an endodermal sinus tumor. Most common papillae with central vessel, lined by columnar cells, are known as Schiller-Duval bodies; these Schiller-Duval bodies are pathognomonic for EST. There are also several microscopic patterns including "reticular" polyvesicular vitelline and "hepatoid"

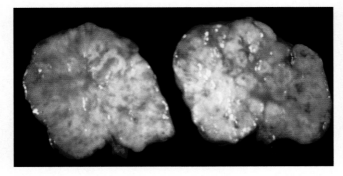

Figure 16–2. A dysgerminoma (bisected).

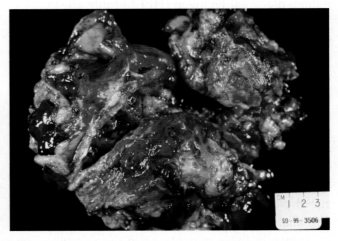

Figure 16–4. A hemorrhagic ruptured stage IC endodermal sinus tumor from a 14-year-old girl (preoperative α-fetoprotein > 10,000 μ/mL).

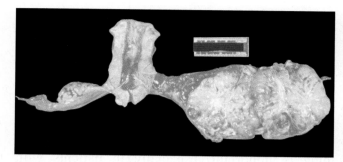

Figure 16–5. An endodermal sinus tumor.

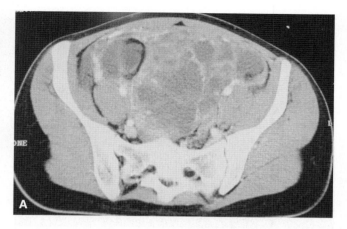

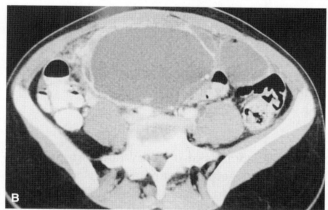

Figure 16–6. Serial section from the computed tomography (CT) scan of a 16-year-old girl diagnosed with an endodermal sinus tumor.

patterns. All patterns contain hyaline pockets that stain for AFP. An elevated level of serum AFP in a young woman with a solid mass is highly suspicious for an EST.

Unfortunately, because of their hemorrhagic nature, many of these tumors rupture prior to diagnosis and create a hemoperitoneum, necessitating emergency surgery. Without a gynecologic oncologist present, unilateral adnexectomy should be the extent of the surgery performed since adjuvant chemotherapy will not only preserve fertility but also cure the majority of patients. Since postoperative chemotherapy will be recommended for the early- and late-stage disease, surgical staging, especially in inexperienced hands, will probably not change the postoperative chemotherapeutic management. It must be particularly emphasized that bilateral salpingo-oophorectomy is almost never appropriate since only 5% of ESTs are bilateral.

Immature Teratoma

The malignant counterpart of a benign cystic teratoma, the immature teratoma (IT) represents about 2% of all malignant ovarian germ cell tumors. ITs are predominantly unilateral and contain both solid and cystic elements (Figure 16–7).

Internally, all germ cell layers (ectoderm, mesoderm, and endoderm), will usually be represented, but the histologic hallmark of the IT is the degree (grades 1 to 3) of immature neuroectoderm, which is closely related to metastatic potential and prognosis.[4]

As with other germ cell tumors, staging is important in cases of IT and should be performed whenever possible; however, most cases can be managed without bilateral oophorectomy since only 5% of ITs

are bilateral. In approximately 10 to 15% of cases, a coexisting mature teratoma will be present in the contralateral ovary; therefore, careful clinical inspection and possible ovarian cystectomy with frozen section may be warranted.

Finally, numerous small benign peritoneal implants may be found at laparotomy. This condition, gliomatosis peritonei, represents mature glia and is not an indication for chemotherapy. Gliomatosis peritonei may develop years after an IT but should not be mistaken for metastatic disease in such a situation. Occasionally, gliomatosis will grow large enough to require surgical excision.

Embryonal Carcinoma

Embryonal carcinoma is a rare type of ovarian germ cell tumor; only a few cases have ever been reported. It is usually seen in a slightly younger population (median, 15 years of age) and usually produces

Figure 16–7. A large immature teratoma in a 19-year-old obese woman (stage IIIC [peritoneal implants > 2 cm], optimal debulking).

HCG and AFP. More commonly, it is seen as part of a mixed germ cell tumor.

Choriocarcinoma

Choriocarcinoma is also a very rare form of a primary ovarian germ cell tumor and is more commonly seen as part of a mixed germ cell complex. In a prepubertal patient, it can present as sexual precocity, androgenization, or abnormal uterine bleeding. In sexually active women, it must be differentiated from gestational trophoblastic disease because the treatment would vary dramatically. Choriocarcinomas are usually unilateral and solid and are typically hemorrhagic. Again, fertility-sparing surgery with staging is the rule in the majority of cases.

Mixed Germ Cell Tumors

Germ cell tumors can present as a combination of two or more malignant histologic subtypes, and do so about 15% of the time. Elevations of LDH, AFP, and HCG are present and may alert the pathologist to the need to perform careful sampling of the primary tumor (one section per centimeter of tumor). Conservative fertility-sparing surgery is the rule although occasionally these cancers can be bilateral.

Polyembryoma

Polyembryoma is the rarest of all ovarian germ cell tumors. It is characterized microscopically by structures known as embryoid bodies. It is found more commonly in mixed germ cell tumors, but when in its pure form, it will manufacture AFP, HCG, and HPL.[5]

SURGERY

A careful, tedious, and meticulous staging laparotomy is important, especially in patients with "apparent early-stage disease," to identify occult microscopic disease. As previously stated, the goal of these operations is to accurately stage the cancer and, in most cases, preserve the uterus and contralateral ovary.[6] The components of a staging laparotomy are listed in Table 16–2.

Unfortunately, even in the 1990s, approximately 80% of patients with "apparent" early ovarian cancers are inadequately staged.[7] The reasons for this are numerous but are mainly financially driven by lack of appropriate referrals from small community hospitals to cancer centers and tertiary care facilities where gynecologic oncologists are more readily available. Unfortunately, these triage decisions may cost young women their lives. Multidisciplinary teams in referral centers are often faced with difficult decisions concerning the consequences of inadequate staging, especially with regard to the amount, schedule, and duration of chemotherapy. Most of the time, reexploration is required to get the

Table 16–2. STAGING LAPAROTOMY FOR OVARIAN CANCER
1. Vertical midline incision
2. Peritoneal cytology
3. Inspection (upper abdomen, pelvis, retroperitoneum)
4. Removal of involved tube and ovary, frozen section*
5. Selective pelvic and para-aortic lymphadenectomy (ipsilateral)†
6. Omentectomy
7. Peritoneal biopsies (pelvis, paracolic gutters, diaphragm)
8. Biopsy of any suspicious areas or adhesions

*Implies disease is grossly limited to one ovary and/or pelvis; biopsy should be performed on any grossly obvious disease that is present on the uterus or contralateral ovary. If disease is confirmed, the involved organ should be removed in most situations.
†Anterior and medial aspects of the external iliac artery and vein and the lymphatic tissue anterior to the obturator nerve should be removed. The limits of the dissection should be the deep circumflex vessels inferiorly and the obturator nerve posteriorly. The lateral and anterior aspects of the common iliac vessels and aorta should be cleared of their lymphatic tissue to the origin of the ovarian blood supply, near the renal artery and vein. Although a complete lymphadenectomy is not recommended, a selective lymphadenectomy should be done. Historically, it has not been possible to accurately "sample" lymph nodes by gross inspection.

most accurate information and to make the best recommendation regarding subsequent chemotherapy.

Similar to the principles of cytoreduction in the treatment of epithelial ovarian cancer, every attempt should be made to debulk germ cell malignancies if there is gross disease remote from the primary tumor. Slayton and co-workers initially reported on the advantage of complete surgical debulking of germ cell tumors.[8] Since then, other studies have confirmed the survival advantage in patients who have had optimal cytoreduction in their initial exploratory laparotomy.[9] As with epithelial ovarian cancer, the concept of second-look laparotomy (SLL) is controversial in regard to ovarian germ cell tumors. In general, the procedure is not necessary, nor does it provide useful information in patients whose tumors were completely resected at their initial surgery. However, patients with incompletely resected tumors, especially if the initial tumor had teratomatous elements (IT), may benefit from secondary cytoreduction.[10]

Surgery continues to be the "gold standard" as initial therapy for germ cell tumors and provides pivotal information for the amount and nature of chemotherapy. These tumors are remarkably curable, even in an advanced state. However, survival depends heavily on an experienced team of physicians, including a gynecologic oncologist, who needs to exercise thoughtful intraoperative skill and judgment; a pathologist, who can accurately and precisely diagnose the disease, and a medical oncologist, who has a particular expertise in these rare tumors and who clearly understands the biology and chemosensitivity of this disease.

GONADOBLASTOMA

Scully and co-workers at the Massachusetts General Hospital described a tumor now known as gonadoblastoma 1953. The tumor was composed of both germ cell and sex cord–stromal derivatives, which resembled immature granulosa and Sertoli's cells. Both occurred in females showing abnormal sexual development. The neoplastic nature of these tumors has been questioned because the tumors are very small and can regress by hyalinization and calcification. Unfortunately, approximately 50% are associated with dysgerminomas and with other malignant ovarian neoplasms in approximately 10% of cases. Fifty percent of the phenotypic females are virilized, and this unfortunately does not regress after excision of the tumor. Most of the time, gonadoblastoma is associated with gonadal dysgenesis although there have been reported cases of normal pregnancies following excision of a dysgerminoma containing a small focus of a gonadoblastoma (Figure 16–8). Almost all patients with gonadoblastoma who have had karyotypes tested were found to contain a Y chromosome. Although exceptions have been reported, this tumor occurs exclusively in patients with pure or mixed gonadal dysgenesis. The gonadoblastoma is classified with benign germ cell tumors although the dysgerminoma does have the propensity to undergo malignant degeneration. It can be bilateral in up to 30% of cases. The rare patient may have a normal karyotype, but most patients are sex chromatin negative and have a 46 XY, 45 XO, or a mixed 46 XX/46 XY karyotype.

Because of the risk of malignant degeneration, both ovaries should be removed at the time of surgery. Rare exceptions have been documented.[2] The clinician should be careful not to consider a streaked ovary enlarged by a gonadoblastoma to be a normal ovary.

FERTILITY AND FOLLOW UP

At several times in this manuscript we have suggested that fertility-sparing surgery is the standard

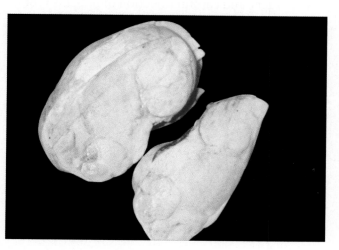

Figure 16–8. Gonadoblastoma.

of care in germ cell malignancy whenever possible. Recently, Zanetta and colleagues reported outcomes of 169 women who had a variety of malignant germ cell neoplasms of the ovary. Irrespective of subtype and stage, conservative surgery followed by chemotherapy was found to be extremely effective in both dysgerminomas and nondysgerminomas of the ovary. During follow-up, 12 untreated and 20 treated patients had 55 conceptions. Forty pregnancies were successfully delivered at term and there were six elective terminations and nine miscarriages. Four congenital malformations were observed; however, only one malformation was seen in 14 conceptions of patients who had not received prior chemotherapy and three were observed in 41 conceptions of the treated patients. The conclusions of this study were that fertility seemed only marginally effective and miscarriages were in the expected range of the general population. The malformation rate was slightly higher than in the general population but there did not seem to be a difference between patients who did or did not receive chemotherapy. The survival with a median follow-up of 67 months was 94% for dysgerminomas, 89% for endodermal sinus tumors, 100% for mixed germ cell tumors, and 98% for immature teratoma. For women who received conservative surgical treatment, survival rate was 98%, 90%, 100%, and 100%, respectively. Several women (two) had adnexal recurrences and both received salvage treatment. All but one patient had return of menses within nine months of completing therapy. Based on this information, we believe that conservative surgery and careful selection of patients requiring adjuvant chemotherapy should be the rule rather than exception in patients with malignant germ cell tumors of the ovary.

REFERENCES

1. Gordon A, Lipdon D, Woodruff JD. Dysgerminoma: a review of 158 cases from the Emil Novak ovarian tumor registry. Obstet Gynecol 1981;58:497.
2. Hart, WR, Burkons, DM. Germ cell neoplasms arising in gonadoblastomas. Cancer 1979;43:668–78.
3. Gershenson DM, Del Junco G, Herson J, Rutledge FN. Endodermal sinus tumor of the ovary: the M. D. Anderson experience. Obstet Gynecol 1983;61:194–202.
4. Norris MJ, Zirkin HJ, Benson, WL. Immature (malignant) teratoma of the ovary. Cancer 1976;37:2359–72.
5. Takeda A, Ishizuka T, Goto T, et al. Polyembryoma of ovary producing alpha-fetoprotein and hCG: immunoperoxidase and electron microscopic study. Cancer 1982;49:1878.
6. Low JJ, Perrin LC, Crandon AJ, Hacker NF. Conservative surgery to preserve ovarian function in patients with malignant ovarian germ cell tumors. A review of 74 cases. Cancer 2000;89:391–8.
7. National Institutes of Health Consensus Development Conference Statement. Ovarian cancer: screening, treatment, and follow-up. April 5–7, 1994. Gynecol Oncol 1994;55 Suppl:S4–14.
8. Slayton RE, Park RC, Silverberg SG, et al. Vincristine, dactinomycin and cyclophosphamide in the treatment of malignant germ cell tumors of the ovary: a Gynecologic Oncology Group study (a final report). Cancer 1985;56:243.
9. Williams SD, Blessing, JA, Moore DH, et al. Cisplatin, vinblastine, and bleomycin in advanced and recurrent ovarian germ-cell tumors. Ann Intern Med 1989;111:22.
10. Williams, SD, Blessing JA, DiSaia PJ, et al. Second-look laparotomy in ovarian germ cell tumors: the Gynecologic Oncology Group experience. Gynecol Oncol 1994;52:287.
11. Zanetta G, Bonazzi C, Cantu M, et al. Survival and reproductive function after treatment of malignant germ cell ovarian tumors. J Clin Oncol 2001;19:1015–20.

17

Ovarian Sex Cord–Stromal Tumors

PATRICIA L. JUDSON, MD

MATTHEW P. BOENTE, MD

Ovarian sex cord-stromal tumors represent 5% or fewer of all ovarian neoplasms. Histologically, these tumors are classified as malignant neoplasms. Their natural history, however, is indolent and their prognosis is similar to that of low malignant potential tumors. The peak incidence of these cancers is in women beyond the age of 50, but a significant portion also occurs in premenopausal women. Many of these tumors, up to 30%, can produce estrogen, testosterone, or androgens. These tumors develop from the intraovarian matrix that supports germ cells, hence the excessive estrogen or androgen production.[1–5] (Table 17–1).

TYPES OF OVARIAN SEX CORD–STROMAL TUMORS

Granulosa-Stromal Cell Tumors

Granulosa Cell Tumor

Granulosa cell tumors (GCTs) represent approximately 2% of all ovarian neoplasms, and approximately 50% of these cases develop in postmenopausal women.[4] Histologically, the adult-type GCT has different pathologic characteristics than the juvenile type. These tumors are typically large and, in most cases, 10 cm or more in diameter (Figure 17–1). The adult-type GCT represents 95% of all GCTs. Many patients will develop bloody ascites or a hemoperitoneum secondary to rupture, as they are prone to internal hemorrhage. Patients may also experience severe pain secondary to torsion or hemorrhage. Abnormal uterine bleeding is also common, secondary to the endometrial stimulation by these estrogen-secreting tumors.

Retrospective studies evaluating the endometrium in patients with GCTs show that atypical adenomatous hyperplasia is present in 40 to 55% of patients and that frank carcinoma is present in 15 to 22% of patients.[6–8]

Eighty to ninety percent of granulosa cell tumors are stage I at initial diagnosis. These neoplasms have a rather indolent behavior, and although they can metastasize and recur, they have, by and large, a favorable biology. All patients with a known GCT should undergo surgical staging including lymph node dissection, omentectomy, peritoneal biopsies, and peritoneal cytology. Inhibin levels can be elevated with these tumors and can be predictive of recurrence. Patients with stage I disease have a 5-year survival rate of between 90 and 100%.[9] Stage I tumors can be treated with surgery alone. Patients with more advanced stages should be considered for chemotherapy with bleomycin, etoposide, and platinum. The surgical stage of the disease was the most significant prognostic factor in a large retrospective review of 454 case studies from the Johns Hopkins

Table 18–1. CLASSIFICATION OF SEX CORD–STROMAL TUMORS
Granulosa-stromal cell tumors
Granulosa cell tumors (adult and juvenile)
Thecoma and fibroma
Fibrosarcoma
Sclerosing stromal cell tumor
Sertoli-stromal cell tumors
Sertoli-Leydig cell tumor
Sertoli cell tumor
Leydig cell tumor
Lipid cell tumor
Sex cord tumor with annular tubules
Gynadoblastoma

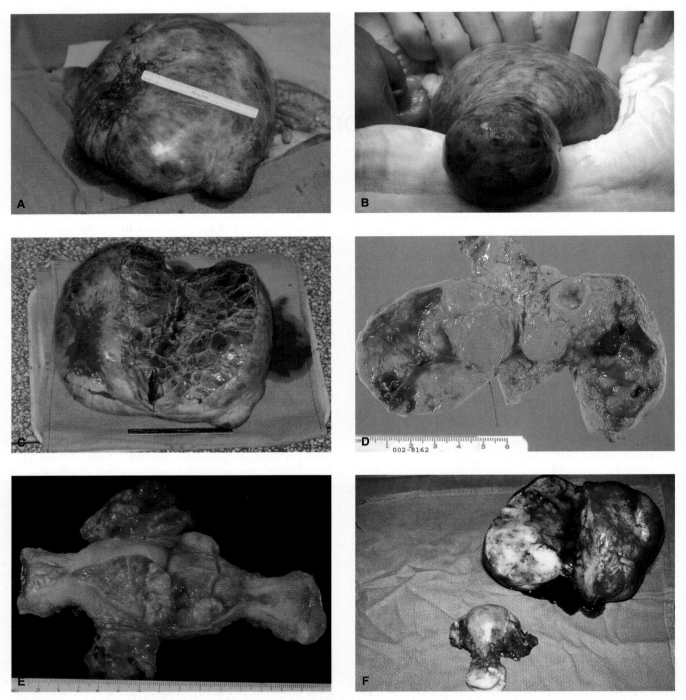

Figure 17–1. *A*, Granulosa cell tumor (30 cm × 30 cm × 25 cm). *B*, a large, Stage 1A granulosa cell tumor in a 48-year-old woman who presented with pelvic pain. *C*, granulosa cell tumor, bisected (fresh). *D*, granulosa cell tumor, bisected (fixed). *E*, adenomatous hyperplasia associated with granulosa cell tumor.

Hospital. They reported a mortality rate of at least 40% when the tumor had spread beyond the ovary.[10] Recurrences can be late, and several reports in the literature show a mean interval from diagnosis to recurrence of 8 years.[11] Survival for patients who have recurrence is poor. With aggressive surgical cytoreduction followed by chemotherapy; between 30 to 50% of patients can be significantly palliated.

Although the survival rate for patients with early-stage GCTs is greater than 90%, only 3 of 13 patients with advanced disease (stage II through stage IV) have been reported to survive.[5] Young and co-workers at the Massachusetts General Hospital have reported that the most important prognostic factor is stage at the initial surgical exploration, followed by tumor size, mitotic activity, and nuclear atypia.

Juvenile-type GCTs (JT-GCTs) are most often diagnosed in prepubertal girls. The diagnosis is usually made on the basis of a physical examination that documents isosexual precocious pseudopuberty. These symptoms include breast enlargement and the development of pubic hair as well as other secondary sex characteristics. In addition, serum estradiol is usually elevated.[12] Rarely, the patient with a JT-GCT will present with virilization. As with the adult type, more than 90% are stage I at the time of diagnosis. Traditionally, although serum estradiol levels and pelvic imaging studies have been used to detect juvenile granulosa cell tumors, more recently müllerian inhibitory substance and inhibin have been documented to play a pivotal role in diagnosing this tumor in young girls.[13] Pathologically, these tumors are distinguished from the adult type by their rounded nuclei. Call-Exner bodies, which are typically seen in the adult type, are rarely encountered in the juvenile type of GCT. Juvenile granulosa cell tumors also carry a very poor prognosis when diagnosed in advanced stages, or at the time of recurrence. Recently, however, multimodality therapy with surgery, platinum-based chemotherapy, and pelvic radiation has provided long-term survival in patients with these malignancies.[14]

Unlike the adult type, most recurrences of JT-GCTs occur within 3 years of the initial diagnosis, and there has not been a reported occurrence to date beyond 3 years.

Thecoma and Fibroma

Thecomas account for approximately 1% of ovarian neoplasms. They are usually diagnosed in the patient's sixth decade of life, are rarely bilateral (2%), and typically present as a pelvic mass. These tumors can be hormonally active, and abnormal uterine bleeding is encountered in as many as 60% of patients. As with GCT patients, between 25 and 40% of these patients with thecomas will have concomitant endometrial hyperplasia or adenocarcinoma at the time of diagnosis. These are benign tumors and require only surgical excision.

Pure fibromas are the most common sex cord–stromal tumors. They are usually diagnosed in the patient's fifth decade and can be identified on pelvic examination as a firm mobile mass (Figure 17–2). Approximately 15% will be associated with ascites. Meigs' syndrome (pelvic mass, ascites, and pleural effusion) is seen in approximately 1% of patients with fibromas.[15] Fibromas require no additional therapy after surgical removal.

Fibrosarcoma

Rarely, fibromatous tumors will exhibit greater than 10 mitotic figures per high-power field, increased cellular density, and nuclear atypia. In these circum-

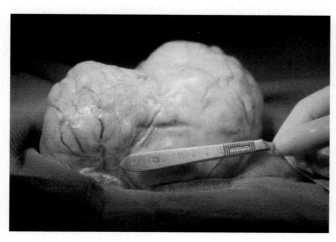

Figure 17–2. Fibroma.

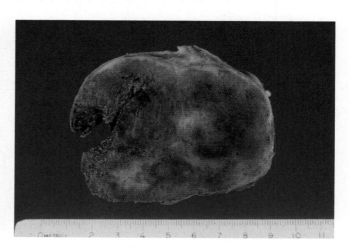

Figure 17–3. Fibrosarcoma with necrosis.

stances, these tumors are known as fibrosarcomas and can exhibit highly aggressive behavior (Figure 17–3). Tumors that have between three and ten mitotic figures per high-power field are also fibrosarcomas, but depending on the degree of cellular density and the nuclear atypia, they can behave as tumors of low malignant potential. As compared with cellular fibromas, fibrosarcomas appear to have a higher proliferative index as well as a higher MIB-1 immunostaining. In addition, fibrosarcomas exhibiting trisomy 8 cells were observed in all cases of fibrosarcomas, but in none of the 8 patients with cellular fibromas.[16]

Sclerosing Stromal Cell Tumor

Sclerosing stromal cell tumors are rare and account for less than 5% of sex cord–stromal tumors but are histologically distinct from the other tumors in the thecoma-fibroma family. They are most commonly found in the patient's late teens and twenties and usually present with pelvic pain or abnormal uterine bleeding. Histologically, they exhibit a pseudolobulation of cellular areas, and these areas are separated by edematous connective tissue and increased vascularity (Figure 17–4). The overwhelming majority of these tumors behave in a benign and indolent fashion.[17]

Sertoli-Stromal Cell Tumors

Sertoli-Leydig Cell Tumor

Sertoli-Leydig cell tumors are rare stromal cell tumors most commonly seen in the second and third

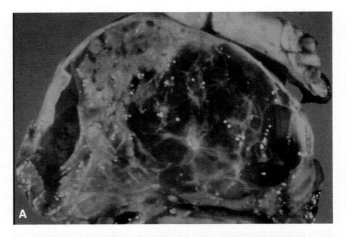

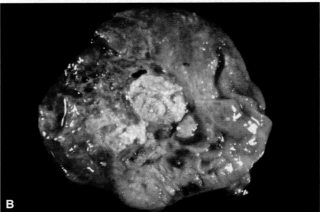

Figure 17–5. *A*, Sertoli-Leydig cell tumor with hemorrhage. *B*, Sertoli-Leydig cell tumor (bisected).

decades of life. They represent less than 1% of all ovarian tumors. These tumors tend to be unilateral and < 5 cm in size (Figure 17–5). Approximately 30% of these tumors are androgen producing and can produce signs and symptoms related to an overproduction of testosterone.[18] Symptoms may include oligomenorrhea or amenorrhea, breast atrophy, acne, hirsutism, temporal balding, and clitoromegaly (Figure 17–6). The prognosis of these tumors is dependent on the degree of differentiation. Well-differentiated tumors tend to be benign whereas poorly differentiated tumors are malignant.

Sertoli Cell Tumor (Pick's Adenoma)

The pure Sertoli cell tumor is very rare and is more likely to be feminizing than virilizing.[19] Presentation is in the patient's third decade, with abdominal distention and/or pain. The average size is 9 cm.

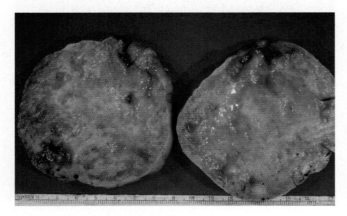

Figure 17–4. Sclerosing stromal cell tumor.

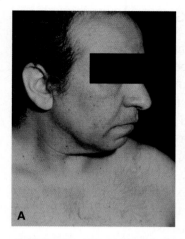

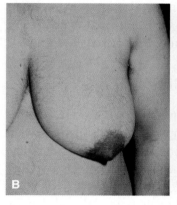

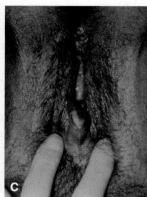

Figure 17–6. A 57-year-old woman with an androgen-producing Sertoli-Leydig cell tumor, showing the following symptoms: *A*, temporal balding and hirsutism; *B*, hirsutism; and *C*, clitoromegaly.

Leydig Cell Tumor

Leydig cell tumors, formerly known as hilum cell tumors, are also androgen-producing tumors that develop in the ovary. These tumors are usually small and solid in nature. Grossly, they are yellowish orange, and the microscopic pathognomonic sign of these tumors is known as Reinke's crystals. When these structures are present, these tumors usually behave in a benign fashion.

Lipid Cell Tumor

Lipid cell tumors, formerly known as adrenal rest tumors, are malignant in about 20% of cases. They can be very difficult to differentiate from Leydig cell tumors but usually occur at a younger age (Figure 17–7). Rapid and extensive virilization is the hallmark of these tumors, and Reinke's crystals are usually absent. The malignant nature is characterized by extreme cellular atypia and mitoses, which are seen microscopically.

Sex Cord Tumor with Annular Tubules

The sex cord tumor with annular tubules (SCTAT) is associated with Peutz-Jeghers syndrome approximately one-third of the time. Peutz-Jeghers syndrome is an autosomal dominant syndrome that is associated with oral and cutaneous pigmentation, gastrointestinal polyps, and multiple cancers. Fortunately, SCTATs are usually benign when associated with this syndrome (Figure 17–8). Adenoma malignum of the cervix occurs in approximately 15% of these patients. Therefore, a thorough evaluation of the cervix is required in the preoperative work-up. Rarely, this clinical syndrome has been associated with malignant ovarian sex cord tumors with annular tubules.[20,21] The tumors also occur independently of Peutz-Jeghers syndrome, and approximately 20% will be malignant in this setting.[10] Treatment is surgical resection.

Gynandroblastoma

Gynandroblastomas are extremely rare sex cord–stromal tumors that appear microscopically as a combination of granulosa cells and tubules of Sertoli's cells. They can be associated with either androgen or estrogen production. Strict morphologic criteria are used to make the diagnosis. These tumors are usually unilateral and are generally tumors of low malignant potential.

TREATMENT

Ovarian stromal tumors should be managed according to the childbearing potential of the patient. In postmenopausal women, they should be surgically managed with hysterectomy and bilateral salpingo-oophorectomy. Surgical staging including bilateral pelvic and para-aortic lymph node dissection, omentectomy, peritoneal biopsies, and peritoneal cytology should be performed in the following tumors: adult and juvenile granulosa cell tumor, intermediate and poorly differentiated Sertoli-Leydig cell tumor, SCTAT, and steroid tumors.

Frozen sections are notoriously unreliable in this group of ovarian neoplasms. Therefore, a unilateral salpingo-oophorectomy and a staging procedure are recommended in the young patient, with conserva-

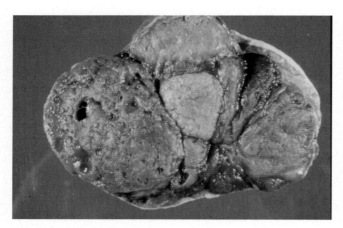

Figure 17–7.   Lipid cell tumor.

tion of the uterus in the contralateral ovary. If the disease is metastatic, cytoreductive surgery is beneficial. If a patient wishes to preserve her reproductive capacity, consideration should be given to a dilatation and curettage as endometrial hyperplasia or endometrial adenocarcinoma can coexist when these tumors are estrogen producing.

Chemotherapy

Bleomycin, etoposide, and cisplatin (BEP) appear to be the most effective chemotherapeutic agents in patients with advanced ovarian sex cord-stromal tumors with measurable disease. Most of the data compiled are from patients with advanced stage or recurrent granulosa cell tumors. There is a paucity of data on other ovarian sex cord tumors. There is no data to suggest that adjuvant chemotherapy with BEP is advantageous in patients with early stage disease whose tumor is completely resected at their initial surgery. In a relatively large study, the GOG reported a 37% objective response rate in patients treated with BEP who ultimately underwent a second-look laparotomy in whom measurable disease was left behind after their initial surgery. Patients who completely responded had a 24-month progression-free interval. Interestingly, 18 of the 75 patients entered in this study were ineligible at the final analysis following surgical pathologic review, underscoring the need for expert gynecologic pathology review.[22] Sertoli-Leydig cell tumors have also been reported to respond to both radiation therapy and VAC (vancristine, actinomycin-O, cyclophosphamide).[23,24]

PROGNOSIS

The efficacy of adjuvant therapy in patients with early-stage disease has been difficult to assess. Due to the rarity of these tumors, there have been few prospective randomized trials. In general, the prognosis for GCT has been good, and survival ranges between 75 and 90% for all stages. Similarly, juvenile GCTs are usually cured with surgery alone, particularly stage I disease. Survival in stage I disease has ranged from approximately 98% for patients with stage IA disease to approximately 85% for patients with stage IC disease.

Sertoli-Leydig cell tumors also have an excellent prognosis with the 5-year survival rate being reported as between 93 and 97% for stage I disease.[19]

CONCLUSION

In general, sex cord–stromal tumors are rare, and for this reason, solid or complex adnexal masses, when discovered by examination or pelvic ultrasonography, should be referred to gynecologic oncologists so that appropriate management may result. Many of these tumors have a low malignant potential and can be cured with conservative surgery (ie, with retention of the uterus and contralateral ovary) and staging procedures. Since frozen sections can frequently be inaccurate, a great deal of experience is needed in the operative theater so that the appropriate surgery is performed. Many times, too little or too much surgery is done because of an inexperienced team of physi-

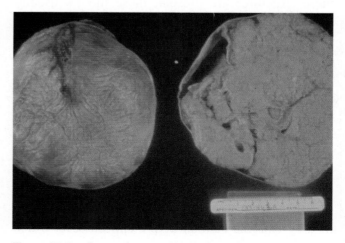

Figure 17–8.   Sex cord tumor with annular tubules.

cians. With appropriate surgical treatment and proper adjuvant therapy, many of these patients can be cured and can retain their reproductive capability. Additionally, these tumors have a propensity to recur late (beyond 5 years), and aggressive surgical re-debulking is a cornerstone of management in these patients as well.

REFERENCES

1. Aiman J, Nalick RH, Jacobs A, et al. The origin of androgen and estrogen in a virilizing postmenopausal woman with bilateral cystic teratomas. Obstet Gynecol 1977;49:695–704.

2. Aiman J, Forney JP, Parker CR Jr. Secretion of androgens and estrogens by normal and neoplastic ovaries in post menopausal women. Obstet Gynecol 1986A;68:1–5.

3. Aiman J, Forney JP, Parker CR Jr. Androgen and estrogen secretion by normal and neoplastic ovaries in premenopausal women. Obstet Gynecol 1986B;68:327.

4. Teilum G. Special tumors of the ovary and testes and related extragandal lesions. In: Comparative pathology and histologic identification. 2nd ed. Philadelphia: JB Lippincott; 1977.

5. Young RH, Scully RE. Ovarian sex cord-stromal tumours: recent advances and current status. Clin Obstet Gynecol 1984;11:93.

6. Gusberg SB, Kardon P. Proliferative endometrial response to theca-granulosa-cell tumors. Am J Obstet Gynecol 1971;111:633.

7. Evans AT, Gaffey TA, Malkasian GD, et al. Clinicopathologic review of 118 granulosa and 82 theca cell tumors. Obstet Gynecol 1980;55:231.

8. Norris JG, Taylor HB. Prognosis of granulosa-thecal tumors of the ovary. Cancer 1968;21:255.

9. Piura B, Nemet D, Yanai-Inbar I, et al. Granulosa-cell tumor of the ovary: a study of 18 cases. J Surg Oncol 1994;55:71.

10. Cronje HS, Nieman I, Bam RH, Woodruff JD. Review of granulosa-theca cell tumors from the Emil Novak ovarian tumor registry. Am J Obstet Gynecol 1999;180:323–327.

11. Stenwig JT, Hazelkamp JT, Beecham JB. Granulosa-cell tumors of the ovary. A clinicopathological study of 118 cases with long-term follow-up. Gynecol Oncol 1979;7:136.

12. Plantaz D, Flamant F, Vassal G, et al. Tumeurs de la granulosa de l'ovaire chez l'enfant et l'adolescente. Arch Fr Pediatr 1992;49:793.

13. Silverman LA, Gitelman LE. Immunoreactive inhibin müllerian inhibitory substance, and activin as biochemical markers for juvenile granulosa cell tumors. J Pediat 1996;129:918–21.

14. Endreich-Epstein A, Monforte HL, Lavey RS, et al. Successful multimodality therapy. Recurrent multifocal juvenile granulosa cell tumor of the ovary. J Ped Oncol 2002;24:229–33.

15. Meigs JV, Armstrong SH, Hamilton HH. Further contribution to the syndrome of fibroma of the ovary with fluid in the abdomen and chest: Meigs Syndrome. Am J Obstet Gynecol 1943:19.

16. Tsuji T, Kawauchi S, Utsunomiya T. Fibrosarcoma versus cellular fibroma of the ovary, a comparative study of their proliferative activity and chromosome aberrations using MIB-1 immunostaining, DNA flow cytometry, and flourescence in situ hybridization. Am J Surg Pathol 1997;21:52–9.

17. Healey DL, Burger HG, Mamers P, et al. Elevated serum inhibin concentrations in postmenopausal women with ovarian tumors. N Engl J Med 1993;329:1539–42.

18. Young RH, Scully RE. Ovarian Sertoli-Leydig cell tumors: a clinicopathological analysis of 207 cases. Am J Surg Pathol 1985;9:543.

19. Young RH, Scully RE. Ovarian Sertoli-cell tumors: a report of 10 cases. Int J Gynecol Pathol 1984;2:349.

20. Lele SN, Sawh RN, Zaharopolous P, et al. Malignant ovarian sex cord tumor with annular tubules in a patient with Peutz-Jeghers Syndrome: A case report. Moder Pathol 2000;13:466–70.

21. Scully RE. Sex cord tumor with annular tubules: A distinctive ovarian tumor of the Pentz-Jeghers syndrome. Cancer 1970;25:1107–21.

22. Homesley HD, Bundy BN, Hurteau JA, Roth LM. Bleomycin, etoposide, and cisplatin combination therapy of ovarian granulosa cell tumors and other stromal malignancies: a Gynecologic Oncology Group study. Gynecol Oncol 1999;72:131–7.

23. Gershensen DM. Management of early ovarian cancers: Germ cell and sex cord-stromal tumors. Gynecol Oncol 1994;55:S62–72.

24. Berek JS, Hacker NF. Sarcomas of the female genital tract. In: Eilber FR, Morton DL, et al editors. The soft tissue sarcomas. Orlando (FL):Grune and Stratton; 1987. p. 229–38.

Index

Page numbers followed by f indicate figure. Pages numbers followed by t indicate table.